VOICES OF FREEDOM

VOICES OF FREEDOM

AN ORAL HISTORY OF THE CIVIL RIGHTS MOVEMENT FROM THE 1950s THROUGH THE 1980s

HENRY HAMPTON
AND STEVE FAYER
WITH SARAH FLYNN

BANTAM BOOKS
NEW YORK · TORONTO · LONDON · SYDNEY · AUCKLAND

D961:IV master voices of freedom

VOICES OF FREEDOM

A Bantam Book
Bantam hardcover edition / February 1990
Bantam trade paperback edition / February 1991

Grateful acknowledgment is made to reprint photographs appearing at the opening of chapters 1, UPI/Bettmann; 2, © Don Cravens; 3, Thomas McAvoy, Life *Magazine © Time Inc.; 5, UPI/Bettmann; 6, UPI/Bettmann; 7, UPI/Bettmann; 8, © 1963 Charles Moore/Black Star; 9, © 1989 Mary Lee Moore; 10, A. Philip Randolph Institute; 11, AP/Wide World Photos; 12, UPI/Bettmann; 13, © 1989 Flip Schulke; 14, © 1984 Robert L. Haggins; 15, © 1975 Flip Schulke; 16, © UPI/Bettmann; 17, UPI/Bettmann; 18, © Michael Sullivan/Black Star; 20, © 1989 Stephen Shames/Visions; 21, UPI/Bettmann; 22, AP/Wide World Photos; 23, © Washington Post/Matthew Lewis; 24, UPI/Bettmann; 25, © Jill Freedman 1968/*Old News: Resurrection City*; 26, © 1989 Fred W. McDarrah; 27, UPI/Bettmann; 28, New York State Police; 29, Chester Higgins, Jr./Photo Researchers, Inc.; 30,* The Boston Globe*/Charles B. Carey.*

Grateful acknowledgment is made for permission to quote from "Malcolm" by Sonia Sanchez in Homecoming *(Detroit: Broadside Press, 1969), p. 32, and for permission to quote from "The Drum Major Instinct" and "I See the Promised Land" by Martin Luther King, Jr., in* A Testament of Hope: The Essential Writings of Martin Luther King, Jr. *(Harper & Row, 1986), © 1986 by Coretta Scott King, executrix of the estate of Martin Luther King, Jr. Reprinted by permission of Joan Daves.*

Library of Congress Catalog Card Number: 89-18297.

ISBN 0-553-35232-6

Published simultaneously in the United States and Canada

Bantam Books are published by Bantam Books, a division of Bantam Doubleday Dell Publishing Group, Inc. Its trademark, consisting of the words "Bantam Books" and the portrayal of a rooster, is Registered in U.S. Patent and Trademark Office and in other countries. Marca Registrada. Bantam Books, 666 Fifth Avenue, New York, New York 10103.

PRINTED IN THE UNITED STATES OF AMERICA

RRH 0 9 8 7 6 5 4 3 2

People pay for what they do, and still more, for what they have become. And they pay for it simply: by the lives they lead.

—James Baldwin

CONTENTS

PREFACE

TOWARD A MORE PERFECT UNION

I have a good, though complex, friend—Rutledge Adam Waker, black in every sense, South Carolina smart. I have watched him solve Rubik's Cubes and Boston politics by first sitting and watching and then, seemingly from nowhere, bursting into full and complete action. He has spent thirty years of his life buying land for himself and trying to create affordable housing for the poor, mostly the black poor. He inspires, confuses, and sometimes frightens whites, elevating them with his passion, putting them off with his anger. But he is as likely to take me on, poking fun at the black middle class, attacking our unreadiness for the revolution. He has taught me much about being black in America.

He called me early one bright, crisp fall day and with his peculiar urgency demanded of me, "How much would it cost to rent a helicopter?" He knows I am a pilot. Playing along, certain that he will get to it eventually, I tell him four hundred dollars an hour. There is this game between us in which he will not say why. I must ask. Finally, I can stand it no longer. I concede. "Rudy, what do you need with a helicopter?" I can feel his grin over the phone at his small victory. "To surrender," he says. He has me now.

"Look at the Japanese, look at the Germans. They lost to America and both surrendered. Look at them now, look at the money America poured onto them. We made a mistake. We should have just surrendered and then America could deal with us."

I can't argue with his logic but wonder about the helicopter. "I want to bring it right here to a vacant lot in the South End of Boston"—a formerly poor section now being rapidly gentrified—"call the news media, and announce that we've lost and want to come to terms, then climb on board the helicopter and depart."

I smile at the theatricality of the image. We'd make every prime time news show. He's right, of course. Black Americans don't know how to surrender. Surrender is not the stuff of innocence, belief, and idealism. Surrender is not possible when too large a price has been paid. And finally, Americans cannot surrender to themselves.

Rudy's instinctual ploy reaches deep into the Black American soul. His voice is like so many others that seem to understand our quandary.

Voices that tell us stories, tell us of our history, of the pain and joy, voices that guide us through this grand, tragic—and unfinished—American chronicle, the struggle of Black Americans for equity and the continuing challenge to redeem democracy in America.

* * *

This book, *Voices of Freedom,* is an outgrowth of the "Eyes on the Prize" project centered around a television history of America's civil rights years. We began work on the project in the late 1970s. The goal for the public television series and print materials was to capture the American civil rights movement in the voices of those who were there, and thereby give younger citizens who had not lived that struggle, or those who never understood, some idea of the raging torrents that had engulfed America in the fifties, sixties, and seventies and that came to be known as the civil rights and black consciousness movements.

The "Eyes" process was to collect the voices of the participants in this history and to have them tell us the stories they carried within them. Because of the difficulty of raising funds and the cost of the effort, we had to divide the project into two phases. In the first, consisting of six one-hour television programs, we covered the years from the mid-1950s (the death of Emmett Till and the trial of his killers) to 1965 (the Selma marches and the passage of the Voting Rights Act). In the second stage, consisting of eight one-hour programs, we began with the movement spreading into the North and covered the emergence of Malcolm X and the years of remedies, rights, and power from the mid-1960s to the 1980s.

Voices of Freedom encompasses both phases of the project. Only a fraction of the material we gathered over the last decade—in interviews done on tape, on film, and over the telephone—could be used in the television series, because the medium imposes such stringent time limitations. It was this realization that led us to review the thousands of pages of interview transcripts and weave them into a book of oral histories.

We are aware of the danger in presenting history that may not have fully settled into clear perspective, but I think the risk is worth it. The times are too urgent to have generations ignorant of strategies tried, the role of leaders, the failures and successes of our recent racial history. Our times seem to be ones of retreat from the dearly won gains of earlier generations. That is why the lessons of these voices are so important.

While the headlines of racial violence are frightening, nothing is more disturbing than to listen to young men and women who appear to have no sense of what brought us to where we are. How can you enter the debate if you fail to consider what has happened?

In the pages you are about to read there is history that has and will define our future as a nation. Because America is what it is, our battle has implications far beyond our shores. And if there are lessons to be gained from these years, one is surely the importance of history to a disenfranchised people. Its importance was assured when it was systematically taken from African-Americans. Looking back, it is clear to me that history is the high ground in the battle for self—and without a sense of self, one's freedom is forever in the hands of others.

Finally, I must take responsibility for a decision. We are in a time of linguistic transition, and the term "black" is increasingly being replaced by "African-American." And that is the term we used when it seemed appropriate. However, for most of the period of these interviews most persons used the word "black," and the convention of the period, as it is now, was to lowercase the word. We have followed that. However, I feel strongly that when "black" specifically identifies the racial group, as in Black American, it should be capitalized, just as we capitalize Irish-American or Italian-American. This may be an inelegant solution, but we trust that the reader will appreciate our dilemma.

HENRY HAMPTON

ACKNOWLEDGMENTS

Going from interviews on tape to the book you now hold in your hands was an unusually challenging task. It required a sensitive, intelligent, and dedicated team of people.

While this book belongs to none of us and to all of us, surely there are two people without whom it would not exist. Sarah Flynn has committed most of her waking hours for an entire year to the herculean task of wading into the transcripts, reading, researching, and editing them into storylines with which we all could work. In a world where egos are not always small, Sarah kept her eyes on the task of doing what was right for the book. If there was a choice of sleeping or finishing, Sarah stayed awake and worked. This book is as much hers as anyone else's. It is impossible to credit Robert Lavelle adequately for his contribution. He had the original idea and carefully kept it alive as we moved from notion to manuscript. He served as Blackside's project director, hiring all the other members of the team, reviewing our work, monitoring the schedule and the budget, and jumping in to research, write, edit, cajole, and support as needed. He was our visionary, cheerleader, and taskmaster. But mostly, when all the rest of us flagged, he was the one to keep us going.

Bennett Singer helped remarkably with this project (while somehow simultaneously working on the films), and he did so with tremendous skill. Whenever work needed doing, from interviewing, editing, researching, or writing, to racing to the airport with an overnight package, Bennett completed the task at hand with a professionalism far in excess of his years.

Suzette Malveaux came for a few weeks and, luckily for us, stayed a year. Our key researcher, she organized the research staff, tracked down facts, figures, photographs, names, addresses, and dates—and she did so tirelessly. She also coordinated the transcribing of telephone interviews. Throughout the development of the manuscript, she supplied us with the benefit of her boundless enthusiasm and sincerity.

Other key members of the team include Derrick Evans, who helped us with research and helped also to compile the list of books for further reading, and Samantha Langbaum, who graciously provided much-needed general assistance, helping with research, transcribing interviews, and being available to do whatever needed doing.

Judy Richardson has worked on the project since the late 1970s. She conducted many of the interviews from 1979 through 1989. She also reviewed the manuscript and offered her strong opinions. She wanted us never to lose sight that it was the African-American spirit that drives this history. And while all of us felt and knew it, Judy made certain. We remain in her debt.

Those who logged or transcribed the interviews were Christian Du Lac, Cathy Hinton, Maia Harris, Sharon Epperson, Sandy Martin, Kim McClain, Patrick Keenan, Leah Mahan, Ken Jacobson, and Mary Tabor. Debra Rose Mecca also did a good deal of the transcribing and evidenced an abundance of grace under pressure.

The interviews on which this book is based were conducted by members of several "Eyes on the Prize" production teams. The interviewers were Prudence Arndt, Orlando Bagwell, Sheila Bernard, Carroll Blue, Callie Crossley, Howard Dammond, James A. DeVinney, Steve Fayer, Paul Good, Henry Hampton, Maia Harris, Barbara Howard, Henry Johnson, Kirk Johnson, Laurie Kahn-Leavitt, Madison Davis Lacy, Robert Lavelle, Susan Levene, Suzette Malveaux, Louis Massiah, Sam Pollard, Judy Richardson, Terry Rockefeller, Dale Rosen, Jackie Shearer, Bennett Singer, Romas Slezas, Llewellyn Smith, Paul Stekler, Judith Vecchione, and Noland Walker.

Bantam has been a wonderful publisher with which to undertake this project. The company not only believed in us enough to contract for this book, it supported us throughout the process. We are indebted to Henry Ferris, who acquired the book, Ann Harris, who edited it with remarkable intelligence, insight, and patience, Don Weisberg, who showed such great enthusiasm for the project, and all of the others at Bantam who have helped us. We'd also like to thank Peggy Leith Anderson, a thoughtful and gifted copy editor, and Marilyn Rash of Editorial Inc., who coordinated the final production stage of the manuscript.

Our literary agent (and friend) Doe Coover offered us her professional assistance and personal encouragement.

We particularly thank the people whom you are about to meet for sharing their experiences with us. The interviewees showed a remarkable generosity, even to their adversaries, in recounting their history.

We've been lucky enough to have several academic advisers for this book: Darlene Clark Hine (Michigan State University), David Garrow (City University of New York), Steven F. Lawson (University of South Florida), Rosalyn Terborg-Penn (Morgan State University), and James Turner (Cornell University) all provided invaluable advice. In addition, Michael Thelwell of the University of Massachusetts at Amherst, teacher and movement participant, read the manuscript with a gifted storyteller's eye and offered much-needed encouragement, insight, and eloquent analysis.

In such a project there are many special people, but we must give special recognition to four: Vincent Harding, Ruth Batson, Thomas Layton, and Jack Mendelsohn have provided extraordinary support, for which we can only say thank you.

All of these wise and talented men and women helped us enormously, and we have listened carefully to their criticisms and followed many of their suggestions. However, with so many advisers and colleagues working on the project, we feel it is especially important to point out that while we are grateful for everyone's assistance, final responsibility for *Voices of Freedom* rests with the authors.

* * *

It is impossible to complete these acknowledgments without giving due credit to all of the funders, advisers, and production staffs of the fourteen programs that make up the television series "Eyes on the Prize." They are listed in the back of this book, and without them *Voices of Freedom* would not be as rich or as comprehensive.

Working tirelessly on the films, many of the producers took time to review chapters and advise the authors, and their contributions were invaluable. Since they had often just returned from location, they brought fresh insight and nuance that might otherwise have been missed.

The funders of "Eyes on the Prize" ranged from the foundations and corporations that provided millions of dollars to contributors such as the students and faculty at Newton South High School in Newton, Massachusetts, who granted us a most inspiring twenty-five dollars. All of these men, women, and children who so often found creative ways to gain support for the project should feel proud, knowing that without their efforts our work would not have been possible.

It has been twelve years since this project began to occupy our professional lives, and it has been an extraordinary experience, primarily because of the people involved. If we have one regret at this writing, it is simply that we cannot bring you all together for one grand and glorious "Thank you."

HENRY HAMPTON
STEVE FAYER

PROJECT NOTES

This book is based on an archive of some one thousand interviews conducted for the television series "Eyes on the Prize." The series and all of the related materials were produced by Blackside, Inc., an independent multimedia production company based in Boston. It is important to note that *Voices of Freedom* is an event-driven oral history, which is to say, our interviewers did not gather life histories of movement participants; instead, people were asked to tell us what they saw, heard, did, or felt at specific moments in history. As much as possible, we have tried to let the voices speak for themselves, believing, as Studs Terkel has said, that "in their rememberings are their truths. The precise fact or the precise date is of small consequence." Where the precise fact or date is in the judgment of the authors significant or helpful, we have edited around erroneous statements, balanced them with information elsewhere in the text, asked the interviewee for a correction, or footnoted the data.

This is not a comprehensive history of America's civil rights years. It is a collection of stories, told by many of the participants themselves. In no way was the civil rights movement confined to these episodes. Rather, the stories told here illuminate one or more themes of the continuing struggle for freedom. Further, this is not a book of facts, dates, and places. Voting records, patterns of migration, legislative or judicial actions and reactions—all are alluded to here, but at the heart of this book are the experiences of people who fought for civil rights for African-Americans. For more comprehensive and factually specific accounts of the civil rights movement, the reader is encouraged to see "For Further Reading" at the end of the book.

In each chapter, we introduce the interviewees by describing who they were in relation to the story being told (not who they became in subsequent years). Likewise, during our interviewing process, we asked participants to take themselves back to the time of the event—and as much as possible not to reflect on it with the benefit of hindsight. But we are aware that all oral history is by nature revisionist history, and that hindsight may have changed participants' perspectives.

We have given the names of interviewees as they are now most commonly known (or as they requested us to list them) and have expanded on this format only when we thought it would assist the reader, for example, Kwame Ture (Stokely Carmichael).

We edited the interviews with caution and respect. Primarily, we worked with large passages of interview material, arranging the excerpts according to the intent of often long and rambling conversations. When we edited by stringing sentences and phrases together to make a particularly long discussion shorter and more coherent, we sent the edited transcript to the interviewee for review and approval. Relevant transcripts of the telephone conversation excerpts were sent to interviewees as well. Occasionally they made changes, always minor, and even those requesting changes were the exception.

For the record, the authors do not always agree with all the voices in the book. To borrow a legal term, the authors include "testimony against interest," allowing people from both sides of the battle line to speak whenever possible (and whenever they would consent to an interview) and letting readers draw their own conclusions.

While we aspire to fairness, we do not pretend neutrality. In such a struggle, with such stories, that would be impossible.

ROBERT LAVELLE
Vice President, Publishing
Blackside, Inc.

Voices of Freedom

PROLOGUE

When the First Continental Congress met in Philadelphia in 1774, it established as one of its goals "to wholly discontinue the slave trade." But during the next decade the leaders among the "free Persons" in the United States had a change of heart. When codifying the laws of the new nation in 1787, the framers of the Constitution did not abolish slavery; instead, they wrote slavery *into* the law, declaring that each slave, for purposes of taxation and representation, would count as three-fifths of a person.

Eighty years later, after the Civil War, America was offered another opportunity to live up to its ideals. "Forty acres and a mule" was the cry from Pennsylvania congressman Thaddeus Stevens. He and Senator Charles Sumner of Massachusetts sought the seizure of slaveholders' property and redistribution of the land to the slaves as compensation for generations of unjust treatment. They sought a true reconstruction of the South. But again, America backed away from the moment. There was no radical redistribution of the wealth created by slavery and there was no compensation to the slaves. The Reconstruction years, which began at the end of the Civil War, witnessed a temporary realignment of political forces, in which black citizens were able to vote and were elected to local and national offices. But by 1877, the North proved incapable of stopping southern white resistance and pulled out its troops. Reconstruction, which had already proven weak in many areas of the Deep South, collapsed. In the 1890s, poll taxes and literacy tests succeeded in disenfranchising all but a handful of southern blacks. America had once again walked away from an opportunity to achieve justice. In place of slavery came "Jim Crow" laws that governed almost every aspect of life for Black Americans living below the Mason-Dixon line. The insidious Jim Crow caricature of the Negro became a powerful barrier to legal and social equality.

This book is about another moment in American history when the country was forced to decide whether it would live up to its principles. In it you will hear the voices of people who pushed the country to change, and the voices of those who resisted.

The U.S. Supreme Court, in a case known as *Brown* v. *Board of Education of Topeka,* in 1954 overturned the doctrine of "separate but equal" in the area of education, which had forced segregation of the races in schools for generations. With that decision was set in motion social change that would alter countless lives. The decision came to an America that had been profoundly transformed by World War II, and to a black citizenry changed both by the war itself and by their veterans returning from service.

Of the 16 million Americans who served in the segregated armed forces during the years 1941–1945, more than 1 million were black. Those veterans, and their dreams, would have a profound influence on the awakening of black people to the potential within themselves to effect change in American society.

James Hicks was among the black officers who served in World War II. In the United States he became one of the black press's leading journalists.

JAMES HICKS

I think that when black veterans of World War II returned home, they were really an influence on their communities. They were activists and they had been trained, and of course when they said, "No more of this Jim Crow" or what have you, the people, that is the black people, picked it up.

I think there was extreme resentment among the black veterans when they came back, because they felt, "I paid my dues over there and I'm not going to take this anymore over here."

After serving three years in the army, including fifteen months of combat duty in the South Pacific, one black soldier was taking a bus home to North Carolina from his camp in Georgia. The year was 1946 and Isaac Woodward was the veteran who, on the way through South Carolina, made the "mistake" of taking too long to return to the bus from a rest stop. The bus driver called the local police and after a severe beating, Woodward was left blinded. His case was widely publicized by the National Association for the Advancement of Colored People (NAACP) and presented to President Harry Truman as evidence of the need for civil rights legislation.

The NAACP, founded in 1909 by a biracial group of activists, among them W.E.B. Du Bois, Mary White Ovington, and Oswald Garrison Villard, had evolved during the first half of the century into an institutional defender of the rights of Black Americans. In the 1940s, Constance Baker Motley was an attorney with the NAACP Legal Defense and Educational Fund.

CONSTANCE BAKER MOTLEY

The issue of segregation loomed large during the war and the war effort. Here we were as a nation involved in a war to make the world safe for democracy, and one of the embarrassing features was that blacks were segregated in our armed forces, and they resented it. And here we were trying to represent ourselves as a democratic nation. The NAACP's membership almost doubled during that period from membership applications from black servicemen who recognized that the NAACP was the only organization they could turn to for assistance with what they believed to be a very pressing problem for them. And that is that they received disproportionately harsher sentences than white servicemen for any crime which they committed. They felt this was a tremendous grievance that something had to be done about. When I first went to work at the NAACP Legal Defense and Educational Fund, in the summer of 1944, we had court-martial records stacked to the ceiling that had to be reviewed and appeals taken to military review boards in Washington, so our legal efforts were concentrated in the area of trying to get these servicemen's sentences reduced, if not the conviction reversed.

After World War II, as a result of the activity of black servicemen, really, the whole attitude in the country about the race relations problem changed. I think people became more aware that something had to be done about the fact that black servicemen were overseas dying for this country, and when they would be coming home, they would be coming home to a situation that said, in effect, You're a second-class citizen. You can't go to school with white children, or your children can't. You can't stay in a hotel or eat in a restaurant because you're black. And I think that gave the momentum, particularly in the black community, for what became the civil rights movement of the 1950s and 1960s.

The NAACP's strategy for attacking segregation through the Legal Defense Fund was revitalized and extended after World War II. It had been in the making prior to the war but was abandoned during the war, when all the attention was focused on black servicemen. Eventually, it led to the Supreme Court's decision in the *Brown* case in 1954.

Black veterans were not the only people who realized how the war had dramatized the need for social change. Harry Ashmore served in the army in Europe during World War II and returned to his native South to take a job as editor of the *Charlotte* (North Carolina) *News*. He was to become one of the few white southern newspapermen to openly support the civil rights movement.

HARRY ASHMORE

When I was growing up in South Carolina, it was predominantly an agrarian region. Most people still lived on the land, and most of the people who lived in the towns were dependent on the land. But all that was changing and changing very rapidly. People were leaving the land and, of course, agriculture was being mechanized. The first great technological revolution was in the fields, and that was displacing blacks and whites. They were coming to the cities in the South and they were going on beyond, in a great flood. They were going to the North and to the West Coast, where there had been few blacks before. The whole great out-migration was beginning.

Political patterns were changing and the pressure, although not then directly against segregation as such, was beginning in other significant ways, such as the demand for the vote, for service on juries, and all those civil rights that had been denied, either by legal means or by custom, in the South. And it seemed to me quite early that we had to yield on those, that those had to go first.

Most people were not recognizing the depth of this. They were still whistling, they were pretending there's nothing really going on, the black people are satisfied with what they've got, the system's working, just a few outside agitators are coming in, stirring things up. It wasn't so much a matter of conscious race prejudice, though that was a big element of it, but another big part of it was the status quo. This was the only thing they knew, they had never known anything else. This is the way it had always been. This is the way they thought it was supposed to be.

Then came along what I have always thought was the most significant of the changes, and that was the court cases brought by the NAACP—the cases that began in systematically attacking voting, jury service, that sort of thing—which began taking these things one at a time, getting into federal court, where obviously they couldn't stand a constitutional test, and then taking these cases all the way up.

> The Congress of Racial Equality (CORE), founded in 1942, was another interracial organization demanding change for Black Americans. Bayard Rustin, who had worked with labor and civil rights leader A. Philip Randolph, accepted a position as CORE's first field secretary.

BAYARD RUSTIN

I think the beginning of this period from 1954 has its roots in the returning soldiers after 1945. There was a great feeling on the part of many of these youngsters that they had been away, that they had fought in the war—that they were not getting what they should have. Already, black and white soldiers coming home from the war were sitting anywhere they wanted in the buses and they were being thrown in jail. There was a great feeling that the A. Philip Randolph movement to stop discrimination in the armed forces had been helpful but it was not enough. There was a building up of militancy, not so much by going into the streets as by a feeling of "We are not going to put up with this anymore." What was lacking was that they did not have the Supreme Court backing them. But when the Supreme Court came out with the *Brown* decision in '54, things began rapidly to move. Some of us had been sitting down in the front of these buses for years, but nothing had happened. What made '54 so unusual was that the Supreme Court in the *Brown* decision established black people as being citizens with all the rights of all other citizens. Once that happened, then it was very easy for that militancy, which had been building up, to express itself in the Montgomery bus boycott of '55–'56.

The *Brown* decision marked a turning point in America's race relations. But the opposing and parallel forces that led to *Brown* and that carried the implementation of that decision into virtually every corner of American life were the forces found in the American people, white and black, North and South. For many Americans in the 1950s, particularly Black Americans, the conflict between those forces came into clear focus in a small town in the Mississippi Delta in August 1955.

1

Emmett Till, 1955

"I Wanted the Whole World to See"

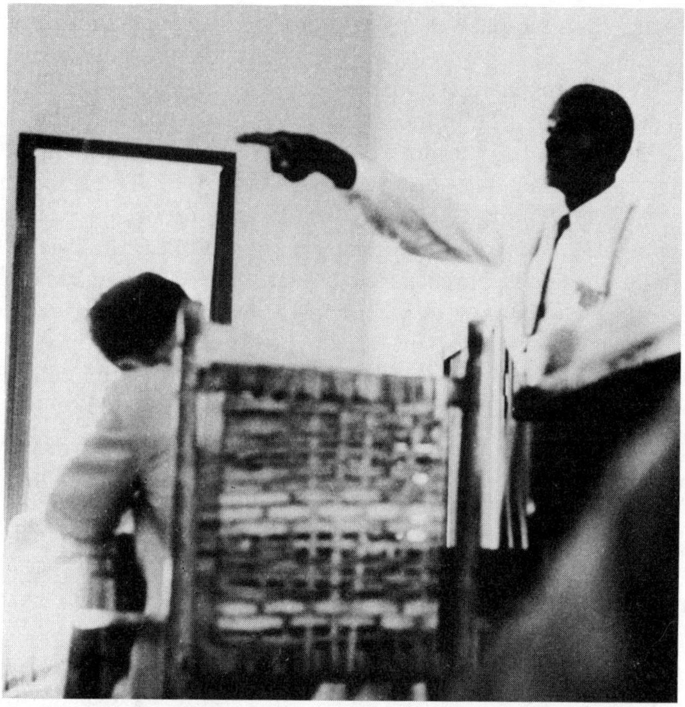

On the witness stand in Sumner, Mississippi, Mose Wright, sixty-four, points to the men accused of abducting and murdering his grandnephew, Emmett Till.

On August 20, 1955, Emmett Till, a fourteen-year-old from Chicago's South Side, almost missed the train that would carry him to a summer visit with relatives in the Mississippi Delta. Emmett, nicknamed Bo, was supposed to meet his seventeen-year-old cousin, Curtis Jones, at LaSalle

Street station. Young Till didn't show up at LaSalle Street, but with only seconds to spare, out of breath and stammering with excitement, he boarded the train at Englewood, more than seven miles away.

In the forty years since World War I began, Chicago's black population had grown from some forty thousand to half a million. Many blacks had moved up from the South, seeking jobs and a better way of life. Of those, 75 percent hailed from Mississippi. Emmett Till was part of the emigrant community and was closing the circle that summer, traveling back to his family's home place.

Money, Mississippi, was a dusty crossroads, population fifty-five, with the Tallahatchie River at its back door. Emmett's mother had warned the boy to mind his manners with whites down there. No one expected a fourteen-year-old to be in mortal danger, but anyone black had to be careful. More than five hundred black people had been lynched in the state since these statistics were first compiled in 1882. Thousands more racially motivated murders were never officially reported. Now, in the summer of 1955, the death toll was beginning to build again, particularly in the Delta, the northwest corner of the state, where Money was located.

In some Delta counties, blacks constituted 80 percent of the population, and the outnumbered whites were bent on intimidating any blacks who wanted access to a better education or to the ballot box. Three months before Emmett's trip, the Reverend George Lee from the Delta town of Belzoni was killed by a shotgun blast to the face. Local authorities ruled his death a traffic accident. Lee had been the first black to register to vote in the county.

On August 13, just a week before Emmett's arrival, Lamar Smith, a black man who had voted in the state's Democratic primary earlier in the month, was shot to death at high noon in front of the courthouse in Brookhaven. Again, there were no arrests.

For almost seventy years, the U.S. Supreme Court had supported southern insistence on second-class citizenship for blacks. With the *Brown* v. *Board of Education* decision in 1954, the Court signaled that it was changing its position regarding the legality of segregating black and white schoolchildren. Reaction in the South was swift, particularly in Mississippi. Leaders of the white supremacist Ku Klux Klan exhorted their followers to resist the "mongrelization" of the white race. White Citizens' Councils were formed to exert political and economic pressure on black activists and their white sympathizers. Segregationists James O. Eastland and John Stennis, Mississippi's two U.S. senators, worked to further consolidate the white monopoly of political power. Governor J. P. Coleman stated flatly that Negroes weren't fit to vote. Ten years after the end of World War II, many whites in the Delta felt that Mississippi was now in another war to protect its way of life.

Emmett arrived in Mississippi with his cousin Curtis Jones on August 21, 1955.

CURTIS JONES

We was going to Money, Mississippi, to have a good time. I'd never picked cotton before and I was looking forward to that. I had told my mother that I could pick two hundred pounds, and she told me I couldn't. Emmett Till was fourteen years old, had just graduated out of the grammar school.

My grandfather in Mississippi was a preacher. He had a church and he had a little raggedy '41 Ford, if I'm not mistaken. And he took all of us to church that day, including my grandmother, my three uncles, myself, my cousin Emmett, and my cousin Willa Parker. While he was in the pulpit preaching, we get the car and drive to Money. Anyway, we went into this store to buy some candy. Before Emmett went in, he had shown the boys round his age some picture of some white kids that he had graduated from school with, female and male. He told the boys who had gathered round this store—there must have been maybe ten to twelve youngsters there—that one of the girls was his girlfriend. So one of the local boys said, "Hey, there's a white girl in that store there. I bet you won't go in there and talk to her." So Emmett went in there. When he was leaving out the store, after buying some candy, he told her, "Bye, baby."

I was sitting out there playing checkers with this older man. Next thing I know, one of the boys came up to me and said, "Say, man, you got a crazy cousin. He just went in there and said 'Bye, baby' to that white woman." This man I was playing checkers with jumped straight up and said, "Boy, you better get out of here. That lady'll come out of that store and blow your brains off."

It was kind of funny to us. We hopped in the car and drove back to the church. My grandfather was just about completing his sermon.

The next day we was telling some youngsters what had happened, but they had heard about it. One girl was telling us that we better get out of there 'cause when that lady's husband come back gonna be big trouble. We didn't tell our grandfather. If we had told our grandfather, I'm sure he would have gotten us out of there. That was Wednesday. So that Thursday passed, nothing happened. Friday passed, nothing happened. Saturday, nothing happened. So we forgot about it.

Saturday night we went to town. The closest town was Greenwood. We must have stayed there till approximately three o'clock that morning. We returned and—my grandfather didn't have but three rooms, the kitchen and two bedrooms—it must have been about three-thirty, I was awakened by a group of men in the house. I didn't wake completely, youngsters, they sleep hard, you know. When they came, my grandfather answered the door and they asked him did he have three boys in there from Chicago? And he stated yes. He said I got my two grandsons and a nephew. So they told him get the one who did the talking. My grandmother was scared to death. She was trying to protect Bo. They told her get back in bed. One of the guys struck her with a shotgun side of the head. When I woke up the next morning, I thought it was a dream.

I went to the porch and my grandfather was sitting on the porch. I asked him, "Poppa, did they bring Bo back?" He said, "No." He said, "I hope they didn't kill that boy." And that's when I got kind of scared.

I asked him, "Ain't you going to call the police?" He said, "No, I can't call the police. They told me that if I call the sheriff they was going to kill everybody in this house." So I told him, I say, "*I'll* call."

That happened Sunday.

> When Curtis Jones called the sheriff that Sunday, he also placed a call to his mother, Willie Mae Jones, back in Chicago. She in turn got in touch with Emmett's mother, Mamie Till Bradley, a thirty-three-year-old schoolteacher.

MAMIE TILL BRADLEY MOBLEY

Willie Mae was hysterical. I could barely get any sense out of her. But I finally pieced out that Emmett had been taken from her father's house. I said, "Mama, Willie Mae said someone had taken Emmett from Poppa Mose's house." Well, Mother comprehended the situation immediately. And that of course alerted me that there was real danger.

By Wednesday we knew it was beyond the shadow of a doubt—the thing had really come fallin' in place. We knew about the men who had taken Emmett. We knew the alleged crime. We knew that something was highly amiss that Emmett hadn't turned up by then. He had an uncanny sense of direction, and I don't care where you took him, he could get back home. And he hadn't called. We knew the situation was serious, and we just couldn't name it—that he had been killed. You just couldn't put it into words, but deep down in our hearts we were fearing that.

> Based on information that Mose Wright and Crosby Smith gave the sheriff, two men were arrested for kidnapping— Roy Bryant, husband of the woman in the store, and his half brother, J. W. Milam. That Wednesday, Emmett Till's body was discovered in the Tallahatchie River. A cotton gin fan was tied to his neck with barbed wire. Milam and Bryant now faced murder charges.

CURTIS JONES

Wednesday I was over at some relatives' house. We was out there picking cotton. One of my uncles drove up there in that 1941 Ford. He said, "Curtis, they found Bo." I say, "Is he alive?" He said, "No, he's dead."

MAMIE TILL BRADLEY MOBLEY

I understand the order came from the sheriff's office to bury that body just as soon as you can. And they didn't even allow it to go to a funeral parlor and be dressed. He was in a pine box. Well, we got busy. We called the governor, we called the sheriff, we called Crosby, my mother's brother. We called everybody we thought would be able to stop the burial of that body. I wanted that body. I demanded that body because my thoughts were, I had to see it, to make sure, because I'd be wondering even now who was buried in Mississippi. I had to know that was Emmett. Between Crosby and the sheriff in Mississippi who went with him and the undertaker here who contacted the undertaker there, we were able to stop the burial.

After the body arrived I knew that I had to look and see and make sure it was Emmett. That was when I decided that I wanted the whole world to see what I had seen. There was no way I could describe what was in that box. No way. And I just wanted the world to see.

> The boy's body was so mutilated that Mose Wright had been able to identify Emmett only by the ring on his finger. The black press was outraged. *Jet* magazine ran a photograph of the corpse that Mamie Till Bradley had resolved all the world should see. Her son's face was swollen and disfigured. He had been beaten severely. One eye was gouged out, and one side of his forehead was crushed. A bullet was lodged in his skull.
>
> The *Chicago Defender,* one of the country's largest national black weeklies, gave the Till case and the open-casket funeral prominent coverage. The story of the lynching also received unusual attention in the national white media, with newsreel and television cameras on the scene in the Delta.
>
> Medgar Evers, the first field secretary for the National Association for the Advancement of Colored People (NAACP) in Mississippi, traveled to the Delta for the trial of Bryant and Milam. Myrlie Evers worked with her husband at the NAACP office in Jackson, the state capital.

MYRLIE EVERS

The Emmett Till case was one that shook the foundations of Mississippi, both black and white. With the white community because of the fact that it had become nationally publicized, with us blacks because it said that even a child was not safe from racism, bigotry, and death.

Medgar was the field secretary for the NAACP. He and Amzie Moore and others had the responsibility of going into these areas, wherever there might have been problems, and investigating these cases. I can recall so well that Medgar cried when he found that this had happened to Emmett Till. Cried out of frustration and anger. I myself felt anger, frustration, almost a hopelessness at that time, that things were going to continue to happen.

Medgar and Amzie Moore and a few others dressed as sharecroppers to go on the plantations and ask people about the accused murderers. What had happened? They made contact with the local officials. They got the press out. It was a very dangerous job. Medgar was also responsible not only for finding witnesses, but helping them get out of town. I remember one very distinct case where he used a casket, put a person in a casket in conjunction with a mortuary, and got the person out of the state, across the border to Tennessee.

Charles Diggs of Detroit, one of the first black congressmen since Reconstruction, traveled from his district in Michigan to attend the murder trial, which began in Sumner, Mississippi, on September 19.

CHARLES DIGGS

When I read about the Emmett Till case, I became immediately interested. First of all, because it was Mississippi, the bottom line for archsegregationists in the United States. Secondly, because it was the home state of my father and grandfather and all the people on the Diggs side of the family. And thirdly, I thought, being a pioneer member of Congress, that I had a special security there that could serve the purpose well.

I think the picture in the *Jet* magazine of the Till boy, showing his mutilation, after he was removed out of the river, I think that was probably one of the greatest media products in the last forty or fifty years, because that picture stimulated a lot of interest and a lot of anger on the part of blacks all over the country. And the fact that the Till boy was just a child also added to this matter.

Simeon Booker's coverage of the case for *Jet* magazine began as soon as news of the kidnapping broke.

SIMEON BOOKER

The unusual thing was, it was the first time the daily—meaning white—media took an interest in something like this. I remember one of the jokes among our press corps down there was that, hell, they'd go lookin' for Till's body, they would find bodies of a lotta other blacks who'd just been thrown in the river. Because that was the custom, that was the procedure.

Well, after it broke in Chicago and when the boy's mother demanded that the body be brought back, they had thousands that viewed that body, and that really brought it to the international circuit.

When Diggs went down to that trial those blacks had never seen a black congressman. In fact, many of them never knew there was a black congressman, because they didn't have any communication, have any black newspapers down there, they didn't have any radio or anything that gave them information about what was going on outside of Mississippi.

> The National News Association, a black wire service, sent reporter James Hicks to cover the trial. Like the other black reporters, Hicks stayed in Mound Bayou, an all-black town about twelve miles from Sumner. There he met Dr. T.R.M. Howard, a physician who earlier that summer had organized a voting rights rally attended by thousands of black people.

JAMES HICKS

Dr. Howard, I'll never forget him. He was a prominent man. Having made his money down there, they, the white folks, looked at him as, I think, the nearest thing "like us." So that when the trouble came they looked to him. They said, "Quiet them down over there." It turned out he wasn't in the mood to quiet them down. He said, "Well, you're not doing right."

I asked him, "Are they going to arrest these men? When are they going to sentence them? You think they'll get the chair?" And he said, "Chair, are you kidding?" He said, "I can tell you this. A white man in Mississippi will get no more of a sentence for killing a black person as he would for killing a deer out of season."

He was saying around that this was just the worst thing. So he became a target. Howard saw that it was time for him to go. They had threatened him. So I said, "I'll drive you."

He had a lot of money and he put it in a pillow slip, in cash, with his valuables. We put it in the back of this you-drive-it car. I drove him to Memphis and he flew on to Chicago.

There was a white fella on the Jacksonville daily newspaper, and I struck up a friendship with him in covering the trial, even though blacks and whites were frowned upon when they talked to each other. Farnsworth, that was his name. He told me that he knew where the propeller around the boy's neck had come from. He knew what cotton gin it had come off. I said, "Well, look, I am not a ballistics expert, but if there was a propeller revolving on a cam on any machine, whether it was a propeller on a boat or a cotton gin, it would leave certain grooves on the inside of the propeller that it was attached to, just like a bullet has rifling marks on it so you can match it with the barrel of the gun." I'd been in the army so I knew a little bit about it.

He said, "That's right, and I'll tell you where the cotton gin is. That gin fan come right out of J. W. Milam's barn." So I said I'd sure like to get over there and see that.

That night, with Ruby Hurley, who was a field representative of the NAACP, and a few others, I went as close to J. W. Milam's house as we felt we could go. And Farnsworth went up to a certain point where he could point out the barn to me and he said, "You go on up there and you sneak into that barn."

I was concerned about dogs because this house was sitting out in a cotton field and the road leading up to it was so narrow. I had my flashlight with me, but I didn't use it. I wondered what a cotton gin might be like. I didn't know just what to expect. It was this big, big machine. I finally reached enough courage to put my light on to see where the motor was. I saw it. I had the light on and bent down to feel the shaft from which the propeller had come. I got out of there in a hurry and made it back to the car. I wrote a story in which I pointed out that this cotton gin on Milam's farm did not have a fan belt or a propeller on it and that the FBI could simply take this thing they found on the boy's neck and match it against the cam of the cotton gin machine. They could tell instantly whether or not it came from there.

The Council of Negro Newsmen wrote a letter to J. Edgar Hoover and pointed out how glaring this evidence was and asked that Hoover order somebody to check it out. The next thing I get is a communication forwarded to me from Hoover saying that he had an agent down there. And would I get with the agent? The first thing I wanted to know was where did this FBI agent come from? Was he out of Washington or was he a homegrown FBI agent? It turned out that he was homegrown and I said, "Oh no, I'm not going to go near *him*." 'Cause I didn't even want him to know who the hell I was. They never did connect the thing up. But it was so plain to be done.

Amzie Moore, one of the early NAACP organizers in Mississippi, attended the Milam-Bryant trial.

AMZIE MOORE

Some days in the summertime in Mississippi, the weather is so hot you can almost see it. If the wind doesn't blow every once in a while and just bring you a little cool air, you look like you might be getting yourself ready to be burned to death.

I don't think I could give you an accurate description of what the courtroom was like, because we could not stand in the halls, nor could we sit down in there, because the people in the courtroom, with very few exceptions, were white and they didn't leave much room for blacks.

JAMES HICKS

I had covered courts all over this nation, but I never saw anything like the Till case before. First of all, it was a segregated courtroom, and all the white veterans in town were deputized. The press table was denied to blacks. We had to sit at a bridge table far off from the jury, whereas the white press sat right under the judge and the jury, right up front at a reserved section. The laxity in the courtroom was something you couldn't imagine. I mean, they drank beer in the jury box.

Mamie Till Bradley traveled to Sumner to testify that the body fished out of the Tallahatchie was her son's.

MAMIE TILL BRADLEY MOBLEY

I remember I was concentrating very hard on using the proper language, the "yes, sirs" and the "no, sirs." And I was certainly not treated very gentle on this day and on the witness stand. Particularly when I was so adamant about that being Emmett's body. I knew that if they could just get me to say this wasn't Emmett, then they could get off scot-free. But I couldn't say that, because I knew that was Emmett.

JAMES HICKS

Somebody had said that Mose Wright had told them from the git-go that he wanted to testify. He wanted to tell how these people got Emmett Till out of his house that night. All the people in Mound Bayou were saying, "Look, this is it. This man gets up there and identifies J. W. Milam and this other man, Bryant, we don't know what's going to happen. His life won't be worth a dime if he testifies against these two white men." We had been told that this was going to happen, this was a point when the stuff would hit the fan. We black reporters devised our own plan. We were seated in this Jim Crow setup, near a window. On this particular day, every able-bodied white man you saw in the courtroom had a .45 or a .38 strung on him. They were expecting something to happen. One of these young deputies who was wearing a gun, there was only an aisle between us. I said the first thing I will do is grab that .45. Snatch that safety off and then battle as far as we could, because it was almost hopeless. I didn't know if it would come out too well, but if you blasted a few of them, then somebody might think you meant business.

When Uncle Mose testified, electricity came over the courtroom. This elderly, gray-haired man sitting up there. The prosecutor said, "Now, Uncle Mose, I am going to ask you, is it a fact that two men came to your house? Now what did they say?"

"They asked, 'You have a nigger here from Chicago?'"

And he told them, "My little nephew is here from Chicago."

"And what did they say then?"

"He ask me where he was, and I said he was in there in the bed 'cause it was nighttime, and so they said get him up. I got him up and then he, they took him away and they said, 'I'm going to take this nigger with us.' I couldn't do anything."

The key point came when they said to him, "I'm going to ask you to look around in the courtroom and see if you see any man here that came to you and knocked on your door that night." And so this old man—I mean, talk about courage—he looked around and in his broken English he said, "Dar he," and he pointed so straight at J. W. Milam. It was like history in that courtroom. It was like electricity in that courtroom. The judge, he was pounding on his gavel and he was saying "Order, order," like that. There was a terrific tension in the courtroom but nothing happened. I mean, no outbreak came. I think that was because of the judge.

The trial lasted five days. In addition to Mose Wright, two other black witnesses took the stand: Willie Reed, who testified he had seen Till in the back of Milam's pickup truck and heard a beating in Milam's barn, and Reed's aunt, Amanda Bradley, who had heard the beating victim cry out, "Momma, Lord have mercy, Lord have mercy." In spite of the eyewitness testimony, the all-white jury returned a verdict of not guilty, having deliberated for one hour. The black witnesses were all moved quickly out of state for their own protection by Medgar Evers, James Hicks, Congressman Diggs, and others.

Two months after the trial, William Bradford Huie, a white journalist and novelist from Alabama, met with one of the several attorneys who had defended Milam and Bryant.

WILLIAM BRADFORD HUIE

John Whitten was thirty-six years old. He knew who I was. I knew his cousin Jamie Whitten, in Congress. So we quickly established a rapport. I told him I wanted to find the truth over there. I thought it would be better for the community if the truth were told. All sorts of myths were being published. Forty or fifty reporters from all over the world had been down there, a highly publicized trial, and because nothing had been established since the trial, all kinds of rumors were being published as truth about great congregations of white men who had beaten somebody in a barn or something. So I told John Whitten, "John, the truth, whatever the truth is, ought to be told." And I said, "I assume these two white men that you defended——."

And he said, "Well, you know that we all defended them. All the attorneys in town defended them." He said, "You know, my clients, some of them were interested in it. They wanted me to defend them, and in a sense I could charge them a little extra—I'm talking about farm equipment companies and that sort of thing—to defend these boys."

And I said, "Well, I assume they killed the boy, didn't they?"

And John Whitten looked at me and he says, "You know, Bill, I don't know whether they did it or not. I never asked them."

I said, "You mean you defended them in court for a crime here, and you never questioned them?"

He says, "I didn't want to know. Because my wife kept asking me if they killed him. And I kept telling her no." And he says, "I didn't want them to tell me that they did, because then I'd have to tell my wife, or tell her a lie, so I didn't even want to know."

And I said, "Well, did any of them?"

And he said, "No, none of us questioned them. See, all we did was defend them, which the community wanted us to do."

I said, "Well, John, I want these two men to come in here and tell me the truth, because I think it's the best thing. They're not in jeopardy any longer and I don't see why they shouldn't. I want to make a film about it. And so I'm willing to buy what we call portrayal rights, and I'm willing to pay four thousand dollars for their portrayal rights if they'll come in here and tell me the truth. They must give me ways so that in the daytime I can go out and verify that they're telling me the truth, and if I find them telling me a lie, I won't pay them a damn thing."

I met Milam and Bryant. We had this strange situation. We're meeting in the library of this law firm. Milam and Bryant are sitting on one side of the table, John Whitten and I sitting on the other side. I'm not doing the questioning. Their own lawyer is doing the questioning. And he's never heard their story. Not once. He becomes as interested in the story as I am. I said, "Now, I'm going to take notes and then during the day I'm going to do two things. I'm going to be roughing out this story, and I'm also going where you say you went and I'm going to find evidence."

Milam did most of the talking. Now remember, he's older. Milam was then thirty-five or thirty-six. He was a first lieutenant in the U.S. Army Reserve at that time. And so Milam was a bit more articulate than Bryant was. Bryant did some talking, particularly when they talked about what they were told had happened in the store. But J. W. Milam did the killing. He fired the shot when they took Till down on the river and killed him.

They did not intend to kill him when they went and got him. They killed him because he boasted of having a white girl and showed them the pictures of a white girl in Chicago. They had him in the car trying to scare him and that sort of thing for about three hours. Young Till, he never realized the danger he was in, he never knew. I'm quite sure that he never thought these two men would kill him. Maybe he's in such a strange environment he really doesn't know what he's up against. It seems to a rational mind today, it seems impossible that they could have killed him. But J. W. Milam looked up at me and said, "Well, when he told me about this white girl he had," he says, "my friend, that's what this war's about down here now. That's what we got to fight to protect." And he says, "I just looked at him and I said, 'Boy, you ain't never going to see the sun come up again.'"

They were told that they had inherited a way of life. They were told that for a young black man to put his hand sexually on a white woman was something that could not be allowed. They were told that with the beginning of the Supreme Court decision this was a war.

WILL CAMPBELL

I was the director of religious life at the time, at the University of Mississippi. I knew that whoever had committed this murder would never be convicted. But the two men who were charged with this murder were at the time heroes. Now the strange part of it is, as soon as the trial was over, Mr. William Bradford Huie wrote a story for *Look* magazine showing the check that he had made out to tell the real story, where they said, Yes, we took him down there and we beat him and then killed him and threw him in the Tallahatchie River. Those people were nobodies after that. They were disgraced. Which is a strange dichotomy in southern society, that while they were being accused of this crime, we have to rally to their defense and take up money and hire lawyers and all the rest. But then when it's over, "Look, why did you have to disgrace us like that? Now get out of town, we really don't want to see you again."

For several years after her son's death, Mamie Bradley traveled the country speaking for the NAACP.

MYRLIE EVERS

I bled for Emmett Till's mother. When she came to Mississippi and appeared at the mass meetings, I know how everyone just poured out their hearts to her, went into their pockets when people had only two or three pennies, and gave that—some way to say that we bleed for you, we hurt for you, we are so sorry what happened to Emmett.

It was a sad and terrible time. And perhaps it's too bad to have to say that sometimes it takes those kinds of things to happen, to help a people become stronger and to eliminate the fear so that they have to speak out and do something.

2

THE MONTGOMERY BUS BOYCOTT, 1955–1956

"LIKE A REVIVAL STARTING"

The Reverend Martin Luther King, Jr., twenty-six, discusses the Montgomery bus boycott. The Reverend Ralph Abernathy and Rosa Parks are seated (center).

Frederick Douglass, born into slavery in Maryland around 1817, fled to New Bedford, Massachusetts, twenty years later. He soon became one of the North's leading abolitionists, fighting to end slavery. In his autobiography he described one of his experiences on a segregated train car: "My treatment in the use of public conveyances about these times was extremely rough, especially on the Eastern Railroad, from Boston to Portland. On that road, as on many others, there was a mean, dirty, and uncomfortable car set apart for colored travelers called the Jim Crow car. Regarding this as the fruit of slaveholding prejudice and being determined to fight the spirit of slavery wherever I might find it, I resolved to avoid this car, though it sometimes required some courage to do so. The colored people generally accepted the situation and complained of me as making matters worse rather than better by refusing to submit to this proscription. I, however, persisted, and sometimes was soundly beaten by conductor and brakeman. On one occasion six of these 'fellows of the baser sort,' under the direction of the conductor, set out to eject me from my seat. As usual, I had purchased a first-class ticket and paid the required sum for it, and on the requirement of the conductor to leave, refused to do so, when he called on these men to 'snake me out.' They attempted to obey with an air which plainly told me they relished the job. They however found me much attached to my seat, and in removing me I tore away two or three of the surrounding ones, on which I held with a firm grasp, and did the car no service in some other respects."

There was black resistance to segregated travel long before the Montgomery bus boycott in 1955 and 1956. Toward the end of the nineteenth century, blacks had boycotted streetcar lines in more than twenty-seven cities. Montgomery, the capital of Alabama, witnessed a boycott of Jim Crow car lines that lasted for two years, from 1900 to 1902. And although the local transportation companies gave in to the boycotters' demands, segregated seating was soon reinstated through city ordinances.

By 1955, segregation on Montgomery's bus lines was an entrenched and complicated arrangement. Black passengers paid their fares at the front, then left the bus to board at the rear. Blacks sat at the rear, whites in the front. And, by practice if not by law, an entire row of blacks would be asked to give up their seats if one white person was standing.

In 1955 the Reverend Ralph Abernathy was twenty-nine years old and the pastor of the First Baptist Church in Montgomery.

RALPH ABERNATHY

In the mid-1950s, life was most difficult for all poor people, but it was much better for poor white people than for black people in the South. Blacks were permitted to hold only the menial jobs, domestic workers and common and ordinary laborers. The only professional jobs that were open to blacks were the field of pastoring a black church and the schoolteaching profession, which was open because of segregated schools. White teachers didn't normally teach black students. In the whole state of Alabama we had probably less than five black doctors. And we didn't do anything but dig ditches and work with some white supervisor that told us everything to do. We were the last to be hired and the first to be fired.

All of the restaurants were segregated, the hotels and motels were segregated. Meaning that black people were not permitted to live in these hotels. Even in the public courthouse, blacks could not drink water except from the fountain labeled "Colored." You could not use a filling station that was not designated with a restroom for colored. You had a restroom for white males and a restroom for white women, and you had a restroom for colored. Meaning that colored people had to use the same restroom, male and female. And the janitor never would clean up the restroom for the colored people.

Rosa Parks, forty-three, an experienced activist in the black community, worked in downtown Montgomery.

ROSA PARKS

Having to take a certain section [on a bus] because of your race was humiliating, but having to stand up because a particular driver wanted to keep a white person from having to stand was, to my mind, most inhumane.

More than seventy-five, between eighty-five and I think ninety, percent of the patronage of the buses were black people, because more white people could own and drive their own cars than blacks.

I happened to be the secretary of the Montgomery branch of the NAACP as well as the NAACP Youth Council adviser. Many cases did come to my attention that nothing came out of 'cause the person that was abused would be too intimidated to sign an affidavit, or to make a statement. Over the years, I had had my own problems with the bus drivers. In fact, some did tell me not to ride their buses if I felt that I was too important to go to the back door to get on. One had evicted me from the bus in 1943, which did not cause anything more than just a passing glance.

On December 1, 1955, I had finished my day's work as a tailor's assistant in the Montgomery Fair department store and I was on my way home. There was one vacant seat on the Cleveland

Avenue bus, which I took, alongside a man and two women across the aisle. There were still a few vacant seats in the white section in the front, of course. We went to the next stop without being disturbed. On the third, the front seats were occupied and this one man, a white man, was standing. The driver asked us to stand up and let him have those seats, and when none of us moved at his first words, he said, "You all make it light on yourselves and let me have those seats." And the man who was sitting next to the window stood up, and I made room for him to pass by me. The two women across the aisle stood up and moved out.

When the driver saw me still sitting, he asked if I was going to stand up and I said, "No, I'm not."

And he said, "Well, if you don't stand up, I'm going to call the police and have you arrested."

I said, "You may do that."

He did get off the bus, and I still stayed where I was. Two policemen came on the bus. One of the policemen asked me if the bus driver had asked me to stand and I said yes.

He said, "Why don't you stand up?"

And I asked him, "Why do you push us around?"

He said, "I do not know, but the law is the law and you're under arrest."

After being booked by Montgomery police, Mrs. Parks telephoned E. D. Nixon, a Pullman car porter and a leader within the city's black community. Nixon headed the Progressive Democrats, who opposed the all-white Democratic party in Alabama. He also ran the local chapter of A. Philip Randolph's Brotherhood of Sleeping Car Porters and the local branch of the NAACP. Nixon and Parks had worked together closely over the years.

E. D. NIXON

I made bond for Mrs. Parks and got her out. Fred Gray, our local lawyer, who had just come out of law school about a year, was out of the city at the time. So I turned to a white lawyer that I had known for some years, Clifford Durr. I went by, and his wife come runnin' down the stairs with him, so the three of us went down there. Mrs. Parks's husband came up, and we followed them to her house. I talked to her for a couple of hours and I ended up by saying to her point-blank, "Mrs. Parks, with your permission we can break down segregation on the bus with your case. If I wasn't convinced that we can do it, I wouldn't bother you by it."

She asked her mother what she thought about it. She said, "I'll go along with Mr. Nixon."

And her husband, he said, "I'll support it."

Then I went home and I said to my wife, "Baby, we're going to boycott the Montgomery buses."

The next morning at five o'clock I went to calling people. Number one, I called Ralph D. Abernathy. And he said he'd go along with it. Second, I called the late Reverend H. H. Hubbard. And I called Reverend King, number three. Reverend King said, "Brother Nixon, let me think about it awhile and call me back." Well, I could see that. He's a new man in town, he don't know what it's all about. So I said, "Okay." So I went on and called eighteen other people, and I called him back and he said, "Yeah, Brother Nixon, I'll go along with it," and I said, "I'm glad of that, Reverend King, because I talked to eighteen other people, I told them to meet at your church at three o'clock." So then I talked to a Methodist minister. And I asked him to preside in the meeting. I couldn't be there that evening. I had to go to work.

> The Reverend King whom Nixon called was twenty-six-year-old Dr. Martin Luther King, Jr., the minister of Dexter Avenue Baptist Church. Atlanta-born, King had taken the appointment in Montgomery a year earlier, returning south after doctoral studies in theology at Boston University. In Boston he had met Coretta Scott, a native of Marion, Alabama, whom he married in 1953.

CORETTA SCOTT KING

Martin and I were home together when the phone call came in from E. D. Nixon, who was a leader in the community. Mr. Nixon had worked very actively on some of these problems and had called for black people to rise up and do something about them. He felt that this was an opportunity, with these young ministers being in town. Dr. King was at Dexter and Reverend Abernathy was at First Baptist Church, and they were very good friends and working together. He called both of them and suggested that there ought to be a boycott of those buses. They decided that they would call together the ministerial group and some leaders. They had the meeting at Dexter and things didn't go well, but somehow they got through it. The plans called for a one-day boycott of the buses on December the fifth. They sent out leaflets all over town.

> The person behind the mimeographed leaflets was Jo Ann Robinson. A teacher of English at all-black Alabama State College, she was president of the Women's Political Council, an organization of black professional women, mostly teachers, founded in 1946. The WPC had, in fact, met with the city fathers about the bus situation almost two years earlier.

JO ANN ROBINSON

Fred Gray told me Rosa Parks was arrested. Her case would be on Monday. He said to me, "Jo Ann, if you have ever planned to do anything with the council, now is your time." I called all the officers of the three chapters, I called as many of the men who had supported us as I could reach, and I told them that Rosa Parks had been arrested and she would be tried. They said, "You have the plans, put them into operation." We had worked for at least three years getting that thing organized.

The Women's Political Council had begun in 1946, after just dozens of black people had been arrested on the buses for segregation purposes. By 1955, we had members in every elementary, junior high, and senior high school, and in federal, state, and local jobs. Wherever there were more than ten blacks employed, we had a member there. We were prepared to the point that we knew that in a matter of hours, we could corral the whole city.

I didn't go to bed that night. I cut stencils and took them to the college. The fellow who let me in during the night, John Cannon, is dead now, but he was in the business department. We ran off thirty-five thousand copies. After I had talked with every WPC member in the elementary, junior high, and senior high schools to have somebody on the campus during the day so I could deliver them, I took them to school with me in my car. I taught my classes from eight o'clock to ten o'clock. When my ten o'clock class was over, I took two senior students with me and I had the flyers in my car, bundled and ready to be given out. I would drive to the place of dissemination, and a kid would be there to grab them. I was on the campus and off before anybody knew that I was there.

Most of the people got the message, but there were outlying areas that didn't. And one lone black woman, who was so faithful to her white lady, as she called it, went back to work and took one of the circulars to this woman so she would know what the blacks had planned. When the woman got it, she immediately called the media. After that, the television, the radio, the evening newspapers told those persons whom we had not reached that there would be the boycott. So the die was cast.

Monday morning, December the fifth, 1955, I shall never forget because many of us had not gone to bed that night. It was the day of the boycott. We had been up waiting for the first buses to pass to see if any riders were on them. It was a cold morning, cloudy, there was a threat of rain, and we were afraid that if it rained the people would get on the bus. But as the buses began to roll, and there were one or two on some of them, none on some of them, then we began to realize that the people were cooperating and that they were going to stay off the bus that first day. What helped us to keep them off, too, was that the police department had decided that they would put a police on a motorcycle with a white cap who would accompany the buses and any of the blacks who wanted to get on. They would help them to get on without what they called "the goon squads" keeping them from riding. And that helped out the cause because those few blacks who were going to ride were afraid that the police who were following the buses would hurt them. So they didn't ride. As a result, a very negligible number of riders rode that first day.

CORETTA SCOTT KING

The Monday night, December the fifth, there was to be a mass meeting at the Holt Street Baptist Church. In the afternoon of the fifth, there was another meeting of the leadership. And that was the time when they decided to form the Montgomery Improvement Association and to select a spokesperson. When E. D. Nixon proposed Martin's name, Martin said, "Well, I'm not sure I'm the best person for this position, since I'm new in the community, but if no one else is going to serve, I'd be glad to try."

He came home very excited that he had to give the keynote speech that night at the mass meeting. He only had twenty minutes to prepare his speech.

When he got there, he told me, there were so many people, they couldn't get near the church. They almost had to be carried over the shoulders of people, he and Reverend Abernathy, in order to get to the pulpit. He made a speech that really did determine which direction the movement would go, as well as the tone. It was to be a nonviolent movement. He called for Christian love, and to not retaliate with violence. He called for unity, and said he felt that future generations would have to pause and say that there lived a people, a black people, a great people, who injected a new meaning into our civilization.

Because he was new to Montgomery, not many outside his congregation knew much about Dr. King. As he spoke that night, Rosa Parks occupied a seat of honor behind the pulpit.

Among the thousands of bus passengers in the mass meeting was Donie Jones, a forty-seven-year-old mother of six who cooked and cleaned for white families across town at Maxwell Air Force Base.

DONIE JONES

When we had the first meeting, the church was so full, there were so many people. It was like a revival starting. That's what it was like. And Reverend King prayed so that night, I'm telling you the goddam truth, you had to hold people to keep them from gettin' to him. Reverend King was a God-sent man, and he was a good man. He was friendly to the white and the black.

Joe Azbell of the *Montgomery Advertiser* prided himself on sources and friendships within the black community. He had been given the boycott story by E. D. Nixon and had run it Sunday on the front page, adding the newspaper's circulation to the impact of the handbill campaign. On Monday night, the young city editor visited Holt Street Baptist Church to see if the mass protest would continue.

JOE AZBELL

I was the first white person there. The preachers were preaching as I came in, and that audience was so on fire that at last this was going to be lifted off of them. And I recognized that. There was a spirit there that no one could ever capture again in a movie or anything else, because it was so powerful. The next day, in a special column, I wrote that this was the beginning of a flame that would go across America.

The mass meeting voted unanimously to continue, but the boycotters did not call for an end to segregation on the buses, only for a more polite version of Jim Crow. Their three demands were for more courteous treatment by the drivers; first-come, first-served seating, with whites starting from the front of the bus and blacks from the back; and the hiring of black drivers for routes in black areas. The ministers and leaders of the newly formed Montgomery Improvement Association would negotiate for the community.

Gussie Nesbitt, a fifty-three-year-old domestic worker and NAACP member, belonged to the Holt Street Baptist Church. She was among the forty thousand boycotters who refused to ride the buses.

GUSSIE NESBITT

I walked because I wanted everything to be better for us. Before the boycott, we were stuffed in the back of the bus just like cattle. And if we got to a seat, we couldn't sit down in that seat. We had to stand up over that seat. I work hard all day, and I had to stand up all the way home, because I couldn't have a seat on the bus. And if you sit down on the bus, the bus driver would say, "Let me have that seat, nigger." And you'd have to get up. A lot of times that we'd go to the front, he wouldn't let us in the front. He'd take our money at the front, and then before we could come on through the back door he'd drive off and leave us standing there. He done took our money and gone. That's how it was and that's why I walked. I wanted to cooperate with the majority of the people that had on the boycott. I wanted to be one of them that tried to make it better. I didn't want somebody else to make it better for me. I walked. I never attempted to take the bus. Never. I was tired, but I didn't have no desire to get on the bus.

To take the pressure off the walkers, black-owned taxi companies agreed to carry passengers for the regular bus fare of ten cents per person. But the city regulated taxi fares and threatened action against the black drivers. King turned to the Reverend Theodore J. Jemison of Baton Rouge, Louisiana, veteran of a ten-day bus boycott two years before. Jemison advised setting up a volunteer car pool.

Rufus Lewis was the director at a black funeral home and a founder of the Montgomery Improvement Association.

RUFUS LEWIS

I think I was made chairman of the transportation committee because I had access to cars at the funeral home. When we needed cars, I could get a car right then, and go and do what was necessary. But to organize the transportation was a much bigger job. Therefore, we asked for persons who had cars and would voluntarily put them in the transportation pool to let us know. The people who worked in the various outlying areas of the city would register their place of working and the time they'll get off and where they would be for cars to pick them up. And those folks who had cars would register them in the pool, and register the time that they would be usable, and from that we could serve the people.

We had a transportation center downtown, a parking lot. The cars that came from the various sections of the city, they would bring all the people in that area, and there would make the transfer. People would call in, say, "I'm out here on Cloverdale Road in such-and-such a block, and I'll be ready at such-and-such a time." This was being done all through the day. And we would know what time they was to go to be picked up, and where they were. When we bring them to the center, then all of those people who lived in North Montgomery would get into a car and be carried to their place in North Montgomery.

The car pool began on December 13 with some three hundred vehicles. While blacks carpooled or walked, negotiations with the city produced no results. By Christmas, just three weeks into the strike, Montgomery Improvement Association leaders were talking about preparations for a twelve-month bus boycott. By the third week in January, the city announced a "get tough" policy. Car pool drivers would be arrested for overloading their vehicles. Passengers waiting on city streets would be arrested for loitering.

Not all whites in Montgomery opposed the black protest. Among the supporters was Virginia Durr, who had accompanied her husband, Clifford, and E. D. Nixon to bail out their mutual friend Rosa Parks on December 1.

VIRGINIA DURR

The strange thing that happened was a kind of a play between white women and black women, in that none of the white women wanted to lose their help. The mayor of the town issued an order that all the black maids had to be dismissed to break the boycott. Well, their reply was, "Tell the mayor to come and do my work for me, then." So the white women went and got the black women in the car. They said they did it because the bus had broken down, or any excuse you could possibly think of. And then the black women, if you picked one of them up who was walking, they'll tell you that they were walking because the lady that brought them to work, her child was sick. So here was this absurd sort of dance going on. I saw a woman that worked for my mother-in-law, and they were asking her, "Do any of your family take part in the boycott?" She said, "No ma'am, they don't have anything to do with the boycott at all." She said, "My brother-in-law, he has a ride every morning and my sister-in-law, she comes home with somebody else, and they just stay off the bus and don't have nothing to do with it." And so when we got out of the room, I said to Mary, "You know, you had been really the biggest storyteller in the world. You know everybody in your family's involved in the boycott." And she says, "Well, you know, when you have your hand in the lion's mouth, the best thing to do is pat it on the head." I always thought that was a wonderful phrase.

The boycott took off some of the terrible load of guilt that white southerners have lived under for so many generations, such a terrible load of shame and guilt that we won't acknowledge. But you can't do things like that to people and pretend to love them too. It's created such a terrible schizophrenia, because when you're a child, particularly if you have blacks in the house, you have devotion to them. Then when you get grown, people tell you that they're not worthy of you, they're different. And then you're torn apart, because here are the people you've loved and depended on. It's a terrible schizophrenia. That's why I think so much of the literature of the South is full of conflict and madness, because you can't do that to people. You can't do that to children. At least under the Nazis they never even pretended to like the Jews, but in the South it was always that terrible hypocrisy. You know, We love the blacks and we understand them and they love us. Both sides were playing roles which were pure hypocrisy. So I thought the boycott was absolutely marvelous.

White opponents were not retreating. To show where they stood, Mayor W. A. "Tacky" Gayle and the entire Montgomery City Commission joined the white Citizens' Council. Shortly thereafter, on January 26, Dr. King was arrested and briefly jailed on trumped-up speeding charges. Four days later, his house was bombed.

RUFUS LEWIS

When King's house was bombed, it affected the whole black community, because they acted as though *their* house was bombed, and crowds of people gathered right down the street where he lived. Soon as they heard it, it was a mass of people in the streets. That's the way they responded to him. Now, King had to come out to tell them that his wife and child were safe, and they could go home. But they didn't respond to that. They wanted to do something to make amends for someone bombing his house. That was the way they felt. And later on, during the night, they gradually went back home.

The damage wasn't bad, but it was intended to intimidate. It did just the opposite of intimidating. It roused the Negroes in the community to stand up, not to run and hide. They lost in their effort to intimidate. They only gave more courage to King's family and the blacks in the community to stand up with him.

On February 1, Fred Gray and other attorneys for the Montgomery Improvement Association filed suit in U.S. District Court challenging the constitutionality of bus segregation. Later that month, the city made what was afterward viewed as a tactical mistake. It indicted King and more than ninety others for conspiring to conduct a boycott, an action illegal under Alabama law. The trial and subsequent conviction of Martin Luther King made him a national figure and the boycott a major story for newspapers and national television newscasts.

The boycotters were undeterred. Like Rosa Parks, Georgia Gilmore had been arrested on a Montgomery bus.

GEORGIA GILMORE

You know, you can take things, and take things, and take things. We were dealing with a new generation, and this new generation had decided that they just had taken as much as they could. They decided that they wouldn't ride the bus until there be Negro bus drivers and something could be done about the way that the people would be treated. They decided that they was tired of it and they wouldn't do it again no more. Sometime I walked by myself and sometime I walked with different people, and I began to enjoy walking, because for so long I guess that I had had this convenient ride until I had forgot about how well it would be to walk. I walked a mile, maybe two miles, some days. Going to and from. A lot of times some of the young whites would come along and they would say, "Nigger, don't you know it's better to ride the bus than it is to walk?" And we would say, "No, cracker, no. We rather walk."

I was the kind of person who would be fiery. I didn't mind fighting you. I didn't care who you was, white or black, but listening to Reverend King I began to realize some of the things that my mother had taught me in the past. That you think twice before you do some things, because some things you do, you will regret it later.

The maids, the cooks, they were the ones that really and truly kept the bus running. And after the maids and the cooks stopped riding the bus, well, the bus didn't have any need to run.

In order to make the mass meeting and the boycott be a success and keep the car pool running, we decided that the peoples on the south side would get a club and the peoples on the east side would get a club, and so we decided that we wouldn't name the club anything, we'd just say it was the Club from

Nowhere. I had a lot of white people who contributed. The Club from Nowhere was able to collect maybe a hundred and fifty or maybe two hundred dollars or more a week. I collected the money and I'd always report it at the mass meetings, the same day that they would give it to us, so there never was any conflict.

CORETTA SCOTT KING

What happened throughout the mass meetings is that there were songs interspersed. They had an order of service, and so sometimes they would do what you call the long meter. Someone would come and sing, without an instrument at all. Then they would have someone who played the piano or the organ, and they would start, just like they start at the church services. And they would sing the songs and the hymns of the church. "What a Friend We Have in Jesus," "What a Fellowship, What a Joy Divine, Leaning on the Everlasting Arm." They'd sing spirituals like "Lord, I Want to Be a Christian in My Heart," and "Oh, Freedom Over Me, Before I Be a Slave, I'll Be Buried in My Grave, and Go Home to My Lord and Be Free." Or they would sing "Go Down Moses, Way Down in Egypt Land." They would end, of course, after Martin's message, with a song and a prayer, a benediction and prayer. And everyone would go home feeling good and inspired and ready to go back the next morning to a long day of hard work. But I think they could take it a little better, really—even the work that had been difficult became easier. It was something about that experience that gave all of us so much hope and inspiration, and the more we got into it, the more we had the feeling that something could be done about the situation, that we could change it.

JO ANN ROBINSON

Every black person would get a traffic ticket two and three times a week. Everybody had been told, "Drive carefully, don't speed. Stop." One time, I stopped at the corner right above the college where I lived, and a policeman drove up and said, "Well, you stayed there too long that time." And the next day or two I'd come up, "Well, you didn't stay quite long enough this time." There was no need of arguing, we just took them. We just paid them. I got thirty tickets, and there were other people who got I don't know how many. When the buses were finally put out of business, and the bus drivers were out of work, they were employed as policemen. So they had a continuation of income. And many of those policemen would give just hundreds and hundreds of tickets every day to black people who were not violating any traffic laws, but they were doing it to help to raise the salaries they had lost.

I never reached a point during the boycott where I was sorry. I reached a point where I was scared.

One night I was sitting up there in the house. Fred Gray and his wife were with me because I had gotten a lot of threatening telephone calls. Someone threw a brick in my picture window, and the man next door saw them. He didn't know the police had sent them out. He drove down to the police department and reported these men. He had the car's number and everything and said, "I was looking at them when they threw this brick in that woman's window." The police commissioner said to him, "Listen here, boy, do you want to live?" He said, "Yes, sir." He said, "Then you go back home and shut your mouth." The man came back in tears and knocked on my door and said, "Mrs. Robinson, I saw them do it, but there's nothing I can do about it."

About two weeks after they had broken my picture window, I heard a noise on the side where my car was—a new Chrysler parked under the carport—and I went and looked out the window in the dark, and there were two policemen scattering something on top of my car, on the hood of the car. I didn't know what it was. I saw them when they went back and got in their car and drove away. The next morning my car was eaten up with acid. I had holes as large as a dollar, all over the top of the car, all over the hood and the side of the car—that body was just eaten up with those holes. At first I thought it was a terrible tragedy.

I cried, and then I said, "Well, you know, these are beautiful spots." Everybody wanted to know what ate that car up, and I had pleasure in saying, "Well, the *police* threw the acid on it and burned it up, but it became beauty spots."

The boycott continued. By February 1, 1956, downtown merchants claimed losses over $1 million. The bus company estimated it had lost 65 percent of its income. By late April, Montgomery City Lines announced it would no longer enforce segregation. The city countered with a threat to arrest bus drivers who did not abide by Jim Crow laws, and followed through with a court order restraining the company from desegregating its buses.

In June, the U.S. District Court ruled for the Montgomery Improvement Association in its suit against bus segregation. The city of Montgomery immediately appealed to the U.S. Supreme Court. In mid-November, the Supreme Court reaffirmed the district court's decision and declared segregation on Alabama's buses unconstitutional. But implementation was delayed. Meanwhile, the city had obtained a state court injunction against the car pools. People no longer had a choice. They had to walk until the Supreme Court decision took effect. That happened on December 20, 1956.

GEORGIA GILMORE

I was cooking and I was listening to the gospel music when they made the announcement on the radio. They stopped to say that the boycott would be ended and we would have a mass meeting. I was just so excited, I just didn't believe it, so I ran and turned the TV on. Just as I turned the TV on, they were telling that the boycott had ended and that we would have the mass meeting at seven o'clock. And I ran outside, and there's my neighbor and she said yes, and we were so happy. We felt that we had accomplished something that no one ever thought would happen in the city of Montgomery. Being able to ride the bus and sit anyplace on the bus that you desire was something that hadn't ever happened before. And it was a queer feeling. In the beginning you thought, well, maybe it wouldn't last. But still you would give it a try. And we did.

JO ANN ROBINSON

We did meet after the news came through. All of these people who had fought for thirteen months got together to communicate and to rejoice and to share that built-up emotion and all of the other feelings that they had lived with during the past thirteen months. And we just rejoiced together. We had won self-respect. We had won a feeling that we had achieved, had accomplished. We felt that we were somebody, that somebody had to listen to us, that we had forced the white man to give what we knew was a part of our own citizenship. If you have never had the feeling that this is not the other man's country and you are an alien in it, but that this is your country, too, then you don't know what I'm talking about. But it is a hilarious feeling that just goes all over you that makes you feel that America is a great country and we're going to do more to make it greater.

CORETTA SCOTT KING

Martin helped the following to understand that when you have a victory, or when you achieve the goal that you've set, that you take it humbly. He said,When we go back to the buses, we're not going to go back bragging about the fact that we won, but that we try to win those people who were not friendly with us before, because part of the process of nonviolence is to achieve a reconciliation when the struggle has been won. And if you do it nonviolently, it is easier to have that kind of reconciliation take place.

Reconciliation was not to be achieved easily. Although Jim Crow could no longer be practiced legally on the buses of Montgomery, segregation continued at hotels, restaurants, lunch counters, restrooms, water fountains, and in employment. Montgomery remained a thoroughly segregated town.

After the boycott was settled, riders still faced harassment—even if the harassment was no longer sanctioned by law. Buses were shot at; Ralph Abernathy's home and his church were bombed, as well as the homes and churches of several other ministers.

But the Montgomery bus boycott became an example to blacks throughout the South of what could be accomplished with organized protest. Dr. King, who had often traveled through the North during the boycott, raising funds to continue the struggle, had become a nationally known figure. Shortly after the bus boycott, the Reverends Theodore Jemison of Baton Rouge, Ralph Abernathy and Martin Luther King of Montgomery, Fred Shuttlesworth of Birmingham, Joseph Lowery of Mobile, C. K. Steele of Tallahassee, A. L. Davis of New Orleans, Sam Williams of Atlanta, and several other activist ministers created an organization that was to become known as the Southern Christian Leadership Conference. They elected Martin Luther King, Jr., as their president.

3

The Little Rock Crisis, 1957–1958

"I Had Cracked the Wall"

Daisy Bates, president of the Arkansas NAACP and adviscr to thc Little Rock Nine, watches as armed troops prepare to escort the black students to Central High School.

In the world media, the crisis at Little Rock in the fall of 1957 began on September 4, when a long line of Arkansas National Guardsmen with drawn bayonets turned a fifteen-year-old girl away from the entrance to Central High School and motioned her back into an angry mob that threatened to lynch her. It continued when Governor Orval Faubus traveled north for a solemn confrontation with President Dwight D. Eisenhower. And it ended three weeks later with the cool professionalism of paratroopers from the 101st Airborne Division making a show of federal power in a southern state.

But in the memories of the nine black children who lived it, the real battle was fought out of range of news cameras, and it lasted for a full school year. The school itself was an integral part of the drama, a structure so large thousands could riot at one end of its campus and not be heard at the other.

Central was a segregated school, for whites only. In 1954, when the Supreme Court ordered such schools to desegregate, the Little Rock School Board was the first in the South to announce that it would comply, although Superintendent of Schools Virgil Blossom felt that "the people of Little Rock, a vast majority of them, were not in favor of integration as a principle." It was that kind of ambivalence that would help fuel the crisis over the Little Rock schools.

As resistance to desegregation grew among whites, Daisy Bates—editor in chief of the black newspaper the *Arkansas State Press* and president of the Arkansas NAACP—was in the forefront of black community efforts to force integration. When the schools opened in the fall of 1957, her home became the rallying point for the black students involved.

Harry Ashmore was executive editor of the *Little Rock Gazette,* the more moderate of the city's two daily newspapers.

HARRY ASHMORE

The situation in Little Rock in 1957 was that the city school board had accepted the fact that it had to desegregate the schools. The school board had announced shortly after the *Brown* decision in 1954 that they would meet with the black leadership, such as it was, and work out a voluntary desegregation plan. Well, it took them three years to work it out, and it was, to say the least, about as minimal as it could be. For political reasons, they felt they could control it if they started at the top with Central High School, and kept the black high school running and limited severely the number of blacks who would come into Central. And that's what they did. But the plan did have, as far as anybody could measure it, local support within the city school district.

Harold Engstrom, a product of the Little Rock school system, was the youngest member of the Little Rock School Board and its president.

HAROLD ENGSTROM

Little Rock was certainly not a dedicated southern city, like in Alabama or Mississippi. On the other hand, we in Little Rock were not as liberal as some of the other parts of the state—like the northwestern part of the state, which had always been a little more closely tied to Missouri and to the Midwest. Little Rock was in between. We had a moderate, median attitude about things.

When we got the interpretation of what the integration decision was, the key words were "with all deliberate speed." And we could understand that that was a contradiction. We could understand that there probably was a lot of compromise, within the Supreme Court, on the ruling, and that there were no precedents for what "all deliberate speed" was and was not. So we had to come up with our interpretation, and we felt, like anyone in our position, that it would be related to our problems in our community.

As we approached the first day of school in 1957, there were certain anxieties about having everything in order for the plan to start smoothly. The key point was what would the police do, what would the governor do? Or the dissidents, the ones that did not agree with us. The NAACP was not at all satisfied with our construction of what deliberate speed was. The people who were against integration, especially integration on a voluntary basis, were saying it wasn't necessary. So we needed some help from the officials—the state officials, the county, the city—and primarily from Governor Faubus, as to what he told the people, whether it was the law or not. Could we get him to say that regardless of what his opinion was, it was the law of the land? The governor of North Carolina had done that. So we delegated Mr. Virgil Blossom, our superintendent of schools, to make direct communication with Governor Faubus. And it was done on an informal basis, at the mansion, in the afternoon, just visiting one-on-one. And whenever Mr. Blossom could get an appointment, why, they'd continue the discussions. It felt like there'd been a dozen such meetings. And each time Mr. Blossom would come back and report to us. Blossom was confident that in the end Governor Faubus would come down with a statement more or less to the effect that integration was the law of the land. And that the deliberate speed that we had construed was reasonable, and that integrating under a controlled situation, instead of a forced situation, would be satisfactory for our particular community. He wouldn't have to say it for the whole state, just for our particular community. But as the world all knows, it went the other way. The last thirty days [before school was to open], Governor Faubus began to get much stronger pressures from other people, a lot of them outside the community. And he finally came down with his decision that he would not publicly take the position to support us. But we did not get any information that he would forcefully prevent it, either. And we were in a meeting—we met morning, noon, and night—we were in a night meeting and saw on television Faubus calling out the guard and the pictures of the guard being put around Central High. And so we failed in our objective of getting support from the governor.

> Orval Faubus was not considered an avid racist. But for southern politicians, resistance to integration had long been considered a surefire way to get votes. The governor ordered the Arkansas National Guard to prevent the entrance of the nine black children who had volunteered to go to Central High School. These students, aged fourteen to sixteen, were Carlotta Walls, Jefferson Thomas, Elizabeth Eckford, Thelma Mothershed, Melba Pattillo, Terrance Roberts, Gloria Ray, Minniejean Brown, and Ernest Green.

ERNEST GREEN

In early August, the newspapers ran the names of the nine of us who were going to Central. And I'll never forget what happened when I went to work the next day. This young guy, he was about my age, his folks were members of the Jewish country club where I worked as a towel boy, and he came up to me and said, "How could you do it?" I said, "What do you mean, how could I do it?" He said, "You seem like such a nice fellow. Why is it you want to go to Central? Why do you want to destroy our relationship?" For the first time it began to hit me that going there was not going to be as simple as I had thought when I signed up. I was still committed to go, but it made me know at that time that it was going to mean a lot to a lot of people in that city. Particularly to white folks. From then on, events started to cascade.

There hadn't been any trouble expected, given the fact that there had been other schools in Arkansas that had been integrated—Fort Smith, Arkansas, and some others. The buses in Little Rock had been desegregated without any problem. The library was integrated, the medical school, and the law school at the University had admitted some blacks. So there was an expectation that there would be minimal problems, but nothing major that would put Little Rock on the map. The first inclination that I had of it was the night before we were to go to school, the Labor Day Monday night. Orval Faubus came on TV and indicated that he was calling out the National Guard to prevent our entrance into Central because of what he thought were threats to our lives. He was doing it for our own "protection." Even at that time that was his line. He said that the troops would be out in front of the school and they would bar our entrance to Central—for our protection as well as for the protection and tranquility of the city. So it was only that Monday night that I knew that I wasn't going to be able to go to school the next morning.

MELBA PATTILLO BEALS

I wanted to go to Central High School because they had more privileges. They had more equipment, they had five floors of opportunities. I understood education before I understood anything else. From the time I was two, my mother said, "You will go to college. Education is your key to survival," and I understood that. It was a kind of curiosity, not an overwhelming desire to go to this school and integrate this school and change history. Oh no, there was none of that. I just thought it'd be fun to go to this school I ride by every day. I want to know what's in there. I don't necessarily want to be with those people; I assumed that being with those people would be no different than being with people I was already with. My getting into Central High School was somewhat of an accident. I simply raised my hand one day when they said, "Who of you lives in the area of Central High School?" That was two years before, in 1955. And they said, Who had good grades? and I had excellent grades. It was an accident of fate.

In late August, I was sitting in Cincinnati, Ohio, with my mother on a couch, and Walter Cronkite came on television and said that Central High School was going to be integrated in Little Rock, Arkansas, that they were already beginning to have difficulty with the white Citizens' Council and the Ku Klux Klan, and that these were the children who were going, and he mispronounced my name. My mother said, "What did he say?" And that was it, my mother started making phone calls back home. Then we came back to Little Rock and I began to be involved in the preparation that the NAACP was making for us to go to Central High School. But before that I had no real consciousness that I was going to go.

NAACP lawyer Wiley Branton had filed suit on behalf of thirty-three black children and their parents in Little Rock to speed the integration process and to broaden it to include all school grades. In the summer of 1957, he watched the city begin to back away even from the token high school integration it had proposed.

WILEY BRANTON

Under the so-called Blossom Plan of gradual desegregation, nearly three to four hundred black children were supposed to enroll at the high school level in Little Rock beginning in 1957, because of where they lived. But as the summer went by, and Little Rock decided, "Oh my God, this thing that we've been pushing is on us," they started putting up all kinds of barriers. They required black children who wanted to go to white schools to register. Approximately seventy-five black kids signed up to go to Central High School. Then as the opening of school approached, the number went down to just twenty-five. And they made darn sure that they did not include a single one of the plaintiffs who had been selected by the NAACP. Those whom we recognize in history today as the Little Rock Nine were the nine children whose parents, and themselves, decided they were going to go. But you could not have selected, even if we had done it, nine finer youngsters.

We became concerned about the board's watered-down dilution of their own court-approved plan, and we were on the verge of going into federal court seeking to compel the Little Rock School Board to do what it had represented that it was going to do, when Faubus pulled the rug out from under everybody.

From a political standpoint, Faubus was then in his second term of office, and the term at that time was only two years, and only one governor in the history of the state had ever been elected for a third term. Faubus was not a lawyer, he was not much of a businessman, he had nothing to fall back on other than to be governor, hopefully, and when he saw what [Governor] Marvin Griffin was doing in Georgia and some of the other places, somebody told him, "If you can whip up this thing and holler 'Nigger' loud enough, you can be elected for a third term." So much of what he did was due to his own political desires to have something to retain him in office. And it worked.

ORVAL FAUBUS

I don't think anyone can fully understand the complexities of the situation that existed in Arkansas and many places in the nation at the time. But I can say that at the beginning of the Little Rock crisis in Arkansas in 1957, I was on excellent terms with all citizens of the state. And my relations with black citizens were especially good for a number of reasons. I had placed leading black citizens on the Democratic State Central Committee, the policy-making body of the Democratic party in Arkansas, for the first time in the modern history of the state. I had served as governor while all the institutions of higher learning were being integrated. My staff meetings were integrated and this was somewhat unprecedented in Arkansas at that time. We were in the process of equalizing salaries of blacks and whites in state government, which hadn't been done, and in the public schools throughout the state. And I was known as the most understanding man in the history of the state in relation to programs that benefited the poor people.

Many, many of the black people understood when I explained to them that my objective in the Little Rock crisis was to prevent violence and death in the disorders that became imminent. There would have been small, well-organized groups there that morning that school opened, armed to the teeth with repeating rifles and other firearms, determined to halt by extreme means if necessary the entry of the black students into the school. Now, one group—and I have personal knowledge of this and I can even name some of the individuals—unloaded their weapons at a town a short distance east of Little Rock when they learned that the National Guard had been placed on duty. Now, if the guard had not been placed, these determined, armed men would have been there and the well-directed volley from such a well-armed group long skilled in the use of firearms could have left many dead and wounded people. Now, I was not nearly as concerned, which was all in the press, with the protestations of the Mothers' League, a group formed to oppose integration in Little Rock, or the speeches of the segregationist leaders, as with the intentions of the small, well-armed groups who didn't proclaim their intentions publicly and kept them well concealed.

Now, who was most in danger if such occurred? Well, the blacks themselves would be in most danger. But once it started, everyone would be in danger.

> On the first day of school, the school board asked that black students stay away from Central "until this dilemma is legally resolved." Within hours, a federal judge ordered Little Rock to proceed with integration. There would be no breathing space. The black students were to be admitted the next day, September 4.

ERNEST GREEN

The morning that we went to school, Daisy [Bates] had called us all up to meet at her house. And eight of us showed up. Elizabeth had missed the call—she didn't have a phone, I think—so she wasn't there. At the Bates's house, there were a number of ministers that had been involved in trying to lay a groundwork to have the integration of the schools reasonably accepted by the people in the city. So that morning, we went by car to Central. We got to school. We were at one end of the school, Fourteenth Street, and Elizabeth was at the other end, Sixteenth Street, neither group knowing where the other was. Because it's a big place. Two blocks separating it. And we just made a cursory kind of attempt to enter school, but we were denied access. Elizabeth attempted to go through the guards and have the mobs behind her. It had to be the most frightening thing, because she had a crowd of a hundred, two hundred, white people threatening to kill her. She had nobody. I mean, there was not a black face in sight anywhere. Nobody that she could turn to as a friend except this white woman, Grace Lorch, came out of a crowd and guided her through the mob and onto the bus and got her home safely. None of us knew that until we met at Daisy's house. Elizabeth was there; she was in tears. The rest of us had not experienced anything like that.

Craig Rains was a white student at Central, a senior and an officer in the student council.

CRAIG RAINS

There really wasn't anything like Central High anywhere in the country, back in 1957. When the building itself was built in 1928 it was named the most beautiful high school in America. The facilities were unlike anything in this part of the country. We were unique in that we had two or three thousand students going to one school. Central was like a small city.

I don't remember exactly when I first realized that the school was going to be integrated, but I do remember that one of the things that bothered me was that we were being told to do something that we might or might not want to do. I was a student of the Civil War, and Robert E. Lee was, and still is, one of my ideals, and he was a man that believed equally in local government having a closer knowledge and awareness of what the people wanted, as opposed to the federal government. So my first thought was not that we were going to have to go to school with blacks, that didn't bother me, but that we were being told by the federal government to do something and we didn't have any say-so in that.

One of my jobs as an officer in the student council was to raise the flags outside. That gave me an opportunity to see what was going on outside the school, to see the anger. You could cut it with a knife, the tension outside the school, with these people who had come in from other parts of the state, other states. There were license plates from out of state. Very few people from Little Rock were there causing these problems, that I could see. But it was an ugly attitude. Especially when Elizabeth Eckford came to try to get into school. And the crowd began to heckle her, and cheer and shout, as she walked along. I was just dumbfounded.

I had my camera at the time; I ran up and took a picture of it. And then as she went on I thought, Well, I can't believe people would actually be this way to other people. I began to change from being somebody who was a moderate, who, if I had my way, would have said, "Let's don't integrate, because it's the state's right to decide," to someone who felt a real sense of compassion for these students. I also developed a real dislike for the people that were out there that were causing problems. It was very unsettling to me.

The mobs at Central High School became an international story.

On September 14, Governor Faubus met with President Eisenhower at the summer White House in Newport, Rhode Island. Ike was cordial but refused the governor's request to help defy the federal court order to integrate. Instead, the president wanted Faubus to use the Arkansas guard to protect the black students.

The governor had a different plan. A week later, he went on television to announce his removal of the troops from Central. The following Monday, September 23, the guard was gone. So was Faubus, who had left for a governors' conference in Georgia. But the mob had returned.

The nine black students, who still had not taken their classroom seats, were scheduled to enter the school under police escort. James Hicks was assigned by the *Amsterdam News,* the New York-based black weekly, to cover the story.

JAMES HICKS

Three of us black reporters—me, Alex Wilson, Moses Newsome—traveled by car to Central High School. Daisy and the Little Rock Nine were in back of us in another car. When we arrived at the school there was a mob already out in front. From that point on, we didn't see Daisy and them until afterwards, because they didn't come right in the front door, they went into a side door. Pretty soon we were out there on a mall in front of the school and the word got to the crowd outside that the niggers are in the school. And so they said to us, "Did you decoy? Did you lead these people in? You come out here as a decoy and let other people slip into the side of this building?" So I said, "Hell," like that, and the rest of us said this was ridiculous. But now, this was a mob all around us; we were outnumbered I guess about five hundred to one. And so they started getting smart and whatnot. And pretty soon this one man, he was a one-armed man, he put his arm around my neck, and the others started attacking me. But I was able to look up and see that whereas I was being held and my clothes torn off, Alex Wilson was being attacked by somebody who had a brick in his hand. Instead of throwing the brick, 'cause he was too close and he didn't want to, I guess, throw it, he hit Wilson up the side of his head with this brick. I mean a full brick. He picked it up and slapped Wilson like that. Wilson was more than six feet tall, and an ex-marine. He went down like a tree. Newsome, he was mauled. I was mauled. One thing that I remember was that when I bent over because I was in pain, a man was circling me to see if he could get up underneath me. I mean, I'm bent double and he was trying to kick me in my stomach, in the groin. We started running, but there was hardly anywhere to run because they were surrounding us. We saw the FBI, who did nothing, but we finally ran away and got down to the black section of Little Rock.

MELBA PATTILLO BEALS

The first day I was able to enter Central High School, what I felt inside was terrible, wrenching, awful fear. On the car radio I could hear that there was a mob. I knew what a mob meant and I knew that the sounds that came from the crowd were very angry. So we entered the side of the building, very, very fast. Even as we entered there were people running after us, people tripping other people. Once we got into the school, it was very dark; it was like a deep, dark castle. And my eyesight had to adjust to the fact that there were people all around me. We were met by school officials and very quickly dispersed our separate ways. There has never been in my life any stark terror or any fear akin to that.

I'd only been in the school a couple of hours and by that time it was apparent that the mob was just overrunning the school. Policemen were throwing down their badges and the mob was getting past the wooden sawhorses because the police would no longer fight their own in order to protect us. So we were all called into the principal's office, and there was great fear that we would not get out of this building. We were trapped. And I thought, Okay, so I'm going to die here, in school. And I remember thinking back to what I'd been told, to understand the realities of where you are and pray. Even the adults, the school officials, were panicked, feeling like there was no protection. A couple of kids, the black kids, that were with me were crying, and someone made a suggestion that if they allowed the mob to hang one kid, they could then get the rest out. And a gentleman, who I believed to be the police chief, said, "Unh-uh, how are you going to choose? You're going to let them draw straws?" He said, "I'll get them out." And we were taken to the basement of this place. And we were put into two cars, grayish blue Fords. And the man instructed the drivers, he said, "Once you start driving, do not stop." And he told us to put our heads down. This guy revved up his engine and he came up out of the bowels of this building, and as he came up, I could just see hands reaching across this car, I could hear the yelling, I could see guns, and he was told not to stop. "If you hit somebody, you keep rolling, 'cause the kids are dead." And he did just that, and he didn't hit anybody, but he certainly was forceful and aggressive in the way he exited this driveway, because people tried to stop him and he didn't stop. He dropped me off at home. And I remember saying, "Thank you for the ride," and I should've said, "Thank you for my life."

President Eisenhower's chief adviser during the Little Rock crisis was Herbert Brownell, his attorney general.

HERBERT BROWNELL

President Eisenhower was well aware of the political costs of intervening in the Little Rock situation—or not intervening. He knew for one thing that the leadership in the Congress, both the Senate and the House, would be antagonized if he decided to send troops into Little Rock. That, of course, was important to him, because he had worked fairly closely with the leaders in both houses, which were southern oriented. But he knew that not going into Little Rock would mean that he would be charged, and rightfully charged, with not enforcing the Supreme Court decision in the *Brown* case. Upholding the Constitution was his duty as president, so on balance he never had any hesitation once the crisis developed.

After their meeting in Newport on September fourteenth, President Eisenhower felt let down when Governor Faubus went back to Arkansas and decided against allowing the black children to enter the high school. And the southern governors who had consulted with President Eisenhower to work for a peaceful solution at Little Rock felt let down, and they supported President Eisenhower when he took a firm position.

The FBI was on the spot at Little Rock when the crisis occurred and black children were not allowed to enter the high school there. They gave us hourly reports on what was happening. We felt that it was necessary for local officials to appeal to Washington for assistance before the federal government would send in troops. The mayor of Little Rock did appeal to Washington on the ground that the rioting and the threatened rioting there meant that local law enforcement authorities could not handle the situation. That gave the legal authority which, under the Supreme Court cases, we thought was necessary to have. And that's when the president acted swiftly and surely by sending the troops up the main street of Little Rock and arriving on the scene before anyone realized it. The crisis was solved peaceably without any deaths or any casualties.

He federalized the National Guard to be sure that they were directly under his command. And he had selected the 101st Airborne Division, first, because he had known them and their capabilities when he was commander in chief during World War II and, second, because they were close by and they could be transported quickly and efficiently.

We felt that this was the test case that had to be made in order to dramatize to everyone that when it came to a showdown the federal government was supreme in this area. The situation was as close as you could get to an irreconcilable difference between the North and the South. There'd been nothing like it since the Civil War.

With the 101st Airborne protecting them, the Little Rock Nine went to school on September 25.

ERNEST GREEN

There was more military hardware than I'd ever seen. We went to school in an army station wagon, and I think if anything stays on my mind as long as I live, this does. The colonel in charge of the detail escorting us to school was from South Carolina. And that seemed, from what I knew about southerners, so incongruous—that this guy with this deep southern accent was going to provide us with our protection. When we got into the station wagon, the convoy that went from Mrs. Bates's house to the school had a jeep in front, a jeep behind, they both had machine gun mounts, and there were soldiers with rifles. Then when we got to the front of the school, the whole school was ringed with paratroopers and helicopters hovering around, and we marched up the steps with this circle of soldiers with bayonets drawn. Walking up the steps that day was probably one of the biggest feelings I've ever had. I figured I had finally cracked it.

MELBA PATTILLO BEALS

I went in not through the side doors, but up the front stairs, and there was a feeling of pride and hope that yes, this is the United States; yes, there is a reason I salute the flag; and it's going to be okay.

The troops were wonderful. There was some fear that they were dating the girls in high school, but I don't care what they were doing: they were wonderful, they were disciplined, they were attentive, they were caring. They didn't baby us, but they were there. So for the first time I began to feel like there is this slight buffer zone between me and this hell on the other side of this wall. They couldn't be with us everywhere. They couldn't be with us, for example, in the ladies' bathroom, they couldn't be with us in gym. We'd be showering in gym and someone would turn your shower into scalding. You'd be walking out to the volleyball court and someone would break a bottle and trip you on the bottle. I have scars on my right knee from that. After a while, I started saying to myself, Am I less than human? Why did they do this to me? What's wrong with me? And so you go through stages even as a child. First you're in pain, then you're angry, then you try to fight back, and then you just don't care. You just, you can't care;

you hope you do die. You hope that there's an end. And then you just mellow out and you just realize that survival is day to day and you start to grasp your own spirit, you start to grasp the depth of the human spirit and you start to understand your own ability to cope no matter what. That is the greatest lesson I learned.

THELMA MOTHERSHED WAIR

We would meet at Daisy Bates's house every morning, then we'd go back there in the evening for our parents to pick us up. That's when we gained our support from each other—who had done what and what had happened to who and this sort of thing.

Most of the faculty were helpful, but there were a few that weren't. My homeroom teacher was kind of strange. She just did little strange things. I remember that when we were absent, we'd have to go to the office and get a readmittance slip. When I would come in to give her my readmittance slip, she wouldn't take it. So I would just put it down on the desk, and then she would sign it and put it in the book and slide it back across to me. Now, that was really strange. I guess she had to do something to show her class that she wasn't particularly happy about me being in there. And then she—well, they set us in alphabetical order and in the row where I was, there were about two seats behind me—and she started the next person at the front seat in the next row, because she knew nobody wanted to sit behind me. She just kept those two chairs empty. So she did little strange, subtle things—subtle as a ton of bricks.

ERNEST GREEN

For a couple of weeks there had been a number of white kids following us, continuously calling us niggers. "Nigger, nigger, nigger," one right after the other. Minniejean Brown was in the lunch line with me. I was in front of Minnie, and there was this white kid, a fellow who was much shorter than Minnie. Minnie was about five foot ten. This fellow couldn't have been more than five five, five four. He reminded me of a small dog, yelping at somebody's leg. Minnie had just picked up her chili, out of this line. The help in the whole cafeteria was black, all black. And before I could even say, "Minnie, why don't you tell him to shut up," Minnie had taken this chili, dumped it on this dude's head. There was just absolute silence in the place. And then the help, all black, broke into applause. And the other white kids there didn't know what to do. I mean it was the first time that anybody, I'm sure, had seen somebody black retaliate in that sense. It was a good feeling to see that happen, to be able to let them know that we were capable of taking care of ourselves. With that the school board suspended Minnie. Part of it was the attitude at that time, which was somehow we were supposed to be so stoic that we weren't to retaliate to any of this. Finally, after the suspension, they moved to remove her from school, and Minnie went to school in New York, finished up the other semester outside of Little Rock.

Marcia Webb Lecky was secretary of the senior class.

MARCIA WEBB LECKY

When I think of my senior year at Central, most of my memories are the real fun ones—homecoming, cheerleading, research papers, the dances, the people you dated, slumber parties, all the fun things that seventeen-year-olds should be doing. And even though we were making headlines, it was a fun year.

You would see the soldiers in the hall. You would see them at cheerleader practice, or gym, or football games, but they never bothered us, and we thought they were there because Faubus was causing problems, and I think most of us were glad when the resolution came with President Eisenhower taking charge.

I didn't see much of the black kids. If you didn't have any classes with any of the nine, one really didn't know if they were in the building or not. And the school is so large. Occasionally I would see Ernie Green. He is the only one of the Little Rock Nine who was a senior, and in my class, and the one that I knew by name. I would say, "Hi, Ernie," but that was it. One didn't have time to stand around the hall and talk to anyone. But it would be the smile, and the "Hi." Now I can see it from their perspective, not knowing what was going on in the minds of the other students, and yet we did not go enough out of our way to seek them out. I'm sure those students had some teachers that they felt comfortable with, and I know that Mrs. Bates offered a lot of support for them, but there were a lot of us who could have helped, and I wish we had.

ERNEST GREEN

Graduation was the end of May. I had been there nine months and had thought that all I needed to do was to graduate, just get out of there, so that it would be impossible for white people to say that nobody black had ever graduated from Central High School. I was having difficulty with one course, it was a physics course, and almost up to the last minute I didn't know whether I was going to complete it successfully so that I would get out of there. But as things were, I got a fairly decent grade out of it.

The interesting thing about graduation was, being the only senior, I'd given up all the graduation activity that had gone on in the black high school—the school play and the prom and all of those kinds of things. Sometimes because of not having that activity, I would really feel isolated, because I wasn't going to Central High School's prom, and I wasn't going to be invited to be in the school play at Central. But all of the black students at Horace Mann, which was the school that I would have graduated from, invited me to all the activities, included me in all of it, really made me feel a super part of it. So that I had the best of both worlds. I had cracked this white institution and still had all of my friends who were supersupportive of what I was trying to do.

At the graduation ceremony, one of the guests was Martin Luther King. He was speaking in Pine Bluff, Arkansas, at the black college there. And he came up to sit with my mother and Mrs. Bates and a couple of other friends in the audience. I figured all I had to do was walk across that big huge stage, which looked the length of a football field. I'm sure it was very small, but that night before I had to walk up and receive my diploma, it looked very imposing. I kept telling myself I just can't trip, with all those cameras watching me. But I knew that once I got as far as that principal and received that diploma, that I had cracked the wall.

There were a lot of claps for the students. They talked about who had received scholarships, who was an honor student, and all that as they called the names off. When they called my name there was nothing, just the name, and there was this eerie silence. Nobody clapped. But I figured they didn't have to. Because after

I got that diploma, that was it. I had accomplished what I had come there for.

In September 1958, three months after the first black student graduated from Central High, Orval Faubus closed all the public high schools in Little Rock; they were not to reopen until August 12, 1959, after the U.S. Supreme Court ruled the closing unconstitutional and called the action to prevent integration an "evasive scheme."

Not all Americans agreed with the Court's position. In December 1958, Faubus was named one of the ten most admired men in the world, according to a Gallup poll. Others on the list were President Eisenhower, Sir Winston Churchill, Dr. Albert Schweitzer, General Douglas MacArthur, and Dr. Jonas Salk.

4

Student Sit-ins in Nashville, 1960

"A Badge of Honor"

On February 1, 1960, the student sit-ins exploded out of the American South, capturing the imagination of an entire generation of young people.

There had been sit-ins before: at lunch counters and restaurants in Chicago by members of the Congress of Racial Equality (CORE) in 1943; in St. Louis and Baltimore in 1949 and 1953; and in some sixteen southern and border cities in the late 1950s as the push for civil rights began to heat up. The media and the nation had not paid much attention. But in 1960, the gathering energy of the movement forced the sit-ins into the American consciousness. For several years, representatives of CORE and the Fellowship of Reconciliation, NAACP youth organizers, and ministers from the Southern Christian Leadership Conference (SCLC) had been training young people in nonviolent direct action.

One of the cities where nonviolence training took place was Nashville, Tennessee. Nashville was considered a moderate southern city in its racial attitudes. But the pattern of local segregation was marked by inconsistency. On the positive side, the parochial and public schools were integrated. Blacks served on the board of education, the city council, and the police force. Blacks and whites sat side by side on desegregated city buses. But libraries, theaters, hotels, and restaurants remained segregated. As a contemporary report prepared for the Nashville Community Relations Conference indicated, "In downtown Nashville Negroes have no adequate facilities for eating. Welcomed as customers for merchandise, they are refused service as customers for food."

In 1959, thirty-one-year-old James Lawson was one of the few black theology students at Vanderbilt University.

JAMES LAWSON

In early 1959 we decided that we needed to begin a movement to desegregate downtown Nashville. We planned a series of workshops on nonviolence to begin to start that process. Through those workshops in the fall came adults in the community and students from Tennessee State and American Baptist Theological Seminary and Fisk University.

We met weekly for much of September, October, November. We tried to give people a fairly good view of nonviolence, and we mixed that with role-playing of various kinds. We also added to it the first series of forays into downtown to test which restaurants we would decide to work on. In November, everyone who attended the workshop was given the experience of going to a Nashville restaurant and sitting in. These were very small groups, no more than usually four people. And they were not supposed to be arrested. They were supposed to sit, ask for service, and if it did not come—which of course it didn't—then talk with customers around them, and talk with the waiter, waitresses, see what their attitudes were, and then ask to see the manager or somebody in authority and talk with them about the policy of the place.

Why use nonviolence? The most practical reason is that we're trying to create a more just society. You cannot do it if you exaggerate the animosities. Martin King used to say, "If you use the law 'An eye for an eye, a tooth for a tooth,' then you end up with everybody blind and toothless," which is right. So from a practical point of view, you don't want to blow up Nashville downtown, you simply want to open it up so that everybody has a chance to participate in it as people, fully, without any kind of reservations caused by creed, color, class, sex, anything else. So going past any theoretical notions for nonviolence, which many of us hold, is the practical issue. How do you achieve a community where people are people, where they have a fair chance?

Diane Nash, a Chicagoan, was a student at Nashville's Fisk University.

DIANE NASH

I was really feeling stifled that fall. My goodness, I came to college to grow and expand, and here I am shut in. In Chicago, I had had access, at least, to public accommodations, lunch counters and what have you. So my response was, "Who's trying to change these things?" Paul LaPrad, a white Fisk student, told me about the nonviolent workshops that Jim Lawson was conducting. They were taking place a couple of blocks off campus.

Jim Lawson was a very interesting person. He had been to India and studied the movement of Mohandas Gandhi. He also had been a conscientious objector and had refused to fight in the Korean War. He conducted weekly workshops, where we would do things like pretend we were sitting in at lunch counters. We would practice things such as how to protect your head from a beating and how to protect each other. If one person was taking a severe beating, we would practice other people putting their bodies in between that person and the violence, so that the violence could be more distributed and hopefully no one would get seriously injured. We would practice not striking back if someone struck us.

As 1959 ended, students from four black educational institutions in Nashville—Fisk, Meharry Medical College, Tennessee State University, and American Baptist Theological Seminary—were poised to confront the city about the morality of segregation. Nashville was not only an educational center with thirteen colleges and universities, it was also headquarters for several Protestant denominations and publishing companies. For a city alternately billed as the Protestant Vatican and the "buckle of the Bible Belt," the impending moral confrontation would no doubt occasion special soul-searching. While Nashville prepared, Greensboro, North Carolina, leaped ahead. On February 1, 1960, four students from North Carolina Agricultural and Technical College sat down at a lunch counter in Woolworth's and refused to leave when denied service.

Joe McNeil was one of the four students sitting in in Greensboro. All had been members of the NAACP Youth Council.

JOE MCNEIL

I was particularly inspired by the people in Little Rock. I think if we had to have done that in the area where I was growing up at the time, I would have volunteered to participate. I was really impressed with the courage that those kids had and the leadership they displayed. I think children my age in general felt that way. We knew what they were going through was not easy, but somehow many of us wanted to make a contribution and be a part of something like that.

In 1959 I was fortunate enough to get an academic scholarship to A and T. Junior Blair and I were roommates. Frank McCain lived down the hall from us. David Richmond lived in the city. We were all in the same algebra class and we gravitated to each other and became friends. We would get together and discuss current events, political events, things that affected us—pretty much as college kids do today. Bull sessions. The question became, What do we do and to whom do we do it against? There were many conspicuous forms that we could have chosen, but Woolworth seemed logical because it was national in scope and somehow we had hoped to get sympathies from without as well as from within.

I don't think there's any specific reason why that particular day was chosen. I had talked to a local merchant [Ralph Johns] who was extremely helpful to us in getting things rolling, in giving us some ideas. We had played over in our minds possible scenarios, and to the best of our abilities we had determined how we were gonna conduct ourselves given those scenarios. But we did walk in that day—I guess it was about four-thirty—and we sat at a lunch counter where blacks never sat before. And people started to look at us. The help, many of whom were black, looked at us in disbelief too. They were concerned about our safety. We asked for service, and we were denied, and we expected to be denied. We asked why couldn't we be served, and obviously we weren't given a reasonable answer and it was our intent to sit there until they decided to serve us. We had planned to come back the following day and to repeat that scenario. Others found out what we had done, because the press became aware of what was happening. So the next day when we decided to go down again, I think we went down with fifteen, and the third day it was probably a hundred and fifty, and then it probably mushroomed up to a thousand or so, and then it spread to another city. All rather spontaneously, of course, and before long, I guess it was probably in fifteen or twenty cities, and that's when we had our thing going.

> In the first week, sit-ins flared in neighboring Durham and Winston-Salem. Within two weeks, as word passed from campus to campus, the wave of nonviolent protest spread to communities in South Carolina, Virginia, and Florida. On February 13, it was Nashville's turn. One of the Lawson-trained leaders was John Lewis, a twenty-year-old black student who had left his family's farm near Troy, Alabama, to attend American Baptist Theological Seminary.

JOHN LEWIS

We had on that first day over five hundred students in front of Fisk University chapel, to be transported downtown to the First Baptist Church, to be organized into small groups to go down to sit in at the lunch counters.

We went into the five-and-tens—Woolworth, Kresge's, McClellan's—because these stores were known all across the South and for the most part all across the country. We took our seats in a very orderly, peaceful fashion. The students were dressed like they were on the way to church or going to a big social affair. They had their books, and we stayed there at the lunch counter, studying and preparing our homework, because we were denied service. The managers ordered that the lunch counters be closed, that the restaurants be closed, and we'd just sit there, all day long.

DIANE NASH

The sit-ins were really highly charged, emotionally. In our nonviolent workshops, we had decided to be respectful of the opposition, and try to keep issues geared towards desegregation, not get sidetracked. The first sit-in we had was really funny, because the waitresses were nervous. They must have dropped two thousand dollars' worth of dishes that day. It was almost a cartoon. One in particular, she was so nervous, she picked up dishes and she dropped one, and she'd pick up another one, and she'd drop it. It was really funny, and we were sitting there trying not to laugh, because we thought that laughing would be insulting and we didn't want to create that kind of atmosphere. At the same time we were scared to death.

JOHN LEWIS

The first day nothing in terms of violence or disorder happened. This continued for a few more days and it continued day in and day out. Finally, on Saturday, February twenty-seventh, when we had about a hundred students prepared to go down—it was a very beautiful day in Nashville—we got a call from a local white minister who had been a real supporter of the movement. He said that if we go down on this particular day, he understood that the police would stand to the side and let a group of white hoodlums and thugs come in and beat people up, and then we would be arrested. We made a decision to go, and we all went to the same store. It was a Woolworth in the heart of the downtown area, and we occupied every seat at the lunch counter, every seat in the restaurant, and it did happen. A group of young white men came in and they started pulling and beating primarily the young women. They put lighted cigarettes down their backs, in their hair, and they were really beating people. In a short time police officials came in and placed all of us under arrest, and not a single member of the white group, the people that were opposing our sit-in, was arrested.

That was the first time that I was arrested. Growing up in the rural South, you learned it was not the thing to do. To go to jail was to bring shame and disgrace on the family. But for me it was like being involved in a holy crusade, it became a badge of honor. I think it was in keeping with what we had been taught in the workshops, so I felt very good, in the sense of righteous indignation, about being arrested, but at the same time I felt the commitment and dedication on the part of the students.

DIANE NASH

After we had started sitting in, we were surprised and delighted to hear reports of other cities joining in the sit-ins. And I think we started feeling the power of the idea whose time had come.

Before we did the things that we did, we had no inkling that the movement would become as widespread as it did. I can remember being in the dorm any number of times and hearing the newscasts, that Orangeburg had demonstrations, or Knoxville, or other towns. And we were really excited. We'd applaud, and say yea. When you are that age, you don't feel powerful. I remember realizing that with what we were doing, trying to abolish segregation, we were coming up against governors, judges, politicians, businessmen, and I remember thinking, I'm only twenty-two years old, what do I know, what am I doing? And I felt very vulnerable. So when we heard these newscasts, that other cities had demonstrations, it really helped. Because there were more of us. And it was very important.

The movement had a way of reaching inside you and bringing out things that even you didn't know were there. Such as courage. When it was time to go to jail, I was much too busy to be afraid.

C. T. Vivian was an adviser to the students. He had been involved, with Jim Lawson and others, in organizing the workshops. A minister, Vivian had graduated from American Baptist Theological Seminary two years before, and worked as an editor at a black religious publishing house.

C. T. VIVIAN

Now, many of the parents were afraid, thought that their children's lives would be destroyed forever because of what would be on their record. Many telephone calls were coming from everywhere. Pressure was on the college presidents and the vice presidents and staff. But students made up their minds what they were going to do. It was a great point of their own development.

The police knew that they represented the city, the merchants, the thugs, more than they represented us. Yet here is the importance of nonviolence, that they did not want to appear too demanding, too brutal. They wanted to stop us, but when we would not stop, then they had to begin to work on the thugs, because the thugs will bring out the worst of segregation in a racist society, so that it even shames the people who are themselves racists and who keep the system going. They were caught in that dilemma and they were waiting for their orders from the businessmen.

The city fathers themselves had to see their relationship to the businessmen. Businessmen saw their relationship to profits. And the black people were beginning to respond all over, "What to do?" So the boycotts start, to force the businessmen to deal with the issue. As one of the businessmen put it, nobody came downtown. Blacks wouldn't come downtown, whites were afraid to come downtown, so the only people downtown were green people and there weren't many of them, all right? As a result, the businessmen began to lose money and they began to ask for a change. Remember, though, we were meeting with them, we were talking with them, trying to get them to understand, think for themselves, or react without our presence. We were constantly negotiating with them.

Leo Lillard, a Nashville native attending Tennessee State University, had become involved in the sit-ins as soon as they started.

LEO LILLARD

It was no longer just the students, it was clear that the town had declared war on racism, and we had all the troops in every little nook and cranny in Nashville. The boycott said, Stay out of town. And Nashville as a whole, black and white, did stay out of town. The white folks didn't go downtown because of the potential violence. There were some black folks who went to downtown to try and break the boycott; we had to send some educating committees to downtown to convince them that that was not the thing to do. We didn't hurt them, but we did kind of snatch their bags and tear things away from their arms and let them fall on the ground and say, "Stay out of town." And of course the word got around pretty quick you don't go downtown anymore.

All the intellectuals or people who put the sit-ins together were from out of town. Once the sit-ins started, it was my chance to get back at Nashville, it was my chance to not have any adult lie to me about what the problem was, it was my chance to make the problem different, to correct it. Being a Nashvillian, I felt I had *clear* obligations, clear reasons to put my body on the line, put my mind on the line. It appeared to me that if I was going to pursue an engineering career in Nashville, pursue a degree at TSU, then it was also equally important to spend as much time as I could involved with the movement in Nashville. It was basically our movement, it was a city movement, even though students from out of town started it. It was clear to me that the people who were going to be the leaders of Nashville had to be born and bred here. The people who were going to take over the reins after the students left—and they would surely leave—had to come from Nashville, and I felt that that's where I belonged.

Most of the people who were on the line were young—nineteen, twenty, twenty-one. Some high school students were there. It was clear that we had little to lose, we had no jobs to lose, we had no houses to lose, we had no cars to lose. Of course, in those days, credit and the ability to buy things was just becoming accessible to some black folks. A lot of black folks treasured those things. We knew that the adults were not going to get that much involved, so we had to do things and escalate the whole conflict to the point where they had no choice.

By mid-April, seventy-eight cities and towns in southern and border states had become part of the sit-in phenomenon. Fifty thousand black students and white sympathizers had participated. Two thousand had been arrested. In northern cities, demonstrators had thrown up picket lines around five-and-tens operated by chains that were discriminating in the South.

On the weekend of April 16, 1960, one hundred twenty student leaders met at Shaw University in Raleigh, North Carolina. The conference had been conceived and organized by the SCLC's acting executive director, Ella Baker, one of the few women in that organization's leadership. At forty-five, Baker was a seasoned civil rights activist who, in the 1940s, had traveled throughout the South organizing NAACP chapters.

DIANE NASH

I remember receiving the invitation to attend the conference that would bring together student leadership from many campuses where sit-ins were going on. Ella Baker saw how important it was to recognize the fact that the students should set the goals and directions and maintain control of the student movement. I never had to worry about where Ella Baker was coming from. She would speak her mind honestly, and I turned to her frequently, because she could emotionally pick me back up and dust me off. She would say things like, "Well, so-and-so is concerned about his fund-raising, maybe that's why he took that position," and it would make things click and fall into place. She was just tremendously helpful. I think she was constantly aware that the differences that the students had were probably not as important as the similarities that we had, in terms of what we were trying to do. So, very often, she was the person who was able to make us see, and work together. I think her participation as a person some years older than we were could really serve as a model of how older people can give energy and help to younger people, and at the same time not take over and tell them what to do. She really strengthened us as individuals and she also strengthened our organization.

Marion Barry, a graduate student in chemistry at Fisk University, attended the Raleigh conference.

Marion Barry

Dr. King was there, also a number of people we hadn't seen, just heard about, people in Birmingham and in Montgomery and North Carolina and South Carolina who had gone through hell—probably much more than we had gone through in terms of the white folks and the jails. It was just good to come together. Dr. King was trying to convince students they ought to become part of SCLC. The students decided they didn't necessarily want to make that move, so a lot of caucusing was going on among various delegations. The Nashville group became very close to the Atlanta group—I guess there were a lot of similarities in Atlanta.

Then there was the whole question of nonviolent direct action, what that meant. And Jim Lawson was the foremost proponent of the philosophical construct around nonviolence. Most of us were doing it as a tactic. I never felt any real deep philosophical sense that we ought to do it this way except that was the best way to do it at the time, and so I could argue that and feel comfortable with it.

Julian Bond was in his junior year at Morehouse College in Atlanta when his friend Lonnie King showed him a newspaper article about the Greensboro sit-ins. That same day King and Bond called a meeting on the Morehouse campus. The first Atlanta sit-in took place on March 15 and involved Bond and several companions who later attended the Raleigh conference.

JULIAN BOND

Somehow or other we knew that Ella Baker had extended the invitation from [Martin Luther] King to come to this meeting. I remember her presence at Raleigh. Very regal. Always had a business suit that she'd wear—a long skirt, and it had a long jacket. She was sort of matronly in a not-dominating way. Like "Don't do that, be careful, don't do that." In a very nice way, but very much your mom.

I remember she kept pushing, and first I remember her speech "More Than a Hamburger." And I can remember it being an eye-opener to me, because I really had not thought about much more than a hamburger. We were doing lunch counter sit-ins, we wanted to integrate the lunch counters, and that was the deal. I knew that racial problems extended far beyond lunch counters. But I didn't see *us* doing anything like that, till she mentioned it there. So it was a real eye-opener, a real big step, a big leap for me. And I think it was for a lot of the other people too.

I can remember her warning against entanglement with adults. Not political entanglements, not against leftists or anything like that. But just to keep our movement pure. That we had started it, we had carried it forward, and we could carry it on by ourselves. And she didn't say that directly; you got the feeling that that's what she meant. She didn't say, "Don't let Martin Luther King tell you what to do," but you got the real feeling that that's what she meant. You know, "He's a good man and so on, but don't let him tell you what to do."

And then of course Lawson spoke and we had this real sense of friendly rivalry between Lawson and King. Not any personal animosity between them, but Lawson was like the bad younger brother pushing King to do more, to be more militant, to extend nonviolence—just to do more. I remember his as being a thunderous, militant speech with a much more ambitious idea of what nonviolence could do than I had ever heard before. He envisioned a militant nonviolence, an aggressive nonviolence. You didn't have to wait for the evil to come to you, you could go to the evil.

I remember how well dressed a lot of the people were. And I don't mean expensively dressed. Not all, but many of the men in sort of the preacher's uniform, dark suits, knee-high black socks, black shoes. Very much in the image of the young up-to-date minister about town. And I remember how mature all these young people seemed in comparison to the run-of-the-mill student, in comparison with my fellow students at Morehouse, the people that I went to school with, and at Spelman, how mature they seemed. Not because they were older, but because they had these leadership qualities, these abilities to command attention in a respectful way. I was impressed with their maturity, their command of themselves.

At Raleigh, as you began to meet these people from all these various different sit-in places and you said, "Oh yeah, I remember reading about what you all did there," the idea began to seep in that we might be real hell-on-wheels in Atlanta, but if we can coordinate what we're doing in Atlanta with what they're doing here, we would really be tough stuff. So if we had an informational connection and a coordinational connection, we'd be so much better off than we are today. This feeling built that we needed some kind of structure, some kind of network that would connect Raleigh with Atlanta with Nashville, and so forth and so on.

That weekend the students formed an organization that was soon to be named the Student Nonviolent Coordinating Committee (SNCC).

Back in Nashville, on April 19, the home of Z. Alexander Looby, a prominent black attorney and politician who had represented the arrested students, was destroyed by dynamite. Miraculously, Looby and his wife survived the blast with only minor injuries, but the black community had had enough. The attack had occurred in the early morning. By noon, students and members of the community were marching on City Hall.

LEO LILLARD

The morning that Looby's house was bombed, it was clear that the racists in the town were out to get a symbol of the movement. They couldn't get a student because they had already beaten us up. That wouldn't work, so they decided to attack an adult symbol. This worked to the benefit of the movement, because once you attack Looby—a pillar of the community, a councilman, a professional—what that did was send a signal to Nashville as a whole that no longer is it going to be a student-only movement. That the adults—professors, workers, teachers, all the spectrum—had to make some physical presence shown on that march. I think the march following Looby's house bombing was very gratifying, because not only was it spontaneous, but it had quantity for a change. Oftentimes, we would have to cajole people to come down, convince them, but in this case the march didn't need that.

C. T. VIVIAN

The march on April nineteenth was the first big march of the movement. It was what, in many ways, we'd been leading to without knowing it. We began at Tennessee A and I [Agricultural and Industrial] at the city limits. Right after the lunch hour, people began to gather, and we began to march down Jefferson, the main street of black Nashville. When we got to Eighteenth and Jefferson, Fisk University students joined us. They were waiting and they fell right in behind. The next block was Seventeenth and Jefferson, and students from Pearl High School joined in behind that. People came out of their houses to join us and then cars began joining us, moving very slowly so they could be with us. We filled Jefferson Avenue: it's a long, long way down Jefferson. After a while there was a certain bit of singing, and as we came closer to town, it was merely the silence of the feet. We walked by a place where there were workers out for the noon hour, white workers, and they had never seen anything like this. Here was all of four thousand people marching down the street, and all you could hear was our feet as we silently moved, and they didn't know what to do. They moved back up against the wall and they simply stood against the wall, just looking. There was a fear there, there was an awe there. They knew that this was not to be stopped, this was not to be played with or to be joked with. We marched on and started up the steps at City Hall, and we gathered on the plaza that was a part of City Hall itself. The mayor knew now that he would have to speak to us.

The leadership came up front, and we didn't know how it was going to come out, but the mayor was standing there and I gave him a short speech. The idea was that we have come here before you because we are outraged that this bombing could happen in our city. We are tired of the fact that segregation and racism has ruled our lives, and we do not feel it's necessary either for us to live this way or for you to be oppressors of this sort.

Following that, Diane Nash read a statement. It was a challenge to the mayor as to what he was going to do, and the mayor was listening. I remember very clearly that I felt that the mayor wanted to answer with the normal political talk. But then the questions came: Are you against the segregation? Are you for what is happening in this city? He looked out across the expanse of four thousand people and he said, "No, no, I'm not for it. I do not think racism is right," or words to the same effect. We then asked him the question, Would he work to end it? And he said yes, he would.

DIANE NASH

C. T. Vivian presented our position to Mayor Ben West on the steps of City Hall. He was an eloquent spokesperson. His fire was very much in evidence. He has a certain commitment in his personality that really pervades the things he does and says, and that was his role that day.

Then I confronted Mayor West with what his feelings were as a man, as a person. I was particularly interested in that, as opposed to his just being a mayor. I have a lot of respect for the way he responded. He didn't have to respond the way he did. He said that he felt it was wrong for citizens of Nashville to be discriminated against at the lunch counters solely on the basis of the color of their skin. That was the turning point. The Nashville newspaper reported his statement in the headlines the next day, and it was one more step towards desegregating the lunch counters. That day was very important. One of the things that we had learned from Gandhi's movement was to turn the energy of violence that was perpetrated against us into advantage. So when attorney Looby's house was bombed, that was used as a catalyst to draw many thousands of people to express their opposition to segregation.

Bernie Schweid was a white bookstore owner sympathetic to the sit-in movement.

BERNIE SCHWEID

When Mayor Ben West said, "Well, in my heart, I have to say I think it's wrong," that seemed to be kind of a turning point. I think the merchants were afraid to move on their own, were almost looking for an excuse to say, "Well, if that's what the mayor thinks, then maybe we ought to go ahead." And they decided to go ahead and start integrating some of the lunch counters. And the skies didn't fall in when that happened.

Three weeks later, on May 10, six Nashville lunch counters that had been sit-in targets began serving blacks. But this was just a beginning; further demonstrations had to be conducted before theaters, hotels, and restaurants in Nashville were desegregated.

Across the South, sit-ins took place in more than a hundred cities in 1960. The rallying cry became "Jail, no bail." The movement spearheaded by black students in the South ushered in a decade of activism on the part of the country's young people, both black and white.

Postscript: "A Suitcase Full of Votes"

Martin Luther King had moved back to his native Atlanta early in 1960, taking up a position as co-pastor to his father at Ebenezer Baptist Church. This move also enabled him to devote more time to his job as president of the Southern Christian Leadership Conference. On October 19, Atlanta students persuaded King to participate in a department store restaurant sit-in they had organized. He and thirty-five other people were arrested. King was sentenced the following week to four months on a Georgia road gang. The severity of the sentence shocked many people across the nation, including Harris Wofford, a white lawyer who was working in the small civil rights section of Massachusetts senator John F. Kennedy's campaign for the presidency. Wofford had known King since the bus boycott victory in Montgomery, and had been in contact with him about supporting Democrat Kennedy against the Republican candidate, Vice President Richard Nixon.

HARRIS WOFFORD

King didn't want to be arrested in Atlanta at that time. He really thought that it would be better not to have a racial crisis during the election campaign. He had wanted to be meeting with Kennedy somewhere in the South, and negotiations had gone on, but each time something went wrong. King said, "I'll also have to invite Nixon to meet with me," and Kennedy would say, "Well, then, why should I go out on a limb to risk my southern support if you're then going to meet with Nixon?" The meeting that had been almost scheduled in Miami got canceled and King had no excuse for not being in Atlanta. The students were starting the sit-in of Rich's Department Store. And King didn't have a reason to be away. So he joined it and he got arrested.

The whole country was then galvanized, not just by the arrest of King but by the fact that the judge then sentenced him to four months on a hard labor gang because he had had a previous arrest for driving with an out-of-state license. It was a shocking sentence and it went like waves across the country, particularly among black people. But I think the whole American people realized that that was an absurd sentence.

So the question then was, What would you do about it? We initially drafted a very strong statement that Kennedy liked, opposing what had happened to Dr. King and calling for his release. And then Governor [Ernest] Vandiver of Georgia called and said, "Look, I'll get the son of a gun out of jail if you won't issue a public statement. Believe me, I'll get him out." So Kennedy called me and said, "Look, we can't issue the statement." But then the governor dragged his feet. Whether he was going to do it, or not really going to do it, or how long it might take, nobody knew. Day after day the question was, What would you do? And Kennedy, having promised not to issue the public statement, was sort of locked for those days.

The idea came to me, and was backed by others in the civil rights section of the campaign, that why shouldn't he just call

Mrs. King? She was pregnant. She was very anxious. She had been on the phone to me telling me about how worried she was, and the thought came, Why can't Kennedy at least just call her and say, "We're working at it, we're going to get him out. You have my sympathy." A personal, direct act. We then said, How do we get this to him? He was in downstate Illinois then, we couldn't get through.

Finally we called Sargent Shriver, Kennedy's brother-in-law, and said, "Look, here's an idea, but nobody wants to hear from us in the civil rights section right now because we've been bothering them too much." And he said, "That's a wonderful idea. I'll get to O'Hare International Inn, where Kennedy is for another hour and a half, and I'll put the idea to him." Shriver got there. He looked around, he saw the strategists of the campaign, and he said to himself, If I bring it up it'll never go through because the wise guys will all have reasons why it shouldn't be done. So he waited until Ted Sorenson went off to work on a speech and Pierre Salinger went to meet the press and Kenneth O'Donnell went into the bathroom. Finally Shriver said to Kennedy, "Why don't you just call Mrs. King? You wanted to know what you could do. Give her your support and sympathy." Kennedy looked up and said, "That's a wonderful idea," with a big grin on his face. "Do you have her number?" Shriver had her number, dialed her, [Kennedy] talked to her.

CORETTA SCOTT KING

I was very depressed about Martin being in jail and being so far away, knowing I couldn't get to see him in less than a whole day's journey and back, and suddenly I got this very unexpected but uplifting telephone call from Senator John F. Kennedy. And he was campaigning and was at O'Hare Airport, and called and said, "Hello, Mrs. King, this is Senator Kennedy, and I'm calling because I wanted to let you know I was thinking about you. How are you? I understand you are expecting your third child." I was amazed that he even said third child. Someone of course had to tell him, but anyway, it was a very personal touch. He said, "I'm thinking about you and your husband, and I know this must be very difficult for you. If there's anything I can do to be of help, I want you to please feel free to call on me." And I didn't quite know what to say, except to thank him and say, "Well, I really appreciate this and if there is anything that you can do, I would deeply appreciate it." And of course, knowing the implications of all of this—it was toward the end of the month of October, and the election was just a few days away—I didn't quite know what to make of it.

HARRIS WOFFORD

Later in the morning Kennedy started telling his strategists what he'd done, and Robert Kennedy's first reaction was, "You've lost the election. We had three southern governors tell us that if you support Khrushchev, Castro, or Martin Luther King, we're going to throw our votes to Nixon." Robert Kennedy called my black colleague in the civil rights section, Louis Martin, and me in, and he gave us hell. He said, "Close down your civil rights section. You've shot your bolt. You've probably lost the election." I've never been chewed out by anybody as angrily as I was by Robert Kennedy. Then that very night Robert Kennedy called the judge in Georgia and told him to get King out of jail. And we asked Bob Kennedy, "After you were so angry, why did you do that?" He said, "Well, as I went up to New York on the plane and thought about King in jail with that sentence, and screwing up our politics in this country and maybe losing the election for my brother, I got so mad that I got that judge on the phone."

Of course, this had an enormous impact on black voters and lots of other people in those last weeks of the campaign. It wasn't just the action that had the impact, though, because the press didn't pay an enormous amount of attention to it initially. But Louis Martin said, "We've got to get this out to the whole black constituency in this country." So a little pamphlet was printed that featured Nixon's remark on the whole thing, which was "No comment." The pamphlet said, "No-Comment Nixon versus a Candidate with a Heart." All the pamphlet had were the remarks by Coretta King, by Martin King, Jr., by his father, and by Ralph Abernathy of the Southern Christian Leadership Conference, King's number-two colleague. These were wonderful strong statements, such as Daddy King saying, "As a Baptist I was going to vote against John Kennedy because he was a Catholic, but if he had the courage to wipe the tears from my daughter-in-law's eyes then I have the courage to vote for him, Catholic or not. And I've got a whole suitcase full of votes that I'm taking up and putting in the lap of John Kennedy." Probably a million and a half, two million, pamphlets were distributed at black churches in the key cities of the country on the Sunday before the election.

CORETTA SCOTT KING

That call from Kennedy was a very important call. I think it did turn the tide, because Martin was released the next day. And then we went to a mass meeting that night, as we usually did, to go to our churches to have a meeting, and Daddy King said this was the first time we'd had a Catholic to run for president, and most black people were like most other Americans about Catholics, I guess. We were not sure about Nixon, but Nixon had befriended a lot of people. And so Daddy King said, "I have a sackful of votes, and I'm going to place them at Senator Kennedy's feet." And of course, essentially what he was saying was he was going to vote for him. And actually, I think the difference in that election, which was very close, had to do with Kennedy's intercession in Martin's case.

HARRIS WOFFORD

Right up till election night people worried that there were more white people who had been turned away from Kennedy by it than black people who were drawn to him. But it didn't turn out that way as far as anybody can tell. The enormous turnout of black votes in critical states was said to have been the margin of victory.

> Kennedy defeated Nixon with a margin of less than two-thirds of 1 percent of the popular vote; it was one of the closest presidential elections in American history. John F. Kennedy had begun his campaign for the Democratic nomination as the least popular candidate among registered black voters. But on election day, at least seven out of ten blacks who went to the polls voted for him.

5

Freedom Rides, 1961

"Sticks and Bricks"

Outside Anniston, Alabama, Freedom Riders escaped through an emergency exit seconds before their Greyhound bus burst into flames after a firebombing.

Candidate John Kennedy's statements on civil rights had given hope to many in the movement. During the campaign, in Kennedy's first televised debate with Richard Nixon, his outline of the plight of the Negro in America seemed to give evidence of an understanding of black people and black issues. Soon after his victory, the president-elect announced his intention to appoint Robert Weaver administrator of the Housing and Home Finance Agency, the highest position ever held by a black in a federal administration. But Kennedy knew few black people and had little firsthand experience with black issues. His discourse on civil rights in the debate was the product of a thorough briefing by his civil rights advisers. After the inauguration in January 1961, civil rights had low priority, and civil rights leaders knew it. James Farmer, director of the Congress of Racial Equality (CORE), an old-line northern-based rights organization, said: "Many of us felt that Kennedy's commitment to civil rights was political, that it was a device to get him elected."

In 1961, as the new president took office, Black Americans were still forced to ride in the back of interstate buses in the South and were excluded from "whites only" waiting rooms and terminal restaurants. The Supreme Court had first banned segregation on interstate buses and trains in 1946. The next year, an interracial group of sixteen civil rights activists had undertaken a Journey of Reconciliation through the South to test compliance. Several on the journey were members of the Fellowship of Reconciliation (FOR), a pacifist organization founded in Britain in 1914 and inspired by the work of Mohandas Gandhi. Others had worked with CORE, an offshoot of FOR founded in Chicago in 1942. During the two-week journey through the upper South, twelve of the riders were arrested. James Peck, one of the white activists, was also beaten by an irate cab driver.

Some thirteen years later, just weeks before Kennedy's inauguration, in a case known as *Boynton* v. *Virginia,* the Supreme Court ruled against segregating interstate passengers not only on buses and trains but in the terminals. The question was, Would the executive branch of the federal government now force the South to comply?

> In January 1961, one black and one white veteran of the sit-in movement, Tom Gaither and Gordon Carey, were returning to CORE headquarters in New York City. The two field secretaries had been conducting nonviolent training workshops for CORE in Rock Hill, South Carolina.

GORDON CAREY

There were several things that had happened shortly before this time. One was that the Supreme Court had ruled that not only should the interstate buses be integrated but also facilities for those buses had to be integrated. Tom and I happened to be riding on this bus when we got caught in a snowstorm, stranded on the New Jersey Turnpike for something like twelve hours. I opened my briefcase and the one book I had to read was Louis Fischer's biography of Gandhi. Tom and I were reading and talking about it, and a combination of sitting on a bus, the recent Supreme Court decision, and reading about Gandhi's march to the sea got us talking about an analogous march to the sea in the South. We began talking about something that would be a bus trip, and of course we were also inspired by the Journey of Reconciliation, which CORE and the Fellowship of Reconciliation had sponsored back in '47. Somehow the drama of the whole thing caught us up, and the two of us planned most of the Freedom Ride before we ever got back to New York City. Tom knew the black colleges in the South very well and laid out a potential route for the trip. We planned to go to New Orleans because that was the ocean and that was analogous to Gandhi's salt march to the sea. So we went back to the CORE office and talked to some people there.

James Farmer, one of the founders of CORE, became its director on February 1, 1961.

JAMES FARMER

Federal law said that there should be no segregation in interstate travel. The Supreme Court had decided that. But still state laws in the southern states and local ordinances ordered segregation of the races on those buses. Why didn't the federal government enforce its law? We decided it was because of politics. If we were right in assuming that the federal government did not enforce federal law because of its fear of reprisals from the South, then what we had to do was to make it more dangerous politically for the federal government not to enforce federal law. And how would we do that? We decided the way to do it was to have an interracial group ride through the South. This was not civil disobedience, really, because we would be doing merely what the Supreme Court said we had a right to do. The whites in the group would sit in the back of the bus, the blacks would sit in the front of the bus, and would refuse to move when ordered. At every rest stop, the whites would go into the waiting room for blacks, and the blacks into the waiting room for whites, and would seek to use all the facilities, refusing to leave. We felt that we could then count upon the racists of the South to create a crisis, so that the federal government would be compelled to enforce federal law. That was the rationale for the Freedom Ride.

We recruited a small group, thirteen persons, carefully selected and screened, because we wanted to be sure that our adversaries could not dig up derogatory information on any individual and use that to smear the movement. Then we had a week of arduous training, to prepare this group for anything.

They were white, they were black, they were from college age up to their sixties. One professor from Wayne State University in Michigan, Dr. Walter Bergman, was sixty-one. His wife was approximately the same age. At least two of the college students had participated in the sit-in movement: John Lewis from Nashville, and Hank Thomas, who was a senior at Howard University and had participated in the sit-ins in Washington, D.C.

Following the Gandhian program of advising your adversaries or the people in power just what you were going to do, when you were going to do it, and how you were going to do it, so that everything would be open and above board, I sent letters to the president of the United States, John Kennedy; the attorney general, Robert Kennedy; the director of the FBI, Mr. J. Edgar Hoover; the chairman of the Interstate Commerce Commission, which regulated interstate travel; and the president of Greyhound Corporation and the president of Trailways Corporation. Those were the carriers that we would be using on this bus ride. We got replies from none of those letters.

We hoped that there would be protection. Indeed, that was one of the reasons we sent a letter to the FBI. We had thought that the FBI would provide protection for us, would see to it at each stop that we were not brutalized or killed.

> Plans called for two interracial groups to travel south by Trailways and Greyhound bus from Washington, D.C., to Atlanta, then through Alabama and Mississippi to arrive in New Orleans on May 17, 1961, the seventh anniversary of the Supreme Court's *Brown* decision. After the week-long training session, James Farmer hosted a send-off dinner. Sit-in veteran John Lewis had postponed graduation from American Baptist Theological Seminary to participate.

JOHN LEWIS

This group of thirteen Freedom Riders, seven blacks and six whites, had a dinner at a Chinese restaurant in Washington, D.C. It was my first time having Chinese food. Growing up in the South and going to school in Nashville, I'd never had it before. To me this meal was like the Last Supper, because you didn't know what to expect going on the Freedom Ride.

I remember getting on the bus at the Greyhound station in Washington, D.C., on May fourth, and my seatmate was an elderly white gentleman named Albert Bigelow. He was from Cos Cob, Connecticut, and he was a pacifist. He had been the skipper on a little ship called the *Golden Rule* out in the South Pacific protesting against testing the atomic bomb. He was very committed to the philosophy and the discipline of nonviolence. We went through parts of Virginia—through Lynchburg, Petersburg, and other places—without any problems. In Charlotte, North Carolina, one of the riders attempted to get a shoeshine and a haircut in a so-called white barber shop. He was arrested and went to court the next day and the jury threw the case out. We went on to Rock Hill, South Carolina, and Albert Bigelow and myself got off the bus. As we started in the door of the white waiting room, we were met by a group of white young men that beat us and hit us, knocked us out, left us lying on the sidewalk in front of the entrance to the waiting room. In a few minutes the Rock Hill police officials came up and asked if we wanted to press charges and we said no. I left the ride the next day because I had to fly to Philadelphia for an interview with the American Friends Service Committee. I had applied to go abroad as a volunteer in an international program in what is now Tanzania. I planned to rejoin the ride in Birmingham on Mother's Day, the second Sunday in May.

The buses proceeded from Rock Hill to Atlanta. There, on May 13, James Farmer learned of the death of his father. The following day, Mother's Day, Farmer made plans to fly to Washington for the funeral, and said good-bye to the other riders just minutes before they boarded two buses, a Greyhound and a Trailways, bound for Birmingham.

White Journey of Reconciliation veteran James Peck was on the Trailways bus. The only scheduled stop en route was Anniston, Alabama.

JAMES PECK

When we left Atlanta for Birmingham on May 14, 1961, we knew that we were in for a very rough reception upon arrival, because we had telephoned to Reverend Fred Shuttlesworth, who was to be our host in Birmingham. He told us that the Klansmen had been preparing this reception for a full week. But we did not anticipate that the violence would start two hours before we would get to Birmingham, at Anniston. When our bus pulled into Anniston, as we were waiting in the station, a group of six Klansmen boarded our bus and bodily threw the black riders into the backseat. Walter Bergman and I were sitting on the backseat, so we decided to go up front and intercept with our bodies. We got clobbered on the head. I didn't get it so bad, but Bergman got it so bad that he later had a stroke and has been paralyzed ever since.

These Klansmen who boarded the bus told the driver to drive on. When we arrived in Birmingham, we saw along the sidewalk twenty men with pipes. There was no cop in sight. Well, we got out of the bus. Charles Person, a black student from Atlanta, and I had been designated to try to enter the lunch counter. Of course, we didn't get there. This mob seized us and I was unconscious, I'd say, within a minute. I came to in an alleyway. Nobody was there. A big pool of blood. I looked at that pool of blood, and I said, I wonder whether I'm going to live or die? But I was too tired to care. I lay down again. Finally I came to again, and I looked up and a white GI who had come up to me said, "You look in a bad way. Do you need help?" And I looked the other way and Bergman was coming, so I said, "No, my friend is coming, he'll help me out." So Bergman took me in a cab to Shuttlesworth's home, and when Shuttlesworth saw me, he said, "Man, you need to go to a hospital." And so he called the ambulance and they took me to the hospital and put fifty-three stitches into my head.

The next day, Bull Connor, the notorious police chief, was asked why there were no police on hand. He replied that it was Mother's Day and they were all visiting their mothers. Also that next day, the FBI wanted to talk with me. My attitude was, What's the use? But the other riders wanted me to go, so I went. I told the agent my story, and when I was finished, he didn't have any questions. Shows how interested he was, you know? He didn't have a single question. You'd think he would have at least asked a question like, "Would you recognize any of the people who beat you?" Any question. Just for form—but no question.

The other vehicle, the Greyhound bus, never reached Birmingham.

JAMES FARMER

When the Greyhound bus arrived in Anniston, there was a mob of white men standing there at the bus terminal. The members of the mob had their weapons—pistols, guns, blackjacks, clubs, chains, knives—all in plain evidence. The Freedom Riders made a decision on the spot that discretion was the better part of valor in this case, and that they were not going to test the terminal facilities at Anniston. To do so would have been suicide. They told that decision to the driver, who prepared to drive the bus on. Before the bus pulled out, however, members of the mob took their sharp instruments and slashed tires. The bus got to the outskirts of Anniston and the tires blew out and the bus ground to a halt. Members of the mob had boarded cars and followed the bus, and now with the disabled bus standing there, the members of the mob surrounded it, held the door closed, and a member of the mob threw a firebomb into the bus, breaking a window to do so. Incidentally, there were some local policemen mingling with the mob, fraternizing with them while this was going on.

The riders managed to escape the bus before it was totally engulfed in flames. Photographs of the burned-out vehicle were quickly circulated in the national and world press. For Burke Marshall, the assistant attorney general in charge of civil rights under Robert Kennedy, the violence provoked astonishment "that people—presumably otherwise sane, sensible, rational—would have this kind of reaction simply to where people were sitting on a bus."

But for federal men on the scene in Alabama, the Klan's violence came as no surprise. The FBI had informed local police of the Freedom Ride itinerary, including the police in Anniston and Birmingham. The FBI was further aware that at least one officer in the Birmingham police department was a member of the Ku Klux Klan and that the Klan planned to use violence at the Birmingham terminal.

BURKE MARSHALL

The FBI had information, it turns out, that was quite specific about what was going to happen in Birmingham. They might have had similar information about what was going to happen in

Anniston, but I'm not sure of that. But they clearly had advance information from Klan sources that the Freedom Riders were going to be attacked in the bus station at Birmingham, and that the Birmingham police were going to absent themselves and not do anything to protect the riders. The Bureau knew that. The Bureau didn't pass that information along to anybody in any other part of the Justice Department. They didn't inform the civil rights division, they didn't inform the attorney general, they didn't inform anyone until after the event. Now, the reason that they didn't do that may be partly that they didn't understand what was going on in the country. It may have been in part a bureaucratic FBI reaction to the protection of informants, because if they had done something, it probably would have become clear to the Klan that someone in the Klan was peaching. And the danger to that person, had he been identified by the Klan, would have been very great. So that might have been another reason. A third reason is that I think Mr. Hoover personally was totally out of sympathy with the civil rights movement and especially the degree to which it focused on demonstrations and direct action.

Alabama governor John Patterson had been a Kennedy supporter but split with the president and the attorney general over the issue of protection for the Freedom Riders.

JOHN PATTERSON

I thought that the Freedom Riders should stay home and mind their own business and let us try to work out our problems down here in some legal way. I even asked the attorney general and the president to ask these people to mind their own business and obey the law. The whole thing would have been over if they would have done that. But of course they didn't want to do that.

These were not bona fide interstate travelers by any means. These people were buying tickets from town to town within states. And they were getting off the bus at various terminals and going into restaurants and waiting rooms and cafeterias that had been traditionally segregated. They were deliberately going in there and rubbing up against people and pushing into the places and deliberately trying to create trouble and cause fights to get the publicity. Of course, you can start a fight anywhere that way—New York or anywhere you want to go. If you start that kind of conduct in a public place, you're goin' to have a fight. And that's what these people were doing. They were deliberately doing this in order to create trouble, violence if necessary, to bring publicity to what they were doing.

Violence continued to track the Freedom Riders. Monday afternoon, May 15, with their departure from Birmingham blocked by a new mob of Klan members at the Greyhound bus terminal, the riders changed plans. Instead of traveling by bus to Montgomery, they would fly to New Orleans for the desegregation rally on May 17.

The rides were becoming an international embarrassment to the Kennedys. The administration was primarily interested in defusing the protest and avoiding further violence. John Seigenthaler, Robert Kennedy's administrative assistant, was assigned to help the Freedom Riders from both buses get out of Birmingham. They had moved to the Birmingham airport, and the mob had moved with them.

JOHN SEIGENTHALER

That first wave of Freedom Riders had difficulty getting out of Birmingham after they were brutalized. They were stymied in the airport, surrounded by an angry mob, and there were bomb threats every time an airplane would take off. The attorney general heard by telephone from Simeon Booker, the reporter who was with them, and he could tell from Booker's voice that things were desperate. I think Booker had doubts that they would ever get out of there. So the attorney general, after talking to the president, decided to send me down to try to get them from Birmingham by air on to New Orleans. I don't remember ever feeling more welcomed by a group of people. They were almost reaching out to touch me. It was a simple matter to work out with the airline a procedure whereby we got them on the airplane. We simply cut off telephone calls [so bomb threats couldn't get through] for a period of several minutes prior to announcing the flight. So we managed to get them out of there and to New

Orleans, where they were met by friends who took them into their care.

DIANE NASH

We [in the Student Nonviolent Coordinating Committee] had heard about the Freedom Rides when they were starting, and we all agreed with their purposes and agreed that it was really an important thing for CORE to do. We also were very aware that they would probably meet with violence a number of times. So we decided that we would watch them; if there were ways that we could help, we'd stand by and be available. Since there was such a close kinship between us and the Freedom Riders, we understood exactly what they were doing, and it was our fight every bit as much as theirs. When that bus was burned in Alabama, it was as though we had been attacked.

I strongly felt that the future of the movement was going to be cut short if the Freedom Ride had been stopped as a result of violence. The impression would have been given that whenever a movement starts, all you have to do is attack it with massive violence and the blacks will stop. I thought that was a very dangerous thing to happen. So, under those circumstances, it was really important that the ride continue.

A contingent of students left Nashville to pick up the Freedom Ride where it had been stopped. Some of the students gave me sealed letters to be mailed in case they were killed. That's how prepared they were for death.

The students who were going to pick up the Freedom Ride elected me coordinator. As coordinator, part of my responsibility was to stay in touch with the Justice Department. Our whole way of operating was that we took ultimate responsibility for what we were going to do. But it was felt that they should be advised, in Washington, of what our plans were. Some people hoped for protection from the federal government. I think Jim Lawson cautioned against relying on federal protection.

I was also to keep the press informed, and communities that were participating, such as Birmingham, Montgomery, Jackson, and Nashville. And I coordinated the training and recruitment of more people to take up the Freedom Ride.

John Lewis was with the contingent of reinforcements organized by SNCC that traveled from Nashville to Birmingham.

JOHN LEWIS

After the Mother's Day incidents, Attorney General Robert Kennedy said there must be a cooling-off period. Well, as one of the participants in the original effort and as someone who had been involved in the Nashville student movement, I felt and others felt that the rides should continue. We got the necessary resources, and we went from Nashville to Birmingham. Outside of Birmingham, two of the riders that were sitting near the front of the bus—I think maybe the very first seat behind the bus driver—were arrested and taken to jail. The other riders, we were taken to the city and into a waiting room. The Birmingham commissioner of public safety, Bull Connor, informed us that we were being taken to jail. We were not being arrested, but we were being placed in protective custody, for our own safety.

We went to jail that Wednesday night, May 17, 1961. We stayed in jail Thursday night, and we went on a hunger strike, refused to eat anything, refused to drink any water. About two o'clock Friday morning, Bull Connor and several members of the Birmingham police force came to our cell, took us out of the jail, and said, in effect, that they were taking us back to the college campuses in Nashville. We got in the car—we didn't go in a voluntary way, we went limp, so they literally picked us up and put us in the car—and we started back up the highway toward the Tennessee state line. It was about one hundred twenty miles from Birmingham and maybe about the same distance from Nashville.

They literally dropped us out on the highway near a railroad crossing and said, "A bus will be coming along or a train will be coming along and you can make your way back to the city of Nashville." We were frightened. We didn't know anyone in that part of Tennessee. And we went across the railroad tracks with our baggage and came upon the house of an elderly black couple. They were afraid to let us in, but they did. When daylight came, the man went and bought food from several different places because he didn't want to indicate in any way that he had some unwanted guests in this small town. The people had heard on the radio about the Freedom Riders from Nashville going to Birmingham. In the meantime, we made a telephone call to Diane Nash and told her what had happened. She said, "What do you want to do? Do you want to come back to Nashville? Do you want to go back to Birmingham and continue the ride?" We told her that we wanted to continue the ride. She sent a car to pick us up and she informed us that ten other packages had been shipped by other means. She was telling us through a code that ten other Freedom Riders had left by train to join us in Birmingham. See, the people in Nashville and around the country thought we were still in jail. When the car arrived, seven of us and the driver got back to Birmingham and met with Reverend Shuttlesworth and some local people and one student in particular, Ruby Doris Smith, who made it from Spelman College in Atlanta to join the ride.

We attempted to get on the bus about five-thirty P.M. I will never forget what this bus driver said. It was a classic statement. He said, "I have only one life to give, and I'm not going to give it to the NAACP, not to CORE." This was a white bus driver in Birmingham, Alabama. Didn't have any black bus drivers at that time.

In the meantime, we understood from some of the reporters that Robert Kennedy was negotiating with the officials of Greyhound to get us out of Birmingham that night. But no bus drivers would drive, because they were afraid of what could happen, since the Klan had surrounded the bus station and they were throwing stink bombs. Police officials there were trying to keep the Klan from getting to us inside this so-called white waiting room, and they had police dogs. But it was not until eight-thirty Saturday morning, May twentieth, that we understood that an arrangement had been worked out between the Justice Department and the officials of Greyhound and the officials of the state of Alabama.

FLOYD MANN

After what happened in Anniston and Birmingham, as Alabama's director of public safety, I certainly knew that we had a tremendous problem on our hands. So did the governor. So did Attorney

General Kennedy apparently, because at that point he began to send people into Alabama, like Mr. John Seigenthaler, also Byron "Whizzer" White, who's now a member of the Supreme Court, and others.

The attorney general wanted to get Governor Patterson publicly committed to guaranteeing the safety of these people throughout Alabama. I'd heard that several attempts had been made to contact the governor by the attorney general, which had failed. That is, the governor did not take the calls and was unable to be found. Governor Patterson was in a terrible political situation because the various people who had so actively supported him strongly and openly were some of the people that were very critical of the Freedom Riders coming into Alabama. So I felt Governor Patterson was in a situation where he would rather not make that commitment.

Eventually, several meetings were held, one in the governor's office. Mr. John Seigenthaler attended, and he wanted the assurance from the governor that law and order would prevail in the state.

JOHN SEIGENTHALER

When finally Governor Patterson agreed to meet, he had me into his office, with his whole cabinet seated around this great conference table. He lectured me for the better part of half an hour, at times pounding the table, telling me how these outside agitators had to get out of that state, that this state was not about to permit the federal establishment to move in and to assert the rights of those people, that this was an Alabama matter and that I in fact was an intruder. It was none of my business nor the president's business nor the attorney general's business.

At one point he pounded on the table and told me how much more popular he was than Jack Kennedy. He said he was sorry he ever supported Kennedy for president. And he made it clear that if we thought we were going to use federal power against state power, blood would flow in the streets.

The cabinet sat there in silence and listened to the lecture, a few of them smiling, a few nodding encouragement to him. But Floyd Mann was stoic and solid and reserved. At one point, the governor gave me an opportunity to respond, and I said that my duty as a federal officer was to inform him that if the state could not protect citizens of the United States, either in the cities or on the highways, that it was a federal responsibility and we were prepared to assert it, but we hoped we would not have to. He said he was not sure that safe conduct could be given to these agitators, as he called them. Floyd Mann then broke in and said, "Governor, as your chief law enforcement officer, I assure you if you give me the responsibility, I can protect them."

I found myself looking to Floyd Mann first of all with some skepticism. He was part of this monolithic silent cabinet till that moment. At the same time, he was the one voice of reason in that room, so I leaned to him and we engaged in this colloquy and we quickly worked out an arrangement whereby the attorney general would be notified that the governor of Alabama said, "I can protect all the travelers in the state of Alabama, those who are citizens of this state and those from outside." And Mann was told the state police would protect those travelers from city limits to city limits and the city police would protect them inside the city.

JOHN LEWIS

We would board the bus with other passengers, and there would be two officials of Greyhound. A private plane would fly over the bus, and there would be a state patrol car every fifteen or twenty miles along the highway between Birmingham and Montgomery, about ninety miles.

We got on the bus and a great many of the riders took a nap. I sat on the front seat right behind the driver, with Jim Zwerg, a young white guy. I was a spokesman for this particular group of riders, and we did see the plane. But I would say about forty miles or less from the city of Montgomery, all sign of protection disappeared. There was no plane, no patrol car, and when we arrived at the bus station, it was eerie. Just a strange feeling. It was so quiet, so peaceful, nothing. And the moment we started down the steps of that bus, there was an angry mob. People came out of nowhere—men, women, children, with baseball bats, clubs, chains—and there was no police official around. They just started beating people. We tried to get all of the women on the ride into a taxicab. There was one cab there, and this driver said he couldn't take the group because it was interracial. One of the Freedom Riders was a young black female student who said something like, "Well, I will drive myself. I will drive the cab." And the driver said no, but finally he did drive off with all of the black women—and the white women started running down the street. Then the mob turned on members of the press. One cameraman, I believe from NBC, had one of these heavy old pieces of camera equipment on his shoulder. This member of the mob took the equipment, bashed this guy, knocked him down, bashed his face in. So they beat up all of the reporters, then they turned on the black male members and white male members of the group. I was beaten—I think I was hit with a sort of crate thing that holds soda bottles—and left lying unconscious there, in the streets of Montgomery.

Also confronted by the mob was Fred Leonard, a black freshman at Tennessee State University in Nashville. As a high school student in Chattanooga, he had participated in sit-ins a year earlier.

FRED LEONARD

Everybody was feeling comfortable going into the terminal in Montgomery. We didn't see anybody, but we didn't see any police either. And then, all of a sudden, just like magic: white people, sticks, and bricks. "Nigger! Kill the niggers!" We were still on the bus. I think we were all thinking maybe we should go off at the back of this bus, because we thought that if we had gone off at the back maybe they wouldn't be so bad on us. But we decided no, no, we'll go off the front and take what's coming to us. We went out the front of the bus. Jim Zwerg was a white fellow from Madison, Wisconsin—he had a lot of nerve. I think that's what saved me, Bernard Lafayette, and Allen Cason, 'cause Jim Zwerg walked off the bus in front of us and it was like those people in the mob were possessed. They couldn't believe that there was a white man who would help us, and they grabbed him and pulled him into the mob. When we came off the bus, their attention was on him. It's like they didn't see the rest of us for about thirty seconds. They didn't see us at all, and we were held up by this rail—parking lot down below, cars down there—and then when they did turn toward us, we had a choice. We could stand there and take it, or we could go over the rail. Over the rail we went—me and Bernard Lafayette and Allen Cason, who always carried his little typewriter. Over the rail he went, on top of a car, hit the ground, took off, ran into the back of this building. It was the post office and the people were in there carrying on their business, just like nothing was happening outside. But when we came through there, mail went flying everywhere, 'cause we were *running*.

Later we heard the news about Jim Zwerg, about John Lewis, about William Barbee. William Barbee was damaged for life, really, Jim Zwerg for life. It's amazing that they're still living; they could have been killed. I think what saved them was this white fellow who was in the crowd shot a gun in the air, and if it was not for him, they would be dead. Jim Zwerg would be dead, Bernard Lafayette—all of us would be dead.

The man with the pistol was Floyd Mann.

FLOYD MANN

When they left Birmingham we had sixteen highway patrol cars in front of that bus and sixteen patrol cars behind the bus, with troopers. Also we had small aircraft running reconnaissance, watching for bridges, where someone might try to sabotage that bus. During that period of time, I received some confidential information that when they arrived at the bus station in Montgomery the police had planned to take a holiday and there'd be no one present. So I ordered a hundred state troopers into Montgomery immediately. We quartered those troopers at the Alabama police academy because it was a policy of the state police in 1961 not to ever enter a city unless they were invited or it became very apparent that law and order had broken down.

When the bus arrived at the Montgomery bus station, only the assistant director of public safety, Mr. W. R. Jones, and myself were there. Just as soon as the riders began to get off the bus I noticed these strange people all around the bus. I knew immediately they were Klansmen. No sooner had the Freedom Riders gotten off the bus than a riot evolved. Mobs of people began to appear at the bus station, just coming out of everywhere, and then it certainly became obvious to me that law and order had broken down. And there were no police around the bus station. We immediately sent for those hundred state troopers. But before they could arrive, cars were set on fire, people were attacked. Newspaper people were beaten, cameras busted. Those Freedom Riders, some of them were being beaten with baseball bats. Therefore, we had to threaten to take some lives ourselves unless that violence stopped immediately. So I just put my pistol to the head of one or two of those folks that was using baseball bats and told them unless they stopped immediately, they was going to be hurt. And it did stop the beaters.

After one of the Freedom Riders was knocked unconscious we got him to a car, sent him to a hospital. Then it was called to my attention that another person had been knocked unconscious and had been taken to the hospital, and I retrieved his credentials—they had fallen out of his pocket in front of the bus station—and I saw it was Mr. John Seigenthaler.

JOHN SEIGENTHALER

My colleague John Doar and I left Birmingham immediately behind the bus. The Freedom Riders had insisted they weren't going to ride this bus unless it was a local. They wanted to test the bathroom facilities, the dining facilities, in every little out-of-the-way bus stop. Well, the driver was scared out of his wits. He knew what had happened in Anniston the week before. So he drove the bus as an express. Doar and I didn't know that. We made a couple stops—for gas, maybe for a cup of coffee.

We arrived at the Federal Building in Montgomery, which adjoins the bus station, about two or three minutes after the bus. As John got out of the car, you could hear the shouts and screams from across the way. Doar ran for the Federal Building and I drove up the street and quickly through an alleyway on the back side of the bus station. As I came down the far side, I saw this almost anthill of activity. The Freedom Riders emerging from the bus were being mauled. It looked like two, three hundred people just all over them. As I drove along, I saw two young women who were Freedom Riders being pummeled to one side. A woman was walking behind one of them. She had a purse on a strap and she was beating the young woman over the head, and a young skinny blond teenager in a T-shirt was sort of dancing backward in front of her [the Freedom Rider], punching the young woman in the face. Instinctively, I just bumped up onto the sidewalk, blew the horn, jumped out of the car, came around, grabbed the one who was being hit, and took her back to the car. The other young woman got into the backseat and I opened the door, pushed this young woman, whose name I later learned was Susan Wilbur, and said, "Get in the car." And she said, "Mister, this is not your fight. I'm nonviolent. Don't get hurt because of me." I almost got away with it. If she had gotten into the car, I think I could have gotten away, but that moment of hesitation gave the mob a chance to collect their wits. One guy grabbed me by the arm, wheeled me around, and said, "What the hell are you doing?" And I said, "Get back, I'm a federal man." I turned back to Susan Wilbur and the lights went out. I was hit with a pipe over one ear.

I woke up half an hour later. Beside me was a police officer. He had my notebook with all sorts of phone numbers in it—like Fred Shuttlesworth, the black leader, Bull Connor, the White House, the Justice Department, John Patterson—and he told me, "Well, you've had some trouble, buddy. Is there anybody I can call for you?" I had enough wits about me to say, "Yes, if you would call Mr. Kennedy." "Which Kennedy would that be?" he replied. And I said, "Either the president or the attorney general," and he said, "Who the hell are you, buddy?" And I said, "Well, I'm the attorney general's administrative assistant." He said, "We've got to get you to a hospital," and he got me out and I passed out again. The next thing I knew I was in the hospital on the operating table and the doctor was talking on the telephone to Byron White, who was deputy attorney general. A few minutes later, I woke up again in the room and the attorney general was calling.

Robert Kennedy felt betrayed by Governor Patterson's failure to protect the riders. Kennedy ordered six hundred federal marshals into Maxwell Air Force Base outside Montgomery. The next day, May 21, groups of angry whites continued to roam the streets of Montgomery. And Martin Luther King was scheduled to speak in support of the Freedom Riders.

JAMES FARMER

A rally had been planned in Ralph Abernathy's church. Dr. King was flying in from Atlanta, and Abernathy was going to speak there too. So was Wyatt Tee Walker, who was executive director of the Southern Christian Leadership Conference. After the funeral of my father in Washington, I flew to Montgomery. When I arrived at the airport, Reverend Fred Shuttlesworth was there to meet me. He drove me toward the church, telling me we would be encountering a mob, because there were hundreds of white men marauding through the streets beating up blacks, and that mob was approaching the church, probably would be holding the church under siege. His prediction was correct.

We approached the church, and a mob blocked the car and began to rock it, trying to turn it over. Fortunately, Shuttlesworth had enough traction to get the car in reverse and back away. He tried another approach through another street and had the same result. Then he stopped by a black-owned taxi stand to inquire how we could outflank the mob. He was told he should drive around to one side of a graveyard, park the car, walk through the graveyard, and try to enter the church through a back door. However, the mob had gotten there first. The [back] door was blocked by members of the mob. Shuttlesworth, who didn't know the meaning of fear, it seemed to me, said, "Well, Jim, I've gotta get you to that church, so we're going to have to walk through that mob." I said, "We're going to have to do what?" He repeated it and proceeded to walk through the mob. Now, Shuttlesworth is a rather small man, slight, not too tall, and he walked through the mob, saying, "Out of my way, step aside, let me through," and members of the mob complied with his request. They stepped aside and here was big me trying to hide behind Fred Shuttlesworth as we walked through the mob. I told Shuttlesworth that really was an example of the "crazy nigger" syndrome. A member of the mob says, "Don't mess with that nigger, he's crazy." That's the reason we got through. Well, we rapped on the back door of the church and the door opened and we were in.

By early evening, U.S. marshals ringed the church to protect the fifteen hundred people trapped inside.

FLOYD MANN

Outside the church, the crowd just continued to build, and at one time there were just thousands of people there. Some of those marshals were just about as inexperienced at handling a crowd like that as some of the police were in Alabama. They began to throw tear gas, and they threw it against the wind. And the gas began to affect the marshals more than the people they were trying to control. We just had an awful situation there for a while.

Tear gas from the battle outside began to seep into the church. Some inside were armed. They prepared to defend themselves if the mob broke through the line of marshals. King was on the telephone to Robert Kennedy. Kennedy in turn called Governor Patterson. While Fred Shuttlesworth condemned the governor from the pulpit as "the most guilty man in this state," a reluctant Patterson finally declared martial law and sent in the Alabama National Guard to disperse the crowd.

With the church crisis over, Attorney General Kennedy called for a cooling-off period. He was not to get his wish. On May 24, just two days after the all-night siege at the First Baptist Church was lifted, twenty-seven Freedom Riders boarded buses in Montgomery. They were bound for Jackson, Mississippi.

JAMES FARMER

That ride from Montgomery to Jackson was like a military operation. Our theory had been right that once we allowed the racists to create the crisis by bloodying us, then the federal government would have to provide protection, and it did. Bobby Kennedy had persuaded Governor Patterson of Alabama to declare martial law and bring in the National Guard. Kennedy had also sent in U.S. marshals. Now as we rode on the bus, there were Alabama National Guardsmen with us, about six of them with bayonets fixed on their rifles. There were helicopters chopping around overhead. There were police cars screaming up and down the highway with their sirens blaring. There were federal, state, and county police. That did not ease our fear. If anything, it increased it. We didn't know which way the National Guardsmen would point their guns in the event of a showdown.

We got to the border between Alabama and Mississippi and saw that famous sign, "Welcome to the Magnolia State," and our hearts jumped into our mouths. The bus pulled off the road, stopped, the driver left the bus, another driver got on. The Alabama guardsmen left the bus, the Mississippi guardsmen replaced them. The Alabama director of public safety came onto the bus and whispered something to one of the reporters. Reporters were there too, because this was the big story of the day and they wouldn't miss it, even though they were risking their lives. That reporter then passed that message to other reporters on the bus. All but one of the reporters left the bus then. I asked him what the message had been. He said, "The director of public safety has told us that he has received word from usually reliable sources that this bus is going to be ambushed and destroyed inside the Mississippi border."

Well, the bus moved on across the Mississippi line and shortly we passed through a heavily wooded area—forests on both sides with great oak trees growing up out of the swamp, moss hanging from the branches—and we could practically see Harriet Tubman more than a century ago tramping through the swamps with runaway slaves as they ran from bloodhounds. But I shook my head, came back to reality, and there were Mississippi National Guardsmen flanking the highway with their guns pointed toward the forest on both sides of the road. As the bus barreled along, an official of the National Guard shouted, through a bullhorn, "Look behind every tree." Apparently this was where they expected the ambush, but the ambush did not materialize and the bus proceeded on into the environs of Jackson. As we got to the suburbs of Jackson, one of the Freedom Riders broke into song, and this was as it had to be. His words went something like this:

> I'm taking a ride on the Greyhound bus line,
> I'm a-riding the front seat to Jackson this time.
> Hallelujah, I'm a-travelin',
> Hallelujah, ain't it fine?
> Hallelujah, I'm a-travelin'
> Down Freedom's main line.

All the Freedom Riders picked up the chorus, then we pulled into Jackson itself.

FRED LEONARD

When we got to Jackson, we didn't see anybody except the police. Oh, we stuck our chests out then, 'cause we didn't see a mob. We walked on off the front of the bus, the police were standing there, said, "Just keep moving." And they had a little line right there to go to the waiting room, 'cause they knew where we were going, so we walked on through the white waitin' room. As we walked through, the police just said, "Keep moving." We never got stopped. They passed us right on through the white terminal, into the paddy wagon, and into jail. There was no violence in Mississippi.

The next day, we went to court. The prosecutor got up, accused us of trespassing, took his seat. Our attorney, Jack Young, got up to defend us, as human beings having the right to be treated like human beings. While he was defending us, the judge turned his back, looked at the wall. When he finished, the judge turned around—*bam*, sixty days in the state penitentiary—and there we were, on the way to Parchman, maximum security.

> Robert Kennedy had struck a deal with James O. Eastland of Mississippi, chairman of the Senate Judiciary Committee. The U.S. attorney general had agreed not to enforce the Supreme Court decisions desegregating interstate travel. Mississippi authorities, in turn, had guaranteed there would be no violence.
>
> The certainty of a jail sentence did not stop the Freedom Riders. By summer's end, 328 had been arrested in Jackson. More than half were black. One quarter were female. Most were college students and from the South. Most served time in the state penitentiary.

JAMES FARMER

In Parchman, the male Freedom Riders were in one very large horseshoe-shaped cellblock. As a way of keeping our spirits up, we sang freedom songs. The prison officials wanted us to stop singing, because they were afraid our spirit would become contagious and the other prisoners would become Freedom Riders as a result of our singing. They said, "If you don't stop singing, we'll take away your mattresses." Now, the mattresses were the only convenience we had in those little cells. They were our link to civilization, so to speak. Everything else was cold and hard and the mattress was no more than an inch and a half thick, and straw, but at least it was something. So it was a real threat to have nothing left to sleep on. People were quiet for a while, until finally Jim Bevel, who was a Bible student at the time, made a little speech pointing out, "What they're trying to do is take your soul away. It's not the mattress, it's your soul." Then everybody said, "Yes, yes, we'll keep our soul." One Freedom Rider then yelled, "Guards, guards, guards," and the guards came dashing out to the cellblock to see what was wrong. He said, "Come get my mattress. I'll keep my soul." And everybody started singing,

> Ain't gonna let nobody turn me round, turn me
> round, turn me round.
> Gonna keep on a-walkin',
> Gonna keep on a-talkin',
> Keep on walkin' to the Promised Land.

They came in and took the mattresses away and people sang as they had never sung before. We thought we were winning the battle, they were on the run.

FRED LEONARD

The next night they gave us our mattresses back. So, we start singing again. They threatened us again. "We will take your mattresses and you will have to sleep on that steel without a mattress." That steel was cold, and you only had a pair of shorts and a T-shirt on. We kept singing freedom songs: "Freedom's coming and it won't be long." Stokely Carmichael was my cellmate. I told Stokely, "I'm not letting my mattress go." Everybody was peaceful, and let their mattress go, but I remembered the night before, when I had to sleep on that steel. So they came in to take my mattress. I was holding my mattress. They drug me out into the cellblock. I still had my mattress, I wouldn't turn it loose. They were using black inmates to come and get our mattresses, and I mean the *inmates*. And there was this guy, Peewee they called him, short and muscular. They said, "Peewee, get him." Peewee came down on my head. *Whomp, whomp*—he was crying. Peewee was crying. And I still had my mattress. Do you remember when your parents used to whup you and say, "It's going to hurt me more than it hurts you"? It hurt Peewee more than it hurt me. I still wouldn't turn my mattress loose, and they had these things they put on my wrists like handcuffs, and they started twisting and tightening them up—my bones start cracking and going on and finally I turned my mattress loose.

That summer, while Fred Leonard and the other riders served their sentences, Robert Kennedy petitioned the Interstate Commerce Commission for regulations banning segregation in interstate travel. In late September, the ICC issued the regulations that would enable the federal government to enforce the Supreme Court ruling of nine months earlier.

C. T. VIVIAN

Parchman prison was a national action, in that now we were challenging states' rights, we were challenging the laws across state lines, and people came from all over the country. That's the first time people had come from all over the country into a major movement. The treatment, the atmosphere, the police, the nature of the prison, all of that was proof to them of how negative everything was there.

The feeling of people coming out of the jail was one that they had triumphed, that they had achieved, that they were now ready, they could go back home, they could be a witness to a new understanding. Nonviolence was proven in that respect. It had become a national movement and there was no doubt about it, for common people in many places in the country. And there was a new cadre of leaders.

6

Albany, Georgia, 1961–1962

"The Mother Lode"

Demonstrating for integration in Albany, Georgia, activists led by the Reverend Samuel B. Wells (right) conduct a pray-in as local policemen stand by.

W.E.B. Du Bois, in his classic book *The Souls of Black Folk* (1903), described Albany, Georgia, in the early 1890s as "a wide-streeted, placid, Southern town, with a broad sweep of stores and saloons, and flanking rows of homes, —whites usually to the north, and blacks to the south. Six days in the week the town looks decidedly too small for itself, and takes frequent and prolonged naps. But on Saturday suddenly the whole county disgorges itself upon the place, and a perfect flood of black peasantry pours through the streets, fills the stores, blocks the sidewalks, chokes the thoroughfares, and takes full possession of the town." It was the "center of the life of ten thousand souls."

Seventy years later, Albany was still the seat of Dougherty County, but by then its population had increased to twenty-three thousand black residents and thirty-three thousand white. It remained a completely segregated town.

Albany was surrounded by fields of cotton and peanuts. Workers from those fields and plantations would come to town to conduct business, buy supplies, attend church, and search out entertainment. The music of Albany, from Ray Charles (a native) to the Shiloh Baptist Church a cappella choir, was an integral part of the city's life. As Bernice Johnson Reagon would later say of her hometown, "There is a point in the gold mine where you have the richest part, and that's called the mother lode. That's what Albany is to black people in terms of just the concentrated essence of the spirit of the people. If you can imagine black people at our most powerful point, in terms of community and peoplehood, then that's Albany, Georgia, during the Albany movement. The singing is just an echo of the society."

In the summer of 1961, the first workers from the Student Nonviolent Coordinating Committee arrived to conduct a voter registration project in southwest Georgia, basing themselves in rural Terrell County—known to local blacks as Terrible Terrell—just outside Albany. Charles Sherrod was twenty-two, and Cordell Reagon was eighteen. Both young men were already veterans of direct action protests such as sit-ins and Freedom Rides. By fall they had relocated in Albany.

> When the two young men arrived, Bernice Johnson was a student at all-black Albany State College and was secretary of the local NAACP Youth Council.

BERNICE JOHNSON REAGON

In the fall of '61, I was at Albany State and Charles Sherrod came up to me and said, "What do you think about Terrell County?" And I said, "It's a little bitty county." Then he turned to Otis Turner and asked him. Otis was from Terrell County and he started to run down what it was like to be black in Terrell County in terms of black people and white people. And I remember thinking, God, I wish that I'd not been so flip, and had taken the time to take Sherrod seriously. I didn't know who he was. That was my first contact with SNCC.

The first problem I had with SNCC was the name. They said they was the Student Nonviolent Coordinating Committee. Now I had problems with two words in there. I understood *student* and

I understood *committee*. I had read *coordinating*, but I'd never said *coordinating* in my life, so that was not a functional word for me. *Nonviolent* I had never really read in my life. I just told them I thought it was a stupid name, that half of their name was totally beyond me. I used to ask them, what was nonviolent? And Cordell Reagon would say, "Nonviolence is love, love for your fellowman," and it just clicked a blank in my head.

But one thing was very clear: they were there full-time, and they were from the movement. I knew that because Cordell talked about being on the Freedom Rides. Charles Sherrod talked about what he was doing. They had already been to Terrell County and had decided they couldn't stay, and if they were going to do anything to overthrow the white power structure in those counties that have more black people than white people, they had to start in Albany, Georgia.

They were for freedom. I understood that, and I had been waiting.

> SNCC, a young organization determined to develop new and nontraditional leadership at the grass roots, was stirring things up. Within weeks of the SNCC workers' arrival in Albany, the goal for that city became not just the vote but total desegregation of the way life was lived. With several groups competing for funds and support in the black community, local leaders felt the need for a more united front, and for more control. An umbrella organization called the Albany Movement was formed, with osteopath William G. Anderson as its president.

WILLIAM G. ANDERSON

Albany was a typical small town in Georgia. In 1961 it had nearly sixty thousand, so it's not small by rural Georgia small-town standards, where the population may be as low as five hundred. But it was a semirural community and in part dependent upon farming. There was very little industry. It was a rather close-knit town in that people knew each other. It was totally segregated. Blacks held no positions in any of the stores downtown as salespersons, clerks, or what have you. Of course, there were no black policemen, and blacks held no political office. As a matter of fact, we weren't even called blacks. We were called Negroes by the ones who were more liberal and benevolent, and we were called more unsavory things by others. You couldn't say that it was a community where you could experience racial harmony. The interplay was nonexistent. Most of the people who had lived in Albany all of their lives had sort of come to accept things as they were, or at least there was no outward expression of opposition to things as they were.

I first got the impression that we were caught up in what was happening nationwide when the SNCC representatives came into Albany. They sort of infiltrated all the social, civic, and religious organizations in the community and became a part of us.

Charlie Sherrod looked like the typical college kid who had been caught up with the excitement of the times. He was very dedicated, very well motivated, and he was received very well.

As a result of the catalytic reaction created by the SNCC students, a number of the black civic and social organizations got together and decided all in one night that the people in the community apparently are ready for whatever is happening. We are their leaders. And we are not ready for what the people appear to be ready for. We decided it would be better for us local leaders to give some direction to whatever is happening. So the Albany Movement was sort of a spontaneous thing.

CHARLES SHERROD

Now, we had been walking them dusty roads, and talking to the young people, and the old people. They had a very good feeling of our presence. We had become, in a sense, one with those that we had been talking with. Then came this ICC ruling, that interstate travel should be desegregated effective in November, and I said to myself, Wow, this is it. Here we go. I had anticipated moving into sit-ins or something else later on. But when this ruling came through, we were ready. So we got some students from Albany State College. We picked out this nice little innocent but big-mouthed girl—she could talk, and she could sing. Bertha Gober, I remember her very clearly. And a fellow by the name of Blanton Hall. We told them that they would be the beginning, and we had people ready to go to the station right after they would be arrested, if they were to be arrested. Actually, some of us really didn't think they would get arrested, because this was a federal mandate. I mean, we had constitutional rights. They mess with us now, they're going to get the federal government on them. Nobody is going to mess with the federal government, we thought.

We walked in there, and we had five students. They each understood that we would be nonviolent, we'd been slapped around and kicked around and pushed around in workshops, so they were accustomed to what might happen. They were accosted by the police, they really wanted the students to leave. The police tried to scare them, they tried to cajole them, they tried all kinds of ways of getting them out of there, aside from arresting them. But the young people stayed. I wasn't in there, this first arrest. Bertha, and the other, Hall, went limp, so they had to drag them out. This was all planned, of course.

The students were arrested on November 22 for entering a white waiting room and for attempting to eat in the bus terminal's dining room. But Police Chief Laurie Pritchett was anxious to avoid a confrontation with federal authorities.

LAURIE PRITCHETT

Those students were not arrested on a federal charge, they were arrested on a city ordinance of failing to obey the orders of a law enforcement officer. It had nothing to do with interstate commerce. They were violating a city ordinance. They were asked to leave. They was not on any bus. They were not eating at any counters. They were obstructing the flow of pedestrian travel in and out of the bus station. They were asked to disperse, they failed to do so, and they were arrested.

The next wave of arrests occurred in early December. Nine Freedom Riders traveling from Atlanta were charged with trespassing at the Albany train station. As far as the city government was concerned, segregation of the races was permanent and nonnegotiable.

WILLIAM G. ANDERSON

When the Albany Movement was organized, we drafted a purpose for the organization, which was to seek a means of desegregating the city of Albany, and we presented it as a petition to the city council. I went to the next city council meeting to get a response to our petition. The council conducted its business as usual on that evening, and Mayor Asa Kelley, who chaired the council, announced that the meeting was about to adjourn. Whereupon I asked for a hearing. This was granted, and I asked about our petition. I said, "We have petitioned the city council to set into place some mechanism whereby we can seek means of desegregating the city of Albany. And we gave all the reasons why we felt this should be done."

Well, Mayor Kelley said: "We discussed this in the executive session of the city council and we determined that there is no common ground for discussion, and did not deem it appropriate to have it as an agenda item. Adjourned."

Before I left I said, "It is regrettable. This is not in the best interest of Albany." And I left.

The next day the local newspaper, the *Albany Herald,* edited by our "friend" Mr. James Gray, who was at that time state Democratic chairman, had on the front page of his newspaper that the Albany Movement demands complete and total desegregation of the city of Albany. And it went on to relate my attending the city council meeting and "storming out"—he described it as storming out of the meeting—indicating that this was not in the best interest of Albany. I might add that he put in that same article not only my address but my phone number. This led to a series of events that coincided with the arrival of the Freedom Riders. They came into Albany on a Sunday. I can remember very vividly. They were arrested as they got off the train. That night we had a meeting of the Albany Movement and decided that we would not let these people stay in jail alone, we would fill up the jails.

That next morning, at breakfast, I was advising my wife and my kids that their husband and father would very likely wind up in jail before the week was out, because the Albany Movement had decided that the best way to respond would be mass demonstrations. You'd have to understand that going to jail was probably one of the most feared things in rural Georgia. There were many blacks who were arrested in small towns in Georgia never to be heard from again. We have every reason to believe many of these were lynched. So going to jail was no small thing. It was nothing to be taken lightly by any black. Because there were all kinds of horror stories of atrocities that had been suffered by blacks in jails.

On this Monday morning following the arrests on Sunday, we met at a church, and we started a march downtown, and we were going to walk around the courthouse and go back to the church. We made it around the first time, and I was at the head of the line with my wife. After we made it around the first time not getting arrested, I went on to my office, but the group went around the second time to make this impression that we are united behind these people that you have unjustly arrested. The second time around they were arrested. And some seven hundred were arrested before they stopped.

When we had this many people in jail, we had a meeting of the Albany Movement that night, and we all recognized that we had no experience in what we were doing. We had never been involved in mass demonstrations, mass arrests. We had no provisions for bonding. No provisions for taking care of families of people who were in jail. Recognize that this was not a select group. These were common, ordinary, everyday people—housewives, cooks, maids, laborers, children out of school. We had made no provisions for these people going to jail because we did not anticipate the mass arrests. So we concluded that night that we really need some expert help here, someone who has had the experience.

I knew Dr. King from years earlier. I knew him well enough that if I were to call him he would come down and help us. Needless to say, there was not total agreement initially with issuing this call. Because recognizing that now SNCC was on the scene and, by virtue of the Freedom Riders coming through, CORE was on the scene, and they did also have established organizations. We also recognized that to the extent that they received some publicity it helped to further their cause, and they would be able to raise money to continue their activities. But anyway, we were able to get a unanimous decision of the Albany Movement to call in Dr. King. I called him personally. And he merely asked if this is the desire of all involved. And I said, "Yes, it is." And he asked that I send him a telegram to that extent. I indicated on the telegram all the organizations that were represented now in the Albany Movement. And he responded to that call.

Andrew Young, a twenty-nine-year-old minister who had recently gone to work at the Southern Christian Leadership Conference headquarters in Atlanta, traveled the two hundred miles to Albany in the company of King and other SCLC staffers.

ANDREW YOUNG

The Albany Movement had asked Martin to come down just to make a speech, and he went only to make a speech. But people came from all over the region, and there were two big churches right across the street from each other that were filled, and people were all out in the streets in between. Dr. Anderson got carried away, and in public asked Martin to demonstrate, to lead the march with him. And he agreed, and then he got put in jail, with no plan, no thought of what we were going to do.

King and more than 250 demonstrators were arrested on December 16. He vowed to stay in jail until the city desegregated.

CHARLES SHERROD

When the decision was made by the movement to call in Dr. King, we had about five hundred to seven hundred people already in jail. I was in jail, and Cordell was in jail. There was only one of our group left out. I was in jail to stay, and I had programmed everybody to follow me in jail. We were going to break the system down from within. Our ability to suffer was somehow going to overcome their ability to hurt us.

It was the frustration on the parts of the adults who were then in charge while we were in jail that made them feel like they needed Dr. King. In jail all kinds of things happen. Kids are being hurt, females had physical needs, somebody's getting smacked. All kinds of pressures are brought upon the leadership. But pressure is also being brought against the opposition, which is the intention of the whole thing. One old person said, "Pressure make a monkey eat pebble," and we just pushed: pressure, pressure, pressure. Sometimes we don't know who controls this, who controls the other. So we stomp and stomp, and see whose feet we get. And then somebody's going to holler, "Oh, you got me." So then, when he hollers, that's the direction we go in. And that was the general strategy. We didn't know what we were doing. We'd never done it before. Nobody had never got that many people to go to jail. And

I'm not talking about just the hoi polloi, I'm talking about the upper crust. The great people in Albany. Even some white folk went to jail with us, from Albany. So we were steamrolling. After the fact, they come up with all these theoretical things about what happened in Albany. And perhaps some of them were true. Sure, there were conflicts. When you get a personality—I'm soft-spoken now, for the most part, till you get me riled up, you know—but when you get a soft-spoken personality, but a stout personality, like myself, coming head to head with Dr. Wyatt Tee Walker, who was the executive director at that time of SCLC, you going to have a few fireworks. So what? What's most important? They don't talk about the unity we had. About the strength we had, for the first time.

> The Reverend Wyatt Tee Walker was no stranger to Charles Sherrod. They both came from Petersburg, Virginia, where Sherrod had been a member of Walker's church.

WYATT TEE WALKER

In Albany we in SCLC were like fire fighters. The fire was already burning and, I try to say this as charitably as I can, SNCC was in over its head. They wanted the international and national attention that Martin Luther King's presence would generate, but they did not want the input of his organization, nor his strategy, which was considerably different from the methodology and strategy of SNCC.

Dr. King felt he was between a rock and a hard place. He could not say at Dr. Anderson's invitation that it won't work into my schedule, or I can't come, because nonviolent struggle is what Dr. King was about, and it was under the aegis of his leadership that it was introduced on the American scene. It had been introduced before, but Dr. King introduced it on a mass scale. So it was a natural place for him to be. But without having organizational input and control it was a very difficult campaign for him.

LAURIE PRITCHETT

After the SNCCs came into Albany, I had information from a law enforcement agency, a federal agency, who I worked with quite close. They informed me that Dr. King's intentions were to come into Albany and join the Albany Movement. Upon learning this, I did research. I found his method was nonviolence, that his method was to fill the jails—same as in India. And once they filled the jails, we'd have no capacity to arrest and then we'd have to give in to his demands. After learning this and studying this research, I started orientation of the police department into nonviolent movement—no violence, no dogs, no show of force. I even took up some of the training the SNCCs originated there—like sitting at the counter and being slapped, spit upon. I said, "If they do this, you will not use force. We're going to out-nonviolent them," and this is what the police department and the other people did.

Prior to King's arrival, I had sat down and took a map and went fifteen miles. How many jails was in a fifteen-mile radius, on up to maybe a fifty- or sixty-mile radius. I contacted those authorities, and they assured us that we could use their facilities. When the mass arrests started, we'd have marches and there'd be two hundred, three hundred—at one time there I think we had almost two thousand—but none in our jail. They were in surrounding counties under our supervision, so as nothing would happen to them. We never had any in our jail, they were all in surrounding counties. So when these mass marches started, we were well prepared.

My position was chief of police. It didn't deal in segregation or integration. My responsibility was to enforce the ordinances and laws of that city and state. As I told Dr. King many times, I did not disagree with his motives or his objectives, it was his method. I believed in the courts, he believed in the streets. So I've never been classified as a segregationist, and not as an integrationist. I was administrator of the city of Albany's police department.

WYATT TEE WALKER

Laurie Pritchett posed as a sophisticated law enforcement official. A more apt description would be slick. He was not nonviolent, as I've seen some people write. He was nonbrutal.

He developed the reputation that he was using Dr. King's nonviolence to blunt Dr. King's campaign, which was not true. The foil for our nonviolent campaigns in the South had been the anticipated response of segregationist law enforcement officers such as Bull Connor in Birmingham, Alabama. Laurie Pritchett was of a different stripe. He probably had finished high school, and he did have enough intelligence to read Dr. King's book on the Montgomery boycott. He culled from that a way to avoid confrontation in inducing the great ferment in the national community by being nonbrutal rather than being nonviolent. It's bizarre to say that a segregationist system or a law enforcement official of a segregationist system could be nonviolent, because, first of all, nonviolence works in a moral climate, and segregation is not a moral climate.

CHARLES SHERROD

Some people say Chief Pritchett was nonviolent. How could a man be nonviolent who observed people being beaten with billy clubs? One young lady was dragged up the steps of the courthouse, after being arrested, by her hair. Another man, Reverend Samuel Wells, was dragged into the courtroom by his gonads. One person was hung in the jailhouse by his thumbs. All under the direction and authorization and officiating of this nonviolent police chief, Laurie Pritchett. I just don't understand how they could come up with this, but it has been the case.

I remember a statement that Chief Pritchett made to me one time. "You know, Sherrod," he says, "it's just a matter of mind over matter. I don't mind, and you don't matter." That statement was certainly true of people that he sent to Terrell County and Baker County, 'cause I witnessed it myself. The deputy sheriff slapped me almost unconscious, just because I said yes and no. Those were the early days when I didn't know that you just didn't say yes or no to these white folks, you had to say yes, sir, and no, sir. And the same things were done a thousand times all over. They took the heat off us in the winter, and wouldn't give us any blankets or mattresses, and they stuffed forty people in cells.

BERNICE JOHNSON REAGON

What I can remember is being very alive and very clear, the clearest I've ever been in my life. I knew that every minute, I was doing what I was supposed to do. That was the way it was in jail and on the marches. In "We Shall Overcome" there's a verse that says "God is on our side," and there was a theological discussion that said maybe we should say, "We are on God's side." God was lucky to have us in Albany doing what we were doing. I mean, what better case would He have? So it was really like God would be very, very happy to be on my side. There's a bit of arrogance about that, but that was the way it felt.

I think Albany settled the issue of whether to go to jail. Songs helped to do that, because in the songs you could just name the people who were trying to use this against you—Asa Kelley, who was the mayor, Chief Pritchett, who was the police. This behavior is new behavior for black people in the United States of America. You would every once in a while have a crazy black person going up against some white person and they would hang him. But this time, with a song, there was nothing they could do to block what we were saying. Not only did you call their names and say what you wanted to say, but they could not stop your sound. Singing is different than talking, because no matter what they do, they would have to kill me to stop me from singing, if they were arresting me. Sometimes they would plead and say, "Please stop singing." And you would just know that your word is being heard. There was a real sense of platformness and clearly empowerment, and it was like just saying, "Put me in jail, that's not an issue of power. My freedom has nothing to do with putting me in jail." And so there was this joy.

There's a song that a Reverend Hollaway would do, and it's called "Shine on Me." [*Begins singing.*] "Shine on me, shine on me, let the light from the lighthouse shine on me. Shine on me, shine on me, let the light from the lighthouse shine on me." It's like claiming your space. We had been too long out of the light. It was our time. It still is.

On December 18, 1961, two days after King's arrest and vow to stay in jail until the city was desegregated, the city and the Albany Movement announced a truce. According to the oral agreement, the movement would call off mass demonstrations in return for concessions from the city government. It felt like a victory for Albany's black community, so King and most of the prisoners accepted release from jail.

The bus and train stations were, in fact, desegregated. But with King returned to Atlanta and the national reporters gone, the city began to drag its feet on most concessions and, ultimately, refused to negotiate further. The movement, in turn, boycotted the segregated bus line and the stores downtown.

As the months wore on, small skirmishes like sit-ins replaced the head-on assault of the earlier mass marches. One of the Albany Movement's great frustrations was the apparent inability, or unwillingness, of the federal government to intervene.

WILLIAM G. ANDERSON

We never at any time got any of the Justice Department officials [from the civil rights division] to come in, to my knowledge. Even as observers during the arrests or the court hearings. There were FBI agents on the scene, but no one from the Justice Department. I would have expected a representative from the Justice Department to be on the scene as an observer if nothing else. Because civil rights were being violated. For example, we were not permitted to demonstrate at all, even following all the guidelines that had been set forth by the city. We attempted picketing of selected stores in small numbers, widely spaced, not blocking any ingress or egress. We would do that and still get arrested. I was arrested on several occasions just walking down the street holding a piece of paper in my hand, under the pretext of passing out literature without a permit or something to that effect. I'm saying that Justice officials were not there as observers, and if they were there, mind you, they were not identified as such. To my knowledge, no action was taken relative to the violation of our civil rights.

BURKE MARSHALL

My recollection with Albany, Georgia, is that the city claimed they weren't arresting people to enforce segregation. They were arresting them for some other purpose. So that was a dispute. I have no doubt about which side of the dispute was right, but there was a dispute and an argument. When the movement in Albany moved out of the bus station where it started from and into other areas of the city and other problems, we didn't have the authority we could wave at the city of Albany that we had in the case of the bus stations.

The FBI had a mindset—I don't know whether I'd call it a southern mindset, I would call it a Hoover mindset. And the

Hoover mindset was anti–civil rights movement. For reasons that may have been pure racism. It may have had other motives in it, I don't know. Mr. Hoover at that time was not showing good judgment about anything, in my opinion. That is not, however, the complete explanation for the reasons that the civil rights movement complained about the behavior of the Bureau.

Wholly apart from Mr. Hoover's feelings about the civil rights movement, he had for a long time stuck to the notion that the Bureau was purely an investigative agency. It worked in his highly bureaucratic mind this way: if there was reason to believe that what happened violated a federal law, wasn't just wrong or unjust, or hurt somebody, but violated some federal law that you could name, then some lawyer in the Justice Department—civil rights division in this case—would write him a memo, addressed to Mr. Hoover, saying please make a preliminary investigation or please make a full investigation of the following matter. Then he would insist on knowing what federal law had been violated.

So just speaking very broadly, if somebody beat somebody up on the streets of Albany, that violates justice. It violates a city ordinance in Albany, it may violate the law of the state of Georgia. But it doesn't violate, normally, any federal law, so the FBI will say that it's none of their business. And it will say that it's none of their business not only to investigate it afterwards, but that it's doubly none of its business to interfere with what's going on at the time, since Bureau agents are not policemen, they're investigators. Their job is to produce evidence to go into court later and not to interfere. Now that's the position. Of course, he didn't hold to that position with, say, bank robberies, so it's not a coherent or consistent position. But as I understood it, that was his position throughout the period.

When King and Ralph Abernathy returned to Albany in July 1962 for sentencing on their December arrests, the two men chose forty-five days in jail rather than admit guilt by paying a fine. With King in jail, the conflict in Albany was once again national news. The mass marches resumed, and black youngsters stoned Pritchett's police cars.

For the second time, King vowed to stay in jail. Also for the second time, Pritchett and the city fathers maneuvered to get him out.

LAURIE PRITCHETT

I knew that if Dr. King stayed in jail, we'd continue to have problems, so I talked to some people. I said, "We've got to get him out, and once we do, I think he'll leave here." An arrangement was made. Frankly, I don't know who the man was that paid the bond, but it was done at my request.

It sort of surprised Dr. King. This was the only time when it seemed he didn't know which way to go. 'Cause, see, when we went back and got him, he thought he was being transferred to a better jail in Americus, Georgia. When I said, "No, you're leaving," he said, "I can't go, Chief Pritchett. I'll lose face if I go." I said, "Well, you've got to go, Dr. King." Later on, after it was all over, we discussed this, and he told me, "This is one time, not only did you out-nonviolent me, but you outsmarted me." You know, it was a shrewd move, but it accomplished what we wanted to do.

After King's release, the campaign to immobilize him continued when the city attorney on July 21 obtained a federal court order that enjoined King and other leaders from demonstrating.

CORETTA SCOTT KING

In Albany we had a federal injunction placed against us. And when the federal court started ruling against us, that created a whole different thing in terms of what strategy do you use now? Because up to that point, Martin had been willing to break state laws that were unjust laws, and our ally was the federal judiciary. So if we would take our case to the federal court, and the federal court ruled against us, what recourse did we have? So we were working in concert with the federal laws, all the time, in the South, up to that point. [Now] he was asking President Kennedy, and the attorney general, Bobby Kennedy, for an intercession in Albany. He was asking the Justice Department to intercede as a friend of the court, so that injunction could be lifted. Because if you break the federal injunction, that would be a problem.

CHARLES SHERROD

The injunction didn't have a great immobilizing effect on us. We had a mass meeting that very night. I remember it very clearly. Reverend Samuel B. Wells got up in the mass meeting—we had talked before, because we talked about these things before we did them, most of the time; a lot of things were spontaneous, but not everything—Reverend got up there, we called him black Jesus, he was a beautiful black man, big. He got up there and he held up the injunction that the judge had handed down. He said, "I see Dr. King's name, and I see Dr. Anderson's name, and I see Charles Sherrod, and I see this, but I don't see Samuel Wells, and I don't see Mrs. Sue Samples, and I don't see Mrs. Rufus Grant. Now, where are those names?" And with that, and two or three other very colorful expressions, taken out of the great tradition of our church, he marched about seventy-five folk out of that church, and they went to jail that night. So the movement did not stall. We did not stop doing anything that we had been doing.

Now, I can't help how Dr. King might have felt, or Wyatt Tee might have felt, or Bernard Lee, or any of the rest of them in SCLC, NAACP, CORE, any of the groups, but as far as we were concerned, things moved on. We didn't skip one beat.

SNCC never did consider Albany a defeat. But for King and the ministers of SCLC, the small city in southwest Georgia had become a morass. After the brutal beating of a pregnant black woman, Mrs. Slater King, at one of the outlying jails in Laurie Pritchett's rural network, blacks in Albany again responded by hurling bottles and bricks at Albany police, a rejection of King's nonviolent credo. To reassert moral leadership, King went to jail in Albany for the third time, but again he was soon released.

Mass meetings and protests would continue in Albany for most of the decade. But King's participation ended when he left the city in August 1962.

ANDREW YOUNG

When Martin left Albany he was very depressed. But he knew what had happened. He really felt that it was a federal judge that called off that movement. He had a very emotional exchange with Burke Marshall over that, because he felt that the Kennedy administration had helped to undercut the possibility of continuing in Albany.

The weakness of the Albany Movement was that it was totally unplanned and we were totally unprepared. It was a miscalculation on the part of a number of people that a spontaneous appearance by Martin Luther King could bring change—that it wasn't just a spontaneous appearance by Martin Luther King, it was the planning, the organizing, the strategy that he brought with him that brought change. The weakness was not understanding that.

The strength was that I don't know that there were any more powerful and beautiful people. Albany was one of those areas where blacks seemed to be still intact culturally. The singing, the folklore, had a kind of indigenous power to it that meant you couldn't walk away from Albany, Georgia.

WILLIAM G. ANDERSON

The Albany Movement was a qualified success. Qualified in that at the time the movement came to an end—and it didn't come to an abrupt end; it was sort of phased out, marked by the cessation of the mass demonstrations and the picketing—none of the facilities had been voluntarily desegregated. The buses had become desegregated, the train station, the bus station. But these were being desegregated by federal edict. It was not a voluntary move on the part of the people of Albany. But the lunch counters, the parks, and other public accommodations were not desegregated and there were no blacks employed as clerks in the stores at the time the Albany Movement came to an end, that is, in the sense of no more mass demonstrations.

But the Albany Movement was an overwhelming success in that, first of all, there was a change in the attitude of the people: the people who were involved in the movement, the people involved in the demonstrations, because they had made a determination within their own minds that they would never accept that segregated society as it was, anymore. There was a change in attitude of the kids who saw their parents step into the forefront and lead the demonstrations. They were determined that they would never go through what their parents went through to get the recognition that they should have as citizens.

Secondly, the Albany Movement was a success in that it served as a trial or as a proving ground for a subsequent civil rights movement. It gave some direction. The mistakes that were made in Albany were not to be repeated. For example, that settlement on a handshake in December 1961. That would never be repeated anytime in the future.

Bringing in Dr. King was probably the smartest thing that we ever did. Not only did we get the benefit of having a well-established, well-experienced civil rights organization as a part of the Albany Movement, but it also brought in world attention. The eyes of the world were focused on Albany primarily because of Dr. King. There was not a major newspaper in the world that was not represented in Albany. Not a major television network in the United States that was not represented in Albany. Having seen the results of his coming there in terms of the increase in the number of media people present, I know that they came there because Dr. King was there. He was a media event. We needed the media attention because we thought that we could not get what we were looking for by appealing to the local people. There would have to be outside pressure, and the only way we could get the pressure would be for the media to call to the attention of those outside people what was happening in Albany.

In 1976, fifteen years after he first arrived, Charles Sherrod was elected to the city commission of Albany, Georgia.

CHARLES SHERROD

Some people talk about failure. Where's the failure? Are we not integrated in every facet? Did we stop at any time? What stopped us? Did any injunction stop us? Did any white man stop us? Did any black man stop us? Nothing stopped us in Albany, Georgia. We showed the world.

7

James Meredith Enters Ole Miss, 1962

"Things Would Never Be the Same"

James Meredith, accompanied by Justice Department official John Doar, attempts to register at the University of Mississippi. Lieutenant Governor Paul Johnson (left) bars his entry.

On the last day of January 1961, almost seven years after the *Brown* v. *Board of Education* decision, James Howard Meredith, then a student at all-black Jackson State College, applied for admission to the University of Mississippi. Officials at Ole Miss returned his application and his ten-dollar room deposit fee. Meredith, it seemed, like the four blacks before him who had sought admission to this all-white institution, would have to go elsewhere to complete his schooling.

Meredith was determined to take his case public. In May 1961, lawyers from the NAACP Legal Defense and Educational Fund, Inc., an organization that provided legal services for civil rights–related cases, filed suit on his behalf in U.S. District Court. The suit charged that he was refused admission "solely because of his race." After more than a year of legal battles and appeals, on September 10, 1962, the U.S. Supreme Court upheld Meredith's right to be admitted to Ole Miss. Just three days after the court's ruling, Mississippi governor Ross Barnett announced to a statewide television audience that "there is no case in history where the Caucasian race has survived social integration." Barnett pledged that the state "will not drink from the cup of genocide."

The Supreme Court decision had come just ten days before registration day at Ole Miss. On September 20, Barnett had himself appointed university registrar and personally blocked Meredith's admission. Joining the effort to stop Meredith, the Mississippi state legislature passed a law barring admission to any state school of any individual "convicted of a state crime and not pardoned." While he attempted to register at the campus in Oxford, Meredith was tried in absentia by a justice of the peace in Jackson and convicted of the crime of false voter registration.

The Kennedy Justice Department was growing impatient with the state's evasion. That week, federal marshals unsuccessfully attempted to register Meredith a total of four times. On Saturday, September 29, the governor addressed the halftime crowd at the Ole Miss–Kentucky football game and continued his public stand against the "tyrannical" interference of outsiders in Mississippi's affairs. But privately, Barnett continued to negotiate with Attorney General Robert Kennedy.

A deal was struck. At 6:00 P.M. on Sunday, September 30, Meredith was flown into Oxford and secretly escorted onto the campus. Stationed on or near the campus to protect him were 123 deputy federal marshals, 316 U.S. border patrolmen, and 97 federal prison guards. Within an hour, they were under attack from a mob that would eventually number more than two thousand. Under orders not to shoot back, the marshals were assaulted throughout the night by guns, bricks, bottles, Molotov cocktails, and a bulldozer. The marshals fought back with tear gas. With the arrival of federal troops ordered in by President Kennedy, the mob finally retreated into downtown Oxford around six the next morning. It had been a shooting war. Two people were dead. Twenty-eight marshals had been shot and 160 injured.

At eight o'clock in the morning, James Meredith became the first black student to register at Ole Miss.

NAACP field secretary Medgar Evers had been one of the four blacks who sought admission to Ole Miss prior to 1961. To Evers's wife, Myrlie, Meredith was "a very private person, not one to talk or brag about himself too much," but at the same time a man with a "sense of mission and responsibility and duty."

MYRLIE EVERS

When Meredith finally enrolled in Ole Miss, it was a triumph. It was something that many people had worked for. It validated the legal system, and it validated the NAACP's approach to this issue. It validated Medgar's involvement and the sacrifices, the hard work, that he had put forth to try to help Meredith get in, and I think it validated Meredith in his ability to stick to it, and see it through. It was a major breakthrough. It said, indeed, that there is hope, and that we are moving forward and that perhaps the sacrifices that had been made had been worth it, because we are talking about not just one man's education, but what will happen for the rest of other generations yet to come. And we celebrated.

One of the reasons that Ole Miss was such a difficult university to desegregate was the emphasis that the Mississippi press gave to the desegregation of Mississippi. I can recall one of the newspapers having a front-page editorial with a broad black band around it that called for blood to flow in the streets if the school was desegregated. Of course, the governor took a very active role in talking about the threats that the state would make on its blacks who would try to enter the school. It was an effort to instill fear in the hearts of blacks, and it was also an effort, and a very successful one, to arouse fear and a kind of frenzy in the white community to fight back against the change within their system. We were hitting them at the very heart of it, in the educational system. The media played up all of the negatives that could possibly happen. The radio stations continually played the Rebel songs. You had the Rebel calls, and almost every five minutes you had a message from the governor saying that we must resist, that the federal government is an enemy of ours, that we are, if you will, kind of an island unto ourselves. It really took one back into the days of the Civil War. It was a maddening time. But it was also a time that gave us, as a people, more determination to follow through.

Jan Robertson was managing editor of the Ole Miss student newspaper, the *Mississippian,* which warned that rioters "are bringing dishonor and shame to the University and the State."

JAN ROBERTSON

People in Mississippi had a very strong emotional response to Meredith. It was just Mississippi and Ole Miss against the world: "They're not going to tell us what to do. We're not going to be pushed around." It was a gut-level response. Ole Miss just happened to be the battleground. And this was the chance to fight for states' rights, for the southern way of life, and for all those people that just wanted to fight back, they chose Ole Miss as the place to do it.

Assistant Attorney General Burke Marshall played a major role in the negotiations between the Kennedy administration and Governor Barnett.

BURKE MARSHALL

Governor Barnett was intransigent and he was also stupid. He had a narrow political vision. He knew that Meredith was going to the University of Mississippi, he just didn't want it to be his fault. So that if you could give him a way of acting like a governor and performing a governor's duty and at the same time say, I couldn't help it, then Governor Barnett's very narrow, short-range, stupid political values and political goals would have been achieved. What we were trying to do in the negotiations between President Kennedy and Governor Barnett—which may read like silly conversations now, because they were with a silly man—was to try to give him an out of that sort. It almost worked, and the trouble is that Governor Barnett didn't have the confidence of anybody. He didn't have the confidence of the students, he didn't have control of the police force, or if he did have control of the police force he didn't exercise it. He pulled the state police out at a critical moment during the riot, and so in the end we did what we were always determined to do when necessary, which was to use federal, physical force.

Of course, the president's gonna win in the end. He's got the whole armed forces of the United States. He can call in the air force, he can bring navy ships up the Mississippi River, he can call out the army as he did, he can drop parachuters in. I suppose he could shoot missiles at Oxford, Mississippi. So he's gonna win at the end.

Wiley Branton had served as attorney for the NAACP in the Little Rock school desegregation case. He was director of the Southern Regional Council's Voter Education Project at the time of the Meredith case.

WILEY BRANTON

When I hear all this stuff about the Kennedys, I think about the fact that throughout this period, the most defiant judges we had to encounter in the South were Kennedy appointees—the people who almost led the movement in defying civil rights. I must admit, I get angry. I had great admiration for Burke Marshall, but at the same time we used to quarrel all the time. I was at Oxford on the night of the riot, not because I was then working for the Justice Department, I joined the Justice Department later, but because I wanted to be there to say to the Burke Marshalls and to the others the role that I thought they should be playing. Yes, ultimately the president will win. But why in the hell don't they say that in the beginning? And why don't they come out with all the might and power of the United States government? We would not have had these kinds of problems if they had.

John Doar, an attorney in the Justice Department, was assigned by Robert Kennedy to serve as Meredith's escort during the confrontation between the United States and the state of Mississippi.

JOHN DOAR

Would the Justice Department of the United States government ever have done it that way again? No, they wouldn't have. Did the state of Mississippi have any justification for the way it behaved?

Absolutely not, there was total lawlessness. The people that came up there to get into the riot, did they have any right to come up from halfway across Mississippi, or halfway across Alabama, to get into that thing? No. But I suppose that with power and authority you have to take the responsibility for doing it right, and I'm sure that everybody in the Justice Department believed that if you were going to be confronting something like this again you had to do it with a lot more force than two or three hundred marshals, and you couldn't depend on the state police force of Mississippi. You just could not depend upon 'em. That would not work. So when we went in with Vivian Malone to the University of Alabama in 1963, we went in in quite a different way. There was lots more military power.

When James Meredith was registered that next morning, everybody was worn out. There was a lot of physical destruction. The Lyceum building was pretty well messed up 'cause of all the people moving in and out of there, there was debris around, and I had no feeling of elation about what had been accomplished. It seemed to me that it was just another step in a long, long effort to break the caste system. There was no feeling of satisfaction, no feeling that a heck of a lot had been accomplished, but a feeling that the government did what it said it was going to do.

William Simmons was editor of the newspaper published by the Mississippi Citizens' Council and one of the chief spokesmen for the organization. The Citizens' Council, formed by whites in 1954 in the wake of the *Brown* decision, had helped elect Ross Barnett to the governor's office in 1959.

WILLIAM SIMMONS

When Meredith was brought in to Ole Miss by the U.S. marshals and the riots broke out, I was in the Citizens' Council office in Jackson. We were kept aware of what was going on through radio reports. There was a lot of excitement because rumors were flying that Governor Barnett would be arrested by United States marshals. Many people, probably several thousand, surrounded the governor's mansion in downtown Jackson and stood there. It was very orderly, not too excitable, but they stood there as a sort of human barrier, to protect the governor and to simply show solidarity with him in support for his position in trying to protect the integrity of the university.

We thought the use of marshals was pretty bad. We viewed the whole episode as an attack on the authority of the state. It was apparently politically mandatory for President John F. Kennedy and Attorney General Robert Kennedy to put a black in Ole Miss. They had been suffering from a bad defeat when the Freedom Riders had tried to invade the state. So it appeared politically necessary for them to show some results. Mississippi was a good whipping boy and also the symbol of resistance to the Supreme Court's decision, so why not humiliate the state and show the fist? And that's exactly what happened.

After it was all over, the next day was a beautiful fall day, bright sunshine, blue sky. I looked out the window of our office overlooking the governor's mansion. We were on the third floor, and my wife was standing there beside me. We looked at people walking down the street, normally going about their everyday affairs, and I turned to her and I said, "These people have just been deprived of the power of self-government, and they don't know it." That's the shock. The realization came to me that the enormous usurpation of power by the federal government had succeeded and from then on things would never be the same.

JAN ROBERTSON

The day after the riot, I remember getting up and going to brush my teeth. There was a ravine behind the sorority house, and I looked down and there were men in military uniforms encamped there. I was very relieved to see them there, because it had been a very frightening night; you heard the sound of gunfire, but you really didn't know what was going on. Most people were back in their dormitories or their fraternity or sorority houses. There was tear gas everywhere. Most people just really didn't go out. There were a few classes that met. I tried to go to one, but the tear gas was so bad you couldn't stay there. There was a stunned silence. You saw very few people out on the campus, very few students or faculty. A lot of people went home. Their parents wanted them to get home. You didn't know what on earth was going on, but at that particular time you could believe anything could happen.

There was some anger, but there was just this stunned disbelief that this had happened on our campus.

I think something was won by Meredith's enrollment: the right of a person regardless of race to attend the school of his choice. But I think innocence was lost. I don't think that most of the students thought that it would ever come to real violence.

Constance Baker Motley, an attorney for the NAACP Legal Defense Fund, represented James Meredith.

CONSTANCE BAKER MOTLEY

What really happened in the Meredith case when the state decided to resist was that they were playing out the last chapter of the Civil War. You have to understand that everyone expected that Mississippi would resist. Mississippi had long been the state which offered the most resistance since the Civil War to the idea of equality for blacks.

The case demonstrated to the American people how the system really works. The Supreme Court does not have any means by which to enforce its own decisions, and it's rare indeed that a state government says, in effect, "We're not going to abide by a decision of the United States Supreme Court." Except for Arkansas [the Little Rock crisis] and Alabama [the Freedom Rides], the American people had never had to confront the issue of how a Supreme Court decision is to be enforced if there is resistance, and so they learned that it is the sworn duty of the president to uphold the law, and that he has the armed forces of the United States at his disposal to put down any physical resistance such as we had in Mississippi to the enforcement of a lawful order of the federal court. Under our system, the federal court is supreme to any state government, and the South was not agreeing to that proposition when it came to the rights for Black Americans. So our Constitution was put to the test and survived. Our country is stronger now for having had that demonstration of what the Constitution means in practical application.

James Meredith graduated from the University of Mississippi in 1963.

8

Birmingham, 1963

"Something Has Got to Change"

By order of Bull Connor, Birmingham commissioner of public safety, fire fighters turn their hoses on demonstrators, slamming them into a building.

"I draw the line in the dust and toss the gauntlet before the feet of tyranny . . . and I say segregation now . . . segregation tomorrow . . . segregation forever." These were the words of George C. Wallace when he was inaugurated governor of Alabama on January 14, 1963.

Many whites in Birmingham took heart. With a population of 350,000 in the 1960s, Birmingham was Alabama's largest city and the largest producer of iron and steel in the South. Some called the city's blue-collar roughnecks "millbillies." With its smokestack skyline and having been founded some six years after the end of the Civil War, Birmingham was not considered a typical southern town. But, in some quarters, it clung hard to the underside of what was considered the southern way of life. The Ku Klux Klan had sympathizers in the police department and local government. Birmingham's Eastview 13 Klavern of the Klan was believed to be one of the most violent in the South. One of its members was Robert Chambliss, known around town as Dynamite Bob. Since the end of World War II, as many as fifty bombings had rocked the city. Many black churches had been targets, and two synagogues. One black section of town was attacked so often people called it Dynamite Hill. The city itself was often referred to as Bombingham. So strong was the segregationist influence that the city had closed down its system of public parks and its professional baseball team rather than admit blacks.

Almost 40 percent of Birmingham's residents were black. Since the 1940s, several businessmen had attempted to establish a dialogue between blacks and whites but with little success. The city was run by a commission form of government and the three commissioners were in favor of the hard-line segregationist position. The Klan attack on the Freedom Riders at the Birmingham bus terminal in 1961, and the collusion that day between the Birmingham police, the Klan, and Public Safety Commissioner Eugene "Bull" Connor, pushed the city's moderates to action. In the 1963 election, voters threw out the old commission form of government, eliminating Bull Connor's power base. Connor also lost his bid for the newly created office of mayor. Albert Boutwell, formerly a leader in the white Citizens' Council but considered a relative moderate (for Birmingham) on racial issues, won that position in a runoff election.

Fred Shuttlesworth, the black civil rights activist and minister of Bethel Baptist Church, had fought the segregationist forces of the city for seven years. His own home had been bombed twice. When he had attempted to enroll his daughter in a white grammar school, he had been chain-whipped outside the school by angry whites. Shuttlesworth was the founder of the Alabama Christian Movement for Human Rights (ACMHR), established to replace the NAACP when that rights organization was banned by the state of Alabama during the Montgomery bus boycott. He was also one of the founders of SCLC.

From Shuttlesworth's embattled perspective, Birmingham segregationists made up "a three-tiered society. If the Klan didn't stop you, the police would stop you. And if the police didn't, the courts would." He felt Birmingham would be the ideal target for SCLC's next campaign.

FRED SHUTTLESWORTH

Coming out of Albany, which many people considered not a victory, Dr. King's image was slightly on the wane. The SCLC needed a victory.

In Birmingham, we'd been fighting for seven years. We had desegregated the buses and the terminals, and done many other things. Birmingham was suing me a lot, but also I was suing them—*Shuttlesworth* versus *Birmingham* got the parks desegregated, but then they closed the parks. So we won victories but we couldn't cash in on them. We needed something more than we were doing.

The SCLC needed something and we needed something, so I said, "Birmingham is where it's at, gentlemen. I assure you, if you come to Birmingham, we will not only gain prestige but really shake the country. If you win in Birmingham, as Birmingham goes, so goes the nation." So we invited Dr. King and the SCLC into Birmingham to confront segregation in a massively nonviolent way, with our bodies and our souls.

Wyatt Tee Walker was executive director of SCLC.

WYATT TEE WALKER

After Albany, Dr. King decided he wasn't going into any situation again where he was not in control. But the most valuable lesson we learned from Albany was that our targets were too numerous. We diluted our strength by going after everything that was segregated. Up to that time we had been trying to win the hearts of white southerners, and that was a mistake, a misjudgment. We realized that you had to hit them in the pocket.

When we started planning for Birmingham, I wrote a document, probably seven or eight typed pages, called "Project C"—it meant confrontation.

My theory was that if we mounted a strong nonviolent movement, the opposition would surely do something to attract the media, and in turn induce national sympathy and attention to the everyday segregated circumstance of a black person living in the Deep South. We targeted Birmingham because it was the biggest and baddest city of the South. Dr. King's feeling was that if nonviolence wouldn't work in Birmingham then it wouldn't work anywhere.

Learning from the Albany circumstance, I targeted three downtown stores. Since the Sixteenth Street Baptist Church was going to be our headquarters, I had it timed as to how long it took a youngster to walk down there, how long it would take an older person, how long it would take a middle-aged person, and I picked out what would be the best routes. Under some subterfuge I visited all three of these stores and counted the stools, the tables, the chairs, et cetera, and determined what the best method of ingress and egress was. Now, it occurred to me that we might not get into the stores downtown. They might block us from getting to downtown, so we had to have secondary targets. I then targeted the federal installations, the Social Security office, the Veterans Administration, where there were some eating facilities. For our tertiary targets, I had gone out into the surrounding suburban areas and looked at variety stores in shopping centers. And I felt that with those primary, secondary, and tertiary targets we would be able to do something. In addition to that, I spent time with the lawyers, mainly Arthur Shores, to be absolutely familiar with the laws of the city of Birmingham, Jefferson County, and the state of Alabama, so that we could anticipate what the legal moves would be on the part of the law enforcement officials.

The Reverend Joseph Ellwanger was a white Lutheran minister supportive of the civil rights movement in Birmingham.

JOSEPH ELLWANGER

Birmingham in 1963 was about as segregated a city in the South as you can find. There were still signs over water fountains. There were no black clerks in downtown stores. There were no blacks in the police or fire department. And there were a lot of open threats on the part of the police commissioner, Bull Connor, against any attempt to gain some of these rights. There was not even a single forum where blacks and whites regularly came together except for the Birmingham Council on Human Relations, which was suspect as some kind of communist organization by virtue of the very fact that blacks and whites came together. That group numbered about forty or fifty on paper, and when we actually met we were about fifteen to twenty-five.

There was not only the belief in the white community that blacks were inferior, but that belief was clearly articulated and was assumed as the basis for the segregation that had existed all these years. To break down the barriers of segregation is to permit, in that way of thinking, an inferior race to mix with a superior race, and the inevitable result would be—and this was a phrase that was even used in public—a mongrelization of and a pulling down of that white superior race. That underlay both the fears and the wild threats and the commitment that the KKK had to enforcing its viewpoints. Many members of the KKK had that as almost a religious belief in their hearts, that we've got to maintain that kind of purity of the race or otherwise we're dooming ourselves and our future generations.

As we think about what white people were afraid of in terms of the possibility of an integrated society, part of it was simply the fear of the unknown. Perhaps even deeper was the fear of the Ku Klux Klan and their threats becoming a reality. In Birmingham, we had had something like forty bombings in the previous ten years, so it was not an idle threat. And so among whites there was literally the fears for their lives and the kind of convulsions they expected in society if integration were attempted. There just would be open warfare in the streets.

My role in the Birmingham demonstrations was basically being part of a committee of twenty that met to do the planning. We met in the A. G. Gaston Motel, and I can still remember those sessions with Dr. King and Ralph Abernathy and Andrew Young, and it was an amazing experience of an openness towards everybody's ideas. There was no one who was not given the opportunity to help participate in the planning.

In contrast to Ellwanger's enthusiasm for King, many blacks and whites in the city's reform movement felt that progress could be made without forcing a racial confrontation. Meanwhile, in a last-ditch move to retain power, Bull Connor was challenging the legality of the new city government in the courts. White attorney David Vann and other members of the reform movement asked for just a little more time to deal with the city's problems. But King and SCLC would wait no longer. Project C began on April 3, 1963, with demonstrations downtown.

DAVID VANN

The day we swore in the new mayor and council, the headline said, "A New Day in Birmingham," and before the day was over, we discovered we had two mayors, two city governments, and Dr. Martin Luther King and the SCLC starting marches up and down the street. At first, there was a lot of resentment, both in the black community and the white community. I felt that I had set out to prove what you could do through the democratic process, and how you could bring substantial change even in tough things like race. Some of the black leadership had worked hard on electing a new mayor, defeating Connor. They felt they had commitments from the new government, and Dr. King was trying to pick up their crackers, you might say.

JOSEPH ELLWANGER

With Albert Boutwell having just been elected as mayor of the city of Birmingham—he was supposed to be a more liberal, more progressive mayor—leaders in both the black community and the white community were saying, "Please give Boutwell a chance to make the changes and he'll do it. Why are you pressing the issue with these proposed demonstrations coming right after he was elected?" That was a real struggle, because Boutwell had made some promises about fairer government but they were all generalities, and most thinking people recognized that unless Albert Boutwell had some real help in making those changes, he would meet with the same resistance that had been shown down through the years.

FRED SHUTTLESWORTH

The only difference between Bull Connor and Albert Boutwell was that Bull was a bellowing bull and Boutwell might have been a crying, trembling bull. We didn't think that any system of government at that time would do what we needed to do. To the outside it looked like it meant change, but to us it had been superficial.

A. G. Gaston, a millionaire black businessman, was the owner of the Gaston Motel and a member of the Chamber of Commerce. He was not entirely pleased with the decision to go ahead with Project C, but he had over the years provided financial help to the local movement.

A. G. GASTON

My interest in the civil rights movement wasn't so much helping myself, it was helping the other fellow so we all could survive. It wasn't a selfish movement, it was for all of us. Arthur Shores did quite a bit of the legal work, but I was fortunate enough to have had a little money, and I did the financing, most of it.

We didn't anticipate the need for Martin King at that time. We had a fellow named Shuttlesworth that was raising sand around here. Shuttlesworth was a leader. I got him out of jail many a time. He was a brave young man. He was the one who led the organization that brought King over here from Atlanta. Them folks had no place to stay when they started coming from Atlanta and Montgomery, and that's when I put them up at the motel.

I was with the movement, but my idea of approaching it was somewhat different from some of the folks that you might call radical. My place on the chamber there got some of the leaders to move. They were willing to do some things for me that they wouldn't have done for Martin King or Shuttlesworth.

Birmingham's business establishment did not want to spark a confrontation between King and Connor. The downtown sit-ins soon fizzled because most department stores simply shut down their lunch counters instead of calling police and generating mass arrests.

Frustrated by the lack of headlines, SCLC strategists switched to phase two, calling for mass protest marches. But few blacks in Birmingham volunteered to fill Bull Connor's jails. And Connor obtained an Alabama court order that enjoined King and other leaders from taking part in more demonstrations.

King would violate the orders of a state judge if he had to. But with fewer than 150 demonstrators in jail, with the local and national media virtually ignoring the protests, Project C was in serious trouble. On Good Friday, just nine days into the campaign, King and his advisers were confused, and facing defeat.

ANDREW YOUNG

We'd raised money. We had people in jail, but all of the money was gone and we couldn't get them out of jail. The black business community and some of the white clergy were pressuring us to call off the demonstrations and just get out of town. We didn't know what to do. Martin sat there in Room 30 in the Gaston Motel, and he didn't say anything. He listened to people talk for about two hours. And then finally he got up and he went in the bedroom and he came back with his blue jeans on and his jacket, and he said, "Look, I don't know what to do. I just know that something has got to change in Birmingham. I don't know whether I can raise money to get people out of jail. I do know that I can go into jail with them."

Not knowing how it was going to work out, he walked out of the room and went down to the church and led a demonstration and went to jail. That, I think, was the beginning of his true leadership, because that Sunday a group of white ministers published in the newspapers a diatribe against Martin, calling him a troublemaker and a communist, and saying that he was there stirring up trouble to get publicity. And he sat down and took that newspaper—he had no writing paper and he was in solitary confinement—and he started writing an answer to that one-page ad around the margins of the newspaper. By the time it came out three days later, it was what we now know as the "Letter from a Birmingham Jail." He put in concise form exactly what the problems were, the moral dilemma of segregation and racism.

King addressed his letter to the eight white clergymen who had attacked him for "unwise and untimely" demonstrations. About the issue of timeliness, he wrote, "When you are humiliated day in and day out by nagging signs reading 'White' and 'Colored'; when your first name becomes 'nigger,' your middle name becomes 'boy' (however old you are) and your last name becomes 'John,' and when your wife and mother are never given the respected title 'Mrs.'; when you are harried by day and haunted by night by the fact that you are a Negro, living constantly at tiptoe stance, never quite knowing what to expect next and plagued with inner fears and outer resentments; when you are forever fighting a degenerating sense of 'nobodiness'—then you will understand why we find it difficult to wait."

Despite its eloquence, King's letter did not receive much local or national attention when released, and worries continued to mount within SCLC about the campaign's impending failure. King accepted release on bond after spending eight days in jail.

The Reverend James Bevel, an SCLC organizer and veteran of the Nashville sit-ins, had been called to Birmingham by King. It was Bevel who initiated the third and most controversial phase of Project C.

JAMES BEVEL

Up to this point, about five to ten, maybe twelve people would go and demonstrate each day. My position was you can't get the dialogues you need with a few. So the strategy was, Okay, let's use *thousands* of people who won't create an economic crisis because they're off the job: *the high school students*. Besides, most adults have bills to pay, house notes, rents, car notes, utility bills, but the young people—wherein they can think at the same level—are not hooked with all those responsibilities. A boy from high school, he can get the same effect in terms of being in jail, in terms of putting the pressure on the city, as his father—and yet there is no economic threat on the family because the father is still on the job.

We started organizing thc prom queens of the high schools, the basketball stars, the football stars, to get the influence and power leaders involved. They in turn got all the other students involved. The black community as a whole did not have that kind of cohesion or camaraderie. But the students, they had a community they'd been in since elementary school, so they had bonded quite well. So if one would go to jail, that had a direct effect upon another because they were classmates.

We held workshops to help them overcome the crippling fears of dogs, and jails, and to help them start thinking through problems on their feet. We also showed the "NBC White Paper" [a network television documentary] about the Nashville sit-ins in all of the schools. Our approach to the students was that you are responsible for segregation, you and your parents, because you have not stood up. In other words, according to the Bible and the Constitution, no one has the power to oppress you if you don't cooperate. So if you say you are oppressed, then you are also acknowledging that you are in league with the oppressor; now, it's your responsibility to break the league with him.

The first response was among the young women, about thirteen to eighteen. They're probably more responsive in terms of courage, confidence, and the ability to follow reasoning and logic. Nonviolence to them is logical: "You should love people, you shouldn't violate property. There's a way to solve all problems without violating. It's uncomfortable, it's inconvenient to have an immediate threat upon you; however, if you maintain your position, the threat goes away." Then the elementary students, they can comprehend that too. The last to get involved were the high school guys, because the brunt of the violence in the South was directed toward the black male. The females had not experienced that kind of negative violence, so they didn't have the kind of immediate fear of, say, white policemen, as the young men did. So their involvement was more spontaneous and up front than the guys'.

WYATT TEE WALKER

James Bevel had one of the best tactical minds in our movement, one of the best facilities for analyzing segregation as a system and what it does to black people. He is a native of Itta Bena, Mississippi, and anybody who grew up in Mississippi in his generation certainly had all of the emotional and psychological scars of what segregation does to them. So he was hypersensitive to it, and he drew very strong analogies as to how you had to fight the enemy. There was no one any better at mobilizing young people than James Bevel. Had it not been for him and the support of Dorothy Cotton with her leading skills and Andrew Young to some extent, the influx of the schoolchildren into the Birmingham equation might not have taken place. We knew we were right to use the children. One of the basic tenets of the nonviolent philosophy is that it is the kind of struggle in which everyone can participate—young, old, children, adults, blind, crippled, lame, whatever—

because it is a moral struggle. I think someone quoted me as saying six days in Jefferson County Jail would be more educational to these children than six months in the segregated Birmingham schools that they were attending.

> Bevel and his colleagues launched the next phase of the campaign on May 2, dubbed D Day by SCLC. As the children marched out of Sixteenth Street Baptist Church, Bull Connor arrested more than six hundred, ranging in age from six to eighteen. The next day, as another thousand children gathered at the church, an angry Connor called out the police canine units and ordered his firemen to rig high-pressure hoses. At one hundred pounds of pressure per square inch, the fire hoses were powerful enough to rip the bark off trees.

DAVID VANN

Bull Connor brought the police dogs to the scene of the marches. He was also the head of the fire department, and he had the firemen and their hoses come to the scene, and I remember I was talking to A. G. Gaston on the telephone, and he was expressing a great deal of resentment about King coming in and messing up the thing just when we were getting a new start, and then he said to me, "But, lawyer Vann, they've turned fire hoses on those black girls. They're rolling that little girl there, right there in the middle of the street now. I can't talk anymore." And there in a twinkling of an eye, the whole black community was instantaneously consolidated behind King.

While many people probably think these marches took place over many blocks, very seldom did they march further than from Sixteenth Street to Seventeenth Street. It was a masterpiece of the use of media to explain a cause to the general public of the nation. In those days, you had fifteen minutes of national news and fifteen minutes of local news, and in marching only one block they could get enough news film to fill all of the newscasts of all of the television stations in the United States. And of course, when the police dogs arrived and they started the hoses, the water, that just created very dramatic pictures. There was no way Dr. King could have bought that kind of thing.

The ball game was all over, once the hoses and the dogs were brought on.

Patricia Harris was one of the youngsters involved in the demonstrations.

PATRICIA HARRIS

My mother and my brother, they were locked up, the dogs were put on 'em and water was skeeted on 'em, and this type thing. But at that time, I guess by me being so young, my mother just didn't want to get me off into it. The serious violence, I wasn't involved in that, just the verbal abuse is mainly what I came in contact with. But some of the times that we marched, some people would be out there and they would throw rocks and cans and different things at us. I was afraid of getting hurt, but still I was willing to march on to have justice done. I was really afraid, because I had seen and heard about the real bad things that could happen. I used to wonder if things really got out of hand, what would I do? Where would I run to? So many people and everybody trampeding over everybody else. What would happen to me? And yet I was willing to continue and just go on and see what happened. I was really afraid, but I wasn't afraid enough to just say, "Well, I don't want to go on any longer," because actually I marched quite a bit.

On Saturday, May 4, more black children were knocked down by blasts from Connor's fire hoses. For adult onlookers at Kelly Ingram Park, this was too much—it was time to defend the kids. The crowd pelted the police with rocks and, as Bevel describes it, "began to organize their guns and knives and bricks." These were not the people schooled in nonviolence by SCLC organizers. In a surprise move, Bevel crossed the police lines, grabbed a bullhorn, and wheeled to face the crowd.

JAMES BEVEL

I took the bullhorn and I said, "Okay, get off the streets now, we're not going to have violence. If you're not going to respect policemen, you're not going to be in the movement." It's strange, I guess, for them: I'm with the police talking through the bullhorn and giving orders and everybody was obeying the orders. It was like, wow. But what was at stake was the possibility of a riot. In the movement, once a riot breaks out, you have to stop, and it takes you four, five days to get reestablished. I was trying to avoid that kind of situation.

By May 6, two thousand demonstrators had been jailed. The next day, a serious confrontation erupted at Kelly Ingram Park when police again turned on the fire apparatus. Across the street, the hoses slammed Fred Shuttlesworth against the wall of the Sixteenth Street Baptist Church. He was hospitalized with injuries.

The following day, a truce was declared so that negotiations could continue between the movement and the white merchants. The goal of movement negotiators was the desegregation of downtown stores, the hiring of black sales clerks, and ultimately the desegregation of other areas of the city's daily life. Black leaders believed it was the businessmen and not the politicians who held the real power to change law and local custom.

BURKE MARSHALL

The demonstrations were over jobs and lunch counters, over private establishments; they weren't over voting rights, they weren't over school desegregation. They were over private business behavior. There wasn't any magic lawsuit we in the Justice Department could bring. I had a discussion with the attorney general. He said, "Do you think you should go down there?" and I said, "I think I should." So I went down there, not knowing quite what I was going to do, but that I was going to try to get in the middle of it and see if it couldn't be resolved. The negotiations were prolonged and, like labor negotiations, a lot depended on just stamina. The way the negotiations worked was that the white businessmen wouldn't meet with Martin King because they called him an outsider—some of them wouldn't meet with any blacks at all—so that there had to be a sequence of meetings. I participated in all of them, in order to try to get some kind of agreement between people that often wouldn't talk to each other at all. I don't mean that the blacks wouldn't talk to anybody, but I mean there were many whites that wouldn't talk to any blacks and there were many more whites that wouldn't talk to certain blacks, and there were no whites, I think, except for David Vann, who would talk to Martin King. Andy Young was Martin King's closest aide during that period, and he was there at all of those meetings.

I remember an all-night session in which there was a disagreement, a very deep division of opinion, between Martin King and Fred Shuttlesworth about whether or not to accept the propositions that were then on the table from the white businessmen. It was a moment of difficulty and drama, but in the end, Dr. King exhibited enormous patience and enormous prudence, and he concluded that the movement should accept the agreement, which involved some lunch counters and some jobs by the white business establishment, and suspend the demonstrations to see if that worked.

FRED SHUTTLESWORTH

Martin's position was, we got to call it off. "Well," I said, "why we got to call it off?"

"The merchants said they can't negotiate with the demonstrations going on."

I said, "Well, hell, they been negotiating with them going on." And they had. I said, "No, we can't call it off."

See, I had a disagreement to begin with. I never thought Burke Marshall should negotiate with us and then go and negotiate with the whites. I thought that the whites and blacks should do it together. You never know with somebody going and talking to somebody and then come talking to you, what they're really doin'. So I reminded King that I didn't agree to that at first, but my thing was that we were not gonna call it off, regardless. I said, "But I tell you what you do. You go ahead and call it off, and I know we've got around three thousand kids over there in the church. When I see it on TV, that you have called it off, I will get up out of this, my sickbed, with what little ounce of strength I have, and lead them back into the street. And your name'll be Mud, it won't be Dr. King anymore."

Burke Marshall said he had made promises. I said, "Burke, any promise you made that I did not agree to is not a promise." Then they all realized they had to get my consent before they called it off. See, I really think that the merchants were gonna use Burke Marshall to get us to call it off. If we had just called it off without an agreement, the merchants would've said, "Well, we never agreed to anything." And we would not have gotten a victory. And King wouldn't've been immortal today, as simple as that sounds.

> The two ministers did eventually reach agreement and jointly announced a desegregation settlement the next day, May 10. Also resolved was the release of the three thousand demonstrators still in jail. The following night, after one thousand Klansmen held a meeting to denounce Birmingham's businessmen for negotiating with blacks, the city was ripped by explosions—at the home of King's brother, A. D. King, and at the SCLC headquarters at the Gaston Motel.
>
> Although no one was seriously hurt by the bombs, many were injured by Alabama state troopers under the command of Colonel Al Lingo. The troopers, ordered to disperse crowds gathering at the motel, were breaking heads as they moved in, and a full-scale riot ensued as blacks began to fight back. By morning, forty people had been injured, and seven stores set afire.

WYATT TEE WALKER

The night the Gaston Motel was bombed is a very ugly night in my memory. The agreement had been formally reached early Friday morning, and Dr. King and Shuttlesworth and Abernathy had issued a statement. This was the Friday before Mother's Day. The task then before me was to dismantle the Birmingham campaign. I had not been home to see my family in eleven or twelve weeks, and Martin, almost as an afterthought, said, "Wyatt, everybody's leaving, and somebody from the national staff needs to be here," and he asked me to stay.

I said, "I haven't seen Ann and the children in eleven weeks."

He said, "Well, I'll tell you what, SCLC will pay for them to come to Birmingham."

So my wife and four children were in Birmingham. My wife and the two youngest children were in the motel and the two eldest were staying with friends.

Saturday night, I heard this explosion and someone called and said it was A.D.'s house. While we were there, we heard another explosion, and I feared the worst. It was the motel. In the midst of that, the state troopers told the people to go to where they lived, and my wife turned to go to her motel room and this state trooper hit her with a carbine, split her head open, sent her to the hospital. And of course they had been in the motel when it was bombed. I was there within a matter of minutes. A UPI reporter from Mississippi, Bob Gordon, who was a segregationist up to this time, saved my life, because I asked him which state trooper had hit my wife. He pointed him out, and I started for him. Then Gordon tackled me and threw me to the floor and held me down. Then it occurred to me that this guy would take this automatic rifle and shoot me as quickly as he had brained my wife. Well, if Bob Gordon had not wrestled me to the floor, I think aside from me probably losing my life or being seriously maimed or injured, it would have done irreparable harm to the nonviolent movement. Because here was Dr. King's top lieutenant, his chief of staff, attacking a police officer. And I certainly would have been the aggressor. That's the way it would have appeared. However, I just wasn't thinking about anything except that my wife had been injured and hit with the carbine and that was the man who did it.

Rocks had been thrown the year before in Albany, Georgia. Now, in Birmingham, Alabama, buildings were set afire, a signal that black anger would not be forever contained in orderly marches led by nonviolent ministers. In the spring and summer of 1963, civil disturbances in American cities created an angry prelude to long, hot summers still to come.

9

ORGANIZING IN MISSISSIPPI, 1961–1963

"THE REALITY OF WHAT WE WERE DOING HIT ME"

After Amzie Moore (second from right) suggested that volunteers from outside Mississippi participate in political organizing in the state, Bob Moses (far left) worked to put the idea into practice. Other key organizers included Julian Bond (second from left), E. W. Steptoe (far right), and Hollis Watkins (left of Moore).

In the relative prosperity of postwar America, Mississippi continued to be both the poorest of all the states and the core of Deep South resistance to the black movement for civil rights.

In Mississippi, any black man or woman who attempted to register to vote might be met by retaliation from the police, the Citizens' Councils, the Klan, or the Democratic party state organization. Also, within some sectors of the black community itself, there was the generations-old belief that voting was strictly "the business of the white man."

The NAACP had been seeking legal remedies since it moved into the state in 1916 but with little success. Amzie Moore, head of the Cleveland, Mississippi, NAACP chapter, was a longtime veteran of that struggle. In 1960 he met Bob Moses, a twenty-five-year-old Harlem-born, Harvard-educated black schoolteacher working for SNCC, and presented a plan to help blacks resist the terrorism that had kept them powerless.

Moses soon learned that only 5 percent of voting-age blacks in Mississippi had been allowed to register, and that in some of the eighty-three counties, no blacks were registered at all. But the bleak statistics only hinted at the intimidation that had created them. The state in which Emmett Till had been killed in 1955 still had an arsenal of violence at the ready as the 1960s began.

BOB MOSES

In the summer of 1960, I was on a trip for SNCC. Ella Baker had written ahead to Amzie Moore, and I stopped in to see him in Cleveland, Mississippi. Amzie laid out what was to become the voter registration project for the Delta of Mississippi. He wanted SNCC to come in and do it. In fact, he was the only person in the leadership of the NAACP that I met at that time that was willing to welcome SNCC. I think he saw in the students what had been lacking—that is, some kind of deep commitment that no matter what the cost, people were going to get this done. They were actually going to get out there and do the job. He didn't want the legal procedures that he had been going through for years. He wanted to get the work done. So I agreed to come back and help on that project.

When I think about Amzie and his relationship to the movement, one of the things which I keep coming back to is his insight into Mississippi, into the consciousness and the mentality of white people who lived in Mississippi, and what it was that would be the key to unlocking the situation in Mississippi. He wasn't distracted by school integration. He was for it, but it didn't distract him from the centrality of the right to vote. He wasn't distracted at all about integration of public facilities. It was a good thing, but it was not going straight to the heart of what was the trouble in Mississippi. Somehow, in following his guidance there, we stumbled on the key—the right to vote and the political action that ensued.

AMZIE MOORE

I knew Bob was a graduate from Harvard and had taught [at Horace Mann high] school in New York. I felt like if a man was educated, there wasn't very much you could tell him. I didn't think you could give him any advice. To be honest with you, Bob was altogether different. Bob believed me and was willing to work with me. When I found out he was honestly seeking to help, then, in any way I could, I was willing to help him.

I was vice president of the state conference of the NAACP branches. I had worked with [Mississippi NAACP president] Aaron Henry; I did everything I knew how. Every time we moved, we had to move according to law. Unless we were advised to do certain things, we didn't do it. But when SNCC came, it didn't seem to matter what these white people thought. When SNCC moved, SNCC moved in SNCC's way. I'll tell you one thing—the only thing in the twentieth century that gave courage and determination to the blacks in the South is SNCC.

Bob Moses returned in July 1961 to set up SNCC's first voter registration project in Mississippi. The young organizer moved into Pike County in the southwest section of the state. Pike had two hundred registered black voters. The more rural, bordering counties, Amite and Walthall, had none (or, according to local legend, one black registrant between the two).

Headquarters for the SNCC project was the city of McComb, population thirteen thousand, some twenty miles north of the Louisiana line.

BOB MOSES

The first project started in McComb. We faced organized resistance at the state level. For example, we took people down to register in Liberty, in Amite County. On our way back, the highway patrolman who had been at the office all the time we were there flagged us down. He began talking to the people who had tried to register. When I got out of the car to ask him a question, he arrested me and brought me to the county jail in Pike County. I spent a couple days in jail when I refused to accept the sentence of the judge.

In Amite County, most of the people were afraid to go down to the courthouse to try to register. We had workshops for several weeks before we could get a handful who would agree to go if we went with them. Our position was that if the people wanted us to go with them, then we would go with them; if they wanted to go by themselves, then that was fine. I think they felt some sense of security, and clearly we were acting as a kind of buffer, because the initial physical violence was always directed at the voter registration workers. That was the first stage. Now, when that didn't work, you began to get violence directed at the local people who were involved. The first being Herbert Lee.

Justice Department attorney John Doar traveled to Mississippi to investigate conditions for voter registration. In Jackson, he met with NAACP field secretary Medgar Evers.

JOHN DOAR

Early in 1961, we had several counties under investigation for voter discrimination, but we had not done much investigating in Mississippi. We arranged to meet Medgar Evers at his house on a Saturday morning, I think, it was in the spring of 1961. We flew down to Jackson and went to his house early the next morning, and sat around the table with him and Mrs. Evers, and showed him the counties that we were interested in, principally, on that trip, in southern Mississippi. And we asked him who were the black persons in those counties who had attempted to register to vote, and where did they live? And he was able to give us the names of one or two black leaders in each county, and pretty well on his fingertips the efforts that they had made to try to get registered to vote in those counties.

So then we set out across southern Mississippi to find out where these people were, and locate them. On the second or third trip down there, I asked about efforts by white persons to keep blacks from registering, and one of the examples I got was from Mr. E. W. Steptoe. He said that there were people coming to the meetings taking down the license numbers of the people that attended. Taking down the license numbers suggested that there might be an effort at economic intimidation. I asked Mr. Steptoe if he saw the people that were taking down the numbers, and he said he didn't but Herbert Lee did. I asked him who the most powerful white person was in that area, and he said it was a man named Hurst, who was a state legislator.

Well, then we went down the road to try to find Herbert Lee. When we got to Lee's house, he wasn't there. I had to go back to Washington, and when I got back at ten o'clock the following night, there was a note on my desk that Herbert Lee had been killed. I learned that Mr. Hurst claimed that he'd been attacked with a tire iron and he had to respond by killing Lee.

A coroner's jury called on the day of Lee's killing, September 25, 1961, absolved State Representative E. D. Hurst of responsibility. Voter registration efforts were brought to a standstill. But McComb did not stay quiet for long. Demonstrations resumed in early October when high school students Brenda Travis and Ike Lewis, arrested for sitting in at the local Greyhound bus station, were expelled from the black high school after their release from jail.

To protest this decision, as well as the death of Herbert Lee, more than one hundred students marched to McComb City Hall. They were joined by several SNCC workers, including Bob Moses and Bob Zellner.

Zellner, a young white activist raised in Alabama, had been sent from SNCC headquarters in Atlanta by the organization's executive secretary, James Forman.

BOB ZELLNER

My job description at SNCC was going to be as a campus traveler, primarily to white southern campuses. To recruit and to bring the gospel of the movement to white campuses. I was so new myself that I kept bugging Jim Forman about how I was going to do this project, and he said, "Well, for one thing, you're gonna have to know a lot about SNCC. You're gonna have to know the people and the things that are going on, and the best way to do that is to go to a SNCC meeting." So I went to McComb for the purpose of attending a staff meeting. And my view was still that I'm going to a cut-and-dried staff meeting where I will listen and maybe meet some people. I had no idea it was going to be my baptism by fire.

Well, the meeting proceeded to discuss the voter registration campaign. The meeting had a strange atmosphere about it because we were meeting there in the upper room of the black Masonic Temple and we had the distinct feeling that the real action was somewhere else. We knew that the students were protesting the expulsion of Brenda Travis at the high school. So we sort of had this meeting with an ear to the outside, as it were. And like in any good movie, sometime in the middle of the afternoon we heard singing, faint strains of "We Shall Overcome." Everybody stopped what they were doing and we listened. It got louder, and soon the stairs were filled with young people coming up, setting about the business of making picket signs.

I immediately began to consider my relationship to it. I said, Well, I'm here to serve and they'll tell me what to do. Of course, I didn't realize that the whole modus operandi of SNCC was that nobody told anyone what to do. When that dawned on me, I said, That's no problem for me because I can't go on this march. They intended to march to protest the killing of Herbert Lee and also the expulsion of Brenda Travis. I knew that if I went on the march I'd be the only white person. They might put me in the newspaper. If I went, I might provoke more violence than would occur otherwise. My parents would get in trouble. My father would lose his church. My mother might not get a teaching job. This all happened during the time they were making signs. Then they started in on the stairs. It wasn't a question of, "Are you guys going to go with us?" They were going and everybody sort of made their decisions. All in a flash I said, I have to go. How can I not go? These are young people here in Mississippi. They're going to go on the first-ever demonstration like this and they can be murdered. What's going to happen to *their* parents? Are they going to lose their jobs? I went.

Hollis Watkins, twenty years old, was one of the students on the protest march.

HOLLIS WATKINS

As a native Mississippian, there were many things that I was risking. One thing I risked—and did face—was being ostracized by my family. From the time I participated in the first sit-in demonstration at Woolworth's lunch counter, my relatives would see me walking down the street and then they would pass over on to the other side rather than meet me on the street. Because they was afraid of what white people might do to them because they were my relatives. This is aunts, uncles, first cousins and, you know, close relatives. In addition to that, I put on the line the whole thing of being able to ever get a job in Mississippi, put on the line the whole thing of whether I would ever be able to get an education in Mississippi. Or whether that mark would go through onto my children and their children—or onto my mother and father, who was living, who had to support me at that time.

When we marched downtown to City Hall, we attempted to pray on the steps, but each time someone stepped on the steps, they were arrested. Then everybody that was on the march was just herded into the jail. Bob Zellner was one of the ones that was attacked and beaten. Others arrested were people like Curtis Hayes, Brenda Travis again, Ike Lewis again, and myself.

BOB ZELLNER

People just couldn't believe it when they saw me. They went into a level of hysteria. Their hysteria continued to grow and they would reach a certain peak and you would think they wouldn't get any more frenzied, and then they would. I began to observe one thing that was interesting: the interaction between members of the mob and the police. There was a vanguard of the mob, about ten or a dozen white men, and they began to gather round me and hit me. They would take a swing at me and they would not look for my reaction but they would look for the reaction of the cops. And the cops very clearly with their body language and everything else said, "Sure, get that son of a bitch." While this was happening, I was also aware that Charles McDew and Bob Moses, and maybe others, too, came to where I was and attempted to stand between me and these white people that were after me. And the first action of the police was to come over and get them and beat them with blackjacks. I remember the sound of the blackjacks as they hit the heads of Bob Moses and Charles McDew.

The mob dragged McDew and Moses off, and I was more and more isolated. They had just every kind of weapon you can imagine: baseball bats, pipes, wrenches. They started shouting to the men who were beating me more and more now. They said, "Bring him here, we'll kill him." They were screaming just absolutely like animals. I was holding this Bible and they started dragging me out in the street, and I realized that if they got me in the street, no matter what the cops did, nothing was gonna stop that mob from killing me. So I put the Bible down and grabbed ahold of the railing that went down the City Hall steps. I resisted. I don't know if I would have done that if I'd had a lot of nonviolent workshops. But I hadn't had very many nonviolent workshops. I remember thinking to myself, God helps those who help themselves. So I helped myself to the railing, and then it became a contest.

The crowd started screaming in a high-pitched, shrill scream that sounded like grief to me. It was just unreal. I hadn't seen the movie *Invasion of the Body Snatchers,* but it was that kind of sound. My hands were on the railing and they got two, three guys on each leg. They held me round the belt. And they would all pull. And I would hold on. They'd pull and they couldn't get me loose. And then they got even more excited and they started trying to hit my hands with the objects that they had: pipes and so forth. I would have to move my hand just very, very quickly back and forth on the pipe while holding on to keep them from really knocking my fingers off. Then one of the guys got behind me, got very hysterical, and came over the top of my head. This is a very grisly part, but he started putting his fingers into my eye sockets and he actually would work my eyeball out of my eye socket and sort of down on my cheekbone. And I remember being amazed that it would stretch that far. He was trying to get my eyeball between his thumb and his index finger so he could get a grip on it and really pull it out. He intended to gouge my eye out. So what I would do is, I would wait until he had maneuvered it into a good place and before he could clamp down, I would move my head in such a way that it would make him lose his grip. And my eyeball would slip between his fingers and pop back in my head, with a thunk.

During the protest, 119 students and 3 SNCC workers were arrested. Bob Zellner was taken to jail in Magnolia, the county seat.

BOB ZELLNER

A little bit after I got there, the sheriff came and took me out of the cell. He said, "The FBI's here to see you." There were four FBI agents all neatly turned out in their suits and ties. And they took me outside the building to take pictures of my head, my eyes, my face.

One of them sort of sneaked over out of earshot of the sheriff and he said, "It was pretty rough out there on the City Hall steps, wasn't it?"

And I said, "Yeah, you know it was nip and tuck there for a while."

And he said, "We didn't want you to think that you were out there by yourself. We were there. We got it all down."

And I never had the slightest misapprehension about the FBI from that point on.

Moses, McDew, and Zellner were sentenced to four months in prison. Brenda Travis was sent to a juvenile detention center for six months. By December 1, 1961, SNCC's voter registration project in McComb had come to an end.

The following year, SNCC joined forces with CORE, SCLC, and the NAACP to form the Council of Federated Organizations. COFO soon received financial help from an unexpected quarter. The Kennedys, after the political problems created by the sit-ins and the Freedom Rides, were eager to steer the movement away from direct action and into activities considered less confrontational. Foundation funding was arranged for a Voter Education Project under the auspices of the Atlanta-based Southern Regional Council. COFO received VEP monies and expanded its voter registration effort throughout the western half of Mississippi and into the Delta.

Lawrence Guyot, a twenty-three-year-old native Mississippian, was a SNCC field secretary who helped organize COFO.

LAWRENCE GUYOT

COFO was organized twice. In 1954, it was organized to deal with the 1954 Supreme Court decision. It was disbanded and remained dormant until 1962. It was then reestablished by Medgar Evers, Dave Dennis, Bob Moses, and Aaron Henry, who was made the titular head of it. We understood when we were organizing it that Aaron Henry would be the titular head and the spokesperson, but that SNCC—which provided more manpower than anyone else—would determine policy. We had that fight, that internal, friendly fight, out in Clarksdale, Mississippi.

There was no question about Medgar's commitment to COFO, no question about it. We invited Medgar to a meeting in Greenwood, Mississippi. See, for some thirty-two years, the NAACP had existed in Mississippi, before COFO was established, and before SNCC became active. But activism on a statewide basis, and involving people other than paid personnel of civil rights organizations—we started that. Medgar could identify with that, when he saw the kind of support we got from people in the Delta, Greenwood specifically.

Dave Dennis, a field secretary for CORE, had come to Mississippi in 1961 from Louisiana.

DAVE DENNIS

Bob Moses and I were codirectors of COFO. And once the organization was formed, we sort of merged everybody in to call ourselves COFO workers. SNCC workers were COFO workers, CORE workers were COFO workers, and those were the primary two groups that participated at that time. We did not see ourselves as other than COFO workers. We didn't organize SNCC chapters, we didn't organize CORE chapters. The national offices of CORE and SNCC didn't like that, but that's the way we felt we could keep from having any real competition among the organizations.

JOHN DOAR

In 1962, while the Meredith case was going on, and while Meredith was in his first year in the university, there were continued efforts by the SNCC kids to register voters. They had moved up into the Delta, and they had settled pretty much in the headquarters at Greenwood. Greenwood was a tough place, a really tough place. And they started to have demonstrations there at the courthouse and in Greenwood and people got arrested. We brought suits against the county officials and the state officials, and they were in court on these cases of intimidation. At the same time, we were trying to get more registrars to open up the rolls. We were battling. We weren't making any significant progress, but we had a lot of presence in Mississippi.

To retaliate against the growing voter registration movement, the Leflore County Board of Supervisors in Greenwood voted in October 1962 to cut off its participation in a federal program that distributed surplus food to needy families. That winter, twenty-two thousand residents—mostly black—were in danger of starving. SNCC responded by organizing a food drive of its own. Ivanhoe Donaldson became involved in SNCC as a student at Michigan State University.

IVANHOE DONALDSON

We raised food in various communities that we knew a lot of people in. A guy by the name of Ben Taylor and myself collected food at East Lansing and at Ann Arbor, Michigan, and we brought it down. We drove our truck down to Clarksville where Doc [Aaron] Henry was. He was the head of the NAACP in Mississippi, had his base in a drugstore. Everyone called him Doc Henry, but he was a pharmacist.

Prior to Christmas of '62, Ben and I arrived in Clarksville with a truckload of food in the wee hours of the morning, around two or three A.M. The store was locked and we didn't remember how to get to Doc's house, so we simply parked the truck in front of the drugstore and went to sleep. About two or three hours later the police woke us up. We were harassed and juggled around and thrown in jail. The charges were that we were taking narcotics across state lines, but what we had were aspirins and bandages as parts of first aid kits for people who might need medical help. We were locked up for about five days before anybody even knew that we were locked up. In the county jails in Mississippi, the prisoners did local labor. One of the jobs was to collect money out of the parking meters. I met this guy who was in the bunk beside me who was going to collect money on Fourth Street where Doc's store is. I gave him a little note saying, "Doc, I'm in jail, help. Ivanhoe." We were eventually gotten out of jail by a writ of habeas corpus by the NAACP Inc. Fund [the Legal Defense Fund]. The adventures of a SNCC field secretary!

I made about thirty-odd round trips to Louisville, to Detroit, round trips from Clarksville and Greenwood, back and forth, and also to Chicago during that period. In fact, one of the interesting points about the food drive was that a prominent young black comedian named Dick Gregory got involved with the movement and it totally changed his life. Dick Gregory, Harry Belafonte, and Sidney Poitier came to Greenwood, and Dick became quite a politicized person from that experience and became quite involved with SNCC.

Also politicized were the black residents of Leflore County. People who had been reluctant even to talk about registering to vote now lined up by the hundreds at the courthouse in Greenwood.

But for every black action there was a strong white reaction. As Moses had known all along, the idea that a voting project would provoke less violence than a Freedom Ride was totally out of touch with the reality of white Mississippi. In late February 1963, he was driving with two colleagues, SNCC worker and local Mississippian Jimmy Travis and Randolph Blackwell from VEP, when three white men pulled alongside and opened fire. Young Jimmy Travis was rushed to Jackson, where doctors removed .45 caliber slugs from his head and shoulder. Miraculously, he survived.

BOB MOSES

Medgar came to Greenwood after Jimmy Travis was shot on the highway, just gunned down, and addressed a mass meeting there. And I remember how he spoke to the people. Greenwood did something to him that made him feel that he needed to go back to Jackson and to really start working. That is, if people up in Greenwood could get themselves together and move in the way they had, then there was no excuse for Jackson, because Jackson of course had always been thought of as the leadership around civil rights in the state. So he went back determined to move Jackson.

At great risk to his own safety, Medgar Evers began leading an NAACP boycott of downtown stores in Jackson in May. Myrlie Evers often worked side by side with her husband in the Jackson office.

MYRLIE EVERS

When the students came along, with their spontaneity, with their willingness to be heard and to strike back if necessary, I think it was a kind of turning point for Medgar. I think it was that group of college students that helped light the fire, to make it burn more in him, to do something that would make things work a little faster. Medgar was very moved by the young people that volunteered to sit in the restaurants, who were beaten, who were spat upon, and who were thrown in a kind of concentration camp in the fairgrounds of Jackson, Mississippi. He was also moved by the Freedom Riders. He saw that this country as a whole, and particularly the South, was becoming more violent, and questioned whether that violence should not be met with violence of some sort—yet the other part of him realized that nothing could be solved by violence but more violence. And that had not quite jelled in his mind as to exactly what he was going to do.

Medgar did make a decision that the legal procedures that the NAACP had been following in the state of Mississippi were beginning to be somewhat outdated and that the movement had to accelerate its efforts. Medgar tried to get the support from the national office to endorse the sit-ins and other kinds of activities; he found that he had come up against a roadblock. The national office did not feel that those strategies and techniques were the ones that the organization should be pursuing. As a result, Medgar had some difficult days trying to decide whether he should actually remain with the NAACP or not. The NAACP was more than an organization; it was a family, people who worked very closely together and loved each other. But he also realized that things were changing, and the organization had to move along with it. He being the key spokesman, really the only person with his neck stuck out there, realized that he had to make a decision to move the efforts along. And he was prepared to do that even if it meant, as he told me, leaving the NAACP and starting his own movement.

Because of the success of the economic boycotts, because of the media attention that was given to our efforts, and specifically to Medgar as a leader of this movement, he became much more vulnerable, in terms of his safety and his life. Our home was firebombed; we received threats on almost an hourly basis at home. He received threats through the mail. It was a life of never knowing when that bullet was going to hit. It was something that he knew, but as he said to me, and as he said to his followers in the mass meetings, we can't let that stop us. I have to go forward, there's a job to be done.

Medgar was an absolutely marvelous father. He could talk to the children and tell them what was happening, and he devised a game with them where they decided where was the safest place in the house to hide if something happened. The children made a decision with their father that the bathtub was. They could not understand everything that was happening, but they were well aware that their father's life was in danger, and at their young ages—three, eight, and nine—they worried constantly about that.

Now, we had guns in every room of our house. I slept with a small revolver next to me on the nightstand. He slept with a rifle next to him. We had one in the hall, we had one in the front room. We often talked about it, and he said: "Yes, I will use it if it's necessary to protect myself, to protect my family, to protect my friends."

DAVE DENNIS

Medgar Evers and I were very good friends. He was one of the first people other than Bob Moses and others to befriend me when I first got to Mississippi. We was tight friends and we did things together, go out together, eat together. He was a very strong-willed person, very committed to the movement. A person who always had the fear, or feeling about death. When I say fear, it's that he wasn't afraid of dying. He felt he was close, and from what he did on a day-to-day basis, he knew he was a marked man. But his commitment was extremely strong, and you couldn't find a better human being. And he was more committed to Mississippi and the people as a whole than he was to any type of real organization. He had some very strong conflicts with the national office of the NAACP because of that. But at the same time, he was a firm and strong worker for the NAACP.

Medgar was not a nonviolent person. He did not feel that he should be aggressive, but he felt that he should defend himself. One of his reasons for not being willing to participate in a lot of things that we did as CORE people and SNCC people and COFO people was that he felt he could not be nonviolent. Medgar used to carry guns, you know, in the trunk of his car, for his own protection. I used to tease him about that too, because what are you gonna do with these in the trunk of your car, how you gonna get to it if the guy comes? We used to laugh, and he said, "Well, if I put it in the car and the cops catch me, I'll go to jail, or they'll claim that I had pulled a gun on them." So the gun was always in the trunk of his car.

MYRLIE EVERS

We came to realize, in those last few days, last few months, that our time was short. It was simply in the air. You knew that something was going to happen, and the logical person for it to happen to was Medgar. It certainly brought us closer during that time. As a matter of fact, we didn't talk, we didn't have to. We communicated without words. It was a touch, it was a look, it was holding each other, it was music playing. And I used to try to reassure him and tell him, Nothing's going to happen to you, the FBI is here—laugh—everybody knows you, you're in the press, they wouldn't dare do anything to you.

When he left that morning of June 11, 1963, and went out of the door, he told the children how much he loved them, turned to me, and said, "I'm so tired. I don't know if I can go on, but I have to." And I remember rushing to him and holding him, and he kissed me and said, "I love you," and he walked out of the door. I told him how much I loved him, too, and that it was going to be all right. And we clung to each other and he walked out of the door and he came back in and said, "I love you. I'll call you." During that day, he called two or three times, which was a little unusual with all of the activity that was going on. And each time he said, "I love you. I want you to know how much I love you."

And I told him the same thing. And he said, "I'll see you tonight." I said, "Fine."

DAVE DENNIS

Medgar and I had traded cars that day. He had my car and I had his car, all day and night. I'd used his car because I was doing some work in Canton, and I knew that every time I went in my car, the police would come and stop me. On the evening when we got back together, he told me that he had almost been run down by a car while he was trying to get into my car. He was teasing me about the fact that a man could get killed in this car. And I told him that I had had an incident too. I'd been stopped by some Klan members. And then he said, after the rally we will go to his house. I told him no, a person could get killed, you know. So we laughed about it.

> That night, as Medgar Evers attended a meeting in Jackson, Myrlie Evers and her three children watched at home as President Kennedy spoke on national television. It was Kennedy's strongest speech on civil rights, unexpected, powerful, and encouraging to movement leaders. Medgar, working until midnight, apparently missed it.

MYRLIE EVERS

Late that night, he came home. The children were still up, I was asleep across the bed, and we heard the motor of the car coming in and pulling into the driveway. We heard him get out of the car and the car door slam, and in that same instant, we heard the loud gunfire. The children fell to the floor, as he had taught them to do. I made a run for the front door, turned on the light, and there he was. The bullet had pushed him forward, as I understand, and the strong man that he was, he had his keys in his hand and had pulled his body around the rest of the way, to the door. There he lay. And I screamed, and people came out. Our next-door neighbor fired a gun, as he said, to try to frighten anyone away, and I knew then that that was it.

When Medgar was felled by that shot, and I rushed out and saw him lying there, and people from the neighborhood began to gather, there were also some whose color happened to be white. I don't think I have ever hated as much in my life as I did at that particular moment anyone who had white skin. I screamed at the neighbors, and when the police finally got there, I told them that they had killed Medgar. And I can recall wanting so much to have a machine gun or something in my hands, and to stand there and mow them all down. I can't explain the depth of my hatred at that point. And it's interesting how Medgar's influence has directed me in terms of dealing with that hate, then and over the years. He told me, as well as his children, that hate was not a healthy thing.

> Medgar Evers, aged thirty-seven, died in the early morning hours of June 12, 1963. The one fingerprint on the murder weapon belonged to Byron de la Beckwith, a fertilizer salesman and member of the white Citizens' Council in Greenwood. Murder charges were dropped after two trials in which juries failed to reach a verdict. A local hero to many Mississippi segregationists, de la Beckwith later ran for lieutenant governor in the Democratic primary. He was unsuccessful.

JOHN DOAR

I went to the funeral because I knew Medgar. I was his friend. His friends, people from all over the country, came to the funeral and wanted to have a march up the main street in Jackson. The police officials didn't want them to do that. They said they could only cross Main and then walk into a side street where blacks congregated. There was a street for whites and a street for blacks; the black street was a second-class street. The police put up a roadblock, put up a line of people and blocked, and said, You can't walk, you can't march on the main street of Jackson, Mississippi. And so you had a line of police and you had a line of kids, or three lines of kids, they were two or three feet apart, and the kids were singing and agitating, and yelling and shouting and complaining, and then, who pushed who first I can't tell you, but the police started to reach out and grab one, five, six of these kids and throw them in the paddy wagon. They got that stopped. And then they decided they would clear the street.

DAVE DENNIS

On the day of Medgar's funeral, there was violence. There was no way to predict it. There was a different element of people who had never participated in the movement before. They didn't want to have anything to do with us, because they felt that they could not cope with the nonviolence. It's not that they disagreed with the movement, but with the tactics that we used. These guys off the street were just angry, you know, and that day they decided to speak up. The police department and others came there. They actually antagonized the people. They were there in full riot gear, with guns, and they were being pretty rough with the people on the street. And the people just said, "We're not gonna take that. This is a funeral of our leader and here they are, you know, harassing us, and the white folk killed him."

That started a violent reaction. John Doar attempted to stop it. He was one of the few people that we found had a very strong commitment, a real commitment, to make the government respond in a positive manner. He made a genuine effort to do what he could to stop the violence, because he felt that what was gonna happen here was mass slaughter. At one point, as he rounded the corner, a black guy—it just so happened I knew him—came around with a rifle and put it right on Doar and was about to kill him. I was able to stop that guy. John said thank you and took a bullhorn from one of the police officers and got the crowd more controlled.

After Medgar's death, the reality of what we were doing just really hit me. And I was extremely angry, not knowing what to do. After that incident, things became very automatic for a while to me. I became extremely cold. I was more like an army sergeant. I had sent some people over into Natchez to pick up some affidavits that we needed for some lawyers. They came back, and their car had been shot up and they were very upset. My first reaction was, "Did you get the affidavits?" They said no. I told them, "As soon as you get something to eat, take the keys to the other car. I want you to go back and get those papers, because we need them. I don't want to wait." I didn't realize what I had done until later on that evening when one of the workers came up and asked how I could have done that.

In the weeks after Medgar Evers's assassination, several SNCC workers participated in preparation for a march on Washington, D.C., scheduled for August. In Mississippi the COFO field staff continued the dangerous work of organizing for voter registration and for an event that would become known as a Freedom Vote, to be held that fall. Among the lessons the civil rights workers learned was how to live with fear.

IVANHOE DONALDSON

Fear was always a major reality that you had to live with. You learned how to live with it, how to function with it. Almost every organizer in the Deep South was constantly faced with harassment. They'd been beaten, they'd been shot at. Some were shot.

I remember Charlie Cobb and I, who were active organizers along the river a long time in Mississippi and the Delta counties. Charlie is a very happy, sophisticated poet who is always in an upward kind of attitude. Always smiling. One of the few times in four or five years I ever saw Charlie stop smiling was when we were coming out of Mayersville, Mississippi, and we were trying to make a telephone call into Jackson. We were in trouble. In fact, we were in serious trouble. I was on the phone with Jackson, trying to tell them that I was having this trouble, and that we were going to be late getting in. And Charlie came and whispered in my ear that this is a party line, the police are listening, let's get out of here.

So we left the store, jumped in the car, and were heading down the road and a pickup came up behind us, and I think they popped off a couple of shots. I looked at Charlie and he was deadly serious. There was no smile on Charlie's face; he was sitting tensely in his seat, ready for us to roll. This was an everyday kind of occurrence. Every once in a while they'd catch up with you and you had to figure out a way to gird it into your system and move on. If you showed fear, it affected the community around you, so you had to show this was just a regular part of life. And people, if they saw you had confidence, developed confidence. It was important for an organizer never to transmit fear to anybody, even though there was fear there and we all knew about it.

10

THE MARCH ON WASHINGTON, 1963

"THEY VOTED WITH THEIR FEET"

March on Washington leader A. Philip Randolph (center) seated with the march's deputy director, Bayard Rustin (left).

Over the years, mass marches on Washington had not been welcomed by American presidential administrations. Leaders of Coxey's Army of the jobless in 1894 were arrested and jailed upon arrival. In 1932, thousands of World War I veterans in the Bonus Army were teargassed and driven out of town by U.S. soldiers under the command of General Douglas MacArthur. A decade later, black labor leader Asa Philip Randolph, founder of the Brotherhood of Sleeping Car Porters, was angry enough to ignore the precedents. In the summer of 1941, as a surge in military spending began to lift white America out of the Depression, the needs of the black unemployed were being ignored. Randolph threatened President Franklin Roosevelt with a mass march by 100,000 Negro citizens. Their goals: equal employment opportunities in America's defense industries and desegregation of the armed services.

Roosevelt brought all his forces to bear—his own personal charm and his outrage, the good offices of his wife, Eleanor, and of liberal Mayor Fiorello La Guardia of New York City, and appeals to patriotism from all quarters—but Randolph had heard the rhetoric in the last great war, and was no longer buying it. With only a week to the July 1 march deadline, Roosevelt created the first national Fair Employment Practices Committee, and Randolph postponed his protest—for more than two decades.

In 1962, the seventy-three-year-old elder statesman of the civil rights movement was heard from again. With black unemployment at double the rate for whites, and with civil rights still unrealized, Randolph proposed a new march "for jobs and freedom." Working with him was Bayard Rustin, the antiwar and civil rights activist who had participated in the plans for the original march in 1941. By the long, hot spring and summer of 1963, other black leaders were taking the idea of a new march seriously. And Washington, contemplating still another siege,. was unsure of its ability to control the petitioners.

From its point of view, the Kennedy administration had cause for concern. In May, massive black demonstrations in Birmingham had culminated in the night of rioting around the Gaston Motel. Other parts of the country were ready to blow. Bob Moses, testifying before a House subcommittee on the president's civil rights bill to ban discrimination in public places, education, and employment, warned congressmen they were facing a situation in Mississippi that could be "ten times worse than Birmingham."

In mid-June, there had been a near riot at Medgar Evers's funeral in Jackson. On June 19, in Savannah, Georgia, police used tear gas against a large civil rights demonstration. On the same day, police battered demonstrators with fire hoses and nightsticks in Danville, Virginia. In Gadsden, Alabama, local police and state troopers used electric cattle prods. Closer to Washington, in Cambridge, Maryland, the governor called out four hundred National Guardsmen to restore order. On the streets of Harlem, blacks battled police. In Americus, Georgia, not far from Albany, thirty-five were wounded in racial disturbances, and one black man was killed. There had never been anything like this angry year in American history. More than nine hundred demonstrations in more than one hundred cities, more than twenty thousand arrested, at least ten related deaths.

In late June, President Kennedy met with thirty civil rights leaders in an attempt to call off the march. But he had even less success than

Roosevelt. Unlike 1941, this was not a quid pro quo situation. Blacks were not asking Kennedy for an executive order. They were instead offering their support for legislation the president had already proposed to Congress. And whether Kennedy liked it or not, they were going to bring their bodies to Washington to make their witness in August.

To raise funds, march organizer Rustin had distributed buttons featuring a strong black and white handclasp to participating organizations. Given the reaction of many in the government and the media, the interracial symbol seemed a precursor to the red flag of anarchy. For August 28, 1963, all leaves were canceled for Washington's 2,900 police and for 1,000 police in nearby suburbs. Also called to duty were 2,000 National Guardsmen. As backup, several thousand U.S. troops were standing by in Maryland and Virginia, and paratroopers were on alert at bases farther south.

Publicly, the Kennedy administration was looking for ways to turn the event to the president's advantage. But the March on Washington hardly seemed destined to become a moment when millions would share a dream of the reconciliation of the races in America.

BURKE MARSHALL

The politicians in Washington—I'm not speaking of the president or the attorney general at the moment, I'm speaking of Congress—were scared to death of the march, just totally irrational. I don't know what they thought a march on Washington was going to be. I guess they thought people were going to march down Constitution Avenue throwing stones at them or something like that. There were congressmen who would call up the White House and say, We'd better have troops all over the place. No troops, we said.

We were in constant touch with the organizers of the march, especially Mr. Rustin. We wanted it to be a success. The president was as interested in having it a success as the organizers of the march were, because of the effect it would have politically, on the movement, on momentum in the House of Representatives, particularly on the civil rights bill. I remember that Dick Gregory came into my office and he said to me, "I know these senators and congressmen are scared of what's going to happen. I'll tell you what's going to happen. It's going to be a great big Sunday school picnic."

Actor and playwright Ossie Davis had testified before Congress in 1962 on racial discrimination in show business. He and his wife, actress Ruby Dee, were both longtime supporters of the civil rights movement.

OSSIE DAVIS

Bayard Rustin had asked Ruby and me to serve as masters of ceremonies at the Washington Monument part of the program and we had agreed. And when the time came for us to go down to Washington, the night before the march, a part of our responsibility was to report to a hotel room where Bayard was going to run all of us through what the program would be for the next day. A. Philip Randolph was there. Whitney Young [of the National Urban League] was there. Martin Luther King, Roy Wilkins [of the NAACP], John Lewis, were all there. Everybody except Jim Farmer was in that particular room.

Now, when Ruby and I came to the hotel and we got off at the floor where the conference was to be held and we were going through the hallway to get to the room, to our great surprise, there, standing in the hallway talking to a reporter, was Malcolm X. And this amazed us because Malcolm had made statements against the March on Washington. How this integration, these so-called Negroes then made a deal with the Kennedys and all that sort of thing. Here was Malcolm in the hallway. And we listened to the reporter, who was baiting him. "Why did you show up?" And Malcolm was saying, "Well, whatever black folks do, maybe I don't agree with it, but I'm going to be there, brother, 'cause that's where I belong."

We went on into the room and participated in the meeting, getting ready for the next day. The reporter came in and after there was a break announced that Malcolm X was out in the hall and he was castigating the black leadership and talking about the march and how did we feel about that? How did Martin Luther King feel? Roy Wilkins, of all people, told the reporter, "Hey, look, we know Malcolm X and we're not surprised that he's out there, and whatever he says you know it doesn't insult or hurt us. We have business to take care of, and if that's all you can bring from the meeting with Malcolm X the conversation is closed. Please leave. We got work to do." They understood, although nobody articulated it then, that a part of what Malcolm was involved in was a part of a grand strategy. Martin and the regular civil rights leaders were presenting to America our best face. Our nonviolent face. Our desire to be included into American society. And we wanted to show the world that we had no evil intentions against anybody. We just wanted to be included. But they also understood that America in spite of our reassurances would be frightened and hesitant to open the doors to black folks. So Malcolm, as the outsider, as the man they thought represented the possibilities of violence, was the counter that they could use. They would say to the powers that be, "Look, here's Martin Luther King and all these guys. We are nonviolent. Now, outside the door if you don't deal with us is the other brother, and he ain't like us. You going to really have hell on your hands when you get to dealing with Malcolm. So it behooves you, white America, in order to escape Malcolm, to deal with us." That was the strategy. And to some degree it worked. And Malcolm was always involved somewhere in the struggle.

Unlike Martin Luther King, Jr., Malcolm X found his strongest constituency in the urban ghettos of the North. A minister in the Nation of Islam, he did not see himself as part of the integrationist tradition and preached a message of black nationhood that appealed to a far broader audience than his own Black Muslim congregation. Malcolm saw separatism as self-determination, and he criticized reliance on whites to achieve black progress. In a speech called "Message to the Grass Roots" delivered later that year, he called the March on Washington "a sellout" and "a takeover." "They told those Negroes what time to hit town, how to come, where to stop, what signs to carry, what song to sing, what speech they could make, and then they told them to get out of town by sundown."

At the time of the march, Cleveland Sellers and other members of the Nonviolent Action Group, a support organization for SNCC at Howard University, ran into Malcolm X at a Washington coffee shop.

CLEVELAND SELLERS

Malcolm talked about the changes in the march. At first, he said, it was supposed to be a civil disobedience and now it was not. Malcolm talked about how at first it was supposed to be primarily a black thrust march and now it was integrated. Malcolm raised a lot of questions about the internal organization and the compromises that were being made. And he was raising that in the context of raising questions in our own minds so we could begin to observe and analyze the march from that particular perspective.

Courtland Cox was one of several young SNCC activists who had made contributions to a militant speech that SNCC chairman John Lewis had written for the march. There were already fears in some quarters about allowing rhetoric this fiery on the march platform, though as the day dawned, organizer Rustin's biggest concern was the empty Mall.

COURTLAND COX

The March on Washington was supposed to be a huge, big event. Bayard Rustin and I went out to the monument grounds around eight o'clock in the morning and there were, I think, fifty people out there. And our question was, Is anybody going to be out here? Everybody kept saying, Well, there's no one out here because nobody could get into Washington because the roads are all jammed. By ten o'clock there was a sea of humanity. We felt we were really going to make an impression this day.

In the midst of that, probably about eleven o'clock, we got a message that Archbishop [Patrick] O'Boyle had stated that if we did not change John Lewis's statement, he was going to withdraw from the march. We told Bayard that you'd have to change the speech over our dead bodies. He went down into the crowd and got A. Philip Randolph. And A. Philip Randolph said, "I have waited twenty-two years for this. Would you young men please accommodate an old man?" Randolph must have been about seventy-five, and here we were, one-third his age, and he was asking us to do this for him. He said, "I've waited all my life for this opportunity. Please don't ruin it." And we felt that, for him, we had to make some concessions.

But I think the real question about John's speech was the whole question of how Kennedy wanted to be perceived in terms of the black community. Remember, Kennedy came to the presidency on a lot of votes from the black community, and he wanted to be perceived as someone in front of this march, allowing it, wanting it, encouraging it.

As one of the "Big Six" leaders in the civil rights movement, John Lewis had participated in the top-level planning for the march along with A. Philip Randolph, Martin Luther King, Jr., Whitney Young, Roy Wilkins, and James Farmer.

JOHN LEWIS

During the early discussions about the march, it was never our design to come to Washington to support any particular piece of civil rights legislation. But before the march, by the time we got to Washington, some of the people, particularly the representatives of the Urban League, the NAACP, and maybe a segment of organized labor, wanted the march to support proposed legislation. We in SNCC took exception to that. In one part of the speech I had prepared with my colleagues, I suggested that we could not support the Kennedy legislation because it did not guarantee the right of black people to vote. President Kennedy and his administration took the position that if you had a sixth-grade education you should be considered literate and then you should be able to register to vote. We disagreed with that; we felt that the southern states had denied people a right to a decent education and now it's wrong for them to come back and say you must be able to pass a literacy test in order to be able to register to vote. SNCC, and I think the southern wing of the movement, took the position that the only qualification for being able to register to vote should be that of age and residence.

During the time leading up to the preparation of my speech, there was an article in the *New York Times* with a picture of a group of women in Rhodesia who had signs saying "One man, one vote." In my speech I said something like "One man, one vote, is the African cry. It must be ours too." Some of the people objected to that.

In another part of the speech we suggested that there was very little difference between the major political parties, that the party of [Jacob] Javits is the party of [Barry] Goldwater, that the party of Kennedy is the party of Eastland. Then I raised the question, "Where is *our* party?" I suggested that as a movement we could not wait on the president, on members of the Congress, we had to take matters into our own hands, and I went on to say that the day might come when we would not confine our marching to Washington, that we might be forced to march through the

South the way Sherman did, [but] nonviolently. Some people suggested that was inflammatory, that it would call people to riot, and you shouldn't use that type of language.

> Among the phrases that caused the most controversy were "The revolution is at hand and we must free ourselves of the chains of political and economic slavery. . . . We will not wait for the President, the Justice Department, nor Congress, but we will take matters into our own hands. . . . We will march through the South, through the heart of Dixie, the way Sherman did, leaving a scorched earth with our nonviolence." The line about General Sherman had been contributed by SNCC executive secretary James Forman. With only hours to go before speechtime, Forman went back to the typewriter.

JAMES FORMAN

The rewriting took place at the Lincoln Memorial, and it was done out of a spirit of unity. We wanted the March on Washington to go forward, and we wanted SNCC's participation to be very visible. We certainly weren't interested in withdrawing from the march. The three of us—John Lewis, Courtland Cox, and myself—huddled together, and I was the person mainly responsible for redrafting the speech. As representatives of SNCC, we were attempting to make the march work. We wanted to make sure that no one left the march, especially the Roman Catholic representatives. We wanted to try to meet whatever objections they had to the speech. And as we were attempting to do this—A. Philip Randolph was there—someone objected to the words *masses* and *revolution,* so A. Philip Randolph said, "There's nothing wrong with those two words. Those words don't have to be changed, because I used them myself."

We didn't feel in any way intimidated. The Student Nonviolent Coordinating Committee always operated from a position of strength. We always felt very secure about what we were doing and we knew we were right, so we didn't in any way feel that we were being compromised or that we were under the gun. A lot of people talked about how we had to change these things, but these things were not great changes to us. It was a question of unity for us. We felt that the speech was much stronger after meeting the objections and redrafting it. I'm very serious about that.

FRED SHUTTLESWORTH

I did not think it was necessary for John Lewis's speech to be changed. I didn't think we went up there to be little sweet boys. We were suffering. People were going to jail, people were dying and would be dying. So I didn't think we should gloss over that and act as if everything was pie in the sky, that we should be so thankful that we could come to Washington that we shouldn't say what was wrong with this country.

Even with modifications—the line about General Sherman, for example, was changed to "By the force of our demands, our determination, and our numbers, we shall splinter the segregated South into a thousand pieces, and put them back together in the image of God and democracy"—John Lewis's speech was the most radical of the day.

But it is Martin Luther King's articulation of his dream for America that most people identify with the march. In addition to the 250,000 participants gathered on the Mall, millions of television viewers watched the day's events on CBS, which had pre-empted its programming to provide continuous coverage. The United States Information Agency also covered the event, for exhibition overseas. Before King approached the podium, both NBC and ABC broke into their programming to broadcast the speech.

". . . I say to you today, my friends, so even though we face the difficulties of today and tomorrow, I still have a dream. It is a dream deeply rooted in the American meaning of its creed, 'We hold these truths to be self-evident, that all men are created equal.' I have a dream that one day on the red hills of Georgia, sons of former slaves and the sons of former slave owners will be able to sit down together at the table of brotherhood. I have a dream that one day even the state of Mississippi, a state sweltering with the heat of injustice, sweltering with the heat of oppression, will be transformed into an oasis of freedom and justice. I have a dream that my four little children will one day live in a nation where they will not be judged by the color of their skin, but the content of their character. . . . "

William H. Johnson, Jr., a World War II veteran and New York City policeman, had traveled to Washington as head of the Guardians, a group of more than 1,500 who provided security for the march.

WILLIAM H. JOHNSON, JR.

I was enthralled by Dr. King's speech. Oh, my God, it just seemed to move you almost off the platform, off the earth. A big ole ox like me, it made my eyes water a little bit. It made me reflect upon my army service. It made me angry about what I had suffered overseas at the hands of my white compatriots, white Yankees. It made me reflect upon how, as a sergeant, I had told my men during an army orientation, "Don't be deceived by this big second war to fight for democracy. Things are not necessarily gonna be any different when you get back home. You better take advantage of all the free time we get, all the rest periods and all the army information education courses that they give us, to do your best to improve your lot when you get home."

Oh, my mind went crazy. I thought about the fact that I had had the nerve to write to my girlfriend, who is now my wife, that I wanted to join the paratroops, and she let me know I was crazy. She was back here hearing the nasty things that were being done, things that were being said, and what was thought about the things between white and black troops and even things that were going on right here in the United States. She thought I'd gone stark, raving mad. But Dr. King brought to life the hope that someday we could walk together hand in hand, that despite all this, one day we could smooth out our differences. It was a matter of being inspired and moved. It was an awfully sentimental and spiritual experience for me.

IVANHOE DONALDSON

I think that a lot of people felt, because of the drama and the vast greatness of it all, that somehow we had turned the mystical corner, that a new era of humanity and social consciousness and social justice was now on the table. That didn't happen.

So the rhetoricians and the activists are correct when they say there was no major accomplishment because of the march, but at the same time, it does represent a continuum in the struggle, and the need from time to time to create exclamation points and question marks and commas, so that people can define themselves in some time frame, which is also important to an organizer, to bring something to a culmination, to take people to a next step.

BAYARD RUSTIN

It wasn't the Harry Belafontes and the greats from Hollywood that made the march. What made the march was that black people voted that day with their feet. They came from every state, they came in jalopies, on trains, buses, anything they could get—some walked. There were about three hundred congressmen there, but none of them said a word. We had told them to come, but we wanted to talk with them, they were not to talk to us. And after they came and saw that it was very orderly, that there was fantastic determination, that there were all kinds of people there other than black people, they knew there was a consensus in this country for the civil rights bill. After the March on Washington, when Kennedy called into the White House the leaders who had been resistant before the march, he made it very clear to them now he was prepared to put his weight behind the bill.

The march ended for me when we had finally made sure we had not left one piece of paper, not a cup, nothing. We had a five-hundred-man cleanup squad. I went back to the hotel and said to Mr. Randolph, "Chief, I want you to see that there is not a piece of paper or any dirt or filth or anything left here." And Mr. Randolph went to thank me and tears began to come down his cheeks.

I think it was the greatest moment in my life. A. Philip Randolph in my view was the greatest leader of the twentieth century, in terms of the basic analysis and program for blacks. He is a man that history does not record so well as many others. But to me, he was a giant. And to see this giant with tears in his eyes moved me to want to do everything I humanly could do to bring about justice, not only for black people but for whoever is in trouble.

RALPH ABERNATHY

The March on Washington established visibility in this nation. It showed the struggle was nearing a close, that people were coming together, that all the organizations could stand together. It demonstrated that there was a unity in the black community for the cause of freedom and justice. It made it clear that we did not have to use violence to achieve the goals which we were seeking.

I went back to the grounds about six or seven o'clock that evening. There was nothing but the wind blowing across the reflection pool, moving and blowing and keeping music. We were so proud that no violence had taken place that day. We were so pleased. This beautiful scene of the wind dancing on the sands of the Lincoln Memorial I will never forget. This was the greatest day of my life.

11

THE SIXTEENTH STREET CHURCH BOMBING, 1963

"YOU REALIZED HOW INTENSE THE OPPOSITION WAS"

The four children killed when the Sixteenth Street Baptist Church in Birmingham, Alabama, was bombed on September 15, 1963. From left: Denise McNair, Carole Robertson, Addie Mae Collins, and Cynthia Wesley.

Eighteen days after the euphoria of the March on Washington, four hundred worshippers crowded into the Sixteenth Street Baptist Church in Birmingham for Sunday services. Only months earlier, the church had been the rallying point for the marches against Bull Connor's police dogs and fire hoses. On September 15, 1963, a group of young girls had just finished a Sunday school lesson and were in the basement changing into their choir robes.

A few blocks away, but within sight of the church, a white man stood waiting on the sidewalk. He was Birmingham truck driver and one-time city employee Robert Edward Chambliss—the man whom friends in the Eastview 13 Klavern of the Alabama Klan called Dynamite Bob.

At 10:19 A.M., fifteen sticks of explosive blew apart the church basement and the children in the changing room. The four who died were Addie Mae Collins, Carole Robertson, and Cynthia Wesley, all fourteen; and Denise McNair, eleven. Some twenty others were injured.

JAMES BEVEL

My first reaction when I heard about the bombing of the church was anger, rage. The bombing felt almost like a personal insult; the reactionary forces of the Klan, or whoever, were trying to teach us a lesson. Then I got information to the effect that some of the guys involved in it were from the sheriff's department, and then I was thinking about killing people. I had to do a lot of thinking about that. That's when I started thinking about what would be the appropriate response to that kind of situation. I think it's natural for human beings to get angry when there's an intense violation, and I think if a person doesn't have the capacity to get angry, they don't have the capacity to think through fully the implications of that which causes them to be angry. Under the nonviolent Christian thing, what you do is you relax and you work through the cause and address the cause. Well, we figured that if the sheriff was involved in that and the deputy sheriff was involved in that, then the way we can stop the bombings is to give black people the option to put sheriffs and irresponsible lawmakers and law-enforcing agents out of office, since they're elected by the people. So, other than being mad and asking for Kennedy to send the army down and those kinds of things, let's take it to the people, since all of the people feel the shock of this violation. Let's take to the people a strategy and a plan for working on the right to vote. What was interesting was all of the people bought into it, but the leaders had a problem with it. By leaders I mean the NAACP people, the Urban League people, the CORE leadership, and, in fact, some of the people in SCLC. They had problems with it because it demanded a new commitment, it demanded an involvement, it demanded that we become engaged in the confrontation over the question of the right of black people to vote. And I think that all of them were aware that most of the violence perpetrated toward black people was specifically for the purpose of disenfranchising them. So they thought that if we moved in that direction, we would probably reap a whole lot of unprecedented violence, and I think that most of them were unwilling to face that.

DIANE NASH

My former husband and I, Jim Bevel, cried when we heard about the bombing, because in many ways we felt like our own children had been killed. We knew that the activity of the civil rights movement had been involved in generating a kind of energy that brought out this kind of hostility. We decided that we would do something about it, and we said that we had two options. First, we felt confident that if we tried, we could find out who had done it, and we could make sure they got killed. We considered that as a real option. The second option was that we felt that if blacks in Alabama had the right to vote, they could protect black children. We deliberately made a choice, and chose the second option. At that time, we promised ourselves and each other that if it took twenty years, or as long as it took, we weren't going to stop working on it and trying, until Alabama blacks had the right to vote. So we drew up that day an initial strategy draft for a movement in Alabama designed to get the right to vote. Bevel continued working in a local voter registration campaign we were involved in, and my job was to get on an airplane and have a meeting with Dr. King and Fred Shuttlesworth, and encourage them to have a meeting with the staff to make a decision on what to do.

FRED SHUTTLESWORTH

The bombing of the Sixteenth Street Baptist Church was a reaction on the part of the Klan. They felt like we were making some headway, and the law enforcement agencies couldn't cooperate with them and let them do their thing. It was tragic, but in every war innocent people get killed. President Kennedy said that to me when we went up to see him one time and I asked him about it. I said, "Mr. Kennedy, those girls were in Sunday school, studying the Bible," and he said, "Reverend Shuttlesworth, as tragic as it is, in every war, some people have to die." But maybe that's why we win, because Dr. King said unearned suffering has to be redemptive.

CORETTA SCOTT KING

I was shocked by the bombing. It happened right after the March on Washington, which was such a great experience. It was a great moment of fulfillment, when Martin gave his "I Have a Dream" speech, and we really felt the sense of progress, that people came together, black and white, even though the South was totally segregated. We felt that sense of oneness, and we had the feeling that the dream could be realized. And then, a few weeks later, came this bombing in Birmingham, with four innocent little girls. Then you realized how intense the opposition was, and that it would take a lot more than what was being done to change the situation.

DAVID VANN

I first learned of the bombing of Sixteenth Street Baptist Church just about five minutes to noon, when I was leaving my church on southside, Howard Methodist. I have a feeling someone from the mayor's office was there, because Mayor Boutwell belonged to the same church I did, and said that there was a bombing at the church. I immediately drove down to see what had happened, and they had all roads blocked off, so you couldn't get within a block of the church. I was driving south on Nineteenth Street, which was two blocks from the church, and there on the corner stood Chambliss, a known Klansman, watching all of the commotion and excitement and fire trucks and things that were coming and going. I remember thinking that he looked like a firebug watching his fire.

Of course, several years later he was convicted of being a participant in the bombing. One of the main reasons it was a long time before he was brought to trial is the FBI was called in by the city to do the initial investigation, and there was such a degree of distrust between the Birmingham Police Department and the FBI that the FBI and the Justice Department would never give any of the records to either the state of Alabama or the city of Birmingham. Having been a counterintelligence agent myself, I know the policy of protecting informants had a great deal to do with the FBI policy in those days. But it wasn't until after Jimmy Carter became president that the attorney general of the state, Bill Baxley, and I put all the pressure we could on the new U.S. attorney general, and they did agree to allow a review of those records by the state attorney general's office. Within about six months, prosecution was begun of Mr. Chambliss. Unfortunately, in the meantime, the FBI at least claimed that they had lost all of their records, and most of the physical evidence that the FBI collected at the scene that day was nowhere to be found.

BURKE MARSHALL

There was a feeling of real, bitter outrage at the killing of those four little girls in the church bombing. Of course, there was an enormous reaction in Birmingham. The president asked me to go down there and I went immediately. When I got to Birmingham, I thought I was in a city under siege. The black community had set up guards to prevent people from coming into it. They didn't know what would happen. They were afraid the Klan had gone wild and they would come in with other violence. So you had to go through a cordon in order to get into the black community. When I got there, I called Martin King immediately and arranged to meet him. He was in a house in the black community. The Bureau didn't want to take me there, because there were no black Bureau agents and driving white, cop-looking people into the black neighborhood at that time was sort of like an act of war. So somebody arranged for some black civil defense workers who were acting as guards to come get me at my hotel. They gave me a white helmet and sort of shoved me down in the backseat so that my face couldn't be seen, and drove me to the house where Martin was staying.

Then we had a long meeting about what to do. The president had choices to make that were important. Should he do something militarily? The city might explode and it would be possible to do something militarily. Martin King, I think, favored that notion at first. I was against it, because I knew that if the military came in, they would declare martial law, and blacks as well as whites would be confined to their houses. Nobody would be able to protest anything, and having the military run a civil rights movement is a terrible step to take if it can be avoided. The president did move some troops down near Birmingham as a sort of symbolic gesture of federal force, if the state authorities didn't behave themselves. Then, of course, the other thing that we could do was get the Bureau out in full force. Now the Bureau, I think, knew who did that bombing. It certainly turned out in the end that they knew who did the bombing. They never gave the Department of Justice a case to prosecute, or identified to the civil rights division the person that did the bombing. He was eventually prosecuted by the state authorities.* But that was a terrible event, a terrible event because of its cruelty, its futility, senselessness, and everybody in the administration felt just the same way that everybody, at least every sensitive, civilized person, in Birmingham—white just as well as black—thought of it. It was a horrifying event.

*Robert Chambliss was convicted of first-degree murder on November 18, 1977.

12

Mississippi Freedom Summer, 1964

"Representation and the Right to Participate"

Fannie Lou Hamer addresses the 1964 Democratic National Convention in Atlantic City, New Jersey.

Fannie Lou Hamer embodied what the Student Nonviolent Coordinating Committee hoped to achieve in Mississippi. She was local, from the grass roots, someone awakened to her own power to lead and to effect change, and strong enough not to be intimidated by her enemies. The youngest of twenty children born into a sharecropping family in Montgomery County, Mississippi, Mrs. Hamer (as she was always known by the SNCC staff) lost her job as a timekeeper on a cotton plantation when she attempted to register to vote in the summer of 1962. With her job she also lost her home on the plantation. As Mrs. Hamer explained it to Congress in 1964: "I traveled twenty-six miles to the county courthouse to try to register to become a first-class citizen. I was fired the thirty-first of August in 1962 from a plantation where I had worked as a timekeeper and a sharecropper for eighteen years. My husband had worked there thirty years. I was met by my children when I returned from the courthouse, and my girl and my husband's cousin told me that this man my husband worked for was raising a lot of Cain. I went on in the house, and it wasn't too long before my husband came and said this plantation owner said I would have to leave if I didn't go down and withdraw. About that time, the man walked up, Mr. Marlowe, and he said, 'Is Fannie Lou back yet?' My husband said, 'She is.' I walked out of the house at this time. He said, 'Fannie Lou, you have been to the courthouse to try to register,' and he said, 'We are not ready for this in Mississippi.' I said, 'I didn't register for you, I tried to register for myself.' "

Mrs. Hamer left the Marlowe plantation and set to work registering other black voters. It was something that she did extraordinarily well.

SNCC field secretary Lawrence Guyot helped set up many of the early voter registration meetings in Mississippi.

LAWRENCE GUYOT

Mrs. Hamer was a great gospel singer and a natural leader. She flowed out of the plantation system, she was a timekeeper, a position of trust and honor, if there is such in the plantation schema. James Bevel did most of the talking at the first meeting that Mrs. Hamer attended. Bevel was a great speaker and was a minister. Our being able to use the church as a meeting place, and to have a minister speak the social gospel about why we should register to vote, what impact that would have on our lives, influenced Mrs. Hamer and twenty-one other people. She decided to go with us the next day to Indianola to register to vote.

Now, registering to vote at that time meant that you filled out a twenty-two-question questionnaire. One of the questions was, interpret any of the two hundred eighty-six sections of the Mississippi constitution to the satisfaction of the registrar. Now, you have to bear in mind that some of those registrars couldn't read or write, but that didn't matter, they could still determine who should be registered, if that person happened to be black. Because all whites who attempted to register were registered. After we went through the process of filling out the questionnaire, we knew that all of the applicants' names would be posted in the newspaper, serving notice to their creditors and employers that here's someone who had done something wrong.

As soon as we left the courthouse in Indianola, the bus driver was arrested. He was charged with having a bus that was too yellow. This was a school bus. It was a frivolous charge, but that's what he was charged with at the time. Upon returning to the plantation, Mrs. Hamer was told that she had a choice. She could take her name off and stay on the plantation, or she could leave her name on and she'd have to leave. She said, "I didn't register for you. I registered for me." And I think the act of registration, and making that statement, was the beginning of a history that changed the South.

Unita Blackwell also attended a voter registration meeting held in a church in Sunflower County, Mississippi.

UNITA BLACKWELL

In 1963, we had heard that there were supposed to be these Freedom Riders, that's what they called it, coming to Mississippi. Nobody thought they would ever show up, you know. Everybody talked about it—maybe they would come to Jackson or someplace like that. But I didn't think they would ever show up in Mayersville, Mississippi, a little small town in the Mississippi Delta. It wasn't even a town at that time.

And then they showed up. It was two guys, two black fellows. They came walking down the road and I knew they were different, because they was walking fast. We didn't walk fast at that time. They just waved, you know, and says hello. We didn't say that either. We always says, "How y'all feeling?" So we knew that that had to be some of them. That evening, we saw the highway patrols and police coming off the highway looking around, so we had an idea that this must be some of these Freedom Riders.

Two Freedom Riders came to Sunday school that morning, and they were pointing the finger at me, saying, "Just like that lady talking back there in the Sunday school class says that God help those who help themselves, you can help yourself by trying to register to vote." That's the first time in my life that I ever come in contact with anybody that tells me that I had the right to register to vote.

The white people knew what it meant. The black folks didn't know that much what it meant. I was only told when I started off that if I registered to vote, I would have food to eat and a better house to stay in, 'cause the one I was staying in was so raggedy you could see anywhere and look outdoors. My child would have a better education. At that particular point, our children only went to school two to three months out of the year. That was what we were told. It was the basic needs of the people. The whites, they understood it even larger than that in terms of political power. We hadn't even heard that word, "political power," because it wasn't taught in the black schools. We didn't know there was such a thing as a board of supervisors and what they did, and we didn't know about school board members and what they did.

Bob Moses was a little bitty fella. And he stood up to this sheriff and Bob said, "I'm from SNCC." I had never saw that happen before. From that day on, I said, "Well, I can stand myself."

People remember them people. SNCC went where nobody went. They was about the nuttiest ones they was. Ended up in some of the most isolated places and drug people out of there to vote.

Mrs. Fannie Lou Hamer said to me, "Girl, these here young people know something, don't they?" And I said, "Yeah, they sure do."

Victoria Gray was from Hattiesburg, in southeastern Mississippi.

VICTORIA GRAY

I applied for voter registration six times before I was able to be accepted. I was only able to be accepted after we had taken our registrar to court. In fact, all of my applications were used by the Justice Department in trying to have the registrar establish why I had not been registered in the beginning.

Of course, the very next step after becoming registered is to exercise that right to vote. For those few of us who had managed to become registered voters, we naturally wanted to begin participating at the earliest possible time. So when the time came for [the Democratic party] precinct meetings and county meetings, we were all set to attend, but there were all kinds of games played. The schedules and the places were always deliberately misrepresented. You would get there and there was nothing happening there. Or in many cases, people did actually get there and the meeting was going on, but we were not permitted to go in, pure and simple. We just weren't permitted to come in. And we realized that even with the vote, you're not gonna get anyplace if you can't participate in these meetings. And so, out of the frustration of not being able to participate at the precinct and county levels, was born the idea of holding our own elections.

With blacks barred from the processes of the all-white Democratic party in Mississippi, COFO held its own mock election in the fall of 1963. NAACP state president Aaron Henry was the candidate for governor and white Tougaloo College chaplain Edwin King the candidate for lieutenant governor. In late October, one hundred white students from Yale and Stanford (recruited by Allard Lowenstein, a former dean at Stanford) took two weeks off from school to help canvass black neighborhoods for the Freedom Vote. On election day, some eighty thousand blacks cast their ballots. The Freedom Vote proved that black political apathy was a myth. And the presence of the white volunteers helped draw attention from out of state. But national attention to the Freedom Vote was soon overshadowed by the assassination of President Kennedy in Dallas, Texas, on November 22. The movement had mourned the murder of another young leader, Medgar Evers, just months earlier. Now many sorrowed along with the rest of the nation as a young president was put to rest. In Mississippi, the SNCC workers felt an urgency to continue their own struggle despite the dangers. Given the results of the Freedom Vote, they decided to expand the registration effort.

Although the use of white volunteers during the Freedom Vote had been successful, the further recruitment of whites was troubling to some in SNCC.

BOB MOSES

There had grown a concern within SNCC and the movement about the involvement of white students in the Deep South as actual organizers and workers in the field. This was first demonstrated in southwest Georgia. In 1962, Martha Prescod and Jean Wheeler, who had been working in southwest Georgia and were two young black girls, left that project and came to Mississippi because of the presence of too many white people who were working there. They mirrored a kind of concern which existed within the Mississippi staff, which was predominantly people who grew up and lived in Mississippi, were from Mississippi, had spent their lives under the Mississippi condition, which was strict segregation and living in this closed society, so they had very little working contact with white people and they weren't anxious to introduce them into the project, which they viewed—and rightly so—as *their* project, something which they had created out of nothing and at great risk to themselves.

They had voted down the attempt in SNCC in the beginning of 1963 to introduce white people into Mississippi as part of the Mississippi staff. Then, when the Freedom Vote came and the question arose of bringing in white volunteers, they reluctantly agreed, since they were going along with the campaign, with what Aaron Henry and Ed King wanted, and since they knew that it was only going to last for a couple of weeks. The volunteers from Yale and Stanford would be coming down for a couple of weeks, working with them, mobilizing the vote, and then they would be gone.

Immediately after the Freedom Vote, which was successful, there came the question of should we do this in the summer of 1964. Al Lowenstein proposed that we bring down students from all across the country, from the nation's most prestigious schools. The discussion then arose within the staff as to do we want to do this or not. And we were split. We met for months over this question. You had the staff on the one hand, and the people that we were working with on the other. Mrs. Hamer was an excellent case in point. She wanted the students to come back, and so we were at loggerheads.

SNCC staffer Hollis Watkins had strong reservations about the impact of whites on a grass-roots black movement.

HOLLIS WATKINS

The summer project to bring students down in Mississippi was a tough issue. Some felt that it would bring out more publicity to get more whites involved, that it would serve as a deterrent to keep the whites in Mississippi from doing things. There were others of us, from Mississippi especially, that was looking at this effort in terms of a long-range project. We felt that even though it would do this, that ultimately it would destroy the grass-roots organizations that we had built and were in the process of building.

For the first time, we had local people who had begun to take the initiative themselves and do things. For the first time, we had local Mississippians who were making decisions about what moves to make next. And where the organization should be going and how the organization politically and economically would work and where it would end up. We felt that with a lot of students from the North coming in, being predominantly white, that they would come in and overshadow these grass-roots organizations, causing the organizations to go on a different course than that which had been started.

At the same time, by the local indigenous people knowing that most of the students would be more educated than themselves, they would feel, "Since they are more educated than I am, maybe I should listen to them, do it their way, do what they say." Because of that, they would become complacent, they would feel inferior and fall back into the same rut that they were in before we started the grass-roots organizations. And ultimately, when the people from the North would go back, people from Mississippi would have to start all over again, and go through that same rebuilding process. All of us knew that it is much harder to rebuild something than to keep it in motion. We wanted to keep what we had in motion rather than stand the risk of destroying it and have to rebuild.

BOB MOSES

What was in the offing was whether SNCC could integrate itself, as it were, and live as a sort of island of integration in a sea of separation. And SNCC was trying to work itself out as an organization which was integrated in all levels. The question of white volunteers, or white SNCC staffers, came up in this context. Are they to be confined to the Atlanta office? And they're pushing, those that are there, to get out in the field. If they come over to Mississippi, are they to be confined to Jackson? Is there a way for them to work in the field? There was constant pressure about what the goals of the organization were.

I think it was January 1964, and we were in Hattiesburg having a demonstration, picketing the courthouse. Mrs. Hamer was there and staff from all around the state, and we were taking up the question again. We got a telephone call that Louis Allen [black witness to the 1961 shooting of Herbert Lee] had been murdered on his front lawn in Liberty. I went over there to speak to his wife, who then moved down to Baton Rouge, and in the process of helping her and thinking through this, I felt like I had to step in and make my weight felt in terms of this decision about the summer project. Because up to then I had just been letting the discussion go on. I guess what I felt was that, as we were going now, we couldn't guarantee the safety of the people we were working with. There were larger things that were happening in the country: there was the 1963 civil rights bill. Mississippi was reacting to that, and we were feeling the backlash that was growing in Mississippi against gains that were being made nationally but which were not having any immediate effect in Mississippi in terms of people being able to participate in some of those gains. But what they were feeling was the oppression, the backlash that was rising up in Mississippi—burning churches, the murder of two boys from Alcorn State occurred at that same time, Louis Allen down there in Liberty. We felt that we had to do something. And I felt that in that context that I had to step in between this loggerhead between the staff on the one hand and the people that we were working with. And so that's how the decision was made to invite the students down for the summer of 1964.

Tom Hayden, an early member of the northern-based Students for a Democratic Society, founded in 1960, served as a liaison between SDS and SNCC.

TOM HAYDEN

I was in Mississippi when there were very few white students or northern whites there at all. I remember the thinking was that if this simply remains a black thing, where the white official violence is visited upon black sharecroppers or black civil rights workers, how will a country that is significantly prejudiced respond? What's going to make them interested? The conclusion was that for all the problems, it would be necessary to bring down the white sons and daughters of the country's middle class, from the liberal North. By the hundreds, by the thousands if possible, to experience the true nature of southern segregation. It was kind of like a political civil war. If you mobilized the North, then pressure would be put on Congress and on the administration and then they would finally do something about these strongholds of segregation in the South. I think there was some truth to that strategy.

In a span of seventy days, the summer project planned to build parallel institutions for blacks who had been shut out of a closed, white-dominated society. Volunteers would help establish Freedom Schools and community centers, and deliver medical and legal services. They would also canvass the state to build support for a new political party. Established in the spring of 1964, the Mississippi Freedom Democratic party was a direct response to the exclusion of blacks by the all-white Democratic party regulars in the state. Lawrence Guyot was MFDP chairman; Fannie Lou Hamer was vice chairman. The goal: to elect an integrated slate of delegates to the national Democratic convention in Atlantic City in August, and to present the MFDP as "the only democratically constituted body of Mississippi citizens worthy of taking part in that convention's business."

In June, the first of some seven hundred student volunteers met in Oxford, Ohio, for a COFO training program funded by the National Council of Churches. They would later be joined in the summer project by a volunteer corps of several hundred doctors, lawyers, and ministers.

Sandra Cason, who during the early 1960s was married to Tom Hayden, was a white SNCC worker who had moved into Mississippi the year before at the request of Bob Moses.

SANDRA CASON (CASEY HAYDEN)

I had a lot of contact with northern students previous to my work in Mississippi because I'd been doing fund-raising for SNCC out of Atlanta. I was what was called northern coordinator, so I handled all the correspondence with northern college students that came into the office. And they all wanted to come to where the action was, you know? I mean, what was happening in the South was so dramatic and heroic. You've got to remember, this was the early sixties. Kids on college campuses were reading the existentialists. The black students were like heroes. They were like existentialist heroes, and people wanted to get close to this. It was beautiful, it was happening. And it drew white intellectuals. It was more real, or more profound, than most anything else happening. They wanted to get close to it.

Peter Orris was a freshman at Harvard when he heard about plans for Freedom Summer.

PETER ORRIS

I grew up in New York City. I had been raised in a family where being Jewish was important in terms of identifying with the underdog, with people who were suffering repression and discrimination. I had come into contact with SNCC organizers the summer before, when I worked in the national office of the March on Washington for Jobs and Freedom in 1963. I was seventeen at the time, and was very impressed with the SNCC workers that were involved in that organization as well as those that I met in Washington at the time of the march.

Sometime in the spring of my freshman year at college, four of us from the civil rights coordinating committee at the college went to Atlanta for a regional meeting of SNCC and heard about what was going on. We met many people who were involved in voter registration and direct action from the southern states, and it was tremendously impressive and exciting. For me, it was a tremendous privilege to be allowed to participate in this movement for racial justice. At eighteen years old, to be able to be involved in this kind of a struggle was very important to me.

In June of 1964, I arrived in Oxford, Ohio, for the training session for the summer project. I was selected to be part of a group that was going to the southwest area of Mississippi and to do voter registration in that area. A farmer had been killed a short time before for being involved in voter registration efforts, and violence had been ongoing in that area. We were a group of fifteen or sixteen people, and we spent many hours with Bob Moses and a variety of other leaders of SNCC who had been in the South and in that area.

Additionally, it was to give us a feeling of exactly what kind of a tense atmosphere we were going into, what kind of violence we should expect, how to avoid the violence, as well as nonviolent responses to violent situations. We playacted situations where angry groups of people, mobs, would be attacking us and how we would handle ourselves in that situation where our life was threatened. The experienced SNCC workers were sure that we were going to meet situations like these during the summer, and they wanted to guarantee that we were going to respond in a nonviolent manner. Then a group of us were asked to go to Washington to make a direct appeal to the deputy attorney general, Nicholas Katzenbach, and others in the government, that they should pay special attention to what was happening in Mississippi this summer, as we felt, and the organizers felt, that our lives would certainly be at risk for engaging in this activity.

> The press in Mississippi called the influx of northern students an "invasion." A hostile state legislature passed more than twenty laws in anticipation of the students' arrival. In the capital city of Jackson, Mayor Allen Thompson doubled the size of the police force, then purchased 250 shotguns and a large armored truck that soon became known as the Thompson Tank. The white Citizens' Councils in Mississippi, whose principal spokesman was William Simmons, were also publicly opposed to "hippies" coming in from out of state.

WILLIAM SIMMONS

Black people have had voting rights in this state all along. The Citizens' Council has always taken a position that anyone who is qualified to vote should register and vote and be a good citizen. But there had to be certain qualifications. The objective of this student invasion was to eliminate all of the qualifications. To have mass voting and, frankly, to advance black political power. They were asked to vote not as American citizens, but to vote as blacks. It was a very racist objective. And as such, it was opposed.

I would say the summer project of 1964 was less of a high point in emotion than the Ole Miss events because it was so much less dramatic and did not represent the use of government force.

It was more of an annoyance than anything else. When the civil rights workers invaded the state in the summer of 1964 to change us into their own image, they were met with a feeling of some curiosity, but mostly resentment. They fanned out across the state, made a great to-do of breaking up our customs, of flaunting social practices that had been respected by people here over the years. That was the time of the hippies just coming in. Many had on hippie uniforms and conducted themselves in hippie ways. They were not exactly the types of models that most people that I knew wanted to emulate. Also, the arrogance that they showed in wanting to reform a whole state in the way they thought it should be created resentment. So, to say that they were not warmly received and welcomed is perhaps an understatement.

The first wave of student volunteers left for Mississippi from Oxford, Ohio, on June 20. Andrew Goodman, a white twenty-year-old from Queens College in New York City, rode with two experienced civil rights workers from CORE, twenty-one-year-old James Chaney, a black native of Meridian, Mississippi, and white twenty-four-year-old Michael Schwerner from Brooklyn, New York. On June 21, their first assignment took them to a small town near Philadelphia, Mississippi, and the site of a church that had been burned. As a safety precaution when on the road, the three young men had been trained to maintain regular telephone contact with the COFO organization.

SANDRA CASON (CASEY HAYDEN)

Mendy Samstein and I were in the Freedom Summer office in Jackson, which was a storefront. Somehow we'd gotten this storefront together back during the Freedom Vote, and for the summer we'd put in a lot of telephones and a lot of desks. We had these cubicles. It was real hot, super hot. I remember somewhere later in the summer we got fans, which was a big deal.

So it was very hot and the phone was ringing. People were calling in with reports, and we got a call that these guys had gone out and hadn't called back. We had a system where people were to call in every half hour, or to call in at appointed times. And if the call-in didn't come, then within 15 minutes, whoever was receiving the call-ins was supposed to call the Jackson office. We had a security system we would then put into operation which involved calling the FBI and calling the Justice Department and calling the local police and in this case, calling back up to Oxford, where people were still training. So we did that and we asked the people to call back in half an hour to let us know what was happening. They did, and nothing was happening. At that point, Mendy was in the office and we assumed that they were either in real danger or dead. We got the folks in Oxford on the phone and said, "Well, it's almost an hour now and we really think that this is trouble." And Bob started trying to do what he could from Oxford and started calling Washington to try to put pressure on the FBI to send some people to check it out.

We had anticipated that there would be violence, but I remember thinking, Boy, they're really quick, you know. We had a lot of fear. I remember talking to Bob and saying, "You have to tell people to be very careful." And I remember hearing the way I sounded and thinking, This is so silly, it doesn't matter how careful they are, you know. There was nothing you could do. There was just nothing you could do.

PETER ORRIS

Those of us that had gone to Washington returned to Oxford, Ohio, in the middle of the second week of the training session. We had driven thirty hours straight, and we arrived in Oxford late one evening to find the college in a state of extreme remorse. In front of the dormitory area, there was a large circle of volunteers and SNCC organizers. They were in the dark and they were singing freedom songs. They had linked arms. We asked what had happened, and they described the situation to us. Three civil rights workers—Andrew Goodman, James Chaney, and Michael Schwerner—had disappeared. Our reaction was horror. The sorrow that went through the camp was profound.

BOB MOSES

Mickey [Michael Schwerner] had come down I think in 1963 to work for CORE as a volunteer from New York and had been based in Meridian for almost a year or so before the summer project. He had gotten James Chaney to join him. James was black, from Meridian, and his family lived there. He became a part of the

CORE staff and of Mickey's project there. They had some exposure to Mississippi and the conditions. Mickey had been there over a year; James, of course, all his life. When they went to Oxford, they took Andrew Goodman back with them. He had just come to Oxford and knew nothing about Mississippi. The three of them went back to Neshoba County to try and look for some housing for volunteers and for some churches, I think, for meeting places.

We heard that they had been arrested by the sheriff in Neshoba County and then we heard that they had been taken out of the jail. I remember Rita Schwerner, who was Mickey's wife, was still at the orientation session and spoke to the volunteers about that incident. And then she left and she was very emotional, and she was asking for students to help put pressure on the Justice Department and so forth. I spoke after her. I waited until she left, because we had to tell the students what we thought was going on. If, in fact, anyone is arrested and then taken out of the jail, then the chances that they are alive were just almost zero. We had to confront the students with that before they went down, because now the ball game had changed. We talked to them about the fact that as far as we could see, all three of them were dead. And that they had to make the decision now as to whether they really wanted to carry through on this and go down. We sang a couple of songs, and for a while I was worried because no one was leaving. But finally a few of them did leave, so I did think that the message had gotten through. You couldn't think that all of those who came to that orientation session were prepared to face the actual murder of their fellow students.

JAMES FARMER

It was two or three o'clock in the morning when I got a call from one of the CORE staff people in Meridian, telling me that Schwerner, Goodman, and Chaney were missing, and that I should come down immediately. I told them I would be on the next plane. I called Dick Gregory in Chicago and woke him up—he had just gotten back in the country and was jet-lagged—but his reaction was, "Hey, Big Daddy, what's happening?" Then I told him what had happened and he said, "When are you going?" and I said next flight—seven o'clock in the morning. Dick said, "Well, I'll get the first plane I can out of Chicago, and I'll meet you down there." We went to Philadelphia in Neshoba County and actually talked with Sheriff [Lawrence] Rainey and his deputy, [Cecil] Price, about the disappearance. They of course denied they knew anything about it. They had arrested the men for speeding, they claimed, and finally had taken them out of jail and headed them back toward Meridian.

JOHN DOAR

On the second day after the disappearances, Burke Marshall came into my office one night and said that President Johnson had decided to have Allen Dulles go down, the [former] head of the CIA, to make an investigation of the situation in Mississippi and give his recommendations. And Mr. Dulles came to the Justice Department the next morning, and the attorney general had me come up and talk to him because I was more familiar with Mississippi than most anyone, probably anybody else in the department. I went to Mississippi with Allen Dulles, and out of that trip the Justice Department made a recommendation that the FBI increase its force in Mississippi substantially. And Mr. Hoover opened an office in Jackson and put some very excellent FBI investigators in charge of that investigation. They were not only good, but there were a lot of them and they worked all that summer and solved that murder. The performance of the Justice Department was something that I am proud of in that respect.

PETER ORRIS

Following the disappearance of Goodman, Chaney, and Schwerner, there was a decision made by the SNCC leadership that those of us that were going to go to the southwest area of Mississippi shouldn't go right away, because the situation was too tense and the possibility of mass violence and many more deaths was present. So they decided that we should go in the interim to Holmes County in the Delta and do the voter registration there. So we went to a town called Mileston, which was outside of Tchula, in Holmes County. And we spent two to three weeks there, working on voter registration. What that meant was going to people's houses who we knew were not registered to vote and we would begin to talk to people about the Freedom Democratic party, about registering to vote, about the programs that were being put forward, about being ready to drive people to the courthouse, and going with them while they registered.

When we'd go to a new farmer's house, the first problem was that we were white northerners there on a mission, so to speak—all of those things were fraught with danger for the people that we were talking to. You'd get there, and the people would be sitting down and you'd shake their hands. Now, that was an unusual thing for a white person to do to a black person in Mississippi at that time. The next thing was that you would avoid a situation in which you were standing over and talking down to people—a body message about the power relationship. So we would always sit down, we'd sit on the steps, walking up to the porch. We'd either be on an equal eye level or on a lower level. We were much younger than many of the people we were speaking to, and it was necessary to establish a relationship or an understanding of the respect that we paid to them for their age and their situation. Frequently, people would respond by not looking us in the eye. At the end of every phrase there would be a "ma'am" or a "sir," depending on who was there. And they would say yes to everything we said. We'd say, "Would you like to be involved in the voter registration project? Will you go down to vote?" "Yes, sir." And we knew we were not getting across, we knew they were just waiting for us to go away because we were a danger to them, and in many ways we were. We had much less to risk than they did. This was their lives, their land, their family, and they were going to be here when we were gone.

> On July 2, President Lyndon Johnson signed the Civil Rights Act of 1964 into law. Although the act was a victory in that it represented a federal response to the ongoing civil rights demonstrations, it had little immediate impact on Mississippi.

SANDRA CASON (CASEY HAYDEN)

We wanted to break Mississippi open. It was a kind of blitzkrieg. Previous to that summer, we had been weaving, trying to weave, a network or a community of people who could work to change the system. But it was so slow and so many people were getting picked off one by one, the local leaders were getting murdered, people were being evicted, and the white power structure was so strong that it really seemed like we needed an enormous amount of outside support to punch a hole in the whole system of segregation.

We didn't have much money, you know. I mean, I can remember a lot of nights we didn't have gas to get home, so I slept in offices an awful lot of times. We were eating off the generosity of local black restaurateurs who were feeding us. We wanted to try to create actual human interactions between blacks and whites, which was impossible under the social structure as it was in that day. We wanted to break it open on a personal level in local communities.

UNITA BLACKWELL

For black people in Mississippi, Freedom Summer was the beginning of a whole new era. People began to feel that they wasn't just helpless anymore, that they had come together. Black and white had come from the North and from the West and even from some cities in the South. Students came and we wasn't a closed society anymore. They came to talk about that we had a right to register to vote, we had a right to stand up for our rights. That's a whole new era for us. I mean, hadn't anybody said that to us, in that open way, like what happened in 1964.

There was interaction of blacks and whites. I remember cooking some pinto beans—that's all we had—and everybody just got around the pot, you know, and that was an experience just to see white people coming around the pot and getting a bowl and putting some stuff in and then sitting around talking, sitting on the floor, sitting anywhere, 'cause you know, wasn't any great dining room tables and stuff that we had been used to working in the white people houses, where everybody would be sitting and they'd ring a bell and tap and you'd come in and bring the stuff and put it around. We was sitting on the floor and they was talking and we was sitting there laughing, and I guess they became very real and very human, we each to one another. It was an experience that will last a lifetime.

BOB MOSES

There was quite a group of support that was organized around the summer project. In fact, every day we had what we called the COFO Shuttle, which flew over from Atlanta to Jackson and quite literally they filled the plane. There were lawyers representing different lawyers' groups—the [NAACP] Legal Defense Fund, LCDC [Lawyers Constitutional Defense Committee], National Lawyers' Guild—there were doctors from the Medical Committee for Human Rights, which Al Poussaint was heading up. There were church people organized around Bob Spike. There was the Free Southern Theater, which Gil Moses and John O'Neil had organized. Through the Freedom Schools, we tried to develop the idea of alternative education, that is, that what's important is that the young people in Mississippi have a forum in which they could really think through and discuss problems which were really important for them. And they did. They met in little hot rooms all through the summer and did a lot of things—discussion and education about the problems in Mississippi. They came out with some statements about Vietnam. They came out with some statements about the politics of Mississippi and lack of representation.

DAVE DENNIS

During the time they were looking for the bodies of Chaney, Schwerner, and Goodman, they found other bodies throughout the state. They found torsos in the Mississippi River, they found people who were buried, they even found a few bodies of people on the side of roads. As soon as it was determined that these bodies were not the three missing workers, or one of the three, those deaths were forgotten. That's what we were talking about in terms of what the Freedom Summer was all about, in terms of why it was necessary to bring that attention there. Because people forgot, and if it had just been blacks there, they would have forgotten again. It would just have been three black people missing.

Rumors had circulated about Chaney, Goodman, and Schwerner all through the summer. The white opposition claimed they were in Cuba with Fidel Castro and the communists. Another story had them hiding out in Chicago, laughing at the efforts to find them. The search, and the rumors, ended on August 4. The FBI, after paying an informer, found the bodies of the three young men buried in an earthen dam on a farm near Philadelphia. All three had been shot. James Chaney, the black Mississippian, had been savagely beaten, with bones broken and crushed.

DAVE DENNIS

After the bodies were found, there was basic concern about cooling things down because the country was angry. I had been told I was gonna give a eulogy at the church, in Meridian, for James Chaney, and I had been approached by my national office of CORE and others to make sure that the speech that's given is calm. They don't want a lot of things stirred up and everything else like that, and I said okay, fine, that's good. Then when I got up there and I looked out there and I saw little Ben Chaney [James's eleven-year-old brother], things just sort of snapped and I was in a fantasy world, to be sitting up here talking about things gonna get better, and we should do it in an easy manner, and with nonviolence and stuff like that. It's because this country—you cannot make a man change by speaking a foreign language, he has to understand what you're talking about—this country operates, operated then and still operates, on violence. I mean, it's an eye for an eye, a tooth for a tooth. That's what we respect. So I just stopped and said what I felt. And there was no need to stand in front of that kid Ben Chaney and lie to him.

Two days after the discovery of the bodies,* the MFDP met in state convention to select delegates for the Democratic National Convention in Atlantic City.

Joseph Rauh, a white lawyer active in the liberal wing of the national Democratic party, volunteered to help the MFDP

*In December 1964 nineteen white men, including Neshoba County's sheriff and deputy sheriff, Lawrence Rainey and Cecil Price, were arrested on conspiracy charges connected with the deaths of Chaney, Goodman, and Schwerner. The charges were subsequently dropped in state court, but seven of the men were sentenced to prison in 1967 for periods ranging from three to ten years after being convicted of violating federal civil rights laws.

unseat the all-white party regulars from Mississippi, who had excluded blacks from the delegate-selection process.

JOSEPH RAUH

I was general counsel of the Leadership Conference on Civil Rights, a group then of, say, sixty civil rights organizations. I had been in the various fights for civil rights. For example, in 1957 I had been the chief lobbyist along with Clarence Mitchell for the 1957 Civil Rights Act. That was a pretty pale one, but it was better than nothing. It dealt with voting rights. In 1963, I lobbied for the bill that was passed the next year. I helped with the March on Washington.

In March of 1964, I first heard of the MFDP and their challenge. There was a meeting of the National Civil Liberties Clearinghouse—it's now defunct—and we were having a discussion of the whole problem of black voting. Out of the audience rose a man I had never met, Bob Moses. I was the chairman of the panel that they had at that moment, and Bob rose from the audience and said, "Mr. Rauh, we are thinking of taking a challenge to the lily-white Mississippi delegation at the upcoming convention in August. What do you think our chances would be?"

Well, I thought for a second and I said, "I think your chances are pretty good, and the reason I think that is there's not going to be any excitement at the convention. Johnson's going to be renominated for president. He's going to choose the vice president. He's going to write the platform. This might be the one thing that would stir up the convention. I think you've got a good chance." That's where I first saw Bob Moses. I liked him, he liked me. And we started in partnership there for the August fight.

I went to the convention of the MFDP in early August. It was in Jackson, at the Masonic Temple on Lynn Street. I'll never forget it. It was practically all black. There may have been a couple of white ringers, but it was a black party.

When I returned from Jackson, the pressure was incredible. President Johnson was a man who believed every man has his price. And he had two things on me which he could squeeze with. One was that I loved Hubert Humphrey, and I wanted Hubert to be vice president and hopefully one day president. The other was that I was general counsel of the UAW [United Auto Workers], and Walter Reuther could have some effect, he figured. So they would call and sort of say, "The president is very angry—Joe, you've got to stop it." And Walter would be very serious. He'd pound on me, and I'd say, "Walter, I just can't give up. I believe in this, Walter. After all, I'm an employee of the UAW, but I'm not operating that way here." With Hubert, it was a little bit different. It was more fun. He'd say, "Joe, just give me something to tell the president!" And I'd say, "Why don't you tell him that I'm a dirty bastard who is absolutely uncontrollable." And he says, "Well, the president wouldn't like that if I told him I couldn't control you." And I said, "Well, then, you'll have to think of what you want to tell him yourself, because that's the only thing I can think of telling him."

VICTORIA GRAY

We went to Atlantic City with lots of optimism, because at this point we were still idealistic enough to believe that the constitutional rights were all there to be ours as soon as we met the requirements. So we had documented, in all of the ways possible, the fact that black people in particular in Mississippi were being denied the right to participate, were being denied the right to representation. You know the old story: taxation without representation. And so we were indeed off to Atlantic City for the Democratic National Convention.

The difference between the regular Democratic party delegation and the Mississippi Freedom Democratic party delegation was that the election process within the MFDP was open at every level to the total populace, whereas in the regular Democratic party, this was not the case. The delegation from the regular party was almost totally unrepresentative of the populace of Mississippi; our delegation was representative of blacks, whites, the spectrum.

I think one of the things that made the delegation of the Mississippi Freedom Democratic party so hopeful, so expectant, was the fact that people had made a discovery that there is a way out of much that is wrong with our lives, there is a way to change it, and that is through the execution of this vote. We can't get past these people at the state level, because they've locked us out, but we just know that once we get to the national level, with all of the proof that we had been locked out and the fact that we've had the courage to go ahead and create our own party, then we feel like we were going to get that representation that we'd been denied for so long. That's the way we arrived in Atlantic City—really excited about the fact that we were at long last going to be able to participate, to be represented.

UNITA BLACKWELL

The bus ride to Atlantic City was full of enthusiasm. We had done this. We had had our own elections. We had our delegates. And we were going to challenge the regular party. I remember one man, he was supposed to have been nonviolent, but he was sitting there with an old rusty gun and he said, "Well, if the Klans come at us, I think that's when I'm going to have to take care of business this time." We were going with that feeling of nonviolence, but trying to see what we could get. When we left Jackson, Mississippi, to pick up people and head toward Atlantic City, we went saying we were coming at all of the seats or half . . . nothing less. And we kept to that.

COURTLAND COX

What happened in Atlantic City was that we went through all the processes that the Democratic party said one had to go through in order to be credentialized, though the white delegation from Mississippi went through none of the processes and violated all of them. So the question was, would the Democratic party obey its own rules, or would it favor those whites who had been in the party all the time? The credentials committee would make a decision as to who would be able to represent the state of Mississippi on the floor. A presentation was made by both groups. Now, what happened was that the MFDP in that environment in 1964 had a tremendous sympathy among white liberals, the black community, the church community. The person who seems to symbolize that, who thrust out from Mississippi, was Mrs. Fannie Lou Hamer. Fannie Lou Hamer spoke on television, was very effective in her presentation of what was going on in Mississippi. And what Johnson did at that time when she was beginning to ruin his congress, he called the TV stations and preempted her in the middle of her speech, literally preempted her in the middle of her speech. I think he spoke about his trip to the hospital or some other foolishness—his beagles, or something inconsequential.

After that, Johnson called Humphrey up and told him, "Hubert, if you want to be vice president of the United States, you've got to stop these people from Mississippi." Humphrey called Walter Reuther from the UAW and a number of other people and said to them that these people had to be stopped.

We knew that if we could get eleven of the hundred and ten delegates on the credentials committee, ten percent of them, to vote that the Mississippians had a valid case, then it could be brought to the floor for the entire convention to vote on. And Johnson knew that in fact if that happened, then it was all downhill in terms of his convention. So what Johnson did is he got a Negro congressman to "befriend" the group. We had a strategy session in the convention hall, deep in the bowels of the convention hall. Mrs. Hamer was there, Edith Green [congresswoman] from Oregon, Bob Moses, Dona Moses. We had a list of delegates who we felt were solid. The Negro congressman asked us for the list, and Bob did not want to give it to him. I said to Bob, "Do you think this man is going to steal this list of names?" And the congressman said, "Yes, I want to give this list of names to [credentials committee chairman David] Lawrence, to show him we have the strength to pull a minority vote on the floor."

In my ignorance, I pressed Bob to give him the list so that he could show that we had some clout. Bob gave the list reluctantly, and what happened next was something unbelievable. Every person on that list, every member of that credentials committee who was going to vote for the minority, got a call. They said, "Your husband is up for a judgeship, and if you don't shape up, he won't get it." "You're up for a loan. If you don't shape up, you won't get it." And you began to see how things worked in the real world. I mean everybody, including a number of the people in the civil rights movement, a number of people in the religious community, a number of people in the liberal community, all came out and tried to blunt the thrust of the MFDP to take its rightful place as the lawful delegation from Mississippi.

Walter Mondale, the young attorney general of Minnesota, was asked by his political mentor Hubert Humphrey to develop an acceptable solution.

WALTER MONDALE

We started out with that vast credentials committee—there must have been a hundred people there. It couldn't handle that kind of burden. So we set up a subcommittee, which I chaired, and I think we had seven or eight members. And we tried for the better part of two and a half days, maybe three, to come up with a resolution that would satisfy everyone.

They were pushing against an open door in terms of the objective of civil rights and preventing any future lily-white, segregated delegations. We expected the all-white delegations from Alabama and Mississippi to walk out. That was almost preordained. And that was fine by us, because you couldn't justify what they'd done. The tough question was, How do we handle it? One theory was you just take the black delegation and seat them, kick the white delegation out, and that's all you needed to do. Well, that didn't solve any long-term problems. It didn't establish any rule of law for civil rights, and if all it's going to be is blacks or whites, one winning, one losing, then there was no hope for a healthy political party, an integrated party.

Everybody was trying to think of something that was simple, that would solve it, and would satisfy everybody. The problem was there was no such solution. We'd go around and around and around, and everybody would try this and try that, and writers would see if they could write around the problem, and philosophers see if they could dream of something to dream over the problem. It wouldn't go away. It had to be resolved. It had to be compromised, I think, in the way we did it. And it was inevitable that some people would be unhappy.

JOSEPH RAUH

There was a stalemate. On Tuesday morning, about three in the morning, Walter Reuther comes in, Johnson orders him in. He's actually in negotiations, I think with General Motors. Johnson orders him to come. You know, Johnson's a pretty tough character. So Reuther comes in and they make the deal that they offer us. Namely, two delegates-at-large. They promised us that no lily-white delegation would ever be seated again. And that they would set up a civil rights committee of the Democratic National Committee so that no lily-white delegation could ever be seated again.

We're about to have a meeting of the credentials committee and I get a call from Reuther. He said, "This is what the convention has decided." What he meant was, this is what he and Johnson had agreed to, and I want you to accept it. He tells me that's it.

Well, I thought it was wonderful. I mean, it is wonderful. It's the basis from which the whole Democratic party has been opened up, to blacks, to women, to Hispanics, to everything. It was a great, great, great victory, but I couldn't accept it. I said, "Walter, look, I cannot accept this without talking to Aaron Henry. We have a deal sealed in blood that neither of us will ever take anything without talking to the other. You get me a postponement. Tell me where Aaron is. We can possibly make this unanimous." Walter said he would.

So I went back into the credentials committee room and said to David Lawrence, the chairman, "I want a postponement for this purpose." And he said, "Well, go ask Mondale, who is the chairman of the subcommittee which is walking up the stairs there." So I did, and Mondale says, "Well, of course, Joe, you can have a postponement." And some little punk, I think his name was Sherwin Markman, from Iowa, says, "No postponement. We're going ahead." He was the one Johnson had put in there to watch Mondale, to be sure Mondale wasn't fair. So Mondale says, "Well, Joe, that's the way the ball bounces."

They all went in. I tried to get the floor for a postponement. So then Mondale announces what the compromise is. He made it sound so favorable to us, and he would interject all the time about how much I had won, and that made it harder to fight. But I got up and said, "I'm not arguing whether this is good or bad. Life alone will tell that. But what I am saying is we ought to have a postponement so Aaron Henry's views can be injected here and we can decide probably that we're all in agreement." It was like a lynch mob: a hundred people shouting "Vote, vote, vote!" while I'm talking. I finally had to say, "It's your rudeness that's the problem. I've got a right to speak. I've got the floor. You ought to shut up." "Vote, vote, vote!" I moved for a postponement. I moved for a roll call. I moved for everything, but I didn't get it. Then they take a vote on the Mondale proposal, the proposal that I knew in my heart was a victory, but I had to vote no. There were eight of us who voted no. It was a ragtag eight. They had gotten the rest of them away from us.

While I am in the credentials committee, trying to get the postponement, Reuther, Humphrey, and others from the administration are talking to Martin Luther King, Bayard Rustin, Abernathy, Moses, Henry, and a few others from the MFDP. While they're talking, the television is going, low. Somebody shouts out, "It's all over. It was unanimous for the compromise." Bob Moses lost his cool. It was like hitting him with a whip, like a white man hitting him with a whip, everybody had ratted on him. It wasn't true, of course. The fact is, I had even voted no. It was not unanimous. We went outside and Mondale and I had a little pushing match for the television cameras. The cameras really wanted Mondale. They want the majority before they get the minority, and I understood that. So I waited. Mondale filibustered a little bit. He was savoring his victory. He was having a good time talking. So I didn't get the floor for about fifteen minutes. And then I blew up the idea that there was any unanimity. I said we may try to get enough votes so that we can go to the floor tonight. Bob was angry. This had struck him like a bolt of lightning. That evening, we were on the evening news. I said we would continue the fight. But I also said—it was my position—that this is a great victory which is going to end up with a new Democratic party because of their promise that there will never be a lily-white group again. Bob got on and said, "You cannot trust the political system. I will have nothing to do with the political system any longer."

COURTLAND COX

All the people that you thought were on your side began to crumble. I mean, the liberals began to crumble. The labor movement began to crumble. A number of the civil rights leaders began to crumble. The only people who did not crumble in the final analysis were the people from Mississippi. They're the people who stood firm. Mrs. Hamer stood firm. And the people whose lives depended upon the benevolence of either the Democratic party, the labor movement, or the liberal movement, they caved in under the pressure, because that's where their bread and butter lay.

UNITA BLACKWELL

Here we were at first, we wasn't recognized at all. And then they said they was gonna give us two seats. So these leaders talked to us and tried to show us what we ought to do. Take these two seats, and at least then we would have somethin'. Roy Wilkins, he told us that we was ignorant. Dr. King was there, too. He didn't call us ignorant. He just said we should seriously think about taking the compromise.

And we told them we might be some ignorant folks from the sticks in Mississippi, but our people was also back there, ignorant and from the sticks. And we promised them that we would not take the compromise. Praise God today, we did not take that compromise. And there was a group of people that stood up in this country. And stood up to the payoffs and buyoffs and so forth.

VICTORIA GRAY

Those who are unable to understand why we were unable to accept that compromise did not realize that we would have been betraying the very many people back there in Mississippi whom we represented. They had not only laid their lives on the line, but many had given their lives in order for this particular event to happen. They said to us, "Just take this this time, and then next time, you know . . ."

I thought about the many people for which there was not gonna be a next time, and I think so did the majority of the delegation. We came with nothing, and we realized that it made no sense at all, with all the risk that had been taken, to accept what we knew for certain to be nothing and to go back there to God only knows what. You may get home and not have a house. You may get home and a member of your family might be missing. You may not get home at all, and so you know we are not going to accept anything less than what we came after, which is the real thing—representation and the right to participate. And if we don't get that, then we'll go back and take our chances and regroup and come to fight another day, and that is precisely what we did.

In November 1964, President Lyndon Johnson, who had chosen Hubert Humphrey as his running mate, defeated Republican Barry Goldwater in a landslide.

At the next Democratic convention, in 1968, the MFDP would join a new challenge to the all-white Mississippi delegation in front of the credentials committee. This time the challengers would win. As Aaron Henry said, speaking of the 1964 MFDP challenge, "It wrote the beginning of the restructuring of politics in this nation."

Postscript: "A Trip to Africa"

Entertainer Harry Belafonte was an early supporter of SNCC. He saw that they played an important role as "provocateurs" and that they were "a radical voice," "the voice of noncompromise." Belafonte was one of the principal fund-raisers for both SNCC and SCLC. After Freedom Summer, he raised funds for SNCC workers to take a trip to Africa. They chose among themselves, and Bob and Dona Moses, John Lewis, Jim Forman, Prathia Hall, Julian Bond, Ruby Doris Robinson, Bill Hansen, Donald Harris, Matthew Jones, and Fannie Lou Hamer left on September 11, 1964, for Guinea.

HARRY BELAFONTE

I had become sensitive to the fact that many of the people in SNCC were on burnout. They had been on the front line for so long, doing so much and many had been beaten and battered. What became clear to me was that they really needed a hiatus. They needed to get away. After much thought and discussion I concluded that if it were acceptable to the leadership, the most meaningful and creative thing to do would be to arrange for as many as possible to go to Africa. Having visited the continent with some regularity, I felt the most appropriate place would be Guinea. I was most taken by the young spirit of the country, which had just recently gained its independence from France, and in those early years the clearsightedness of its leader Sékou Touré held great promise for Africa's future.

All this was at the time when Schwerner, Goodman, and Chaney were reported missing and everyone suspected they had been murdered. At a meeting with SNCC leaders it was decided that the summer voter registration project, which was to have officially ended that summer, would be extended through the fall and many students agreed to stay on, missing the fall school semester provided I would fund the extension. I agreed to do this and at the same time personally fund the Africa trip. I raised the required sixty thousand dollars for the extension of the voter registration project and in addition the ten thousand dollars for the transportation to take those chosen who were the most in need of the change of scene. It was a difficult choice to make, but it had to be made and among those selected were Jim Forman, Ruby Doris, Julian Bond, John Lewis, and Fannie Lou Hamer.

For most this was a first time out of the United States. I think the person who early on appeared to be the most affected by the trip was Fannie Lou Hamer. When we arrived in Guinea, the Guinean government put us up as their guests. We were given the best places to live and Guinean citizens were there to help meet the needs of the guests.

Upon our arrival we were told we were to meet [President] Sékou Touré the next day at a reception, but he was noted for doing his evening thing, which was to, at random, drop in unannounced on friends for informal exchanges. We were one of those so selected. Fannie Lou Hamer was in the middle of taking a bath when Sékou Touré drove up to meet us. I had to go over to tell Fannie Lou Hamer that the president had arrived. It was the only time I could remember Fannie Lou Hamer getting totally rattled. She said, "What, no, no, no, you all playing a joke. I'm having a bath. I'm definitely not ready to meet no president." When she understood that we were telling the truth, she hurriedly dressed and came to the meeting. It was a moving experience. After the meeting, Fannie Lou started to cry and said that she didn't know quite what she would do with this experience. For so long she and a lot of poor black folk had tried unsuccessfully to meet with the president of her own country, the United States of America, where we were citizens, and we could never see him. And here in Africa a head of state, President Sékou Touré, came to see her with great words of encouragement and hope and a declaration that this Africa was their home and its people their family.

I don't think that anybody who was on that trip ever saw life in quite the same way again.

JOHN LEWIS

I saw Africa as a place of independence, a place of freedom, particularly in West Africa, and East Africa, where we visited as members of the Student Nonviolent Coordinating Committee. For the first time, you saw a group of black men and women in charge. Growing up in the southern parts of the United States of America, we had been talking and speaking a great deal about one man, one vote. In Guinea, in Ghana, in East Africa, in Zambia, we saw people making it real, making it happen. It was a source of inspiration, for us to be in a country, on a continent, where there was a greater sense of freedom, and a greater sense of appreciation for human dignity.

We met Malcolm X at the New Stanley Hotel in Nairobi, and it was by chance that we met. It was one of the most moving meetings that I ever had with Malcolm, and probably the longest meeting. For more than two days, we discussed not just the problems and the issues in Africa, but we spent a great deal of time speaking about the problems in America. This was right after the Democratic convention in 1964. So the whole question of the right to participate in the democratic process was on the mind of Malcolm, as it was on the minds of my colleagues in the Student Nonviolent Coordinating Committee.

He kept warning us and telling us to be careful. I remember on one occasion, while we were meeting in a little coffee shop at the hotel, he said, "Always sit with your back to the wall, so you can look out and see who is watching you." He told us to be careful, but I had a feeling from my discussions with him that Malcolm was in the process of becoming a changed person, a changed man, because he kept saying over and over again that he really wanted to be helpful and be supportive of the civil rights movement. And he wanted to visit the South.

He also told us over and over again to keep fighting. "Don't give up," he said. "This is an ongoing struggle. Be prepared for the worst, but keep it up, keep fighting. People are changing, there are people supporting you all over the world."

In December of that year, while Fannie Lou Hamer and other representatives of SNCC and the MFDP were in Harlem on a tour of northern cities, Malcolm X agreed to speak at one of their rallies. In return, Mrs. Hamer and the SNCC Freedom Singers (a group consisting of Bernice Johnson Reagon, Cordell Reagon, and others who traveled the country performing freedom songs) attended a meeting of Malcolm X's Organization of Afro-American Unity.

Later that month, while speaking to a SNCC-sponsored group of teenagers visiting New York from McComb, Mississippi, Malcolm X said that the greatest single accomplishment of the 1964 struggles was "the successful linking together of our problem with the African problem, or making our problem a world problem. . . . It is important for you to know that when you're in Mississippi, you're not alone. As long as you think you're alone, then you take a stand as if you're a minority or as if you're outnumbered, and that kind of stand will never enable you to win a battle."

13

SELMA, 1965

"TROOPERS, ADVANCE"

Alabama state troopers armed with tear gas, cattle prods, and clubs await demonstrators attempting to cross the Edmund Pettus Bridge in Selma, Alabama, on Sunday, March 7, 1965.

There were many signals that the civil rights movement was in danger of coming apart. The riot in Birmingham at the end of Project C demonstrated that many black people were not buying into the creed of nonviolence, which had been key to the movement's legislative victories. The summer of 1964 began with a four-day riot in Harlem, reinforcing the challenge to the traditional movement from within the black community itself.

On another front, soon after the announcement that Martin Luther King was to receive the 1964 Nobel Peace Prize, the FBI's J. Edgar Hoover stepped up his personal campaign to discredit King and drive a wedge between the SCLC leader and his allies in government. Adding to the tension was the difference in operating philosophies between the Southern Christian Leadership Conference under King and the younger, more militant activists in the Student Nonviolent Coordinating Committee. The ministers of SCLC took great pride in King's ability to deliver victories and to bring national attention to local movements. SNCC, on the other hand, attempted to develop leaders at the grass roots rather than to bring them in from the outside.

As 1965 began, the greatest victory of all—the right to vote—had eluded all of the civil rights organizations. For white segregationists, the political and economic consequences of opening a lunch counter or a front seat on a bus to blacks were relatively small. The consequences of allowing blacks to vote were enormous. White southerners foresaw an end to the political system they had dominated for almost one hundred years, and a possible end to economic hegemony as well. The white resistance had proved that it would kill to keep blacks from the polls. There was little reason to believe that it would not kill again.

The stage was set. SNCC had been laboring in Selma, Alabama, a city of twenty-nine thousand, for almost three years. When Amelia Boynton and the Dallas County Voters League appealed to SCLC to help Selma's black residents win the right to vote, local SNCC staffers were frustrated and angry.

As Martin Luther King, Jr., and his SCLC entourage entered Selma in January 1965, the many conflicting forces of the civil rights decade, white and black, began to converge on this small southern town.

Amelia Boynton was a longtime Selma resident and community leader. Before 1965 she was one of the few blacks in Dallas County allowed to register to vote.

AMELIA BOYNTON ROBINSON

In 1930, when I was at Tuskegee Institute, I was not a registered voter because I was barely twenty years old. When I reached the age of twenty-one, my late husband, who at that time was a county agent, brought me to the county courthouse to register. I was acquainted with becoming a registered voter and the political way of doing things because when the women were given the right to vote in 1920, my mother with a horse and buggy used to get people to go down to the registration office and help them to register in Savannah, Georgia. When my husband took me down to register, I had no trouble whatsoever, because I was a single person, just one.

During the time before the civil rights movement started, which was between twenty-five and thirty years before the whole country became interested in registration and voting for the more downtrodden people, my husband and I decided that we were going to help people to register. At that time, they had two pages to fill out. These two pages were questions that were pretty hard for the average person, terribly hard for those who were illiterate. But we would teach people how to fill these blanks out. We could not do it by coming out in the open, so we started with the people with whom we worked, the rural people. My husband as a county agent, and I as a home demonstration agent, would have meetings in the rural churches, and even in the homes. Each person that came down to register had to have a voucher with him. At that time, my husband was a registered voter and a voucher. He was supposed to tell the registrars that he knew these people, he knew where they lived, he knew their ages, he knew that they were people who had contributed whatever they could for the benefit of the city, or the county, and if he could tell all of that, saying that they were "good Negroes," as it was said, then they would consider letting them become a registered voter.

When my husband began to bring three and four people at a time, then the registrar became very upset and said, "You're bringing too many people down here to register. Why is it you're bringing these people down here? We have been registering and voting them all the time. Now you are doing the wrong thing by bringing these large numbers of black people to register and vote." So he said, "They would like to be citizens."

After my husband died in 1963, I became a voucher. The sad thing about it is the registrar had only been through the eighth grade, and he could not read many of the applications that were sent down for people to register and vote. I remember very vividly one man who asked me to vouch for him. We went up to the registrar, and as he began to write in a very unsteady way—he wrote his name across a line—the registrar said, "Now, you're going across the line, old man. You failed already, you can't register, you can't vote, you just as well get out of line." The old man looked at him and said, "Mr. White Man, you can't tell me that I can't register. I'll try anyway. For I own a hundred and forty acres of land. I've got ten children who are grown and many of them are in a field where they can help other people. I've got a man who's a preacher and a man who's a teacher and all of them out there, and I took these hands that I have and made crops to put them through school. If I am not worthy of being a registered voter, then God have mercy on this city." With that I stepped back. I figured he had said it all. They let him go on and fill the blanks out, but he didn't become a registered voter, and neither did many others, for in eight years' time, we had less than twenty-five people who became registered voters.

Perhaps no federal official had more firsthand experience with Alabama's resistance to change than Deputy Attorney General Nicholas Katzenbach. In 1963, when Governor George Wallace blocked the doorway of the University of Alabama in defiance of a federal court order to integrate, it was Katzenbach who confronted Wallace and engineered the successful admission of the school's first black students, James Hood and Vivian Malone. Katzenbach also went to federal court in an attempt to break the color line at the ballot box.

NICHOLAS KATZENBACH

The problem in the South of voting was primarily the problem of the literacy tests and the way in which they were administered. You had black Ph.D.'s who couldn't pass a literacy test and you had whites who could barely write their name who had no problem being registered to vote.

The Justice Department was empowered by earlier legislation to sue, but it had to sue on behalf of individuals who were discriminated against when they attempted to register to vote. This meant, essentially, that you had to bring a separate lawsuit for each person who was discriminated against, and there were thousands. It would take years to get them registered to vote. It simply was not a solution to the problem.

Impatient with the lack of progress, the Student Nonviolent Coordinating Committee offered its own solution. SNCC's attempt to mobilize local leadership in Alabama began in early 1963, when Bernard and Colia Lafayette inaugurated a voter education project in the city of Selma. That fall, chairman John Lewis and other SNCC staffers mounted a drive to register black voters by the hundreds. As FBI agents looked on and took notes, Dallas County Sheriff Jim Clark and his deputies attacked the SNCC activists and some reporters covering the story.

JOHN LEWIS

Freedom Day in Selma, Alabama, on October 8, 1963, I believe was a turning point in the civil rights movement. We had witnessed at the March on Washington the Student Nonviolent Coordinating Committee call for one man, one vote. We went to Selma to test that idea. We had witnessed the bombing of a church in Birmingham a few weeks earlier where four little girls were all killed, and we had made a commitment; we felt we had an obligation, a mandate really, to go to Selma, where only about 2.1 percent of the black people of voting age were registered to vote. On this particular day, hundreds of blacks lined up and stood at the county courthouse for most of the day, and at the end of the day only about five people had made it in to take the so-called literacy tests. I can never forget that day. We met hostile law enforcement officials. Sheriff Jim Clark and others stood there and later some of us were arrested. But mostly elderly black men and women stood there all day in line, and as several people from the outside observed—James Baldwin, Professor Howard Zinn, a historian, and others—it was the turning point in the right to vote.

Despite the dramatic start, the black leadership in Selma grew dissatisfied with SNCC's progress. In the fall of 1964, the locals asked SCLC and Martin Luther King, Jr., to step in. Andrew Young was SCLC's newly appointed executive director.

ANDREW YOUNG

Our thinking in going into Selma was that we had a lot of experience in Albany and Birmingham that we would apply to Selma. But I think we knew enough about people and we knew enough about the political situation to know that you couldn't prepackage a movement, that a movement had a life of its own. The people had a dynamic, and you had to get in and work with those people.

The local black leadership in Selma was really responsible for the Selma movement. Selma was not a place that we picked out. We did not choose them, they chose us. We had trained some of the people, including Mrs. Boynton, in our citizenship education program some years before. But Mrs. Boynton's background goes all the way back to the early NAACP days, before the NAACP was outlawed in Alabama.

Jim Clark was a near madman. It just infuriated him for anybody to defy his authority, even when they just wanted to vote. If he said you couldn't vote, you were supposed to go away. And just to stand there enraged him. John Lewis and Bernard Lafayette, with the Student Nonviolent Coordinating Committee, had gone down to attempt to register voters. They were beaten up pretty badly. Then the local courts put a total injunction on the city, where it was unlawful for more than three people to even walk down the street together. No more than three people could be in a public meeting without permission from the sheriff's office. It was really a very repressive situation. Mrs. Boynton came to the SCLC board meeting, just after Dr. King won the Nobel Prize, and she told us about this situation, and she asked us if we would come over there to work with her.

There was a traditional Emancipation Day service scheduled that year for the second of January [1965]. To hold that Emancipation Day service was a violation of this particular injunction. We decided that that would be the way to come to Selma. We would let everybody know well in advance that we were going to hold it, and we would publicly announce that we were going to defy this injunction and from that time on begin to work in Selma.

Martin had a way of making fun out of any dangerous situation. He talked about going down to Selma. We knew the kind of people that were there. And he started preaching everybody's funeral. He was saying, "We were lucky in Birmingham, all of us got out alive." But some of us weren't going to make it out of Selma. And he'd go around the room sort of saying, "Well, Ralph, now if they get you . . ." and then he'd preach Ralph Abernathy's sermon for about five minutes. He just made fun of saying all the embarrassing things he could think of saying, pretending that he was preaching our eulogies and our funerals. That was the way that we dealt with the anxiety and the fear and the tension, by joking about it and laughing about it.

Frederick Reese, a local minister, a schoolteacher, and president of the Dallas County Voters League, had joined Mrs. Boynton in inviting SCLC to Selma. The January 2 service was held at Brown's Chapel.

FREDERICK REESE

I remember vividly how it snowed and there were those who felt that many people would not show up at that meeting because of fright, fear of being jailed. However, at three o'clock, January the second, that church was packed with people sitting in the windows. The law enforcement agencies, instead of arresting us for meeting, they only directed the traffic around the church to make sure that everybody had a parking space. There were so many people there that having to arrest that number of people would have been a liability on the city to fit all those people in jail. We kept meeting from that point on.

ANDREW YOUNG

We never wanted racists to retaliate. That was not an SCLC plan. What we did say was that we would put so many people in jail that we would bring the system to a halt. And that our emphasis was on noncooperation and economic withdrawal.

There has been a rumor that the plans for Selma were already out in 1964 and that Public Safety Director Wilson Baker took copies of them to Washington to Burke Marshall to try to get him to intercede or to stop the campaign. I don't know that to be a fact, but it's quite possible. In fact, it's even probable that that was the case. During the Selma movement, the John Birch Society and the white Citizens' Council had people in our meetings, taping our meetings and making films. And we didn't put them out. We knew who they were. We would take the microphones off from wherever they would hide them, under the pulpit, and put them right out on top. Reverend Abernathy got quite famous for preaching to "the little doohickey," which is what he called the bugging device. It didn't disturb us that everybody knew our plans. We wanted them to know our plans.

> King moved from mass meetings to direct action in mid-January, when he led four hundred marchers to the Dallas County Courthouse in Selma. Clark was there to meet them. So were hecklers from the American Nazi party. But there was no violence. Joseph Smitherman, Selma's new mayor, reasoned that if Clark restrained himself, the press would see little reason to remain in Selma. But despite differences in tactics, the mayor, like the sheriff, was a segregationist.

JOSEPH SMITHERMAN

I was elected at age thirty to the city council. It was all white, obviously. I was a Rebel with all those other council members—we were all segregationists—but I really got in politics to try to get industry, pave the streets, install streetlights. Segregation was not an issue, because everybody was a segregationist. I could do very little in the council and I was determined I wanted to be the mayor. That's where you had a lot of authority. So at age thirty-four I ran for the office of mayor. I put together a coalition of people, moderate low-income and middle-income whites and some of the upper-income financial institutions. After being elected on October 1, 1964, I was on a cloud, having run on these progressive steps. And I thought we could handle the racial situation. I called three prominent black leaders down to my office, and I tried to make a deal with them. I said, "I've got some state money. If you three will come out publicly and demand I pave a road"—back then, practically all the streets in the predominantly black area were dirt—I said, "you'll get credit for this and I'll respond. We don't need this Martin Luther King in here." He was announcing from Atlanta he was coming to the most segregated, biased city in the South. He would make these announcements, while we did what we thought was a good job trying to defuse it and keep him out of here.

They picked Selma just like a movie producer would pick a set. You had the right ingredients. I mean, you would've had to see Clark in his day. He had a helmet like General Patton, he had the clothes, the Eisenhower jacket and the swagger stick. Then Baker was very impressive—a dynamic figure, a professional law enforcement officer and a moderate—and I guess I was the least of all. I was a young mayor with no background or experience, one hundred forty-five pounds with a crew cut and big ears.

Smitherman had recently appointed Wilson Baker as Selma's public safety director, with authority over all law enforcement in the city except for Clark's jurisdiction in and around the county courthouse. Baker was expected to keep Clark under control, but on January 19, the second day of SCLC demonstrations, Sheriff Clark could control himself no longer.

AMELIA BOYNTON ROBINSON

I left the courthouse with the intention of going to my office. I was vouching for some people. I was going back and Jim Clark said to me, "You get in this line." And that line was one where he had sixty people standing up. He had planned on taking them upstairs in the courtroom, cursing them out, and saying, "If you do this again, you will go to jail." I would not get in the line. But when he grabbed me, I didn't know whether I should go limp or whether I should turn around and knock him out or whether I should just fall to the ground and let him take me. These people who were standing there said to me, "Go on, Mrs. Boynton, you don't have to be in jail by yourself. We'll be there." So it gave me courage, and I let him almost pick me up off of the ground by grabbing me, throwing me in the car.

JIM CLARK

Amelia Boynton led the group to the courthouse and directed them to come inside and to take over the offices and to urinate on top of the desks and throw the books on the floor. She was telling them what to do and how to do it, and I went and tried to persuade her to leave the premises. She would not, and I laid my hand on her shoulder to indicate that I was putting her under arrest and she started trying to run out from under my hand, screaming "Where are the cameras? Where are the cameras?

Take my picture, take my picture." And so, to quiet things down, and since she was a leader, I was forced to arrest her.

She was a tall woman. It may look like she was a tiny woman from the angle of the cameras, and that I was taking advantage of her. But there was no violence there at all.

> The next day, the *New York Times* and the *Washington Post* ran photographs of Sheriff Clark pushing Mrs. Boynton down the street with his billy club.
>
> Four days after the first march, Frederick Reese led Selma teachers to the courthouse.

FREDERICK REESE

We were going down to the county courthouse to ask the board of registrars to have the board office open so teachers could get registered. We knew that on Friday the board is not open. In fact, the board only was open on the first and third Mondays of each month, but I had written a letter to the chairman of the board of registrars requesting that the office be open, because I felt that if we could go to the courthouse to pay our taxes any day of the week that we ought to be able to go and get registered any day of the week.

Ninety-nine percent of the teachers participated in the march. When we got there we encountered Sheriff Jim Clark and his deputies, who had formed a line across the door at the courthouse. Clark informed me that I was making a mockery out of his courthouse. I was asked to take those teachers back to the school where they came from. I reminded him that that courthouse did not belong to him, it belonged to us also, and we were there as citizens to see if the board of registrars was in session as we had requested. We had a right to go in the courthouse and I would not back down from that right.

He gave us one minute. At the end of that one minute he and his posse took their billy clubs and knocked us down the steps. We regrouped and went back a second time. Again he gave us another minute and then he knocked us down the steps again. We tried it a third time. He gave us another minute, and after about forty-five seconds someone came and pulled Jim Clark's coat and took him into the courthouse door. I don't know exactly what they told him, but I could imagine. He was told not to arrest those teachers. So he came back out of the courthouse and jabbed us down the steps again. I saw he was not going to arrest us, as I really wanted him to do.

This march by the teachers, the largest professional group in the city and the county, enlisted others to come and join the movement. There were all kinds of groups after the teachers' march. The undertakers got a group and they marched. The beauticians got a group and they marched. Everybody marched because the teachers had more influence than they ever dreamed in the community.

The black teachers, whose jobs were controlled by the white school board, had taken a significant risk. Marching with them was a little black girl—eight-year-old Sheyann Webb, who lived across from Brown's Chapel, which had become the marchers' informal headquarters. She was by now a regular participant in the Selma movement.

SHEYANN WEBB

What impressed me most about the day that the teachers marched was just the idea of them being there. Prior to their marching, I used to have to go to school and it was like a report, you know. I had to report to my teachers because they were afraid. They were just as afraid as my parents were, because they would lose their jobs. And it was amazing to see how many teachers participated. I remember one teacher who was one who wasn't afraid, Mrs. Margaret Moore. She used to always tell me, "Baby, don't be afraid. You're young, but just don't be afraid." She say, "Sooner or later, we're going to have some followers," and they did follow us that day. It was just a thrill.

As the number of marches increased, so too did national press attention. On February 1, Martin Luther King and 250 marchers from Brown's Chapel were arrested and jailed. Within the next two days, 800 schoolchildren marched and were taken into custody. A congressional delegation of fifteen left Washington to investigate. Among them was Charles Diggs of Michigan, the congressman who had attended the Till trial ten years before.

CHARLES DIGGS

Many of these members of Congress had never been south before. They certainly had no real understanding of segregation. I was the only black member of that delegation. The other members came from districts that were not predominantly black, and I think that the very presence of a group of that type in Selma impacted upon the local people. It gave credibility to our crusade, and I think that it inspired the congressmen when they returned to Washington.

SNCC invited Malcolm X to speak in Selma on February 4 at a mass meeting to be held in Brown's Chapel. When he arrived, King was still in jail. SNCC staffer Cleveland Sellers had attended Howard University, where he heard Malcolm X debate Bayard Rustin in 1962. He and others in SNCC listened regularly to tapes of Malcolm's recent speeches delivered weekly in the Audubon Ballroom in Harlem.

CLEVELAND SELLERS

Our idea was to expand on Malcolm's identification with our struggle and young people in the South but at the same time get young people to begin to appreciate the leadership and the efforts on the part of other leaders who were not as popular in the press. We had done that with the youngsters from Mississippi that we had taken up to Harlem in the early part of December of 1964, and we had Malcolm talk to them about the world struggle and how black people fit into that struggle. Malcolm also talked about his appreciation for the efforts on the part of the civil rights workers in the Deep South. What we were able to do is join the struggle and get people to understand that because you're in the North you were no less discriminated against than if you were in the South. That became very important to people, to see themselves not in isolation. Malcolm talked about the fact that the persons in the South should not see their struggle as independent and separate from what he was trying to do in New York. And that our struggle was not separate from Kenya and Liberia and Angola and Southwest Africa and places like that. So it became important for us to continue to try to raise those issues, even though they might have been unpopular in the press. The people that we came in contact with needed to begin to understand that they could play a role in shaping and changing their conditions.

ANDREW YOUNG

I knew Malcolm well and Malcolm quite often stopped by the SCLC headquarters. So my concerns were minimal. I think what we had to address was the concern being fostered by the press, and that was getting to the kids, that Malcolm X was coming and the promise was that—or the threat that they were describing was that—he would stir up sentiments of violence and make it difficult for us to control the movement.

I had heard Malcolm speak and knew that he was a very effective speaker up north, but I figured the kids down south that were involved with us really at that time didn't know him and didn't understand him very well. So Malcolm spoke up, sandwiched between James Bevel and Fred Shuttlesworth, two experienced southern preachers who know all the southern language and style. He made a very good speech but no negative impact at all on the movement.

Also on the speakers' platform at Brown's Chapel was Coretta Scott King.

CORETTA SCOTT KING

When I arrived in Selma and went to the church where the noontime mass meeting was being held, Andy Young said, "Malcolm X is here and he just made a speech. He has really aroused the people. You're going to have to speak and talk about nonviolence and invoke the whole nonviolent spirit, because the people now have been turned a different way." And I said, "Andy, I really don't want to speak." He said, "You really got to do it, we just need it." So I said okay.

As I was sitting on the platform, Malcolm X leaned over toward me, because we sat next to each other, and he said, "Mrs. King, will you tell Dr. King that I'm sorry I won't get to see him? I had planned to visit him in jail, but I have to leave. I want him to know that I didn't come to make his job more difficult. I thought that if the white people understood what the alternative was that they would be willing to listen to Dr. King."

I didn't know how to take it, because prior to that, I had my own perception of Malcolm, and I thought of him as being a really violent-type person. But he was so meek and he was so different, as most people are when you get to know them. He had begun to turn around, after having gone to Mecca and understanding what true Islam is.

Martin Luther King was released in early February after an SCLC advertisement, entitled "Letter from a Selma Jail," was published in the *New York Times*. That week, three thousand more were arrested. In midmonth, SCLC's C. T. Vivian led another march to the courthouse. When the sheriff refused to let the group enter, the sharp-tongued Vivian began comparing Clark and his deputies to Hitler and the Nazis. "You're racists in the same way that Hitler was a racist." That was enough. Clark punched the minister so hard the sheriff later needed treatment for a fractured bone in the finger of his left hand.

Three days later, Vivian was asked to address a nighttime rally in support of James Orange, an SCLC worker jailed during a voter registration drive in nearby Marion, in rural Perry County. Albert Turner, a Marion native, was one of the rally's planners.

ALBERT TURNER

We had formed a demonstration that day for the United Methodist Church and had decided we would walk from that church to the jail—which was a short span, maybe a block—and sing to James, to let him know that we cared. The mayor of the town had prepared a story, and gotten the state troopers to be on hand that day, by telling the governor that we had intended to go to the jail and break James out of jail.

C. T. VIVIAN

When they called me I told them, "Look, now, I will come over and give the speech, but I've got to get right back to Selma. I can't lead the demonstration." So I came on over and gave the speech.

When I finished I went out the back door, walked down the little steps, and got in the car to get on back to Selma. When I got to a place where you turn, there was a state policeman standing there with a flashlight directing cars. About a half dozen state cars had already passed us—zoom, zoom, zoom—and we figure, What's this all about? Boy, they were coming.

Richard Valeriani was covering the Selma campaign for NBC News.

RICHARD VALERIANI

Nighttime marches were always more dangerous than daytime marches. I went to Marion and the crowd was particularly nasty that night. A lot of townspeople had gathered around, and we knew we were in for trouble right away because people came up and started spraying the cameras with paint. Then they'd insist we put the cameras down.

ALBERT TURNER

As we went out of the church to begin the actual march—we got about half a block from the door—the sheriff and several troopers halted us. We were told that we was an unlawful assembly and that we had to disband the demonstration and go back into the church. We had planned already to have a prayer at that point. We had Reverend [James] Dobynes who got down to pray. And they took Reverend Dobynes, who was on his knees immediately behind me, and they just started beating him right there on the ground. That was probably the viciousest thing I had ever seen. They beat him, and they took him by his heels and drug him to jail. At that point, they had state troopers all over the city, and plainclothes people, a lot of citizens really was involved. They beat black people wherever they found them.

As we attempted to go back to the church, they started whipping people. All of us tried to get back into the church. The line of demonstrators still was in the door; the demonstration never did get all of the way out of the church. The whole town was surrounded by auxiliary police, state troopers, sheriffs, and everybody who wanted to come in, who felt like beating folk up. Some of us tried to go back in the front door and some of us just went where we could.

Billy clubs was broken on people's heads. I got in the back door of the church. But Jimmy Lee Jackson was not able to make it back in the church. He went down the hill below the church into a small café.

RICHARD VALERIANI

It was very tense and we were all very frightened. I guess in the excitement somebody walked up behind me and hit me in the head with an ax handle. Now, very luckily, he hit me with a roundhouse swing instead of an overhead swing. It caught me on the thick bone part of the back of my head, instead of crushing the top of my skull.

Before I left, a state trooper walked up, took the ax handle away from the guy who hit me, threw it on the steps of City Hall, and said, "I guess you've done enough damage with this tonight." But he did not arrest him. Then another white man walked up to me and he said, "Are you hurt? Do you need a doctor?" I was stunned, and I put my hand on the back of my head and it was full of blood. I said to him, "Yeah, I think I do. I'm bleeding." And then he thrust his face right up against mine and said, "Well, we don't have doctors for people like you."

ALBERT TURNER

In the melee in back of the church, Jimmy's grandfather was hit in the back of the head with a billy club and his skull was bust. He left the church and went down to the café to have Jimmy carry him to the hospital. Jimmy immediately tried to rush out, forgetting about what was going on, to take his grandfather to the hospital. As he attempted to go out of the door, these troopers met him and forced them back into the building. Of course, Jimmy kind of insisted that he wanted to carry his grandfather to the doctor and they insisted that he did not go. From that they ganged him, simply physically subdued him and put him on the floor of the café. There they started to whip him up pretty bad. His mother was in the café also. She had come down with her daddy. She just couldn't stand it no longer, so she took a drink bottle and tried to knock people off her son because they was going to kill him right there on the floor, it appeared. When she hit them, then they knocked her out. And then they took Jimmy and pinned him against the walls of the building and at close range they shot him in the side. After shooting him, they ran him out of the door of the café. Some of the remaining troopers was lined up down the sidewalk, back towards the church. He had to run through a cordon of policemen, then, with billy sticks, and as he ran down, they simply kept hitting him. He made it back to the door of the church, and just beyond the church, he fell. Of course, at that point, he was picked up and carried to the hospital.

Only three days after the brutality at Marion, on February 21, Malcolm X was assassinated in Harlem.

CLEVELAND SELLERS

I was just very distressed and frustrated, because I thought that Malcolm was beginning to see not civil rights but human rights as being something that he could be involved in. He had said that he would assist with voter registration. We even had a kind of commitment from Malcolm to go into Mississippi to speak to the Mississippi Freedom Democratic party. We saw a growth on both parts. We saw Malcolm growing. We saw SNCC growing. And that was important, because during that period of time there wasn't a lot of intellectually stimulating kind of speakers on the scene. Malcolm was that. And Malcolm raised our consciousness. No question about it. He encouraged and motivated us to continue to struggle, be dedicated, be committed, be disciplined. We looked at Malcolm in terms of Malcolm's whole, and the fact that Malcolm had changed. He, at first, was one kind of person. He was able to change, discipline himself, educate himself, move forward. That was the real essence of what we found to be the best of what Malcolm was all about.

The Student Nonviolent Coordinating Committee sent myself and John Lewis to Malcolm's funeral. It was a kind of sad occasion but it was also inspirational in that we felt like we were bringing a message to Malcolm, and that message was: We heard you, we were listening, and in essence we have taken the best of what you offered and we will continue to incorporate that in our movement and our struggle.

Jimmy Lee Jackson died in his hospital bed on February 26. When he heard the news of Jackson's death, SCLC's James Bevel was recovering from pneumonia contracted as the result of a beating.

JAMES BEVEL

I had to preach, because I had to get the people back out of the state of negative violence and out of a state of grief. If you don't deal with negative violence and grief, it turns into bitterness. So what I recommended was that people walk to Montgomery, which would give them time to work through their hostility and resentments and get back to focus on the issue. The question I put to them was, "Do you think Wallace sent the policemen down to kill the man? Or do you think the police overreacted? Now, if they overreacted, then you can't go around assuming that Wallace sent the men down to kill. So what we need to do is to go to Montgomery and ask the governor what is his motive and intentions."

It's a nonviolent movement. If you went back to some of the classical strategies of Gandhi, when you have a great violation of the people and there's a great sense of injury, you have to give people an honorable means and context in which to express and eliminate that grief and speak decisively and succinctly back to the issue. Otherwise the movement will break down in violence and chaos. Agreeing to go to Montgomery was that kind of tool that would absorb a tremendous amount of energy and effort, and it would keep the issue of disenfranchisement before the whole nation.

The whole point of walking from Selma to Montgomery is it takes you five or six days, which would give you the time to discuss in the nation, through papers, radio, and television and going around speaking, what the real issues were.

SCLC scheduled the march from Selma to Montgomery for Sunday, March 7. Most of the SNCC leadership was reluctant to participate. The growing rift between the two organizations reminded insiders of the tensions in Albany, Georgia, two years before. SNCC workers complained of an SCLC effort to build a cult of personality around King (privately, some in SNCC called him "de Lawd") and worried that the SCLC ministers would abandon Selma before a final and permanent victory had been obtained.

JOHN LEWIS

On a Saturday night, March the sixth, the SNCC executive committee met all night in the basement of a restaurant in Atlanta, debating whether we should participate in the march. It was the decision of the committee that we shouldn't participate in this matter. Some people felt a lot of people would get hurt. Some people started saying the SCLC would have this march and then they would leave town, and the people would be left holding the bag. I took the position that people we had been working with in the heart of the Black Belt for more than three years wanted to march and we should be there with them. The decision was made that if I wanted to go, I could go as an individual but not as a representative of the Student Nonviolent Coordinating Committee. I felt I had an obligation; I had gone to jail in Selma on several occasions. So I made the decision with three other members of that committee to leave Atlanta early Sunday morning, and we drove to Selma.

Governor Wallace prohibited the march, contending that it would be impossible to protect the demonstrators. But some six hundred marchers, many from Marion, assembled at Brown's Chapel, determined to proceed. Martin Luther King and Ralph Abernathy were in Atlanta, preaching at their churches. John Lewis and SCLC's Hosea Williams were selected to lead the marchers over the Edmund Pettus Bridge and on to U.S. 80, the road to Montgomery.

JOHN LEWIS

When we arrived at the apex of the Edmund Pettus Bridge, we saw a sea of blue: Alabama state troopers. About six hundred of us were walking in twos. It was a very peaceful, orderly protest.

The moment we got within shouting distance of the state troopers, we heard one state trooper identify himself. He said, "I'm Major John Cloud. This is an unlawful march. It will not be allowed to continue. I'll give you three minutes to disperse and go back to your church." In about a minute and a half he said, "Troopers, advance." And we saw the state troopers and members of Sheriff Clark's posse on horseback. The troopers came toward us with billy clubs, tear gas, and bullwhips, trampling us with horses. I felt like it was the last demonstration, the last protest on my part, like I was going to take my last breath from the tear gas. I saw people rolling, heard people screaming and hollering. We couldn't go forward. If we tried to go forward we would've gone into the heat of battle. We couldn't go to the side, to the left or to the right, because we would have been going into the Alabama River, so we were beaten back down the streets of Selma, back to the church.

AMELIA BOYNTON ROBINSON

The men came from the right side, from the left side, from in front of us. They came upon us and started beating us with their nightsticks, they started cattle-prodding us, they started gassing us. The troopers were ahead of us, and I said to the lady who was with me, "What in the world do these people mean?" I remember having seen a horse, a white horse, and then I saw several other horses. One of the officers came to me, a state trooper, and he hit me across the back of my neck. I made a slight turn and he hit me again, and I fell to the ground.

Eight-year-old Sheyann Webb marched to the bridge that day.

SHEYANN WEBB

As we approached the bridge, I was getting frightened more and more, and as we got to the top of the bridge, I could see hundreds of policemen, state troopers, billy clubs, dogs, and horses, and I began to just cry. I remember the ministers who were at the front of the line saying, Kneel down to pray. And I knelt down and I said to myself, Lord, help me. Once we had gotten up, all I could remember was outbursts of tear gas, and I saw people being beaten and I began to just try to run home as fast as I could. And as I began to run home, I saw horses behind me, and I will never forget a freedom fighter picked me up, Hosea Williams, and I told him to put me down, he wasn't running fast enough. And I ran and I ran and I ran. It was like I was running for my life.

Amelia Boynton, unconscious from tear gas, and John Lewis, whose skull had been fractured, were among the seventeen demonstrators hospitalized for injuries. Another forty were given emergency treatment at Good Samaritan Hospital and released. Brown's Chapel was also used as an infirmary for several hours after the attack. That night, the ABC television network interrupted *Judgment at Nuremberg*, a film about Nazi racism, to show Alabama police attacking American citizens on the Pettus Bridge.

FREDERICK REESE

There was a great question in the minds of many people whether or not the nonviolent method really should be employed continually in the movement. There was some indication there were those who really wanted to take up whatever arms they had and retaliate with violence. Of course, this had to be subdued and discouraged. About six o'clock that evening Dr. King called me at Brown's Chapel and he said, "I understand that you had a little trouble." I said, "Dr. King, that is the understatement of the year." I said, "We have encountered a lot of trouble down in Selma." Of course, he was being somewhat facetious, because he had heard what really had happened. But he told me that he had sent out a call to people in America, those who wanted to come to Selma to share in and participate in the struggle that we were engaged in. About ten-thirty, eleven o'clock that night, we were still at the church. If you can, imagine a congregation being somewhat subdued and the spirits low. And all these question marks whether or not we should continue in this same vein. Then you hear the door of the church opening and there is a group of people, black and white, who came from New Jersey. They had chartered a plane. And they walked into the church, down the aisle to the front, and said to us, "We are here to share with the people of Selma in this struggle for the right to vote. We have seen on the television screen the violence that took place today, and we're here to share it with you." There was a round of applause in the church and you could feel a change in the atmosphere—a spirit of inspiration, motivation, hope, coming back into the eyes and into the minds of these people—and then renewed commitment to the nonviolent method.

On Tuesday, March 9, two days later, 2,000 marchers, including 450 clergy who had traveled to Selma in response to King's call, gathered at Brown's Chapel. They were determined to cross the line the police had drawn on "Bloody Sunday."

The marchers, led by King, returned to the crest of the bridge. They were unmolested by state troopers waiting there but nonetheless turned around and marched back to Selma.

The Reverend Orloff Miller, a Unitarian minister from Berkeley, California, was among the marchers on Tuesday.

ORLOFF MILLER

We waited and waited at Brown's Chapel for the word to come that we could finally march. When it finally came, we were ready, we were eager, and we marched. I had not seen downtown except very quickly through a car window as we came into town, so it was all very new to me. I remember looking up at that bridge, which just seemed huge. It had this bend that goes up over the river and you couldn't see the other side. We marched up, wondering, What's on the other side? What are we going to confront? And as soon as we got to the top, we could see the line of state troopers with their blue helmets. And so we knew there was going to be a confrontation. What we didn't know was how far we could get. We remembered the television shots of the horses, the beatings, and we didn't know whether the same sort of thing lay in wait for us. Within the front lines of the march, Senator Paul Douglas's wife was there, and of course leaders of various religious groups, with Martin Luther King at the head. I had just gotten off the bridge—I was a third to halfway back in the march—and the order came back in the lines to stop and kneel down on the highway. Apparently a prayer service was beginning. So we knelt and we prayed. Then we stood back up, and all of a sudden I realized that the people in front were turning around and coming back, and I was aghast. What is going on? Are we not going to go through with this confrontation? What's happening? It was very frustrating to simply be one of the troops, so to speak, and not know what was going on, but we were well disciplined to follow what was suggested by the leadership, so we turned around too and marched back over that bridge with a terrible sinking feeling. It felt just awful. I had come to lay myself on the line just as much as people in Selma had done only forty-eight hours before. And here I was in a turnaround march.

When we got back to Brown's Chapel, we waited to hear Dr. King's explanation of why this had been. He did attempt to explain, though we never fully understood what had gone on behind the scenes. But we did understand his saying, "As many of you as can, could you stay a few more days, could you remain?" Well, most of us had come without even a toothbrush, because we thought it was a one-day event, but a number of us decided to stay.

ANDREW YOUNG

We had gone into court, to ask Judge Frank Johnson for a restraining order to restrain the police from stopping us and giving us permission to march. Judge Johnson was a fair judge, but he enjoined us against attempting to march until he had time to hear the case and settle it.

For us to march we would have been in violation of a federal court order from a judge who had always been fair with us. So we were in the delicate position of having people who had come down wanting to march, but for them to march would have meant that we would have turned the movement around. Since the police—the troopers—weren't going to let us march anyway, we worked out a compromise that we would go up to the place where people were beaten, have our prayers, and then turn around and come back. There were some people who wanted to insist on another confrontation. But Martin made a deliberate distinction between federal judges and state court judges. He said that from 1954 the only ally we've had has been the federal courts. And we have to respect the federal courts, even when we disagree with them. So he just refused to violate any federal court order.

> While most of the ministers backed King, many of the young SNCC activists, who had come to Selma after hearing of Sunday's events, decided not to stay. They called it "Turnaround Tuesday" and denounced it as a sellout. They moved to Montgomery to stage protests separate from SCLC.
>
> The night of Turnaround Tuesday, Orloff Miller joined fellow Unitarian ministers Clark Olsen and James Reeb, both from Boston, for dinner at Walker's Café, a restaurant in the black community where activists were free from harassment by local segregationists.

CLARK OLSEN

The three of us sat, ate, and had good conversation. Then we wanted to go back to the chapel for the evening meeting, where King was going to speak again. Instead of turning in the direction from which we had come, through the black community, we thought we would take a shorter walk back to the chapel, turning right as we came out the door rather than turning left. We walked past a little alleyway and then we were going toward the end of the block, when three white men came across the street at us. It was just the three of us walking together; nobody else was on the sidewalk at the time, certainly not in our direction. The three of them came across the street, one of them carrying some kind of a club or a pipe or baseball bat. From across the street they shouted at us, "Hey, you, niggers." And we whispered to ourselves, "Just keep walking." Orloff and Jim Reeb, arriving earlier that day, had received some instructions about how to behave, and one of those instructions was that if you get attacked, threatened, fall down on your knees, huddle down, with your hands over your head, protecting your head with your arms. We weren't sure what these fellows were going to do. Jim was on the side of the sidewalk closest to the curb and I was nearest the building, with Orloff between us. I looked around at them as they were coming up behind us in such a threatening way. Just in time I perceived one of them swing that club-type thing at Jim Reeb's head, hitting him over his left ear. It was a terrible sound. Jim fell to the ground.

Orloff Miller dropped to the ground per instructions. And I, not having gotten those instructions, ran away. I only ran a few steps, however. One of the fellows chased me and he hit me a few times, knocked my glasses off, but I was not really hurt.

Orloff was down on the ground and one of the fellows had come up to him and hit him or kicked him a few times, fortunately not using the pipe or club. They went away in short order. Whether they went quickly because they realized they'd dealt such a serious blow to Jim Reeb or what, I don't know. They did not put up more than a few seconds' fight against us. So I went back, and Orloff was able to get to his feet okay. Then we went to Jim Reeb, who was clearly the more seriously hurt. And after a few moments we helped him get to his feet. He could not speak coherently. And he leaned against the wall, trying to clear his head some. Of course, we felt it important to get out of there if we possibly could. So, Orloff and I stood on either side of Jim Reeb, put his arms around our shoulders, and walked him around the block to the Boynton Insurance Agency. There was a cot there, so Jim was able to lie down on that.

Reeb's heart stopped twice and was twice revived as he lay in a coma in Birmingham's University Hospital. When he died two days after the attack, both President Johnson and Vice President Humphrey made calls to the Reeb family. A memorial service was held in Selma. Groups of clergy demanded federal action. Thousands protested in northern cities. The movement mourned Reeb. But some compared the national outrage with the relative silence surrounding the death of the young black man Jimmy Lee Jackson, the first fatality in the Alabama project.

SNCC field secretary Stokely Carmichael was a veteran of the Mississippi Freedom Summer project. Born in Trinidad in 1941 and raised in New York City, he graduated from Howard University in 1964.

KWAME TURE (STOKELY CARMICHAEL)

It seemed to me that the movement itself was playing into the hands of racism, because what you want is the nation to be upset when anybody is killed, and especially when one of us is killed. It's almost like, for this to be recognized, a white person must be killed. Well, what does that say? We've died out of proportion to numbers, and yet even today when people speak they will tell you once again about Goodman and Schwerner. Everybody forgot about Chaney. The names are recorded—Jimmy Lee Jackson, Herbert Lee—and so many many many names are not even known. Even the names of the children blown up in the church in Birmingham, Alabama, are not as well known as the names of Chaney and Goodman and Schwerner. Of course, we're still bitter to this day about it, because it still means that our life is not worth, even in death, the life of anybody else—that their life is still more precious.

On March 13, two days after Reeb's death, President Johnson met with Governor Wallace in anticipation of the federal court lifting its ban on the march.

BURKE MARSHALL

The president asked Governor Wallace to come up, because he wanted Governor Wallace to enforce law and order in the state of Alabama, which governors are supposed to do. In the meeting, the president totally snowed him. Governor Wallace didn't quite grovel, but he was so pliant by the end of the two hours, with President Johnson putting his arm around him, and squeezing him, and telling him it's a moment of history. And how do we want to be remembered, as petty little men, or do we want to be remembered as great figures that faced up to our moments of crisis? Then he led Governor Wallace out, in the hopes that Governor Wallace—who was, by that time, like a rubber band—would give a press statement that confirmed his determination to protect the marchers at Selma, and act like a responsible governor. Well, between the time that the president stopped squeezing him in the Oval Office and the time that the governor got before the television cameras with the reporters, he took a small, mental cold shower, so that when his statement actually came out, it was very ambiguous, and by the time he got back to Alabama, he'd recovered from the presidential treatment and was back to being George Wallace again. He said he didn't have any money, he couldn't preserve the peace, this was all a federal plot, and he wasn't going to have anything to do with it.

GEORGE WALLACE

Well, listen, Lyndon Johnson is a most personable, easy man to be around as a president. He put his arms around you and say, "Come on here, George, and sit down. Let's talk." I was not shivering and shaking. He makes you feel at home. Most personable president you probably ever knew. I stayed with him three and a half hours but we talked about everything under the sun, from education to the welfare program to national defense, Vietnam, and all those things.

I told him that if the march was big enough we might not be able to contain it. We were worried about it, that we didn't have what it took to give a hundred percent protection between fifty miles of marching. And when we left there we felt like we could, but then when I got a report from my own public safety department, it required five hundred policemen, several thousand National Guardsmen, twenty-five helicopters, so many mobile toilets, et cetera. We didn't have the money to put out that kind of defense, so I called on him to send troops to help us be sure that no one got a hair on their head harmed.

I think it angered him, though, because then it was his troops that if anybody had to be knocked in the head, it would be Lyndon Johnson's troops, but I did not want anybody to. I went on television. I asked people to stay away from the march. They had a right to march. Let them march in peace.

While the Justice Department was hurriedly completing a voting rights bill to present to Congress, Judge Frank Johnson was conducting his hearings in Montgomery to determine whether the SCLC-sponsored march should proceed.

Two days after meeting with Wallace, President Johnson went before a full session of Congress to present the voting rights bill. In that speech, he vowed, "It is not just Negroes but all of us who must overcome the crippling legacy of bigotry and injustice. And we shall overcome."

C. T. VIVIAN

When we heard LBJ give that famous speech, we were all sitting around together. Martin was sitting in a chair looking toward the TV set, and when LBJ said, "And we shall overcome," we all cheered. I looked over toward Martin and Martin was very quietly sitting in the chair, and a tear ran down his cheek. It was a victory like none other, it was an affirmation of the movement, it guaranteed us as much as anything could that we would vote and that millions of people in the South would have a chance to be involved in their own destiny.

On March 17, Judge Johnson issued his ruling.

NICHOLAS KATZENBACH

The blacks wanted to continue their Selma-to-Montgomery march, and so they brought a lawsuit. It was decided by Judge Frank Johnson, U.S. District Court, a man of great courage, who decided that they did have the right to do so and should be protected throughout the march. The Department of Justice's point of view was Please, Dr. King, please don't violate any law or court injunction. You'll get it overturned, but comply with the law. And that was vindicated, I think, when Judge Johnson did order that the march continue. Then Governor Wallace didn't want to pay that much money to protect them, so he ended up telling President Johnson he was unable to guarantee their safety, so it ended with federalizing the National Guard, the Alabama Guard, and the U.S. government paying for the protection.

Thirty-two hundred marchers left Brown's Chapel on Sunday, March 21, crossed the Edmund Pettus Bridge, and set out along Route 80, bound for Montgomery.

RALPH ABERNATHY

The final march was enjoyable and it was tension-filled all at the same time. We knew that victory was in sight. We had to march on one side of the highway, and the cars had to move on the other side. A great deal of profanity was yelled from the passing cars, and the old farmers came out, mostly white people, and they looked at us with utter disdain. But we knew that the victory was in sight.

We were very much aware of what was taking place in Washington, and we were eagerly looking forward to the passage of the voting rights bill. We got information from congressmen. We had reporters right there on the scene and they would keep us informed. People also had radios who were a part of the march.

JOHN LEWIS

I was very happy, really. I was honored to be able to walk with the people that participated in the effort, with Martin Luther King, Jr., and others. I think we all walked those days with a sense of pride and with a sense of dignity. I will never forget a little song that one of the guys would sing—"Pick 'em up, put 'em down"—all the way from Selma. It was like a holy crusade, like Gandhi's march to the sea. You didn't get tired, you really didn't get weary, you had to go. It was more than an ordinary march. To me there was never a march like this one before, and there hasn't been one since. It was the sense of community moving there—as you walked you saw people coming waving, bringing you food or bringing you something to drink. You saw the power of the most powerful country on the face of the earth, the United States government. The United States military provided protection for this nonviolent crusade. It was almost a contradiction, really, that these unarmed few nonviolent soldiers—some of us carrying a book, an apple, an orange, or something in a bag—were being guarded by men with guns and riding jeeps.

Only three hundred people were allowed to march and camp overnight once U.S. 80 narrowed to a two-lane highway.

ANDREW YOUNG

The march from Selma to Montgomery, from my perspective, was a job. We had three hundred people to feed every day. We had to find a place to pitch tents, and we had to be concerned about security all along the road. There was absolutely nothing romantic about it. I was running back and forth, mostly with Ivanhoe Donaldson of SNCC, trying to keep the march together and solving problems from one end to the other. I figure anytime they marched ten miles, I did closer to forty.

KWAME TURE (STOKELY CARMICHAEL)

I wasn't very enthusiastic about the march itself. But it was a fait accompli—King was going to have it, and there was no way to stop it. So all you have to do now is make a positive out of a negative. Consequently, I marched along with the marchers, but I wasn't considering myself part of the march. When it entered Lowndes County I would seek out all the people from Lowndes County who came to the march. I would write down their names, record their addresses, and tell them, "Listen, we're going to stay in Lowndes County. We're not just going to pass through," and they'd be excited to hear that.

On March 25, the three hundred marchers reached Montgomery and joined with supporters from around the nation for a rally on the steps of the state capitol.

CORETTA SCOTT KING

It was great, it was a great moment to go back to Montgomery. For us it was returning to Montgomery after ten years. And I kept thinking about how, ten years earlier, we were visibly just blacks, and when you looked at that march, you had Catholic priests and nuns, you had other clergy, and you had a lot of white people. It was really a beautiful thing to pass Dexter Avenue and go toward the capitol marching together, even though it was a dangerous march. We never felt that we were safe at any point, even coming into Montgomery that day, because they had National Guardsmen on buildings, and all around, and as we came through certain sections, the staff people surrounded Martin and even held up their hands around his head, to make sure that if there was a bullet it would be deflected. There were threats of his assassination all the way through that march, though when we got down to Dexter and were going up toward the capitol, it was safer. There was a great feeling of exhilaration when you looked back and saw what we thought was at least fifty thousand people, with a lot of entertainment personalities and so on.

ANDREW YOUNG

When we got to Montgomery, John Doar came to me and said, "Look, we understand that there's a plot on Martin Luther King's life. We can't search every house in Montgomery. We'd like for you to drive him from the city limits down to the capitol, not let him walk through this entire town." Well, we normally didn't discuss things like that with Martin. And we just told him we thought that he needed to ride and didn't tell him the reasons. And he said, "No." He wanted to walk. He was going to walk in with everybody else. And so finally then we told him what the situation was, and he said that he didn't care. He still wanted to walk.

Martin always wore the good preacher blue suit. I figured since we couldn't stop him from marching, we just had to kind of believe that it was true when white folks said we all look alike. So everybody that was about Martin's size and had on a blue suit I put in the front of the line with him. Of course, I had on my blue suit. We all just lined up. But there were some very important people who felt as though they were being pushed back. All of the preachers loved the chance to get in the front line with Martin Luther King, but I don't think to this day most of them know why they were up there.

It created a kind of tension, where you're looking around and you never know where a bullet's coming from, walking all through town for an hour or so. And when you finally got downtown to the state capitol and past the Dexter Avenue Baptist Church, you knew you'd made it. I think then I just—I just really then felt filled with joy.

The Reverend Dana Greeley, president of the Unitarian Universalist Association, came to Selma from Boston shortly after the attack on his colleague James Reeb and stayed for the march.

DANA GREELEY

Standing on the capitol steps in Montgomery, I think we had both a great sense of victory and a great sense of frustration. You couldn't help feeling so much had been accomplished. That successful march and so many people gathered, tremendous crowds. The sense of frustration and near hopelessness was as a result of seeing the Confederate flag still flying on the capitol building and not being able to get the governor, for whom you had a certain sense of disdain at that point, to negotiate or be visible even. But that combination of a great sense of achievement and of victory plus frustration was almost an epic-making experience.

SHEYANN WEBB

I felt real good at the last march. It was like we *had* overcome. We had reached the point we were fighting for, for a long time. And if you were to just stand there in the midst of thousands and thousands of people and all of the great leaders and political people who had come from all over the world, it was just a thrill.

I asked my mother and father for my birthday present to become registered voters. They took me to the polls with them to vote. I would never forget it. I was very excited and, you know, what even made it so unique to me was the fact, just something being so simple, just a check on the ballot at that particular time, they didn't have machines. I thought it was a long, drawn-out thing because of how people had to really fight for that, you know. And it was just a matter of walking over to a building and making that check. It was very exciting. And it was exciting for them to have that right as well as for me to see them do it.

14

Malcolm X (1925–1965)

"Our Own Black Shining Prince!"

On a cold Nebraska winter night in 1925, night riders of the Ku Klux Klan converged on a small house in Omaha's black community. They were met by an obviously pregnant black woman who announced that her husband was not home. The Klansmen contented themselves with breaking windows and warning the family to stop spreading trouble among local Negroes or get out of town.

The Reverend Earl Little and his wife did neither. On May 19, 1925, their youngest son, Malcolm, was born in Omaha. Almost thirty-five years later, that manchild would burst into the national consciousness as Malcolm X, militant spokesman for the Nation of Islam and chief apostle of its Messenger, the Honorable Elijah Muhammad. For some, Malcolm would be the uncompromising teller of unpleasant truths, an incorruptible symbol of black pride and self-reliance, and a staunch advocate of self-defense. For others, he was a hate-mongering black racist, a harbinger of racial conflict and violence. But no matter how he was perceived, whether hated or loved, in the early 1960s in America, he was a presence haunting the often violent national argument over race. That argument was well under way at the time of his birth.

The year Malcolm was born, Marcus Garvey, pan-Africanist and advocate of black independence of whites, had been jailed by the U.S. government. It was Malcolm's parents' work as effective organizers for Garvey's vision of a black nation that had attracted the attention of the Omaha Klan. A year after Malcolm's birth, the work was continuing. *Negro World,* the international organ of Garvey's Universal Negro Improvement Association, reported that "the Omaha division held its regular mass meeting on Sunday, May 8. Mr. E. Little gave the principal address. This division . . . is much alive to carrying on the great work." The paper reported Elder Little presiding over meetings on May 23 and July 13, the reporter being Mrs. Louise Little.

In 1927, the family was in Milwaukee, where the paper noted that the "wonderful progress under the leadership of Elder E. Little" was "an asset to the division." The family moved to Lansing, Michigan, in 1929. There the four-year-old Malcolm attended meetings of Garveyites. He remembered "my father saying several times, and the people chanting after him, 'Up, up, ye mighty race, and accomplish what ye will.' "

The parents' activism exacted a price. Earl Little found it necessary to carry a gun for defense of his person and family. In 1929, two white men burned down the Littles' home in Lansing. In 1931, Earl Little died after being run over by a trolley car, a reported accident that many in Lansing's Negro community believed to be a lynching. Six years after his death, Louise Little suffered a breakdown and was institutionalized. The remaining family of eight children was split up. In Lansing, the young Malcolm, now living with family friends, graduated from junior high school at the top of his class and had been elected class president by his white peers. The election was extraordinary. It was still an era when blacks were not allowed on the streets of many towns in Michigan after dark. When Malcolm told a teacher he wanted to become a lawyer, the response was: "You've got to be realistic about being a nigger." Malcolm dropped out of school.

In a career that recapitulated the experience of many urban black youths in the 1940s, Malcolm drifted into menial jobs in New York's Harlem and Boston's primarily black Roxbury section. Calling himself Detroit Red, he moved into petty hustling and drug dealing, and finally into a full-time life of crime as head of a burglary ring. He later said that the best thing that happened to him was that he was arrested early.

In February 1946, he was sentenced to ten years in prison. There he discovered and converted to the Lost-Found Nation of Islam, a then-obscure sect founded in the 1930s that became known as the Black

Muslims and headed by Elijah Muhammad. The Muslims proselytized vigorously among black inmates in America's prisons. In 1952, after a period of intense self-education and spiritual rehabilitation, the youthful hustler was paroled from Norfolk Prison in Massachusetts, reborn as Malcolm X, minister of Islam.

Intense and single-minded, he began preaching the gospel of the Nation with an incandescent and bitter eloquence. As enunciated by Elijah Muhammad, the Georgia-born son of former slaves, it was in part a doctrine of theological fundamentalism, antiwhite mythology, and total racial separation as the means to black redemption. Even more frightening to whites, the message was framed by black images of authoritarian discipline and unfathomable intention. The antiwhite rhetoric attracted some to the Nation, but more were drawn by such things as the bearing of its members; its schools, stores, and restaurants; and its newspaper, *Muhammad Speaks,* which carried news of the African-American community. The lean, austere Malcolm became not only its best-known spokesman but, by virtue of his own transformation, its personification.

Malcolm was the message made manifest. As he described it, he had gone from ghetto criminal—without vision, purpose, or future, without knowledge or respect for God, himself, or his people—to the supremely disciplined, self-confident, self-knowing, and self-respecting black man who eschewed the evils of tobacco, liquor, drugs, crime, and the flesh of the swine. What Allah had done for one, could he not do for a nation? Purposeful and erect, Malcolm X was for many supporters a walking metaphor for the possibility of an entire people's redemption.

On the question of race, Malcolm and Martin Luther King, Jr., came to symbolize the choices facing black and white America. On the one side was King's forbearant example and integrationist vision. On the other was a vision of the Nation of Islam, in which the white man was not a brother subject to the healing force of love and redemptive suffering. He was instead a blue-eyed devil, the militant creation of a mad experiment, with whom integration was unthinkable. For the Nation, nonviolence was suicide, and the acceptance of suffering masochistic folly.

In the end, so grim a vision would prove far too apocalyptic for the restlessly inquiring intelligence of Malcolm X. (Even when he bitterly criticized the methods and goals of those in the southern civil rights struggle, he evinced respect for their courage and spirit and particularly admired the SNCC students and Dr. King himself.)

Malcolm broke with Elijah Muhammad and the Nation in late 1963, and in 1964 he made a pilgrimage to Mecca, toured Africa, reevaluated his perception of *all* white people as blue-eyed devils and began to link the struggles of African-Americans with those of Africa and other Third World countries, and created a new activist association, the Organization of Afro-American Unity. On February 21, 1965, Malcolm was assassinated. Three black men, all Muslims, were convicted and sentenced for the murder. However, in light of the number of people, groups, and institutions who considered Malcolm X dangerous, many continue to debate from whence came the orders to gun him down. The teachings of Malcolm X continue to have a far-reaching impact on people throughout the world.

> Alex Haley, just beginning a civilian writing career after twenty years' service in the U.S. Coast Guard, met Malcolm X in 1959. Haley had heard about the Nation of Islam from a friend whose family in Detroit had converted. His first article on the Black Muslims was published in *Reader's Digest* in early 1960. He later wrote articles on Malcolm X for the *Saturday Evening Post* and Playboy and, in early 1963, began work on *The Autobiography of Malcolm X.*

ALEX HALEY

When I came first to know Malcolm, my perceptions were that most white people—probably nearly all, from the exposure I had—ranged from being very, very apprehensive about Malcolm to hating Malcolm, the image of Malcolm which had been purveyed by the media, of course. That was not too far afield of probably the majority of black people also. Nowadays you might hear a lot of people talking about how they followed him and so forth, but my perception at that time was that the large majority were frightened by the things Malcolm said. They were so extreme, it seemed, and so radical by comparison with what others were saying. But there were those who were empathetic with the Nation of Islam, or were feeling that Malcolm was having the courage to say aloud, publicly, things which they had felt or which they wished somebody would say. So the blacks' reaction was a mixed one, from some who were terrified by what he was saying to those who cheered and applauded when his name was mentioned, let alone when he came into sight.

My own perception of Malcolm bordered on fascination, because I was looking at him and reacting to him as a subject. I was a young writer, with the usually requisite fifteen years getting rejection slips for the most part, and finally was beginning to get assignments. I saw him as someone who was hard to top as a subject. I like to say of Malcolm he was just simply electric.

Almost everything he did was dramatic—and it wasn't that he was trying to be, it was just the nature of him.

Here was a man who in the eighth grade in Michigan, at a school where I think he was the only black in his class and one of the very few in the school, had been a straight-A student, and in fact the president of his class. Obviously he had to be exceptional to be those things. So you had that quality, which was a facet of him: the brains, the innate ability to learn and to acquire and utilize knowledge. And then you had the Malcolm who had left school and who had gone to Roxbury, Massachusetts, where he had gotten his first exposure to what might loosely be called hustling. I remember him telling me with great seriousness about an older person who came from where he had come from in Michigan and who had called him Homeboy. And this man had taught him his first hustle: that to be a shoeshine boy was okay. He would get, say, fifteen cents or maybe twenty cents per shine, but if he learned how to make the rag pop loudly—there was a way you could use the rag kind of loosely and then jerk it down on the shoe and it would make a popping noise—people somehow liked that and they would give Malcolm as much as a quarter tip. And so he became the poppingest shoeshine boy in town. This type of thing, the hustler world, became part of him. Later he was into more serious things, crime-type things. All of these sharpened his wits and his ability to connive and to do cunning things. Finally, he was in prison, and the world of the prisoner is one that is quite educational in its way. So that was another part of him.

But one should not talk about Malcolm without making reference to the Nation of Islam, colloquially the Black Muslims. It is said—I certainly agree—that Malcolm lived more than the average ten men in his relatively few years. And nobody knew about him except the people right around him in all those earlier years. It was only via the Nation of Islam and its drama that Malcolm came to the public notice. I know that he, in turn, thought of himself totally as the embodiment of the Nation of Islam and what it could achieve. He loved to tell about how other people's lives had been changed—but "none so dramatically," he would say, "as my own."

I don't think Malcolm uttered five sentences in the period that I first knew him without saying, "I have been taught by" or "All that I know" comes from the Honorable Elijah Muhammad. And he was, in fact, at least according to what he testified and said and volunteered, taught virtually everything he knew in the area he was famous for by Mr. Muhammad. What Malcolm became was the extremely effective public figure, the man who could go out and face the audiences and rivet and galvanize people and make people stop and think.

I remember there were Nation of Islam ministers—neatly groomed young men with perfectly clean shirts, their hair cut short—who would stand outside Baptist and Methodist churches Sunday morning and pass out cards and politely invite people: "Would you care, since you like good preaching, to come over and hear ours?" And then these people who were old-line members of Baptist and Methodist churches with southern backgrounds, some of them would come to the Muslims' storefront church, and there would be Malcolm. You really missed something if you never saw Malcolm operate like this. The people would file in. Here was Malcolm standing up there looking as if he was a pent-up volcano, which he was, in a metaphoric sense. On the stage with him would be a lithograph in color of Jesus Christ. Malcolm would say something like, "Brothers and sisters, we're glad you have given up your time to come be with us this afternoon, and I want to say at the first, we may say things—we *will* say things—that may not be something you ever heard before. And all we ask is not that you join, or not that you agree with us, but that you go home and think about what we talk about here." And then he would say, "Who is this?" pointing with a pointer at the lithograph, and you'd hear these old-line Christians in the back say, "That's my Jesus, that's Jesus Christ." And Malcolm would listen to all this, and then he would say, "Isn't it interesting that this person to whom you pray—you do pray don't you?" And then you'd hear, "Oh yes, I do, every night," and so forth until they all agreed. And then he would say, "Isn't it interesting that this person to whom you get on your knees in your most private of sessions at night and you pray, doesn't even look like you? Your eyes are not blue, your hairs are not this color," and so on. And he was doing it in the sense of someone exhorting people to just think about it, what they were doing. And then he would say things like, "Now, do we correctly understand that all who believe in this person are the same, that that's what he teaches, that you are all the same? You and those of the race who believe in him too?" And you'd hear a little weaker, "Well, that's what it says," and so forth. And then he'd say, "Well, you know, ladies and gentlemen, we are going to be closing our little service here shortly, but I'd just like to ask one thing. When you leave here, you who are equal in His sight with the others who believe in Him, you go get on the subway and you go downtown and you walk around and look at the houses the other Christians live in, and the factories they own, and the businesses they own, and then you get on the subway and you come back up here to where you live and walk around and look at where you live, and what you have, and what you own. And then go home tonight, brothers and sisters, and think about it, if you are indeed equal in his sight." And Malcolm would quickly bring the meeting to a close. No collection. And people began to defect from the old-line Protestant churches. There were churches which split. One part of the congregation went to the Nation of Islam, the other remained Baptist and Methodist, but even then kind of shakily. And so that is why I say Malcolm was the point of the plow.

In 1959, black reporter Louis Lomax approached television newsman Mike Wallace about producing a series of five-minute news segments on the Nation of Islam for WNTA-TV, a local New York City station. Like most whites, Wallace was totally unaware of the black religion and its message. The two men soon expanded their nightly news reports into an hour-long documentary with the controversial title "The Hate That Hate Produced."

MIKE WALLACE

The meaning of the title "The Hate That Hate Produced" was there is hatred, suspicion on both sides. If indeed the Muslims hated the whites, and they acknowledged that they did, Malcolm was very eloquent about that. Elijah Muhammad was very eloquent about it. They were racists. They were separatists. They wanted to separate the blacks from the whites in this country. If they felt that hatred, it was in reaction to the hatred that they felt had been directed against them. Therefore, "The Hate That Hate Produced."

Following the hour-long program that night on Channel 13, we had a panel with Jackie Robinson, Roy Wilkins, [the Reverend] Gardner Taylor, Arnold Forster from the Anti-Defamation League, and a black woman, Anna Hedgeman [first female member of a New York City mayor's cabinet]. A couple of them, especially Roy Wilkins, and Jackie Robinson to some degree, suggested that we had overstated about the Black Muslims, that they weren't as important as we had made them by devoting this hour to the subject.

White journalism at that time didn't know who Malcolm was, who Elijah Muhammad was, had no conception of the Black Muslims. So there was no attention being paid at that time. It took some time following that for major publications—white publications, if you will—the *New York Times, U.S. News and World Report, Detroit Free Press,* to come forth and begin to pay attention, to put reporters on it and find out that the Black Muslims were indeed a substantial group and a group that had to be dealt with.

Ossie Davis and Ruby Dee were among the thousands of New Yorkers who watched "The Hate That Hate Produced."

OSSIE DAVIS

I don't remember very much about the documentary except that young man with his flaming—well, it wasn't red—hair, lean and gaunt and quite capable of using language to open wounds. I was amazed at his capacity to communicate and at the naked honesty with which he expressed his feelings about black people, about white people. He scared me. I'm sure he intended to. But certainly after I saw him in "The Hate That Hate Produced," I knew I would never forget this man.

Now, I had known a little bit by reading and other things that there was the Black Muslims. I had heard about them in general terms, but it was that film that brought it into focus. Plus the fact that Ruby and I knew Louis Lomax. I had grown up as a boy in Georgia in the same town that Louis came from and knew his family and his uncle. And we also got to know Mike Wallace on a personal basis, and they talked to us about what was happening behind the scene and everything like that. But the film did make an impact on everybody and introduced Malcolm to a national audience, which gave him a great opportunity which he took full advantage of.

In 1962, Stokely Carmichael was one of the student leaders in the Nonviolent Action Group, a SNCC affiliate based at Howard University in Washington, D.C. He and other activists developed a program called Project Awareness to sponsor debate on social issues.

KWAME TURE (STOKELY CARMICHAEL)

Our first debate was Malcolm X versus Bayard Rustin. There were great divisions within the movement, and Bayard Rustin and Malcolm X posed these divisions, with their approaches toward the solution. Of course, Bayard Rustin's approach was one of total commitment to nonviolence as a philosophy, with the aim of integrating into the American capitalist system, almost. Well, he questioned the capitalist system, but not to a profound degree. Malcolm, of course, was the total opposite, not seeing nonviolence as a philosophy, almost denouncing it as a tactic, if you will, calling for violent clash of arms against the American capitalist system and not for integration into it, but separation from it, while seeking its destruction, either through our hands or the hands of Allah, as he himself would say it. So, the Malcolm X and Bayard Rustin debate had a profound effect upon the Nonviolent Action Group and consequently on SNCC, because of the role that the Nonviolent Action Group played in SNCC, and, of course, consequently on the country because of the role that SNCC played in the country.

Marian Wright, a native of Bennettsville, South Carolina, first met Malcolm X when she was a student at Yale Law School in the early 1960s.

MARIAN WRIGHT EDELMAN

Malcolm had come to the law school to speak. I was sitting in the back of the audience. He walked up to me and said, "Marian Wright, I'm Malcolm X." I thought, How does this man know who I am? I then looked at some of these handsome black men standing behind him, and I recognized a number of people who were his followers from my hometown. But he knew almost everything about me and wanted to sit down and talk.

When he spoke that night at Yale Law School's auditorium, he was absolutely mesmerizing. He was brilliant. He was funny. He expressed the rage that all of us continued to feel about the slow pace of change in the country, but he did it in the cleverest and the funniest way you could imagine. I just remember laughing uncontrollably at some of the ways in which Malcolm would answer questions and put down whites who were trying to trick him at that point. So, he was a new outlet for the anger and the frustration. But he sure was smart.

Malcolm had the same kind of audacity that I think I had been taught by adults in very many different ways, all of my life. Because again, it had never occurred to me, either as a black or as a woman, that I couldn't make a difference or that I couldn't be anything. Malcolm sort of elevated that to a different level, because he was blunt where King was tactful. They were both smart, both extraordinarily eloquent and articulate. He could say the anger, while King could do the softer encouraging, persuasion, pushing, prodding. Malcolm was a reinforcing person and responded to a different need in us. It was always hard to try to be half as good as Dr. King. Even though we believed in nonviolence, it was also very good to have somebody vent the other side. There always need to be multiple voices with multiple strategies pursuing social change.

In 1962, Ossie Davis and Ruby Dee met Malcolm through Dee's brother.

OSSIE DAVIS

Malcolm had created a lot of excitement in the black community, but we also were aware or felt that it was somewhat dangerous to be too closely associated to Malcolm. He was saying some pretty rough things, particularly about whites. And those of us who wanted to keep peace with the white world—some of us, you know, had our jobs out in the white community—we didn't really want to get too close to Malcolm. And also you must remember that in the fifties and during the red-baiting period, everybody had learned to be a little wary of everybody else. Ten-foot poles was the style of the social intercourse in those days.

We had gone to the mosque, to the restaurant at the mosque, and had met him for lunch and discussed various things and were impressed with him. We'd ask him questions and we said, "Hey, a lot of people want to know what you really are about. They are afraid to come to the restaurant or to the mosque, but they're still curious." And he jumped at that. Nothing pleased him more than going out to proselytize and to convert. He was a missionary of the first order, and any opportunity he had to talk to anybody, he grabbed it.

So we invited him to come out to our house in Mount Vernon one afternoon. He came and he brought [Elijah Muhammad's son] Herbert Muhammad with him, who had his camera and went around taking pictures. And Sidney Poitier, he was there, and [writer] John O. Killens was there, [singer] Lonnie Satin and his wife, Tina, were there, and a few other people. But we got Malcolm to the house and we felt we had him cornered. And we asked him all the questions that we thought were pertinent. You know, What is your program offering black people, really? Do we all have to join and become Black Muslims to participate in your kingdom? Or is there a program that you have that affects all black folks? He never really answered that question. We learned later on, of course, that whatever economic program they had was a rather limited one and wouldn't really have solved all of our problems. And he had some thoughts but he was very careful not to let his thoughts get ahead of what he thought was Elijah Muhammad's thoughts and policies on the question. And when we would run him into a corner, he would say, "Well, the Honorable Elijah Muhammad says——"

"Hold it, brother, hold it now. We're not talking to the Honorable Elijah Muhammad. We're talking to you. What do you think, Malcolm, we should do?"

On one occasion he said, "Look, I am like the man who goes inside the lion's cave to rescue the brother that is supposed to be the lion's next meal. Now, the brother wants to know what you going to do. And I can't tell the brother what my plans are, how I intend to rescue him, because the lion is listening. So we have ideas, we have plans, but we can't tell everybody now, because the enemy will find out." Well, the truth was that they had not worked out a sufficiently broad economic plan. But it did indicate to us the kind of person Malcolm was. And those of us who were there became his friends, 'cause we knew there was an honest, earnest, dedicated young brother. And we had seen many leaders, white and black, and had been able to gauge their integrity, their honesty, and their degree of commitment. And while we loved all the leaders and we worked for all the leaders, Malcolm was by far morally the most pure person that we ever ran across.

Let me say something else that happened in '62. At that time we were doing *Purlie Victorious,* my play, on Broadway, and the Muslims did not believe in theater. They did not want their membership to participate in theater or go to those places which were a waste of time. Malcolm somehow managed to come and see a matinee. He came by himself. And I think he sort of sneaked away, because Elijah Muhammad probably wouldn't have wanted him to show up at the theater. He saw *Purlie Victorious,* which of course had a lot of laughs in it, and he came back and he said, "You know, I think you're trying to do with laughter what I'm trying to do by 'any means necessary.' You're really zinging the Man, and I appreciate that." He said, "Man, I saw the play and I liked it. I'll do anything I could to help you, except that if I said something in favor of the play no white folks would ever show up at the box office again. So the best thing I can do for you is to keep my mouth shut. But I really enjoyed the play."

In the early 1960s, poet Sonia Sanchez lived in Harlem and was active in the Congress of Racial Equality.

SONIA SANCHEZ

I was in an organization called New York CORE. I and some other people had made that trek down to Washington to listen to Martin talk about his dream. We came back very much involved with that dream and also with being the people who were going to do some real work in this country. I continued to be involved with that whole movement of New York CORE. But I viewed what was happening as necessary for the South, not necessarily necessary for us in the North. I mean, we were doing okay, although a part of us knew we were not doing okay. There was some part that knew something was wrong every time we experienced that peculiar subtle segregation that New York was about.

People quite often want to make you believe that Malcolm was some terrible, terrible man who never smiled and who was always scowling and demanding something that was obscene almost. When I first saw Malcolm on the television, he scared me also. Immediately the family said, "Turn off that television. That man is saying stuff you ain't supposed to hear." [*Laughs*.] And so of course we did. But you know when the sun comes in the window and you kind of jump up to get it, to close the blinds or pull down the shade, before you do that the sun comes in? Well, before each time we turned the television off, a little sun came in. And you'd be walking someplace and it would resonate in the air, what he said. And you would say, "No, I can't listen to that because I'm in New York CORE. I can't listen to that because they say he's a racist. So don't listen."

The first time that I really listened to Malcolm was when CORE was doing a large demonstration. And Malcolm had sent out a directive to all of the civil rights organizations that you cannot have a demonstration in Harlem unless you invite me to speak. So in our office at 125th Street, we moaned and groaned and said, "Who is that man? Imagine that man saying such a thing. Who does he think he is?" Of course, we had to say yes.

So we went to this big demonstration. Malcolm came with his bodyguards. I shall never forget that day. It was a day where it was cloudy. There was no sun. And in New York City when it's cloudy and rainy, you finally see the colors of the buildings. The yellow came out on the buildings and the reds came out on the buildings. And when Malcolm got up on this man-made stage the reds on his face came out. The red in his hair came out, that kind of blond-red thing. I was standing on the island there looking at him, and my friend said, "I'm going back to the office." I said, "I'm going to stay because I like the rain." There was this kind of quiet drizzle that was happening there. And I looked up and looked around determined not to look at him. Determined not to listen. But he started to talk. And I found myself more and more listening to him. And I began to nod my head and say, "Yeah, that's right. That makes sense. That's logical. Uh-huh," whatever. And the audience was like, "Yeah, Malcolm, yeah man, uh-huh, Malcolm. Amen. Yes, uh-huh, right on, yes brother, uh-huh." When he came off the stage I jumped off the island, walked up to him, and of course when I got to him the bodyguards moved in front. He just pushed them away. I extended my hand and said, "I liked some of what you said. I didn't agree with all that you said, but I like some of what you said." And he looked at me, held my hand in a very gentle fashion, and said, "One day you will, sister. One day you will, sister." And he smiled. After that, every time he was speaking in New York City I was there.

The reason why Malcolm was so effective was because the moment that he came into an audience, he told them exactly what he intended to do with them. What he said to an audience is that we are enslaved. And everyone looked at first and said, "Who? We are enslaved? We're free." And he began to tell us and explain to us in a very historical fashion just what our enslavement was about. The moment he did that, he always had some new information for you. As a consequence, he drew an audience towards him. Malcolm knew how to curse you out, in a sense, and make you love him at the same time for doing it. He knew how to, in a very real sense, open your eyes as to the kind of oppression that you were experiencing. On the one hand, he would say something in a very harsh fashion. And then on the other hand, he would kiss you and hug you.

I've never seen anyone appeal to such a broad audience. The joy of Malcolm is that he could have in an audience college professors, schoolteachers, nurses, doctors, musicians, artists, poets, and sisters who were housewives. Sisters who worked for people in their houses. Brothers who were out of prison. Brothers who were on drugs and were coming off drugs. Brothers who were workers. Brothers who were just hanging on the streets or were waiting outside the temples to get inside. And he understood the bottom line is that if you tell people the truth, then it will appeal to everyone. If you tell them all about their oppression, in a fashion they ain't never heard before, then they will all gravitate towards you. He cut through all the crap. You see, what he said out loud is what African-American people had been saying out loud forever behind closed doors. The reason why initially we cut off the televisions is that we were scared. What he did was he said, "I will now"—in a very calm fashion—"wipe out fear for you." He expelled fear for African-Americans. He says, "I will speak out loud what you've been thinking." And he says, "You'll see. People will hear it and they will not do anything to us necessarily, okay? But I will now speak it for the masses of people." When he said it in a very strong fashion and this very manly fashion, and this fashion that says I am not afraid to say what you've been thinking all these years, that's why we loved him. He said it out loud. Not behind closed doors. He took on America for us. He assumed the responsibility of father, brother, lover, man. He became again Martin Delaney's Blake, the first black revolutionary character in literature. He came out and he became the person that we wanted to see. The man that we needed to see in the North and in the South. He became the man that most African-American women have wanted their men to be: strong. "See, I want to take you on, America. Here I is. Look at me. I'm going to say the things that you've wanted people to say." That's why the men and women loved him. That's why we all loved him so very much. Because he made us feel holy. And he made us feel whole. He made us feel loved. And he made us feel that we were worth something finally on this planet Earth. Finally we had some worth.

The point is that the message that he gave was a message that came out to men and women. And each one of us took that message and went on to do the work that needed to be done. I never, in a very real sense, allowed myself to be relegated. Or, if I saw people relegating me into an arena, I complained about it. I think that most of the women who were involved with that movement did it. I mean, they would do things like get coffee. But at some point they recognized the fact of what they were doing. So, Malcolm's message was a message that came out to men and women. It did not say, "Now, woman, you be this woman." Rather, his message was quite often, "I want to say this to the men: be the men that I want you to be." But also, he made women feel like they were queens of the universe. It was a queen not that set on a throne and did nothing. It was a queen that worked. A queen that talked. A queen that led. A queen that was very much involved with the movement. So, yeah, you said, "Hey, I am pretty. Look at here, look at these big lips. Aren't they full? When you been kissed by these lips, you know you been kissed by these lips—that's why they so full. No one kisses like these lips kiss." I mean, it was that kind of beauty. And, if your nose was wide, yeah, your nose was wide, simply that you could breathe well in the summertime when it was hot. And the hair was what it was, simply because it jumped back when we went swimming. All those things we began to integrate from his word. So when he began to talk to us about our beauty, we understood that beauty, but it was not to relegate us in an arena that we got quiet and didn't say anything. I mean, my listening to Malcolm was like,

Here are the words, here's the message, now go forth and spread the message. And that's what we did, listening to him.

Peter Bailey grew up in Alabama. In 1962, on his second day in Harlem, he went to hear Malcolm deliver one of his Saturday streetcorner lectures. A year later, Bailey was witness to an extraordinary demonstration of Malcolm's leadership.

PETER BAILEY

Sometime in late September of 1963, there was a rally on 125th Street in front of the Hotel Theresa, which is where all the major rallies were held in Harlem. What had happened was that the Sixteenth Street Baptist Church was bombed in Birmingham and four little girls were killed. The person who seemed to have put the rally together was Jackie Robinson. Now, when he broke into baseball, he was my childhood hero, but I kind of forgot about that when he became very hostile to Brother Malcolm, and I switched my allegiance.

Malcolm X was the first speaker. I guess maybe eight or nine other speakers spoke—including Eartha Kitt, who was at the Apollo Theatre at the time—and when it was over Jackie Robinson thanked everyone for coming. And the crowd started yelling, "We want Malcolm." They kept saying, "We want Malcolm X," and they wouldn't leave. And Jackie Robinson kept saying, "Well, the rally's over, everybody should go home." And then the crowd started really getting belligerent. And they were jumping on cars and stopping traffic and Brother Malcolm—who had been kind of leaning up against the Chock Full O' Nuts, which was right there at the bottom of the Hotel Theresa—got up on the platform again and said to the crowd, "Brothers and sisters, let's don't do this. The rally was for a very important cause and we've had it and I think everyone should now go home." And immediately the crowd just quieted down and moved on out. They just faded away. All of the ruckus and all the jumping and screaming and yelling stopped and everybody just left. Within a few minutes, the air was cleared. I had never seen anything like that before. He had a certain kind of integrity that people responded to and that was that. It always stayed etched in my mind. At this time I had not met him. I was still just following around wherever he went and if I could be there I would go and listen. I was not a Muslim and had no intentions to become a Muslim.

In December of 1963, Brother Malcolm was suspended from the Nation of Islam. This came about as a result of statements in the press trying to imply that he had rejoiced over the assassination of President John Kennedy, which occurred on November 22, 1963. The statement that Brother Malcolm had made was that it was a case of the chickens coming home to roost. Now, if you go through the South, like I did, you know that everyone knows that statement. You hear it all the time from the older people. What he was basically saying was what he had been saying all along, that the whole violent atmosphere that had been created as a result of the movement—the bombing in Birmingham and all the other things that had gone on, and the government not doing anything about this, and in this case Kennedy was the president at the time—finally this violence had reached the White House. Well, of course, the press used this and reported it as though he was rejoicing over Kennedy's assassination.

After he was suspended by the Nation of Islam, in the latter part of December or early January, a friend of mine approached me and said, "How would you like to be part of a new organization?" "Fine," I said. "What kind of organization?" And she gave me some very, very brief details. I said I would be very interested, so she said, "I'm going to call you on Saturday morning around eight o'clock and I'll tell you where." It was all very secretive. She called me, told me where to meet and what time. It was a motel in Harlem at 153rd Street and Eighth Avenue. When I got over there I saw [historian] John Henrik Clarke and John Killens. There were a couple of other people that I had seen around but I didn't really know. My curiosity was aroused, and so I'm wondering, What is going on here? We sat around and talked for a while. And then in walks Brother Malcolm. Now, when he walked in I said to myself, This is going to be serious. I had no idea until he walked through that door that he was going to be involved. That's when I found out that he was planning on forming an organization where people like myself, who were non-Muslims, would work with his program.

Nothing significant happened that first day. I was just another one of the people there, but I remember thinking I had finally found an organization that was beginning to appeal to the types of things that I was thinking about. I had been in the NAACP youth group, CORE, the Harlem Rent Strike Committee, and eventually I would pull out of these groups because I used to get frustrated with them. But I felt this organization sounds like it's going to be very interesting.

Over the months, we discussed the organization, and we developed a constitution. The Organization of African Unity had been formed about the same time over in Africa, so we called ourselves the Organization of Afro-American Unity. We publicly announced the organization in early June of 1964.

Shortly after that, Malcolm went off to the Organization of African Unity meeting in Cairo. It was the first time that an African-American had been allowed to sit in on an OAU meeting. He did not participate. He was not allowed to speak. But he was allowed to sit in as an observer. And while there as an observer he distributed documents outlining his position and trying to make the Africans see where it was in their best interest to have a strong relationship with us, as it was in our best interest to have a strong relationship with them. The OAAU, unlike some of the other organizations at that time, had a foreign policy, and Brother Malcolm was our secretary of state and our foreign minister. One of the results of his spending time over there was a statement issued by the Organization of African Unity denouncing what was happening in Mississippi. This was the summer of '64, when Chaney and Goodman and Schwerner were killed. There had been bombings going on. The Mississippi Freedom Democratic party was being organized and was trying to replace the racist Democratic party in Mississippi, and they refused to seat them at the Democratic Convention in Atlantic City. So all of this was happening at this time. And for the Organization of African Unity to issue a statement recognizing what was happening was a very, very important step. The foundation was laid by what Brother Malcolm did at that OAU meeting. Later in the summer, when the situation broke in the Congo, where some Belgian nationals were killed and there was a big to-do over there about those terrible Africans killing Europeans, some African diplomats at the United Nations connected the situation that was happening in the Congo to the situation that was happening in Mississippi. And they did this because of the foundation that Brother Malcolm had laid. So our foreign policy was beginning to connect up, and I think that that was when he began to be considered seriously dangerous.

What he ultimately was aiming for on a foreign policy level was to have the U.S. government have to defend its inaction, in terms of the racist attacks that were going on, before the UN Commission on Human Rights and take it before the World Court. Now, we all know that whatever the World Court decided, the American government could say, "We don't have to pay any attention to that. We are powerful. It doesn't mean anything." But if they had had to go and do that, it would have been a tremendous propaganda loss, and they did not want that to happen.

For Harry Belafonte, Malcolm X, like Dr. King, was "part of the glue that held the movement together." After Malcolm's return from a pilgrimage to Mecca in April 1964, Belafonte noted a change in his views on relationships between the races.

HARRY BELAFONTE

Malcolm's having gone to Mecca gave him the perfect basis on which to unhinge himself, to remove himself from a rather forceful, sharply defined racial position that he had taken—that all whites were intrinsically evil, that they were possessed of the devil, and that there was no basis on which one could strike a harmonious existence with them, and certainly no basis on which to rely on them to help us with our cause. In reality, however, there were whites who were deeply committed to our struggle and were demonstrating on the front line this commitment. Although we had not mobilized the large masses of whites in this country, certainly there were many whites in the movement who on a daily basis were giving of themselves and their lives.

I think Malcolm began to realize that, and at Mecca, there was the undeniable fact that people came in every color that exists in the human species. I remember him coming back saying that he had been to Mecca and had seen not just black, not just white or yellow or red, but had seen all people and in the eyes of Allah they were one. Malcolm made use of that, but I don't mean without integrity. It was a major shift from a past position and Malcolm knew that this shift would have profound ramifications. It would create grave problems, but he was a man of enormous courage; he would not deny his sense that a new alliance would have to be forged, that more than ever there was a need for the movements to come together.

Ossie Davis

Juanita Poitier set up a meeting at her house in early 1965 for the regular civil rights leaders to meet with Malcolm X to work out the differences between us so we could come from that meeting with a common platform. A. Philip Randolph was there, Whitney Young was there, Dorothy Height [of the National Council of Negro Women] was there, Malcolm X was there, several others were there. Martin Luther King couldn't make it, but he sent a representative. And we spent that day discussing Malcolm's philosophy, the mistakes he made, what he wanted to do now, and how he could get on board the people's struggle that was taking place. You know, he moved, he grew, he developed. And at that meeting we saw that Malcolm was truly dedicated to the progress of black people, and to the point where he was prepared to modify even his philosophy to the best of his ability, to take back what he had said against the white folks, although he did say, "You know, I do not think all white folks are evil now, but some of you are, and I'm going to keep on at it until you, whoever you are, grant us the respect that we're due as fellow human beings."

Nobody was trying to shoot Malcolm down because, remember, he himself had just gone through a very devastating time. He had been run out of the Nation of Islam and was suffering a great deal from his rejection by Elijah Muhammad, so nobody wanted to take advantage of that. What was discussed was the practical ways in which Malcolm could begin to get on board with the regular civil rights leaders but at the same time retain enough threat to serve his old purpose, how Malcolm can be a part of us and at the same time serve the function of being outside, saying, "Look, if you don't deal with them, you're going to have to deal with me." So tactics were at issue. He was a brilliant man, he could be an overpowering man, but at that meeting he was very deliberately astute, listening and asking very polite questions to those leaders, but determined at the bottom line to be included. He wanted to be a part of that struggle.

Malcolm was killed on February 21, 1965, while giving a speech at the Audubon Ballroom in Harlem.

OSSIE DAVIS

When we heard the news, we sat stunned, as everybody was stunned, and that night we went into the Harlem community to walk and mingle with the people. And as we passed people, some who were even strangers, we would stop and greet each other and say what this man had meant to us. And I felt, in Harlem, a determination to say something about who the man was, because at that time the headlines were so full of so many awful things. He was being described as a mad dog whose violence had killed him, and that sort of thing. There was a feeling in the community that this was not so. That we had to do something to let the world know what we in Harlem thought of this man. That we loved him, respected him, and admired him.

The week after his death, we in the community went around trying to come up with something by way of the funeral that would refute all of this negativity and say once and for all who this man was. I was approached ultimately by [*Muhammad Speaks* columnist] Sylvester Leaks and [New York state assemblyman and Malcolm's attorney] Percy Sutton, who said that they wanted me to give the eulogy at Malcolm's funeral. I said, "Why me? I'm not a member, I'm a friend, but why me?" "Well, you're the least controversial person we can think of. The Muslims would accept you. The left wing will accept you. The right wing will accept you. The black folks will accept you. The white folks will accept you. So you're it." I said all right and accepted that.

Meanwhile, we went around with Sister Betty Shabazz's blessings trying to find the house where we could hold the funeral. A lot of the churches in Harlem, though the ministers knew and admired Malcolm, would not open their doors, and we could understand why. Because Malcolm was killed on a Sunday and on Tuesday night the mosque was firebombed, and everybody feared that at the funeral some big explosion was going to take place and nobody wanted his church to be the place. Finally there was a place on Amsterdam Avenue that opened up, but their expectations that violence was going to take place pervaded the whole atmosphere. You know, it was like an armed camp.

Ruby and I arrived that Saturday morning for the funeral. Walked through the community, which was quiet and still, and the police were everywhere, and we went into the church and the body was there, but there were police there and we didn't know what was going to happen. As a matter of fact, the night before the funeral, Ruby's brother had called and said, "From what I hear on the streets, I don't know what's going to happen. I suggest that you guys maybe shouldn't go." And we sat up in that kitchen until three or four o'clock in the morning deciding whether we would go. We decided to go, and I sat down and wrote a few words that I would say. And we went in, and our job was to sort of announce who was speaking next and where this telegram came from and various other things.

Then it was my moment to deliver the eulogy to Malcolm, and there he was lying before me and all of us—this beautiful, magnificent spirit—and it was all I could do to keep my own personal emotions out of what I was saying, because of all the leaders that I knew and loved and admired and have walked with and have walked behind, this one had been the closest to me. I felt I was losing a son. But I had an assignment. And that assignment was to say something that would let the world know what Harlem felt at this moment and about this brother. To dignify the occasion in a way that was worthy of a man who stood with the greatest leaders we ever produced. And so it was that I said what I had to say at that time, and I suppose that in terms of the total effect it did the job. It seemed to me that Malcolm spoke directly to the emasculation of the black male in particular. And Malcolm wanted to heal that emasculation. He wanted to teach us how, in spite of that, to be men again. So I thought that I would like my children and generations to come to know this aspect of Malcolm X.

> Ossie Davis said in his eulogy: "Many will ask what Harlem finds to honor in this stormy, controversial, and bold young captain—and we will smile. . . . They will say that he is of hate—a fanatic, a racist—who can only bring evil to the cause for which you struggle!
>
> "And we will answer and say unto them: Did you ever talk to Brother Malcolm? Did you ever touch him, or have him smile

> at you? Did you ever really listen to him? Did he ever do a mean thing? Was he ever himself associated with violence or any public disturbance? For if you did, you would know him. And if you knew him you would know why we must honor him: Malcolm was our manhood, our living black manhood! This was his meaning to his people. And, in honoring him, we honor the best in ourselves. . . . And we will know him then for what he was and is—a prince—our own black shining prince!—who didn't hesitate to die, because he loved us so."

OSSIE DAVIS

We went out to Ardsley, to the cemetery, and when we got there the professional gravediggers were standing there with their shovels, but some of the black brothers said, "No, unh-unh, we can't let you do that. We dig this grave. We cover this brother with dirt." And it was a moving moment and I was proud at that moment to be black. And proud that my community and people, no matter what had been said by the outside world, said to the brother, "We loved and respected and admired you." And so we buried him, and there it is.

> Betty Shabazz met Malcolm X in 1956 when she joined the Nation of Islam's Temple Number 7, in Harlem. They married in January 1958 and had four children. At the time Malcolm was assassinated, she was pregnant with twins.

BETTY SHABAZZ

What should be remembered about Malcolm is his love of humanity, his willingness to work. He stressed the fact that our young people—all young people, not just blacks—need to accept the responsibility to do what is best to salvage civilization. We talk in terms of nuclear warfare, and we think in terms of drugs, and polluting the sea, and everything is destruction. Surely people of goodwill can come together to salvage the world. I wonder now, though, with Malcolm gone, they don't have anyone to point to, and I look at all of the people who were against Malcolm. Somehow they have not gotten together to get rid of all the things that ail us. So that Malcolm is at peace. He did all of the things that he had to do and should have done. I would not have had it any different, but I wonder about all those people who are still involved in a high type of leadership. I wonder where they will lead us. You look at the world, it is really in torment, and Malcolm's dead twenty-five years, so that he was totally correct in his assessment. And I think the people need to know that.

Martin Luther King and Malcolm X met only once, by chance, on March 26, 1964, at the U.S. Capitol.

CORETTA SCOTT KING

I think that Martin and Malcolm agreed in terms of the ultimate goal of the freedom struggle. I don't think there was any difference there. I think it was basically one of strategy. My husband believed that to accomplish the goals of freedom and justice and equality it was necessary to use nonviolent means, particularly in a society such as ours, where we were ten percent of the population. And he believed finally that nonviolence was the only alternative that oppressed people had in this kind of society. I think Malcolm felt that people had a right to use any means necessary, even violence, to achieve goals of their freedom. I think that was the basic difference. Martin, I don't think, ever spoke publicly against Malcolm in any forum. I think Malcolm did against Martin, unfortunately. But Martin never held that against him.

I think they respected each other. I know Martin had the greatest respect for Malcolm and he agreed with him in terms of the feeling of racial pride and the fact that black people should believe in themselves and see themselves as lovable and beautiful. Martin had a strong feeling of connectedness to Africa and so did Malcolm. I think that if Malcolm had lived, at some point the two would have come closer together and would have been a very strong force in the total struggle for liberation and self-determination of black people in our society.

PETER BAILEY

With Brother Malcolm being assassinated, the organization [OAAU]—which, unfortunately, had been built around him, instead of around his philosophy—kind of fell apart. But when I think back over him now and I talk to people who want to know what he was, I tell them he was a master teacher. And there is no greater loss to a community than the loss of a master teacher.

He left us with a new way of looking at this society. He left us with a clearer vision of what had to be done and that we were to develop our power as a group. He talked about self-determination. He talked about self-defense. He talked about education, but the right kind of education. He believed in responsibility. He could be very critical of black folks with some of the irresponsible things that he felt was going on. He insisted that we must be responsible for our own communities. He gave very emotional and very practical reasons why we had to have an international posture. And, like any teacher, he left behind people who then take what he had done and present it to other people to keep it and perpetuate it. He left changed minds.

SONIA SANCHEZ

I began this poem after Malcolm was assassinated. I used to come to it, look at it, hold it, put it down. But the great joy of poetry is it will wait for you. Novels don't wait for you. Characters change. But poetry will wait. I think it's the greatest art. Because it will wait for you in a drawer, in a notebook. And when you open that notebook and say, "I'm ready to finish it," the poem will say, "Welcome, come on, get to it, do it." And I did it.

Do not speak to me of martyrdom
of men who die to be remembered
on some parish day.
I don't believe in dying
though I too shall die
and violets like castanets
will echo me.

Yet this man
this dreamer,
thick-lipped with words
will never speak again
and in each winter
when the cold air cracks

with frost, I'll breathe
his breath and mourn
my gun-filled nights.

He was the sun that tagged
the western sky and
melted tiger-scholars
while they searched for stripes.
He said, "Fuck you white
man. we have been
curled too long. nothing
is sacred now. not your
white face nor any
land that separates
until some voices
squat with spasms."

Do not speak to me of living.
Life is obscene with crowds
of white on black.
death is my pulse.
what might have been
is not for him/or me
but what could have been
floods the womb until I drown.

That poem for him was done almost in one sitting. I walked through it and thought about how to at some point say to people, "Don't talk to me about martyrdom. I know it. I feel it. I taste it. I've lived through it. I don't believe in dying but we're all going to do it." And then go to the man. Talk about this man, this dreamer, this man thick-lipped with words who will not speak again. But in a sense when he spoke we listened and we heard and knew and felt and lived and loved and we were.

15

The Lowndes County Freedom Organization, 1965–1966

"Vote for the Panther, Then Go Home"

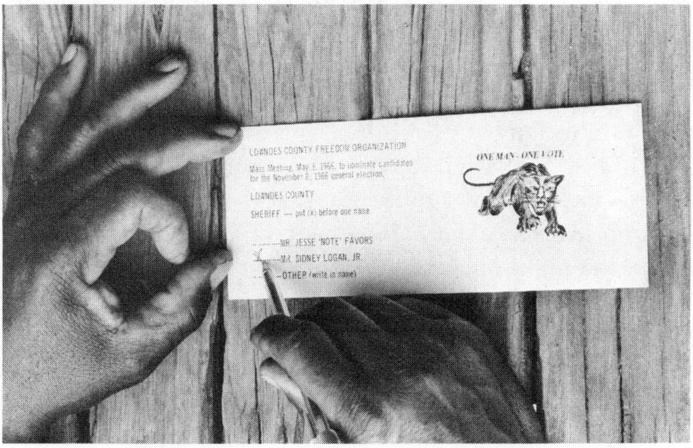

"You turn the other cheek and you'll get handed half of what you're sitting on" was the advice of local activist R. L. Strickland to Stokely Carmichael and the small group of other SNCC workers who, in 1965, quietly moved into the Alabama county they referred to as Bloody Lowndes.

Lowndes County straddled U.S. 80, the route of march from Selma to Montgomery. The county was a living relic of the old South—gum trees and palmetto, low-hanging limbs draped with Spanish moss, the rustle of movement in swamps that smelled of danger.

The local white aristocracy—fewer than ninety families owned 90 percent of the land—was headquartered mostly in Lowndesboro, just north of Route 80, an oasis of large homes in one of the poorest counties in the nation.

Of the county's black population, more than half lived below the poverty line, many in unpainted shacks, along red dirt roads, with wooden shutters instead of glass windows to keep out the weather. Many were sharecroppers or tenant farmers. Half the women commuted daily to Montgomery to work for four dollars a day as domestics.

Blacks in Lowndes County numbered about twelve thousand out of a total population of fifteen thousand. It was no secret that the Democratic party's official motto in Alabama was "White Supremacy." In Lowndes County, whites took that very seriously. At the beginning of 1965, not one black was registered to vote.

In a county that kept black people from the ballot box through economic intimidation and physical terror, a shotgun or rifle in a black farmer's hands was often the key to survival. Many black people had strong admiration for Dr. King and his nonviolent principles but did not feel those principles were incompatible with using weapons for self-defense. The Klan was active everywhere, in the county seat of Hayneville, and in Fort Deposit, the largest town in the county with a population of thirteen hundred, where it was reported the Klan manufactured and stockpiled its supply of crosses.

Few Americans outside Alabama had ever heard of Lowndes County until the night of March 25, after the conclusion of the Selma-to-Montgomery march. Viola Gregg Liuzzo, a white civil rights volunteer from Detroit, and Leroy Moton, a young black man from Selma, were driving back to Montgomery. They had just dropped off some marchers who needed a lift home to Selma and were heading back for others. In the dark of that night, as Liuzzo's car sped across Lowndes County, a car carrying four Klansmen drew alongside.

As Leroy Moton remembers: "I looked at my watch. It was like eight o'clock, and I reached over for the radio and that's when I felt this glass and everything hit me in the face, and the car goin' off the road. Mrs. Liuzzo, last thing she said was, 'I was just thinkin' of this song, "Before I'll be a slave, I'll be buried in my grave."' By the time she got 'grave' out, that's when she was shot. That's when the glass started hittin' me in the face. We ran into an embankment, a ditch, came out of it, and ran into a fence. And I reached over and called her, shook her. She didn't say anything. That's when I turned the motor off and the lights. This other car came back, stopped, and I looked over my left shoulder and I seen it, and I saw the door open and I passed out for about a half hour. I understand they thought I was dead, too. Because the blood was on my face from the glass hittin' me. They figured I was dead. Only the good Lord saved me."

Viola Liuzzo, dead at age thirty-nine, had been shot twice in the face. The next day, with the shooting in the headlines, Stokely Carmichael quietly slipped into Lowndes County to help organize an independent black political movement, something SNCC had been planning for several months. After the refusal of the Democratic National Convention to seat the Mississippi Freedom Democrats' delegation the year before, SNCC workers were determined to build a black political power base outside the Democratic party rather than work for a place inside it.

KWAME TURE (STOKELY CARMICHAEL)

George Wallace was then head of the Alabama Democratic party. The Alabama Democratic party was racist. Its symbol at that time had a white rooster, a white cock, and the words "White Supremacy." That was the official emblem of the Democratic party of Alabama. So here it would be easy for us to tell our people, "Hey, look, this party is not for us. We need our own party."

This was the first time that as SNCC organizers, Bob Mants and myself were able to go into a county with a full list of names—thanks to the march that was conducted by Martin Luther King—of the strongest people, those who were unafraid, willing to participate. This work can take you sometimes as much as six months when you go into a county, to find and to isolate the people, but this was given to us, and it was demographically broken down because the march had gone through the entire breadth of the county. When we sat down to work, it was a matter of deciding which group we wanted to spend most of our time with out of all the strong people we had collected, in order to spread out rapidly within the county.

Most of the people in Lowndes County grew agricultural goods. But some of them, to combine their income, were also workers. For example, maybe the husband would work and the wife and the children would carry on the agricultural work. This was the case of John Hulett, who was a worker in Montgomery and commuted every day. He worked in the Martin Luther King program. He was even a bodyguard of Martin Luther King's house when they dynamited it in Montgomery in '56. Yet, himself and some others who were workers in Montgomery still could not spring a movement in Lowndes County. But since they had this experience and wanted always to get a movement in Lowndes County, the minute we walked in with a program for a movement, and they could see the program was a clear program that would work, they immediately seized the program. Mr. Hulett was extremely instrumental in helping to rally the population of Lowndes County toward the cause of the struggle.

> On March 17, only days before the Selma-to-Montgomery march, John Hulett became the first black person since Reconstruction to register to vote in the county. Two days later, he helped to found, and became president of, the Lowndes County Christian Movement for Human Rights. Andrew Young and James Bevel of the SCLC had encouraged Hulett's efforts, but SCLC did not send in any full-time organizers.

JOHN HULETT

Lowndes County was considered a total rural county. Very poor. Bad roads. The school system was very bad, the worst almost in the nation. There were no jobs available except farming and sharecropping. Most of the young peoples who finished school, they immediately left the South and went north, to try to live, and even to survive.

Most black peoples had to live in fear. We had a sheriff during that time that I can never forget. At nighttime, the young men, if they walked the road and saw car lights coming, would just run in the bushes and hide until they come by. If it was raining, whatever it was, you stayed out there and waited until that car passed. Because they thought the sheriff was coming by and maybe would do something to them. During that time we had a new beginning. We decided ourselves what group we were going to work with. The people of this county chose Stokely Carmichael and his group. They helped us to organize and gave us a kind of leadership and the encouragement that we needed to go through with.

BOB MANTS

Prior to 1965, SNCC had had staff members in Alabama, but the staff was small. Lowndes County had the reputation of being the most violent county in the state of Alabama. It had a long history of violence and repression. It was in Selma that we decided we wanted to tackle Lowndes County. I had just come from south Georgia, working there with SNCC. And Carmichael came over from Mississippi. In other places the civil rights movement for the most part had been built around students, young people. Here was an opportunity, especially with the Voting Rights Act in the making, where it seemed to us that it would be a lot more appropriate to deal with that group of people who were able to register their vote. So this was a major contributing factor to our coming into Lowndes County. That and the abject fear that black people had there.

John Jackson was a high school student.

JOHN JACKSON

After the march had went through, people had a ray of hope, and civil rights workers came in. We were afraid of them, some people wouldn't talk with them. They would come to the schools to see what was happening at the educational level, and I had an opportunity to meet some of them, and I got kind of excited. They were risking their lives coming in, and I wanted to know what I could do. We began to discuss some things that we could do as students, and I found out that they were students, from the Student Nonviolent Coordinating Committee. So I got a little courage, and I got involved with them and began to meet with them to see what we could do as students. And I began to talk to older people that I knew. My parents, my father, got actively involved right after we began to talk to them.

My father was concerned about the civil rights workers—Stokely Carmichael, Bob Mants, and those fellas who were coming in and out. They were afraid: they were being shot at, they were being chased off plantations, they were being run out of Lowndes County. The threat was out that the Ku Klux Klan and the white racists were gonna kill the civil rights workers because they were coming in and stirring up a "mess," that's what they called it. They used to come in and stay late at night and talk to some people, but they were afraid to go back to Selma, because it was so dangerous on Highway 80. We had property, the only vacant house in this area, and finally one day, my father said to them, "Nobody is using the house. You all can stay over there." So they started moving in, and he opened up the Freedom House for them.

Despite the efforts of Carmichael, Mants, Hulett, and others, only 250 blacks registered to vote between the middle of March and the beginning of August, largely because of intimidation by local whites.

JOHN HULETT

They changed the registration place, and took us to an old jail. They didn't want blacks to come to the courthouse to get registered. That was one of the things they done. But there was other intimidation. For example, while I was waiting for people to go in and take their tests, many of the white mens would ride by in pickup trucks with shotguns. In the summertime when it was hot, they cut the water off so we couldn't get water to drink. And they made peoples come over and over and over again, and they would turn them down.

Peoples who lived on plantations and the farms, sharecroppers, they didn't own their own land. If they registered they could not live on the plantation any longer. During the summer months, many families had to leave their crops and move to other places to try to make a living.

On August 6, 1965, President Johnson signed the Voting Rights Act. Lowndes County was one of the first areas to which a federal registrar was sent. The new law banned the use of literacy tests, and blacks began to register in greater numbers. But the law also increased the danger from a threatened white community.

Ruby Sales was aware of the risks. A sixteen-year-old student at Tuskegee Institute, she had been volunteering in Lowndes County for several months before she joined a voter registration demonstration in Fort Deposit on August 14. Also participating were two whites, Episcopal divinity student Jonathan Daniels, from Cambridge, Massachusetts, who had been working in Selma that summer, and Father Richard Morrisroe, a Roman Catholic priest from Chicago who had come south a week earlier to attend an SCLC convention and met Daniels through John Lewis. The night before the demonstration, a planning meeting was held, at which the subject of white participation was debated.

RUBY SALES

One of the things that we were very conscious of is that sometimes in that kind of situation, white presence would incite local white people to violence. So there was some concern about what that meant to jeopardize the local black people. The other question was who should be in the forefront of the movement. People like myself thought it should be the people themselves in Lowndes County, the local black people, who should be in the forefront. I had some serious concerns about what it meant to allow white people to come into the county and what kind of relationship that set up in an area where black people had historically deferred to white people, and whether or not that was in some real ways creating the very situation that we were struggling very hard to change. More fundamentally, I was very afraid of unleashing uncontrolled violence because of Lowndes County's history and the fact that since I had been in the county I had encountered more than one violent incident. But ultimately it was decided that the movement was an open place and should provide an opportunity for anyone who wanted to come and struggle against racism to be a part of that struggle.

When we got to Fort Deposit—we meaning SNCC people, Stokely Carmichael, Bob Mants, myself, Jean Wiley, who came to write up what was happening—suddenly out of nowhere there were white men with guns, with baseball bats, with tops of garbage cans, and they surrounded us. Literally there was no place to go. We were hemmed in. I was on the tail end of the line when that happened. So I was faced with a choice. I could have easily slipped away and pretended that I was a part of the crowd that was standing there, or I could have continued to march around in the circle with the demonstrators. Well, I was really very afraid, but I decided that I would continue to march around in the circle. And I kept watching Jean Wiley because she had been my teacher at Tuskegee and I looked up to her. So I kept watching to make sure that she was okay, because she was outside of the circle. And I looked up and saw her backing away with her front towards us. Later on, I asked her what had happened. She told me that some of the men there with guns had told her that she should leave or they were going to kill her. She decided that she would leave but she would not walk with her back to them, because if they shot her she didn't want her family to think that she had been shot running.

They began to snatch and pull us and threaten us and told us that we were under arrest. And one of the guys there said that if we didn't come with him, he couldn't be responsible for what might happen. So we were all put on this truck and taken to jail [in Hayneville].

We were released after about a week. Suddenly the jailer announced that we were all free to go home, and I was very suspicious of that. I just did not trust that suddenly without penalty we would be allowed to go free, and I questioned that. The jailer told me that we were being released on our own recognizance. That raised a red flag to me because it was just very incongruent with the blindness of their racism that they would release us on our word, when they didn't think we even had a word. The other thing that bothered me tremendously was that there was no one to meet us, because I knew enough about Stokely Carmichael [who had been released earlier] and also the local people, like the Jacksons, that if we were being released from jail, their commitment was such that they would be there to meet us. So that was another red flag for me. But the deputy and the sheriff told us to stop asking questions and get out. So finally we left, but we just didn't feel comfortable because there was no one around. There was a kind of eerie feeling as if suddenly the streets were deserted, and we could not locate a black face anywhere. We were very hot and very tired, and someone decided that perhaps while we were waiting to be picked up it would be a good idea to go and get something to drink. It was one of those hot summer days where you could literally feel the heat coming out of the pavement. And so the group designated Jonathan Daniels, Father Morrisroe, Joyce Bailey, and myself to go and get the sodas. As we were walking, my anxiety was beginning to increase, and I turned to people and said, "I feel very uncomfortable. Something is dreadfully wrong." They said, "No, it's okay. Let's go and get a soda and people will show up."

As we approached the store and began to go up the steps, suddenly standing there was Tom Coleman. At that time I didn't know his name; I found that out later. I recognized that he had a shotgun, and I recognized that he was yelling something about black bitches. But my mind kind of blanked, and I wasn't processing all that was happening. Jonathan was behind me and I felt a tug. The next thing I knew there was this blast, and I had fallen down. I remember thinking, God, this is what it feels like to be dead. I heard another shot go off and I looked down and I was covered with blood. I didn't realize that Jonathan had been shot at that point. I thought I was the one who had been shot. When the second shot went off, I heard Morrisroe crying for water and I realized that he had been shot. I also thought that Joyce Bailey had been shot. And I made a decision that I would just lie there and maybe if I lie there then Coleman would think that I was dead and then I could get help for the other people. He walked over me and kicked me and in his blind rage he thought I was dead. Joyce Bailey had escaped, and she ran back around the store to the side near an old abandoned car and she was calling out our names. "Ruby, Jonathan, Ruby, Jonathan." I heard her and I got up. I didn't stand up, I crawled, literally on my knees, to the side of the car where she was, and when I got to her she picked me up and we began to run across the street, and Coleman realized that I wasn't dead. At that point, he started shooting and yelling things, and Joyce and I were running across the street for dear life and we were screaming and yelling and there was nobody.

Jonathan Daniels was dead and Richard Morrisroe seriously wounded. The two men had managed to pull Ruby Sales and Joyce Bailey out of the line of fire. The white man with the shotgun, Thomas Coleman, was a part-time deputy sheriff (later acquitted by an all-white jury).

Stokely Carmichael had known Daniels for several months and had advised him not to come to Lowndes County but to confine his work to Selma.

KWAME TURE (STOKELY CARMICHAEL)

We'd meet quite often in Selma. Whenever I was there, he would seek me out to spend time together. I had a lot of appreciation for Jonathan. He was different from the regular activists that came. He tried to analyze your problems a little bit deeper, and he too was more interested in lasting solutions rather than the temporary ones.

He was not the first I had seen die. I had seen those much closer to me die. Certainly I had not become immune to death, but I knew that in no way was it to stop or slow down my work. So I was deeply sorry about his death, but only sorry that he was the one who had to go. Then I had to analyze it; someone had to go, and unfortunately it was him. It was one of those things which came to affect those of us in SNCC on the Alabama staff so strongly that our position was correct, that to bring white workers in was just, in fact, to court their death.

> Later that summer, Carmichael and the other SNCC workers learned that Alabama law allowed for the formation of political parties at a county level.

JOHN HULETT

Stokely Carmichael and Courtland Cox and others got together and told us, according to the Alabama law, if we didn't like what the Democratic party or the Republican party was doing in our county, we could form our own political organization, and it could become a political party. During that time, I was president of the Lowndes County Christian Movement for Human Rights. They asked me would I take over the political aspects and resign from the Lowndes County Christian Movement, and I did. And we were able to pull our people together to form our own political organization.

KWAME TURE (STOKELY CARMICHAEL)

Luckily it was very easy to form a third party in Alabama. Since the Democratic party was so sure of its authority, it never paid much attention. All you had to do was give yourself a name. You couldn't call yourself a political party until you had received a certain percentage of votes in the election. But the law stipulated that you had to have a symbol. Perhaps one of the reasons the law stipulated this was because of the high rate of illiteracy in Alabama. And so this high rate of illiteracy meant that people could vote by the symbols of the political parties rather than by reading them.

The new group was named the Lowndes County Freedom Organization. The symbol it chose was a black panther.

JOHN HULETT

The black panther was a vicious animal who, if he was attacked, would not back up. It said that we would fight back if we had to do it. When we chose that symbol, many of the peoples in our county started saying we were a violent group who is going to start killing white folks. But it wasn't that, it was a political symbol that we was here to stay and we were going to do whatever needed to be done to survive.

Those of us who carried guns carried them for our own protection, in case we were attacked by other peoples. That's what the purpose of that idea was. White peoples carried guns in this county, and the law didn't do anything to them about it, so we started carrying our guns too. I think they felt that we was ready for war, but we wasn't violent. We wasn't violent people. But we were just some people who was going to protect ourselves in case we were attacked by individuals.

As the LCFO's voter registration and organizing efforts continued, so did white intimidation. In March 1966, LCFO established a place called Tent City to accommodate some of the sharecroppers who had been evicted by whites after registering to vote. The property was donated by black landowners. One of the fifteen to twenty people who moved there was Josephine Mayes.

JOSEPHINE MAYES

My brother Willie registered to vote, and the man told him that he had to leave. So he moved to Montgomery, and after that my mother, she moved to Montgomery too. I moved to Tent City, with my husband. And after I moved to Tent City I become a registered voter.

It was a great experiment for me in Tent City. The blacks had been hidden behind the white for so long. Now we could make a start for ourself, and get out and register to vote and help others become registered voters. And to find the world for themselves. I put it like that because so much was going on. We got involved with lots of activities to help black peoples to get jobs and learn how to do things for themselves. Like we bought land, and then after we got the land we built a house, something that we had never had before of our own.

The white peoples would come round. They would pull up to the side of the road and they would call us hoodlums and niggers and things like that. They would shoot at us and try to scare us, but we wouldn't let them bother us. We hung in there anyways.

On primary day, May 3, the Lowndes County Freedom Organization was to hold its first convention, at which candidates for seven county offices, including sheriff and school board members, would be nominated. But first the constituency had to be educated about the voting regulations.

BOB MANTS

Our idea was to find a medium in which we could communicate a political message to our constituents. The South is known for its storytelling, so we thought the best way to do that was to create a comic book using the idioms and folk expressions that they were familiar with. We thought it was quite successful.

The other idea was to create a jingle that people could memorize. "Vote for the panther, then go home." They could not vote in more than one political party. They could not vote for the panther and then vote in a Democratic or Republican primary, for example. So we wanted them to vote for the panther, then go home. People would memorize the jingle and associate it with the black panther as the emblem. We had posters all over, and it helped in the number of persons that turned out to vote. There were people who were voting for the first time in their lives. And some of these were elderly people.

The sheriff deputized 550 white men to prevent the Lowndes County Freedom Organization from holding its convention at the courthouse in Hayneville as planned. When word circulated that local blacks were prepared to convene by force of arms if necessary, federal and state authorities worked out a compromise location—the First Baptist Church, only a few blocks from the spot where Jonathan Daniels had been murdered the summer before.

SCLC spokesmen and regular Democrats urged local residents to stay with the established Democratic party. But nine hundred of the two thousand black voters now registered in Lowndes County chose to risk their lives and their livelihoods on May 3. They voted the black panther, and then went home.

JOHN HULETT

This was the first time that the black peoples in this county came together to make the choice of their own candidates for public office. That's why it was important. It was important also because of the numbers of peoples that turned out to that election that day and voted for their candidates and thought that they had done something for themselves to start making changes, the kind of changes they wanted to see happen in the system. Even though in the general election we were unable to elect our peoples to office, it gave the kind of incentive to our people that they ought to turn out to the polls on election day and vote.

The explosion of black consciousness in Lowndes County ultimately had national, and international, impact. The image of the black panther—the snarling black cat ready and able to defend itself—proliferated first throughout the Alabama Black Belt, was adopted by the Black Panther party in Oakland, California, and by the end of the 1960s had reached most of the major cities in America, and some in Europe. Back in Lowndes, the LCFO merged with a reorganized state Democratic party. In 1970, John Hulett was elected sheriff of Lowndes County, the same Bloody Lowndes that had denied him the vote for most of his life.

Events in Lowndes County also created significant change for Stokely Carmichael. In May 1966, just days after the first "vote the panther" primary, Carmichael was elected chairman of the Student Nonviolent Coordinating Committee, defeating John Lewis at a SNCC staff meeting held near Nashville.

KWAME TURE (STOKELY CARMICHAEL)

John's policy was one which was good for SNCC in the early days. But if you took a clear look at John Lewis, he looked more like a young Martin Luther King, Jr., than anything else. A role which he himself was quite happy and pleased with. Because of his policies and the space between SNCC's field workers and himself, he had become alienated from the SNCC staff. So the vote against him represented that. More importantly, it represented the SNCC organizers who understood that the question of morality upon which King's organization depended to bring about changes in the community was not possible. The SNCC people had seen raw terror and they understood properly this raw terror had nothing to do with morality but had to do clearly with power. It was a question of economic power, of the exploitation of our people, and they clearly saw that the route to this liberation came first through political organization of the masses of the people.

We saw the political organization of the masses as the only route to solving our problem. We placed a strong emphasis on the fact that nonviolence for us was a tactic and not a philosophy, as it was for SCLC. Our direction was clear, with a heavy emphasis on nationalism. And strong, as strong as Malcolm had it, as strong as we could get it.

JOHN LEWIS

In the Student Nonviolent Coordinating Committee, in the summer of 1965, coming on the heels of the assassination of Malcolm, after the Democratic convention, after many people had returned from Africa, I think there was a growing sense of black awareness. It was a sense that the organization, not just SNCC but the civil rights movement, had to take on a different role. I continued, as the chairman of the Student Nonviolent Coordinating Committee, to preach the possibility of creating a truly interracial democracy. In SNCC during those days, I think many of us believed in the idea of a circle of trust and a band of brothers. I think some of us felt at the time that the only real and true integration that existed in the American society was within the civil rights movement itself. However, in spite of the feeling that people, blacks and whites, were struggling together, going to jail together, in many instances being beaten together, and some of our colleagues dying together, there was a sense, this feeling, that somehow and some way this movement must be more black-dominated and black-led.

In 1965, Stokely Carmichael, along with two or three other people, did mention the possibility of challenging me for the chairmanship of the Student Nonviolent Coordinating Committee. I was reelected in 1965, and continued to serve until the spring of 1966. I think there was a feeling in SNCC, on the part of some of the people, like Stokely and others, that they needed someone who would maybe be not so nonviolent, someone who would be blacker, in a sense, that would not preach interracial effort, preach integration.

I remember very well, in the spring of 1966, I had been invited to go on a trip, to speak to Scandinavian students, to Sweden, Norway, and Denmark, about the civil rights movement, about the effort to end the war in Vietnam. And when I came back, it was almost like a coup. People were saying that we need someone who will stand up to Lyndon Johnson. We need someone who will stand up to Martin Luther King, Jr. And it was at that time that the real battle for the chairmanship of SNCC took place, and it was May 1966. I made a decision that it didn't matter what happened, I was going to continue to advocate the philosophy and the discipline of nonviolence, that I believed in the interracial democracy, that I believed in black and white people working together.

It was very disappointing—after going to jail forty times, being beaten on the Freedom Ride in '61, almost facing death during the attempted march from Selma to Montgomery in 1965—to be challenged and unseated, to be reelected and deelected the same evening as chairman of the Student Nonviolent Coordinating Committee. It was a personal disappointment. It was a personal loss. But at the same time, I said to myself, and to those that supported me, primarily southern students and a great many of my white colleagues in the Student Nonviolent Coordinating Committee, that the struggle was an ongoing struggle. And I was going to continue to advocate the philosophy, the discipline, of nonviolence, and the sense of community, that all of us, blacks and whites, were in this boat together.

Postscript: The War in Vietnam

Part of SNCC's ongoing struggle would be against American involvement in the war in Vietnam. Even before President Johnson's escalation of the war in the summer of 1965, SNCC leaders had criticized the federal government for sending soldiers overseas while not protecting civil rights workers in the American South. In November 1965, the staff authorized preparation of an official SNCC statement against the war. Then, on January 3, 1966, Sammy Younge, a twenty-one-year-old SNCC worker and navy veteran, was shot to death in Tuskegee, Alabama, for attempting to use a whites-only restroom at a service station. Three days later, SNCC issued its statement, linking the death of Sammy Younge and racism at home with America's wars against peoples of color overseas. SNCC's strong stand on the war helped earn it the enmity of the Johnson administration. The statement also served to further divide the young activists in SNCC from the leadership of old-line civil rights organizations like the NAACP and the Urban League.

16

The Meredith March, 1966

"Hit Them Now"

Martin Luther King, Jr., Floyd McKissick, and Stokely Carmichael on the Meredith March.

James Meredith wore a pith helmet against the Mississippi sun and carried an ivory-headed African cane as he walked down U.S. 51 on June 6, 1966. Just the day before, the thirty-two-year-old civil rights veteran had set out on a 220-mile "March Against Fear" from Memphis, Tennessee, to Jackson, Mississippi. His announced purpose: to encourage blacks in his home state to register and vote. Four years earlier, when Meredith had integrated the Oxford campus of Ole Miss, he had strong support from the major civil rights organizations and the federal government. Then, his was a cause the movement was ready to embrace. Now, at the beginning of his 1966 march, Meredith, a man few could get close to or understand, was ignored by almost all of his former allies. "A black Don Quixote," *Newsweek* called him.

Crossing the state line into Mississippi with only four supporters in his entourage, Meredith seemed to be making an eccentric and empty gesture, marching in a personal crusade at a time when the nation had grown tired of marches. Then, on the second day, a white unemployed hardware clerk from Memphis, forty-year-old Aubrey James Norvell, trampled out a hiding place in a thicket of oak and honeysuckle at the roadside and waited. "I just want James Meredith," Norvell called when the marchers appeared. And then he fired his sixteen-gauge automatic shotgun. Two of three blasts found their mark and sent Meredith sprawling.

An Associated Press photographer snapped Meredith writhing in a pool of blood. In a matter of hours, Meredith's lonely walk became, in the words of one reporter, "the biggest parade since Selma." The first wire service bulletins on the shooting mistakenly indicated that Meredith had been killed. Later, he was reported in satisfactory condition at a Memphis hospital after emergency surgery.

Martin Luther King, Jr., rushed from Atlanta to be at Meredith's bedside. Joining him were Stokely Carmichael, just elected chairman of SNCC, Floyd McKissick of CORE, and the older moderates—the NAACP's Roy Wilkins and Whitney Young of the National Urban League. SNCC program secretary Cleveland Sellers traveled to Memphis with Carmichael.

CLEVELAND SELLERS

In Memphis we met with Martin King and Floyd McKissick from CORE and some of the other leaders who had come in from around the country. In looking at the march we recognized that Meredith was planning to march through what was essentially the second congressional district in Mississippi. That was the area that we had all worked in in the summer of '64 and through 1965. So we felt comfortable that we knew many of the people that could be intricately involved in giving the march some perspective and focus. At that point we seized upon the opportunity to go forward and encourage that the march would continue.

On the first day, Floyd McKissick and Martin King and Stokely and myself and a few other people went out to continue to march. We thought that the theme of the march, March Against Fear, was very important. And we thought that not following through on that would send a negative message to the black community and a very positive message to the white Citizens' Council and Ku Klux Klan types. We also thought that it was an opportunity to begin to raise the question of blacks controlling their own destiny. We were in areas that was almost seventy percent black, and we felt like we could begin to talk about registering to vote, and we talked about empowerment and we talked about using the model of Lowndes County and adapting it to Mississippi. We also believed that it was time for the black community to take the responsibility for assuring that it had a successful march. We had seen Selma and we had seen Albany, Georgia, and we had seen Birmingham, where we had an entourage of press and leaders and once the objective was reached, they would leave behind a vacuum and a lot of frustration. If there was going to be a march, we wanted [local] people to share in the leadership development, share in making decisions on what the march objectives were. We wanted them to share in providing the resources and in the actual marching. We felt the Meredith March could be a showcase, a focal point where we could begin to talk about doing programs differently from the way they had been done across the South prior to that time.

We returned to the Lorraine Motel in Memphis, and at that point we met up with Roy Wilkins and Whitney Young, representing the NAACP and the Urban League. SNCC had some concerns about how the march would unfold. We raised several issues. One was the inclusion of the Deacons for Defense [an armed, black self-defense group from Bogalusa, Louisiana]. We wanted them to be involved in the march. Two, we did not want a national call to be made. We wanted to keep the march indigenous to Mississippi, indigenous to the South primarily. The question of a March Against Fear impacted directly on people in Mississippi, and we felt like in order to make that statement they had to be involved. They had to make the step out and say that I am not frightened by vigilantes and Ku Klux Klans and people who are going to try to oppress me and take advantage of me. What happened then is that those more moderate civil rights leaders, Roy Wilkins and Whitney Young, were reluctant about the inclusion of the Deacons for Defense. They wanted to have a national call and they wanted to bring in people so that they could generate the resources external to Mississippi to carry off the march. We discussed that issue, we were able to lobby Floyd McKissick to our position, and then it came to a vote, and the final decision had to be made by Martin King. Martin King did side with us in the effort to put the march together, and that infuriated Roy Wilkins and Whitney Young. They went through the whole litany of calling us rabble-rousers and saying we didn't understand the dynamics of the civil rights movement and all that, and they slammed their briefcases shut and stomped out of the meeting, going back to New York.

> King agreed to participate, but only after getting assurance that the march would not exclude whites and would be nonviolent. SNCC was successful, however, in arguing for the inclusion of the Deacons for Defense and Justice.

CLEVELAND SELLERS

The Deacons for Defense was a group whose responsibility was to defend their communities or themselves against attack. It was never a group of retaliation. We involved them to protect the marchers. They were in fact armed and their responsibility was to make sure that the march was safe. If they could eliminate an aggressive action or eliminate sharpshooters or people taking advantage of the march, then that's what they would do. We tried to learn from them. They would tell us certain things we needed to know along the way. They would go into the wooded areas. They would check cars out. They would keep their eyes on all of these things, but the spirit was around self-defense. This is something emerging inside of the movement. What we're beginning to see is a shift away from just talking about nonviolence, and in order for you to shift away you see other philosophies and other tactics creeping in. Now we're talking about empowerment. We're talking about black empowerment. Not only registering to vote—we'd already secured the 1965 Voting Rights Act—but how to vote and how to get the kind of power so that you wouldn't have to worry about being a registered voter and the person who you have elected is the one who comes to your house and beats you up and drags you off to jail. We were beginning to raise those kinds of questions and to try to find solutions to the problems that people faced in their communities.

Floyd McKissick had recently succeeded James Farmer as national director of CORE, having previously served as one of its attorneys. In 1951, McKissick had been the first black to receive a law degree from the University of North Carolina. He had known James Meredith for many years.

FLOYD MCKISSICK

When we got on the Meredith March, the Deacons for Defense and Justice came to protect the marchers from attacks when the law enforcement officers would not respond. They were armed. And the question was: Are we going to tell the Deacons to go home? And someone said, "They basically grew out of CORE organization and community organizations in Mississippi. You tell them to go home." I said, "No, I refuse to tell them to go home. I think they have a right to be on the march. I think we should tell them, as we tell everybody else, that we believe in nonviolence, but I'll not tell these people to go home, because they have a right to be here and protect themselves and other people." In other words, I don't believe in a standard for white and a standard for black. I think that violence and nonviolence is equally distributed among all races.

Andrew Young had been opposed to the march on the grounds that King was overextended. Also, unlike Selma, this was not an SCLC-sponsored event, and the role of whites and the role of nonviolence were hotly debated.

ANDREW YOUNG

The SCLC was aggressively nonviolent. But Martin made distinctions between defensive violence and retaliatory violence. He was far more understanding of defensive violence. Martin's attitude was you can never fault a man for protecting his home and his wife. We saw the Deacons as defending their home and their wives and children. Now Martin said he would never himself resort to violence even in self-defense, but he would not demand that of others. That was a religious commitment into which one had to grow.

The role of white people on the march began to be discussed. There was a decision on the part of some of the blacks in SNCC that we don't just want to get people free, we want to develop indigenous black leadership. And one of the ways to force the development of indigenous black leadership is to get rid of all this paternalism. Now, they and we were paternalists ourselves in many ways, because we were outsiders just as whites were. That's the reason SCLC never went along with that. We felt yes, we have to develop local leadership, but you don't want to blame the frustrations of local leadership development on whites alone. We were also partially responsible for usurping some of the leadership.

KWAME TURE (STOKELY CARMICHAEL)

The disagreement over whites was not on having whites. The disagreement was on having white leadership on the march. The question of white leadership in SNCC was one which had already raised conflict since 1963 in the March on Washington. SNCC was very clear here. White liberals could work with SNCC but they could not tell SNCC what to do or what to say. We were very strong about this because of the inferiority imposed upon our people through exploitation that makes it appear as if we are not capable of leading ourselves.

CLEVELAND SELLERS

The three groups—SNCC, CORE, and the SCLC—began to pool our legal resources and contact the people for setting up mass meetings and rallies along the highway. We began to get people involved. The idea of Martin Luther King marching against fear in Mississippi was an idea whose time had come, and many people responded from throughout the state. So we were successful in generating the interest and the crowds that we would not have generated if we had gone the other way and made the calls for a number of people to come in from the North. But we did not want the march to be overtaken by a lot of whites from outside of the community, as had happened in some of the other communities. We thought that it became important, if we are talking about self-determination and pride and effort against fear, for black folk to make that statement.

KWAME TURE (STOKELY CARMICHAEL)

We decided to use the march for an education purpose. Number one, we wanted to push strongly our struggle against the war in Vietnam. It's one of the areas where we started to hit them with it seriously. And of course we wanted to throw out "Black Power" [as a slogan] for the mass of the people. So we prepared the terrain.

Brother Willie Ricks was sent ahead, as the advance scout, and as we grew bigger sometimes he would have twenty or forty people under his direction. His task was to spread them out to plantations, speak to the sharecroppers. Tell them the march was coming through and to give little Black Power speeches to get the reaction. About three nights before Greenwood, about two o'clock in the morning, Ricks came back and he was giving a report. Cleve Sellers was sitting next to me, and Ricks was saying, "We ought to drop it now. The people are ready for it. I said it the other day and they dropped their hoes." And I said to Cleve, "You know, you sent the wrong man out, because we need a clear analysis here and this man is given to exaggerations and talking all sorts of nonsense in hyperbolic terms." Ricks said, "I'm telling you the truth." So as Ricks was telling us about how great the people were, we were moving into Greenwood. Now, I myself had been in Greenwood. I had worked in the [SNCC] project there. I had spent time in the jail in Greenwood so many times the police knew me. The police chief knew me. Everyone in town knew me. So we decided we couldn't go wrong in Greenwood, SNCC's strongest base in the Delta. This is where we will launch Black Power. Unfortunately for the police, we went to set up some tents there and the police had decided to arrest me. So when I got arrested, Ricks was on the side there. He said, "Let them arrest you. We'll get you out of jail, and you come out and make the speech tonight." And he disappears. Anyway, I went to jail but I was bought out, and when I was released it was at night. The speeches were going on, and I was in line. Ricks came back and said, "We have everything prepared. We're ready for Black Power. We've spoke about it all day."

Although no national call had been issued, David Dawley, a student at the University of Michigan, joined the Meredith March along with a number of other whites.

DAVID DAWLEY

That afternoon in Greenwood, I was in a crowd that was listening to speakers from a porch. Willie Ricks from SNCC was introduced, and Ricks was angry and he was lashing out at whites like a cracking whip. And as he talked, there was a chill, there was a feeling of a rising storm. Willie Ricks asked people what they wanted, and they answered, "Freedom Now." Willie Ricks exhorted the crowd to demand not "Freedom Now" but "Black Power." He kept talking at the crowd, and when he asked what they wanted, they answered "Freedom Now," but more answered "Black Power," until eventually "Black Power" began to dominate until finally everyone together was thundering, "Black Power, Black Power." And that was chilling. That was frightening. Suddenly the happy feeling of the march was threatened. Suddenly I felt threatened. It seemed like a division between black and white. It seemed like a hit on well-intentioned northern whites like me, that the message from Willie Ricks was "Go home, white boy, we don't need you."

Around the tents [later that day] after listening to Willie Ricks, the atmosphere was clearly different. There was a surface of more anger and more hostility. There was a release of more hostility toward whites. Suddenly, I was a "honky," not "David." When there was small groups of two or three younger black men who might be talking to each other, where a couple of days earlier we might stand around and listen, now they told us to "move out of the way, honky." Others wanted us to know that there was no danger and that we were welcome. But clearly now there was a division.

In a speech he gave the evening of June 16, in Greenwood, Stokely Carmichael issued the call for Black Power in a more public forum than the porches that Willie Ricks had used earlier.

KWAME TURE (STOKELY CARMICHAEL)

Luckily for us, that night King had to go to do a taped television thing, I think for "Meet the Press," in Memphis. So he was not there. He had other people there, but they were not a threat to us. It meant the whole night belonged to us and we were in Greenwood, in SNCC territory. So Ricks had everybody primed. He said, "Just get to your speech. We're going against 'Freedom Now,' we're going for 'Black Power.' Don't hit too much on 'Freedom Now' but hit the need for the power." So we built up on the need for power and just when I got there, before I got it, Ricks was there, saying, "Hit them now. Hit them now." And I kept saying, "Give me time. Give me time." When we finally got there and we dropped it—Black Power—of course they had been primed and they responded immediately. But I, myself, to be honest, didn't expect that enthusiastic response. And the enthusiastic response not only shocked me but gave me more energy to carry it on further. By the time we got down that night, SCLC was running around everywhere. We knew it was finished. We had made our victory. They could not bring Freedom Now back. It was over. From now on, it was Black Power. We continued with the slogan. King was immediately rushed back. It was too late. We had a meeting the following morning where King tried his best to ask me not to use the term Black Power. But I told him that really I could not do that. That this was an organizational decision, not mine. And like him, I represent an organization and I must represent that organization or I resign from the position which I hold, and I was not prepared to do that, so we would have to use the term.

We expected the press to be completely against us, to use all sorts of terms, but that was not our problem. King was on the march. And since King was on the march, they could not attack the march without attacking King. And King could not leave the march. So their hands would be tied. King obviously could not attack us. If you will look everywhere, King has never attacked Black Power. He said he wouldn't use the term, because of the connotation it conjures up.

FLOYD MCKISSICK

I liked the expression Black Power, and it was not the first time it had been used. It wasn't the first time that Stokely had used it. I had used the expression, and many other people had used it. [Writers W.E.B.] Du Bois and Richard Wright certainly had used the expression of black people getting their power. I think it scared people because they did not understand. They could not subtract violence from power. They could only see power as having a violent instrument accompanying it. In the last analysis, it was a question of how Black Power would be defined. And it was never really defined. We talked in CORE about constructive militancy as Black Power. As we marched, we would give the African cry for freedom. Many people were disturbed because, they said, this is becoming too non-American. We're going back to our roots too much and SNCC was talking about nationalism at that time. These were some of the fuzzy parts of the march, which some of the other national organizations objected to.

> After Greenwood, the media would not let go of the Black Power idea, and neither would Stokely Carmichael. Night after night, he and the SNCC organizers called for Black Power, while King's followers countered with Freedom Now.
>
> Arlie Schardt, a correspondent for *Time* magazine, had been covering the civil rights movement since early 1962.

ARLIE SCHARDT

Greenwood was a kind of milestone because it was there, although Stokely Carmichael had been talking about Black Power from the very beginning of the march, that it was really dramatized. Stokely gave a very, very fiery address that evening, in which he basically told the group that they couldn't count on support or cooperation or help from the white man, and that blacks had to do it on their own, that blacks were being sent off to fight and die in Vietnam and yet they couldn't even vote. They had no rights at all in the communities where they lived, and they were going to have to gather their own courage and not worry about outside help. He began leading the crowd in a chant for

Black Power, which of course many people began interpreting as a call for black separatism.

I wasn't startled by it because I had heard Stokely talking for several days by this time, along the same line. There were talks as we walked along the highway. He made brief little talks, even to the chief of police in Greenwood. We went around during the day and he made calls where there were officials that he knew well and told them that it was a new day and that Negroes—at that time the word *black* was just beginning to be used—were tired of waiting and that they were going to gain their rights on their own. But it was a change, even though I knew him well and we had had many a meal together and walked on marches together. His attitude toward me as a white reporter and toward other white reporters he knew just as well was different. There was a definite barrier between us, and he wanted us to call him "sir" from then on; he wanted a little more formality, at least publicly, in our relationship, which had been very casual in the past because there had been a tremendous amount of dialogue and long interviews and everything. It was "Keep your distance, this is a new day now, and I mean it at all levels." I'm paraphrasing Stokely, but there was a definite change there, no question about it.

The media coverage of the march was interesting because there was a tendency, I thought, to overplay it. There were a couple of reasons for that. One is that there were a lot of reporters who were new to this beat who were coming in from a lot of papers around the country as the march began to pick up momentum and as this Black Power theme began to get some publicity. The second reason was that the theme was never really clearly articulated. Or at least what it meant was never clearly defined. And so it was open to very broad interpretations. There were some whites, for their own reasons, who wanted to take this as a signal of real black hostility and enmity, and there were others who simply didn't know how to read what was being said. Therefore it was left open to the idea that this was a dramatic change in the civil rights movement in which blacks were telling the whites, "Get out and forget it. We're on our own," and that it was antiwhite. But there was a lot of confusion because there was no unanimity about this. Most of the black leaders were still arguing strongly for integration as the only approach to take to achieve justice throughout the country.

ANDREW YOUNG

Martin saw Stokely as a young man with tremendous potential and ability. Black Power itself was something Martin disagreed with tactically. In fact, what he said all the time was "Jews have power, but if you ever accuse them of power, they deny it. Catholics have power, but they always deny it. In a pluralistic society, to have real power you have to deny it. And if you go around claiming power, the whole society turns on you and crushes you." It was not black power that he was against, it was the slogan Black Power, because he said, "If you really have power you don't need a slogan."

DAVID DAWLEY

We left the march a couple of days later. Basically we had come for a few days. We had to return to finals. We were not unhappy to leave the march. When we came, we had felt wanted. We felt needed. When we left, we didn't feel wanted. So we went back to Michigan to fight another war. We were activists. We were interested in changing the United States. So we listened to what SNCC was saying, and there was a sense that this was a time when blacks had the right to define the movement and that blacks would lead the strategy. And the strategy coming out of Black Power from SNCC was that blacks should organize with blacks and whites should organize with whites. I accepted that strategy. My friends accepted that strategy. So we moved on to work with whites on issues that we felt we should work with. In the next year that was not civil rights, that was Vietnam.

Some concerned Americans began to wonder if the call to Black Power was a call for a race war. Vice President Hubert Humphrey, long a civil rights supporter, called Black Power "reverse racism." Roy Wilkins called the new slogan "the father of hate and the mother of violence." Many blacks, however, welcomed the idea. *Ebony* editor Lerone Bennett, Jr., wrote that Black Power "was in the air" before Carmichael made his speech. "It was in the heads and hearts of long-suffering men who had paid an enormous price for minuscule gains."

On June 24, James Meredith rejoined the march in the town of Canton. There had been violence all along the route in Mississippi—near Hernando, when Meredith was shot; in Philadelphia, where King and the marchers were attacked by whites with hoes and ax handles; and in Canton on June 23, when state and local police had attacked with tear gas and clubs—but the protest had not lost sight of Meredith's goal. By the time he led the march into Jackson, three weeks after he first set out, four thousand new black voters had been registered in Mississippi, a state where only 7 percent of eligible black voters had been allowed on the rolls.

The march also provided an electrifying phrase for the movement's lexicon. "Black Power" became a rallying cry heard by blacks far beyond Greenwood, Mississippi. It also inspired fear in a country living through its fourth year of urban unrest. Black Power touched a nerve, in a very nervous white America.

17

Chicago, 1966

"Chicago Was a Symbol"

"White Power" advocates in Chicago demonstrate against integrating neighborhoods.

When Martin Luther King, Jr., decided to take the southern movement north into Chicago, some thought he was pressing his luck. Geography could be overcome. But other factors were gnawing around the edges of the movement's success. Selma had been the last great holding together of traditional civil rights forces. The more radical students and their allies were now going their own way. The right to vote, the last great civil right, had been nominally achieved through legislation. White supporters were beginning to drift away even before Stokely Carmichael's call for Black Power. It was a phenomenon similar to the growing disinterest of former abolitionists after the end of the Civil War. As King said while on a tour of northern cities in 1966, "I am appalled that some people feel that the civil rights struggle is over because we have a 1964 civil rights bill with ten titles and a voting rights bill. Over and over again people ask, What else do you want? They feel that everything is all right. Well, let them look around at our big cities."

White fear and puzzlement were also growing. Watts, the Los Angeles ghetto that to some outsiders had always appeared harmless and suburban compared to Harlem and Chicago's West Side, erupted in violence in late summer 1965. Most unsettling, when King flew into Los Angeles in an attempt to give a nonviolent direction to black discontent, black residents of Watts booed and heckled him. What did these people want?

Martin King thought he knew. He had said in Philadelphia on August 1, just ten days before Watts exploded, "We need massive programs that will change the structure of American society so there will be a better distribution of the wealth." With increasing frequency he began speaking of a need to shift to human rights from civil rights, and a need to struggle for economic justice. But King was laughed at in Watts. Congressman Adam Clayton Powell drew a line around Harlem and told King to stay off his turf. Black leaders in Philadelphia had greeted him with reluctance. Activists in Chicago, however, invited King and SCLC to come in. They felt their own local movement losing direction.

Longtime ally Bayard Rustin thought this unwise. He warned King against going to Chicago. Mayor Richard J. Daley and his Democratic political machine were formidable adversaries. Some of the black leadership in Chicago was part of the Daley machine or beholden to it. The black church, a source of unity in the South, would not be as hospitable in the North. Some Chicago ministers would, in fact, attack King and his program in months to come.

But Chicago was irresistible as a target for black activism. Its black population, which numbered more than 800,000, had increased by 300,000 in the decade 1950 to 1960. Blacks constituted almost one-quarter of the city's residents but were squeezed into areas that had been intended for a far smaller community. In 1959, the U.S. Commission on Civil Rights had called Chicago "the most residentially segregated large city in the nation."

Adding to its appeal as a potential SCLC project, the city boasted a confederation of established civil rights organizations. Chicago's Coordinating Council of Community Organizations (CCCO) had been formed in 1962 to battle the segregationist policies of Superintendent of Schools Benjamin C. Willis. In the organization's first call for a boycott of the public schools, more than 200,000 black students responded and stayed home. Here was grass-roots support on a massive scale. But by 1965 it was evident that CCCO had lost momentum. It was then that the invitation was extended to King. In the fall of 1965, the decision was made to forge an alliance between CCCO and SCLC that would become known as the Chicago Freedom Movement. The battle would be over schools, jobs, housing. But the focus would be on discrimination in housing.

Bernard Lafayette was one of the SNCC activists who had launched the Selma voter registration project in February of 1963. By 1965 he had become urban affairs director for the Chicago branch of the American Friends Service Committee.

BERNARD LAFAYETTE

One of the reasons we were pushing for SCLC to come to Chicago is because there was this myth about the subtlety of the problems in Chicago. People would say that there are problems, but it's not the same as in the South, and it's easier to address the problems in the South, because they're so blatant and obvious, but things in Chicago are sort of beneath the surface, and they are sort of smoothed over, and the real issues are not there. Well, one of the things that Martin Luther King did in the movement was really dramatize the issues by his presence and being able to articulate them in such a way that everything became very obvious.

Chicago was a symbol of things that were happening in places like Newark and Detroit, Philadelphia and New York, and other large metropolitan areas. This was an opportunity to experiment with the whole nonviolent approach to see whether or not we could apply to the North some of the same organizing techniques and principles and strategies that we used in the South. That was the basic reason why we wanted to come to Chicago.

The other reason for choosing Chicago as opposed to some other places was that something like forty-two percent of the blacks in Chicago were either first or second generation from Mississippi. You know, Chicago is right above Mississippi, so people migrate straight up the line. We had a lot of experience dealing with black Mississippians, and here they were transplanted north. Some had very close relationships and would go back and forth and spend time in Mississippi. So there was a good deal of appreciation for what we were doing and a good deal of respect for Martin Luther King.

Mayor Daley was considered a liberal mayor and was very supportive of civil rights in the South. And you had a good deal of black participation in the government.

> Dorothy Tillman was an SCLC staffer who, at seventeen, was working on a voter registration project in Choctaw County, Alabama, when she was asked to move to Chicago. As a child in Montgomery, she had participated in the Montgomery bus boycott.

DOROTHY TILLMAN

I was in Choctaw County when I got this telegram that said that we had to pack up and get ready to come to Chicago. So, like a good soldier, I packed up and came up to Chicago—kicking and screaming. And the first thing I remember, we were riding on an expressway and I said to [James] Bevel, "Ooh, Bevel, what are all these factories doing in the middle of the city?"

"Those are not factories, those are buildings, people live in those."

I said, "How do you expect us to organize that? They're stacked up on top of each other like pancakes."

He said, "We'll do it."

When we got there, the one thing I found was that it was the only city that we'd gone to where black leadership had a press conference and they told us to go back down south where we came from. That blew my mind.

And then we had a very hard time, we were the Southern Christian Leadership Conference, you know, and we always operated out of some church. And we had a very hard time getting black churches to open their doors to us.

If the masses had been like that, we wouldn't've stayed here that long. One of the things I found was that the blacks in this city was worse off than any plantation down south that we had to deal with. You know, down south you lived on the plantation, you worked it, and you had your food, clothing, and shelter. Up here they lived on a plantation with Boss Daley as slave master. Their jobs, their clothes, their shelter, food, that all depended on Boss Daley. And everything was connected. Any little thing they did for you, you had to pay for it. You know, "Okay, Mrs. Jones, I'll move your garbage, now you go down here and vote for so and so."

The six [black] aldermen, they just nodded up and down and would deliver the black community. They kept voter registration down real low. A precinct might have six hundred people eligible to be registered, they tried to make sure they kept it down to two hundred. And that's why you had that machine; that's why you call it the machine. Because the precinct captain could always turn that machine on. And if he had two hundred, you could always bet that a hundred and eighty was gonna vote the way Boss Daley wanted 'em to vote.

Jesse Jackson was a twenty-four-year-old divinity student when he first marched with SCLC in the 1965 Selma-to-Montgomery demonstration. In Chicago he ran SCLC's Operation Breadbasket—a project which, among other economic activities, encouraged businesses to hire more black employees.

JESSE JACKSON

Daley had blacks on his staff and black officials and some black ministers who marched with Dr. King in the South. But on Daley's plantation, they had press conferences and urged Dr. King to leave Chicago, saying there is no place for you here. It really broke his heart.

BERNARD LAFAYETTE

One of the surprises is that we thought that many of the blacks who were part of the Daley machine would have been supportive. But we found that some were very unsupportive, even though they were very supportive of the movement in the South. But when we talked about the kind of issues and problems that exist in their own communities—because they were very tightly controlled, even down to the precinct level—they were people who were very resistant. We came to understand that their jobs were tied to their involvement in the maintenance of the machine, and when we began to challenge some of the conditions and some of the issues in the local communities, then we got severe reactions.

ANDREW YOUNG

We didn't see Mayor Daley as an enemy [at first]. In 1963 he had held one of the biggest, most successful benefits that SCLC had ever had at the time of Birmingham. Mayor Daley and [gospel singer] Mahalia Jackson put it together, and they wouldn't let anybody charge expenses and they made every penny available to SCLC.

Mayor Daley was trying to keep together a political machine. We were trying to break up a political machine. We were trying to get more registered voters. He saw too many registered voters as being more than he could control. He saw the movement as a direct threat to his machine. We saw the machine as the basis of the slums, of the poverty, of the exploitation of black folk. At the same time, I think Martin agreed with [Alderman] Ralph Metcalfe that for black people coming up from Mississippi and Alabama in the Second World War, the political machine had been a very helpful vehicle. Under Congressman [William] Dawson, the organization of blacks in Chicago politics was probably the best in the world. The machine had served the black community well, but its days were over, and we were there to announce that. But Daley wasn't ready to turn loose.

> John McDermott, director of the city's Catholic Interracial Council, added his voice to those inviting SCLC to come to Chicago, but he knew that Daley would be an adversary unlike any King had encountered in the South.

JOHN MCDERMOTT

At the beginning of the marriage between Dr. King's Southern Christian Leadership Conference and the local civil rights movement there were certain frustrations. Dr. King had been accustomed to coming into very overtly hostile southern communities and analyzing the situation in terms of who ran things and raising issues. This is a problem and that is a problem. The reaction of the establishment in those communities almost always was negative. "No, it's not a problem. It's none of your business. Get out of town." And that negativism would arouse the black community and their supporters and help to build the movement. Building a movement is a little bit like jujitsu. You have to use the strength of your opponent. Well, Mayor Daley—I don't think this is fully understood—resented the notion that he and the city of Chicago were like these southern cities. He had a sense that we were Democrats. This was a liberal community. We had a human relations commission going back to the forties. His theory about Chicago was that the system was fair. All you had to do was cooperate with him and it worked for you. And that this was not a hotbed of racism. So when King would raise a problem, he would come up with some kind of remedy, often a superficial remedy but a remedy nevertheless. In the minds of many white people and the press, it became hard to see Daley as some kind of enemy because he would always respond.

Ed Marciniak, director of a city agency, the Chicago Commission on Human Relations, served as Mayor Daley's liaison to the movement.

ED MARCINIAK

The bad housing conditions were there. There was no doubt about it. The housing was deteriorated. The stock was substandard. I think the mayor's point was "You can't hold me responsible for the slums of Chicago. There is a real estate market. There are private landlords. There are private owners. I'm trying to do my best to end these slums, and I'm willing to work with anybody who wants to do something about improving housing." The mayor generally wasn't at home with the expression "slums." And the reason why he wasn't was that he saw very many people who grew up, had a great life, moved out of the area that they had lived in, and then later they were told they had lived in a slum. And so he didn't want to create in people an image of themselves as being slumdwellers.

Bob Lucas was president of the Chicago chapter of CORE and a leader in CCCO. He worked closely with King and the Chicago Freedom Movement.

BOB LUCAS

We have to remember that Daley had a very strong machine and what the machine consisted of was committeemen and precinct captains. And these committeemen and precinct captains were rewarded—at least they thought they were well rewarded—for turning out the vote for Daley. So they used to employ such tactics as telling people, "If you don't vote for the Democratic ticket, you're going to be tossed off of the welfare rolls." "If you don't vote for the Democratic ticket, you're going to be put out of the housing project." And then too, as you know, during that era, there was a lot of vote-buying in Chicago—people just simply and literally sold their vote for almost nothing. And so that's why Daley had a lot of support. Then there were some blacks that felt that Daley was a good mayor and should have been supported.

Clory Bryant's family moved to Chicago from rural Arkansas in 1940, when she was seventeen.

CLORY BRYANT

In the early 1960s, I was running for alderman as an independent against the Daley machine. I had asked a neighbor of mine was she going to vote for me. As a matter of fact, I says, "I know you'll vote for me." And she said, "No, I'm afraid I can't, because my alderman always gives me a Christmas tree for my vote. And I know you can't afford to go around buying these many trees. So I'm just going to vote for him, because I have to have my tree." And so I didn't get her vote.

During this time I was living in Chicago public housing. Having run for public office, a lot of people in the community saw me as a leader. If something would go wrong they would come to me, and one day this group came to me about housing. They were being asked to move. I went to that meeting that night and addressed the group. And in doing so, I said a few things that might have not been right with the powers that be, and by Tuesday, I had a notice in my mailbox that my rent had gone up from sixty-one dollars a month to one hundred seventy-eight.

In midsummer 1966, Stokely Carmichael's call for Black Power followed Dr. King back to Chicago from the Meredith March in Mississippi. The idea had strong appeal for thousands of Chicagoans, including Clory Bryant's daughter, Linda, a member of the city's CORE chapter.

LINDA BRYANT HALL

When I heard Stokely Carmichael say "Black Power" and I saw the picture of him standing there with his fist raised, he drew such an excitement and had such an energy that came to me—and others who were in CORE at the time—that we wanted to say, "Yes, this is what we want, we support you in this, and we don't want to be ashamed of wanting Black Power. Is there something wrong with wanting Black Power? No, there isn't." And we would like to be able to say that to people. I mean, he came with the same kind of energy that Malcolm X came with. That's what we liked, not that we wanted to overthrow our government—and there may have been some who wanted to—and not that we wanted to do anything violent.

In fact, I was one who followed Dr. King's methodology. But when Dr. King decided that Black Power was going to be something that we should hush a little bit, I think that made it even more attractive to us—that somebody would tell you not to harp on it too much, to play it low key. In fact, we decided then that, yeah, that must be the direction that we need to go into, because we're getting too many people who are telling us to go gradually, and to go slow.

On July 10, King spoke to the issue of Black Power at a Freedom Movement rally, which had been postponed in June because of the three-week Meredith March. He endorsed a more militant activism and racial pride but warned against alienating white support. SCLC estimated that a crowd of sixty thousand gathered at Soldier Field with the temperature in the nineties.

Among them was Nancy Jefferson, a community organizer from the city's West Side.

NANCY JEFFERSON

That Soldier Field rally was the height of the excitement of Dr. Martin Luther King coming to Chicago to try to set things right. It was pleasing to see that even though the mayor of this city was trying to thwart having that rally there, there was enough people in Chicago that pushed forward.

Mahalia Jackson sang that day as if the heavens were coming down on Soldier Field. But it was a hot day, and it was just lots and lots of people there. You can't explain that feeling, but you knew then that things are going to change, it must change. You felt that God was with us. It was such an excitement that it's hard to explain, but what was done that day set the tone, the environment, for a real movement in this city.

After the rally, five thousand marchers proceeded to City Hall, where Dr. King was to tape the Freedom Movement's demands to the door of the building. Coretta King and the couple's four children also marched.

CORETTA SCOTT KING

We had planned to not take Bunny because she was three years old and we felt that because it was so hot we would get a baby-sitter—but we took her to the rally. After we got to the rally she started asking if she could march. She said, "I want to march. When are we going to march? Mommy, when are we going to march?" Of course, I was hoping that I could find a way to distract her from the whole thing. Finally Martin said, "Oh, let's take her." So all of the children and Bunny and Martin and myself and the whole crowd of thousands marched toward City Hall. And as we marched toward City Hall, little Bunny got tired, and Andy Young put her on his shoulders and he carried her for a large part of the distance. Of course, I could see her head bobbing up and down on his shoulders as we walked along. And we got to City Hall. The symbolism was very much like that of Martin Luther during the

Protestant Reformation, when he nailed his ninety-five theses on the door at Wittenberg. Bunny did not get to see City Hall because she was fast asleep, but it was a very special occasion since it was the first time that all of us had marched together.

ED MARCINIAK

I was inside City Hall looking out and watching when Martin Luther King and Al Raby put those demands on the door. In the meeting that was held the next day with the mayor and the leadership of the Freedom Movement and Martin Luther King, each of these demands was discussed. And it was very interesting. The Freedom Movement wanted to get a no out of the mayor on each of the demands and he refused. And every time they tried to get a no out of him he'd say, "Well, we could look at it from this perspective, and maybe we could do something over here." The one place where he almost said no was on the demand for a police civilian review board. The mayor's answer was, "Well, I'm against it because my superintendent of police is against it. But I'd be happy to talk to him about it again." I think they were expecting something different. When they came out and met with the press, the Freedom Movement said that they didn't get anything. Well, it's true. They didn't get anything because this was not the meeting in which specific things were talked about. Specific things could have been talked about, but they weren't.

> At the meeting, an angry Al Raby, head of CCCO, told Daley the Chicago movement would move from talk to direct action on the specific issue of housing discrimination. That night, Bernard Lafayette announced a series of mass marches into Gage Park, an all-white neighborhood.

BERNARD LAFAYETTE

We began to see that there were patterns of segregation and discrimination, clear patterns. For example, there were no signs that said "Blacks Cannot Live Here," but it was white only and it was obviously white only. There were reasons why it was white, not because blacks chose not to live in those communities. It's because they were systematically denied, primarily by the real estate agents. Ninety percent of the housing that's sold is by the real estate agents. Therefore, the real estate agents have control. And they were doing what we call blockbusting, where they would allow a few blacks to move into a neighborhood that was all white in order to cause the whites to become fearful. Many of the real estate agents claimed that, "Oh, well, this is just business." Because you had black and white real estate agents working together. This was another thing different from the South. They worked hand in hand in Chicago because they all made money. The blacks were willing to pay more money for overpriced housing because their market was limited. The whites, on the other hand, were afraid of blacks. The real estate agents helped to put the fear in them. Well, whenever the real estate turned over, the banks and the real estate companies and the taxes and everything else went into play. So the slums actually was a way of exploiting both blacks and whites.

One of the things that we recognized is that in the black communities, in many cases, the city did not keep up the same level of services. The parks were neglected, for example, where black people live. The streets were not swept. And, you know, these are basic kinds of things that have something to do with the appearance of the community. So naturally when white people saw the conditions of the community, they assumed that that was going to happen to their community, they assumed it was related to blacks. Well, blacks didn't do it. Because blacks didn't have the power to determine who would sweep their streets and when they would be swept. So everybody was part of the conspiracy.

JESSE JACKSON

It was an attempt to get the nation to make housing segregation illegal, to make certain that no group had the right to use racial covenants in housing, and so as to lock people out. I mean, in Chicago in 1966 there were actual operative covenants. This is Chicago, not Alabama, Mississippi, Georgia. *Chicago*. But there was some covenants that said a black person can only live "in the back of the big house." We had restrictive covenants, plus you had redlining, and real estate brokers would only show you houses in certain areas, or they would do what they call block-busting and simply exploit you economically. I suppose you had twenty-five percent of the people living on ten percent of the land, which meant that the very laws of supply and demand made slum property valuable because people were hemmed up. One concrete manifestation of that is the housing projects like Stateway Gardens, where you got all these people living up on top of each other. All that was a part of a redlining, gerrymandering, political disenfranchisement process.

Chicago continued to swelter that summer. On July 12, with temperatures in the mid-nineties, police shut down a fire hydrant opened by black youngsters on the city's West Side. In the melee that followed, ten people were injured, twenty-four arrested; windows were smashed and stores looted. Mayor Daley called it a juvenile incident. Dr. King called it a riot. On the second night, authorities reported Molotov cocktails, sniper fire, and the stoning of city firemen. Eleven people were injured, including six Chicago policemen. The following night, Thursday, police and snipers dueled on the streets of two black neighborhoods, Lawndale and Garfield Park. Two died.

Movement leaders took to the streets of black neighborhoods to help end the violence.

AL RABY

When the riots broke out on the West Side of the city, Dr. King and Andy Young and I drove around trying to persuade young black people, who were those most involved in the action on the streets, to go into places where we could talk to them collectively. Where that wasn't possible, we tried to talk to them individually and encourage them to get off the streets. We felt that the most dangerous situation was that the police would overreact and the people would in fact be physically hurt or damaged or end up in jail. We understood their frustration, we were trying to address it and find avenues for that energy and frustration and anger to be channeled in a constructive way.

The riots were a threat to the movement and to everything we were trying to do. The only way we had been successful in those goals we had in fact achieved, whether it was voting rights or public accommodations, was by garnering the support and understanding of the broader society. There was no way in which a riot promotes that understanding.

Mayor Daley's accusation that the riots were started by Martin Luther King was absolutely ridiculous. The reason Martin decided to go to northern cities was because he had been acting as a fireman all over the country where riots had started, and he felt that the only way that that could be corrected was to involve himself in trying to rechannel the energies of the black community into constructive, nonviolent social change.

The riots didn't, I think, influence people's attitudes towards blacks as being violent. What they did was make people feel that the problems were insoluble, and that the leadership that couldn't prevent riots, couldn't influence the community, maybe had no relevance or credence anyplace else.

Bob Lucas

The power structure in the city was sitting down with the civil rights leadership, trying to figure out a way to stop the riots. I don't know what they were willing to give up, but I think that they were willing to give up much more than we got. During the discussion about how to stop the riots, one very well known civil rights leader stood up and said, "After all, you remember the riots started because you had black youngsters seeking relief with water from a fire hydrant, so obviously they need swimming pools." Of course, the power structure was delighted with that request, because they didn't have to give anything up. They actually agreed to bring portable swimming pools to many black sections of the city.

As far as I'm concerned, the civil rights leaders should have gotten much more than they did. But I guess being the first time in that kind of situation they really didn't know what to ask for. So they asked for swimming pools and they got swimming pools and the meeting was over.

> Cynicism about the agreement of Friday, July 15, was widespread. Columnist Mike Royko wrote that City Hall was on a crusade "to make Chicago's blacks the wettest in the country." Royko also quoted a civil rights worker who said, "I think they're

hoping we'll all grow gills and swim away." King spent most of Friday night negotiating with leaders of street gangs to help keep the peace. Governor Otto Kerner, taking no chances, ordered fifteen hundred National Guardsmen into the West Side, but by Saturday morning it was clear the riot was over.

That Saturday, the Freedom Movement marches to protest segregated housing practices stepped out into all-white neighborhoods, including Gage Park and Marquette Park. The demonstrations were met by mobs of hostile whites.

On Saturday, July 30, marchers led by Jesse Jackson and Al Raby were pelted with rocks and bottles. Both men were hit. On Sunday, 350 marchers faced a mob of 4,000 in Gage Park. Thirty-one were injured.

That same day, Al Raby led a march into Marquette Park.

AL RABY

The decision to march through Marquette Park was one of several programs that we had. Mayor Daley had said that there were no ghettos in the city and that the racial composition of the city was a result of people's desires. He said you could live really anywhere you wanted to, but people just chose to live where they were. So our decision to go to real estate agencies in white communities and ask to look at available property created an environment in which the white community reacted negatively and threatened us. The attitude of the movement was that we were not going to be frightened out of these neighborhoods, and so we had to march in and out of those neighborhoods until people were convinced that we were not going to be threatened, that we had to be dealt with, and that the city had to admit that there was in fact segregation and initiate programs to remedy that.

We drove that Sunday to Marquette Park, parked our cars, and started marching around the community. Came back to find a number of the cars burning and overturned. We were asked by the police if we wanted to get into paddy wagons and be driven out for our own safety. We refused that, and marched from Marquette Park back to our point of departure in the black community, about seventeen, eighteen blocks. We were attacked constantly by young whites throwing bricks as we marched down Seventy-first Street. Later, on television, there were pictures of a very large contingent of police who were not deployed for our protection and in fact simply sat and waited until everything was over. When that showed on national TV, that embarrassed the city and I think put the mayor on the spot.

DOROTHY TILLMAN

I finally understood what we had to confront over at Marquette Park. I'd never seen whites like these in the South. These whites was up in trees like monkeys throwing bricks and bottles and stuff. I mean racism, you could almost cut it, a whole 'nother level of racism from hatred. And the sad thing about it was that most of those neighborhoods we went to was like first- or second-generation Americans. I mean, they had not been here as long as we had been here. They were first-generation or second-generation Americans. Most of them were fleeing oppression. Down south you were black or white. You wasn't Irish or Polish or all of this. And for me, I learned about the different ethnic groups, Chicago taught me that. The most hostile whites that I found here in Chicago were those ethnic groups who were first-generation. I kind of felt sorry for them and still do, because somehow they believe something that's not real.

> On Friday, August 5, twelve hundred police were ordered to protect six hundred marchers led by Al Raby and Mahalia Jackson. When Martin Luther King arrived, the mob of several thousand whites erupted.

ANDREW YOUNG

I was standing there in the middle of Gage Park when there was just a rain of rocks and cherry bombs. We were ducking because we didn't know whether it was a hand grenade or some more serious explosion, or a rock or bottle. I was standing right next to Dr. King when he was hit. He wasn't hurt, and he just sluffed it off. Then Dr. King told me to go see about something, and I left and put another guy in my place and he was hit in the face with a brick and hurt very badly. It was a dangerous time. In fact, I had just rented a little yellow Ford and it got set on fire and pushed into the lake. It was a rough day where maybe a couple of hundred demonstrators were surrounded by a mob of ten thousand or more. Now, in the South we faced mobs, but it would be a couple of hundred or even fifty or seventy-five. The violence in the South always came from a rabble element. But these were women and children and husbands and wives coming out of their homes becoming a mob—and in some ways it was far more frightening.

NANCY JEFFERSON

When we saw Dr. King go down in that line I didn't realize that I could be so mad at the world. I'm telling you. We were angry because we knew that man was doing nothing. Dr. King was doing nothing but marching, trying to demonstrate we are human beings. And for them to hit that man, I think everybody in that line wanted to kill everybody that was on the other side of the line, to the point that when we got home and really assessed that, it took me days and months to get out of that anger. And I'm still not out of it. I am a citizen of this city. I'm a Black American. I have a right to move wherever I want to move if I have the money to move there. What's wrong with that? I think that's what it was all about. It was that I dare one part of this society to say that you can't move wherever you want to move. I think that was the anger that was in us. And we didn't realize ourselves what it really meant until Dr. King was marching there, and if they could do that to Dr. King, what about me?

JOHN MCDERMOTT

For black people to cross the boundary of Western Avenue into this all-white and then very hostile neighborhood, there had been a familiar experience of fear and intimidation—something you didn't do. But for white people in the march it really was extraordinary because they had never experienced the kind of change from acceptance to hate by crossing the street before in their life. For the first time in their lives they were walking in the shoes of black people. And they really did understand—because when you cross that line, it went basically from friendly territory where people were standing out on the street applauding and waving flags and wishing you well into this very frightened and very hostile neighborhood. As we walked deeper and deeper into the neighborhood, you had a great sense of isolation. Would I ever get out of there? Thank God for the Chicago police who were nearby. I remember we had priests and nuns in our march with the Catholic Interracial Council, and the insults, the vulgar language which they were subjected to—just unbelievable, the expressions of anger and hate, the swastikas which were held up, the housewives who turned their lawn sprinklers on you.

It was a very eerie experience, yet a bonding experience. It was somewhat like war. These were your buddies in the foxhole, and you stuck together for mutual protection. The walk home was like walking out of no-man's-land, out of a war zone. When we crossed Seventy-first Street, there was this tremendous sense of relief, and people began to laugh and hug each other that they had made it. It was an extraordinary experience, extraordinary.

Embarrassed by the national attention to the violence surrounding open-housing marches, the city government searched for a way to bring the demonstrations to an end. A "summit meeting" was scheduled for Wednesday, August 17.

ED MARCINIAK

The mayor wanted to come to the bargaining table right along. He didn't have to be brought there. He was looking for the opportunity to come to the bargaining table to see if these issues could be negotiated rather than settled out in the streets of Chicago. You have to remember that the mayor was a political master. His objective was to win friends and influence enemies. It was not to make enemies. When the religious leaders started taking the initiative to set up the summit conference with the business community, the religious leaders, the leaders of the labor movement, civic leaders, and the leaders of the Freedom Movement, the mayor jumped at it. As a matter of fact, he was the person that brought many of the key principals into that meeting.

ANDREW YOUNG

SCLC went to Chicago to see if nonviolence would work in the North, and so we were doing a number of things. The marches were only one. The marches were part of an open-housing effort. But we were also trying to end slums and create home-ownership opportunities for poor people. We were trying to generate jobs. We were trying to integrate the economic opportunities through Operation Breadbasket, which was Jesse Jackson's project. And all of these were working enough for us to know that we could do many of the same things in the North that we'd done in the South. But Chicago was so much bigger than any city that we'd worked in in the South. We knew we couldn't do them all at the same time. And that we couldn't sustain an aggressive movement much longer. So we were trying to find a way to wind it up, maybe institutionalize it. We wanted to get some settlement and some response and agreements from Daley, and then commit to a slow, long-term change period.

After the initial summit meeting, working committees met over the next ten days to hammer out an agreement. As negotiations went on, so too did the marches and the battle between the movement and the mayor. Daley obtained an injunction limiting marches to only one part of the city per day. The court order also banned marches during rush hour and after dark, limited the number of marchers to five hundred, and mandated that the police be notified twenty-four hours in advance of each demonstration.

AL RABY

The injunction came as a result of the police department's claim that it could not protect multiple marches. We clearly were angered by the seeking of an injunction. We thought it diminished our negotiating power. But it was something we had to learn to live with. And we did that, even though we were still in negotiations.

The movement marches continued under the injunction rules, and also in suburbs unaffected by the order. King was determined to keep up the pressure. If demands were not met, he announced, blacks would march into Cicero, the all-white suburb where just months before a black teenager had been murdered while looking for work. To keep order, Governor Kerner announced he would send in the Illinois National Guard. On Friday, August 26, a ten-point settlement was reached, and the movement called a halt to further open-housing marches.

The agreement committed the city to enforce and support open-housing legislation. The Chicago Real Estate Board pledged to obey the law. Government agencies at all levels, from city to federal, promised to desegregate public housing assignments and to end construction of high-rise public housing ghettos. Banks agreed to end practices which prevented blacks from obtaining mortgage money. Groups from labor and business and the religious community agreed to see that the program was implemented. After the summit meeting, King emphasized the importance of abiding by this agreement by noting that "our summers of riots have been caused by our winters of delay. I want to stress the need for implementation."

By Monday morning, whites were picketing Daley at City Hall, charging that he had sold out Chicago.

Several black activists also voiced discontent.

CLORY BRYANT

Those people who sat in on the summits with the housing department were not the people of our choice. We felt that those people who lived in Chicago public housing, who were emotionally involved and concerned enough to care, for whom Chicago housing was a way of life, should have been involved to say what the problems were. Those are the people we had wanted, because we don't care about summits taking place without us. We don't care about covenants. We want contracts in black and white with some hard answers for us. With some signatures and some people we can hold responsible and some time frames. But none of this was there. It was just another piece of paper.

Others in the Chicago Freedom Movement were enthusiastic.

NANCY JEFFERSON

When Dr. King and Daley signed that accord, it was a great day. It was a great feeling because we understood the hardship that Dr. King went through to get that done. I'm sure to Daley it was superficial. You know, he wasn't real. But one thing that we learned that Dr. King always said so very cleverly is that you cooperate or operate. You get the same result. So we were getting the same result out of Daley having to operate in spite of his noncooperation. And I think it was a great day to us that said just keep on. You can do it. I think that's what it meant to us.

JOHN MCDERMOTT

The negotiators have been criticized for settling for too little too soon. I don't agree with that. I think we got what we could. I thought it was an honorable agreement. What was on the minds of the negotiators for the Freedom Movement was the fact that, in a sense, we had reached our peak. It was, in our judgment, time to get what we could with the strength that we had demonstrated. There is nothing wrong with the summit agreement, in my judgment. It's not a perfect agreement. What people criticize is that many of the promises that were made to us were not kept. But I think that's a problem of implementation and follow-through rather than the agreement itself.

> When King presented the open-housing agreement at a rally, his speech was interrupted by calls for Black Power. SNCC circulated a flyer at the rally which read in part: "WAKE UP, BROTHER! DECIDE FOR YOURSELF—WHO SPEAKS FOR YOU? King says we should celebrate a 'significant victory' tonight because he got some concessions from the city. These concessions were just more empty promises from Daley, a man who has lied and lied to the black man in this city for years. Many people are calling it a sellout . . . WAKE UP, BROTHER! WE GOT TO GET US SOME BLACK POWER—SO THE BLACK MAN CAN SPEAK FOR HIMSELF!"
>
> CORE was also dissatisfied with the agreement and decided to go ahead with the march to Cicero, rescheduling it for September 4.

BOB LUCAS

CORE decided to march to Cicero because we knew that blacks got nothing out of the summit conference. The day the march took place, Dr. King called me at home and said to me, "You know, Bob, we would like to save Cicero to use it later on for something. And I wish that you wouldn't go." I told Dr. King, "Well, Doc, my conscience dictates to me that I must lead that march into Cicero," because as a matter of fact, see, SCLC had threatened to march into Cicero a number of times, and because of that, although blacks did not live in Cicero, blacks worked in Cicero, and people were beginning to beat them up simply because they thought that we were afraid to march in Cicero. So that was kind of another reason why we marched. And I indicated all those things to Dr. King. And after he saw that I was determined to go—you know, Dr. King was a great guy—he said, "Bob, inasmuch as you're going, I wish you the best." So he really in that sense endorsed the march.

CLORY BRYANT

Cicero, you don't know what Cicero meant to people in Chicago. You don't go into the viaduct, honey, because if you do you may not get back. Cicero was on the other side of the viaduct. And you didn't walk through Cicero alone. You didn't let your car break down in Cicero and get out to change a tire. You just didn't go to Cicero if you were black.

LINDA BRYANT HALL

Dr. King's marches in Chicago were usually made up of movement people. This march was community people. These people had not attended any workshops on nonviolence, they had not listened to any lectures on loving your fellow man and all. They were just people who were angry about what was happening and wanted to do something. When they all decided to go on this march, and people started to throw bricks and bottles at us, a couple of people caught the bricks and threw them back. They threw rocks back. These people were saying, "We're going to come to Cicero and we're not going to go limp. We're going to march through Cicero, and we're going to march to the point that we said we were going to march to, and we're going to come back." That in itself was a triumph, because people just didn't do that in Cicero.

JOHN MCDERMOTT

There were people who were not entirely comfortable with the religious dimensions of Dr. King's leadership, with his sense of forgiving the sinner but not the sin, making the distinction between the evil of racism and the basic decency of people and his hope for the possibility of an integrated society of interracial harmony. There were people who were troubled by that, who thought that was too otherworldly and it might not work. And that the way America really worked and the way Chicago worked was that some people had power and some people didn't. Some people were haves and some people were have-nots. And the way they saw civil rights was how quickly can we become haves? How quickly can we become ins? How quickly can we become winners? The talk of Black Power touched that desire.

BOB LUCAS

I felt really good about the blacks catching the missiles and throwing them back, because it sorely indicated to the whole world that nonviolence had worked in the South but it wasn't about to really work in the North.

After Dr. King left the city in late August of 1966, having failed really in Chicago, we began to notice a wider split between the blacks and the whites in the civil rights movement. As long as Dr. King was here, that was sort of held at bay, out of respect for him. But after he left, it really began to manifest itself to the point where blacks literally asked whites to leave the movement and to leave meetings. But, you see, that had really started back around 1964 because of the preachings of Malcolm X. A lot of blacks in the civil rights movement, although they did not become Muslims, they really believed in Malcolm X and Malcolm's preaching. Inasmuch as some people already had those kind of inclinations, it manifested itself in a huge way in the fall of '66 and later.

18

Muhammad Ali, 1964–1967

"I Am the Greatest"

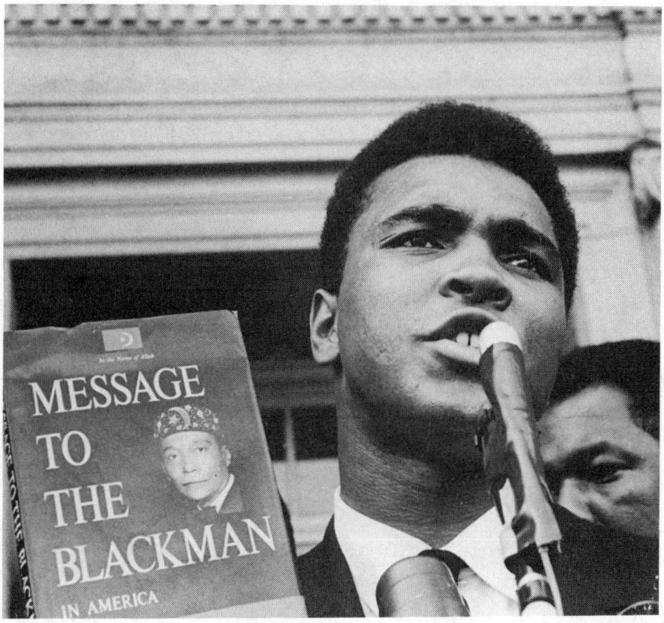

Born in 1942 in segregated Louisville, Kentucky, Cassius Marcellus Clay was so angry when he learned of the murder of fourteen-year-old Emmett Till in Mississippi, he wrote in his autobiography, that he and a friend went out late one night and derailed a diesel engine locomotive in revenge.

Young Clay was taught to box by a white policeman named Joe Martin. In 1958 he won Louisville's Golden Gloves light heavyweight championship. The next year, he won both the national Golden Gloves and Amateur Athletic Union titles. In 1960 Clay traveled to Rome as a member of the U.S. Olympic boxing team, where, still fighting as a light heavyweight, he won a gold medal. Returning to Kentucky, Clay endured the continuing insult of segregation. One night he walked onto a bridge in Louisville and tossed his gold medal into the Ohio River.

But he continued to fight and to mature. He was sharp, handsome, serious, funny—and as gifted a boxer as the sport had seen in decades. Within four years, on February 25, 1964, he upset Sonny Liston to become the world heavyweight champion. One day after the victory, he announced that he had converted to the Muslim faith and had taken a new name, Muhammad Ali. The press treated the conversion as an overnight phenomenon. In fact, Ali had joined the Nation of Islam in 1961.

While many refused to call him by his new name, Ali's insistence on his right to define himself and his identity struck a responsive chord in many Black Americans. Controversy around the young Ali intensified in 1967, when he refused to serve in the U.S. Army on religious grounds.

HARRY BELAFONTE

Muhammad Ali was the genuine product of what the movement inspired. He was the best example. He was the Negro kid who came up in the time of the black movement. Who was Cassius Clay in the beginning and became Muhammad Ali in the end. He took on all of the characteristics and was the embodiment of the thrust of the movement. He was courageous. He put the class issues on the line. He didn't care about money. He didn't care about the quote "white man's success" and the things that the American dream aspired to. He brought America to its most wonderful and its most naked moment. "I will not play in your game of war. I will not kill in your behalf. What you ask is immoral, unjust, and I stand here to attest to that fact. Now do with me what you will," he said. And he was terribly courageous, he was powerful, he was the embodiment of the new day and was very inspirational. I mean he was, in many ways, as inspiring as Dr. King, as inspiring as Malcolm. These men were larger than life, classic leaders. Cassius was a black, young American. Out of the womb of oppression he was our phoenix, he was the spirit of all our young. He was our manhood. He was the future. He was the present. He was the vitality of what we hoped would emerge. The embodiment of all of it, the perfect machine, the wit, the incredible athlete, the facile, articulate, sharp mind on issues, the great sense of humor, which was out of our tradition. He was all of this. He stood courageously and said, "I put everything on the line for what I believe in." They could not break his spirit nor deny his moral imperative.

Edwin Pope was a sportswriter for the *Miami Herald* and a boxing fan. His first great sports hero was heavyweight champion Joe Louis, who won the title in 1937.

EDWIN POPE

Traditionally, writers and fighters have always gotten along together. Fighting has been a treasure trove of material for writers, all the way from Jack London and Ernest Hemingway to Jimmy Cannon and Red Smith. Writers love fighters and fighters love writers. Joe Louis would do anything, sit still for anything you wanted to do and talk to you all day. And suddenly, in Cassius Clay you had a fighter that, I don't know whether "manipulate" is the right word or not, but you had a fighter that wouldn't do exactly what you wanted him to do. He wasn't always at your beck and call. I don't think many of us in the writing business were really comfortable with Cassius Clay joining the Nation of Islam and changing his name to Muhammad Ali.

For the second Ali-Liston fight, which was scheduled for Boston about a year after Ali first dethroned Liston, Ali's people had this idea that it would help promote the fight for him to drive his own bus all the way from Miami to a little place called Chicopee Falls, Massachusetts, where he would train. Well, little did we realize that Ali was going to actually drive the bus. We went over to his house in northwest Miami. There were four white writers—myself, George Plimpton, Bud Collins of the *Boston Globe,* and Mort Sharnik of *Sports Illustrated*. We were all piled on the bus with a lot of fried chicken and soda pop and took off, and Clay is behind the wheel of the bus! He had this terribly disconcerting habit while he was driving along at seventy miles per hour of peering around to address everyone on the bus without looking at the highway. Everybody was constantly on the edge of their seats. Also, he'd lean out the window at every opportunity and wave to people and announce, "I'm Muhammad Ali. I'm the greatest." On that bus trip I gathered a different perception of Muhammad Ali. Up until then I had seen him as sort of a hostile, somewhat bristling person. On that trip it became very apparent that he was enormously sweet-natured, very compassionate, very friendly, and altogether taken with his new role as a Muslim. He would make a lot of jokes about everything but being a Muslim.

We had a lot of things go wrong on that trip. The first night out we stopped at a little place called Yulee, Florida, up in north Florida, and it's really back in the country. They had to pipe daylight in there. Ali didn't want to stop. Everybody else wanted to stop to get some food. Ali said, "I don't want to stop till we get through Georgia, because I don't want anybody having to fool with any Ku Klux Klansmen." Nonetheless, they pulled into this roadside stand in Yulee, Florida, about eleven-thirty at night, and Drew Brown, the assistant trainer they called Bundini Brown, went in to try to get some food to take with us. The proprietor refused Bundini. Said, "You have to go around to the window outside." Well, Bundini got very upset about it. George Plimpton, Bud Collins, and I stepped up and asked how they had a right to do this. Wasn't this the United States? And this man says, "No, this is not the United States." In any case, Bundini got back on the bus in terrible shape. And Ali says, "I told you not to do that. I told you you're in the wrong part of the country for a black person to go in and try to order food." And he picked up his pillow and started beating him over the head with it, half in jest, half seriously. It was a very touching moment, though, Ali seeming wise far beyond his years. He was just a nice person. No matter what preconception you got on that bus with Ali with, it would have been absolutely impossible to get off disliking him.

Ali first met Malcolm X, whom he greatly admired, in 1962 at the Detroit Mosque of the Nation of Islam.

Muhammad Ali

My first impression of Malcolm X was how could a black man talk about the government and white people and act so bold, and not be shot at? How could he say these things? Only God must be protecting him. He was so radical at that time, and yet he walked with no bodyguard, fearless. That really attracted me. What also attracted me, he says, "Why we called Negroes? Chinese are named after China. Cubans are named after Cuba,

Russians after Russia, Germans after Germany. All people are named after their country. What country is called Negro?" I said, "Man, so true."

Malcolm said, "We don't have names." Weinstein, you know is a Jew. Here come Lumumba, Africa. Here come Chang Chow, a Chinaman. Here come Red Cloud, Indian. Here come Jim Washington. He could be black or white. We all got the slave names. We don't have our names. They named us in slavery. So I got me a name from Elijah Muhammad. Muhammad Ali.

When I joined the Nation in 1961, I figured I'd be pressured if I revealed it, so I kept it quiet for about three years. I sneaked to meetings, sneaking in the back door, looking around for the police officers, the press men, before I go in. But after beating Sonny Liston, I was getting more recognition and more power. I revealed it after that fight.

I knew that to draw money to me—people, rich people, mainly the white people at the time, could buy ringside seats—I had to act crazy, supreme. "I am the greatest of all times. I'm pretty. Talk jive and walk in five." They said, "The nigger talks too much. Nigger needs a good whuppin'." That's what made me so attractive. A black man said, "I am the greatest." We weren't taught like that. We were taught the black man had the bad luck. Black was bad and white was good. So me, being black—"I am the greatest. I'm pretty"— it gave more people confidence and it put me in such a spot, I had to fight to back up my words.

I realized blacks was supposed to be humble, meek. They showed us a white Jesus. All the Last Supper is white. All the angels are white. Same with Miracle White. Tarzan, king of Africa, he's white. Angel food cake's white. Devil's food cake chocolate. And here's a black man—"I'm the greatest. I'm supreme." It's a superior attitude. This made me so hated by many of the southerners, whites and blacks. This is confidence and character and different. That's what made me so popular. I liked being who I was because they would put me on television and when I say, "I'm the greatest, I'm pretty," that means that little black children and people who felt like nothing say, "We got a champion. Look what he's doing. Look at him over there."

Former heavyweight champion Floyd Patterson was concerned about the admiration in the black community for Ali. Refusing to call the champion by his Muslim name, he challenged Ali for the title in November 1965 in a fight he called a "moral crusade." Ali, in turn, called Patterson a "white man's Negro."

FLOYD PATTERSON

When I first saw Clay was on television. He was yelling to the top of his voice about what he was going to do to his opponent. I found this very, very funny, in the beginning. But after a while I began to dislike it, because he said mean things about his opponents. And that's something that in boxing I always thought was a no-no. You never down another guy to help yourself. But then as time went on I realized that he was doing this in order to give himself more confidence, convincing himself that he could do it. And Clay, in my opinion, I felt was very, very intelligent. I watched him fight once, and he had predicted that he would knock the guy out in six rounds. And then the guy had something derogatory to say back and he said, "Well, because of that, I'm going to knock you out in four." The fight was in Madison Square Garden. It went the distance. And right away, the TV guy jumped into the arena, put the mike in front of him and said, "Now, you said you were going to knock him out in six, you failed. Then you said you were going to do it in four. What happened?" He said, "What's six and four?" So, what I'm trying to say, that was a very intelligent answer. I got a big kick out of that.

After a while, of course, we had differences as far as beliefs were concerned. And that's mainly why, in the very beginning, we weren't too friendly toward one another, because, well, he has his beliefs, I have mine. I respect his as long as he respects mine, and back then he didn't respect mine. He called me a white man's champion. And I resented that. When I found out that Cassius Clay was a Black Muslim, that he had just joined the Black Muslims, I didn't know that much about them. But it was then that I started listening to Malcolm X on television and then I learned what they were representing. And Clay himself had an awful lot to say about it. I'd always really catch any interview he had made back then.

I'm not a racist in any way. I dislike anyone who's prejudiced, whether they be white or black, see. I don't see any colors. So, as

I said back then, and I'll say again, I think if you put all the KKK's, along with the Black Muslims, on an island somewhere, it would be a better world to live in.

Before our first fight, Cassius Clay had said over TV many times and he had said it to the press at press conferences, he'd beat me so bad he was going to make me call him by the name he wanted to be called. And during the actual fight he did say during earlier rounds, I believe he asked me once or twice, "What's my name? What's my name?" And I said, "Cassius Clay." I distinctly remember the latter rounds, when I was taking a bad beating, he said, "What's my name now?" And my reply was, "Cassius Clay, and that's what it will always be." I'm fifty-four years old now and it's still Cassius Clay. Now, don't misunderstand. I'm not being disrespectful. His mother and father, they still call him Cassius Clay. I ran into his father several years ago and he had said to me, "Do you remember who I am?" So I looked at him and I said, "Well, I don't quite remember. But you look familiar." He said, "Well, I'm Cassius Clay's father." So I said, "Oh, you still call him Cassius Clay?" And he said, "Yeah." So anyway, to get back to what I was saying, Clay and I get along very well now. I mean, I've seen him on several occasions. We talk. We're friends. You know, all that's forgotten about. But he's still Cassius Clay. I'm still the rabbit. He calls me a rabbit.

MUHAMMAD ALI

Me and Floyd Patterson had some fights and I don't say nothing bad about him. I just—he was different. He's different from me, so he would call me Clay. He wouldn't call me Ali. He said, "Muhammad was named Clay, he's going to stay Clay." So I told him, I said, "I'm going to whup you till you tell me my name." And round one, I said, "What's my name?" He doesn't say nothing, so round two, round three, I hit him with my right hand. He said, "Muhammad Ali, Muhammad Ali."

SONIA SANCHEZ

When Muhammad Ali joined the Nation it was a continuation of what we knew was happening already. Everybody had seen Malcolm down in his camp. Everyone knew that he was teaching him, instructing him at that particular time, so when he changed his name, we said very simply, "That's his name." In fact, when people called him Cassius Clay, we would say, "That's not his name. Call the brother by his name. His name is Muhammad Ali. Go on, do it. Get it. Walk on." And we were very pleased and very happy. So it was not a bone of contention unless people wanted it to be. People who said, "I can't pronounce that name," or "I don't want to pronounce that name," or thought it meant, perhaps, at some point, that maybe they thought he had gotten to be too big. But the man knew what he was doing. Could do it. Did it and brought everybody along with him when he did it because he had that sense of himself, that sense that when he said, "I'm the greatest," you say, "Yes, you are. There's no doubt about that, Muhammad Ali. You are indeed the greatest, the greatest that ever done walk on this earth," whatever. And you believed that. Also, this man was a gentle man. I mean, he'd get out of the ring and then would grab your hand and be very gentle with you and say, "Did you like that, sister? Did you like what I just did? Did I tell them really off? Ha, ha, ha." And he'd laugh that laugh, that very infectious laugh, and you would say, "Yes, you did." And that was good.

I don't like fights and fighters, but I love Muhammad Ali. And I love Muhammad Ali because he was not just a fighter, he was a cultural resource for everyone in that time, black students, white students, green students, brown students, blue students. He cut across every race, every religion, because he said, "No, I will not go," and then tried to continue to fight at the same time.

Angelo Dundee met Muhammad Ali in 1958, when Ali, then Cassius Clay, was still an amateur. He was Ali's trainer throughout most of Ali's professional career.

ANGELO DUNDEE

I knew about Muhammad's association with the Muslims about two weeks before the Liston fight. The promoter, Jim McDonald, came to me. He said, "Angelo, unless Cassius Marcellus Clay refutes the reports out of Chicago and says that he's not a Muslim, I'm going to cancel the fight." So I said, "Well, gee, I'll talk to the kid." And I said, "Better still, *you* go talk to the kid." And I made him go off into another area and speak to the fighter. So, Cassius came back and I'm sitting in the office and he says, "Angen, I don't think I'm going to have the fight." I said, "Why?" He said, "Well, because they want me to say I'm not a Muslim and I am a Muslim." "Marvelous, whatever you want to do, you do. I mean, it's up to you." Because what the heck, what's in a name? The thing with me was the individual. But the tough thing about it really was that it was such a pretty name. We had nurtured it and played it up—Cassius Marcellus Clay—and we used to rhyme on it. It was a beautiful name. And then he changed it to Muhammad Ali. People resented that. A lot of people wouldn't call him [Ali]. But what's in a name? To me, he was still the same individual, same guy. Actually, I didn't know what a Muslim was, really, because I thought it was a piece of cloth—and I mean that with all my heart. What the heck's the difference what a guy's religion is? That doesn't project to me what an individual is.

When Ali publicly announced his conversion to the Islamic faith in 1964, his mentor Malcolm X had already been expelled from the Nation of Islam. Elijah Muhammad issued orders that no Muslim was to speak with Malcolm X. Malcolm traveled in Africa that year, after his break with the Nation and during the time that Alex Haley was working on Malcolm's autobiography.

ALEX HALEY

I remember the thing that hurt Malcolm so much was at some place, I don't remember which country, I believe it was in Ghana, he had met Muhammad Ali. Muhammad Ali was like his younger brother, little brother. He was very, very proud of him. I remember Malcolm calling me from somewhere in Florida where Muhammad Ali had just won one of his decisive battles, and Malcolm was boasting about how his little brother had done so marvelously well. And I could hear the noise in the background and Malcolm spoke to Muhammad Ali and said for him to holler something at me over the phone, which he did—it was kind of like a melee backstage after the fight. And now he went to West Africa, and in Ghana he and Muhammad Ali happened to be crisscrossing in their journeys, and now Muhammad Ali did not look in his direction—though they passed right by each other—nor speak. And Malcolm was deeply hurt, wounded, by that.

Kareem Abdul-Jabbar was born Lew Alcindor in New York City in 1947 and took his Muslim name in 1971. Abdul-Jabbar was still in high school in 1964, when Ali announced he was a Muslim. Three years later, when Ali refused induction into the army, Abdul-Jabbar was a star member of the UCLA basketball team.

KAREEM ABDUL-JABBAR

When Cassius Clay changed his name to Muhammad Ali and announced he was joining the Nation of Islam, I was surprised. I thought that he was just a colorful character, and that seemed to show that he had some serious underpinnings.

I think Ali's impact on young people was very formidable. I remember when I was in high school the teachers didn't like him because he was so antiestablishment and he kind of thumbed his nose at authority and got away with it. They didn't like that at all—the fact that he was proud to be a black man and that he had so much talent and could enjoy it in a way that didn't have the dignity that they assumed that it should have. I think that was something that really made certain people love him and made other people think that he was dangerous. But for those very reasons that's why I enjoyed him.

When Ali announced his refusal to accept the draft, I thought it was a very brave stand. I had seen a number of people taking that stand, 'cause while I was at UCLA the draft and a lot of issues around the Vietnam War became very prominent in everybody's lives. People had to really seriously think about what it meant to be in the armed services and go fight in Vietnam. So I knew he would take a lot of heat for it. I definitely thought that Ali was going to have to start dealing with harassment from the federal government, because they were going to use this case as an example. They had tried through sport to make an example of him, and because of his talent and his courage they couldn't get him to lose in the ring. So they had to defeat him in the courts, and use the courts as a means to make him get in line.

A meeting to help Ali was called by black athletes back in 1967. I was a sophomore at UCLA, and I'd gotten to know [professional football star] Jim Brown while I was out here in Los Angeles. He felt that I should be a part of the group to just maybe represent young people, I guess. Being a fan of Ali's, I was very happy to lend my support. I didn't know what we could do to help him, but I wanted to be involved.

I was happy to meet Ali person to person, and it was nice meeting the other black athletes and having some type of solidarity with them. The meeting really was kind of futile in that we really couldn't do anything. But we let black people around the country know that we supported Ali. I think by that time Black Americans understood that their presence in Vietnam was highly disproportionate to their percentage of the American population and that the front-line casualties were being absorbed by Black Americans in much greater numbers than they should have. This impact was obvious to everybody, and I think this kind of heightened that.

When Muhammad Ali reported to the Houston induction center on April 28, 1967, Lieutenant Steven Dunkley was the induction officer in charge.

STEVEN DUNKLEY

The way I felt the day that Muhammad Ali was coming up was that it was definitely going to be a different day at work that day. We were asked to be there early, at six o'clock in the morning, to avoid any problems with the people we were expecting to demonstrate out front. So we were all in. We fortified the induction center and monitored who came in and out. We knew that the whole thing was going to be monitored from the Pentagon on a direct phone line the whole day, all of his activities. A lot of the guys who worked at the center were fans of Muhammad Ali. You know, he was the heavyweight champion of the world and he was coming that day. And it's not every day you get somebody like that come through the induction center, so we were excited about that.

There were three factions outside. You had the Black Muslims, which were concerned with his religious beliefs and that they be respected and everything like that. So they were doing their thing. And you had the draft-card burners, which we referred to as the long-haired hippie dope fiends, and they were burning flags and draft cards and demonstrating and yelling and everything out there, protesting the war in Vietnam. Then you had really kind of the mom and pops. These were basically parents of sons that were in Vietnam already, and they were there basically watching and seeing what was going on. So all three factions were kind of intermixing, and all had their specific territories staked out in front of the induction building.

Muhammad Ali and the people who were to be inducted that day came in. We had this induction ceremony room, had like a podium in it. They were lined up in front of the podium, and then I came in and stood up on the podium and basically told them that they were there for induction in the armed forces of the United States. I explained to them that as I called their name they would take a step forward and that step forward would constitute their induction in the U.S. Army. Okay, so then I started down through the list, starting with the A's and—you know, Army always starts with the A's and ends with the Z's. So I started with the A's, and when I got down to the M's, Muhammad Ali, I said, "Muhammad Ali." I looked him in the eye, wondering if he was going to do it, and he didn't do anything. Then I called "Cassius Clay," and he didn't do anything. Because we wanted to make sure that the name was correct that we were calling. At that time Captain Hall and Lieutenant Hartman took him from the room to advise him of his rights. I continued on with the ceremony, and the rest of the gentlemen in the room took the step forward, became part of the U.S. Army, and then they left. Then we brought Muhammad Ali back in after he had been advised of his rights, and then called his name again. I looked him in the eye again and said, "Muhammad Ali," and he stood there. And then I said, "Cassius Clay," and he stood there. And then we told him that he had in fact refused induction in the United States Army and he was free to go. At that time, we asked him if he wanted to go to the pressroom and talk to the press—because we had a large room full of movie cameras and newspaper people that wanted to talk to him and get his thoughts and his feelings on why he had done what he had just done—or if he wanted to quietly leave by a back entrance that we had. And he said that he wanted to go to the pressroom and talk to the press people. He had a press release that was typed out that he had been carrying through all the processing, and he took it out of his briefcase and gave it out to all the people in the pressroom, which basically gave his reasons for refusing induction. That he was a Muslim minister and therefore was exempt from serving in the armed forces of the United States.

As Muhammad Ali walked out of the center, my thoughts were that he had done the wrong thing. I felt that if he would have taken induction they would have put him in special services. He probably would have ended up coaching the boxing team or something like that. Or, like Elvis Presley was assigned to a special unit in Germany or something like that. I believe, I'm not positive, but I think Elvis Presley made two movies while he was in the service, and so I think for Muhammad Ali probably a couple of fights would have been arranged and also he wouldn't have been stripped of his title as heavyweight champion of the world. So, I felt that he should have taken induction and he should have served his country and that he would have been treated fairly by the U.S. Army, I really do. I think he made a mistake.

MUHAMMAD ALI

When I said, "I ain't got no quarrel with the Vietcong," I said it because it's true. At that time I could see we were wrong. The war was wrong, and my conscience wouldn't allow me to kill them people. But I wasn't the only one. Many people protested. Some went to jail. But me being so famous, it was publicized. I felt bad and felt sorry for the other black men going over to Vietnam and just wished I could talk to them. I wished they believed like I did. Basically, I just felt bad knowing they went there and many got killed, got lame, and then come back. And I said, It's wrong. I saw that early. I said, If America was in trouble and real war came, I'd be on the front line if we had been attacked. But I could see it wasn't right, and what happened to the boys, black and white, when they got back is farther proof that I was right.

That day in Houston in '67 when I went to the induction center, I felt happy, because people didn't think I had the nerve or they don't have the nerve to buck the draft board of the government. And I almost ran there, hurried. I couldn't wait to not take the step. And then when I did that, all the boys looked surprised. The guy that asked me to take the step looked surprised, and we went into the back room and they talked to me, told me what's going to happen. If I go, I don't have to fight, or just do exhibitions and things. I told them I still won't go, because that's leading more boys to death. And I says, I'd rather go to jail. So they say, You're going to get there, and I never did.

How I felt going there? The world was watching, the blacks mainly, looking to see if I had the nerve to buck Uncle Sam, and I just couldn't wait for the man to call my name, so I wouldn't step forward. I enjoyed that day.

Shortly after Ali's refusal to be inducted, a grand jury indicted him. He was soon found guilty and sentenced to five years in prison, but he was released on bail pending his appeal. Stripped of his title, Ali was not allowed to enter a boxing ring. He became a popular antiwar speaker both in the United States and abroad. In June 1970, the Supreme Court overturned Ali's conviction on the grounds that the FBI had placed an illegal wiretap on his telephone. The Court had previously been deadlocked when considering Ali's case on religious grounds.

Muhammad Ali regained his world heavyweight boxing title in 1974.

19

King and Vietnam, 1965–1967

"His Philosophy Made It Impossible Not to Take a Stand"

On March 2, 1965, President Lyndon Johnson launched Operation Rolling Thunder, a major, sustained aerial assault on North Vietnam. That same day, Martin Luther King, Jr., included in a speech he gave at Howard University a call for a negotiated settlement of the escalating conflict in Southeast Asia.

King was morally opposed to the violence of war. His feelings about Vietnam reflected that. Over the next two years, whenever he spoke out, he received criticism from people on both sides of the war debate. There were those in the movement, especially in SNCC, who felt he was too quiet. Others, including his own advisers, warned that statements against the war would jeopardize the civil rights cause at home. In the United States, some who opposed the war were already being called communists and traitors to their country.

Coretta Scott King

Martin agonized really over the decision of whether he should come out sooner than he did. I mean, over those several years. I remember that right after the Nobel Peace Prize, in 1964 in December and in the early part of '65, he made a statement, a fairly strong statement. And of course the press noticed it and sort of attacked him about the statement. And he began to, I guess, kind of weigh his words. But at that time he conferred with his board, because he said that it would affect very directly SCLC and the work that he was doing, in terms of the support that he was getting. "People who were with me on civil rights will not be with me on this issue, and we have to count those costs. And all I want you to do is to allow me to make the statement as an individual, not on behalf of the organization." Now, of course, he had the right to do that on his own, but there was no way the press would make that distinction or the people would make that distinction. Therefore he had to prepare them for what were real consequences. And he, I think, always understood that.

It was very difficult for him, because he really felt very strongly from the very beginning on this whole issue of the Vietnam War, especially because he had studied the conflict, studied it back into the forties, and he was able to see the development of the United States getting more involved and how all that happened and why. You know, we didn't have to get that involved. And then he could see the injustice of it all and how it was affecting the country domestically and how the people who were the poorest people in this country were more directly affected by it.

Vincent Harding, raised in Harlem, had worked full-time with the southern-based civil rights movement. In the mid-1960s, he became chairman of the department of history and sociology at Spelman College in Atlanta.

VINCENT HARDING

I was involved with King as a friend and as a neighbor and as a co-worker. There had been a number of situations where the opportunity for us to talk about what was going on was very important. And I'm fairly certain that it was the SCLC convention of August 1965 when I wrote a fairly long letter to Martin and the convention. I wasn't able to be there, but I had been very deeply involved in studying what was going on in Vietnam for my own edification and came to the conclusion that what was going on was very wrong as far as our country's policy was concerned, and that freedom movement organizations like SCLC and leaders like King needed to say something very clearly about that and needed to put themselves out in the open in solidarity with the suffering of the people of Vietnam. I don't remember that there was any specific response to [my letter], but what I know is that much of what I believed, he believed. And it was simply a question of what do you say and when and where and how.

He'd not only talked with me, but he had spoken publicly on this between '65 and '67. I had occasion periodically to visit Martin's church and there were many references in his sermons—not sermons on, but references in them—to the wrongness of the war in Vietnam, I would say at least from '64 on.

King on many levels was politically advanced over many parts of his organization and saw a perspective that a lot of people simply did not see. And a lot of people were so absolutely single-mindedly focused on one way of dealing with the black condition in America that King's attempt to put it into an international context—not to forget it, not to secondarize it, but to put it into an international context—was just more than they wanted to deal with. You know, one of the major traditional statements by black people on anything that comes on the level of criticizing the government, about the danger of being considered a communist, is "It's bad enough being black without being red, too." So, that's the kind of thing that people were obviously concerned about, especially since the red-baiting was very much a part of both the government's and private citizens' attempts to discredit Dr. King.

The red-baiting seemed to be working. A Gallup poll conducted at the end of 1965 showed that 48 percent of all Americans believed there was "a lot" of communist involvement in the civil rights movement.

Harry McPherson was an aide to President Johnson.

HARRY MCPHERSON

Martin Luther King and Lyndon Johnson had a strained relationship. I remember sitting in the little room off the Oval Office with the two of them one evening. Johnson talked about his problems with trying to get over the agenda that King wanted in the cities and also tried to explain to King why we were unable to bring the Vietnam War to a close. It was a quite civil conversation on both sides. It was strained. And it reminded me as I listened to them that Johnson's relationships, his close relationships with black leaders, had been with those who, like him, were legislative leaders. Roy Wilkins of the NAACP, Whitney Young of the Urban

League, Clarence Mitchell, the lobbyist for the movement on the Hill, A. Philip Randolph of the Sleeping Car Porters, people who were accustomed to dealing with the political machinery of going and lobbying the Congress, working with like-minded or reasonably friendly members to fashion a legislative result. King was out there in the streets. King, I think, was the catalyst for the great movements that were made. King's suffering was the catalyst. His being beaten, his being hosed, his being put in jail, all the suffering that he endured, in every case brought a legislative response. So that the legislators, the Wilkinses and the Lyndon Johnsons, used that national anger and outcry against the treatment that King and his people had suffered at Selma and Birmingham and elsewhere, used that as the momentum builder to get the legislation through.

King had a sedulous enemy in the bureaucracy of the federal government, the head of the FBI, J. Edgar Hoover. Hoover tapped King, had his phone tapped, had his office tapped, and his home I suppose. I think Hoover on more than one occasion brought files to Johnson that were derogatory about King. I don't know how often and I don't know if Johnson believed more than fifty percent of what he read. He might use what he read to belabor those of us who said, "We have to be more understanding of King." Johnson would say, "You ought to see what I've seen about King." But at the same time he was too skeptical of J. Edgar Hoover to have believed everything he saw in FBI files.

The FBI files were about King's personal behavior in some cases and they were about his friends. There were several people who were advisers to King who had long FBI records. The FBI would often send over to the White House a file on a person who was being proposed for some kind of federal job or for a meeting with the president even. And those files would frequently include other people, who themselves had ties to communists. And very often, unless you remembered that they were getting further and further away from the subject, reading those files you got the impression that the subject himself, Martin Luther King, was a communist. This was hardly the case, and Johnson knew better and never proposed to make such a finding. But, oh, Johnson was bitterly disappointed with King's opposition to the war. And he was being told by Hoover that King had lots of procommunist friends who were advising him.

The wiretapping of King and some of his associates had begun under the Kennedy administration.

HARRY BELAFONTE

There were those who sought our confidence and worked their way into leadership positions who in fact were informers and whose specific goal was to assist in those state and federal institutions that were committed to our destruction such as certain forces in the Justice Department and the FBI. We knew we were wiretapped by J. Edgar Hoover and his boys and this fact gave us no end of inventive ways to pass along sensitive information that would circumvent this illegal invasion of the wiretap. However, in some cases there were people who we saw as allies to our cause, who we thought were people of fundamental goodwill, who were involved in wiretapping. People who we had reason to trust. To learn that the Kennedys, Bobby Kennedy and people in the Justice Department's civil rights division, were wiretapping us was a painful discovery. I remember Dr. King saying that if those who are to most benefit from our movement could do this, then imagine what our enemies must be truly like. When the columnist Jack Anderson first informed me of his personal knowledge of the surveillance of my personal life by the government, I was stunned to learn of the Justice Department's involvement. This fact notwithstanding, however, we still continued to do business with all of them, for they were the very government we were forced to do business with and the very government we wanted to win over to our cause.

When SNCC came out against the war in 1966, many other civil rights groups attempted to distance themselves from the antiwar protest. Whitney Young of the Urban League vowed that his organization would repudiate any group that had "formally adopted black power as a program, or which [tied] in domestic civil rights with the Vietnam conflict." Roy Wilkins of the NAACP said that SNCC was "only one of many civil rights groups" and that their statement against the war was "not the statement of other groups or of what is loosely called the Civil Rights Movement." King refused to attack SNCC for its stand on the war.

KWAME TURE (STOKELY CARMICHAEL)

When I was a young man in SNCC, even before taking a position of leadership in SNCC, [the relationship between] Dr. King and I grew on many terms. SNCC had made me in charge of receptions for him in many, many places. In Washington, D.C., while I was a student there, he came to give a talk at a nonviolent seminar where I represented SNCC. I was also given the task by SNCC to represent SNCC in meetings with him and to be of assistance to him there in Washington, D.C. This would be about '62 or '63. Of course, later on in our works we bumped shoulders. When I went into Atlanta I would go and eat in his house. Our relationships were very strong even where we had political disagreements. I'm reminded of the war in Vietnam. You know, the Student Nonviolent Coordinating Committee was the first one to take a position against the war and not only against the war but for the destruction of the draft. Of course, SCLC did not take this position. And at that time I was serving as chairperson of SNCC and, recognizing that we were being isolated politically, I instinctively understood that once King takes a position against the war in Vietnam, we will no longer be isolated. Thus, my task inside of SNCC politically was to put pressure on King to make him take a stand on the war in Vietnam. We understood from the people that I selected to help in this process that here we were going to use nothing but nonviolence, love, with him. You know, the statement was, "We're going to beat them with nonviolence and love." It was clear that his philosophy made it impossible for him not to take a stand against the war in Vietnam.

I remember one time, just joking with him, I said, "You remember"—I forgot the name of the brother, but there was a brother who he remembered and the brother was in Vietnam and got shot—I said, "You remember so and so?"

He said, "Yeah."

I said, "He got shot."

He said, "What? Where?"

I said, "In Vietnam. You told him to be nonviolent in Mississippi. He didn't get shot there. But he got shot in Vietnam. You should have told him to be nonviolent in Vietnam. That's what your problem is. You didn't carry your stuff like you say you're supposed to carry it."

King periodically included his views on the war in statements to the press and in speeches throughout 1965 and 1966. He had not, however, made a speech specifically about the war, nor had he clearly linked the civil rights movement to the antiwar movement. King also continued to speak guardedly when criticizing President Johnson's escalation of the war.

Dorothy Cotton had first become involved with the movement in the late 1950s through Wyatt Tee Walker, who was pastor of her church in Petersburg, Virginia. She joined the SCLC staff in 1960 and, with Andrew Young, ran the Citizenship Education Program.

DOROTHY COTTON

There was a lot of pain as he got negative feedback about his struggle with the Vietnam question. I really do know that it was especially painful when people purporting to be very close to him seemed to, I think rather callously, make comments criticizing the position that he was struggling with and that he was, in fact, taking.

I think at that time people had a rather limited view of nonviolence, first of all. Many of those people were family friends, some people who considered themselves to be deeply involved in the struggle but obviously had not really released their tie to old ways of thinking about things, and indeed did not think in the depthful, almost spiritual kind of way that was very clear in Dr. King's struggle with these questions. So I think some of the comments were rather flippant. That is, they were not thought through. But I think a few people seriously felt that Dr. King had no right to speak about the Vietnam War. Some people would say, "Your work is the civil rights movement. We cannot spread ourselves too thin. Our struggle is the black struggle here in America." Some people even limited it to the South and really were sort of circumscribing his work. Dr. King could not be limited that way. He could not be limited because he was a larger thinker. He was a larger person. He was, in fact, a leader. He didn't follow the crowd. He really did not ask, "Is this a popular position?" Whatever positions he took, he took those positions because he really was convinced that the positions he took were correct.

By April 1966 King had convinced the SCLC board to pass a resolution condemning the war. The SCLC annual convention in August issued a call for the immediate and unilateral de-escalation of the war, but many of King's advisers still discouraged him from linking civil rights to the war and from diverting his attention from the movement.

Marian Logan and her husband, Dr. Arthur Logan, were New York friends and advisers of King's who had provided financial support to SCLC for many years. Marian Logan was on the SCLC board.

MARIAN LOGAN

Most of the other leaders of what we call the Big Six were very against Martin's stance on the Vietnam War. As a matter of fact, frankly, at the beginning so was I. I'm not so sure Dr. Logan was really against it. He was more of a thinker, and he was trying to figure just from where Martin was coming. But we had meetings here at the house, where Whitney and Roy and Bayard, and Dorothy Height, and Martin would get around, and everyone as I remember was against coming out against the war except Martin. But Martin tried to explain, he really was dedicated to his feeling of the lack of morality in the Vietnam War, the same way he was committed to real, true nonviolence. Sometimes that interfered with the thinking or the machinations of others, who had their own agendas, or different agendas, maybe. Martin was very rigid about his nonviolence, and when he finally got around to the Vietnam War he was really bent on it. You could not move him.

SCLC staffer the Reverend Bernard S. Lee frequently traveled with King. In January 1967 he accompanied him on a four-week trip to Jamaica, where King planned to rest and write.

BERNARD S. LEE

He was writing his last book, *Where Do We Go from Here?* It was during a break—his wife, Coretta, and I had seen the [January 1967 *Ramparts*] magazine [article entitled "The Children of Vietnam"] and we just laid it down on the porch—and he saw the magazine and he was so moved by that one picture, seeing this mother and child napalmed in this straw hut and they're framed as they lay. Mrs. King and I were talking about something or other inside of the house. But he came in and said very clearly that he couldn't hold back his opposition to the war any further.

Before he left for Jamaica he had been under the persuasion that he could not speak out against the war because he needed to make sure that his concerns did not impede the progress of SCLC. But after he saw the *Ramparts* magazine, it just became very obvious to him that he'd have to speak out if he was to be the moral force not only in the country but in terms of the morality that rested in his own soul, that he had to be true to it.

King took a more forceful stand beginning with a February 25 address in Los Angeles. He participated in his first antiwar march on March 27 in Chicago, where he and Dr. Benjamin Spock led a group of five thousand demonstrators. King also agreed to speak at a "Spring Mobilization" demonstration in New York City on April 15. Andrew Young was dispatched to New York to iron out details of King's participation in the antiwar march.

ANDREW YOUNG

Coming from the South, where we had a disciplined, very specifically nonviolent movement in the Judeo-Christian religious tradition, the secular leftist radical approaches of the people in the Spring Mobe really shocked me. I thought it was a bunch of crazies for the most part. I mean, people were just so uptight, high-strung, bitter—I wasn't familiar with that. We weren't that way in the South. So I came back saying that he couldn't be a part of that movement as it was. He said he'd made a commitment. So I said, "Well, you won't even get a chance to make a statement there. People will be carrying Vietcong flags, wanting to pit you against Stokely Carmichael, and more than the issues it'll turn into a leadership struggle. You have to make your position clear somewhere." And I suggested that we ask Dr. John Bennett, the president of Union Seminary, to invite Martin to speak to a group of theological students on the war in Vietnam, where he would have a chance to fully develop his ideas. In a mass meeting speech you get five minutes; he needed an hour, hour and a half, to explain to the American people why he held those views. And so Dr. Bennett agreed to work with us. Well, there was so much interest in it, we moved it from Union Theological Seminary across the street to Riverside Church. And [historian] Henry Steele Commager, and Rabbi Abraham Heschel, who had marched with us in Selma, and Dr. Bennett agreed to comment on his speech.

The speech, scheduled for April 4, was sponsored by Clergy and Laymen Concerned About Vietnam.

Vincent Harding had several months earlier prepared a "think piece" about Vietnam for King.

VINCENT HARDING

King had the document and apparently thought that it represented his point of view sufficiently for it to be of help to him. So, when the occasion came that he was invited to speak at Riverside, because of the work that I had done on that piece, he asked me if I would do a draft for the speech. And so that was all part of an organic set of events in which his own point of view was always very clear that the Vietnam War was no good for the Vietnamese or for the Americans. And what I was doing was really simply providing the kind of solid basis for that kind of thing, especially the historical basis, for what he had to say about Vietnam. My sense was that because of who he was and because of what the situation was, that it needed to be as strong as it possibly could. And that it needed to be tied in as fully as possible with his role as freedom movement leader and religious leader and peace leader. The important thing was that this should be a reflection of the unity of his role in the struggle, rather than simply being seen as a kind of anti-Vietnam statement, but that there should be an attempt to indicate the organic nature by which this flowed out of his concern both for the black struggle in this country and for the health of the country at large and for the well-being of the Vietnamese people.

ANDREW YOUNG

Nationally, the reaction was like a torrent of hate and venom. This man who had been respected worldwide as a Nobel Prize winner and as the only person in America who was advocating change without violence, suddenly applied his nonviolence ethic and practice to the realm of foreign policy. And no, [people said,] it's all right for black people to be nonviolent when they're dealing with white people, but white people don't need to be nonviolent when they're dealing with brown people.

Martin gave a brilliant rationale for his position on the war in Vietnam, and as a Nobel Prize winner we expected people to take it seriously and not to agree with it, but to disagree with certain specifics and at least to discuss it as an intelligent position that deserved at least an intelligent answer. We didn't get that. We got instead an emotional outburst attacking his right to have an opinion, quarreling with his attempt to involve himself in foreign policy. It was almost, you know, "Nigger, you ought to stay in your place and your place is acceptable if you're dealing with racial segregation. But when you begin to talk about foreign policy, you don't have any right," and Martin quarreled with that. I mean, he didn't accept that.

HARRY BELAFONTE

[Before giving the Riverside speech, Dr. King] knew that the right wing conservative forces would stop at nothing to create the image of him as a treasonous, unpatriotic, ungrateful man who was not only betraying his country, but his own people and their cause. He was prepared for that eventuality, but he took refuge in his deep belief that responsible, very responsible, forces in this country would give him the platform to debate and define his position as not only morally correct, but to demonstrate that on every level of endeavor it was to America's best interest to support his position. Just a very short time, a matter of days, after his Riverside speech, Stan Levison [a New York attorney and King adviser] and I, in a private meeting with Martin, saw for the first time in a long time that Martin was quite distressed and during the course of our meeting he expressed his anguish over two articles that had been written, one in the *New York Times* and one in the *Washington Post,* that were scathing in their challenge and denunciation of his Vietnam position. He had viewed these journals as responsible instruments of information, but so distorted was their critique of him, he felt that there was now serious doubt that the responsible platform that he thought would be available for open debate and objective examination was now seriously crippled by the prejudiced positions taken by these two powerful newspapers. He knew now that his only hope would be in whatever support he would get from the American people and the moral correctness of his position. The only rage he expressed was at his own naiveté in not clearly understanding that his adversaries would emerge from even the most respected of sources, which he had previously considered supportive.

> On April 15, King spoke to more than 125,000 marchers in the Spring Mobilization demonstration in New York. He had included the war in Vietnam in previous sermons to his own congregation, but on April 30 he returned to the pulpit of Ebenezer Baptist Church in Atlanta to expand on the message he had delivered at Riverside Church.

KWAME TURE (STOKELY CARMICHAEL)

I was in Atlanta on the night before that Sunday King was going to make a statement against the war in Vietnam. He called and said, "What are you doing?"

I said, "Tomorrow's Sunday."

He said, "Are you going to be a good Christian and go to church?"

I said, "Well, like a good heathen, I'm going to work for the people. I've got office paperwork. I'll be working since six o'clock in the morning."

He said, "Well, I want you to come to church."

I said, "Come to church, where?"

He said, "The Ebenezer."

I said, "What's happening there?"

He said, "I'm preaching."

I said, "Well, you know, okay, I can always come hear you preach, you know. Because even though I don't believe in your stuff, you make me tap my feet, you know." We joked.

And he said, "Well, I really want you to come tomorrow."

I said, "Okay, I'll come."

He said, "Because tomorrow I'm going to make my statement against the war in Vietnam." And I think between us there must have been thirty-five seconds of silence.

And then I said to him, "I'm going to be on the front seat of your church."

And the next morning I got Cleve Sellers, I said, "I got good news for you." And we went and we sat in the front row of the church and he gave what I consider to be one of the most profound speeches.

The speech was very beautiful. I say one of the reasons why I have a great deal of love and respect for King was his love for the people and consequently his honesty. King was so honest that he could criticize himself publicly. And sometimes if one would listen to him the words he used were very sharp. In the speech on Vietnam, he has a quote, if I remember it correctly, it says, "There is a point where caution can become cowardice." And here he was speaking about himself, because when asked to make a statement on the war in Vietnam he kept using caution as an excuse.

He used words in that speech that I could never use. I mean, if I were to use those words I would be dismissed as irresponsible. But he said, "The United States government is one of the greatest purveyors of violence in the world today." Of course, you must understand the setting. It's made in his church. So it's his turf. I mean, anything he says here, these people will accept, not for any other reason except for the love they know that he has for them which he himself has demonstrated over years. They know this. From the fact that as a man he could get riches doing many other things, speaking in other bigger churches even, but he totally refused. So, when I say that he's in his turf and they will follow him, I don't want to appear that they will just follow him blindly—no, this blind following which he receives from his congregation, he merits from his service and his love of his congregation.

So you can understand the setting. He can say everything he said. He wants to, number one, first show that nonviolence has to be applied everywhere. It cannot be just segregated to the struggle of our people inside the United States. He wants to also show that it must be a vital force in the world politics and in world struggle. He comes to break down the isolation of our struggle in the States and to show the struggle of a peasant in a rice paddy. So what he comes to do is to link together the struggle of the Vietnamese and our struggle in a clear sense. He comes to show the necessity to stand up against your own government, to take a proper stand against the government if the government is incorrect. So he comes now again to show his law, which he's always said, that there are two laws, man-made laws and God's law. But this is the highest step because his breaking of man-made laws were breaking of southern laws, laws in the South which everybody had to condemn. But going against the United States government is another issue. As a matter of fact, he depended upon the United States government in its contradiction with the South, in his struggle against breaking the laws in the South. But when you go against the United States government, there's nobody upon whom he can call, except God, to help them seriously in his struggle. So here, whether he knew it or not, he was taking the conscience of his people, not just against the southern sheriff, not against Bull Connor, but now against the entire policy of the United States government in its foreign relationship to Vietnam—and obviously Vietnam only represented the top, the entire foreign relationship was the same.

The response was just like a shepherd leading his flock, going to give them water on green pastures. They responded. You know, I'm often amazed. People say, "You know, Dr. King, he speaks with such big words that poor people can't understand." No, King was a true teacher. I mean, he would teach. He would speak. Use all those broad concepts, but they would understand exactly what he was saying. So, his church understood precisely the struggle in Vietnam, the necessity of nonviolence to be applied there. The necessity of them to heighten their consciousness against the war in Vietnam, using their experiences from their own struggle against racism, and they came to understand properly that this position would put him in a most unpopular position and would lead him into complete confrontation with the forces. They understood completely.

20

Birth of the Black Panthers, 1966–1967

"We Wanted Control"

Black Panthers in Oakland, California.

In the 1960s, white police presence in black communities was a source of mounting conflict. Many of the urban disorders of the period were, in fact, touched off by black reaction to police action—the shooting of a fifteen-year-old boy by an off-duty police lieutenant in Harlem in 1964, the speeding arrest of a young driver by the highway patrol in the Watts section of Los Angeles in 1965, the killing of a fifteen-year-old youth shot in the back by a police officer in San Francisco in 1966. The resulting riots, or rebellions as they were called by many blacks, were not simply the community response to a single incident of brutality or perceived injustice. They were, instead, a reaction to years of such incidents, years in which black neighborhoods felt more threatened than protected by cruising police cars. Some activists who were reading the books of Frantz Fanon and others on the revolutionary left began to see their communities not as part of American society but as colonies policed by a white majority. The accumulating grievances against police, the growing suspicion that calls for "law and order" were white code words for more police, and the growing identification with revolutionary movements overseas marked a new kind of awakening in segments of the black community.

In Oakland, California, just across the bay from San Francisco, two young black men, Huey Newton and Bobby Seale, who worked at a neighborhood antipoverty center, were intent on channeling the growing antagonism toward the police while at the same time creating new programs to serve the city's poor. The police department in Oakland was aware of mounting criticism. It had recently circulated a memorandum instructing officers not to use language that "had a derogatory connotation" when in the presence of blacks. Terms to avoid included *nigger, boy, spade, coon, jungle bunny, ape,* and *head hunter*. The department had also organized a seven-person community relations section and instituted special efforts to recruit blacks for the force. Yet by the end of 1966, only 16 of the department's 661 members were black. Newton and Seale condemned that kind of token response and charged the department with continued brutality against black residents. One police captain said that such accusations were part of a "conspiracy against law and order"; another police officer asserted that "the majority of officers think . . . that 99 percent of all complaints [against police] are unsubstantiated."

Frustrated by police inaction, Newton and Seale founded a new political party in October 1966. Members of the new Black Panther Party for Self-Defense, inspired in part by the Lowndes County Freedom Organization in Alabama, would monitor the police and defend themselves by carrying guns, which, under California law at the time, were legal if not concealed.

But "an immediate end to POLICE BRUTALITY and MURDER of black people" was only point seven in a ten-point party program. Topping the list was power to determine the destiny of black communities, followed by the need for full employment, financial restitution for slavery and black suffering, decent housing, education that reflected black history and the black experience, and exemption for black men from military service. The last three points were release of all blacks held in prison, a demand for black juries in cases involving black defendants, and, finally, a demand for land, bread, housing, education, and "a United Nations–supervised plebiscite to be held throughout the black colony in which only black colonial subjects will be allowed to participate, for the purpose of determining the will of black people as to their national destiny."

The party platform and its social programs did not capture the attention of the white media, but the unmistakable uniform of party members did: black leather jackets, blue shirts, black trousers, and black berets. "Berets," Newton explained, "because they were used by just about every struggler in the Third World. They're sort of an international hat for the revolutionary."

The Panthers insisted that "picking up the gun" was a political act designed to galvanize the black community. But the image of young black men carrying guns on the streets of American cities also galvanized the white establishment. Later described by FBI director J. Edgar Hoover as "hoodlum-type revolutionaries," the Panthers had placed themselves on a collision course with the forces of law and order.

Huey P. Newton, twenty-four in 1966, was born in Louisiana and named for populist senator Huey P. Long of that state. The youngest of seven children and the son of a Baptist preacher, Newton was raised in Oakland. In 1966, he was attending law school part-time while working at the North Oakland Neighborhood Anti-Poverty Center.

HUEY NEWTON

It was in 1953, I think, that Oakland had its first black policeman, who was a friend of my father's. His name was Kinner. My father broke friendship with Kinner because of his membership in the Oakland police. Not because he was a policeman, but because at the time the policy was that Kinner could only arrest black people. He could detain a white, but he would have to call a white officer. And my father thought that this was degrading. It was no change from what was happening in the South.

The police, not only in the Oakland community but throughout the black communities in the country, were really the government. We had more contact with the police than we did the city council. The police were universally disliked. In Oakland, in October '66, when the party was founded, there was about one percent blacks on the police department. The police were impolite and they were very fast to kill a black for minor offenses, such as black youth stealing automobiles. They would shoot them in the back and so forth.

Bobby Seale, twenty-nine in 1966, was born in Texas. After service in the U.S. Air Force, he attended Merritt Junior College in Oakland, where he met Huey Newton in 1962. Both were active in the Afro-American Association and the Soul Students Association, and both pushed for courses in black studies. Seale, a comedian, musician, carpenter, and sheet metal worker, was employed at the North Oakland center in the summer of 1966.

BOBBY SEALE

In 1966, numerous acts of police brutality had sparked a lot of spontaneous riots—something that Huey and I were against, these spontaneous riots. And Huey and I began to try to figure out how could we organize youthful black folks into some kind of political, electoral, *power* movement. Stokely Carmichael was on the scene with Black Power.

Huey and I had been involved for some time, off and on, studying black history—what Malcolm had done, where Martin Luther King came from. I was highly influenced by Martin Luther King at first and then later by Malcolm X. Largely, the Black Panther party came out of a lot of readings, Huey and I putting scrutiny to everything going on in the United States of America. Like we must have subscribed to twenty-some-odd different periodicals, offbeat periodicals like *The Liberator, Freedomways,* what have you, even some periodicals out of Africa. We had digested Frantz Fanon's *Wretched of the Earth*. We knew Lerone Bennett's *Before the Mayflower*. I knew about the two hundred and fifty slave revolts that included Gabriel Prosser and Nat Turner and Denmark Vesey. I mean, Frederick Douglass, the Nation of Islam, what had happened in the 1930s, what have you and so on. And there we were with all this knowledge about our history, our struggle against racism.

At that time, Huey and I were working with the North Oakland Neighborhood [Anti-Poverty] Center on the advisory board. We got five thousand signatures for them to go to the city council, to get the city council to try to set up a police review board to deal with complaints of police brutality. Well, the city council ignored us. So that phenomenon was that the city council was just a racist structure which could care less about the forty-eight percent black and Chicano people who lived in the city of

Oakland. So there we are, trying to figure out what to do. We finally concluded through those months that we had to start a new organization.

HUEY NEWTON

Bobby Seale and I used the North Oakland service center as the original work spot to put together our program. They had all the machinery—mimeograph machines and typewriters. The North Oakland service center was a part of the poverty program. The service centers collected names of people on welfare, elderly people who needed aid. We used those lists to go around and canvass the community in order to find out the desires of the community. So we would go from house to house and explain to people our program. We printed up the first program at the North Oakland service center.

Our program was structured after the Black Muslim program—minus the religion. I was very impressed with Malcolm X, with the program that Malcolm X followed. I think that I became disillusioned with the Muslims after Malcolm X was assassinated. I think that I was following not Elijah Muhammad or the Muslims, but Malcolm X himself.

BOBBY SEALE

We sat down and began to write out this ten-point platform and program: We want power to determine our own destiny in our own black community. We want organized political electoral power. Full employment. Decent housing. Decent education to tell us about our true selves. Not to have to fight in Vietnam. An immediate end to police brutality and murder of black people. The right to have juries of our peers in the courts.

We summed it up: We wanted land, bread, housing, education, clothing, justice, and peace. Then we flipped a coin to see who would be chairman. I won chairman.

Huey Newton's title in the new party was minister of defense. Point seven of the Ten-Point Program, the demand for an end to police brutality, also stated, "The Second Amendment to the

Constitution of the United States gives a right to bear arms. We therefore believe that all black people should arm themselves for self-defense." Party rule number five added that "no party member will USE, POINT, or FIRE a weapon of any kind unnecessarily or accidentally at anyone." Other rules stated that no member was allowed to use drugs or be drunk while doing party work, and that no member was permitted to "take a single needle or piece of thread from the poor and oppressed masses."

BOBBY SEALE

We had written the Ten-Point Platform and Program of the organization but yet didn't have a name. A couple of days later, Huey Newton and I was trying to figure out why was it that on a Lowndes County Freedom Organization pamphlet that we had, why they had this charging black panther as the logo. Huey come up with some notion that if you drive a panther into a corner, if he can't go left and he can't go right, then he will tend to come out of that corner to wipe out or stop its aggressor. So I said, "That's just like black people. All the civil rights people are getting brutalized across this country for exercising the First Amendment of the Constitution, which is the law of the land. They can't go left. Other people have tried to control the police with law books and tape recorders and have been brutalized. They can't go right. Even the young whites who were protesting, I saw, who was in support of the black people, can't go left, can't go right. So we just like the black panthers." And in effect Huey Newton and I named the organization the Black Panther party. At first, it was the Black Panther Party for Self-Defense. Later, we dropped the "Self-Defense" because we didn't want to be classified as a paramilitary organization.

HUEY NEWTON

Most of the African countries were liberated during the sixties from colonialism. And we felt there was a need not for a separate nation, but for control of our dispersed communities. We wanted control of the communities where we were most numerous, and the institutions therein. At the same time, we felt that we were due, because of taxpaying, free access to and equal treatment in public facilities.

We felt that the Black Panther party would quickly become a national organization when blacks across the country saw what we were doing in Oakland—driving out what we called the "oppressive army" of police and controlling the institutions in the community. We felt that the government's next move would be to bring in the National Guard to recapture these institutions, and this would connect us to the international workers' movement, the international proletarian movement, such as was happening in Cuba. We were very impressed by the Cuban revolution. At the time of the creation of the Black Panther party, I was introduced to Marxism and I think I had read a book called *Materialism and Imperial Criticism* by V. I. Lenin. At that time, it was pointed out that there were many contradictory social forces, and if you knew what to increase or decrease at a particular time, that you could cause the transformation. So we were trying to increase the conflict that was already happening and that was between the white racism, the police forces in the various communities, and the black communities in the country. And we felt that we would take the conflict to so high a level that some change had to come.

The first action of the Black Panther party was to go down to Santa Fe Elementary School in North Oakland with our arms and be traffic police. I had attended this school. While I was there, many children were hit by cars and so forth. There was no traffic light in front of the school. There was a very busy street, Market Street, crossing the school.

At three o'clock, when the school was let out, we would stop the traffic and allow the children to pass. Of course, this would bring an army of police in the area. They would take over the traffic jam that would occur. And also they would attempt to arrest us for bearing arms. But they would become aware, which they were not, that the law provided for us to bear arms at that time. So we went to the planning commission of the Oakland City Council and asked them to put up a traffic light. They said they had already passed some policy to put up a traffic light but it would be about five years from October '66. We weren't satisfied with that. So we went to the community and gathered a few hundred, or maybe even a thousand or so, signatures. And took those to the city council. When the police were not there, we would police the area. And every time we would try, the police would take over, so the purpose was served anyway. The traffic light quickly went up, in about three or four months.

> The Panthers also began protesting rent evictions, counseling welfare recipients on their rights, and teaching courses in black history. On neighborhood patrols, they carried weapons, tape recorders, and law books. Panthers advised black people stopped by the police of their constitutional rights and used their presence to prevent unnecessary use of force by the police.

BOBBY SEALE

First we had to accept the fact that we might get killed or go to jail. But we were also sensitive to the fact that peaceful demonstrators were being brutalized all across this country. Their rights were being violated. Malcolm X had a particular influence on the Panthers in the sense that earlier he had stated that the civil rights people down south who were exercising the First Amendment of the Constitution, that's what he alluded to, were going to be violated by racists, and every black man who has a shotgun in his home has a right to defend himself. Even the Deacons for Defense in this context had an influence there. [Armed self-defense advocate and author of *Negroes with Guns*] Robert Williams also had an influence there.

You have to remember that we were dealing with clear-cut, fine points of the law. As long as a weapon was not concealed, we felt secure that we weren't violating the law. We studied all the gun laws. We knew them very well.

We started patrolling the police, six or seven of us, and I think we had one sister, she was packing a pistol, and I had a pistol and Huey had a shotgun and our uniforms and we had our Ten-Point Platform and Program and law books. I remember one of these first events when we got out of a car, we saw a policeman, you know, making an arrest of some kind, about twenty or thirty people in the community standing to the side, watching, and the black folks, one of them said, "Hey, who are these people? Hey, man, I'm going to move out of here, these guys got guns." And so Huey says, "No, brothers and sisters, it's not necessary to leave.

It's a new organization, the Black Panther party. We just observe these police in the community to make sure there's not going to be any more police brutality." And little Bobby Hutton passed out some of the Ten-Point Platforms and Programs, which had applications to join.

And it came down to the point where the policeman says, "What are you doing with those guns?" And Huey says, "Well, we've got to defend ourselves and observe you, the police."

"You have no right to observe me."

And Huey, with all this law study, because he was in night law school at the time, says: "California State Supreme Court ruling states that everyone has a right to observe a police officer carrying out his duty as long as they stand a reasonable distance away. And a reasonable distance was constituted in that particular California Supreme Court ruling as eight to ten feet. I'm standing approximately twenty-two feet from you. I will observe you carrying out your duties whether you like it or not."

And the black community is saying, "Well, go ahead on and tell it."

Richard Jensen joined the Oakland Police Department in 1965. He had attended the University of California at Berkeley.

RICHARD JENSEN

It was a hard thing to get to be a policeman. Only one or two out of a hundred applicants got to be. I was very proud of being an Oakland policeman. I was born and raised in Oakland. In my rookie class, there was maybe seventeen of us, from all parts of the country. Maybe five or six people from Florida, and a couple from Michigan that I recall, and a couple of fellows from Baltimore, and only a couple from the Bay Area. I was one of the two people from Oakland.

I tell you, we had a lot of problems in those days, however. We had a lot of militancy going on with the formation of the Black Panther party and also the Hell's Angels were the same kind of thing, only it was another group. We had a lot of problems.

Charles O'Brien was California's chief deputy attorney general.

CHARLES O'BRIEN

Every man is shaped by his experience, and I served as a nineteen-year-old in the infantry in World War II. I didn't think that guns solved an awful lot. I mean, we beat Hitler, but I didn't think that we needed to take World War II to the streets of California. I thought that the use of guns, even if they weren't fired, by these people, was extremely dangerous and could lead to real problems.

It's difficult to say what the reputation of the Oakland Police Department was at that time. I think there were individual officers who might have been somewhat aggressive because of their experience in the streets of Oakland. But I don't think the department, for the San Francisco Bay Area, had a particularly racist reputation. It had a reputation as being a pretty tough police department and perhaps a physical one. But it was difficult, from our point of view, in law enforcement in the Department of Justice of the State of California, to say that a police department should always go with kid-glove rules in a very rough environment. I don't think they had a bad reputation.

HUEY NEWTON

We started to use the symbol of a pig to identify the police. I don't know who first presented that symbol. But I knew that images had to be changed. Most of my young life I was a student. And I know sociologically that words, the power of the word, words stigmatize people. We felt that the police needed a label, a label other than that fear image that they carried in the community. So we used the pig as the rather low-lifed animal in order to identify the police. And it worked. The community picked it up and sort of put the police in another category, a category that was not respected, and a category that the community could deal with. And the police were very offended by it, so it heightened the contradiction between the community and the police.

George Whitfield was president of a black civic organization in San Francisco, the Men of Today, when he first heard about the Panthers. He later became a member of the Oakland Police Department.

GEORGE WHITFIELD

My response when I first heard about the Panthers was, "Well, maybe they are gonna be good for the community. The community needs leadership." The part of Oakland where they centered themselves was a very deprived, underprivileged-type place. So the whole city counted on leadership to come into an area like that to lead it. And it appeared that they might get some leadership from the Panthers.

They had a thing about police officers. That was Huey's whole spiel. His whole thing was that we were pigs. He didn't like the police. He didn't like law and order, more or less. You would stop a guy and he'd talk about you, said that you were an Uncle Tom. They just were not law-abiding people. I think the black policemen took more of his flak. They tried to tell you that you had to do things that white policemen didn't have to do, which was a lot of bull. But that was their style, you know. They tried to piss you off.

Elaine Brown began working with the Panthers in 1967 and became deputy minister of information when the Panthers opened a chapter in Los Angeles.

ELAINE BROWN

The party reached out mostly to men, to young, black urban men who were on the streets, who knew that there were no options somewhere in their lives, who were gang members because that was all you could be in order to find some sense of dignity about yourself. We reached out to these people because we had something for them to do with the rest of their lives. In most cases, they were used to violence, they were used to struggle, they were used to fighting just to keep alive. We offered them the opportunity to make their lives meaningful. Huey used to always quote Mao in saying, "To die for the people is heavier than Mount Tai," meaning to die for nothing is lighter than a feather, but to die for the people is something heavy, something heavy in the sense of meaningful, weighty. And a lot of brothers did make their commitment with that conscious understanding that coming away from the gang was something that they were ultimately building for themselves and for their community.

I was denounced by some of the women's groups because the question of feminism seemed to not allow for this element, this return to the community of the black male. I had grown up in a neighborhood where there were two fathers that I could name off the top of my head, that we knew of, that were still in the home and married or whatever. Most people I knew, and most people in many black communities, had divorced parents long before these statistics were popular. The image that we had, at least, was the father wasn't there. Or the father didn't do this, or there was the black male who was the weak figure, and so forth.

Here were men who were saying, "Listen. We are willing to take charge of our lives. We are willing to stand up." I mean, there was the appeal that Malcolm had in many ways, and it was the appeal that other people have had, but for me the Black Panthers were the ultimate. And so it was the men that I saw and the sense of being part of them and being so happy to see that they cared about me. I was a child who had no father at home, so that had a certain subjective appeal to my psyche and to my emotional need, to say, "Yes, there are men in this world who cared, black men, who cared about the community and wanted to do something and were willing to take it to the last degree."

Emory Douglas, an illustrator and painter, became a Black Panther in 1967.

EMORY DOUGLAS

My decision to join the Panthers was very easy. Once I seen Huey and Bobby and what they were about, and the positive energies and things that they were doing, I was ready to join. It brought a lot of pride. It was like being a part of a movement that you had seen on TV, and now being able to participate and share in that movement. You had heard and talked about Malcolm, seen Malcolm on TV. You had heard and talked about Stokely Carmichael, [H.] Rap Brown [Carmichael's successor as SNCC chairman], SNCC and what have you, and all the different things that were happening. And to become a part of a movement that had encompassed all these different concepts and ideals, in its own creative way, it brought a sense of pride. But there was also the doubts and the fear of whether you were going to survive or exist, which became a part of your makeup, and you, you know, went on and took care of business the way you had to.

My parents, my neighbors, were kind of reluctant or kind of standoffish in their attitudes toward the Black Panther party, because here you had a new, dynamic kind of organization coming out and doing things that never had been done in the history of this country before—carrying guns, standing up to the police, standing up to the power structure, demanding the rights that we were supposed to have.

HUEY NEWTON

A number of people who I knew had just come from Vietnam, and they helped train us in weaponry. Now, I had concluded that our main problem was an economic problem. So we decided to plan a bank robbery, of the main branch of Bank of America, down on Fourteenth and Broadway. We were printing up a little mimeographed leaflet with the Ten-Point Program at the time, and we planned to staple money to the leaflet and drive through the community, throwing the leaflets out. And we were hoping that the community would read the leaflet, that the money would encourage them to read it.

We had cased the bank and everything, and I said [to the people involved], "Who do you want notified in case of your death?" I explained to them that we would only know success coming out of the bank. And that if anyone was wounded in the bank, we would execute that person, so that that person wouldn't suffer a long period waiting for execution, and also so the person wouldn't be pressured to inform.

At that time I was reading Frantz Fanon, and I decided that the people that were involved with me was more important than the money. So while I would insist on being executed if I were wounded in the bank, I didn't think I could execute them. Which upset them very much, and they became violent towards me, because it took them a lot of fortitude to agree to that plan in the first place. They had gotten themselves used to the plan, then I withdrew the action, and they were very upset.

In early 1967, Newton and Seale found a new ally in Eldridge Cleaver, who had been paroled from prison in December 1966, after serving eight years for assault with intent to commit murder. Following his release, Cleaver had become a staff writer at *Ramparts* magazine, and had founded Black House in San Francisco, a center for political and cultural exchange.

ELDRIDGE CLEAVER

Malcolm X was killed while I was still in prison. He had started the Organization of Afro-American Unity just before his assassination. I had been part of the Black Muslim movement in prison, and when Elijah Muhammad and Malcolm X split, I went with those who followed Malcolm X. Black House was actually an attempt to start a local branch to resurrect the OAAU.

By the time I got out of prison, in December of 1966, we had a system-wide black organization going within the prisons. They'd basically shift us from prison to prison to try to break up local organizations. Over the years, it just became a situation where you had a general black rebellion in the prisons and a real strong black consciousness, and all this stuff was new, just beginning to happen outside of the prison, but it had happened earlier *in* the prison and in concentrated, very potent form. Because of the influence of people like Malcolm X.

At that time, they weren't gonna allow the Black Muslim organizations to hold religious services. And we had litigation in the courts trying to win that right, which was later won. But at the time that I was there, the only form of assembly that we were able to win was, we got our organization to have a black history and culture class. And so this became the proving grounds for many individuals who later on, as they got out of prison, joined the Black Panther party. I'm thinking of Alprentice "Bunchy" Carter, who started the Los Angeles branch of the party. He was in Soledad with me and he was part of this class that I just mentioned.

What we did at Black House was really to replicate, with more freedom, the experience that we had in prison. And what we had found in prison was the very powerful psychological effect on blacks when they would come into a controlled environment where black images were on display—black heroes, you know, from Frederick Douglass all the way down to Malcolm X. Literally at that time there was hardly anyplace you could go in the United States where there was a free expression of these images.

And when you came into an environment where black advocacy was very freely put forward along with these images, and everything of a black nationalist orientation, it had a very powerful impact on all those who came in, and it was a recruiting device.

You have to understand that at that time, Elijah Muhammad had put out such a damning opinion against Malcolm X that you risked your life by displaying his picture. Since I really owned Black House, 'cause I had rented it, I forbade Elijah Muhammad's picture to be put up, and put up Malcolm X's picture. And this was really the device that created the sparks for people to come to see. The more radical blacks at that time were of the Malcolm X persuasion, even though it was just coming into their consciousness. And when they were walking through the Black House and experiencing the cultural environment plus the speeches and things that went on there, we were obviously and consciously creating a Malcolm X–type mentality.

Sonia Sanchez was teaching courses in black studies at San Francisco State University when she met Huey Newton and Bobby Seale. She regularly attended meetings at Black House.

SONIA SANCHEZ

Black House was really the western extension of what we had done in a place called New York City, at the Black Arts Repertory Theatre. At the Black House, you saw [Amiri] Baraka's plays and [Ed] Bullins's plays, and we read our poetry, and you saw Emory Douglas's paintings and drawings. You saw people cooperating with each other. You saw students and Panthers and artists coming together there. There was a fantastic coming together. There was a great collage of people from Panthers to so-called cultural nationalists to students to people from black studies, and they supported each other.

ELDRIDGE CLEAVER

I was at a radio program in Oakland, and there were riots going on around the country and I was commenting on this, and really delivered a very radical message, patterned after, you know, Malcolm X. That was my ideal, and I admired the way he was able to handle questioners, antagonists, and the subject matter. Huey Newton and Bobby Seale came down to the radio station while the program was in process. And when it was over, we got together and talked. But it really didn't penetrate, because they did not have on their uniforms or anything like that, and I was meeting a lot of people at that time. I'd just gotten out of prison. I didn't, you know, really understand who they were at that time.

Right after that, we were talking about this meeting to put together the Organization of Afro-American Unity, San Francisco branch. And we were using the anniversary of the assassination of Malcolm X, which was in February. I had gotten together a group of the radical organizations in the Bay Area, and we had gotten so far as to invite Malcolm X's widow to come and give the blessings to a launching of this branch of the OAAU. Sister Betty had not been able to make any public appearances around the country from the time Malcolm X was killed. There was a lot of fear and so forth. This was gonna be the first time that she would make a public appearance. And many people were concerned for her safety. She wanted to be picked up at the airport and escorted to the places that we had designated. And that's when the suggestion was made that Huey Newton and Bobby Seale and the Black Panther Party for Self-Defense could handle that.

Huey Newton and Bobby Seale were invited to the next meeting the next week, at Black House. And so that was the time that I had first really focused on them, having met them at this radio program but not really understanding what they were about.

Oh, I'd say about eight or nine of them came into this meeting room. The whole country was in a form of rebellion and, you know, people were being killed all over the place. And in walks this organized—and I mean disciplined—*armed* group of black men. And it made a very powerful impact on everybody and particularly it got to me. The business at hand, which was to discuss the security of Sister Betty, was turned over to Bobby Seale and Huey Newton, who would meet the airplane at the airport and escort her to *Ramparts* magazine, where I worked at that time. It was on Broadway, the last block before hitting the freeway, in San Francisco. This was the most impressive building that we had access to. That was the reason we went there. We knew that coming from the airport with an armed escort, it would be really hot and smoking. We thought there would be some security in the fact that she was going to this legitimate magazine, because at that time *Ramparts* was very powerful and had a lot of clout.

> When they arrived at the airport, the Panthers were confronted by San Francisco police.

BOBBY SEALE

Some policeman in plainclothes came out and says, "What are you doing with these guns?" Huey said, "That's irrelevant. It's none of your business." So more policemen come out. He says, "Where are you going?" Huey says, "We're going to the airport." The policeman says, "You can't go in the airport lined up with guns like this." Huey says, "This place accommodates over two hundred people. We exercise our constitutional rights, and guns are not illegal. Be quiet. Bobby, let's go."

I say, "All right. Forward. Hup." We start marching. We walked into the airport, walked all the way to the gate, waited for Sister Betty Shabazz. We surrounded her. We came out. Police were walking everywhere. People with their eyes all bugged out. What are these guys doing with these guns?

BETTY SHABAZZ

I had gone to sleep on the plane and I woke up and we were landing. When I got outside, there was all of these police lined on each side of the little area where you walk from the plane to the terminal. And when I saw them all standing there on both sides, shoulder to shoulder, I went, "Oh my God, someone was on the plane"—and I didn't see them, you know. I kind of criticized myself for going to sleep on the plane. And as I walked to the end of the walkway and made a slight right and saw the brothers standing out there dressed militaristically, I went, "Okay, I understand." And there was a young man, reciting part of the Constitution about carrying firearms. And it really did something to me. I just said, "Oh, wow. That's just really fantastic." And so then I got in a car and was swept away. I certainly didn't have any fear.

BOBBY SEALE

We come out. We get into the car and we take off. We go to *Ramparts* magazine for Eldridge Cleaver to interview Betty Shabazz. The police came up, because there's two Panthers standing out in front of *Ramparts*. Several more police came up. Then some police came up and little Bobby Hutton was cussing this policeman out, telling him, "You ain't coming in here. You ain't got no warrant." The brothers begin to know a little law.

As we came out, Sister Betty Shabazz said she did not want any cameras. So Huey had a magazine and he put it up in front of this Channel 7 camera and the guy knocked it down. Huey put it back up. And then the guy hit Huey. And then Huey turned around and popped the cameraman, then turned around and said, "Police officer, arrest this man. He assaulted me." Imagine! Huey was telling the police to arrest this white reporter.

Then the police come around and start grabbing their guns. Huey says, "Spread! Don't turn your back on these m-f's." And the next thing you know, we spread. I put my hand on my gun.

The police says, "Don't put your hand there!"

I said, "Don't you put your hand on *your* gun!"

We spread it and we backed up, a real Mexican standoff. The other guys with the other group were gone with Sister Betty Shabazz. She'd been gone. And we got in our cars and we split and left.

> In February 1967, Newton approached Cleaver about joining the Black Panther party.

ELDRIDGE CLEAVER

Huey started talking to me about putting out the newspaper. And joining the Black Panther party. Well, at that time, my whole mentality was the Organization of Afro-American Unity, and nothing gets in its way. I had come out of prison with this whole plan, then the other people were coming out of prison, and we had taken a kind of a blood oath on this. So the idea of the Black Panther Party for Self-Defense didn't really grab me. I liked the armed action and all that, but I didn't really like the name of the organization. And we had a whole different vision of how we would staff the OAAU.

So what we did was kind of compromise with Huey Newton and Bobby Seale, and I wanted to know what role would I play in there. Huey had already taken the position of the minister of defense. And Bobby Seale was the chairman of the organization. We had a long discussion of, you know, "What's in a name?" To me, there was a lot in a name, and words were very important. So, to be consistent, and logical, we had to have a ministerial bureaucracy of the party, and it was actually in this discussion that I took the title of minister of information. 'Cause I was gonna be in charge of getting these publications together and being in charge of the information, and I wanted a very clear mandate to have control of that.

I agreed to start the newspaper, but if you look at the first issues of the Black Panther newspaper, it says, "Minister of Information is underground." And that was because I was on parole, and I was fearful that my parole officer would violate my parole if he knew that I had put out this newspaper.

Our first printing was ten thousand, and our goal was to reach the fifty-thousand mark. And we very quickly—I think in three issues—went to fifty thousand, and then beyond that, where we were easily reaching a hundred thousand. We had international demand for that paper immediately. And I think we had a very serious operation there. The whole bureaucracy of Black Panther offices started around the distribution of the newspaper. It was one of the most powerful and successful things we did.

Volume one, number one of *The Black Panther,* issued April 25, 1967, consisted of two sheets of legal-sized paper, with typewritten copy on both sides. The bold, handwritten headline asked, "WHY WAS DENZIL DOWELL KILLED?" Dowell, a twenty-two-year-old black man, was shot fatally in neighboring North Richmond by a member of the Contra Costa County sheriff's office. According to the Panthers, a doctor who investigated the killing told Dowell's family that the way the bullets entered the body indicated that Dowell's hands had been raised at the time he was shot. "Denzil Dowell was unarmed," the page-one article in the newspaper stated, "so how can six bullet holes and shotgun blasts be considered justifiable homicide?"

HUEY NEWTON

Denzil Dowell was killed in Richmond by the police, for allegedly tampering with the locks in the back of a store. We talked to the district attorney about his being shot in the back. And we talked to the sheriff, and they claimed that there was a justifiable shooting, because if anyone is suspected of a felony and he tries to flee, then he could be detained or captured, apprehended by any means necessary—including murdering the person. The sheriffs told us if we wanted those laws changed, we could go to Sacramento, to change the law. We said that we would go to Sacramento and talk to the legislature.

To protest the Dowell killing, and to voice their opposition to a bill that had been introduced to make carrying a loaded gun in public illegal, the Panthers planned to visit the state legislature in Sacramento in early May.

CHARLES O'BRIEN

The media, particularly television, liked confrontation. They liked the angry rhetoric of the Panthers. They like people waving around rifles. This made great news copy. The Panthers quickly discovered this. From our point of view in seeking to modulate the dialogue, to reduce tensions, they were terrible. They were absolutely terrible. They fed on each other, and the media was a pain in the butt.

BOBBY SEALE

It was conceived as a media event. The press is always at the California State Capitol. We arrived, all these black men and women—twenty-four males and six females—with guns, and Ronald Reagan, then the governor, was on the lawn with two hundred future leaders of America. You know, twelve- and thirteen- and fourteen-year-old kids. And these kids are leaving his session on the lawn and coming to see us. These young white kids thought we were a gun club.

I began to read a statement. Then I wanted to go inside to the spectator section. When we got in the hall, just imagine, there's a hundred press people. Cameras. Still cameras. Print media people backing up. And I'm saying, "Where's the spectator section?" And the press says, "This way, Bobby." In effect, they led me on the wrong floor and we wound up down on the floor. Some party members got ahead of me, with shotguns, pistols, and wound up on the actual floor of the California state legislature. And the press is not even supposed to go in there. They followed them in, taking pictures of Panthers with guns on the floor. I had to get the party members out of there. I says, "Come on, we're in the wrong place," 'cause I was ready to go to the spectator section.

So we come out. And not until after we left the capitol, two blocks away when we stopped at a service station to get gas and what have you, did we all get busted. In effect, what we did at the capitol was not anything. Later we were charged for disturbing the peace at the senate, which was a misdemeanor. And I wound up in jail for six months.

ELDRIDGE CLEAVER

I accompanied the delegation to Sacramento, but I went there as a reporter for *Ramparts,* and with my parole officer's permission. Although I got busted in Sacramento, they had to let me go because they could not find any TV footage of me with a gun. That's what the whole thing turned on. And then, when I got out, Bobby Seale was in jail, and Huey Newton got arrested, although he didn't go to Sacramento with us, but he got arrested right after that for some smaller stuff.

I began to see that the biggest problem that the Panther party had was its isolation, and the fact that it was not known, except to the police agencies, which was extremely dangerous. There was a need for some public speaking. We needed someone who could really get the message across. We had a need to raise bail real quickly, 'cause we had about twenty-five people who got arrested there. Then we got a whole slew of invitations from all the radical, liberal forums in California, and we were really short on people who knew how to handle that kind of public speaking task. So it kind of fell to me to do that.

CHARLES O'BRIEN

The Sacramento visit was a little upsetting at the time. The force that was up there was California State Police, which are not a state police in the sense of some of the eastern states, but are basically guards on state buildings. And sometimes, unfortunately, pejoratively referred to as "door shakers." And the door shakers, all of a sudden, had a number of armed, black, rather militant and strident types brandishing weapons and pouring in. And the Sacramento police thought this was a very serious problem. And it was. I mean, we didn't know what they were up to and when the calls came in to the state Department of Justice, we said, "What the Sam Hill is this all about? These crazy characters have escalated their actions again." Of course, they guaranteed passage of the Mulford Act, which changed the laws so they could no longer brandish their weapons—which may or may not have been one of the things they intended.

SONIA SANCHEZ

The whole image that went around the world of Panthers going into the assembly with guns was something that said, simply, "Don't mess with me." And I remember talking to some old folks at the time. They said, "Well, girl, that ain't nothing new. We always owned guns. We just kept them in our top drawer, you see." The whole point of the newspaper articles was simply that this was a new phenomenon, that we never thought black men had guns. But if you went south or out west, black folks always had guns someplace in the house. And you were told, "Don't touch those guns that were in the second drawer on the right underneath some shorts someplace."

The Panther party was probably a manifestation of Malcolm on many levels. It gave that sense of "We are men and not boys" in an arena with fathers. Don't call us boy. Call us young men, walking down the street. It was not new to me in terms of look, however, because I grew up in Harlem, where all the very hip people wore the black leather jackets, you know. I wanted to have a black leather jacket because all the so-called bad kids in our school had the black leather jackets and the black berets, and of course I didn't have that and the black skirt. So that was not new at all. That was a familiar kind of scene. And I thought they were very hip because I had always wanted to wear those kinds of things.

HARRY BELAFONTE

The Black Panthers did, in fact, cause quite a tremor in the movement. It wasn't even so much that they appeared to be, quote unquote, very militant and were prepared to bear arms, prepared to go down. That wasn't the problem.

The problem really was that there was such an inordinate level of intelligence that was the endowment of all those young men and women who came together. I mean Eldridge Cleaver, the book that he wrote, *Soul on Ice,* and Fred Hampton and Bobby Seale, all of them. I mean, when these young men spoke, they spoke with such rich vocabulary and such passion and such depth of commitment that Dr. King once said, "Were I able to co-opt those minds into my cause, there is no question that victory would be swift and eternal."

ELAINE BROWN

It meant committing your life. I mean, that's how we saw it. It meant that we had to surrender up something of ourselves, our own lives, because we believed that the struggle that we were involved in, which we thought of as socialist revolution, would take our lives. And so we had to surrender that. We had to make a kind of commitment. Now, whether we realistically thought we would die, most of us, I think, did, after a time. So it meant surrendering our lives to something greater, which was the notion of getting rid of oppression, and all the things that oppression meant and means in this country for black people and other people in the country. It meant not involving yourself in your self and whatever you did as a human being, whatever you were about. It meant really seeing yourself as part of a whole, and part of an entire process, and that you were a soldier in the army. That's how we saw ourselves—as soldiers in the army, and an army that was about bringing revolution, a vanguard army, as we considered ourselves, to introduce socialist revolution into the United States of America.

In July 1967, the California legislature ratified the Mulford Act, making it illegal to carry loaded firearms on one's person or in any public place.

On October 28, 1967, one police officer was killed and another seriously wounded in an early morning shoot-out in West Oakland. Huey Newton, with four bullet wounds in his stomach, was charged with murder, intent to commit murder, and kidnapping. For months to come, the effort to "Free Huey" would be the most pressing item on the party's agenda.

21

DETROIT, 1967

"INSIDE OF MOST BLACK PEOPLE THERE WAS A TIME BOMB"

Michigan National Guardsmen, Detroit, July 26, 1967.

In Detroit in 1967 confidence persisted that the city was immune to the kind of major civil disorder that had swept through Harlem in 1964 and through the Watts section of Los Angeles in 1965. Ron Scott, then a twenty-year-old auto worker, remembers: "The rebellion might not happen, maybe couldn't happen. Everybody was working, those who weren't in Vietnam. It was carefree, I mean, this was Motown, right? Everybody was having a good time. After work, the only thing you had to worry about was to get to the party on the weekend. A lot of money flowing. So people never felt there was anything happening inside of us black people. In fact, there was an article out at that time, I think, talking about the Watts rebellion, where Mayor [Jerome] Cavanagh and Governor [George] Romney said why 'it can't happen here.'"

Viewed from outside the black community, Detroit appeared unusual enough, enlightened enough, to escape a major riot. With two black congressmen, John Conyers and Charles Diggs, Detroit was the only city in the country to send more than one black to the House of Representatives. Many around the country believed that Detroit was a city that worked. In 1966, it was named All-America City by *Look* magazine and the National Municipal League. Since his election in 1962 with heavy black support, Mayor Jerome Cavanagh had been working hard to bring in federal money. Lyndon Johnson's War on Poverty programs had begun in 1964. By 1967, Cavanagh had obtained almost $48 million in poverty funds, and some $200 million in federal grants in all—for jobs, job training, schools, and recreation. Cavanagh was also credited with inventing the federal Model Cities Program. In addition, he had begun the process of integrating the city's mostly white police force.

There were other hopeful signs for a cool summer. The city's black community was organized and active. Detroit's NAACP chapter had the largest membership of any in the country, more than twenty thousand, and it was the most successful fund-raiser. Another civil rights organization, the Detroit Council for Human Rights, had staged a Walk to Freedom in June 1963, led by Mayor Cavanagh and Martin Luther King. One hundred twenty-five thousand Detroiters marched down Woodward Avenue to Cobo Hall, to support King's campaign against segregation in Birmingham, Alabama, and to protest unfair treatment of black people in Detroit. It was the largest civil rights demonstration up to that time, and predated, by two months, the 1963 March on Washington.

But viewed from inside the black community, activism and marches did not always translate into power. Some $38 million of the federal funds brought in by the mayor were for urban renewal, a government program black residents called "Negro removal." The new interstate roadways were resented because they divided and destroyed black neighborhoods, displaced residents, and created a mechanism whereby more prosperous whites could ride over or around the city's black poverty on the way to shop or play or work downtown. Blacks resented that their neighborhoods were further isolated, the easiest to condemn and the easiest to ignore.

Contributing to the discontent was the mostly white force that policed those neighborhoods, called an army of occupation by some black residents. Despite Cavanagh's attempts at reform, the black community continued to accumulate a long list of grievances about abusive treatment. The automobile industry, which had attracted so many black workers to the city in the first place, was also a source of bitterness and anger. The talk on the corner was of black workers being kept in the heat of the foundries and off the assembly lines, and, once on the lines, away from the supervisory jobs that could be the ticket out of the ghetto.

There were still many jobs, neighborhoods, places of business, where blacks were not welcome. To many, Motown was a hostile place.

The discontent in the black community generated a new and more militant leadership. One of the most outspoken activists in the 1960s was the Reverend Albert Cleage, Jr., pastor of the Central United Church of Christ, just west of Twelfth Street. More than a year before Stokely Carmichael issued the call for Black Power heard around the nation, Detroit already had its own Organization for Black Power, formed in May 1965 by Cleage and other activists. By 1966, a new group, the Forum Movement, was meeting at the Dexter Bookstore owned by Edward Vaughn, a store specializing in African-American literature and history. Forum members talked of the need for black revolution, and when the riots occurred in 1967 they would define them in revolutionary terms.

Black Detroit in 1967 was a community of contrasts. Strong mainline civil rights organizations competed for attention with black nationalist and separatist movements. A black community in which more than four out of ten families owned their own homes was in close proximity to more rootless renters, many of whom had been displaced by renewal programs. Black neighborhoods with well-tended one-family homes bordered areas like Twelfth Street's commercial strip, which writers of the time called "an ugly neon scar" and the "nastiest street in town." The tensions were not always black versus white; they were sometimes black versus black, and contributed to growing frustration.

Before the summer of 1967, FBI director J. Edgar Hoover had predicted trouble in eight or nine cities. Hoover's was an underestimate. The summer was to witness disorders in almost 150 American communities. The riot that raged in Newark, New Jersey, from July 12 through July 17 was the worst since Watts. In six days, twenty-six died. In Detroit, beneath the Motown sound, black frustration and anger were also growing. In recent weeks, Carado Bailey, a black, and his white wife had been harassed when attempting to move into Warren, Michigan, a white suburb; Danny Thomas, a black Vietnam veteran, had been murdered by whites in Rouge Park; and rumors (later proved false) were circulating that a white cop had murdered a black prostitute in the Twelfth Street area.

Early on the morning of Sunday, July 23, more than eighty black men and women were gathered to honor two returning black veterans from Vietnam. The party was held at a "blind pig"—an after-hours drinking establishment—called the United Community League for Civic Action, located on the second floor at 9125 Twelfth Street.

Shortly before four in the morning, Detroit police raided the club. The five days of civil disorder that followed were the worst in twentieth-century America in terms of what they cost in lives and in destruction.

RON SCOTT

A lot of people felt it couldn't happen in Detroit, because people had good jobs, they had homes, and generally it was a good time, it was carefree, and people didn't have anything to worry about. But you can't always judge things by how they appear on the surface. Inside of most black people there was a time bomb. There was a pot that was about to overflow, and there was rage that was about to come out. And the rebellion just provided an opportunity for that. I mean, why else would people get upset, cops raiding a blind pig. They'd done that numerous times before. But people just got tired, people just got tired of it. And it just exploded.

> John Nichols was the deputy superintendent of police. In the early morning hours of July 23, he coordinated police activities from department headquarters.

JOHN NICHOLS

The raid on the blind pig was not unusual at all. A blind pig is an after-hours liquor spot. The reason it was raided [after] three o'clock in the morning is that they don't start running until after the bars close at two o'clock. Generally it's a question of somebody going in, making a buy of illegally sold whiskey, notifying the crew, arresting the people, taking them into the station, booking them, and in most instances they're immediately bonded out. So it's a fairly routine thing. This particular time there was more [of a crowd] there than the crew expected. It required shuttling several times from the station to the scene, taking prisoners back and forth, and the crowd became restive and what was kind of a mood of hilarity grew into some derisive talk to the police and ultimately stoning of the cars. The police commander then did what had worked in many, many instances before. He backed the police out of the area, which in some instances had served to enable the crowd to leave without any particular loss of face, and they would mill around for a while and then go back home. In this particular instance, the crowd just increased and increased and increased.

We had had a visit, just a couple of weeks before the riot, from Dr. Martin Luther King, who met with city officials and who indicated that he thought Detroit was a most progressive city. In the areas where they had mixed racial populations, we were heavily into a program of block clubs, which put the police and the citizens into direct relationship with each other. We had had an experience the year before in the Kercheval area—the classical kind of a thing where a scout car made an arrest, there was a fight, and people came charging out of the houses. But at that particular time it was an afternoon shift, the department was at maximum strength. Automatically we saturated the area with police, and the neighborhood watch groups responded. They moved out, dispersed the crowds, and there was a minimal amount of damage. We figured that the system that we had and the modifications that we had made would serve us well. What we didn't figure was that what a young policeman told me on Twelfth Street the morning of the riot was true, that the rioters mobilized faster than the police did.

By 6:00 A.M., Twelfth Street was littered with broken glass and the first looter had been arrested. Police Commissioner Ray Girardin ordered a full mobilization of the department. Police also began calling the city's black leadership, seeking help. One of those contacted was Arthur Johnson, deputy superintendent of schools.

ARTHUR JOHNSON

The black administrative assistant in the police department, Hubert Locke, called me at about six-thirty in the morning. I think he called several people in the community who were regarded as black leaders to come to Grace Episcopal Church. He said we were in trouble. There was a situation developing on Twelfth Street that seemed to be getting out of hand. I was paired with the then young congressman John Conyers, and Hubert Locke passed out bullhorns, so John took the bullhorn and I drove my car.

John Conyers was first elected U.S. representative for Michigan's First District in 1964. He was well known to many in the crowd on Twelfth Street.

JOHN CONYERS

The streets were clogged. We couldn't get people to disperse. There was this mumbling going on, and you could hear in the background sometimes windows being smashed and stores being looted. Houses were being set fire to. The people that were milling around angry and belligerent were my constituents, were people I knew, were friends of mine, were acquaintances, and it was a mean-spirited kind of mood that hung over this. I don't know what impelled me. Someone had a bullhorn and here was a car out in the middle of the street, and I jumped up on it to make an appeal that we should all disperse, that we're going to get to the bottom of this, that we're on the case, and that nothing can be gained from us just continuing this kind of random attacks on our own community. It was after I got off I realized that that was a pretty dangerous situation. I mean, nobody said anything to me directly. They were mumbling and grumbling, "Go ahead on. It's too late for that." I didn't get stoned or drug off there, but you could see that there was a murderous tone about this whole thing. People were letting feelings out that had never been let out before, that had been bottled up. It really wasn't that they were that mad about an after-hours place being raided and some people being beat up as a result of the closing down of that place. It was the whole desperate situation of being black in Detroit and now, all of a sudden, there was no supervening force. There was nobody on top of you.

ARTHUR JOHNSON

Well, as I sat in my car, looking at that scene and listening to that scene, terribly aware that John Conyers is desperately trying to get the attention of people to persuade them to return to their homes, I had many thoughts. One, that there's a terrible distance, and some difference, between me and the people who are doing this. I was seeing something I had never seen before, and that was citizens, in all other respects normal citizens, and young people in particular, who pick up trash cans on the street, break windows of a modest little shop, climb in the window and take whatever they want, cross the street, and nobody's in a position to do anything about it. There was some laughter at some of this.

There was anger being expressed. There was the sound of sirens. I was quite frightened. I had never been so frightened in all of my life, because I'd never been in a scene like this, and I felt that, sitting in my car, I was witnessing a freight train coming at me, and that I was on the track and couldn't move off.

Albert Wilson, age thirteen at the time of the riot, lived near Twelfth Street.

ALBERT WILSON

Early Sunday morning, seven-thirty, which was the usual time for most of the kids in the neighborhood to get out and begin congregating in front of our houses or planning our daily routine or whatever, I came out to find that we didn't have a routine that day. The routine had been altered. There was no smell of chicken frying, which was usually the case on Sunday mornings. Mom's usually frying dinner, and you can smell the gravy and the cornbread. None of this was there that Sunday. My entire family was on the front porch looking in a westerly direction towards the scene of the riot at the corner five-and-dime. All the kids were being warned to stay at home, stay on the porch. I was forewarned myself to stay at home. Don't go. For some reason I went into the house and I snuck out the back door. I went through the alley very inconspicuously in the opposite direction of the houses around the next street to Twelfth Street.

It was kind of like a carnival, a parade, a party, because everybody that was there was laughing. No one was crying or worried. If you saw me running down the street, you saw me running with a smile on my face. I saw people running from stores with televisions but with a smile on their face. Everybody was happy. That's about it. Everybody was happy that day.

I think there was only one restaurant open, Howard's, a black-owned restaurant. All the prostitutes and early morning pimps were in there discussing the matter of how this occurred and everything. Everybody congregated right there. I saw all my neighbors there. And I moved further on down the street to the jewelry shop, where I saw a huge man carrying safes out, and this was all hilarious to us because we never thought those things could be moved. They sat in the middle of the store. No one ever thought they would be able to pick them up, but they did. I entered a couple of the places to see what was going on there—not to take anything out of there, though. One place caught on fire while I was in there, and I was actually trapped for a while with the fire.

After I got out of there I went home and then came back out on Twelfth Street, where I saw my neighbors again and this time we were going towards the five-and-dime. I had no sense of the danger that I was in. I wasn't scared. There wasn't a sense of gaining anything. It was fun exploring and doing something that you'd never done before. I felt kind of grown. I felt like I'm here but the rest of the kids are home, so I'm doing what all the grown-ups are doing. That's really how I felt. I was the only kid in the store.

I'm behind a partition with my neighbors and friends from my block when we hear someone say, "The police are coming." And everyone began to look for a way out. But the bars are on the door so there's no way out. So everyone finds a place to hide, and I was told to find a place to hide too. And I hear this police officer say, "All of you black motherfuckers, come out from back there." Well, I immediately get up and head for the archway of the door to do what he says, when I hear a voice. It was one of my neighbors, I knew it was her voice, and she told me, "Don't go out there. Come back. Come back." And at that time I went to turn to go back and get there next to her behind this bolt end of carpeting. I just remember seeing a flash of light at that time and going back there to lay down on a bolt end.

I woke up, I guess a couple of days later, to hear a doctor tell my mother that the bullet had injured my spine. At that point they had told her that I would live, but I wouldn't walk again. Then I knew that I was [permanently] paralyzed.

Helen Kelly and her family had moved to the Twelfth Street area after losing their home to urban renewal. This Sunday morning, she did not know of the crowds gathering in the neighborhood.

HELEN KELLY

I got my kids ready to catch the church bus and they went to Sunday school. When my daughter got to church she called back and said, "Momma, it's Judgment Day."

I said, "What you mean?"

She said, "Everything is burning."

I say, "Why?"

She said, "They say there's a riot going on."

And I almost had a fit behind that. And I was worried until they brought them back home after church, till they come home, thank God, in one piece. We kept them in the house and told them that you couldn't go outside because we didn't want nobody shooting to hurt them, and so everybody stayed in the house. My husband and all of us, we stayed in the house.

> The first fire flared after dawn in a looted shoe store at Twelfth and Blaine. By 1:00 P.M., four fires burned along Twelfth Street. By midafternoon, the looting and burning were moving west to Linwood. Mayor Cavanagh asked Governor George Romney to send in the Michigan National Guard. Romney agreed. By 5:00 P.M., black homeowners armed with hunting rifles and shotguns were taking up positions in front of their homes as youth gangs attempted to break into houses off Twelfth Street.
>
> By 6:45 P.M., the first National Guardsmen, including Howard Holland, joined police and state troopers on the streets.

HOWARD HOLLAND

They put us in the back of two-and-a-half-ton trucks at the time and we headed for downtown Detroit. I had never really spent any time in downtown Detroit, having lived mostly in the suburbs. I was twenty years old, had been in the guard just barely a year and a half at the time. I really didn't know what to expect, but I'd seen the stories of Watts and Newark on television. Looking out the back of the truck, I did notice that there were fires. The smoke was pretty heavy at that time initially, and there were many fires going on. You'd see occasionally fire trucks running everywhere, hoses laid across Grand River, you know, major highways, and just trucks bouncing over them to get there. I'd see people carrying some things out of stores. Windows had been broken. Some of the stores were on fire and there were still people going into the stores, even with them on fire.

By midnight Sunday, nearly a mile of Twelfth Street was in flames. Fires also dotted a twenty-block stretch of Grand River Avenue. Cavanagh had earlier ordered the closing of all gas stations to cut off the supply of fuel for Molotov cocktails. Now Governor Romney declared a state of emergency for Detroit and two neighboring communities.

Daisey Nunley owned a home near Twelfth Street.

DAISEY NUNLEY

It was getting darker. I was terrified. I didn't know what was happening, because everywhere I looked I could see flames burning. I looked towards Twelfth Street and over St. Agnes Church. I could see the flames just burning. Twelfth Street was just burning, all you could see was just flames. If you looked towards Linwood, all you could see was flames, and in the air you could see the ash just fluttering down. The smell of char, that burning smell, was in the air, and it was just smoky, the whole area. If you looked towards West Grand Boulevard, it was burning. Everywhere you turned and looked you could see nothing but flames. It was like they were just leaping in the sky, at night, and then that was when I really got terrified.

Bookstore owner Edward Vaughn was on his way home from Newark when the disorders began. To Vaughn and to other members of Detroit's Forum Movement, it "felt like the revolution was here. But it also felt like we were going to lose the revolution, because I knew that you could not defeat tanks with bricks."

EDWARD VAUGHN

We were coming from the Black Power conference in Newark, myself and two other brothers, and we heard on the radio that the riot was on in Detroit. And, of course, we were very concerned about it because, you know, our families were here, and we didn't quite know exactly what to do. However, we were not surprised that the riot came, because we knew that the unrest was there—it was seething, it had always been there, and we were not surprised that it happened. But we were concerned about our families and we were detained in Toledo, about forty-six miles from Detroit, for about three and a half hours and then we were allowed to go into Detroit early that morning around three A.M. We went in on back roads and we were able to get to our homes safely, and, of course, the next day the riot was on again.

HOWARD HOLLAND

As I went along through the city, I guess my initial feeling was, you know, how can people be doing this to their own hometown? They have to live there when this is over, and they're burning down homes and businesses and literally putting people out of business. At the time, my mother received a letter from my brother, who was over in Vietnam, and I got a chance to sneak a phone call home one night, just to let my parents know I was all right. And my mother expressed a thought then, and I guess it stuck in my mind ever since. She said, "Here I have one son in Vietnam in a combat zone, and now I'm worried about you in our own hometown, downtown Detroit, and you're getting shot at."

> Governor Romney was a contender for the Republican presidential nomination at the time of the riot. Within twenty-four hours of Romney's initial request for federal troops, Democratic incumbent Lyndon Johnson would use the riot to embarrass the governor politically.

GEORGE ROMNEY

Early Monday morning, after midnight, it was clear that the riot was increasing in magnitude, it wasn't being reduced. And furthermore, it was clear that the National Guard plus the state police plus the local police would probably not be able to handle it. It wasn't certain that they couldn't handle it, but after all we had a group of people out there trying to deal with it who were not trained to deal with riots. The National Guard had arrived late anyway, because the National Guard had been at an encampment up in northern Michigan, so they had to be brought all the way down. Of course, the situation grew worse as they were being transported down to the riot area. So it was in the early morning of Monday that we decided that we might need federal assistance.

Attorney General [Ramsey] Clark indicated when I called that we would get federal assistance, that the troops would be made available. Then he called us back several hours later to indicate that he'd have to have a written statement indicating that the riot was completely beyond our ability to control. The difficulty of that was that it would have nullified all of the insurance policies over the whole area, and furthermore, we didn't know with certainty we couldn't control it. We just felt we might not be able to.

Roger Wilkins, nephew of the NAACP's Roy Wilkins, was director of the U.S. Justice Department's Community Relations Service. On Monday afternoon, July 24, with the riot picking up in intensity, he traveled to Detroit with a presidential team led by former deputy secretary of defense Cyrus Vance. Earlier that day, he had met with President Johnson.

ROGER WILKINS

In the cabinet room, before we were sent to Detroit, the president wanted to make sure that the U.S. troops didn't kill anybody. And he said it in colorful language. He said it to us, who were going out there to direct the operation. He said it to the general who was in charge of the Eighty-second Airborne. "I don't want any bullets in those guns! I don't——. Do you understand me? I don't want any bullets in those guns!!!" He went on and on, and he just got himself all worked up. And he said, "I don't want it said that one of my soldiers shot a pregnant ni——." And he looked at me and his face went red and then he finished his sentence without finishing that word. He then sent us out to go and pack and then go over to Andrews Air Force Base to get a plane. Before I left, he called me over and he took me into his office and he wanted to apologize and he didn't quite know how. He walked me over to the French windows that lead out to the Rose Garden, and he looked at me and he looked down at the floor, and there you saw pockmarks on the floor. They were pockmarks made by Eisenhower's golf shoes. And he said, "Look what that son of a bitch did to my floor." Then he patted me on the back and said, "Have a nice trip."

GEORGE ROMNEY

Cyrus Vance and [Lieutenant] General [John T.] Throckmorton arrived, and in the evening they decided to tour the city. Mayor Cavanagh and I had been urging Vance to get the federal troops on the street, but before doing that he wanted to go out and take another look. And they unfortunately went out at about mealtime, so probably some of the rioters were [*laughs*] getting something to eat, because things had quieted down some. So Vance and Throckmorton decided at that point not to commit the federal troops.

The riot began to pick up after the dinner hour. General Throckmorton and I were covering the figures to indicate the intensity of what was occurring. And as it continued to mount, I became terribly distressed and concerned and asked to see Vance again, and confronted Vance with the necessity of getting those troops out on the street. At that point, he asked me to give the same sort of written statement that Clark had asked me to give him that I was unable to give. So I had to tell Vance, "Look, I've been through that. There's no point in going through that again. We need those federal troops out on the streets. If you want to blame me, blame me, but let's get the federal troops out on the streets." Now, he didn't order them at that point. I'm sure he had to confer with Washington, I think with the White House. I don't know it was the White House, but it was only two or three hours later that he ultimately indicated that the troops were out on the streets. And then President Johnson went on the air and announced that they were going to commit the federal troops.

I was leading contender for the presidency at that point. The polls indicated I was ahead of Johnson and everyone else, so that obviously was a factor in the situation. I felt that President Johnson was taking advantage of the situation politically. I knew that he must have known that the local police and the state police and the National Guard, they're not trained to deal with riots of that intensity. And that he had troops here who could deal with it because they were trained to deal with it. So I was convinced that he was undertaking to shift any blame from himself to me.

Harry McPherson was special counsel to President Johnson and sometimes drafted speeches for him.

HARRY MCPHERSON

The law says that troops can be sent in by the president upon the expression by the governor of the state that there is disorder that he is unable to contain. Johnson wanted Romney to say that before he, Johnson, ordered troops in. All during the night, while fires were breaking out in Detroit and violence was taking lives, Johnson moved troops up from Kentucky to the outskirts of Detroit. But he kept insisting that Romney make that statement. Romney, a potential candidate for president in '68, did not want to make the statement that he could not control the riots. He wanted Johnson to commit the troops and bring order to Detroit without his having to make that statement. There was a standoff for a long time. Johnson had sent Cyrus Vance to Detroit to serve as his representative and had held off all night. There are photographs of me and J. Edgar Hoover and Johnson and [special assistant for domestic affairs] Joe Califano reading the ticker coming back, getting on the phone with Cy Vance, waiting for this statement to be made by Romney. Finally, Romney made a statement which, while not squaring in all ways with the statute, was close enough. I went upstairs in the White House and wrote a speech for the president to make on television. When I got back downstairs, he already had one. I worked with him and some others on the language. We compromised on it, and I thought I was satisfied until I heard the president giving it. He made such a point of Governor Romney not being able to manage things in Michigan that it seemed too political to me. What he was trying to do was to establish that he had complied with the statute that the president only sends troops in when the governor of the state says, "I can't maintain order." But there seemed to be a certain pleasure on Johnson's part in saying that Romney can't maintain order in Detroit and so I've sent troops in.

Escalating violence in the city was brought home to the suburbs via television. Eleanor Josaitis, a white civil rights activist, lived with her husband and five children in Taylor, Michigan.

ELEANOR JOSAITIS

Television showed pictures of people in the street, it showed burning, it showed buildings on fire, it showed total confusion, it showed tanks coming into the city, it showed troops, it showed people looting. It looked like a war-torn zone. That's all you could think of was, my God, this is twenty miles from where I live and they've dropped a bomb. And there was so much fear that there seemed to me to be a sense of hopelessness. And that's certainly what I was experiencing. And again, the negative comments about people, and the name-callings—"animal" was the favorite term.

EDWARD VAUGHN

During the riots, the people who were looting or taking, the people who were in the streets, the people who were making the rebellion, by and large, were people who lived in the community, just average people. I came across a group of brothers, for example, who said they were just fed up and that they did not want to live like they had lived before, and every night they went out with their guns, and they shot at police, shot at National Guardsmen, and of course, went back into their homes. They cut their lights off. They did this on a nightly basis during the curfew. Most of the people were just community people who just had a sense that they were fed up with everything and they decided that they would strike out. That was the way that they would strike back at the power structure.

Howard Becker, an officer in the Michigan National Guard, led a convoy of troops into the Detroit riot zone from the guard training camp in Grayling, Michigan.

HOWARD BECKER

Consistently we were receiving sniper fire from various buildings or from down the street—not always knowing where the firing was coming from unless you happened to see the flash. So we would employ our troops to take cover behind vehicles, behind trees, alongside of buildings, to protect them, first of all, and then for them to be on the watch for snipers. Of course, when the fire department was ordered to evacuate the area, the police officers and the guardsmen stayed fixed in place and still had a mission to relieve the situation by containing the sniper one way or the other to allow the fire department the safety and security to come back and fight the fire.

The tanks provided a lot of security for the guardsmen, because it's heavy armor. Nothing that was being fired at them could penetrate. And so they could button up the tank and drive down the road and not worry about a sniper shooting at them. If somebody did fire on that tank, that also gave us an indication of where the snipers were located. And once locating a sniper, it was pretty easy to hustle them out of the buildings—the police and the guardsmen alike would go in and remove the sniper.

DAISEY NUNLEY

I had got used to seeing the soldiers drive up and down the street in the jeeps, and I had gotten sort of used to seeing the police riding four to a car, back to back, with their shotguns out of the window. I had got used to seeing that. The curfew was on and everybody had to be off the street. I came in the house, and my youngest daughter at the time was still in diapers, and I went upstairs to get a diaper or something for her and to get a washcloth out of the bathroom. And when I heard this helicopter and looked out the window, this helicopter was flying so low, until I could see the soldiers sitting in the helicopter. I could see 'em. And I looked to my right to the alley and saw this tank rolling down, coming down the alley with this big long gun on it. It was absolutely terrifying. It was just lumbering along and then, behind it, came some soldiers in a jeep. I thought, Oh my God, I thought that the tank was getting ready to level out our block. That's what my thoughts were. And I knew my children were downstairs, and I made a jump from the top step downstairs. I was screaming and hollering and I was trying to get them down to the basement, because I just thought that this tank was coming to shoot down the block. One of my daughters was cooking something on the stove—think she was making pancakes or something—but then I made her turn it off and run to the basement. And then we heard gunshots. I couldn't tell where it was coming from. All I knew was that our block wasn't being leveled. All I knew was that I was glad that they weren't shooting down our block.

RON SCOTT

We lived on the fourteenth floor of a fourteen-story building in the Jeffries Housing Projects. One night in July in the middle of the rebellion, my mother, my five-year-old sister, and my three-year-old brother were there. In public housing projects there are about eight apartments on a floor and we knew each other real well, so a lot of times we'd leave our doors open. On this particular occasion, everybody had closed their doors because they didn't really know what was going on outside. A neighbor of ours apparently had brought a rifle into the house and we heard several shots. I was looking out of the window trying to see where the shots were coming from. And the next thing we know, there is a blast of machine-gun fire coming past the building. We fall on the floor and turn out the lights. Next thing we heard, about two, three minutes later, was this pounding, pounding, pounding, pounding on the door. They were knocking like they were gonna cave the door in.

On my side of the door, I'm standing there wondering exactly what's gonna happen when I open that door. When I open the door, there are about four or five National Guardsmen. All young, all white, looking around, with rifles and bayonets. They come in our house, in our living room, they're standing there. And by this time, in the three, four days of the rebellion, there's been people killed. There's been people shot on the street, for no reason whatsoever. By this time, I'm angry, I'm fearful of what's happening. And this one guy says, "We heard some shooting here."

And I said, "There was no shooting here."

He says, "Yeah, we heard some shooting here." And this guy is standing looking at me—at any moment he can blow my head off, my sister's, and my brother's—and I know he didn't come there just to make a courtesy call. He's coming there because he assumes that I had a gun. And I knew that if I was shot, if my family was shot, that they could have closed the door on this apartment and nobody would have ever known what happened. When I looked in his eyes, and he looked at me, it looked to me as if he wanted to kill somebody.

And just then one of the other guardsmen said, "The shooting came from down here." They ran down to the guy's apartment where the shooting had taken place. As they were dragging him down the hall, a couple of them hit him upside the head before they dragged him on the elevator.

When I think about the fact that some guy, from outside of Detroit, who didn't even know us, could've blown us away, it makes me mad. It makes me mad and it makes me realize that, as my mother says, God was protecting us. I believe that if the guy who came in and said that the shooting was happening down the hall hadn't come in, we might not have made it. There wasn't anything I could do.

ROGER WILKINS

Detroit was probably the scariest place I went to during my years in the government. There was a curfew, and you'd hear shooting occasionally as you went around at night. It was eerily dark because a lot of the streetlights had been shot out. You were safest on the east side of town where the federal troops were. They were disciplined troops. They were not afraid. But when you got on the west side of town, which was patrolled by Detroit police, by the Michigan National Guard, and by the state police, you were in trouble. I never really felt that I was in trouble from any black rioters, or threatened. The state troopers were the scariest people because they were from out of town, most of them, and had very little contact with Detroit. They were from little places like Grayling and Zeeland, and here, all of a sudden, they were in big Detroit and there were all these black people that they were afraid of. And frightened people with guns are terrifying.

One of my jobs in Detroit was to go out at night to find out what the level of violence really was, because there was no accurate reporting that we could rely on. And one night a black co-worker and I were driving up Grand River, which is a major artery in Detroit, when a convoy of state police cars went past the other way, and troopers yelled out at us, "Get off the street, get off the street, there's snipers." And we continued up the street and we're going to make a left turn onto Joy Road when all of a sudden this convoy had turned around and had pulled us over and we were surrounded by people screaming at us, "Get out of the car, out of the car, out of the car." And normally I would have stuck my hand in my inside pocket and pulled out my credentials to prove I was from the Department of Justice. But I knew if I did that, somebody'd shoot me. So I came out of the car with my hands up, and I saw I was circled by people with long guns and pistols and they were all pointing at me and they were all nervous people and they were all white. And I'm a black guy and I'm a high government official but I was a nigger. A nigger in white America. And I thought at that moment I was going to be dead, thirty-five years old and dead at the corner of Joy Road and Grand River. Fortunately, somebody heard me screaming. They stopped pulling some other people out of a car where they were tearing their clothes, and they just stopped when they knew they had Justice Department officials around. We explained who we were, and the people [in the other car] explained that the guy was coming from work at an auto plant where he was an essential worker. So they admonished us to be careful and they went away. My legs were shaking. And I got in the car and this other car drove away. It was an old white Buick and it was spewing a lot of smoke, and I heard the guy scream out after the troopers, "Motherfuckerrrrs." At that point my legs stopped shaking and I returned to normal.

JOHN CONYERS

What really went on was a police riot. As a matter of fact, if anything, the addition of state and particularly federal law enforcement agents restrained the Detroit police. Because they saw this as absolutely intolerable conduct that had to be stopped by any means necessary. For example, they would shoot a person on a rooftop. They figured that that person might have a gun and would shoot them. So they would shoot at them first. They were misusing physical force and lethal force because they were angry and they were also frightened.

It was like a war zone. You have U.S. tanks going down neighborhood streets. You had all different kinds of National Guardsmen, police, army, all trying to coordinate. But the Detroit police were unbelievable in their determination to visit excessive violence upon the population. At the police stations, particularly at the Livernois station, they were mopping up blood on the floor.

This was obviously blood of black people that were being detained at the station. The violence was insane. John Hersey captured it in one of his books, *The Algiers Motel Incident*.

The Algiers Motel was situated at Woodward Avenue and Virginia Park, about one mile from the scene of the most serious rioting. On the night of July 25, Tuesday, in response to reports of snipers, Detroit police, state police, guardsmen, and U.S. paratroopers converged on the motel. Early Wednesday morning, three young black men were shot to death inside. Police reports indicated that the three men died in a gun battle. Residents of the motel said the men were unarmed and deliberately killed by police officers. An officer was subsequently tried for one of the killings and was acquitted. Three Detroit police officers and a security guard were later brought up on federal civil rights charges, and again acquitted.

The black community had been the first to hold a trial, called a "people's tribunal," at Albert Cleage's Central United Church, a month after the incident. Jurors included Rosa Parks, of the Montgomery bus boycott, and author John O. Killens. The tribunal found the police guilty of murder.

JOHN CONYERS

During the riots, our office became a sort of ministation in which people were calling in for help, assistance, family members missing, somebody's been arrested. The police stations were all overrun and the jails were filled. So they just created detention centers. And so people were calling up reporting what the police were doing or did or reporting missing people, people wanting to file complaints. Fear, anger. Could this be happening in America? I mean that you look out your window and you see tanks going down the street, and so the thing was an absolute madhouse.

James Ingram was a heavy equipment operator for Chrysler. On the third day of violence on Detroit's streets, restrictions on gasoline sales to private citizens were still in effect. Ingram was in a car with three other black men. They were arrested by state troopers for stopping to purchase gasoline at a service station and then were turned over to Detroit police.

JAMES INGRAM

We were taken to the Seventh Precinct—I knew that because the ride was very short—and the doors were flung open and somebody started yelling, "Run, niggers, run." And an officer started slinging us out of the van. I couldn't see that clearly what was going on in front of me, but I was the last one out of the van and I saw my brother in front of me being swung at. There were National Guardsmen on the right and police on the left, and they were swinging rifles and swinging these brightly painted red pickax handles and I was trying to dodge some of the swings. I don't know how I got through there with only being hit hard one time with a rifle barrel. That's what broke my right arm. We sort of ran, I guess as fast as we could. Some of them were really swinging quite wildly, but it was an experience I'll never forget. It was like I was going to myself, What have we done? I mean, we're guilty of Lord knows what in these guys' minds. I mean, they were treating us like we were hardened criminals or something. And all we were doing was attempting to buy some gas in a gas station. We were in the wrong place at the wrong time.

We were placed in a holding cell, which was rather large but still very crowded because there were so many people in there. At one point we were all talking and they brought in this white kid. I guess everybody at that point was black or Hispanic or whatever. And this young white kid came in, and some of the younger black guys, as soon as he got inside that door and the door was slammed shut, just charged him. He apparently was fairly alert, because he knew right away he was going to be dead meat. He literally climbed the steel bars of the door and climbed almost all the way up to the ceiling. I don't even know how he maintained his balance. At that point, Ross Mitchell and myself and several others just kind of prevailed upon the guys. "Leave the kid alone. He's not bothering anybody. He's in here with us. He may have been doing some of the things we were doing, you know, and he may in fact be innocent, so why are you trying to do something to him?" So, at that point, I began to think that this really couldn't be characterized as a race riot, although there was that white-black thing in terms of the schism between the police and those they were locking up. And I guess they were hurling their resentment of the police back at this one kid. And I didn't think that was fair.

Later on they took us to be fingerprinted and I was taken down this corridor with a young guardsman holding a rifle to my head. And I got to the end of the corridor and this really young kid, looked to be no more than sixteen, put a .45 automatic to my right temple. I was led over to this bench where a police officer grabbed my hand and squeezed it real hard and said, "Relax, nigger."

And I said, "I can't relax, this guy's got——. Why don't you have him take this gun from my temple? What am I, John Dillinger, going to escape? I'm totally surrounded by you guys. I'm cooperating."

And he said, "I'll teach you. I'll show you how to relax," and he put this cigarette out right on my hand. And it was just a pinpoint fire that just seemed to shoot right up my arm. I never knew that kind of pain existed. I mean, it was excruciating. I lost consciousness almost. I remember the one kid with the rifle. He grabbed me and tried to hold me up. And I never was actually fingerprinted.

I left the Seventh Precinct with a burning, raging fury inside of me. These people I'd have thought were guardians of the law and protectors of the people were in fact brutal racist oppressors, and I felt that they had to be wiped out totally. I had a personal mission out of that experience that meant that it was my job in conjunction with others to kill them all and make sure they had no chance of ever reproducing, that they were evil devils, much as the Muslims had said. I along with eleven other people formed something that we called the Order of the Burning Spear, and that was our primary mission—to kill white people, beginning with the police and guardsmen.

In 1967, Grant Friley was one of 227 black police officers in a force of 4,356 in the city of Detroit.

GRANT FRILEY

I was on Hamilton and Puritan, in Highland Park, on my way downtown to work, in plainclothes. I was stopped along with another fellow officer, and we were arrested and thrown in a car and on our way downtown before they realized we were police officers. That was terrifying, because they could have done something to me before they got to my identification. They saw the gun. The bulge of that gun was enough for them to put us in the back of their car and head downtown with us, and that was frightening because I knew what was happening in the city.

We all overreacted by the end of the week. Everybody was walking on pins and needles. It was self-preservation. And the rumors put all of us in a bit of hysteria. It was a very uncomfortable feeling. Whether you were a black police officer or white police officer didn't make any difference—you were very uncomfortable.

Being a black police officer during that time was extremely difficult. Black people would look at you and they'd call you a Tom. "You're a Tom. You're doing your job, but you're a Tom." Your fellow white police officer would look at you to see if you were going to *do* your job, okay? So there you were—here's a white police officer who was concerned about the black officer next to him, as opposed to just being concerned. And then there are the people that you're dealing with who are saying you're an Uncle Tom because you were a police officer. They didn't realize what this was really all about. They looked at the uniform and they saw that you were black and you were in the uniform, so you were the enemy.

I was tired, exhausted, frustrated, but I was a police officer, and I was determined to do the job that I was paid to do. And I wanted it to end. It was an embarrassment for me as a black man. It was an embarrassment for me to know that our city, the city of Detroit, was doing the same thing that the other cities were doing. I wanted it to end and go away, and it wouldn't go away.

It was crazy, to say the least, that you would hear young men and young women damning white people and saying "Down with the honky, damn the honky" over and over, and then you watch them torch their whole block, break in the very stores that they had to shop in. So the logic was crazy to say "Whites are no good," and then burn your own house. I mean, it didn't make any sense, and that blew my mind. I just didn't understand.

HOWARD HOLLAND

I believe it was a late afternoon, it was still daylight but not quite dark. We had gone into this one store. The front had all been burnt out black from soot, and obviously the firemen had already been there. There was water dripping, and we went in to search with the police officers to see if there was anybody in there. We went to the back and there was a storeroom or a meat locker or a cooler of some sort, and we opened it up and there was this guy just huddled up, afraid. He had said basically he'd lost everything, had lost his store. "What did they come back for? I'm the only thing left here that I have." He thought we were more people coming in to do harm to his store or to him. And we assured him that we weren't, and we escorted him outside.

HOWARD BECKER

About the third day of the emergency in Detroit, we discovered that some of our police officers—and this is an isolated incident—had loaded their own weapons, had their own special side arms and their own special shotguns. We heard discussion informally, and it was reported to me and to our intelligence people that they were strictly on a nigger hunt. And that gave rise to a lot of consideration on our part because we had a responsibility here. We followed through on it, and made sure that both police officers were handed over to their command and control and they were removed from the operations.

HOWARD HOLLAND

Our mission was to protect citizens in the city. They were very, very kind to us when we were there. I remember, I had some of the greatest food I ever ate during the disturbance. They would just bring it up to the gates of the schools we were staying at and offer it to us and just not accept money.

Across from Southeastern High School, I had this one lady that would just bring huge platters of pork chops up to the gate and offer it to us. As soon as she finished one platter she'd go back, an hour later come back with another huge platter—it'd be pork chops or fried chicken or something. And it got to the point where people would go over there and ask where she is if she wasn't there for an hour. The people, that was one of the best memories I had.

After five days, the civil disorder was over. It had been seen as a mindless riot by some, as a rebellion against conditions by others. At its peak, it had raged across fourteen square miles of the city, penetrated the business district downtown, and had come close to the wealthy Grosse Pointe suburbs. In all, some two hundred square blocks of Detroit had been involved; and the border to the neighboring Canadian city of Windsor had been closed.

The human arithmetic was bloody. Detroit police put final riot fatalities at 41. Of those killed, 17 were classified by police as looters. Two of the dead looters were white. Estimates of the injured ran from 300 to 600, and included 85 Detroit police officers. More than 4,000 residents had been arrested; more than 5,000 were left homeless and filled dozens of emergency refugee centers. Fire had damaged 682 buildings; 412 were total losses. Property losses reached $45 million. The last of 4,700 paratroopers left Detroit on Sunday, July 30. Governor Romney lifted the curfew on Monday. Two days later, Cyrus Vance declared that "law and order have been restored to Detroit."

In the aftermath, residents took stock.

ED VAUGHN

It wasn't Black Power that caused the rebellion, it was the lack of power that caused the rebellions around the country. People did not see any hope for themselves. People were beginning to be unemployed more and more. We had no access to government. We were still pretty much confined to the ghetto, and then our consciousness was being raised at the same time, and I think the masses of people made a decision that they would do something, and I think that they did.

We felt that we had accomplished something, that the riots had paid off, that we finally had gotten the white community to listen to the gripes and to listen to some of the concerns that we had been expressing for many years. I don't think that it was the call for Black Power that did it. I think it was the lack of power that did it.

After the rebellion was over, there was a strong sense of brotherhood and sisterhood. We saw more and more sisters began to wear natural hairdos, more and more brothers began to wear their hair in the new natural styles. More and more people began to wear dashikis. We saw a very strong sense of camaraderie in the community—that was all very good for us. We enjoyed that feeling.

HELEN KELLY

I don't see where the riot accomplished nothing myself but a lot of burned-up buildings, and people, some of them, lost their homes. So I can't see where it accomplished that much. But one thing I do know, that the people, they couldn't buy a loaf of bread or a quart of milk nowhere in the neighborhood after those riots was all over.

On July 27, even before the troops had pulled out of Detroit, President Johnson appointed an eleven-man commission on civil disorders chaired by Governor Otto Kerner of Illinois. Two days later, the president asked the commission for answers to three basic questions: "What happened? Why did it happen? What can be done to prevent it from happening again and again?"

The Kerner Commission's report was delivered to the president in February 1968. It concluded that "our nation is moving toward two societies, one black, one white—separate and unequal," and then added that "what white Americans have never fully understood—but what the Negro can never forget—is that white society is deeply implicated in the ghetto. White institutions created it, white institutions maintain it, and white society condones it."

Black reaction to the report was generally hopeful, white response was more negative. Vice President Hubert Humphrey questioned the conclusion that America was becoming racially polarized. Republican presidential candidate Richard Nixon said the report "blames everybody for the riots except the perpetrators." President Johnson found the conclusions hard to sell to the Congress and to the public. But privately, he said about the plight of the Negro, "He's still nowhere. He knows it. And that's why he's out in the streets. Hell, I'd be there, too."

HARRY MCPHERSON

The Kerner Commission reported back with a finding and a proposal. The finding was that we were headed toward two societies in America, white and black, affluent and poor. And the proposal was that we come forward on the federal level with a vast budget of social change. Johnson was, I believe, chiefly dismayed by the size of the budget. He was being asked by the Congress to cut the budget that he had submitted to Congress that year in order that there did not have to be a tax increase. And at the same time the Kerner Commission was saying, Don't cut the budget, increase it by thirty to forty billion dollars. He didn't know where he would find the money. He was frustrated and outraged that somebody would be putting that kind of pressure on him. Other people thought the "two societies" description was even more of a problem. Bayard Rustin thought that he would a whole lot rather have a lot of money for social programs than a psychological description.

JOHN NICHOLS

I didn't agree with much of what the commission found. I think that they attempted to do in good faith what was done, but I think that there was a lot of simplistic solutions that were offered as cures for very, very complex problems. For example, they made the point, as I recall it, that unemployment and underemployment was a factor. Most of the people that we arrested were people who had jobs. Most of them had factory jobs that were fairly well paying. Many other things seemed to differ from their findings as to what we knew being on the street scene. They cited a lack of contact with the people. I don't think that was true. I think that Detroit's block club system probably was one of the most sophisticated and the most active ones in the United States at that time. It didn't work on that day. But that is not to say that we were oblivious of the need. The department was moving toward integration. So I think that, all too often, those committees find a format and they put the format down and sweep all the little parts into it until it matches up with what they believe the situation should be, not necessarily always the way it is. This is not to say that they did it deliberately. I think that they did what they considered an excellent job.

It wasn't a race riot, as I see it. It was more of a riot designed to gain people's attention as a secondary thing, and as a first thing to gain property. We wound up with gymnasiums and garages full of stolen property, everything from sixteenth-century broadswords to modern-day washing machines. Some of the items that were stolen would stagger the imagination. Can you believe a guy stealing a two-story circular steel stairway? They caught a guy dragging that down the street. Or an individual with four or five television sets in the back of his car that he didn't know how they got there? Or an individual with a roll of carpeting that must have weighed two tons that crushed the roof of his car, and he didn't know how it got there? Certainly these are not the acts of people who are interested in social reform. They're interested in getting something.

I don't think that a social uprising includes damaging people's property or burning buildings, and certainly it doesn't include stealing. This is where I differ from many people. I think that when social problems get to the point where it results in criminality, then it's a criminal matter, not a social matter. There may be a social solution to it, but the act in and of itself is certainly criminal. A thief is a thief whether it's in a riot or on a day-to-day basis.

ROGER WILKINS

Having watched all the riots from '64 through '67, it was quite clear to me that the riots were an extension of the civil rights movement, not something different. Poor black people in the North had watched their TV sets just like everybody else and had seen progress being made in the South. Their racial feelings had been stirred just like everybody else's when they saw Bull Connor's police dogs, when they saw the rioters at the University of Mississippi trying to keep James Meredith out. Then they saw the Congress pass these laws in '64, '65. When they looked around, they saw that nothing, absolutely nothing, was changing in their lives. They were still poor, they were still jobless, they still lived in miserable housing, their kids still went to lousy schools. What I thought I was seeing in these riots was not what J. Edgar Hoover saw, which was a communist plot, but rather hopeful people who believed that the political system would respond to them. And it was kind of a jagged plea to the political system: Pay attention to us, we're left out, we ache. In a sense it was a hopeful scream, because these people had been awakened from being niggers who were beneath consideration to people who believed that the country could and would pay attention to their plight. Now, that's not to say that there wasn't a lot of thugs among the looters, that there weren't people who were doing it for criminal reasons, but a lot of it, in my judgment, then and now, was people whose racial consciousness had been raised.

I was astonished at what a terrific job the Kerner Commission did. They worked very hard, they were serious, and they issued an extraordinary report that said all the things that I would have wanted said. It was a mandate, had the president chosen to take it and say, "By God, we didn't know how serious the problem was. There is racism in this society, it is deep, and since I have said that I am going to be the president who finishes what Lincoln started," he could use that as a springboard for more social action. Instead, he refused even to have the commission come over and present it to him.

Basically he ignored the report, and that was the end of Johnson and me, really. I wanted to quit. Ramsey Clark, who was the attorney general, persuaded me not to quit on the ground that if I quit they would probably appoint somebody who was awful in my job, and on the ground that I was his closest friend in the department and he really needed me around. So I stayed, but I made a speech that I made sure got into the *New York Times*, attacking the president. And that did get on the front page of the *New York Times*, and the president never spoke to me again while he was president and I worked for him, which was the way we both wanted it.

22

The Election of Carl Stokes, 1967

"We Had to Be Organized"

In the 1960s, a visit to mayors' offices in big cities across the United States would reveal at least one common characteristic—all the mayors were white. In almost two hundred years of American history, a black had never been elected to run a major city. On city streets, however, were large numbers of black people. Although African-Americans represented only 12 percent of the country's population, they made up far larger percentages of big-city residents, a result of the large-scale migrations from rural South to urban North during two world wars.

In Cleveland, a city of 800,000, more than 35 percent of the total, or 300,000 residents, were black. They were mostly poor. At least half were southern-born. And their neighborhoods were surrounded by predominantly blue-collar European ethnic enclaves—of Poles, Germans, Ukrainians, Slovenians, Hungarians, Irish, and Italians. Competition for factory jobs and for turf between blacks and whites was a fact of life, and a source of tension.

Most of the white middle class chose not to compete for turf. As blacks moved into the city, white-collar whites moved out. Cleveland had fewer professionals living within its borders than any other city in the country.

The challenges facing the black community in Cleveland were not much different from those in other major cities. The needs for better schools, jobs, housing, were issues—as were inaction and inattention at City Hall. Also a prime irritant, as in most big cities, was the mostly white police force. Black mistrust of the police up north was at least as great as it had been down south.

In May 1965, relations between the black community and the police and Mayor Ralph Locher became even more strained when the chief of police stated that the death penalty should be reinstated in Ohio. "In Cleveland," said Police Chief Richard Wagner, "we have people saying they intend to overthrow the government of the United States and incidentally shoot all the Caucasians." Each day, for three days, five black leaders tried to meet with the mayor but were refused. On the third day, they sat in at City Hall. They were arrested and jailed. Locher had so alienated the black community that it seemed clear he would not receive the black vote in the 1965 election. The question was, who would?

Ignoring the black vote in Cleveland might prove Locher's undoing. The civil rights movement in the South, the rise of black consciousness and black pride, all had had a catalytic effect. Two black women, Geraldine Williams and Jean Capers, officers of the biracial Nonpartisan Voters League formed in 1964, traveled to Columbus, the state capital, to meet with Carl Stokes.

Stokes was no stranger to making history. In 1962, at age thirty-five, he became the first black Democrat to be elected to the Ohio House of Representatives. And he was no stranger to the street. Born in a Cleveland housing project, he had dropped out of school and literally fought his way up—working factory jobs by day, and fighting for fifty-dollar purses at night at local boxing clubs. Later, after serving in the army, he finished high school, graduated from college, and earned a law degree.

In the fractious world of politics in Cleveland and Cuyahoga County, Stokes had gained a reputation as a coalition builder.

CARL STOKES

I had been elected countywide to the Ohio legislature in a county that had only an eight percent black population. It obviously indicated my ability to put together the white vote that would be needed in a majority-white city. And it's a natural evolution of one who is in a profession to look toward the next echelon. In addition to which, the city of Cleveland was rapidly distinguishing itself as one of the worst examples of the urban crisis that was sweeping the nation, and black people were undergoing, perhaps certainly by degrees, greater deprivations than in other northern cities in the United States. And consistent with my own historical understanding about the evolution of minority groups into the mainstream of America, the next place for us to be was at the helm of one of the major cities.

Geraldine Roberts was a domestic worker and union organizer who moved to Cleveland in the early 1940s.

GERALDINE ROBERTS

I happened to have known Carl Stokes. We were all residents in the projects, in the community government projects. I could often look out my window on Sunday morning and see him and his mother, Louise Stokes, a neighbor of mine up the street where they came from, to pass my door and go in the church. He was not some big guy way out in the Heights. We loved him like a brother. He was like one of us poor persons down here.

I went to a meeting where Carl Stokes was going to be one of the speakers. I had met him when he was in the prosecutor's office there and we were proud of him, our neighborhood person from the projects. A poor Negro guy in this position was quite uplifting to our thinking. We had met him in this meeting, where some tenants of the Garden Valley projects was having some problems, and Carl Stokes came into the meeting. He was invited and he expressed his opinion that the present mayor at the time, he said if this particular mayor ran, he would even throw his hat in the ring if this guy was gonna run again. We felt that the guy wasn't supporting the people. And when he said those very words, myself including others, jumped out of our seats, actually left our seats, we were so excited that Carl said this. And it was the first time, I think, the kickoff point of his thinking in this particular community that he might actually run. And we stood behind him. We didn't want him to change his mind. It was great. And here we are ready for him to do whatever we could to help him. We didn't know what. We had to be organized.

CARL STOKES

The administration of Ralph Locher had been particularly punitive toward the black community in the city of Cleveland. We were faced at that particular time with a thrust from those of us who had been in civil rights and in politics of where to go, and there was a great deal of speculation as to the next step. In the process of all of this, former councilwoman Jean Murell Capers and a small group of people began circulating petitions calculated to draft me to run for mayor. I was not willing to respond to the particular draft by the Capers group, but this had been one of the things I had been considering and talking with people about and people had been talking about my doing. That, however, served as an impetus, from the number of signatures that were gathered, to make it something for me to seriously consider, and it had that purpose and effect.

On June 30, 1965, Representative Stokes presented the Cleveland Board of Elections with a petition signed by fifty-one thousand people to place his name on the ballot for the upcoming mayoral race. Stokes declared that he would run as an independent candidate in the general election.

Thompson J. "Mike" Gaines, a longtime CORE member, volunteered in the 1965 Stokes campaign.

THOMPSON J. "MIKE" GAINES

I went to Washington in 1963 for the march, and I came back inspired by Dr. King's speeches and his philosophy on how to get things done. I was a very angry man at the inequities in our society. And from him, I really began to feel that violence was not the way to redress our grievances. So, naturally, when Carl Stokes announced that he would be a candidate for mayor, myself and hundreds of other people felt that this would be a good way to redress our grievances through the democratic process.

Most of your so-called political leaders went into hiding when this young black man decided to rock the political structure in Cleveland, Ohio. These were the black political leaders. It was very simple: they had been leading the white establishment to believe that they had the black vote under their control and under their command, and in turn, they were getting their rewards—you know, patronage or what have you. But there was nothing coming down to the general black community. And when I say "coming down," the things that we wanted was better police protection, housing code enforcement, and things to maintain our community. We had a number of black councilmen at that time—off the top of my head, I know we had at least six or seven—but only one of them stood up for Carl Stokes. His name was James Bell, and he is now deceased.

So we did things quietly. We didn't call up the television station and say, "We are now trying to register black people today." We just went out and got the job done. And therefore we kind of caught the white community asleep. Because I don't think they realized we had the voting power we actually had. But in 1965, we also had a number of blacks that simply didn't come to the polls, because they simply didn't have the confidence that a black could win.

We would knock on doors and ask for signatures, and the first thing so many people would ask is, "Is he qualified?" Now mind you, here is a young black attorney that graduated from college, had his degree. At one time the president of our council was a high school dropout. And we've also had a mayor who was a high school dropout.

There was a certain segment of people who felt this can't be, the people just won't elect a black man. This is what was so hard in the role that I played, as well as hundreds of others, in knocking on doors to get people to sign petitions or come out to vote. It was just difficult to get people to believe in themselves, that we can do this if you just come out and vote. We brought out the fact that there must be something to the opportunity or the privilege of voting, and we would point out that people in the South were giving up their lives, sacrificing themselves for this right, being abused, driven off of their farmlands, off of sharecropper farmlands, because they were seeking to vote. Now we pointed out to the people that if these people are willing to make this big of a sacrifice to register to vote, and here in the North you have this opportunity, why can't you? And this worked in most cases. This was enough leverage to get the people to register to vote.

Geraldine Williams was Stokes's campaign secretary.

GERALDINE WILLIAMS

Well, in 1965, they thought the whole thing was a joke. They didn't think Carl had a chance, and only one elected official came out for Carl. That was James Bell in Ward Eleven.

In 1965, of course, we didn't have any money whatsoever, so every time a newsman would come, especially from CBS, and want a bit of news, what's happening in the campaign today, we would beg buttons off of him. And I think Carl Rowan was coming out here at that particular time. He said, "What are you doing with all those buttons?" We said, "Well, your buttons are our candidate's initials: Carl B. Stokes." He said, "You wouldn't." We said, "But we are. We're using them."

CARL STOKES

Maybe the most poignant little vignette was when we were in a motorcade coming down East Fifty-fifth Street and my wife, Shirley, and I were sitting on the backseat of the convertible. And a little black kid that was maybe eight years old, probably, came up to us as we were stopped at a traffic signal and he said, "Are you Carl Stokes?" And I said, "Yes." And he just gave a little leap in the air and ran down the street, clapping his hands, saying, "He's colored, he's colored, he's colored." I thought that sort of conveyed the sense of pride that I felt as I went through the black areas of Cleveland. It was also very sobering, I might say to you, because so many of the people were expressing in different kinds of ways about the confidence that they had, both that I would win and that when I won that I'd be able to correct all the wrongs and problems that beset them. And when you realize that people have that sort of feeling about you, that you're going to be some sort of savior from their dilemma, it's very sobering, because it imposes a great responsibility upon you. And I felt that quite keenly through that period.

Charles Butts, a white student at Oberlin College, read a newspaper article about Stokes's candidacy and volunteered to join the campaign. Butts had recently returned to Ohio from two years in Jackson, Mississippi, where he published the Mississippi *Free Press,* a weekly newspaper founded by Medgar Evers and other local activists.

CHARLES BUTTS

The *Free Press* really served the whole state of Mississippi. It didn't have a real large circulation, but it was the third-largest circulating paper in the state, which says a lot more about how many people read in Mississippi than how big it was. I did that from the summer of '62 until the summer of '64. Then I returned north. By then I was married. Certainly, in terms of politics, the cities in the North were where the political frontier was. And so I was attracted to that.

In 1965, the political pundits didn't believe that Carl Stokes was even going to really be a factor. They didn't believe that most blacks voted, and they didn't think that if they did, they necessarily would follow a black candidate. That wasn't the precedent. They had polled—and I did the same kind of polling—blacks that they had encountered just in the course of the day. They said, "Do you think Carl Stokes is going to win?" And the people said, "No." And I think they thought that he probably wouldn't. They didn't ask the second question, though, that I did ask. And that is, "But are you going to vote for him?" And they said, "But you're darned right." And they did. They may have surprised themselves, because their numbers and the intensity of their support resulted in an election that was close enough for a recount.

The recount showed that the incumbent Ralph Locher received 87,858 votes and Carl Stokes received 85,716. Stokes had come within less than 1 percent of winning.

In the spring of 1967, Stokes again tossed his hat in the ring—this time, as a candidate in the Democratic mayoral primary. Many of the same staff members, including Charles Butts, returned to work for Stokes.

CHARLES BUTTS

The strategy was to have the candidate campaign really equally on both the east and west side of town, in both the black and white community. Of course, the campaign relied on doing very well in the black community. And that's where their biggest campaign volunteer effort was.

I'd been able to arrange to get a downtown headquarters that would be the headquarters in the 1967 Stokes campaign—for free, which is the way you want to get it in a campaign. It had some ground-level office space that would have been ideal for our volunteers to do the traditional kind of activities, but it had a larger room that was just down a hall and up the stairs, as I recall. And as I was walking the candidate, Carl Stokes, through that first day and kind of laying out how I envisioned it, I said, "Up in this room, we're going to have forty telephones and we're going to solicit volunteers cold, out of the phone book." And he said, "Well, that's going to cost a lot of money." And I said, "Well, that isn't my part of the campaign." We did in fact have that phone room. We did solicit cold volunteers and ended up with what we called block supervisors.

MARVIN CHERNOFF

Charlie Butts called and asked if I would stuff envelopes, and I did. I put together a couple of what we call stuff-ins, and had my friends come in and stuff envelopes. I just became more and more involved until close to the end, I think, as I best recall, I was practically running it.

I was selling electronic calculators at an office machine company and, you know, I was a pretty good numbers person. I took a look at the number of voters and how we had to organize and they said, "Look, we've got to go around the Democratic organization and establish our own organization, our own precinct workers." And I said, "Well, why don't we do it this way?" And it was just something that came out of the sky. It was just blue sky. Never knew it would work. But we set up—gee, it was amazing, 'cause we had something like forty or fifty phones. And I decided—and it was the best thing I could have done, and I think it was just by mistake—that I'd have 'em all in one room. And we had some trained people who were regular volunteers who acted as supervisors. Gave 'em a script. The other thing we did, we had special phones put in—and this was ingenious—that didn't have hooks. You couldn't hang up. You had to put your finger on a button to hang it up. Okay? So every time you took your finger off the button, you got a dial tone. Which means you couldn't sit around and talk too much. You could joke about the person you just spoke to or make some comment, but you couldn't stand and talk for an hour. So it was really an ingenious kind of thing.

We bought the telephone books in street order, with numbers listed according to the street address. We broke each street down into segments, gave volunteers the assignment of finding somebody on that segment who would be willing to organize their block, to register the voters and get them to the polls. We kept calling down until we found somebody who was a Stokes partisan and would be willing to work. We called them a block captain, communicated with them several times before the campaign, wrote them personal thank you letters from Carl. And we had them report back to us how many people they registered and then had them work election day. It was a very strong organizational effort. It was one of the best I've ever been involved in, and I've been involved in hundreds after it. Never another one like it.

GERALDINE WILLIAMS

Anytime that we gave a gathering, we'd take the names of all the people that were there. Then we'd break them down as to precincts and where they lived, et cetera. And if they were interested enough to come out to a meeting for Stokes, we figured they were interested enough to vote for him.

Then we got the ward books and contacted all the precinct committeemen, especially in the black wards, to see if they wouldn't vote for Stokes. We took a crisscross directory along with our ward books to find out who was registered and who was not. We'd run their names simultaneously. Then we'd find those that were not registered, and we'd send somebody out to register them. We knew we had the votes, but we had to get 'em out.

James Naughton covered politics for the *Cleveland Plain Dealer,* which endorsed Stokes in a page-one editorial a month before the primary.

JAMES NAUGHTON

There was a front-page endorsement in the primary of Stokes which had the effect, as I recall, of saying to the establishment in Cleveland, "We think this guy is a legitimate candidate." This was regarded at the paper as a very bold step. I think there was a concern at the paper that there was gonna be an outcry. In fact, if I'm remembering correctly, they had extra telephone operators on that Sunday to handle what they expected would be an influx of calls about it. And sure enough, they had a lot of calls that Sunday, but it was mostly people complaining that the edition they got didn't have the Cleveland Browns exhibition game final score in it, which, I remember thinking, told me something about the influence of editorials. But it wasn't the general public at that point that I think the editorial influenced. It was the community leadership and chamber of commerce types of people.

Some saw the Stokes campaign as a sort of insurance policy against urban rebellion. During the summer of 1966, violence had erupted in the Hough area of Cleveland after a bar owner posted a sign that said, "No water for niggers." Four people died in the rioting.

CARL STOKES

Obviously, the white business community had never understood the sociological factors, or socioeconomic factors, that were going into the conflagration of the cities, and the only thing that they wanted to know was, "Is there somebody who probably will stop Cleveland from going up in flames?" No matter how often I told them, and others told them, that electing Carl Stokes isn't going to stop riots, they believed that, and since they were so disenchanted with the incumbent mayor and saw no other reasonable alternatives from the other candidates offering themselves, they found it easy to accept me with that very primitive reason.

I never thought I could keep Cleveland cool. I mean, after all, what was happening, the social phenomenon that was expressing itself in the rioting throughout the United States, all of the factors that were basic to that, were more than present in Cleveland and in many other places. So there was never any realistic reason for me to believe that. But from a standpoint of being able to evidence to the black and the poor people of Cleveland that I could do what they most wanted me to do—that is, to have a concern and interest in them, and to apply the resources available to doing something about them—this is what I knew I could do.

On primary day, October 3, 1967, the Stokes campaign sent 903 poll watchers to monitor the 903 precincts and report vote counts to Marvin Chernoff, who tallied returns back at Stokes headquarters.

MARVIN CHERNOFF

The television and radio were reporting the early returns, and the early returns always traditionally in Cleveland came from the white precincts. Early returns were showing Mayor Locher way ahead. I was getting my returns from the precincts, putting them into our machines—they were giant-sized electronic calculators, and all you could do was add and subtract—and I showed a Stokes win. One of the television stations gave the election to Locher. Carl Stokes came up to my suite, where I had ten people working on machines, and this is probably the only thing I really remember well. He said, "Marvin, what are these numbers you're giving me?" Remember, there was great hostility during this election, particularly with the police department. He said, "There are mounted patrolmen outside, the crowds are getting a little hostile, and Dr. King is on 105th and Euclid getting ready to march downtown with a big crowd." I said, "Carl, I know I'm right, and I know they're wrong. And you know, you just gotta stop 'em."

CARL STOKES

When we heard Hugh Danaceau from Channel 5 come on and project that Ralph Locher was going to be the winner, it was a source of great amusement to us because we knew that he certainly didn't have the information that we had. And shortly after hearing the broadcast, I just went out and told him that our own projections are that we would win the election by twenty thousand votes, which was greeted by the media there as that we must have gone off our bonkers or something, because the information available to them was that we were losing badly. Later that night, around one o'clock, in fact, our prediction came true.

Well, in the downtown area, it happens we were near the high-level bridge. And this is a very wide-open business area. And I don't know, there must have been ten thousand people there. As we came outside, they had heard the news. And people were laughing and literally dancing in the street and hugging one another. And crying, some of them, from the emotion of the moment. And when I came out, they just all closed in on me, and it was sort of a scary moment, but you just realized that this was an outpouring of love and affection and happiness at the moment. It was extraordinary. I often tell people the only spontaneous demonstration like that I'd seen in my lifetime was when Joe Louis defeated [Max] Schmeling in the second fight. And the black community just turned out. Just so happy.

> Stokes had defeated Locher in the primary by 18,448 votes, winning 96.2 percent of the black vote and 15.2 percent of the white vote.

GERALDINE WILLIAMS

You see, a lot of people had just registered. And they knew nothing whatsoever about voting. We had stressed so much that you must vote for Carl in the primary or you won't get a second chance. If you don't put him on the ballot, you can forget the whole deal. So they went out and voted for him. I think that was October the third. Okay. We said, "Now, we got to get them back to the polls again November seventh." So we had telephone banks going and we would call them and we would visit them. We'd have the block captains go see 'em, the block supervisors. And they'd tell us, "Already voted for him." We said, "Oh my God. We got to do a voter education campaign." We said, "Yes, but you just put him on the ticket. You've got to go back again and vote to be sure that he's the mayor." And that was a job. Because we had all these new registered voters that had never voted before, and we had a job on our hands.

Seth Taft was the Republican candidate for mayor. Grandson of President William Howard Taft, he was an attorney at a prominent law firm in Cleveland.

SETH TAFT

Frankly, I was very surprised that Carl Stokes won the Democratic primary. I thought at that time the incumbent mayor, Ralph Locher, would win. After all, that would be the normal thing to expect, that an incumbent mayor would win the primary of his own party. And I sort of campaigned on that basis. Now, during that period of the summer, since I was the only person who'd filed in the Republican primary, I had no competition. From the filing deadline in late June, early July, until October—that's July, August, September—the Democrats were having a rip-roaring primary kind of campaign, and I didn't have one. So I had to run my efforts in such a way as to keep me in front of the voters so they would know who I was. The guy who was running the media part of my campaign said, "You got to have something attractive." So we got an elephant and we went around and said, "Remember us in November."

Cleveland, you must understand, is a community that grew up primarily around the turn of the century, when the major immigration to the United States was from eastern Europe. Cleveland is a city full of nationality groups. When I arrived in Cleveland, if you can believe it, there were three or four daily newspapers in eastern European languages. There's one in Polish. There's one in German. There is one in Hungarian. There were probably fifteen or twenty weekly newspapers written in foreign languages. They tended to group in areas, so that there was a Polish neighborhood and there was an Italian neighborhood. Now, these people had come over, had scratched their way up the ladder and finally made it. And they were now happy with their lot. They'd worked hard themselves to make their way. They're all Democrats. I guess it used to be said this was because Franklin Roosevelt "saved our homes" from the foreclosure in the Depression.

These people were Democrats, but they were not comfortable with the newest wave of immigrants, which were from the South—black. Consequently, their attitude was, "Hey, we made it by crawling up the ladder. Why can't these new people make it by crawling up the ladder?" So there was a lot of feeling within the community, within this nationality-oriented community, that somehow the newest group weren't making it on their own. And this was somehow or other that therefore they were not enthusiastic about Carl Stokes. That's what it amounts to.

So right after the primary, we just had thousands of people marching into our headquarters saying, "We want to campaign for you. We think you're the great guy." They'd never heard of me before. So it made a very uncomfortable situation, I can assure you, when a whole batch of people rush into your headquarters and want to work in your campaign when you don't like their motives. On the other hand, if you were running for office and somebody said, "I'll vote for you," and you don't like the reason he's going to vote for you, do you turn him down? Do you say, "Don't vote for me because I don't like *why* you're going to vote for me"? So, uncomfortable as it was, I couldn't see any alternative but to accept those supporters. We fired a whole batch of them that went out and campaigned saying, "Hey, you wouldn't want a black mayor of this city, would you?"

Frankly, both of us ran, I think, a very much affirmative, nonracially oriented campaign. But the racial issue was like one postage-stamp thickness below the surface. It was sort of there all the time. It was very hard to get away from. Partly because there wasn't much difference between the two of us except color.

Carl Stokes

Because of our very close race in 1965, the eyes of the nation were focused on Cleveland in '67 with what seemed to be now to them a probable win here. And there were many people who wanted to be part of it. They ranged anywhere from Vice President Hubert Humphrey, who volunteered to come here or very charitably also said that he would understand if we didn't want him to come. He would either endorse me or oppose me, whichever one would help me. And we told him to do neither, but we did not let him come. Similarly, the national civil rights leaders who recognized the great importance of this election to the whole fight for freedom and equality had wanted to come here. We necessarily rejected them also, because in the delicate black/white balance, we knew that anything representing the Black Power movement would cause a detrimental political effort.

The realities of being elected mayor of the city of Cleveland, which was thirty-five percent black at that time and sixty-five percent white and white eastern European ethnics, was that you couldn't run a civil rights campaign here. You had to run a straight political campaign in which you blurred or eliminated the racial distinctions as much as you could. We had come through a primary election in which the white community had managed to put aside the racial issue. And now we came into the general election with a Seth Taft in which we knew that white people would find it much easier to vote for Seth Taft and that we must, to the extent possible, not inflame their basic prejudices.

In that regard, one morning, when we were reading the morning paper, there was a nationally syndicated story that the civil rights Big Six had met in New York the day before and decided that they would come to Cleveland to help Carl Stokes. I had not invited anyone to come to Cleveland to help me. And I knew that if we had such a group come here with black sloganeering and whatnot, I could forget about being able to capture the needed white votes that I would have to have to win this election. So consequently, my campaign manager, Dr. Kenneth Clement, and I contacted Dr. Kenneth Clark, who served really as an adviser to the major civil rights organizations. Arranged for Dr. Clement and I to go to New York City the next day. We met at the airport hotel. At that time, we explained to [the civil rights leaders] the political realities, that if they came there they would certainly upset the delicate balance that we'd been able to effect. And that we were sure that what they wanted us to do was to win in Cleveland, not turn it into a media event for Black Power demonstrations that would result in a political defeat. Although there was some resistance, Bayard Rustin and Dr. King prevailed and they agreed not to come.

Here in the city of Cleveland, we organized the campaign utilizing the local components of the persons that we did not use on the national level, first as organized labor members, NAACP, or Urban League. Those who were within the Black Power movement. We didn't have a Black Panther organization here, but we did have a Black Afro Set. They were very much an integral part of the campaign, worked very closely with us. Most important, I think, of all of the components of the winning campaign here was the black clergy. They came down out of their pulpit, made each of their churches a veritable political organization of itself, and provided the real winning thrust, I believe, to the whole campaign effort of 1967.

SETH TAFT

Early in the campaign, I had to be sure we had debates because Stokes was the guy who was well known. Polls had shown in early spring that he would beat me three to one in a general election. By June it was down to two to one. By October, it was about three to two in his favor. I knew that I had no chance of success unless I got him on a debating platform.

> Four campaign debates were scheduled. The second debate took place at John Marshall High School on Cleveland's west side.

CARL STOKES

The debate at John Marshall occurred in an area of the city which is a hotbed of hostile racial attitudes and antiblack experiences. The audience that night was about ninety-eight percent white and drawn from the John Marshall High School area. During the course of the debate, for whatever reason it is today—I can't recall—but I recall saying to Seth Taft, "Seth, you've acknowledged to me that as a Republican who doesn't live in the city of Cleveland, that the primary thing that you rely upon in being able to win this race is the fact that you're white and I'm black."

At that moment, there was a great outpouring of protest from this audience I described to you. And when the moderator was able to get them to subside a little bit, Seth Taft, who, I have subsequently learned, had been well coached if some statement like this was made, retorted, "Well, well, well, Carl. So now we really have the real issue out on the table. It's not fair for me to talk about race, but you can talk about it."

And then, of course, there was once again a great reaction from the white crowd there. The next day, the news media focused entirely upon that reaction and termed that I had injected race into the campaign.

This was not a spontaneous statement. I had decided I was going to say that that night. Dr. Clement had been opposed to it from the outset. The campaign press secretary, Al Ostrow, had believed that it should be said, and so Ostrow and I outvoted Clement's decision. It turned out that Clement was right, of course, insofar as what the reaction was. Not the accuracy of the statement, but the subsequent media reaction to it vindicated Clement's belief that we should not have made the statement.

SETH TAFT

Oh, I was armed. Because I had a feeling the race issue might come up. I would never have brought it up, but he finally felt that that was something he had to do, or wanted to do. And I had an old folder of different issues. When he made that statement, I yanked the folder out that said "Race" or something like that.

When I got up, I started off, said, "Well, well, well. So the race issue is with us. Let me tell you about it." So I pulled out a full-page ad from the *Cleveland Plain Dealer,* and all you could read was great big black words that said, "Don't vote for a Negro, exclamation point, vote for a man. Vote for a good candidate. Vote for somebody with confidence. Vote for Carl Stokes." Then I pulled out another one which said the same thing. Just those few words: "Let's do Cleveland proud." And that said do Cleveland proud by overcoming your prejudice and vote for the most competent person. Vote for Carl Stokes. So he had been playing this issue just barely off the most direct way of doing it. And this time, he really got into the middle of it. When that debate was over, that was clearly a potential turning point.

GERALDINE WILLIAMS

We were scared to death. I mean, we wanted to get out of there because you could just feel the hostility of the people. And we wanted to kill Carl for making that remark that would bring on this remark from Seth, because that was his very best remark of the whole night. And I'm sure that by Carl introducing this into the campaign caught him by surprise, but he certainly rose to the occasion, you can believe that.

On the next day, when Carl showed up in the office, nobody spoke to him, because they thought he'd really torn his custom-made britches, you know. I mean, he shouldn't have done that! And he was trying to explain to us why he did, and he always has a reason for everything that he does. Nobody bought it. So we sort of boycotted him that day, we wouldn't speak to him.

CHARLES BUTTS

The following day, Stokes did what I thought was a pretty strategically wise thing. He asked me to get everybody up in that phone room, which was our largest room. And everybody trudged upstairs. And then he spoke to them. He said, "Well, we had this incident last night. It may have been that your candidate made a mistake. But remember, your candidate isn't God. He's going to make mistakes. It's been our one setback, and we feel that the opposition has had a lot. And one mistake won't lose an election unless you let it do so. Just remember, your candidate can make mistakes." And he repeated that he thought that the candidate wasn't God. And it worked very well, because they vented against him for a while, and then kind of began to feel better, began talking about other strategies in the campaign, and the meeting ended.

I remember those people were filing downstairs, and they were stopping to talk with him. Then they had all left, and it was only he just getting ready to go down the stairs. And I said, "Carl, it must have been rather difficult for you to say that the candidate wasn't like God."

And he said, "Yes, it was. But I didn't mean it."

> The last of the four debates took place on Saturday, November 4, at the Cleveland City Club.

SETH TAFT

By this time, the campaign was the hottest subject in town. The debate went very routinely. But right at the very end, after the time we were supposed to go off the air, Carl pulled out a letter that I'd written him back in June. I had gotten charts up there about how much he'd been absent during the session of the legislature that preceding spring.

And he pulled out this letter I had written him in June saying, "Dear Carl: You've done a great job down in Columbus. Keep it up." So it sort of punched a hole in my comment as to how he'd been not attending regularly the sessions of the legislature. My manager said, "Did you write that letter?" I said, "Yeah, I guess I did."

> By election night, November 7, the race was too close to call. In a poll released by the *Plain Dealer* on November 2, 50.1 percent of voters polled had chosen Stokes, while 49.9 percent favored Taft.

CARL STOKES

We were at our suite in the Cleveland Sheraton Hotel on Public Square, and I guess there were probably about thirty-five people there. Some businesspeople. Others whose work had been done and were not in the streets to work that day. And we watched the evening go by, getting reports not just on the television but also reports that were being phoned in to us from the precincts. And as we came down through the evening hours after the polls closed at seven-thirty, and ten o'clock came and he was quite far ahead. And eleven o'clock came and Taft was still ahead. And then around midnight we began closing the gap. And about one-thirty in the morning was when our information came to us that all of our reports were in and we were just a little bit ahead. And about a half hour later, the board of elections announced that all of the precincts were in, had been counted, and I had won by a small margin. It was about two o'clock in the morning.

Of course, we were all exhilarated and we were all congratulating Clement and all the different people who had participated in the campaign. And then we went downstairs to an obviously hysterical crowd. And thanked them for their help and invited them to the inauguration, which would be only a week away. Then we were pleasantly surprised by Seth Taft and his wife, Frannie, who arrived at the celebration. Frannie had a box of roses for Shirley, which I guess that they had had just in the event that the thing went that way. We had a very cordial few moments with them and appreciated Seth for the kind of positive campaign he had run. And then I don't just remember. The rest of the night just goes into a blank, because we were just euphorious, and I don't know what all we did.

GERALDINE WILLIAMS

On election night, when we won, it sort of dawned on me and I think I broke out crying. We had beat the machine. We really beat the machine. It happened.

It was a first! I mean, it was quite important. We had done something that hadn't been done anyplace in the country before, and since folks laughed at us in '65 and we pulled it off in '67, I guess we felt pretty smug about it. And we were very happy about it. We said, "If it can be done here, it can be done other places." And I've always felt that started the trend, and I've always been very happy about that. 'Cause after then, black mayors jumped up all over.

Definitely there was a connection with the civil rights movement. We got blacks to register, to vote, to take part in government. We convinced them that if you don't speak out and ask for things, you're never going to get 'em. You can't just sit there. We taught them that their vote does mean something, that it counts.

> Carl Stokes had put together a winning coalition. With 95 percent of the black vote and close to 20 percent of the white vote, Stokes became the first black mayor of a major American city. He had beaten Taft by 1,679 votes.

CARL STOKES

My election on November the seventh, 1967, had a great deal of meaning to America because this was a city in which the black population was a distinct minority of the city. It illustrated the ability of white people to vote for a black candidate for mayor. To black people, it introduced a whole new echelon of political power. Now, instead of having to go and ask the white mayor for a job, they could go to the black mayor and expect a job. In looking at a police department, now they would know that the police departments were no longer without someone who would have some say over what they did in the black neighborhoods. To black civil rights people who had arrived at the summit by achieving the 1964 Civil Rights Act and the 1965 Voting Rights Act, this represented the next plateau for them to arrive at. And that is the involvement in the political process, which then would enable a system to go into the true economics of the country.

GERALDINE ROBERTS

We loved him. We loved his ideals, the things he was saying. He was hope. He was a change. He was giving life into masses of people who felt that they weren't very much. 'Cause I didn't think I was very much. I always thought that I was black and there was nothing I could do about it, nobody really didn't really love us. We loved our neighbors and each other and the pastor at the church and that sort of thing. And we thought that this was like years and years away. And here this man's gonna talk about this and then he runs. So it was like we were all dancing in the streets and thousands of people came and like we, we *slept* after that campaign. It was real nice to go to sleep and feel proud of yourself. And to walk downtown in Cleveland after he had won the election and see the smiles on the white community faces, white persons look at black persons with a different attitude, a different stare, a little smile like in their cheeks that this is all right. This guy is nice. These people are okay. Like a kid, if he can be accepted, he feels good that his mother and father likes him or likes her. And we felt that the community, for a change—I had kids growing up—that we could really do all the things we hoped. Kids in high school were so proud of themselves. And we always said, "You see, you can do it." Next to all that, maybe if Carl Stokes could run for mayor of the eighth largest city in America, then maybe who knows. We could be senators. We could be anything we wanted. And maybe America wasn't really as bad as we thought it was.

23

HOWARD UNIVERSITY, 1967–1968

"YOU SAW THE SILHOUETTE OF HER AFRO"

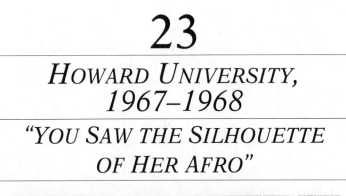

Student Assembly president Ewart Brown addresses protesting students outside the Howard Administration Building, March 22, 1968.

While Carl Stokes was running for mayor in Cleveland in 1967, black students in Washington, D.C., were launching a campaign to change the direction of Howard University. This was a period of ferment and redefinition for many Black Americans, and it was soon evident that electoral politics and cultural politics were different manifestations of the same rising tide of black consciousness.

Howard University had been founded in 1867. In its first century, it had graduated by its own count at least half of the nation's black physicians, dentists, pharmacists, engineers, and architects—all traditional routes to success in American society. But as the university entered its centennial year, some members of its faculty and student body signaled strong discontent with traditional Howard values. On

March 1, 1967, thirty-nine undergraduates disrupted the school's Charter Day ceremonies. One day later, five of its faculty and forty students staged a walkout at the centennial convocation. On March 21, students shouted down the director of Selective Service, Lewis B. Hershey, to protest the draft. The following day, another group of faculty and students announced the formation of a Black Power Committee.

In the months that followed, the number of protesting students would grow to the thousands. The university, they said, stressed white values and largely ignored black and African contributions in its academic and social orientation. They would shut down the school and would demand the resignation of its president, James M. Nabrit, because he was not radical enough. Ironically, this was the same Nabrit who had organized the first course in civil rights to be taught in an American law school, and who had been part of the team of civil rights lawyers who had mounted the legal challenge to segregation that resulted in the Supreme Court's *Brown* decision in 1954. And this was the same university that had graduated many of the other lawyers who had successfully battled civil rights cases for the NAACP Legal Defense Fund. But in the turbulent times of the late 1960s, working for change within the system began to seem out of step with the more radical activism of the day.

The Howard students of 1967 and 1968 were focused on another, younger tradition. They entered college after witnessing numerous examples of students changing the country—the students who braved the mobs at Central High School in Little Rock, the students who waged sit-ins and took part in the Freedom Rides, the students who worked and sometimes gave their lives in Mississippi during the summer of 1964. Many of these young activists were themselves Howard men and women.

This activism among Howard students was nothing new. In the 1940s, Howard students had worked toward integrating the U.S. Army; in the 1950s, they had pushed to integrate buses in Virginia; and in the early 1960s, Stokely Carmichael, Courtland Cox, Cleveland Sellers, and others formed the Nonviolent Action Group (NAG) to support SNCC and to engage in their own movement work.

As protest continued to escalate from 1967 into the next year, Howard students were again destined to lead. In the spring of 1968, while students across the country staged demonstrations against the draft and the Vietnam war, the takeover tactics used on the Howard campus were among the first of their kind in the United States.

Charles Epps, class of '51, was professor of orthopedic surgery at Howard Medical School and chief of orthopedic surgery at the university's hospital in the mid-1960s. His view of Howard and its role in Black America was different from the student protesters'.

CHARLES EPPS

I have very vivid memories of my parents telling me that life was not always fair and because of segregation and discrimination that I would face, I had to work twice as hard as the white man to get to the same point. And I accepted that, and in fact I found it to be true in life. Education was my ticket out of the ghetto.

When I came to Howard University in 1947 it was regarded by people all over the country as the capstone of Negro education. There had been many people who had graduated from Howard since it was started in 1867, and these people had contributed significantly to the life of the country and, of course, to the Negro race. There were still many outstanding people on the faculty in that time. To name just a few, in medicine there was Charles Drew, in physics, Herman Branson, in chemistry there was Lloyd Ferguson, and Percy Julian had been a member of the faculty there. In English there was Sterling Brown; in history, Rayford Logan and John Hope Franklin. In law there was James Nabrit, who later became president. Of course, at that time Mordecai Johnson was president. These were all people who had played a significant role in the life of the university and in the life of the country as well. And so it made me feel very proud to be a member of that academic community, and it afforded me an opportunity to get a first-class education from teachers who were revered not only by the students but who were recognized as authorities by the nation at large.

For a new generation of Howard students, getting a ticket out of the ghetto was not necessarily the reason they came to Howard.

ROBIN GREGORY

When I first went to Howard it was in 1962. The first year was pretty uneventful. I was just studying. One thing I do remember was the sort of provincial mindset that was there. Like, one of the things that first happened when we went there was that all the women had a special assembly. Patricia Harris was the dean of women at that time, and we had this lecture on etiquette, and how we were supposed to dress, and how we were supposed to behave. And we were supposed to be ladies [*laughs*]. I didn't quite accept that for myself, and I didn't feel like I had to conform to that sort of thing either, because I didn't live on the campus. I lived in Washington, D.C.

Most of the students were middle class and they wanted to be good. They wanted to succeed, and they wanted to have a good time. A lot of them were looking for husbands, I remember that. I felt that there wasn't a lot of deep thinking going on among the students that were there when I first went there.

That next summer, I worked on the March on Washington Committee, and I met a lot of people through that. I was in the strategic offices setting the whole thing up, before, during, and after. So that was my first introduction to the movement.

The summer of 1964 I was the liaison in the Washington, D.C., SNCC office for the voter registration project in the South, Mississippi specifically. The liaison part was that people would call me from Mississippi in the office to chronicle some of the incidents that would happen, so that I could contact the attorney general's office and report. That summer was the 1964 Democratic convention. I went to Atlantic City, and some women from Mississippi came up and they were wearing their hair natural. I was real turned on by that statement. In the fifties I had an aunt who was wearing her hair in a natural. It was a real radical thing to do, and everybody in the family always talked about her, so it wasn't something that was completely foreign, the image itself, but it was exciting for me to see that somebody was doing it. I felt it was an affirmation of being who we were. The energy was very high, emotion was very high. Getting a sense of who we were and what we were doing was really acute at the time. And I just decided that I was going to wear my hair that way, and make a statement that way.

When I came back home, and I was wearing my hair like that, my family was pretty horrified. And I got a lot of comments from people on the street. People got angry about it. It was like I was exposing a secret. That was the first reaction. That reaction went a long time, because I didn't have a lot of company. Maybe one or two other people were doing it. Well, there was one person in particular who had worn her hair like that for a year prior to that, or maybe even two, and that was Mary Lovelace, who was Stokely Carmichael's girlfriend at the time. So there was a precedent before that, but the response was pretty negative.

ADRIENNE MANNS

When I first came to Howard in 1964, I came there expecting a black environment. I came out of a white high school and white town; we were in a minority. I was coming to Howard because I wanted black people, black teachers, and positive role models and all of this. When I got there, first of all, I knew I was out of place because my roommates had to have an extra closet brought into the dormitory room. People were going to class in high heels. It was just a totally bourgeois environment, unlike the one I'd come from. I really had never known any middle-class black people except for a doctor and a teacher. So I felt out of place. I felt alone. I didn't have any good friends for about a year and I thought I had made a mistake.

I came looking for black history courses, black literature, black music. It was a kind of void in my life I wanted filled. Black studies is what it was called. Sterling Brown was there, which was very exciting because he was a poet I had admired for a long time, and Arthur Davis. I was expecting to study black literature with Sterling Brown, and what I found was he told us that he could not teach black literature, that it did not fit into the curriculum and it was not offered. There was only one course and that was "Negro History" and you had to be a history major or an upperclassman to take that. And you couldn't fit it in your schedule. After you got finished with all the humanities and the Western Civ. type of courses, you couldn't fit that one course in. It was very hard to get in.

There was no music. You couldn't play jazz in the Fine Arts Building. All you heard when you passed the Fine Arts Building was opera—all day long, opera, opera, opera. And so-called classical music, National Symphony, and this kind of thing. So I was very disappointed and, well, I think they said they were making it the black Harvard or something like that. And it was just not what I wanted.

There were two things that got me involved politically and helped me move out of where I was to somewhat more consciousness. One of them was when one of the students was expelled from school because she had stayed out overnight, violated the curfew regulations. And for this she was not only put out of the dorm, but they put her out of the college altogether. And Jay Greene, who was a law student, he started supporting her and taking up her case. And he would come out at lunchtime in front of the law school and there would be rallies. So I started coming to the rallies. I was working on the newspaper as a reporter my freshman year and we were covering the story. And the editor of the newspaper was interested in it. I think he was friends with Jay. So I started following this case and Jay was saying that we had no rights as students, that she should at least have a hearing, that it wasn't right for her to be put out of school with no hearing. And that was the first time that really I began to think that, well, maybe there were others who didn't like the situation and there were other people concerned and they were willing to do something.

The next thing that happened was second semester, I believe it was, when the Selma campaign took place, and we were in freshman assembly, which was a mandatory gathering all freshmen had to go to on Tuesdays. I think it was like one o'clock. I had to sit there for an hour and listen to, quote, culture. And this particular day they announced that there was a march down at the White House to protest Reverend Reeb's murder in Selma, and if we wanted to go, the student government had rented a bus and we could get out of freshman assembly. Honestly, I just wanted to get out of freshman assembly. I was tiring of sitting there, and some of the other students were going that I knew, so I went along. And when we got down to the White House, first started out picketing, I didn't know much about what was happening, but then across the street the Nazi counterdemonstrators and the Klansmen and other people started counterdemonstrations, and the soldiers moved in. It got very tense, and a couple of my friends said they were going to sneak in the White House and stay there. They were later arrested, I think, and sent to prison. And they kept saying, "Well, let's stay." I said, "My feet hurt. I want to go." And they kept saying, "Oh no. We got to stay." And before I knew it, I was caught up. I was listening. I think I stayed there 'til about two in the morning. And it made sense to me. The civil rights movement never made any sense to me until then, and then it really did. And I said, "Wow."

I heard Stokely Carmichael in the summer of 1966 when I was at Harvard University for the summer school. When he started talking, it was as if I were talking—he was speaking for me, things that I had been feeling and thinking about, he was articulating them so well, especially about the attitude that we should have as black people toward ourselves and the country, and how we shouldn't be begging and pleading for our rights. But we ought to get together and organize and take what rightfully belonged to us. And I liked that. I didn't like the passive kind of beggar mentality that I thought we were into in the civil rights movement. The speech changed me, because when I realized that what I had been feeling and thinking was not just personal, it wasn't just me—somebody else, in fact someone of prominence and stature, felt the same way and could articulate it—I really felt encouraged.

PAULA GIDDINGS

I grew up in Yonkers, New York, in a predominantly white neighborhood, feeling very isolated for many reasons. I really wanted to go to a place where there was a like-minded black community, and I thought Howard would be that place. I had been very affected, growing up, by so much that was going on around me, particularly those Freedom Rides in 1961, that made me ask a lot of questions and made me curious to find out so much more and so many things that I certainly wasn't getting in my own experience in Yonkers. So I was determined to go to Howard in '65.

I was surprised when I first went to Howard. I mean, I expected it to be embroiled in this political ferment, because so much had happened, of course, by 1965.

Freshman assembly was one of those programs that all freshmen had to go to; we didn't have any choice. And they always dragged in these speakers or some kind of cultural program that seemed very, very, very irrelevant to us. You know, the traditional mission of black schools has been not only to educate blacks but to sort of acculturate them and socialize them for the wider industrial order. And those programs symbolized that. So here you would have to drag to this freshman assembly to hear someone give us a very Booker T. Washington, up-from-slavery kind of talk. Here we were in the middle of a civil rights movement. So many important things were happening all around us. Nothing was being explained in terms of the curriculum of Howard University, nothing was being talked about. It was business as usual going on. And here, and in the midst of this, were these assemblies that had nothing to do with what was going on. I mean, this was a period of tremendous ferment, things were changing all the time, all the time. And we'd walk in and hear someone talk about how to dress, how to speak properly, how to fit into some other kind of occupation or job that had nothing to do with black people or helping black people out, except maybe a wage. So most of us found it very, very offensive. I mean, we went partly to get some kind of intellectualized experience of what was happening in terms of the arts, in terms of literature, in terms of social sciences, of political sciences, et cetera. We might not have understood so clearly what we were searching for, but we knew freshman assembly and the rest of those things weren't it.

TONY GITTENS

The whole Howard movement was impacted by what was going on outside of Howard. There was a lot of activity in the South. There were black colleges in the South where students were taking very militant, very firm stands against discrimination. And here there were the students of Howard, who were considered to be very middle-class and sort of away from a lot of that. So there were some students at Howard who believed that that should not be the case and that in fact Howard, if it was to be a leader amongst black universities, should take the firmest of stands. And we pushed to make Howard do that.

There were organizers who wanted to have demonstrations here in Washington, and they would come to Howard to try and get Howard students to participate. And there was always resistance on the part of the administration to such people coming on campus. There were speakers who we wanted to bring to Howard, toward the earlier days, not so much during the later days. And there was always resistance to these speakers being brought to Howard. The university as a whole felt that it should not be in a controversial position. It stated in documents that they felt that a good deal of money was coming from the federal government to support Howard, and Howard students therefore should not be antagonistic toward the government. We, on the other hand, felt that where Howard got its money was its own business and we were adults and able to make our own decisions and take our own stands on things.

In the fall of 1966, an event that raised students' growing black consciousness was orchestrated—Robin Gregory's campaign for homecoming queen.

ROBIN GREGORY

A lot of things were happening in 1966, in terms of where the movement was going. It was just beginning to be the dawn of the whole Black Power movement, getting away from the more conservative approach to change through the way the civil rights movement had been going, into a Black Power consciousness. And it was right on the edge of that. And there were a few students at Howard who were very politically involved in things, and I was one of them. But someone came up with an idea that we should make a statement around the homecoming, because it was such a superificial kind of thing that kept affirming old values that we were trying to resist or trying to overthrow. So I was approached by some men from the law school, actually, and they asked me if I would do it, because they wanted to make a statement about the black aesthetic. And they wanted to resist the whole image. It's kind of hard to describe the atmosphere of the way that it went, but the fraternities would nominate a candidate who would run for the position. It was a popular election, by the way. But you had to be nominated by some on-campus organization. And usually they picked someone who was as close to white as they could possibly get. I mean, it didn't have to be skin color. It was just the whole image of the person. And so they said, "Well, will you do this? We want to run somebody that has a natural hairstyle. We know that you're politically active. Let's take this particular context and use it to make a statement." And so I was willing to do that.

PAULA GIDDINGS

The traditional homecoming campaign was quite a ritual. Each sorority or fraternity, for example, had their candidates, and other organizations had candidates as well. During the days of the campaign, each candidate would appear on campus at certain times of the afternoon. All the candidates, of course, had to get new wardrobes with the latest fashions. They usually came rolling in in a latest model convertible. And everything was color-coordinated. And I remember working on the campaign, you always had to think of what color was the car, then the dress had to match the car, and the flowers had to match the dress that matched the car. So it was all very elaborate, and then there would be a demonstration talking about the candidate.

Of course, Robin Gregory had no car and always looked sharp, but she was certainly not wearing those elaborate dresses. She had an Afro, which of course was the statement that she made physically. And she was always flanked by two very handsome men, very serious, very well dressed in the way that the Fruit of Islam was dressed, with the bow ties. They always had their arms folded and would look straight ahead while Robin talked. And Robin talked about the movement. Robin talked about black politics. Robin was not the traditional homecoming queen candidate. She would also go around to the dorms in the evenings, which was something very, very different.

I was very excited about Robin's campaign. I'd always felt that there was something wrong with that other kind of traditional ritual that was going on. But at the same time I had divided loyalties, because I was a member of Delta Sigma Theta sorority and we had our own candidate, who was a very good friend of mine and who I worked on the campaign with. So many of us had these feelings back and forth. But all of us, with divided loyalties or not, felt very excited about Robin's campaign and about what it symbolized, not just in terms of politics but in terms of what women should be doing as well, the role of women. It was very, very important to us.

I remember being confronted with the kind of situation where when you passed by men, especially as an underclassman, as a freshman, sophomore, they would actually give you a grade. I mean, they would talk among themselves and say, "Well, that's an A," or "That's a B." There was a lack of respect in lots of instances. And there was a terrible degrading sense about all of that. And what Robin did was not only in terms of race but also talking about the role of women and what they should be doing and talking about and being taken very, very seriously, not just because of any physical attributes but because of her mind. And this I think was as important as the racial aspect of her campaign.

I remember very much the evening when the homecoming queen was crowned. I was in Cramton Auditorium, which was filled to the hilt. For the last time all the candidates were announced and went up on the stage in the auditorium. And the way the whole evening was set was very, very dramatic. What would happen after that is that the lights went down and all the candidates went behind the curtain, back of the stage. The ballot was actually secret balloting, so no one in the auditorium knew who was going to win. And the idea was that there was a throne, a high-backed throne, with its back to the audience, behind the curtain, and there was a revolving stage, so whoever would win would sit on that throne and then slowly revolve toward the audience.

The lights went down. The candidates went back. Then you heard the curtains open. And you heard the crank of the revolving stage begin. And as the stage revolved and turned around toward the audience, the lights began to come up at the same time. Well, before you saw Robin, you saw the way the lights cast a silhouette on the curtains, and you saw the silhouette of her Afro before you saw her. Well, the auditorium exploded. It was a wonderful moment. People started jumping up and screaming and some were raising their fists, then spontaneously a chant began. The chant was "Umgawa, Black Power, Umgawa, Black Power," and a chain was created. People started to march to the rhythm of "Umgawa, Black Power," and there was a line that went all the way around the auditorium, and more and more people joined the line. I did too as it went around the auditorium. And finally out the door and into the streets of Washington, D.C., past the campus and still chanting, "Umgawa, Black Power," and that was really the launching of that movement at Howard.

ROBIN GREGORY

The coronation itself was a pivotal point, and it energized a lot of people, causing them to begin to question a lot of the issues that we were bringing forward. And one of the things that happened, that was a big incident on the campus, was the spring after the coronation, the spring of 1967. Someone had invited General [Lewis] Hershey to the campus. And General Hershey was the head of the draft board. And people were just becoming aware of the Vietnamese war, and the fact that people were being drafted and sent to Vietnam, and that a large number of those people were black people. So, when we found out that he was being invited to speak, we decided that we didn't want that to happen, and we staged a demonstration. And, in essence, we didn't allow him to speak. There was a lot of shouting from the audience. There were a number of people that had placards that stormed the stage, and just booed him, essentially, out of the auditorium.

ADRIENNE MANNS

There were a core of young men from Philadelphia who had planned a demonstration. They told me that they were going to do something, they didn't say what, and that I should come. So I came. I wouldn't have come otherwise. They stopped Hershey from speaking. They got up chanting, "America is the black man's battleground." They had placards and Hershey stopped. I remember him looking at them like a grandfather. Like he understood. He just didn't speak. Carl Anderson was dean of students, I think, at that time. He came over to escort him offstage, like he was protecting him. But there was nothing to protect him from. They were chanting but they weren't trying to harm him. They just were trying to stop the program, which they did, and we left. That was all there was to it. But a big thing was made out of it.

Right after the Hershey demonstration there was a polarization among students. One side of the student government leaders and fraternity leaders called a press conference to apologize for the demonstration. And they angered me so, I was so angry. I was the managing editor of the newspaper. And I said how dare they speak for the student body. They said they were speaking for the responsible students. Now, Gloster Current [Jr.] was there, and some others who were leaders in student government. And that really polarized those who supported the demonstration, or at least their right to have it, and those who said it was a disgrace and an embarrassment to the university and so forth. I just made a vow after that. I said, Well, I'll have to get serious about this thing, because the other side is serious.

> Fred Black, son of an army officer, was following a long-standing family tradition by attending Howard and participating in the Reserve Officers' Training Corps (ROTC) beyond the compulsory two years for all male students who were U.S. citizens.

FRED BLACK

I remember thinking that night that this was a major change in the direction of the campus protest movement that had been building momentum. Here's a national figure appearing at Howard that was going to result in many of the so-called outsiders of the university trying to impose their will on Howard. And they could do that very easily financially, since a significant part of Howard's budget came from the federal government. And here was a federal officer, if you will, a lieutenant general in the army, who headed the Selective Service System, who had been mistreated at Howard, at least in the eyes of many. The media was very evident that night, and you never saw the media for most presentations, so you got the feeling that someone must have invited the media because something was going to happen that would be newsworthy, or at least in the eyes of the TV stations. And that, of course, came about. The next day the TVs and the newspapers all made a big deal out of what happened that evening in Cramton Auditorium to General Hershey.

From that point on, the Howard protest received a lot of media attention, and there were days when you just got accustomed to seeing reporters and TV cameras wandering around campus asking people their opinion on various things that were going on. But I think the Hershey incident for the media was a clear signal that something different was happening at Howard University, something that was unlike student protest in days before. This was a serious, issue-oriented protest movement.

One of the things that struck me was that for the first time the media was interested in portraying blacks disagreeing with blacks, whereas the media had covered the civil rights struggle as an example of blacks fighting for their rights—the whole civil rights struggle as we saw it on TV in the evening news. But now, here we have an example of a prestigious black university where the students, faculty, and administration is in conflict, and it seemed like this was a very desirable news story for these folks, particularly here in Washington, D.C., given the tradition Howard has had in this city. It was not unusual from that point on to see negative Howard stories on TV or in the newspaper. And you just wondered whether or not people were interested in what was really happening here or interested in portraying the students, faculty, and administration in a negative light.

The Hershey incident occurred on March 21, 1967. Some students, Robin Gregory among them, were threatened with expulsion for their part in the incident. The rest of that school year saw continued conflict between the students and the administration, including a one-day boycott of classes in May. Over the summer, twenty activist students were either expelled or disciplined. Also, six teachers were not rehired because the administration deemed their influence disruptive.

The spring of 1967 also saw a visit to the campus by Muhammad Ali, sponsored by Howard's newly formed Black Power Committee. Ali's speech was delivered outdoors because Cramton Auditorium was denied him, and 4,500 students came, eager to hear the world heavyweight champion. It was six days before he was to report to the Houston induction center.

By the fall the students had won one victory—ROTC would no longer be compulsory as of February 1968. An umbrella organization of student activist groups was formed at the start of the 1967–1968 school year and given the name UJAMAA (a Swahili word for "familyhood"). Tony Gittens, class of '69 and a writer for the *Hilltop,* the student newspaper, was UJAMAA's political director.

On February 8, 1968, state and local police in Orangeburg, South Carolina, opened fire on a crowd of one hundred unarmed students from two predominantly black universities, South Carolina State College and Claflin College. They had been protesting a segregated bowling alley. Three students died and twenty-eight were injured, most having been shot in the back as they ran.

TONY GITTENS

Some students had been killed in Orangeburg, at a university there. And I went down with some other journalists to look at that. And there we met these students who, because of a demonstration, the same kind of demonstrations that we were having, actually people had been killed and shot. It had a tremendous impression on me. Because these people had been willing to give their lives for something. It was not a game for them; it was not a media event for them. The impact that it had on me and other people who I related it to when I got back was just incredible. And then what we were doing at Howard and the dangers there seemed minimal compared to what other people were willing to face for the same kind of reasons. Those were experiences that just totally changed my view about my role as a student and what I began to define as a role for other students.

A week after the Orangeburg massacre, Tony Gittens, Adrienne Manns, now editor of the *Hilltop,* and other student activists came up with a series of demands—among them the resignation of President Nabrit and Dean Frank Snowden and the reinstatement of those Howard professors who had lost their jobs because of their support of the students. They also wanted Howard to become a center for Afro-American thought with emphasis, in relevant disciplines, on black liberation studies. They presented these demands to the administration and requested a reply within two weeks, by February 29.

TONY GITTENS

After we developed the manifesto, we decided to have a rally to tell students what our demands and our stand was. And we went and we lowered the American flag that was on campus. And then we took the flag and the manifesto over to Dean Snowden's office, just barged into his office. There were a number of us, twenty, twenty-five, fifty students there. And we put it on his desk. He was quite shocked. He was absolutely shocked. He was shaking, he was trembling. And then we just told him that his time had come. That people like himself, focusing on him not as a personality but as a symbol, that people who had the attitudes that he had, that their time had come. It was time for them to sort of move on and make room for more progressive attitudes towards what black people should be doing in this country.

I remember shaking my finger at Dean Snowden. And him just sitting there trembling. He didn't say a word to us. He didn't say a word. He sat there smoking his pipe, in bewilderment, not really understanding. See, they all had this bewilderment. They didn't really know what this was all about. They never really sort of understood what it is we wanted. And that's one reason we made the manifesto. I mean, the Achilles' heel was that they really thought we were children. They really thought we were these kids from the fields. And their job was to keep us in line.

> When the students had heard nothing by March 1, Charter Day (the annual celebration of the founding of the school), they decided to act again.

ADRIENNE MANNS

Right before Charter Day, Tony and I had gone up to see Dr. Nabrit and ask him to respond to the sixteen demands that the coalition of students had drawn up. And we asked him to respond to it either at Charter Day exercises or before. He talked all the time about Amsterdam, his latest trip, so I wasn't very optimistic that he would do it.

UJAMAA, which was a coalition of protest organizations, nonofficial groups, had met, oh, about two days before Charter Day and decided that if Dr. Nabrit did not respond to those sixteen demands during Charter Day exercises that we were going to disrupt the exercises, so we went there with that in mind. There were about fifteen of us who said we would go up on the stage and ask him to respond to our demands, and the rest would hand out leaflets to the audience to tell them why we were doing this and what this was about. We each sat in different places in the auditorium. I think I sat with Tony. And the security guards were there and they had just killed somebody not too long ago who was robbing Punch Out, which was a student hangout, canteen. And one of the security men had shot the man. So all I could see was this guard. I remember this big, tall security guard. He was over six feet and he had a gun. They were all over the auditorium, it looked like. There might have been five or six of them. Anyway, when Dr. Nabrit had finished the preliminaries and got into the program and Dean [Samuel] Gandy got up to give the address, he didn't say one thing about our demands. He sat down and then Dr. Nabrit got up to give the distinguished alumni their awards. So I said, "Tony, I don't think he's going to say anything and the program is going to be over, so we better do something."

And he said, "Well, okay, let's get up."

So I said, "All right." So I got up. We walked toward the stage, and all of the security guards came to the front and stood in front of us, and we were standing there and I said, "Tony, what are we going to do now?"

He said, "Well, let's sit up on the stage."

And finally I said, "I can't get up." I said, "I'm just, I'm just afraid. I can't get up."

So he said, "I'll get up."

So when Tony got up and I said, "Oh, I can't leave Tony stand there by himself," I think Q. T. Jackson got up and some more, and so the rest of us got up there. And we stood on the stage, and Nabrit turned and Tony went over to him and he said something about "Dr. Nabrit, we've asked you to respond to our demands and since you obviously are not going to respond, we feel you should relinquish the ceremonies and let us explain." So, it was a tense moment, and I remember Nabrit saying, "Why are you doing this to me?" or something like that. He looked at Tony and me as though we had betrayed him. And then he walked off the stage and we tried to hold our counter–Charter Day exercises and explain to the alumni. And the faculty jumped up. They were all in their robes. They fled the auditorium. Only about three of them stayed. I think one of the alumni stayed, and we tried to talk. They turned the systems off. We had like a rally, but I was afraid really. For the first time, I think, through the whole thing, I was afraid.

Well, after Charter Day, we got letters. I got one and Tony got one and everybody involved just about, and some more people who weren't involved, got letters from the administration that we were called to a judiciary hearing. And I said, This was it. I had foreseen that, of course. We were going to be expelled. So we decided to hold a coalition meeting of student government leaders and all students really who had been involved. And we met and decided that we were going to have a sit-in, in the Administration Building, to protest these letters because there was no student judiciary. And we said we'd have a rally in front of

Douglass Hall. And then, during the rally at lunchtime, we would announce the sit-in and we'd go into the Administration Building.

The plan was that Ewart Brown was going to speak. He was president of the student government association. And we said, No long speeches. Just tell people what happened, the reason we're having a sit-in, and we're all going to go over there. And we estimated that maybe five hundred would join us.

Well, the day came, I remember it was a very bright day, beautiful day, and I went out after lunch and I told one of our teachers that I liked what was going to happen. I didn't tell him everything. I said, "Stay away from that Administration Building." And I went over to the rally and I couldn't hear what Ewart was saying. I was afraid, really. I said, "What are we going to do? We've got to really do this. Once you say you're going to do this thing, you've got to do it." So I remember Ewart said, "Let's go." And I turned and I was staring at the building and I said, I've got to do this. And I started walking toward it. I wasn't sure how many were coming. I said, It doesn't matter. I've got to do it. I've got to go ahead with it. And, I thought, just a few will come. I was so afraid that we were going to be embarrassed. And I went on in anyway. And I looked behind me and there were all these students coming. The place was filling up, first floor, second floor. I got in the elevator and went on up to the third floor. And went into Dr. Nabrit's office. Right behind me there were enough students to fill the whole floor, the third floor, which is a big area. And there were about ten of us that went into his office. He wasn't there. And we sat down and decided to wait, see what they did next.

His secretary, all the workers, they didn't say anything. They just looked at us and we sat on the floor, and I kept thinking, Where did all these people come from? I just never realized that that many people would support us. But I was afraid all the way over there until I saw the people. And I was afraid then because I said, What will we do now, with all these people? Now that we're over here, what will we do now? So I just sat there waiting. Finally, [after] a couple of hours, they closed up offices and they started leaving. The workers, some of them, said, "About time you all did this." I was surprised. They said, "We were wondering how long it was going to take you to do this. It's about time." And they all went home. And evening started to fall and we said, Well, we've got to do something. So we formed a steering committee that came out of the student leadership and broke down into different areas: communications, food, housing, sleeping quarters for everyone. I've forgotten all of the subcommittees, but we had about eight to take care of things.

That day was Tuesday, March 19. Alfred Babington-Johnson, president of the class of '68 and a self-described "voice of moderation," was one of an estimated twelve hundred students who participated in the sit-in that became a takeover.

ALFRED BABINGTON-JOHNSON

It was probably one of the most wonderful experiences that anyone could ever have. Because it was a time of—especially in terms of the entire group—a time of extraordinary unity. Our students were answering the switchboard. We had daily strategy sessions about how we were gonna deal with things. We had a guard system set up. We had even first-aid accommodations. We had people who set up the logistics for feeding these two thousand people. Everything was very orderly. It was a high just in terms of the fact that we were all there united in one spirit without bickering. I mean, there was another level at which there was some real tension, and that was, you know, as we gathered in the leadership to make decisions about things or respond to things, or to go out and do press conferences, whatever it might be. Now, that's a different level, and the tension obviously has to exist there, 'cause at one point we feared that the National Guard is gonna be here at, you know, eight o'clock. So all those kinds of things were swirling and some student who might say, "Okay, listen, I've got a gun," or whatever. But the bulk of the thing was just such a positive spirit of unity.

PAULA GIDDINGS

The first day I went into the Administration Building after the takeover was really something. I'll never forget it. It was very, very well organized. It was one of the most organized movements I have seen even since. You had to have ID, of course, to get in and out, only students really were allowed, or those who people knew. You walked into the Administration Building, the switchboard now is taken over by students and was running much more efficiently than it ever had before. There was a microphone set up in the front, where there were announcements being made. Different student representatives had different things to say, so everyone would hear it. There was a whole sound system so everyone could hear what was happening. There were separate floors for men and women, for people who were spending the night sleeping over or who wanted to change clothes. So they had one floor for women and one floor for men up in the upper floors. We had the best meals. Of course, every school cafeteria, and Howard was no exception, had the worst meals in the world. But a lot of restaurants and others in the city were sympathetic to the takeover of Howard. So we'd get these wonderful turkeys, whole turkeys were coming in. People were eating three meals a day there and delicious food. There were specified times when there would be cleanup time, and people were assigned to mop floors and keep everything straight and clean. So it was running very, very efficiently. I guess that's when I really consciously knew I had found that black community that I had been searching for. Because you were sitting there in the Administration Building, all of us certainly were very excited about what we had done. Very, very serious, though, about what we had done. The proposals and all were very thought-out of what we wanted the school to do and the administration to do and what kind of courses that we wanted. And we felt very committed to carrying it through and felt very good about ourselves. I guess it was a kind of rite of passage into adulthood in a way, as well.

TONY GITTENS

Cultural groups would come in and say, We want to do something. Can we perform? And there'd be plays and all kinds of things would go on. And people from around Washington would come and give all these supportive speeches and say, Whatever you want, let us know. And then people who could not get into the building, there were all these students outside of the building who were just there. Just there, just willing to participate. And signs were made. "Howard University, The Black University." Then teachers would come up. And they said, What can we do? And we had classes that were going on. Because some students would be afraid they were getting behind. And these faculty members saying, you know, Don't worry about it, we'll take care of it. And people would come in and we'd have seminars. It was amazing. And we met every morning, and we met periodically to take care of the issues. It was just an incredible experience to just show the administration, these people who thought that we were kids, they were just so off key, just so wrong about the whole thing.

CHARLES EPPS

When the undergraduate students took over the Administration Building in 1968 and voiced as one of their concerns that Howard become a black university, I found something incongruous about that—in fact, paradoxical—because Howard had always been a black university. We say "predominantly black," but the fact of the matter was that it was black. In my class of fifteen hundred students, there was one white student. So, there was no question about it being black, but it had a long tradition of training black leaders in this country. And it was, for all practical purposes, a black university. I don't know how it could have been more black. And I'm not sure what they were trying to say, but Howard provided a mainstream education which prepared people to be competitive in every field. I don't recognize and I don't think the world recognizes that there is any black physics. There's no black engineering. There's no black medicine. So that the mission of the university was to train students to be competitive and competent in whatever field, and I'm not sure what they were trying to say. But there was no such thing as Howard becoming more black than it was. It was a black, predominantly black, university.

Three days into the takeover, negotiations between students and trustees began.

ADRIENNE MANNS

There were four of us that were chosen for the negotiating team. And the first problem we had was it had to be done by consensus. And there were maybe a thousand students who had to agree. There was a steering committee of about eleven, who made the nominations to the students. They agreed, but they said, whatever we did, we couldn't do anything without bringing it back to them. So, whatever points that the administration would agree to—at this point, the board of trustees would agree to—we had to then tell them, "We'll take this back to campus." So we were going back and forth, back and forth, on a lot of issues. And it came down to two that were a problem. First was Nabrit's resignation. And the trustees told us that he planned to retire next year. So they felt there was no need to ask him to resign. And second was the matter of the word *black*. We wanted Howard to make a statement about its commitment to the black community, to the welfare of the black community. And the trustees said no, they couldn't do that. It was Kenneth Clark who explained to us that because Howard got so much money from the federal government, they couldn't afford to make an overt commitment to any one group, because that would put them in violation of civil rights laws or fairness or whatever. But they could make a statement saying that they were committed to the general welfare of humanity and so forth. We got everything, agreed to everything, except those two. It took us maybe two days, I guess, of talking, going back and forth from the hotel back to the Administration Building.

On Saturday, March 23, after 102 hours, students ended their takeover.

TONY GITTENS

The negotiating team had come back, and we had gotten a lot of what we had asked for. Students were there. We talked about it that night. And that morning we got up and we went down and we said, "You know, it's time for us to go." And we gave our reasons why we should go. And we asked all the press to leave who were there. We had an open mike so students can come up and say whether they were for it, whether they were against it, whatever the reason. That went on for about an hour, an hour and a half, two hours. We took a voice vote and the agreement was that we should go. We cleaned the building. There was singing. People were singing. And what I felt best about was that no one got hurt. That we were walking out of there. We chose to go in. We were choosing to go out. We weren't forced out. And that we'd gotten a lot of what we went in there for.

I think that experience changed the life of every single Howard student that was on campus that day. Everyone felt proud. And as we walked out, I felt very good. And the students tended to feel very, very good about themselves, and they just felt their whole self-image of what they were as Howard students just changed. They felt part of the whole world of black progress. So it was a wonderful feeling to have ended by choice and in such a positive way.

PAULA GIDDINGS

The takeover and the four years of activity at Howard had tremendous impact on me. I got a new sense of self, a new sense of my black self, in terms of culture, in terms of politics, in terms of the rights to demand certain things, the right to feel good about yourself. And I had always had a good sense of myself but not necessarily a clear sense of myself as a black person. And I think that was the important thing, and it was something I'm sure I was searching for, and I certainly found it at Howard. Certainly, as a person who was always interested in writing, there were all of the debates and all of the editing and the selection of work, the new poetry movement—all that was going on. Certainly, my idea of what the role of a writer should be was formed at Howard. What good literature should be, which I learned in Arthur Davis's class, was formed at Howard. And that certainly stayed with me. I mean, that's a very important legacy that stayed with me throughout my career.

Student takeovers continued throughout the remainder of the academic year following the Howard student action. Groups of white and black students at Columbia University occupied several campus buildings; elsewhere, a group of students seized a building at Bowie State College in Maryland; sixty black students at Northwestern University near Chicago took over the finance building; students at Tuskegee Institute in Alabama held twelve school trustees captive; black students occupied the administration building at Boston University; and students seized the administration building at Ohio State University.

In 1968 campus activism was widespread. Students across the nation demonstrated over such issues as the war in Vietnam, ROTC, university/community relations, and "paternalistic" administrative policies on black as well as interracial campuses. Most black students' demands, however, centered on the call for black studies.

That fall, the first of several conferences exploring the theme of black studies was held at Howard. Called "Toward a Black University," it attracted three thousand students, community activists, scholars, and representatives from a wide range of organizations throughout the country and the world.

24

KING'S LAST CRUSADE, 1967–1968

"WE'VE GOT SOME DIFFICULT DAYS AHEAD"

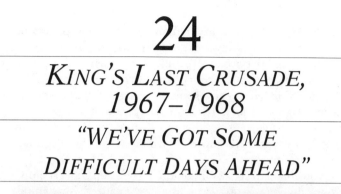

Striking Memphis sanitation workers march past the bayonets of Tennessee National Guardsmen, March 28, 1968.

Like the students at Howard, like Carl Stokes in Cleveland, Martin Luther King, Jr., understood the importance of delivering victories. But for King, there had been no major triumph since Selma and the Voting Rights Act in 1965. He had become skilled at forcing changes in the law. But he and his colleagues were still searching for ways to force changes in the society.

In Chicago in 1966, and throughout the long, hot summer of 1967, King pointed out that the rhetoric of the Great Society and of the War on Poverty had raised expectations that had not been met. He spoke out forcefully against the war in Vietnam, making strong connections between international policy and domestic conditions, and earned the enmity of many in government, including President Lyndon Johnson.

It was a difficult time. The movement could no longer depend on the goodwill of the federal government. Instead, it was being driven to challenge that government. Traditional supporters began to fall away. Within the movement itself, the more militant criticized King for moving too slowly; others hoped he would stop pushing so hard and antagonizing so many.

King continued to speak out, holding true to his moral compass and demanding changes in America. But few realized how radical and far-reaching his vision had become.

Michael Harrington, whose book *The Other America,* published in 1962, has been credited with helping to inspire the War on Poverty, served on Dr. King's research committee, a group that met regularly to discuss pressing issues.

MICHAEL HARRINGTON

In conversations with Dr. King in the last years of his life, we always talked about the fact that to abolish poverty, to abolish economic racism, would require changing the structures of American society. That it meant that you had to have a different kind of occupational structure, that you could not have blacks concentrated among the unemployed, the low-paid, the uninteresting jobs, the jobs without any responsibility. That you had to really change that in a radical way. That you had to change the income structure of American society. You had to redistribute wealth, and now that came out as a demand for more progressive taxation. In private, we could talk in a sense much more candidly, much more openly about the need for really basic democratization of investment decisions, and much more democratic allocation of income and wealth and of work. Then when you go public, then you immediately have to think, How do you phrase this message? And Dr. King had a genius for this. How do you phrase this message so that you don't betray the message but you put it in terms which are understandable and accessible to people on the street? But certainly he wouldn't use radical phraseology in many cases for that reason. And I quite agreed with that. Indeed, in my own book *The Other America* I did not mention the word *socialism* once for precisely that reason. But I always knew that Dr. King, through my conversations, had what I would consider in the good sense of the word a small *d* democratic radical view of what was required in American society.

In March 1967, Marian Wright, a young black attorney with the NAACP Legal Defense Fund and an associate of King's, testified before the Senate Labor Committee's subcommittee on poverty about conditions in Mississippi. The next month, the committee held hearings in Jackson.

MARIAN WRIGHT EDELMAN

The biggest problem then was survival. I mean, we were having major problems of hunger, even starvation. There were people in Mississippi who had no income. The federal government was shifting over to food stamps from commodities distribution. And while the commodities distribution program of the Department of Agriculture was lousy—didn't provide enough food, it wasn't good enough food—it was free. And when you began to shift to food stamps and charge even two dollars per person, there were people in Mississippi who didn't even have that two dollars. It was very hard to get people from Washington to believe that there were families that could not afford a dollar or two. But the poor were struggling. They were being pushed off the plantations because of the mechanization of cotton, because of the use of chemical weed killing. And while it was a literal bondage system, the plantation system in Mississippi, in the forties, fifties, and sixties, where the Senator Eastlands were subsidized in the hundreds and thousands of dollars by the federal government, the peasants or the tenants on those farms literally could not eat and did not have the most basic survival needs in this rich American country.

I tried to bring the senators down to Mississippi because I was trying to figure out ways of getting the country to see. You know, when the white students came down in 1964, that helped the country to see, because it was their daughters and their sons that were there and they were afraid for them. These were not people who necessarily had been attuned to the problems of the black poor in America at that time. So one has to have someone to lift the window. After the young people left at the end of the summer of '64, the problems were still left. They were different. They were changing. We had begun to make a difference. But there was so much suffering that remained to be alleviated. So one was trying to find new ways to capture the imagination and attention of the American public. Therefore, I went to see if I could get the senators to see that it was still bad, and indeed was getting worse in many ways, and that hunger was growing, even though we had the right to vote. The cost of that for many is that they got kicked off the plantations and lost that little bit of money, unjust as it was, that they had had to survive. And so we had to put another means in place.

I told the committee, please come and see for yourselves, because they didn't quite believe me when I talked about how the conditions of life, the poverty, was getting worse and the people really didn't have enough to eat in Mississippi. So they came, and Bobby Kennedy came with them, and while they were there to examine the impact of the poverty program on Mississippi blacks and whites, I used it as an opportunity to tell them about growing hunger in the Delta. And they were shocked and, happily, one or two of the senators agreed to stay over and to go up in the Delta to see for themselves whether it was true that people were starving. Bobby Kennedy agreed to be one of those senators.

I was very moved by what Bobby Kennedy did when we went to visit [a black family] in Cleveland, Mississippi. Without cameras—because he was Bobby Kennedy some newspapermen had come along—we went inside a very dark and dank shack. It was very filthy and very poor, and when we walked through from front to back together, there was in the kitchen a mother who was scrubbing in a tin tub, washing clothes. There was a child sitting on a dirt floor, filthy. And there was very little light there, and he got down on his knees and he tried to talk to the child and get a response from the child. He kept poking or feeling the child and trying to get some response. And I remember watching him in near tears, because I had this complicated feeling. I was moved by it and wondering whether I would have gotten down on that dirty floor. But deeply respectful that he did. He could do almost anything after that and I trusted him from that time on, just as a human being. And then he went out to the backyard where the reporters were waiting. And he was correctly angry. But from that moment on, I knew that somehow he would be a major force in trying to deal with hunger in Mississippi for children.

Later that summer, after watching President Johnson announce the government's military response to the civil disorders in Detroit, Robert Kennedy told an aide, "It's over. The president is just not going to do anything more. That's it. He's through with domestic problems, with the cities. . . . He's not going to do anything. And he's the only man who can."

In August, with urban uprisings still sweeping through America's inner cities, Marian Wright visited Kennedy at his Virginia home, Hickory Hill, on her way back to Mississippi.

MARIAN WRIGHT EDELMAN

It was a gorgeous day and he was lounging out around the pool at Hickory Hill, and we went through our usual small chat about what was going on. And when I was leaving—I had also told him I was going to stop back through Atlanta and see Dr. King—he said, "Tell him to bring the poor people to Washington." That it's time for some visible expression of concern for the poor. I had been expressing to him my frustration that hunger was still going on, and obviously he was still frustrated that the Agriculture Department was so slow in doing something about it or the Johnson administration was hesitant to move, so he thought that there really needed to be some push, some national visible push. But it was a very simple suggestion: Tell Dr. King to bring the people to Washington.

This was a period of white reaction and backlash. It was a period when the war was becoming a much more divisive force, where the problems of black and poor people were being left behind and people thought they were annoyances, and we'd had a lot of violence in northern cities. And Martin King was really depressed. One of the things I always remembered about him from my early student days was how he was able to share his uncertainties, share his not knowing what to do next. I remember his Founders' Day speech when I was a senior at Spelman College, when he talked about taking that one step even if you can't see the whole way and how you just have to keep moving, even if you're slower than you want. If you can't walk, crawl, but keep moving.

He was real down that day [shortly after the visit with Kennedy] when I walked in, sitting in his office, and he was like everybody at that time—Kennedy and me and all of us concerned about the poor and what was happening to civil rights and the country turning itself away from it, about what we were going to do next. And I told him that Bobby Kennedy said he ought to bring the poor people to Washington. And as simply as Bobby Kennedy had said it, King instinctively felt that that was right and treated me as if I was an emissary of grace here, or something that brought him some light. Out of that, the Poor People's Campaign was born.

William Rutherford, a black Chicago native and skilled public relations man who had spent much of his adult life abroad, had organized the Friends of SCLC in Europe in 1966. In the summer of 1967 King appointed him executive director of SCLC.

WILLIAM RUTHERFORD

The staff was really quite busy and quite involved in things when Dr. King looked up and in his reasoning—I'm paraphrasing, of course—he said, "Fine, we now have the right to vote. Fine. We can now go to any restaurant, any hotel, anyplace we want to in America, but we don't have the means. So what good does it do for people to go to any restaurant in the world if you don't have the money to pay for a meal?" So, he says, we've got to attack the whole issue of poverty and economic deprivation. And that was his thinking, his reasoning for pushing for a Poor People's Campaign. But, of course, when this has to impact on people that have been fighting to get people registered and into polling places, people who have been fighting to get education, people who have been fighting for the right to go into public accommodations, the idea of attacking something as vast and as amorphous as poverty, of course, wasn't very appealing. So I'd say that basically almost no one on the staff thought that the next priority, the next major movement, should be focused on poor people or the question of poverty in America.

Andrew Young was by this time executive vice president of SCLC.

ANDREW YOUNG

SCLC was always a battle of egos. We were like a team of wild horses. Each one had very strong opinions and their own ideas about the way the movement should go, and Dr. King encouraged that. And our meetings were loud and raucous, and he sat quietly by until we fought issues out, and then he would usually decide. James Bevel wanted to keep us in northern cities in a movement to end slums. Hosea Williams felt as though we should stay in the South and do voter registration. Jesse Jackson was beginning to develop Operation Breadbasket, which was an attempt to organize nonviolently to get jobs. I was probably more inclined to stay south, because people forget that SCLC at that time had a budget of less than a million dollars.

SCLC board member Marian Logan also was not enthusiastic.

MARIAN LOGAN

When I first heard about it, I was really very apprehensive. I thought that as it began to develop, as I heard about how it was developing, it was becoming much too big and unwieldy for us to be able to handle. And also, considering the tenor of the times, I wasn't sure that we could be a success. I wasn't sure that Congress, and the powers that be in Washington, D.C., would be welcoming—'cause it wasn't like '63, which was such a glorious march, and glorious day. This bringing of poor people to the seat of government was like throwing it in their faces, and I don't think too many of the officialdom of Washington was gonna take that with any great grace. So I had many reservations about it.

In early December, King announced, without specifics, SCLC's intention to bring poor people of all races to Washington around April 1 and to "stay until America responds." Plans remained to be formulated.

CORETTA SCOTT KING

During the fall period he worked very hard, and all into the early part of the year. And in the spring he went all over this country talking about it and promoting the idea, and most people who knew him felt that he was working as if this was going to be his last job. I mean, we were very concerned about him, but the fact is that he could see, I think, a way that this could all come together, and he felt very confident that this could be a real test of how nonviolence can work to change the lives of people economically. When the president asked him, "Dr. King, what if you fail?" he said, "It will not be Martin King, Jr., who failed. It will be America that failed." He believed very firmly, reaffirmed his commitment in nonviolence as the most important weapon available to these people. And he said, "If I be the sole person on earth who clings to the belief and practice of nonviolence, I will be that person."

It was almost like a political campaign three hundred and sixty-five days of the year, but you never take a break, it never ends, it's continuous, year after year. And that's the Poor People's Campaign. It was one of those frantic periods, where it seems that Martin was just continually going, and he had so much anxiety about all this working out and making it happen successfully.

RALPH ABERNATHY

We did a great deal of planning and work while organizing for the Poor People's Campaign. We used cars, and we used small chartered airplanes, and we went all over the states of Mississippi and Alabama where poor people lived, trying to organize and get them aroused.

In Marks, Mississippi, I well remember, we visited a day-care center. And Dr. King was moved to tears there. There was one apple, and they took this apple and cut it into four pieces for four hungry waiting students. And when Dr. King saw that, and that is all that they had for lunch, he actually ended up crying. The tears came streaming down his cheek. And he had to leave the room.

Plans for the campaign began to take shape over the winter. Daniel Schorr, then a reporter for CBS, attended a press conference King held in Washington on February 7, 1968.

DANIEL SCHORR

At this press conference network reporters, including myself, constantly pushed him to try to say something as militant as possible. We were interested in getting the kind of sound bites that would get on the evening news. And in fact, as I went back over the script of that day, I realized that we did get him to say things like the first phase of this march would be educational and then if that didn't work that it would be disruptive, that they were going to stay in Washington until they got a response.

When the press conference was over, I was waiting for my camera crew to pack up and saw Reverend King sitting there looking somewhat disconsolate. And I walked up to him, sitting at the table there, and asked why he seemed to be so mournful and he said, "Well, it's because of what you people in television are doing. I don't know if you are aware of it, but you keep driving people like me, who are nonviolent, into saying more and more militant things, and if we don't say things militantly enough for you, we don't get on the evening news. And who does? Stokely Carmichael and H. Rap Brown. By doing this, you are, first of all, selecting the more militant black leaders to be civil rights leaders, because everybody sees your television programs. And secondly, you're putting a premium on violence." That gave me a lot to think about.

MICHAEL HARRINGTON

The last meeting of the research committee that I attended in the early spring of 1968, we did two things. One was we discussed the general political situation, which we always did at those meetings. And it struck me that Dr. King was very pessimistic, deeply disturbed at the way things were going. On the one hand, he was being increasingly attacked from within the black movement. There was a surge of nationalism. The Black Panthers had begun to come on the scene. There was SNCC, the Student Nonviolent Coordinating Committee. There had been a turn away from nonviolence, so he was being attacked for being too much of a pacifist. Too namby-pamby. Not willing to really fight back. Not willing to use force against racism. On the other hand, he was being attacked by Lyndon Johnson, and even by the Hubert Humphrey liberals, for going too far to the left. For being in the antiwar movement. For taking part in the April 1967 demonstration against the war in New York. And I had the feeling that his sense was that the number of people who really supported him now had really sunk very much.

Within that context, we then talked about the Poor People's Campaign. In a sense, the Poor People's Campaign was certainly no repudiation by Dr. King of his opposition to the war, but it was an attempt to then go back and refocus on basics, and perhaps more importantly, to mobilize a mass movement.

The state of preparation for the poor people's march was very chaotic. That was typical of Dr. King. Careful organization and planning was not his strong suit. He was a genius at improvising. What he did understand was that his strength was in his appeal to masses of people. That he had to mobilize those masses given the defections he felt both to his right and his left. And what I said to him at that meeting was whatever else we do, what we have to do is we have to come up with some demands that we can actually win on. That we can't ask for the moon, or we can ask for the moon and should ask for the moon, but we should also make some demands, and I don't remember the precise ones that I urged, but they would have been winnable demands in terms of legislation. And I would say this is something where Dr. King and I always agreed. That part of his genius was to understand that you could not have a movement simply based on promises of the future. That you had to deliver. And he had delivered on voting rights. He had delivered on public accommodations. He had delivered on the Montgomery bus boycott, and so many other things. And he understood now, above all, was the time to deliver.

> In February, thirteen hundred sanitation workers, nearly all of them black, went on strike in Memphis. Angered by the city's sending twenty-two black workers home without pay because of inclement weather (white workers were not sent home and they received pay), the strikers were demanding that their union be recognized. SCLC's James Lawson, now pastor of Centenary Methodist Church in Memphis, invited King to speak at a rally

in support of the strikers. King recognized the chance to link the economic conditions of the strike with the civil rights movement and arrived in Memphis on March 18 to address a mass meeting.

ANDREW YOUNG

The staff was really disturbed that Martin would even consider going to Memphis. We had charted out fifteen cities that we were going to try to organize. We were trying to organize poor whites, Hispanics, southern blacks, northern blacks—I mean, there was just a tremendous organizing job, and I didn't know how you could take on anything else. And he said, "Well, Jim Lawson has been around for so long and here are garbage workers on strike, he just wants me to come in and make a speech and I'll be right back."

Bill Lucy, an organizer for the American Federation of State, County, and Municipal Employees, had come to Memphis to work with the strikers.

BILL LUCY

In March, when the issue began to be discussed about inviting Dr. King to come to Memphis, it grew out of the frustrations of the city and, I guess, maybe the media really putting a lid on what was taking place in Memphis. We were forty-seven days into the strike and nobody knew it except us and the city of Memphis. Roy Wilkins had come to town, Bayard Rustin had come to town to speak in support of the strike, but still there was no understanding beyond the city as to what was taking place. The invitation to Dr. King to come was that we believed that he would not only lend his moral support to the strike, but he was in the midst of organizing the Poor People's Campaign, and we just really thought that that would be a good movement for him to identify with, that there would be national media with him that would, in effect, take an interest in what was taking place.

What I remember from that night of that first speech was the incredible ability that King had to understand and interpret the issues and what was taking place. He had not been there before, and he had had the most minimal of briefings. But he clearly understood that the struggle was really about a new kind of people, people who worked forty hours a week and still lived in poverty, and he was able to arrange his presentation to demonstrate to the crowd that he understood this, and to give them a sense that their struggle was a legitimate struggle, that they had every right to carry on.

> The crowd at Mason Temple numbered fifteen thousand. King was so moved by their struggle that he decided to return to Memphis to lead a march.
>
> King came back on March 28. Bernard Lee and Ralph Abernathy were at his side when the march took an unexpected turn.

BERNARD S. LEE

I was a little upset that he didn't have some of our national staff in the march organizing prior to its beginning. It was just a mass of people. I don't think the leadership of the march was ever in control. As we marched, I began hearing these noises behind me of glass, broken glass, taking place. And as I continued to look back, and try to jump up over the crowd and see what was going on, I could see and hear that there was tremendous disturbance not very far from us, behind us, in the march. And the people in the march were breaking store windows. And finally we marched, I guess maybe about a block, might have gone two blocks, but I made a decision that Martin Luther King didn't need to be in that march because it had become disruptive. It had become violent internally and the leadership needed to deal with that march and Martin Luther King needed to leave the march.

RALPH ABERNATHY

At that moment, Bernard Scott Lee, who was Dr. King's traveling assistant, stopped a car and asked the young lady if he could use this car to get Dr. Abernathy and Dr. King out of this situation. And the young lady agreed, and she got over, and Bernard Lee became our driver. And we were taken down to the river, the Mississippi River. And we stopped the motorcycle police at that point and asked them if we could use their service to get Dr. King out of the area. And a policeman said, "Where do you want to go?"

And I said, "The Peabody Hotel."

And he said, "We cannot go to the Peabody Hotel, because there's nothing but violence over there."

And we said, "Well, what about the Lorraine Motel?"

And the policeman said, "We cannot go to the Lorraine Motel because there's nothing but violence over there. And tear gas is everywhere." And he said, "Well, I will take you to a place."

And undoubtedly they had radioed ahead, because he took us to the headquarters hotel of the Holiday Inn. It is on the banks of the Mississippi River, and it's a plush hotel. They already had waiting for us a suite that had a living area and two bedrooms, and one was for Dr. King, and one was for Bernard Lee and myself.

> Many stores along the march route were damaged, 280 people were arrested, 60 people were injured, and a black sixteen-year-old boy was killed by police gunfire. Later, the FBI circulated a memorandum to newspaper editorial offices across the country citing the breakdown of the nonviolent march in Memphis as a precursor to possible violence during King's Poor People's Campaign in Washington. Several papers wrote stories that followed the FBI's logic. The *St. Louis Globe-Democrat* virtually reprinted the FBI memorandum as an editorial against the Poor People's Campaign.

BERNARD S. LEE

We went to the motel. He didn't say anything. He just asked where was Jim, Jim Lawson. Jim, I'm sure, was out there trying to deal with the march. I think Andy was with us as well, if I'm not mistaken. But he just, he got on the bed and just rested, just went to sleep. I recall Ralph Abernathy getting a spread and putting it over him and he just slept through it. He just slept. He slept his discontent off. But I knew he was terribly, terribly moved, terribly upset by the events of this march, because deep in his heart and his mind, he knew that he would be criticized for the violent outburst of the march. And he was a victim of circumstances. He had been advised not to go to Memphis in the beginning, that we needed to be going to Washington to try to mobilize and develop the Poor People's Campaign. That this was an aside that he really didn't have time for or shouldn't have taken time for. But responding to a friend, he did so.

When he did awake, he talked about what he saw happening with the press, and he saw this as a tremendous setback for his efforts in Washington. He knew that those who had criticized his developing the Poor People's Campaign would say, You see, this is what will happen in Washington, D.C., if you bring all of these people here. That a similar situation will occur. And he just saw people gloating who were in opposition to the Poor People's Campaign.

Marian Logan was among the millions who had seen footage of the day's events on the evening news. That night, King phoned her.

MARIAN LOGAN

I was upset because I had seen the expression on his face, and I saw Ralph, of course, who was with him, he was distressed. And I just told him, I said, "Martin, I think you need to get your ass out of Memphis."

And he said, "Well, darling," he said, "you know we have to keep going, this is our movement."

I said, "But you haven't prepared those garbage workers." Like we generally have, you know, we'd send Andy in and Bayard, and a few others too. To get people organized in nonviolence and make them understand how important it was. And these garbage workers were not trained like that. And it was really a polyglot group of men, it was a union movement. But Martin wouldn't give in, because he just had to go back and prove that he could lead a nonviolent march of garbage workers in Memphis, Tennessee, in 1968.

King left Memphis after a press conference the next day, Friday, March 29, vowing to return for another march. But this new march would be overseen by SCLC staffers after conducting nonviolent training sessions and working in advance with the local leadership.

That night, King was back in Atlanta at the home of Ralph and Juanita Abernathy.

JUANITA ABERNATHY

He wanted to come here because if you go to a restaurant, then you got to answer questions about, well, what happened to the march? Why the violence? And he was not in the kind of mood to deal with answering those questions, because Dr. King was very sensitive about anything that was in opposition to what his philosophy was. And he didn't want anybody identifying him with the violence that had taken place, 'cause you know some of it was done by us, by blacks. And that hurt. And he just sort of felt that part of his reputation had been damaged and tarnished a bit. So he didn't want to have to deal with answering questions on that. And coming here, he would not encounter that. So we sat that night. And talked about light things. And talked about me. And talked about Ralph. We talked about each other. Talked about the movement. And just chitter-chat. But nothing serious. And we did not talk about Memphis. The news came on. And whenever there was a flash on TV about it, he got very quiet and he was really, really sort of depressed. And I think he was more depressed that night, I believe, than I'd ever seen him.

On Saturday, King held an emergency staff meeting. One of those in attendance was Jesse Jackson, who had been working with SCLC since the Chicago campaign.

JESSE JACKSON

He had this vision we should wipe out poverty, ignorance, and disease, that you couldn't do it on an ethnic basis. That it was never going to be in the plan to wipe out black poverty that would leave the Hispanics in poverty, or whites or women in poverty, or Native Americans in poverty, so we had to pull people together. And on this Saturday morning he said, "I've had a migraine headache for three days, and sometimes because our movement is divided I feel like turning around, just quitting, or maybe becoming president of Morehouse College." And then he said, as if something struck him, "But we will always be able to turn a minus into a plus. We can turn a stumbling block to a steppingstone. Sometimes my works feel to be in vain but then the Holy Spirit comes, I'm revived again." He preached himself out of the depression. He said, "Let us move on from here to Memphis."

> On Sunday, March 31, President Johnson announced to the nation that he would not be a candidate for reelection in November. King found some hope in Johnson's announcement. Perhaps someone more active in helping the poor would soon be installed in the White House.
>
> On Wednesday, April 3, King and Abernathy returned to Memphis to meet with local leaders about the new march, now tentatively scheduled for April 8. That afternoon, a temporary restraining order was imposed against the march. SCLC planned to challenge it in court the next day. King announced he would lead the march whatever the outcome. That evening, King was supposed to address a crowd at Mason Temple.

RALPH ABERNATHY

There was a tornado warning in Memphis that evening. And it was raining, raining, and wind was blowing everywhere. I believe a little tornado came to Memphis also. And he knew that there would not be a big crowd. And he said to me, in the meeting, with the staff around, "I want you to go and speak this evening at the mass meeting." He had become so accustomed to large crowds, and I said, "Oh no, don't send me. Send Jesse or Andy or one of the other fellows." And he said, "Ralph, there is only one person in the world that can speak for me. And that is Ralph David Abernathy. Will you go?" And I said, "Yes, I will go." And so I went. [But] when I got in and was seated, I knew that those photographers and those cameramen were looking for Dr. King. And it was not meant for me. And so I asked, "Where is the nearest telephone?" And I decided that I would go find that telephone and call for Dr. King. And Dr. King said, "Okay, Ralph, I will be right there." And I made a second pitch. I said, "Martin, you know I would not ask you to come ordinarily, but these people want to hear you, and they want to see you," and he said, "David, that is not important. I will be there. Have I ever told you that I would do anything that I did not do? I will be there as soon as the car can bring me over." And when he got over there to the church, in fifteen minutes, the cameramen were glad to see him, and the people were glad to see him, and the presiding officer says to me, "Which one of you wants to be first tonight?"

Abernathy gave a lengthy introduction of his friend, who then delivered a sermon that was to become known as the mountaintop speech. King spoke of the need to march again in Memphis, of the importance of ministers being socially active in what he termed "a relevant ministry." "It's all right to talk about 'long white robes over yonder,' in all of its symbolism. But ultimately people want some suits and dresses and shoes to wear down here. It's all right to talk about 'streets flowing with milk and honey,' but God has commanded us to be concerned about the slums down here, and his children who can't eat three square meals a day. It's all right to talk about the new Jerusalem, but one day, God's preacher must talk about the new New York, the new Atlanta, the new Philadelphia, the new Los Angeles, the new Memphis, Tennessee."

He spoke in some detail about the need for the black community to launch an economic withdrawal from its oppressors. He listed products for his listeners to boycott, banks people of goodwill should support, black insurance companies who should receive the policies of black clients.

His aides had heard versions of it on other occasions, but for the strikers and their supporters, his last words that evening were new: "Well, I don't know what will happen now. We've got some difficult days ahead. But it really doesn't matter with me now, because I've been to the mountaintop. And I don't mind. Like anybody, I would like to live a long life. Longevity has its place. But I'm not concerned about that now. I just want to do God's will. And He's allowed me to go up to the mountain. And I've looked over. And I've seen the promised land. I may not get there with you. But I want you to know tonight, that we, as a people, will get to the promised land. And I'm happy tonight. I'm not worried about anything. I'm not fearing any man. Mine eyes have seen the glory of the coming of the Lord."

BILL LUCY

I guess that you could say the mountaintop speech was perfect for the kind of speech that it was. It was an inspiring speech, one that Dr. King had really given what appeared to be a good deal of thought to. It told about his personal experiences, both high points and low points. It wove into it a message that the strikers were entitled to continue their struggle, and certainly entitled to the broad base of support that they had built across the city. He then went on to talk about the vision that he saw both for them and for himself. And it was one of the most dramatic speeches I've ever heard. It was not negative, it was really very, very high. When it ended, the entire church at Mason Temple just went wild with excitement. I mean, he had touched a chord that was so deeply rooted in all of the people—it went far beyond the strikers to community people—and he had shared with them his view of not only himself but his role in society.

The Reverend James E. Smith was one of the Memphis ministers supporting the strikers.

JAMES E. SMITH

It was an overcoming spirit in Mason Temple that night. We knew that we were going to win. Dr. Abernathy spoke well. But we were waiting for Dr. King. And because he was in town there was an overcoming mood, an overcoming spirit in that place. When Dr. King spoke that night we knew that we were going to win. There was something about Dr. King. A man who could walk with kings, but he was just as simple when he spoke that all of us understood him. Never met a man like that before.

ANDREW YOUNG

The next day I was in the federal court, trying to testify to get the injunction lifted so that we could have a march. I was in court all day long, on the witness stand a good part of that day.

We got the injunction thrown out and we got our permission to march, and I guess about four-thirty or five o'clock I came back to the Lorraine Motel and I found Martin and A.D. [King] and Ralph and everybody gathered there, and they'd been eating, had lunch, and were talking and clowning. And when I came in, Martin just grabbed me and threw me down on the bed and started beating me with a pillow. I mean, he was like a big kid, and he was fussing because I hadn't reported to him, and I tried to tell him I was on the witness stand, I'm here in the federal court, and he was just standing on the bed swinging the pillow at me, and I'm trying to duck with him saying, "You have to let me know what's going on." [*Laughs*.] And finally I snatched the pillow and started swinging back and everybody—it was sort of like after you make a touchdown and everybody piles on everybody. I mean, people just started throwing pillows and piling on top of everybody and laughing and going on. And then he stopped and said, "Let's go, you know we're due at dinner at six," and it was at that time about six o'clock. And he went on up to his room to put on a shirt and tie. I went out in the courtyard waiting for him and started shadowboxing with James Orange, who is about six-five and two hundred eighty pounds. I mean, James could slap me on the ground with his little finger. But I was clowning around with him and Martin came out and asked, "You think I need a coat?" And we said, "Yeah, it's pretty cool and you've had a cold, you better go back and get a coat." And he said, "I don't know whether I need a coat." And the next we know, a shot—well, I thought it was a car backfiring or a firecracker.

RALPH ABERNATHY

I heard what sounded like a firecracker. And I jumped. And when I jumped I saw only his feet laying on the balcony. And I immediately rushed to his side and I started patting his cheek, saying, "Martin, Martin, Martin. Don't be afraid. Don't be afraid. This is Ralph. This is Ralph. This is Ralph." And I got his attention. And he calmed down. His eyes were moving and he became very, very calm.

And finally Andrew Young came up the steps and said, "Oh God. Oh God, Ralph. It is over."

And I became angry with Andrew Young and said, "Don't you say that, Andy. Don't you say that. It is not over."

And Billy Kyles, whom we were going to eat with, came up and I said, "Billy, get me an ambulance." And I heard nothing but a loud cry from our room. And I said, "Billy, keep yourself together. I want an ambulance."

And he said, "Ralph, all of the lines are busy. All of the lines are busy."

[When an ambulance arrived,] I went with him, rode with him in the back of the ambulance. And I committed civil disobedience and I would not leave the operating room. And finally the doctor came over to me and said, "You are Dr. Abernathy? He will not survive. It will be an act of mercy, because he would be paralyzed from his waist down. You may have your last moments with him."

And I went over and took him in my arms. And he breathed his last breath.

With one of his colleagues, William Rutherford had left Memphis after an afternoon staff meeting with King.

WILLIAM RUTHERFORD

We returned to Atlanta by plane. We arrived in Atlanta airport, took a taxi to the SCLC office, and it was a scene of total pandemonium as we arrived at the office on Auburn Avenue. People were screaming and fainting and literally rending themselves, tearing their clothing and so on and so forth, and we said, "What on earth is happening?" And some young woman screamed at us, "Dr. King has been shot. Dr. King has been shot." I said, "Well, that's hardly possible. We just left him. Just left him." So I went in the office and attempted to telephone to Memphis, and of course I couldn't get through for hours. But then we had the radio on and we began hearing the radio broadcast that reported not only that he had been shot, but that he actually had died. That was the way we learned of his death, having left him. All of the senior staff was with him in Memphis, either at the time of his death or very shortly before.

Oh, it took me ages and ages to accept the fact that Dr. King was definitely dead. He was such an active man. He was such a force and a presence, and it was just unbelievable and, I suppose, psychologically unacceptable that he would not be coming back. And in the midst of all this chaos and pandemonium in the SCLC office and headquarters, I kept expecting Dr. King to walk through the door at any minute saying, "All right, come on, this is great. But why don't we stop the nonsense now and get back to work."

As news of King's assassination spread, black communities across the country reacted with violence. Disorders broke out in 110 cities, more than seventy-five thousand National Guardsmen were called out, and thirty-nine people were killed.

HARRY BELAFONTE

The giving in to the loss of Dr. King erupted, but only in moments. The real sense of grieving about him did not come for me, and I think for my wife and a lot of others, until much later. When I flew immediately to Atlanta, there was this bewildering invasion of people, all these faces that we had never seen before, never knew before. All kinds of people, many of whom had come to this tragic moment as if it was a photo opportunity. I don't mean to discredit many who came out of real, genuine concern and goodwill, but there were others who saw in it a time that could be manipulated. So we had to do what we could to sort out those who came with an agenda, who were going to be the manipulators, from those who wanted to help move on with Dr. King's mission, who felt that the momentum of the movement should not falter. In a private conversation I had with Coretta King, we talked about going to Memphis, being there, to meet up with the garbage workers, to carry on the campaign and to do so immediately even before Dr. King was laid to rest. Everybody in the family agreed that it was appropriate. So I arranged for a plane and the necessary support to give Coretta and others mobility to do what had to be done. It was important that this nation know that even in the midst of our grief we were still committed to the objectives of the movement and that the fallen Dr. King did not leave behind a movement that, in the midst of this great tragedy, would lose its courage or its vision.

There was a sense at Dr. King's funeral that we were at a moment in history that was unique. All those hundreds of thousands of people who came there had a sense of oneness that I've never quite experienced anywhere else again.

It's interesting about death. At the March on Washington, a major convening of very diverse groups, Dr. King was alive and we had a great sense of ourselves and our power. It was another thing to be in this other environment, equally dramatic. Dealing with this huge and undefinable loss, very diverse groups of people, on the one hand, feeling close to their fellow humans and on the other hand, a need for perspective. I'll never forget, I was standing, at one point, next to a reporter from the *New York Times,* and he was obviously saddened by Dr. King's death. He was an important writer for the *Times*. Recalling an article on Vietnam and Dr. King, an editorial very critical and highly misleading which helped to fan the flames of discontent with Martin, painting him as unpatriotic, making people quite angry with him and the movement, I could not help but tell him that this grievous moment was in part the result of a climate of hate and distortion that the *New York Times* and other papers had helped create. In particular the way the *Washington Post* wrote its editorial on Dr. King and Vietnam. It was misleading. It was punitive. It was a great disservice to a great cause. And at the funeral when I said this, I didn't say it to him as a personal accusation. I said it because I wanted him to understand that no one could be exempted from responsibility if in the protection of special interests we abandoned moral responsibility. Just coming to grieve the loss was no cleansing of guilt. History would remember what the *Washington Post,* the *New York Times,* and other journals had done to make this moment realizable. I told him that the time would come again when his power and that of his paper would be put to the test. New leaders obviously are going to come. There's going to be a new wave of need for revolt, a new wave of demand and it would even be global.

Two months before his assassination, King had spoken to his congregation at Ebenezer Baptist Church in Atlanta and offered what could be described as his own eulogy:

"Every now and then I think about my own death, and I think about my own funeral. And I don't think of it in a morbid sense. Every now and then I ask myself, 'What is it that I would want said?' And I leave the word to you this morning.

"If any of you are around when I have to meet my day, I don't want a long funeral. And if you get somebody to deliver the eulogy, tell them not to talk too long. Every now and then I wonder what I want them to say. Tell them not to mention that I have a Nobel Peace Prize, that isn't important. Tell them not to mention that I have three or four hundred other awards, that's not important. Tell him not to mention where I went to school.

"I'd like somebody to mention that day, that Martin Luther King, Jr., tried to give his life serving others. I'd like for somebody to say that day, that Martin Luther King, Jr., tried to love somebody. I want you to say that day, that I tried to be right on the war question. I want you to be able to say that day, that I did try to feed the hungry. I want you to be able to say that day, that I did try, in my life, to clothe those who were naked. I want you to say, on that day, that I did try to visit those in prison. I want you to say that I tried to love and serve humanity.

"Yes, if you want to say that I was a drum major, say that I was a drum major for justice; say that I was a drum major for peace; I was a drum major for righteousness. And all of the other shallow things will not matter. I won't have any money to leave behind. I won't have the fine and luxurious things of life to leave behind. But I just want to leave a committed life behind."

25

Resurrection City, 1968

"The End of a Major Battle"

It had always been a tenet of the civil rights movement that it could not surrender to violence and survive. Students and veteran activists on the Freedom Rides were beaten nearly to death, and others rode in to take their places. There were deaths in Mississippi; still more demonstrators came. There were deaths in Selma; still more marched.

Just four weeks after the April 4 murder of Martin Luther King, Jr., SCLC's new head, Ralph Abernathy, set out from Memphis to lead the first group of marchers to Washington, D.C., opening the Poor People's Campaign. By bus, car, foot, and mule train, poor people moved up out of the South, across from the west, and down from New York City to take up residence on the Mall near the Lincoln Memorial, where only five years earlier a crowd of 250,000 had gathered to hear King share his dream.

In Memphis, as the marchers set out, Abernathy said, "For any of you who would linger in the cemetery and tarry around the grave, I have news for you. We have business on the road to freedom. . . . We must prove to white America that you can kill the leader but you cannot kill the dream."

On May 13, on the Mall in Washington, Abernathy welcomed the poor to a settlement he christened Resurrection City. It was a brave name for the city of tents and sheds on public land, and a difficult undertaking for many who still mourned their absent leader.

RALPH ABERNATHY

I felt that I had lost a part of me. I felt that I had to walk this lonesome valley now by myself. I knew all of the people of the Southern Christian Leadership Conference, the staff, I knew them well. And I had worked with them. I had hired most of them. And I knew their weaknesses and I knew their strong points. But I felt that I would have to walk the valley of life the rest of my days by myself without Martin Luther King.

Well, we vowed that we were going to stand together and stick together. Jim Bevel, speaking for the staff of the Southern Christian Leadership Conference, said, "I loved Dr. King. In many respects I loved Dr. King more than I love Jesus. But Dr. King is now dead. But we have our leader. And our leader is Ralph David Abernathy. And we are going on to Washington, but by the way of Memphis."

WILLIAM RUTHERFORD

The purpose and the goal of the Poor People's Campaign was to focus the attention of the nation and the world on poverty. The technique, the tactic being used, was to gather the poorest of the poor in the nation's capital, the heart of the wealthiest country in the world, to camp them, these homeless, hungry people, in the heart of this city and its fabulous malls situated between the Lincoln Memorial and the Washington Monument, take the plea and the complaint of the poor to each of the government agencies. To take them to the Department of Agriculture, where they deal with food. To take them to the Department of Justice, where they deal with laws and the application of laws. To take them to the Department of the Interior, where the Chicanos and the Native Americans have very serious problems of land tenure and so on. The thrust, the tactic of the Poor People's Campaign was in dealing with our own government to focus and attract the attention of the world on these problems, which are everpresent, but which by and large are largely ignored by the masses of Americans or which are not really focused on by the masses of Americans.

HARRY MCPHERSON

The reaction of the White House was a very unhappy one to the notion of people coming across the bridge in their wagons and camping on the Mall, camping in Lafayette Square just across Pennsylvania Avenue from the White House, that image of hundreds and hundreds of people representing the poor but also seeming to be the tools of a political leadership that was seeking to put pressure on the government to bring about change that could not be brought about overnight. Our shoulders sagged. They were going to ask for things that we couldn't provide. They were going to make a lot of people mad, people who were already growing restive. The first effects of the affirmative action programs were being felt in the country. A lot of white workers were getting sore with a feeling that they were being bypassed not through any fault of their own, but in order to advance blacks who had been held down. So the temper was not a good one.

I can tell you that from within the White House, sitting in the West Wing, with the windows open, you could hear people singing "We Shall Overcome" in the tents in Lafayette Square, which was mixed in on occasion with the sounds of people chanting along Pennsylvania Avenue, "Hey, hey, LBJ, how many kids did you kill today?" So you had the antiwar protesters on Pennsylvania Avenue and the antipoverty protesters in Lafayette Square. Both of them asking for immediate change. And out in the country you had the public opinion polls changing pretty radically and people getting more and more angry, more and more looking for a president who would bring the war to a quick end, a president who would enforce order in the cities.

ANDREW YOUNG

Resurrection City was a community that was designed for fifteen hundred, and many, many more people than that showed up. They were fifteen hundred well-trained, well-disciplined demonstrators that were to be recruited from around the country. And in the middle of this process Martin Luther King was killed. So that set us back, both in training and in building of Resurrection City. Everybody wanted to be a part of the Poor People's Campaign after Martin's death. The funeral was the same way. We would have thought that ten, fifteen thousand people coming to Martin's funeral would have been all we could handle. There were probably closer to a hundred thousand people, and yet we made it. But Resurrection City was not just more people than we could house or handle, there were people in Resurrection City who were placed there, I think, to disrupt and create discontent. So we were constantly fighting a battle both inside and outside.

At its peak, Resurrection City housed some 2,500 citizens—most of them black, 200 Native Americans, and a few dozen Hispanics. There was also a group of about 100 poor whites, but many of them complained that they had no voice in the activities and stayed only briefly.

BERNARD S. LEE

And to compound it all, it rained every day. Every day we had rain. And the stench from the rain on the soil, which was fertilized, the fertilizer itself just created a terrible odor. So this compounded our problems. Some people would say, Well, I hadn't volunteered for this. This is not what I envisioned. And that, the rain in itself, the daily rain, created to an extent monumental problems. Because it was very muddy. Sometimes, even though we had placed boards on the ground as a path for people to walk on, still some would wind up in the mud, many times. I recall myself just winding up in the mud, my boots just terribly muddy. And some of the residents didn't have boots. So it was really, it was an awful experience.

But the dividends were there as a result of their having participated and been in Washington in the Poor People's Campaign. The dividends did come, and it was not an activity that was in vain. But we had those human problems, hard to get some services to our people, and it was long sometimes before we could get the money to get some of the things that the residents really needed. But we established a city, and that's the fact that history must always recall. That for good or bad, whatever, however it perceives it, we did establish a city and people did live in that city. And we had all of the problems that any urban city would have. People would get angry with each other and they would commit violence against each other. All of the social and urban problems rested right in that city. We saw the reenactment of a city. We had created it. And in my estimation that was good. I mean, just as you have in the city of Washington or any other city, there were those human problems that existed. Some did not think we had effective leadership. Some felt that we had too much leadership and it did create problems within the city, there's no question about it. But we carried on, we did persevere. And I think we were better for it.

MICHAEL HARRINGTON

I was invited to Resurrection City. When I got to Resurrection City, I already knew from reading the newspaper reports that there had been a lot of violence, a lot of disorganization. That the beloved community was not there by the Washington Monument. And I lectured. Everything was given rather impressive names. And it was called the Poor People's University of Resurrection City. It was a group of people who were coming down and giving lectures during the day.

A group of people were sitting on the ground gathered around and a black man among them, I think with emotional problems, decided that I was the incarnation of white racism. And he wanted to know why I, who had been in the process of giving a talk attacking racism, talking about what was needed in order to end racism and poverty in the United States, was in favor of racism and poverty in the United States. And he got very agitated. And I became concerned that he could physically attack me. The meeting sort of came to a very unhappy ending, where my message didn't get across, and it's very hard to concentrate on your talk when you're worried that somebody might be about to jump you. The man left, and I left to go and catch a plane and to come back to New York, and literally ran away from the meeting. I wanted to get as far away from this place as I could. On the one hand, I was delighted that I was out of this miserable situation and I no longer had to be literally physically fearful. But on the other hand, it dawned on me that this was an end of an entire period of my life that went back to 1954 when I had joined the Harlem NAACP, right after *Brown* versus *Board of Education,* the desegregation opinion. And that one of the most marvelous political movements in America in the form which it took under Martin Luther King from 1955 to 1968 had come to an end. And that the beloved community was gone forever.

By this time Marian Wright had moved to Washington.

MARIAN WRIGHT EDELMAN

I don't recall specific plans for the Poor People's Campaign. They were coming to Washington out of a general and urgent need. They were hungry, there was growing poverty, but they had lost their leader. We were a bit bedraggled as the campaign began, and when I began to meet with them when they came here, it was very clear that the specific position papers and what they would ask each agency to do or what they would ask the president to do needed to be fleshed out. So I got myself an instant job of developing those position papers.

We were all very hurt. We had lost Dr. King. We were trying very hard to carry on. We were determined that the poor would be seen and heard. It was such a struggle. I mean, what I remember most about Resurrection City was the mud and the rain which came along with the poor people, how haphazard the logistics were, and how hard it was to go out and try to get them to be witnesses but how willing and open they always were in a very new setting, about going to do this. And I always have felt somewhat schizophrenic, because on one hand, going out to Resurrection City to identify and talk to witnesses, at the same time to try to craft what they said in a way in which Washington bureaucrats can hear it. So I ran this back-and-forth thing from sort of living out at Resurrection City to hear from them what was needed and then back over to the Pitts Motel, where SCLC staff were staying, where Dr. Abernathy was staying. But it was both a struggle and the poor were so moving, and again so determined to try to do what they could, and so needy, and so I guess my expectation was just to sort of get through the day and to get them heard, to see if the country can't respond.

DANIEL SCHORR

Mired down in mud and misery, the people in Resurrection City clearly needed some action to lift their spirits. So every now and then somebody would come and organize something for them to do.

On this day, late in May, the Reverend Jesse Jackson, of whom I had not been aware before this date, took three hundred of them, they marched up to the Department of Agriculture. He took them down to the cafeteria. They picked up trays. I saw Jackson tell them to go through the line and to give all the checks to him. And so, one by one, they took food, they went through the checkout counter, and they pointed to Jackson, who was standing there, tall, six footer, nodding, smiling, and they said, He's got the check for all of us. And when they'd all gone through the line, Jackson took a megaphone and he announced to everybody, "Okay," he said, "this government owes us a lot. And they've just begun to pay a little bit of it with this lunch."

> Three weeks after the opening of Resurrection City, the Poor People's Campaign lost a powerful ally. Robert Kennedy was fatally shot in the early morning hours of June 5, having just won the California Democratic presidential primary. He died on June 6.

ANDREW YOUNG

Following Martin Luther King's death, immediately after we left the hospital we had a meeting and we said that if you let people stop the dream when the dreamer is slain, then you just encourage people to keep on killing your leadership. So the most important thing was to pick up the movement and keep it going. So we didn't have time to grieve, we didn't have time to even miss Martin Luther King. We had to go on with his work. And so we pushed ourselves even though we were probably all emotionally and internally on the verge of exploding. And we pushed ourselves right on through the early days of the Poor People's Campaign. But then on the sixth of June, right after Martin's death on the fourth of April, Robert Kennedy's assassination just brought everything to a halt, and I think we began to grieve about Martin in the context of Bobby Kennedy's assassination because Bobby Kennedy had been with us in Atlanta at Martin's funeral. And many of us began to see in him a hope for the future. We kind of transferred a little of our loyalty, a little of our trust, and a little of our hope to him, and now he was gone too.

WILLIAM RUTHERFORD

I think the impression that Resurrection City was a failing cause occurred probably two or three weeks into the campaign. That is, we had anticipated a reaction on the part of the American public under the impact of the publicity that we had hoped to generate, that would have helped achieve the goal in focusing attention on the plight of the poor in America. And within two or three weeks after the demonstrations at the Department of Justice, at the FBI Building, at the Department of Agriculture, and so on, it became more and more clear that this was not happening, it was not about to happen. In fact, I would say that the culmination of the Poor People's Campaign, which left thwarted and frustrated the hundreds and thousands of people who had come from all parts of the country, who had no homes to go to, who were deeply buried in poverty and who remained buried in poverty despite the Poor People's Campaign, and were left completely stranded—they were the survivors of what could be described as the Little Bighorn of the civil rights movement.

I think the spirit went out of people. There were people there who had no place to go. People who had come to Washington, had come to Resurrection City, with a great deal of hope and who had none left. When I say it was the Little Bighorn of the civil rights movement, in fact it was the end of the hopes and dreams of many, many people who had come from various parts of the country to participate. It was a very sad, depressed, and depressing scene altogether. We had terrible weather at the time. The city was bogged down in mud and rain. Resurrection City was as bad as any battlefield there could have been in any of the great wars with the foot soldiers slogging through the mud.

There were really very sad scenes. There were people with no place to go clinging to these frame shanties. It was an instant shantytown there. People with very few possessions, poor possessions, things you wonder why or how a human being could have their total worldly goods reduced to such a small lot of almost nothing. Friends saying good-bye, friends being separated. Strangers who had become friends during the weeks of the Poor People's Campaign and Resurrection City. It was a very unhappy and miserable scene from every point of view—the point of view of the weather, the results of the campaign, and so on.

The last day of Resurrection City—I can continue this simile about a camp at the end of a battle or a war—the camp was largely abandoned, very few people were left. They had been warned. They had been given a delay to leave the premises and they were being in effect evicted by the Capitol and Park Police. There was a cap that went off and it sounded like a shot. Of course, everyone was very apprehensive and nervous about possible violence. And of course it was not a shot. I don't know really what the noise was, perhaps a firecracker. But the police in this long blue line moved forward and they actually fired tear gas, and we got a good whiff of tear gas, those of us who were supervising or serving as observers for the evacuation of the camp. And there was the smoke from the tear gas rising from the ground, again, like an abandoned battlefield. As you moved forward across the site, it was literally at the end of a major battle, a battle of the poor, and they had lost.

Resurrection City was torn down on June 24, 1968. Jesse Jackson had served as its unofficial mayor.

JESSE JACKSON

When Resurrection City was closed down there was a sense of betrayal, a sense of abandonment. The dreamer had been killed in Memphis and there was an attempt now to kill the dream itself, which was to feed the hungry, which was to bring the people together, and rather than come forth with a plan to wipe out malnutrition, they were wiping out the malnourished. The first time I had ever really experienced tear gas was in Resurrection City. They drove us out with tear gas. They gassed us. They shot Dr. King. Now they were gassing us. I was determined to keep the struggle moving—if you will, to keep hope alive. I left there with an awful sense of betrayal and abandonment.

Roger Wilkins had been involved in Justice Department negotiations with campaign leaders.

ROGER WILKINS

Right after Resurrection City was emptied out, I was told to go out to Fourteenth and U by the attorney general because there was an incipient riot. When I got there the intersection was all filled with volatile young people who clearly wanted to start a riot. And I looked around, and up on the back of a flatbed truck there was young Jesse Jackson, who was about twenty-six years old at the time. And he was preaching. And he was saying, "I am somebody. If you're somebody, you don't riot. Say after me, 'I am somebody.' If you are somebody, you go out and you build strong black people. Say after me, 'I am somebody.'" What Jesse was doing was preaching the riot out of those people. He's preaching, really, pride. "If you are somebody, you build up, you don't tear down. Say after me, 'I am somebody.'" He kept on preaching, he kept on preaching. He was taking quite a risk. 'Cause to preach nonviolence and to preach no rioting to a group of kids who wanted to tear the place down was taking a risk that you'd be called an Uncle Tom. Jackson took the risk, he preached the people down. They became calm, they went home, there was no riot. It was quite a remarkable performance for a twenty-six-year-old kid.

MARIAN WRIGHT EDELMAN

When Resurrection City was done, I never thought about giving up. I thought about how do I get up and figure out a new way to keep going. I don't think anybody ever has a right to give up on children or give up on the poor. The needs remain. The needs grow. I was raised at a time by black adults—my daddy was a preacher like Dr. King—where, if you saw a need, you tried to respond. And they showed us by personal example how to respond. In my little hometown in rural, segregated South Carolina, there was no playground where black kids could go and play, because we were segregated. So my daddy built a playground behind the church. There was no black home for the aged in South Carolina to take the elderly. So my daddy and mama started one, and we kids were taught to serve and clean and cook. So we learned that it was our responsibility to take care of the elderly. The question was never why, if there was a need, should somebody else do something. We were taught to ask, Why don't I do something? And Dr. King and Whitney Young and others of the sixties reinforced that in college. Dr. King struggled and went through his doubts. He was often discouraged. He was often depressed. He didn't know where he was going to go from day to day, despite the larger vision for what was right for America, and so what right did we have not to try to carry on? None of us had his eloquence and certainly not his goodness, but in our own ways, with our hands and our limited visions, we can try and craft together his dream.

26

Ocean Hill–Brownsville, 1967–1968

"Everything Became More Political"

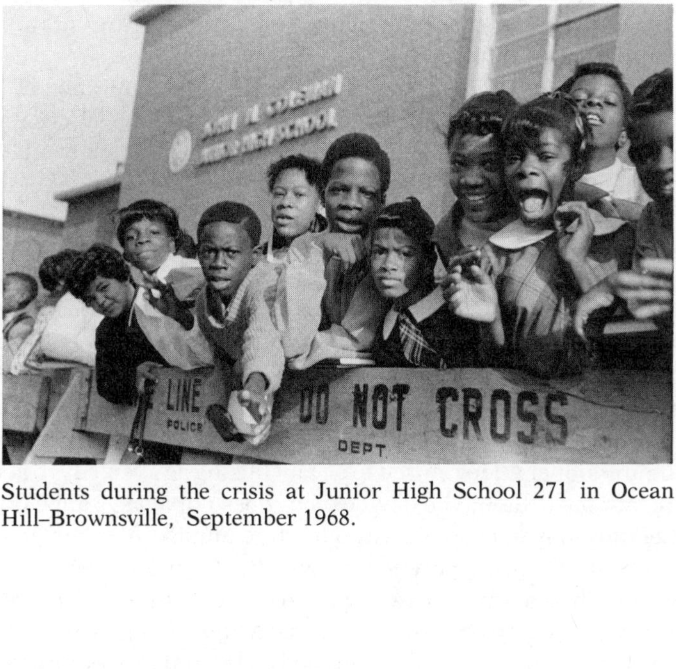

Students during the crisis at Junior High School 271 in Ocean Hill–Brownsville, September 1968.

April 5, 1968—the day after the assassination of Martin Luther King, Jr.—was not a typical day at Junior High School 271 in Brooklyn, New York. "I think right after homeroom period was when all hell broke loose," remembers Karriema Jordan, who was in seventh grade at the time. "We just threw chairs around, wrote on the walls, 'Avenge King! Kill Whitey!' It was almost a riot."

White teachers at the school were told by the principal, who was black, that they might not be comfortable attending a special assembly called to discuss King's death. "The principal said, 'If you want to leave, you may,'" Fred Nauman, a science teacher at the school, recalls. "And many of us left. We were very disturbed by the fact that we had been segregated. This seemed to be saying to the students, 'These people should not be here for this.'"

Controversy over which teachers belonged at the school had been brewing since September, when an educational experiment had begun at JHS 271 and seven other schools in the Ocean Hill–Brownsville section of Brooklyn. Convinced that the schools were not serving the needs of inner-city students, black and Hispanic parents had joined forces to demand the same degree of control that suburban communities exercised over their schools. Parents looked to community control as a means to improve the quality of the education of their children, to boost the self-image of black and Hispanic students, to bring more minority teachers into schools, and to make the curriculum more relevant to minority students.

At schools like JHS 271, where the student population was 98 percent black and Hispanic, community control was an alternative to integration. By the mid-1960s, parents and school officials alike had acknowledged that attempts to integrate New York City schools had failed. State Commissioner of Education James Allen, Jr., issued a blunt assessment of the situation in May 1964: "We must conclude that nothing undertaken by the New York City Board of Education since 1954, and nothing proposed since 1963, has contributed or will contribute in any meaningful degree to desegregating the public schools in this city." Though he advocated integration, Allen was also committed to preserving local neighborhood schools, especially for elementary school students. And like Mayor Robert Wagner and his successor, John Lindsay, Commissioner Allen refused to accept busing as a remedy to achieve desegregation. "It should be obvious, but does not always appear to be, that integration is impossible without white pupils," Allen noted.

Black and Hispanic parents agreed with Allen. In 1964, the board of education had assured parents in Harlem that Intermediate School 201, which was being built to ease overcrowding, would be integrated. But the next year, parents were outraged to learn that this "integrated" school would open with 50 percent black students and 50 percent Puerto Rican students—and that the school's principal would be Jewish, not black or Puerto Rican. "Either they bring white children in to integrate 201 or they let the community run the school—let us pick the principal and the teachers, let us set the educational standards and make sure they are met," declared Helen Testamark, a representative for local parents.

The concept of community control caught the attention of people across the city. In 1967, with funding from the Ford Foundation and the support of Mayor Lindsay, the city's board of education agreed to set up three small experimental school districts—one at IS 201 in Harlem, one on the Lower East Side, and one in Ocean Hill–Brownsville—to test how increased community participation would affect educational progress. Parents and community members in Ocean Hill–Brownsville began by electing an interracial board in August 1967 to govern the new district. The board, in turn, chose Rhody McCoy, a black eighteen-year veteran of the New York school system, as superintendent.

Within months of its inception, the Ocean Hill–Brownsville experiment posed some hard questions about the limits of community control: How much power did the local board really have? Could it hire new teachers? Could it fire old ones? By the fall of 1968, the search for answers had become a full-fledged power struggle. But throughout, local parents insisted that a single concern was driving their fight: the quality of education their children received.

Three of Dolores Torres's children, and a niece she raised, attended public school in Ocean Hill–Brownsville. She participated in early efforts to increase community control of the schools.

DOLORES TORRES

I can't talk about affluent white parents, or even affluent black or Puerto Rican parents. But poor people tend to say, "Well, these are the educated people. They're supposed to know what they're doing." And we just tend to sit back. But see, at the time, there were things going on. If I saw something going on and I knew it wasn't right, I would find out from other parents if they had seen similar things. And it just spread.

What happened was they told us the kids would have to go on double shifts. I had two going in the morning and two going in the afternoon. The school was overcrowded to an extreme. There wasn't much learning, wasn't much education going on. So we started going to PTA meetings, and meeting with other parents to decide what to do about this.

We were going down to 110 Livingston Street [the headquarters of the New York City Board of Education] to complain about the situation in the school. And they would just cut the mikes on us, you know. We would lodge complaints, and nothing was done about it. As I said, the [teachers'] union was dominating the schools. There was nothing done about it. We filed such and such about such and such a teacher, and we find that this has been going on for a little while, and there was nothing they would do.

And we just got fed up with it. One night, we went down there for a meeting, and they started turning off the mikes like they usually did, and we just took over. We took over their seats. That particular night, it was a dramatic thing, but it was something that had to be done. Because we had no voice power. No voice power at all.

I don't think I was surprised. I knew that, eventually, it would happen. Because if you're not getting any kind of satisfaction, and you have kids in the school system and they aren't being taught, then eventually you're just going to rebel. And that's what we had to do. It wasn't something that was actually planned. We just kept saying, "Well, they're not representing us. Maybe we should represent ourselves."

Torres was joined by activists from around the city in the sit-in that started that night in December 1966 at the Board of Education. It lasted for three days. The protesters, who called themselves the People's Board of Education, demanded that the school system "give local parents and community groups effective control over the education of their children."

The Reverend C. Herbert Oliver was pastor of the Westminster Bethany United Presbyterian Church in Brooklyn.

C. HERBERT OLIVER

When my family moved here from Birmingham in 1965, they came from totally segregated schools. The children were all black. The teachers were all black. The principals were all black. One of my sons was above the national average in mathematics. But when he came to the schools here in Brooklyn, within one year he was flunking math.

In Alabama, when I went to a school, I was welcomed. The principal was glad to see a parent there, and I could discuss any problem with my children there. But when I came to the school here in Brooklyn, I couldn't get to see the principal. Someone wanted to know why I came, what I wanted to see him for, and said that he was not available. So I simply said, "I will wait for him." I had expected to see the principal. That was my custom. But here I couldn't see a principal.

In about half an hour, the principal came. And I talked with the principal and told him what the problem was. We went and talked with the teacher. The teacher said my son was doing fine.

I said, "He's not bringing home assignments, and he's flunking math. He came here from Alabama and he was ahead of the national average, and you're telling me he's doing fine. Something is wrong." And that just made me fired up to do something to change the system, because I could see it was destroying children and it was hurting my own child.

There were almost no black principals in the schools. No role models. Tremendous discipline problems. And we found that most of the teachers in the district came into the district, taught, and then went out of the district to their homes. And, of course, this is altogether different from the southern situation, because in the South, the teachers lived among the people. And the principals—all black—lived somewhere among the people, and you got to know them. But this was a vast problem here. And we thought that the best thing that we could do for our young people would be to call for the community control of the schools, and seek through that means to better the education of our children. That's how the cry for community control got under way.

Sandra Feldman was a field representative of the United Federation of Teachers, the labor union that New York City's teachers had chosen as their bargaining agent in 1961.

SANDRA FELDMAN

In 1967, I had just started working for the union as a field representative, but I had come out of an activist background. I had been very active in the civil rights movement. I was a member of Harlem CORE. I had taken part in the Route 40 Freedom Rides [to desegregate restaurants on the Baltimore-Washington corridor in 1962]. I had been arrested right outside of Baltimore on those Freedom Rides. And I spent the summer of '63 as a volunteer organizer for the March on Washington, working closely with Bayard Rustin up in the headquarters at Harlem. So I knew a lot of people in the city and in the community. And I suppose that that was the reason I was sent out there.

Initially, I was asked to go out to a junior high school in Ocean Hill–Brownsville, where a community group had been agitating about improving the school. And when I went to meet with the teachers, first of all, I saw that the school was in bad shape. The school needed a lot in the way of repairs and maintenance and cleaning and supplies. Discipline in the school appeared to be out of control. When I met with the teachers, I urged them not to be defensive. This was a very integrated staff. They had immediately felt defensive because this community group was agitating about the school. And, of course, I had come from a background of nothing but agitation and organization in the civil rights movement. I said, "Look, you know there are problems in this school. It's obvious that there are resources needed here, that there are changes needed here. Why don't we try reaching out to work with this group and see if we can make it a positive experience?" And teachers thought about it and said, "Yes, let's try to do that."

At the beginning, the teachers were excited and enthusiastic about the possibility of really working in a creative way to change the schools. And even though it was very new and people were feeling their way, and I wouldn't say that they were ready to plunge into something totally different, there was a feeling that if we could really have the possibility of the parent support and the community support and get the resources that we need to help the kids, then this could be a very exciting thing. So the teachers were interested in this, and there was a lot of hope at the beginning.

Science teacher Fred Nauman was chairman of the UFT chapter at Junior High School 271.

FRED NAUMAN

JHS 271 was not a prestigious school. It was a ghetto school. But as a ghetto school, it was probably one of the best—at least that's how most of us felt about it. It was a school that had its share of successes, and I know a good many of us felt good about going to work every day.

In the spring of 1967, the teachers had been told that we would be a part of this experiment. Those of us who were involved during the summer found that that just wasn't true. Any suggestions that were made by the teachers were either disregarded or, actually, they were insulted about making them. In addition, Father Powis, who had explained the entire proposal to us at a staff meeting in June, had told us that every school would have a chance to vote in the fall as to its involvement in the program. When we came back in September, we were told, "Well, that's tough. We voted it. It's here and you'll cooperate."

John Powis, a priest at Our Lady of Presentation Church in Brooklyn, was the only white representative on the eleven-member governing board established after a community-wide election held in August 1967. Other board members included Dolores Torres and the Reverend C. Herbert Oliver, who was elected chairman.

JOHN POWIS

You've got to remember, at that time there was no superintendent in the school system that was black. There was maybe one or two black principals. There were no black assistant principals. Maybe a few here and there, but all of a sudden to have a superintendent who was black—New York wasn't ready for that.

School began and McCoy didn't have an office. So he went to 271 and he wanted some room space in 271. And the principal, who was his subordinate, simply told him he wouldn't give him any office space. He then tried some of the other schools, and he got indeed the same reception. He finally had to operate for more than seven or eight months in a storefront on Fulton Street. I mean, a storefront that had no heat. A storefront that had no decent facilities. It was really a disgrace, because any superintendent that was part of the system who had been named the superintendent would just walk into a school and immediately they would give him an office.

Rhody McCoy came to Ocean Hill–Brownsville from his post as acting principal of a Manhattan school for students with special needs.

RHODY MCCOY

I had an idea about education, and my idea was very simple. The schools were not there to teach the skills, i.e., reading, writing, and arithmetic, but to present or prepare a learning environment where youngsters would be educated. Too often, we got caught up in saying, "Our kids can't read and write, and they don't do well on standardized tests," and we lost sight of the fact that we've got millions of our kids who *can* read and write, and who can pass standardized tests, who are basically not educated in terms of what's going on in the real world.

When I talked to Malcolm X as well as [black educators] Herman Ferguson and Wilton Anderson, we had the same idea. It was not skills we were interested in, because the material that they were giving our youngsters wasn't worth the time of day. It wasn't going to do anything for their lives. So what we were looking at is how do we educate our youngsters, and Malcolm's posture, what he said from day one, was, "Wake up. And let's learn, get educated."

> Les Campbell, a history teacher, was a founding member of the African-American Teachers Association. He had transferred into the Ocean Hill–Brownsville district in February 1968, after being suspended in another school district for taking students to a service held to commemorate the assassination of Malcolm X.

JITU WEUSI (LES CAMPBELL)

When I arrived at Junior High School 271, I had very little means of communicating with the student body, with the teachers, and the adults in the school. And I decided that I would use the bulletin board as a means of communication. I constructed a bulletin board and put it in the rear hallway and it was an immediate success. I had on there various pictures of black heroes and heroines. I had various political slogans of the day. Pictures of people like Stokely Carmichael and Rap Brown, who were the heroes of the Black Power movement of that day. We had this large poster of Uncle Sam, with the slogan "Uncle Sam Wants You, Nigger," which was an antimilitaristic poster talking about the fact that the United States government was recruiting young black males to go and fight in Vietnam for freedom that they did not in fact have living in the United States.

Some of the parents did in fact find me too radical. I know one particular parent, Elaine Rooke, who was the PTA president at Junior High School 271, me and her had a number of confrontations as she found my style too black, too political, too militant to teach the students. I remember her son Anthony. She used to tell him, "Stay away from Mr. Campbell, because he'll get you in trouble." So there were parents in the school who found me to be too radical and too militant as a teacher.

Sia Berhan was in seventh grade in the spring of 1968.

SIA BERHAN

Les was a joke. 'Cause he was real tall, and everybody regarded him as some kind of freak. The kids, I mean. It was like, "Come down here and look at this guy, this teacher. You gotta see this guy. He's ridiculous." He was real tall, and he had gray hair, you know—not all gray, but gray in front—and he wore a dashiki. And it was like, this guy is from another planet. This guy is strange. He wasn't one of my teachers. But everybody wanted to know what he was about. Because he wasn't like the other teachers.

The other teachers wore a shirt and tie and jacket. He was the only one to wear a dashiki at that time, and nobody knew what a dashiki was. He broke out in a pair of sandals one day, and it was like, you know, what is this guy into? And then when we would laugh at him, he would say, "The reason why you're laughing is because you don't know who I am." And, of course, I asked him, "What are you? Who are you? What are you about?" And he stopped and talked, to tell us what the dashiki was and what he was about.

Some members of the local governing board wanted to remove Les Campbell and other teachers and administrators perceived to be detrimental to the experimental district. The issue came up at the local governing board meeting in May 1968.

JOHN POWIS

In May, the local board had its regular meeting. I guess we were having meetings at that point about every two weeks. And on the agenda that night, McCoy had put an item to transfer thirteen teachers and also some assistant principals. I guess there were about five or six of them.

We came into the meeting, and of course the issue was such an important issue, we spent an awful lot of time. We really labored over it. We knew that there was really no demonstration district going on because these folks were the ones, the main ones, who were causing us so much sadness because of the way that they just weren't cooperating with the experiment. But we spent a lot of time, we talked it out, we worked it out, we asked people from the community who came into the meeting, and we finally came to a conclusion, so that we could have a demonstration district—this is like eight months after it had begun—we decided some of these people would have to be transferred, would have to go.

Although the school board voted not to transfer Les Campbell, it did decide to send the following letter to thirteen teachers and six administrators, of whom seventeen were white, one Puerto Rican, and one black: "The Governing Board of the Ocean Hill–Brownsville Demonstration School District has voted to end your employment in the schools of this District. . . . This termination of employment is to take effect immediately. . . . You will report Friday morning to Personnel, 110 Livingston Street, Brooklyn, for reassignment."

DOLORES TORRES

We were the local school board. We had hired professionals that agreed, like we agreed, that our children had to be taught. But a lot of the teachers who had been there—not the new people that the governing board had hired—did not feel that. They felt that the union said, "Well, you don't have to do this and you don't have to do that." We went over records of people that had been taught by them. Also, previously we had looked in our classrooms where these teachers were teaching. And we felt that they were there but what they were doing was baby-sitting. We didn't feel that they really had our children's best interest in mind.

We were asking teachers to make an extra effort to get along with our kids, to teach our kids. If there was any problem, to visit in the home. We felt that these people were not doing as we asked. They wouldn't even compromise. We had bells ringing at three o'clock for dismissal, and teachers were out of there before the kids were. So we felt that they weren't making any effort to try to change their way of thinking and teaching. And we felt that we couldn't put up with it anymore.

We felt that these teachers were undermining what we were trying to do. The thing of it was, we did not fire these people. We could *not* fire the nineteen teachers. We had no power over firing. We had power over hiring. We could not fire anybody. So we really didn't have that much power. The only way you can have total power is to be able to hire and fire, as well. Okay? We did not have this power. All we did was dismiss these teachers. We reassigned them to 110 Livingston Street.

FRED NAUMAN

On the evening of May 8, 1968, I received a call at home from Sandy Feldman, the union representative in the district. She told me that she had heard that something was about to happen. She did not know precisely what. The next morning, I was called to the principal's office to receive a registered letter. Some of the teachers had the registered letters delivered to them in their classes. And that letter basically said that the governing board had voted to terminate their employment in the district. That was the specific language.

I'm not sure that I can say my reaction was anything more than I was totally numb. That was the last thing in the world I expected. I had been meeting monthly with McCoy, as part of a group in the union who were trying to work out problems. And at no time had anybody mentioned that there was a problem with my service, or, for that matter, with any of the people who were named, or certainly the majority of them. I didn't know them all. But here was this letter that ordered me out. So all I can tell you is, I was dumbfounded.

RHODY MCCOY

The school system was a bastion of white domination that would never relinquish its control. Never! And the programs and things that it developed and implemented were forms of control. I don't want to get into heavy philosophical things, but let's say "mind control." When you get into this kind of discussion, you're taking on not just the school system, you're taking on white America. So if I say, "Hey, you are not educating my child, and I want you outta here. I don't want you to keep messing with my child's mind," then all of the entities in white America descend on you—i.e., civil service, i.e., equality, i.e., anti-Semitism, you name it. They descend on you.

Albert Shanker was president of the United Federation of Teachers.

ALBERT SHANKER

I did not oppose community participation or even community control. I am against what in those days was called "total community control," which means that we can do anything we want and people don't have any civil rights or human rights or anything else. So we'd better be very careful with what words mean here. Yes, I don't favor a decentralization plan where local community boards can do anything they want, unregulated. We don't have that in our country. A mayor can't do anything he wants, a governor can't do anything he wants. I didn't want school districts to do anything they want.

Rhody McCoy was really saying, "Hey, don't come back to Ocean Hill–Brownsville." Well, if I say to an employee who works for the union, "You're transferred. Don't come back," I'm firing him. I'm not giving him another job anywhere else, because I can't. The only place I can give him a job is right in my own place, which is exactly what Rhody wasn't going to do. So it was a firing. And the very fact that they were called transfers was an indication of the kind of lie the whole thing was. He should have said, "I'm firing you." He should have been honest and above board.

To me, the civil rights movement was a movement for integration and a movement to eliminate segregation. In a sense, this represented a kind of backward step. It represented a step by people in the community saying, "We've given up on integration, so we want to take hold of our own schools."

The governing board's decision to dismiss the nineteen teachers and administrators set the stage for a protracted struggle. The

UFT demanded that its members be allowed to resume their teaching positions; the governing board vowed that the nineteen would not be permitted back.

In the weeks following the dismissals, the teachers, flanked by police, attempted to reenter the schools and were met by angry members of the community. Three hundred and fifty union teachers in the district staged a walkout in support of their colleagues, but the schools in Ocean Hill–Brownsville remained open, with members of the community filling in for the striking teachers.

RHODY MCCOY

When the parents manned the classrooms during the strike, their eyes opened, their hearts opened, and they began to break that myth that there was something mystical about teaching. The parents who are now teachers came to school beautifully dressed and sharp and ready to take on and assume this professional manner. Now these youngsters, who had previously seen ninety percent of their teachers white, are now looking at their parents or the parents of their friends who are teaching. So you already had a change in the learning atmosphere. And this new role model was just fantastic. No more hooky, no more truant playing. Everybody was coming to school.

The school year ended with the UFT teachers still on strike. In August, with the new year approaching, the board of education granted the Ocean Hill–Brownsville board permission to recruit new teachers to take the places of the striking union members.

DOLORES TORRES

In the summer of '68, we knew that we would have to have more teacher coverage in the school than we were going to have with the teachers that stayed, that were not going to be out on strike. We interviewed teachers that summer to come into the schools. And a lot of them were young people. And I guess at that time, well, we called them hippies. They had long hair. The men and the women. We weren't used to that. I mean, our kids went for the Afros, but these were young white people with long hair. They wore jeans. But they seemed like they weren't afraid. They weren't afraid to try something new in teaching our kids to get them to learn. Especially the reading and the math and the sciences. And we thought that they spoke our language. They weren't afraid to come into our neighborhood.

On August 26, Judge Francis Rivers, a black arbiter hired by the board of education to mediate the dispute, ruled that the union teachers had been dismissed illegally and ordered the local governing board to readmit them. The local board refused. In response, the UFT called a citywide teachers' walkout. Between Labor Day and Thanksgiving, three separate strikes kept 1 million students and 57,000 teachers out of school for a total of eight weeks. But schools remained open in Ocean Hill–Brownsville, where, to replace the striking unionized teachers, the local governing board had hired 350 new teachers. Of these, about a hundred were black. The remaining teachers were white; half of those were Jewish.

Karriema Jordan was in eighth grade at JHS 271 in the fall of 1968. She was a member of the school's African-American Students Association.

KARRIEMA JORDAN

I was born Theresa Jordan, that's true. But slave names were out. You know, Jordan was the slave master's name, and Theresa was some—I don't know. So everybody adopted African names. I adopted mine from a book that I read in a summer program. The book was on African civilizations, and one of the women in that book was Nabowiah. So I thought Nabowiah was a great name. She was a woman prophet. My name was Nabowiah Weusi. Weusi meant black. So I adopted that name. Everybody called me Nabi. But I met an African brother who said to me that I was not an African prophet, a woman prophet, and that was sacrilege, you know. So he decided to name me Karriema, which is a person in the Koran who did good deeds for the prophet Mohammed. I didn't oppose it. One name to me was just as good as the other, as long as it was African. So I kept the name Karriema.

During the fall of 1968, I was totally amazed to get up in the morning, walk, meet my friend Sia. Coming from the Howard Avenue side, we had to go through barricades to get to the school. We'd look out on the rooftops, across the street from the school:

the cops were there with their riot helmets and their nightsticks and helicopters, and the playground was converted into a precinct, and walking up to the school you have just mass confusion. You have the community people out there. You have the UFT. You have the black teachers on the inside. You were just amazed. You couldn't believe this was happening, you know, and you just went to school.

[With so many new black teachers at JHS 271], you learned a lot more. You identified more. You learned that teachers were human beings, not some abstract something. They stayed after school. At three o'clock, they didn't run downstairs and punch out. You know, they gave you more time. I mean, you felt more accepted. You weren't an outsider in your own school. They were part of your environment. I mean, they were black. You can identify with them and they can identify with you. It's as simple as that. There's no big mystery, you know.

> During the strike, UFT teachers attempted to return to JHS 271 but were barred by local residents. Striking teachers and community members each set up picket lines outside the school; inside, students attended classes taught by nonunion replacements.

SANDRA FELDMAN

From the point of view of the union, it was a totally basic issue. You're talking about nineteen people who were told, in effect, "You haven't got jobs anymore." It was a dramatic thing, and it was public. So the union really had no choice in the matter in terms of doing whatever it had to do. Especially in view of the fact that the board of ed in the city of New York seemed to have washed their hands of the thing. They just weren't helpful at all. They weren't exercising any authority. And don't forget, the union was still young then. It hadn't at all developed the kind of power that it now has.

I was assigned to go out and stay with the teachers. I was a union presence. I guess I was protecting them or something. There were a number of days when there were a lot of volatile moments, when crowds were being kept away from the school by the police, and teachers had to sort of walk through a gauntlet of shouting, jeering people. It was very painful and very frightening. There were a number of days like that. I used to meet them at a certain point and we'd just sort of walk together to the school where the picketing took place. I think I provided some feeling of protection, somehow. I don't know exactly how, but I wasn't as afraid as they were.

These are teachers who, you know, had spent years and years coming to the school. And suddenly they found themselves so pilloried, so much anger out there at them. It wasn't really anger at them, you know. It wasn't fair in a sense, because these teachers had really tried to do their best for kids, most of them. Not everyone is perfect, obviously. But they tried to do their best. They had worked there all those years. And there was a tremendous conflict taking place, and here they were in the maelstrom of it. And it really didn't have anything to do with who they personally were. The teachers who were supposedly dismissed or transferred, those charges had nothing to do with who they specifically were. They were just picked to be symbols.

KARIMA JORDAN

During the strike, you'd try to have science, you know, but you just can't have a biology class with all the political science going on. So basically, you have political science. Because you, as a student, you have to know why these things are happening. Everything became more political, no matter what it was. If it was Miss McNair's English class, part of the class now is focusing on Langston Hughes. If it was Mr. McFadden's shop class, you know, even while you're constructing whatever you're constructing in shop, you're still talking about what's going on outside. And it was healthy. This information was needed. With white teachers, you didn't discuss these things. You didn't bother to even ask. They didn't volunteer any information, either.

JOHN POWIS

During the strike, every time I went into the schools, particularly 271 or IS 55, I saw something that I thought was so spectacular that I still thought that we were going to win this thing. I mean, I knew the odds were against us. But I think what really made it so difficult was the fact that something was happening in those schools. Here you had mostly new teachers, who were not supposed to have this tremendous experience and all this stuff. But you had schools that were completely orderly, where classes were going on. And people were coming in from the State Office of Education, from the mayor's office, from the board of education, and they were seeing this and saying, "You know, who's so stupid as to destroy this?"

FRED NAUMAN

In the fall of '68, when the city was trying to end the strike, they were dangling all kinds of enticements in front of us. I'm not sure where they were coming from. I was called into the personnel office of the [city] board of education at one point. Ted Lang was in charge of personnel, and we had a nice conversation and he asked me if I wanted to be involved in a computer operation he was establishing at the board, was I at all interested in that kind of work. It was an obvious ploy to see if I would want to move over there. At one point, we were offered a year of study at Harvard. I think that was when Lindsay was getting directly involved.

A lot of times when we wanted guidance, especially from Al Shanker, he almost completely left the decisions of whether we wanted to accept these offers up to us. You have to understand, at this point, we had become sort of heroes to the city—to some of the right people and some of the wrong people. Backing out at this point would have been psychologically difficult. Teachers felt we were fighting a battle for the continuation of the union, the continuation of basic teachers' rights in the city. That kind of support was positive. We got some very negative support from various racist groups. I spoke at a couple of schools out in Bay Ridge, where they wanted me to run for political office. The things that you heard was, "You got the guts. You put the blacks in their place." It was disturbing.

I don't think that we ever lost the support of the black community. I think that an artificial battle was set up by some people who were taking the civil rights movement and using it for personal power, personal aggrandizement. The community of Ocean Hill–Brownsville, the parents of youngsters we had been teaching, did not change a great deal. I think they were friendly to us before, and for the most part friendly to us during and after. What did happen is that a number of people, some of whom had come from outside, some of whom never were part of the local community, had begun to incite students. They incited some of the neighborhood toughs. Also, the relationship with the black teachers with whom I had been friendly deteriorated rather rapidly. We were polarized. Even before this point, a good deal of polarization had taken place. There was a young black science teacher who I had been very friendly with. Dorothy Hopkins was an excellent, excellent science teacher. And we had been very friendly. She became very militant, became a part of the leadership of the opposing group. And I don't think we had two words together after that.

KARRIEMA JORDAN

The police, the UFT teachers, the media—they taught us that we weren't worth anything. What the black teachers did was to broaden us, our perspective of looking at things. We were no longer members of the small community called Ocean Hill–Brownsville. We were broadened to W.E.B. Du Bois, his writings, Langston Hughes, Malcolm X, Marcus Garvey, H. Rap Brown, Mao Tse-tung, the Red Book. I mean, we became international, and it was a good thing, because black people are the Third World. The Third World is much larger than European history. They brought us back to ancient African history, I mean ancient world history, which didn't any longer start at Rome. It started with the Benin society, its melting of ore and silver and gold and things like that. We became much larger than just the community, and still today, when I look at things, I look at it from an international perspective. And that was what those teachers taught us.

JITU WEUSI (LES CAMPBELL)

We had outfoxed Albert Shanker. We had outmaneuvered the United Federation of Teachers. We had shown that this downtrodden community faced with a crisis, using its own resources, could overcome. And there was a feeling of jubilation, and the parents and the community were so much behind us and so supportive of us, this made it feel that much more exhilarating to know that we had community support. I used to walk through the streets of Ocean Hill at that time, and it was so beautiful. Parents used to come up and tell me to come in the house and have some fish or have some chicken or have some coffee or have a cold drink. These were parents who were pouring their hearts out to people who they felt were doing something to educate their children.

The strike was a unifying factor in the black community. Groups that had previously been at each other's throats found themselves together at rallies and meetings surrounding Ocean Hill. It was an issue that, whether you were CORE or the NAACP or the Urban League or the Black Panther party or the Republic of New Africa, you could rally around this community issue. Everybody understood the importance of black children receiving a quality education, and all organizations were willing to rally in support of Ocean Hill–Brownsville. I don't think there's been an issue in New York City that has gotten the total support of all elements of the black community as this educational issue.

> On October 6, the city's board of education suspended the Ocean Hill–Brownsville governing board for thirty days for refusing to allow the transferred teachers to return to the classroom. Two days later, the superintendent of schools relieved Rhody McCoy of his duties as unit administrator; McCoy rejected the directive and remained at his post. Thousands of supporters gathered at City Hall in solidarity with McCoy.

RHODY MCCOY

We went down and met at City Hall. And from that, spontaneously, some of the parents—Mrs. Hanson and Mrs. Torres and Reverend Oliver—suggested that to demonstrate for the city, that we walk over the bridge. We'd cross the bridge and be right in front of board of ed headquarters, taking this entire community and showing both the mayor and the school system that they were in support of the program and didn't want it to change.

Walking across the Brooklyn Bridge was, in my judgment, the greatest moment in my life. I was amongst the people who felt I was doing a good job and supported it and who were committed to the education of black kids. And there were just so many youngsters there. I mean, a lot of youngsters, cheering and orderly and in support of the program and the project and their parents.

C. Herbert Oliver

It was racism, northern-style, that we had to deal with. Bureaucratic racism. It was institutionalized in the North, but more disguised. It was more open in the South: there it was. You could just go right after it and fight it. But here, it was much more disguised. You'd work on one part of the bureaucracy, and it may cave in, but another thing would crop up with as much racism—or more.

The union was our greatest foe, I would say, and they eventually won the day by discrediting the governing board. They painted us as anti-Semites. The union took some writings of a black anti-Semite, I don't know who it was, and attached it to the name of Ralph Poynter, who was one of the activists supporting community control in our district. Said that he was an anti-Semite, and this is what he wrote. And they sent thousands of those all around the city. Apparently, people believed we were anti-Semites, because that is what eventually undercut our support. Mayor Lindsay never accepted that we were anti-Semites. He knew better. He had two advisers who were with us, and they knew better. But the charge was so thoroughly put out, and the newspapers carried it also. And then the Jewish community, they became very much alarmed.

The American Civil Liberties Union came to our support, as well as the Jewish teachers in the district. They took out an ad in the *Times* paper, saying this is not an anti-Semitic governing board. But that didn't have any effect on the line that went out.

> During the strike period, some union teachers found an unsigned leaflet in their mailboxes at JHS 271. It read, in part: "If

African American History and Culture is to be taught to our Black Children it Must be Done By African Americans who Identify With And Who Understand The Problem. It Is Impossible For the Middle East Murderers of Colored People to Possibly Bring To This Important Task The Insight, The Concern, The Exposing Of The Truth That is a *Must* If the Years Of Brainwashing And Self-Hatred That Has Been Taught To Our Black Children By Those Bloodsucking Exploiters and Murderers Is To Be OverCome." The UFT reprinted 500,000 copies of the flyer. A note at the bottom of the reprint asked: "IS THIS WHAT YOU WANT FOR YOUR CHILDREN? THE UFT SAYS NO!"

FRED NAUMAN

I had never felt, and I know there are people who disagree with me, that our being Jewish had anything to do with our being fired. That was a coincidence caused partly by the fact that a good number of the whites in the district were Jewish. There was obviously a black/white confrontation, but the fact that many of the teachers who were fired were Jewish, I think, was incidental. It became more serious when a gentleman who was not a part of the district, who usually came where there was troubles, produced a leaflet and somehow got it distributed in everybody's mailboxes in many of the schools. That, of course, was picked up by the press and became a cause célèbre.

ALBERT SHANKER

The question wasn't so much how widespread is anti-Semitism. The real question was that in the past, if somebody were to make a remark calling somebody a kike or a nigger or a spic or something else, everybody else who was respectable would stand up and would denounce it. But here, when these things were done by some people in the black community, everybody started saying, "What a beautiful expression this is of the anger of the community. The rest of you had better be sensitive to this." I mean, there have always been bigots—people who were antiblack and people who were anti-Semitic. That wasn't surprising. They exist today, and unfortunately, they always will. The whole thing was not, "Do they exist?" Or, "Do they constitute a majority?" The whole question is, "What is the moral atmosphere of an entire community? Does it condemn this sort of thing or does it justify it one way or another?"

A lot of liberals and a lot of Jewish people felt, "Look. We are for human and civil rights. That's why we were in the South, and that's why we'll be anywhere else where people's rights are violated." But now, there are substantial numbers of people within the black community who say, "No. Civil rights doesn't mean that everybody has a right to a fair trial. Civil rights to us means black rights—and Black Power." This is a thing that Bayard Rustin and I and Phil Randolph just cried over a lot. The reason I [had originally] wanted Martin Luther King to come up was not to help our teachers. I wanted him to come up in order to maintain a coalition between blacks and whites. And say, "Look. Wouldn't it be wonderful if blacks rallied around a white being discriminated against because of his race?" This would solidify the civil rights movement. It would keep it going. It was not a question of each group supporting its own kind.

On December 26, 1968, Les Campbell appeared on a WBAI radio talk show hosted by Julius Lester, a veteran of SNCC. At Lester's request, Campbell read a poem written by Sia Berhan entitled "Anti-Semitism."

JITU WEUSI (LES CAMPBELL)

I don't regret having read it. I think the response is raw. The child had very little knowledge of the whole, total picture of Jews, the history of Jews. In fact, she had been taught most of her life by Jewish teachers who had taught her about the Holocaust, had taught her about injustices to the Jewish people, and she was just finding it unusually strange that now some of these Jewish people were performing injustices to her people. That was what she was saying in the poem.

Nothing big came out of that radio broadcast until approximately three weeks later, on January fifteenth, when Albert Shanker revealed to the world that, you know, this poem was an indication of the anti-Semitic response of Ocean Hill–Brownsville and that teachers like myself were teaching these youngsters anti-Semitism within the school system, particularly within the experimental project at Ocean Hill–Brownsville.

SIA BERHAN

I had decided that I wanted to be a writer. I used to write a lot of poems, but I never used to show them to nobody except my buddy Theresa [Karriema Jordan]. I used to read them to her, show them to her. She knew that I wrote; she was the only one that did. I had whole bunches of them. We were up in the African-American Teachers Association office, and she snatched the poems and said, "Read this," and gave it to Les. And he was shocked. Because he didn't know what I was doing. He was surprised that I was a writer. He said, "I didn't know you could do this. I didn't know you could write anything." I said, "You know, yeah. So what?" It was just something that I did.

Let me tell you about that poem. The title of that poem is "Anti-Semitism." That's the name of the poem, and the subtitle, in parentheses, says "Dedicated to Albert Shanker." Now, the reason for the title is that I had found out, doing reading and listening to some of those people that came to the school, that the original Semites were black. That the Falashas in Africa, East Africa, were the original Semites. I felt that instead of saying that we in the black community were anti-Semitic, I felt that the UFT, Albert Shanker, were anti-Semitic.

The community wasn't anti-Jewish. It's true that a lot of the teachers were Jewish. It was something you looked at every day. But see, you shopped on Pitkin Avenue, you shopped on Belmont Avenue, you shopped on Delancey Street. You wasn't anti-Jewish.

> Following the strike settlement on November 17, 1968, Fred Nauman and other teachers who had been removed by the local governing board returned to teach in Ocean Hill–Brownsville schools.

FRED NAUMAN

I had been a strong supporter of the civil rights movement, strong supporter of Martin Luther King, and, obviously, not of the militant black movement. I didn't support the Black Panthers, but I supported the civil rights movement. Every time there was a confrontation of some type between black and white, I tended to side with the black. This was the first time, because I was personally involved, that I discovered this revelation that it was possible to be black and to be wrong. And that this naive attitude I had previously was just that—naive. I think I'm better for it, that I can judge things today based on the individuals rather than on the skin color.

RHODY MCCOY

To the best of my recollection, I don't think there were any mistakes made by the board. You've got to understand that the members of the community board were community people who were disenfranchised with the system, who were nameless and faceless, who had never been incorporated and included, even though their children were mandated to go to school. For them to take on that responsibility was tremendous. And they did a herculean job.

The problems that I think we made as professionals, and me included, was that we had been in the system too long. We were imbued with the bureaucratic system. We had to do things according to certain criteria which we'd learned or had been subjected to in our careers. And we didn't have the resources to do it independently. So we were really in a sense dependent on the school system. We did not have the kind of coalition that the teachers' union would have or that the nonblack community had. We had only our resources, and they were just meager.

SANDRA FELDMAN

I think people wanted to be pulled together. That was my sense of it—that this was not a conflict that was being enjoyed by the people involved in it. There may have been some people who, you know, got off on it in some way. But most of the people involved in it wanted it to end, and it was very difficult to see how it could be ended without some overarching, credible authority pulling it together. And we just didn't have that.

RHODY MCCOY

I'm sure that there were several possibilities for a truce with the UFT. One would be to get rid of me. If I would step down, they would support the project. There was no question about it. If we would take the teachers back and let them have their regular assignments, there would be no problem. If we'd get rid of Les Campbell and Al Vann, there'd be no problem. There were all kinds of offers from the union, if we had done any or all of this combination of things. But then, what would you have? You wouldn't have had a project. You'd have a shell. You'd have some semblance of a project.

As the 1968–1969 school year drew to a close, New York governor Nelson Rockefeller signed a new decentralization bill into law. The bill was a compromise measure that had the support of minority legislators, the UFT, and conservatives, who saw it as a way to protect neighborhood schools. Rhody McCoy called it "a prelude to the destruction of public education," while Mayor Lindsay labeled it unconstitutional. The new law mandated the abolition of the three demonstration districts, including the one in Ocean Hill–Brownsville, but it did authorize the city to establish up to thirty-three districts and provided that each district would be governed by its own local school board. The law, however, did not give the local boards the autonomy the Ocean Hill–Brownsville board had demanded.

Rhody McCoy and the local governing board in Ocean Hill–Brownsville staged one last effort to keep the experimental district alive: they urged residents to boycott the school board elections of March 1970 in the hope that they could persuade the city not to merge the eight schools in the experiment into a larger Brooklyn district. But it was too late for persuasion. After the election, the Ocean Hill–Brownsville experiment was officially over.

27

THE BLACK PANTHERS, 1968–1969

"HOW SERIOUS AND DEADLY THE GAME"

Black Panther leader Fred Hampton.

On August 25, 1967, FBI director J. Edgar Hoover began a new phase of a counterintelligence program known as COINTELPRO. "The purpose of this counterintelligence endeavor," Hoover explained in his confidential memo to FBI offices, "is to expose, disrupt, misdirect, discredit, or otherwise neutralize the activities of black nationalist, hate-type organizations and groupings, their leadership, spokesmen, membership, and supporters, and to counter their propensity for violence and civil disorder." In a follow-up memo, dated March 4, 1968, Hoover outlined five "long-range" goals for his program. Goal number two directed FBI agents to "prevent the rise of a 'messiah' who would unify, and electrify, the militant black nationalist movement. Malcolm X might have been such a 'messiah'; he is the martyr of the movement today. Martin Luther King, Stokely Carmichael and Elijah Muhammad all aspire to this position."

The Black Panther party was not on Hoover's original list of "Black Nationalist-Hate Groups" (SCLC, SNCC, and the Nation of Islam were). But in September 1968, Hoover called the Black Panther party "the greatest threat to the internal security of the country. Schooled in the Marxist-Leninist ideology and the teaching of Chinese Communist leader Mao Tse-tung, its members have perpetrated numerous assaults on police officers and have engaged in violent confrontations with police throughout the country." In all, of the 295 COINTELPRO actions directed against black groups, 233 targeted the Panthers.

By late 1968, there were Black Panther party chapters in twenty-five cities, including Los Angeles, New York, Denver, Des Moines, and Jersey City. Membership numbered more than one thousand. But with Huey Newton, the highest-ranking Black Panther leader, in jail awaiting trial for the October 1967 killing of an Oakland policeman, the party was under severe pressure. Newton claimed he was unconscious at the time the policeman, John Frey, was shot. To garner support for Newton, the party organized dozens of "Free Huey" rallies and established alliances with white and black groups alike. Nevertheless, many expected Newton to die in the gas chamber.

Although the Panthers received the most attention from the FBI, they were by no means the only perceived "threat to the internal security of our country." A variety of radical groups, including the Young Lords, the Progressive Labor Movement, and Students for a Democratic Society, were perceived as security threats by local, state, and federal officials. With police and FBI agents already feeling besieged, the anti-Panther dicta from J. Edgar Hoover bolstered the position of those who viewed the party as a threat.

Wayne Davis was a special agent assigned to the FBI's Washington, D.C., office.

WAYNE DAVIS

There was a perception by the FBI, and perhaps other Department of Justice officials, that there was the seed of a threat to national security in some of the more radicalized or extremist movements. I can't say exactly when that occurred, but the beef-up, the concentration of efforts investigatively, probably started occurring sometime around 1964. And I think some of the things that set off that additional concentration of efforts were the urban disorders that began in New York in 1964. Later, you had the Detroit riots. I think those were the things that led investigative agencies in the federal government—and local as well—to start enhancing their efforts at intelligence and to see just exactly what was going on here, whether these urban disorders were being initiated and fed by interests that didn't have the vitality of the U.S. system at heart.

There's a question about whether or not there was a threat posed to national security, and I think that depends on how you look at it. Some of the groups certainly were attempting to mobilize the communities in which they were located to achieve their ends—and this is a phrase that is familiar to you—"by any means necessary." And "by any means necessary" is regarded as inclusive of violent, revolutionary action. So that, I think, is probably what concerned the majority structure. When you had the Student Nonviolent Coordinating Committee, the Black Panthers, and other groups who were using that kind of phraseology, then you really can't exclude violent, revolutionary means.

As I recall it, there was a great deal of fear about the Panthers' philosophy. And I think that fear went back to the Huey Newton/Bobby Seale faction out on the West Coast that had gone to the state capitol armed. My recollection is that there was an advocacy of violence by the organization in general, and undoubtedly by its branches as well. Probably their use of language also had some impact. In referring to the police as "pigs," that verbiage carried with it, when viewed by the general law enforcement structure, a perception of disrespect for law enforcement authorities and, therefore, law enforcement in general. I think that the law enforcement and the government structure saw this as perhaps the beginnings of a breakdown in respect for law enforcement and obedience to the laws—and perhaps the seeds of anarchy.

Kathleen Neal Cleaver, a SNCC veteran, had married Eldridge Cleaver in 1967 and joined the Black Panther party.

KATHLEEN NEAL CLEAVER

The murder of King changed the whole dynamic of the country. That is probably the single most significant event in terms of how the Panthers were perceived by the black community. Because once King was murdered, in April '68, that kind of ended any public commitment to nonviolent change. It was like, "Well, we tried that, and that's what happened." So even though there were many people, and many black people, who thought nonviolent change was a good thing and the best thing, nobody came out publicly and supported it. Because even nonviolent change was violently rejected. So it's like the Panthers were all of a sudden thrust into the forefront of being the alternative, and maybe weren't quite anticipating as much attention as they got—neither the media attention nor the police repression. 'Cause they sort of went hand in hand. The more repression, the more media attention; the more media attention, the more repression.

While Huey Newton was being held on charges of murder, attempted murder, and kidnapping at the Alameda County jail, he continued to issue Panther directives by sending tape-recorded messages to the party via his lawyers.

HUEY NEWTON

After Dr. Martin Luther King was assassinated, the police across the country were prepared and expecting an uprising in the community. We felt that to protect the community from the kind of brutality that we anticipated, we would ask the community not to have an open rebellion. At the time, I was in the county jail awaiting trial for murder of an Oakland police officer and attempted murder on another. And I communicated with the party that we should encourage our chapters across the country to try to contain the community from open resistance.

According to a report for the National Commission on the Causes and Prevention of Violence, a study group established in 1968 at the Center for the Study of Law and Society in Berkeley, California, the Panthers deserved credit for "keeping Oakland cool after the assassination of Martin Luther King." Nevertheless, there was at least one outbreak of violence. At the time, the Panthers claimed they were ambushed by police. Twenty years later, Eldridge Cleaver says the Panthers had planned the shoot-out.

ELDRIDGE CLEAVER

We found out that King had been assassinated, and everybody all day was talking about taking some action. That night, a group of us met, and the idea was we were gonna just go out and shoot up the town. Shoot up the cops. But everybody discussed it and said, "Well, this is no way to go about doing anything. This is a spontaneous, irrational, and unorganized activity." And so what we did was, we just postponed this stuff for a day and discussed it, and rationalized it and organized it.

So we put together a little series of events to take place that next night, where we basically went out to ambush the cops. But it was an aborted ambush because the cops showed up too soon.

Officer Richard Jensen was in his patrol car the night of April 6, 1968.

RICHARD JENSEN

That whole week, police were working twelve-hour days, and days off were canceled. I was working my day off, on a beat I wasn't familiar with. Along about ninc o'clock at night, just as it started to get dark, we were driving down Twenty-eighth and Union, and we saw a car parked in the middle of the street—a light blue '53 Ford. The car appeared to be empty, but it was parked on the street with the lights on and the doors open. As we drove up behind it, we saw a young black man take a look at us. He was standing by an open car door, and he ran toward the houses.

We pulled up behind the car. I reached for the microphone to run the plate—it was a Florida plate—and just as I was reaching, I got shot in my arm, in my back, all kinds of bullets, just like Fourth of July firecrackers going off. I must have been shot four or five times, and I slumped to the seat of the car. The firing just continued, bullets just flying over, glass flying everywhere. My head and arms and everything is all full of glass, and my partner got out of the other side of the car and returned a couple of shots with his .38. Came back in the car to get to the radio, to tell other units where we were and what was happening, you know. Then you hear all these sirens coming. You know that help was coming. The next thing I remember was being lifted out of the car by some people, a couple of them were crying, some police sergeants I used to work for, and they thought I was dead. I had been shot maybe nine different times, and they thought I was dead. I wasn't, but the firing continued. It was like a war going on. We found out later there was thirteen people shooting at us. Our car, black-and-white car, they counted a hundred and fifty-seven holes in our car. I don't know how many missed or how many went through the windows, but a hundred and fifty-seven of them hit our car.

ELDRIDGE CLEAVER

The cops came down the street, two cops in a car, shining this spotlight, and they see all these black guys in these three cars with guns. I was driving the lead car, and they came upon the other cars behind me first because they were coming from that direction. You had guys getting out of the back cars, running up to our car, telling us, "Hey, here come the cops!" We all could see the cops coming, so this frightened the cops as well as frightening the convoy.

We waited until the cop car got really in the middle of the three cars. Then we got out and just started shooting. That's what happened. People scattered and ran every which a-way. Bobby Hutton was in the car with me, along with other people. He and I stuck together and ran in the same direction. We ended up in the same place in the same house. In the basement of this house. I guess we had a gunfight that went on for about an hour and a half. Because this was a cement basement, with cement stairs and so forth, it provided protection from the bullets. What I remember is the police started shooting gas bombs into the house to gas us out. And some other kind of little firebomb to set the house on fire. It hit me right in the chest and it kind of knocked me unconscious.

It was dark in this basement, and Bobby Hutton tore my shirt off of me, looking for a wound, see? That's how I came to be partly undressed. When they set the house on fire, it got so hot in there that that's when we decided to surrender. And it was after we had surrendered and came outside of the house that the cops beat us at first, and then after that, they shot and killed Bobby Hutton.

Bobby Hutton, the seventeen-year-old party treasurer, was killed by police fire. The police said that he was running away when they shot him in the back.

HUEY NEWTON

Bobby Hutton was the first member of the Black Panther party. He was recruited at the North Oakland service center in October '66. I believe he was fifteen at the time. He was our first recruit, and we made him treasurer. He was like my little brother that I never had. He was the inspiration of the party. Because the party was very youth-oriented. And while he worked at the North Oakland service center, we tutored him and politicized him.

Until he was killed, I really couldn't imagine—not really imagine—any of our party members being murdered. Even though I knew that that risk took place. I was in the county jail at the time of his murder, and after he was killed, then I felt that the party was vulnerable.

Huey Newton's murder trial began on July 15, 1968. Eight weeks and four thousand pages of testimony later, a jury convicted Newton of voluntary manslaughter in the killing of police officer John Frey but found him innocent of shooting officer Herbert Heanes, who had been wounded in the same exchange of gunfire. Newton was sentenced to two to fifteen years in prison. "It makes no sense," Charles Garry stated in response to the decision. "He either had a gun or he didn't."

Following the verdict, the Panthers intensified their effort to free Newton, whom they viewed as a political prisoner. From prison, Newton began to advocate a new direction for the party. (He would stay in prison for twenty-two months, until his conviction was reversed by a unanimous decision of the California State Court of Appeals.)

HUEY NEWTON

During the period of '68 to '69, the federal government had declared all-out war on the party. They were breaking into chapter headquarters across the country and filming weapons and saying, "Look. They have guns." It was never mentioned that the guns were legal weapons. They were doing everything to make the community afraid of the party. And of course you can't organize when people were afraid of you. So I was inclined to try to develop more local politics, to run local members for various offices, and develop our Ten-Point Program, which was housing and food and health programs.

I wanted to emphasize the community development aspect of the party. We were planning our creation of a community school. We were having busing programs to prisons, where we would pick up community people and take them to the various penal institutions [to visit relatives]. I thought that the arms had served their purpose as far as being a catalyst to gain the enthusiasm of the community. I felt that we should turn away from the arms because too much had been made of them.

In November 1968, Bobby Seale announced a number of community programs designed to "serve the people." These included the creation of several free health clinics and a program of free breakfasts for children.

Panther members were also running for a variety of political offices in 1968 elections. Huey Newton was a candidate for U.S. Congress, Kathleen Cleaver and Bobby Seale ran for seats in the California state legislature, and Eldridge Cleaver ran for president. All were candidates of the Peace and Freedom party, a biracial political party founded in California. Cleaver garnered close to 200,000 votes nationwide.

The winner in a campaign dominated by the theme of law and order was Republican Richard M. Nixon, who narrowly defeated Democrat Hubert H. Humphrey to become the thirty-seventh president of the United States. Nixon won by a margin of 500,000 votes out of 70 million cast. Also on the ballot that year was third-party candidate George Wallace, former governor of Alabama, who received 13.5 percent of the popular vote.

Shortly after the presidential election, two young black activists, Fred Hampton and Bobby Rush, opened the Illinois chapter of the Black Panther party in an office building on Chicago's West Side. On November 25, J. Edgar Hoover issued the following instructions to fourteen FBI field offices: "To exploit all avenues of creating further dissension in the ranks of the Black Panther Party, recipient offices are instructed to submit imaginative and hard-hitting counterintelligence measures aimed at crippling the Black Panther Party."

Though he was only twenty, Fred Hampton had previous experience as a civil rights leader. As president of the NAACP Youth Council in Maywood, a Chicago suburb that was approximately 50 percent black, he had led protests against the local high school, which he charged had racist policies. He also lobbied in favor of a town swimming pool, since Maywood's black residents were denied access to pools in the neighboring white communities. Fred Hampton was also known to the FBI, which in 1966 had placed him on its "Rabble Rouser Index." He was arrested in 1967 during demonstrations for the swimming pool and again a year later, for allegedly stealing seventy-one dollars' worth of ice cream from a Maywood vendor.

Don Williams, president of the NAACP in Maywood, had recruited Hampton into the NAACP Youth Council.

DON WILLIAMS

Malcolm X, Rap Brown, Stokely Carmichael—that rhetoric was inflammatory. And they, of course, were very critical of the staid, laid-back, if you will, NAACP/Martin Luther King kind of stand. That wasn't where it was at. And I think Fred viewed it that perhaps the former view had possibilities of achieving more, and more quickly. We had dialogue frequently, and it was clear to me that we had divergent views. But he was always respectful. And he told me that he recognized that I had very much the same objectives that he had, but our methodologies were different.

He started moving away from Maywood. He was involved in other communities, and at the state level. We heard things from time to time. And we were very apprehensive for his safety. You don't like to see gifted people, talented people, on a course that is very likely to injure them very seriously. But there really wasn't anything we could do about it. He was caught up, at that juncture, in the philosophy of that particular group, which was a more militant group. So you just had to kind of accept it.

BOBBY RUSH

I went out to Oakland, I think it was about October of '68, and I met with Bobby Seale, [chief of staff] David Hilliard, Eldridge Cleaver, and a guy by the name of D.C. I told them that we wanted to form a chapter of the Panther party in Chicago. When I talked with Bobby and David, they indicated that there was already a chapter existing here in Chicago and they didn't need another chapter. But I knew what was going on. I was from Chicago, and I just thought that was kind of arrogant of them to say that there was already a chapter here, because the fact of it is that I knew that the people who were claiming to be Panthers weren't really doing anything. They weren't organizing the community, they had no office, no one was able to reach them or anything like that.

When I got back to Chicago, after they had turned me down out there, I said, "Well, we're going to continue to organize, because we know what's going on." Plus, Stokely was supporting us. So the first thing we did was to try to locate an office. About the same time, early part of November '68, I was on the Madison Street bus, and I saw this big building that was vacant and a "for rent" sign on it. So I immediately jumped off, went to the liquor store next door, and inquired about the building. They said it was for rent. I went back to one of our supporters, Alderman Sammy Rayner, who was a member of the city council and also a prominent businessman. I asked him to rent the building for us. He did—in fact, he signed his name to the lease and also got the gas turned on. So we had a functioning office with a functioning telephone.

Around December of '68, there were two Panthers, members of the central committee from Oakland, California, traveling from New York back to Oakland. I guess they were having some discussion on the plane, and they asked the stewardess whether or not the distance from New York to Oakland was the same as the distance from New York to Cuba. And this stewardess got hysterical, ran to the captain, and the captain called in and they landed that plane here in Chicago. They swept these guys off the plane, because they thought these guys were getting ready to hijack the plane, okay? They put them in a county jail.

We got a call from Oakland, California, saying, "Look, we got two Panthers there in jail, and you're the only telephone number that we have in the city of Chicago, so would you see what's going on and take care of those guys that's in jail?" That's how we became the official chapter of the Black Panther party in the state of Illinois, because of that incident.

Fred Hampton became chairman of the Illinois chapter of the Black Panther party; Bobby Rush became minister of defense.

Deborah Johnson joined the new branch of the Panther party soon after it opened.

DEBORAH JOHNSON

I first found out about the Black Panther party when my brother brought a flyer home with a black panther on it. It seemed like it was walking across the page. And it said, "The Black Panthers are here." I had heard about the Black Panther party. They were doing some things at Chicago State University. And trying to organize free breakfast programs in the community. I was really impressed. I thought it was good that black people were standing up and demanding our rights.

I had seen Fred Hampton and Bobby Rush and Iris Shinn, and I think her husband, on a talk show. From that, I was really impressed with Fred. He had a really good knowledge of history. He seemed to really be sincere, believing in what he was doing. And their ideas at the time were in agreement with what I believed in and thought in terms of black people's struggle.

When Fred came over to Wright City College, it was the first time that I actually met him. Afterward, I introduced myself to him. Fred was very dynamic, charismatic. I think the success of his leadership, not only in being charismatic, but in being a very personable person, was that he believed in what he was doing. And the sincerity came across. He would never tell anybody, "Well, listen, brother, you can sell these papers. Listen, sister, you can sell two hundred papers." Fred would get out there. Although he was the leader of the party in the state of Illinois, he would get out there, and in the middle of the street. "Hey, sister, you want to buy a Black Panther newspaper? This is the people's party!" And he would just engage people in conversation. Just to see that, to be a part of that, would send chills. It was a really good feeling.

William O'Neal grew up in Chicago.

WILLIAM O'NEAL

I was with a guy one night, a friend of mine. We were drinking beer and we decided to go on a joyride. We jumped in a car and stole it. We were driving around the city of Chicago for, oh, forty-five minutes, and we decided to leave the state and go and visit a relative in another state. We walked into a pool hall and were shooting pool. At the door, you had to register your phone number and address, and we wrote down our names and phone numbers, then went in and shot a game of pool. We came out and had an accident, and we fled the accident on foot. We messed around in the city awhile, then caught a bus back to Chicago.

About three, four months later, I got a call from this FBI agent by the name of Roy Mitchell. I think I was about nineteen—eighteen, nineteen years old. He told me that he knew what I had done, and we talked. We went around a couple times, then he said something like, "Well, you know, there's no need in your trying to bullshit me. I know you did it. But it's no big thing." He said, "I'm sure we can work it out."

A few months passed before I heard from him again. And one day I got a call and he told me that it was payback time. Roy said, "I want you to go and see if you can join the Black Panther party. I understand they are recruiting Panther members. So why don't you go down to their office and see if you can join, and if you get in, give me a call back."

The next day, I got on the bus and went down to the office of the Black Panther party. It was located on Western and Madison. I walked in the office, and about three or four Panthers were in the office. I think I was about the fifth member in the Chicago chapter to join. They had this big office building up on the second floor. They had about five or six offices, and very little personnel to run things. So it was easy to get a position. They wanted me as the security captain.

The day I joined, I was pretty sure it was just another gang, not unlike the Blackstone Rangers or the Cobras or something. I had no idea of anything about their politics. Almost immediately after I joined the Panthers, probably within ten days, I began to realize that the Black Panther party was a little bit more sophisticated than a gang. I think the first set of reference books I saw inside the Black Panther party was the selected works of Mao Tse-tung, which I had begun to associate with communism. It wasn't too long thereafter that I started to see books like the *Communist Manifesto* of Karl Marx, and the collected works of Lenin. And every night, after the office had closed, the Panthers would sit down and they would study these books. We'd go through political orientation, and we would read certain paragraphs, and then Fred Hampton and Bobby Rush would explain to us, the new membership, basically what it meant and what was happening. And they'd draw parallels to what was going on in the past revolutions in the various countries, for instance China or Russia. So I understood them to be a little bit more sophisticated than a gang. I expected that there'd be weapons and we would be out there doing turf battles with the local gang members. But they weren't about that at all. They were into the political scene—the war in Vietnam, Richard Nixon, and specifically freeing Huey. That was the thing.

Father George Clements was the pastor of Holy Angels Catholic Church.

GEORGE CLEMENTS

The thing I really loved about the Black Panthers is that they refused to be ignored. It was very easy to ignore black people back then, because everybody figured, "Well, it's just a lot of talk and they're not going to do anything. They'll just go on and on and on, moaning and groaning about how terrible everything is. At the best, they just might get involved in some acts of nonviolence. But that's about it. Business as usual."

You couldn't have business as usual with the Black Panthers. The Black Panthers were definitely going to be heard. They had these things they would say, like, "by any means necessary." And you know, that shook people up. People said, "Ooh, ah, these are some serious black folks." That appealed to me very, very much, because I have always said, you know, "Love Clements, or hate Clements, but just don't ignore me. Just don't treat me like I'm a nonentity, as though I don't exist." And that, for all practical purposes, was what was happening with the black community.

Certainly politically, we were considered to be in the back pocket of Mayor Daley. We were really ineffectual. Nobody had to really respond to anything we were going to say, because Boss Daley had us very much in check.

WILLIAM O'NEAL

I grew up wanting to be a policeman, admiring and respecting policemen, although I always thought it was outside of my reach. But stealing a car and all of a sudden having a case with the FBI—the thought of really going to jail got my attention. So when Mitchell asked me to join the Black Panther party, he never used the word "informant." He always said, "You are working for me." And I associated him as the FBI. So all of a sudden, I was working for the FBI, which in my mind at that point, I associated with being an FBI agent. So I felt good about it. I felt like I was working under cover for the FBI, doing something good for the finest police organization in America. So I was pretty proud.

I've been to Mitchell's home. I've held his child in my hands, in my arms, when he was one year old. I have been through the offices of the FBI wearing sneakers and a dirty T-shirt, with Mitchell. I've rode around with him in his car during that time, three or four months after I became a Panther. I've eaten at his table, his dinner table. At one point, he was a role model for me. When I needed one. I mean, we had very few role models back then. We had Malcolm X. We had Martin Luther King. We had Muhammad Ali. And I had an FBI agent.

Mitchell wanted me to build up some credibility within the Black Panther party, so he gave me a lot of room, a lot of leash at that point. He let me become a Panther before I became an FBI informant. I mean, I didn't go right in rifling drawers. He directed me into the Panthers, and then when I got there, he backed off, and he let them work on me awhile. And slowly, it worked. I became a Black Panther in a way. I forgot the scope of my being there. In fact, I didn't really know why I was there. I just knew I was to report. But I really didn't have anything to report early on in the game, so I concentrated mainly on Panther duties. I lived the life of a Panther.

O'Neal was one of several paid FBI informants in the Chicago branch of the Black Panther party and one of more than sixty informants in party offices around the country. As chief of security for the Chicago chapter, he was Fred Hampton's personal bodyguard.

WILLIAM O'NEAL

A typical meeting between my FBI contact, Mitchell, would be downtown Chicago, at eleven or twelve noon, down in the basement at some bar, some dark bar. I would meet him at the bar, he would already be there when I got there, and he'd have a drink and I'd have a drink, and we'd sit there and talk for fifteen to twenty minutes. And it was very casual. I'd come in and he'd say, "Oh, whatcha up to?" And then I'd say, "Well, I'm going down to Champaign on a speaking engagement with Fred. And I'm taking such and such with me. And we're carrying guns, and we're driving this car." And I'd just rattle it off, ten or fifteen minutes. I'd tell him everything I knew. He didn't have to say very much, because when I joined the Black Panther party, most of the information that I was giving to him at that time was new information to him. So as I grew inside of the party and began to learn things, he grew also. He knew the members better than I did. We'd talk about the girlfriends and who was, you know, pregnant, and who had a venereal disease, you know, and this was just casual conversation between he and I. He wasn't always right. What he put in his files, I still don't have the benefit of. But I know that after a while, he and I became friends, and we talked in casual conversation about what I was doing in the Black Panther party.

Mitchell was part of a squad, in my opinion, of about five or ten agents, and each one of them had their little activities within the Black Panther party. Mitchell's questions were confined mainly to my area. He never asked me how many newspapers someone else was selling, or who got the Kellogg's for the Breakfast for Children program, or who's gonna open up the medical center. He wasn't concerned with that. He was concerned with my activities in the Panthers, which at that point was exclusively security issues.

I'd say from about February 1969, activities within the party was high-speed. We were in our bloom. We had various members of our party going to the colleges all over the state. Speaking engagements. Donations were coming in. But at the same time, the Chicago police had stepped up their activities also. A lot of our members were being arrested on petty charges. So the money we were bringing in on the one hand in donations, money that came through the mail anonymously—bank checks and money orders—was going right out in bail money. It was intense.

Black Panther Elaine Brown was based in Los Angeles.

ELAINE BROWN

I met Fred in Chicago, when David Hilliard sort of took me there directly from the gravesite of another Panther. We were at a funeral, we got on a flight to Chicago, and met Fred. The first thing you remember about Fred is that he was down in the trenches with everybody. And his house, that house on the West Side, was a horrible place to live. But he didn't live above, or elevate himself above. He lived like the rest of the comrades in the party, which was pretty poorly—except by that time, this unique thing was that big bed that he and Deborah had. Everybody laughed about the big bed that they had.

We got up with him in the morning. We had come in around two in the morning. He was up all night, which was apparently typical, and around six in the morning, we got out, we drove along to some schoolyard or something, and there were like two hundred, three hundred people waiting for Fred to show up. And the phenomenal part was that, I mean, these are all people from the streets, who are not going to get up and go to work, or anything else, and never had no discipline, and never would, but there they were. And it was six, six-thirty in the morning, freezing Chicago weather. And Fred would have them out there doing push-ups and jumping jacks and getting themselves energized for the day's work. Which included making the breakfast, which included selling papers, which included working in the medical clinic, which included a bunch of stuff. It was a very day-to-day thing, the Black Panther party.

You'd have Fred out there, rallying them. He'd say, "All right, all right, all right, power to the people!" He'd say, "Now, I'm not going to die on no airplane."

Everybody'd say, "No."

"I'm not going to die slipping on some ice."

They'd say, "No."

He'd say, "I'm going to die for the people. Because I'm going to live for the people."

They'd say, "Right on."

He'd say, "I'm going to live for the people because I love the people."

They'd say, "Right on."

He'd say, "I love the people. Why?"

They'd say, "Because we're high on the people, because we're high on the people."

That was Fred Hampton. This was twenty-one years old. He was unbelievable. You could not not be moved by Fred Hampton. It was like Martin Luther King. You just had to see Fred Hampton mobilize people who wouldn't have moved for anything else that I could imagine on the planet, much less to get up and cook breakfast.

Howard Saffold joined the Chicago police force in 1965. He was a member of the Afro-American Patrolmen's League, an association of black policemen founded with Father George Clements's encouragement.

HOWARD SAFFOLD

Around '68, pressure from the black community began to be applied to black officers, because police brutality was rampant. I mean, it was not uncommon for black women who were out after dark to be treated as if they were prostitutes. Black men driving big cars legitimately—ministers, businesspeople—stopped and searched in public, as if there were no constraints, no distinctions between them and the criminal. People had begun to ask, "What are you part of? I mean, what is that institution about really? Are you just pawns, are you part of the oppressive South African–type army? Are you part of an occupying army?"

I was given an opportunity to go into the gang crime unit. They were bringing black guys in because young black gangs had started to spring up and were getting rather rambunctious in terms of committing crimes against each other, committing crimes against businesses in the black community, et cetera. My intent was to be a part of curtailing that and trying to bring some safety back to my own respective communities.

At the same time, the Panthers were pursuing an ideology that said, "We need to take these young minds, this young energy, and turn it into part of our movement in terms of black liberation and the rest of it." And I saw a very purposeful, intentional effort on the part of the police department to keep that head from hooking up to that body. It was like, you know, "Do not let this become a part of what could ultimately be a political movement."

BOBBY RUSH

We wanted alliances with all progressive groups that we could work with toward a common goal. Here in Chicago, early on in the history of the Panthers, we developed a very, very close relationship with the Young Lords, a Hispanic group of gang members. And not only ex-gang members, but they were also middle-class students and things like that, too. They were an organization we decided to work closely with under Cha Cha Jimenez. We also developed a close alliance with the Young Patriots, a young white organization that was involved in Uptown. They were young Appalachian whites. Bob Lee, who was one of the field lieutenants within the Panther party, actually came from the North Side and he was familiar with some of these groups. He worked very hard to pull us closer together. And we developed what we called the Rainbow Coalition. It was the first time that the Rainbow Coalition was used. We actually had buttons, different colors on it, that were promoting the Rainbow Coalition. We also worked very closely with SDS, and other organizations throughout the city of Chicago. We thought that there was a role that needed to be played by all these groups, especially in their own neighborhoods, in their own communities.

By late 1968, Hampton and Rush were close to sealing an alliance between the Panthers and the Blackstone Rangers, a South Side gang headed by Jeff Fort. In a memorandum dated January 13, 1969, Marlin Johnson, the special agent in charge of the FBI office in Chicago, suggested a proposal that might "intensify the degree of animosity between the two groups and occasion FORT to take retaliatory action which could disrupt the BPP or lead to reprisals against its leadership."

Johnson's office sent an anonymous letter to Fort. "The brothers that run the Panthers blame you for blocking their thing," the letter said, "and there's supposed to be a hit out for you. . . . From what I see, these Panthers are out for themselves, not black people. . . . I know what I'd do if I was you."

WILLIAM O'NEAL

A meeting was arranged with Jeff Fort of the Blackstone Rangers. They were the largest street gang at that time. They had about two thousand members and were well armed. At the meeting, we were in a Catholic church, I remember, that night. We were setting up, and Jeff Fort told Fred Hampton, "There's not gonna be any Black Panthers in this city of Chicago. You guys either join the Blackstone Rangers or get out of the city." Hampton came away from that meeting feeling like we were gonna eventually have to do battle with these guys. There was no compromise. The Blackstone Rangers couldn't associate our purpose politically with their gang turf thing. So we were gonna have to deal with them. Word went out to me to basically start buying weapons.

We also knew that the state's attorney had declared war on us. And pretty soon, we were gonna face a raid in one of our offices. The mentality at that time was, "We know it's coming. Our job is to set an example for the people. We must be ready." So we started fortifying the offices and buying guns, and training our soldiers, our security people.

In late May, Hampton was convicted on the year-old charge of stealing ice cream from a Maywood Good Humor vendor. He was sentenced to two to five years in jail and was denied an appeal bond because he advocated "armed revolution."

On July 31, 1969, two months after Cook County state's attorney Edward Hanrahan declared "war on gangs," Chicago police raided the Panther office. Five policemen and three Panthers were wounded.

DEBORAH JOHNSON

When Fred went to prison, there was a lot of dissension in the party. A lot of people didn't have faith in the leadership that was in place there. The belief in the sincerity level of some of the people that were in leadership positions was really questioned, you know. Fortunately, though it was a long time him being incarcerated, it wasn't years. So the party managed, once he got out of prison, to pull back together.

I think everyone that was in the Black Panther party kind of understood—it was a given—that we would have wiretaps, that we would be followed, that we would be harassed, locked up, even beaten by the police.

I remember particularly one day when there was a raid on the office. I was walking to the office, and I see the policemen jumping out of the police car. And I'm really concentrating hard on not showing any emotion, that I'm not connected with this, because the fear was there that they might just start shooting: "Oh, there goes a Black Panther. Shoot her."

I remember thinking of someplace just totally removed from where I was and walking past there. They're shooting up the office and then I walked down the street and I come back, you know? Just like I'm casually walking down the street, and they're dragging people out and beating them, and I'm fighting back the tears. I don't want to cry because I don't want them to know that I'm a part of this. Because I know I have to call somebody and let them know that these people have been arrested and what happened with this raid. So I guess all that is to say that you know things are going on around you, but you have to be able to take yourself out of that place and do what you gotta do. It's necessary for your own survival.

In early 1969, Bobby Seale announced a membership purge to rid the Black Panther party of infiltrators and informants. Until further notice, no new members would be accepted into the party.

BOBBY SEALE

In 1969, practically every branch and chapter of the Black Panther party throughout the United States was attacked not less than once and as much as five times, particularly in Chicago. The Chicago chapter was attacked several times. And one particular time, I remember, they raided the Black Panther party office and they had a short shoot-out. And, of course, we had a rule that we would take an arrest. But what the police did is they went in like Eliot Ness with sledgehammers. I mean, our press, all of our IBM typewriters that had been donated by the white radicals, our newspapers, our mimeograph papers by the caseload, and then set the whole building on fire. This is what the FBI and the Chicago police did. The idea on the part of the police was to psych the community up. To terrorize us out of existence.

They called me up the next day. I says, "Is the office open?"

"Well, no, the police boarded the place up."

I says, "Open it back up. You got the lease to the place."

"What?"

I says, "Open it up. Take all that boarding down. Paint that place."

And the Black Panther party members started working for a couple of days. Next thing you know, the community started bringing wood, paint, and everything. And opened that Black Panther party office right back up.

> After four months in prison, Hampton was released on a ten-thousand-dollar appeal bond. He organized weekly rallies for Bobby Seale, who, as one of the Chicago Eight, was on trial for conspiring to disrupt the 1968 Democratic National Convention.
>
> Meanwhile, throughout the fall of 1969, O'Neal met regularly with Roy Mitchell, his FBI contact.

WILLIAM O'NEAL

The whole nature of the relationship changed right around November thirteenth, when two police officers were killed by a Black Panther member named Jake Winters on the South Side of Chicago. That night, as I understand the gun battle, Jake Winters straddled one of the officers who were wounded in the shoot-out and performed a coup de grace, a mercy killing. He straddled the officer after the officer was down, and put the shotgun to his head and put him out of his misery. Or at least that's the way the newspaper described it. And I think the Black Panthers took the rap for that one when they really didn't deserve it, because Jake Winters was out there on his own. He wasn't out there on any official mission for the Black Panther party, he was out there on his own. He got into an altercation with the guy, and the guy called the police, and the police came, and the shoot-out broke out, and two police officers were killed, and Jake Winters was killed. But the Panthers took the heat because Jake Winters was a Black Panther.

I noticed, maybe a couple of days after these officers were killed, Mitchell had this grim, solemn atmosphere about himself. And I could tell he was looking for specifics—he wanted specific criminal violations. He wanted something that he could move on. And I think he may have implied, or even expressed that, at one or two points. He expressed his anger over what had happened, the total disregard for life, and I mean, it was the first time I ever saw him express a personal opinion about what he thought the Black Panthers were doing.

Mitchell wanted to know the locations of weapons caches, he wanted to know if we had explosives, he needed to know who was staying at what locations, who spent the night where. His information didn't change so much as he requested more detail. And I knew why. The shoot-out on the South Side had pretty much laid the foundation within the party, within the Black Panthers; we knew that the police would react in some type of way. We could just feel the stepped-up surveillance, we could feel the pressure all the way around. And we knew something bad was going to happen. And I think we were all prepared for it.

I felt like at that point what they wanted to do was catch Fred with weapons and seal his conviction. If he'd been caught with the weapons out on appeal, he would've went straight to jail. I can't recall any specific conversations I had with Mitchell about the raid, but we had such a unity of minds, so to speak. Our efforts were basically one. I understood what was going on. He didn't have to tell me. He described to me going to the funeral of two police officers who got killed. And I knew he was hurt by that. And I knew he was gonna do what he could to help the police department do something about it.

In October, Fred Hampton and Deborah Johnson, now engaged, had rented an apartment on West Monroe Street. Johnson was pregnant with their child. In late November, the Illinois Supreme Court denied Hampton's appeal and ordered him back to prison by the end of 1969.

DEBORAH JOHNSON

On the night of December 3, 1969, there was a political orientation class held at the People's Church. I didn't attend the class. I was at home that night. Fred was to come home after the class was over, and we were to go out to his mother's house. Of course, the class went on and on, and then some of the people ended up going back to the office. I would talk to Fred at different times, and he kept telling me, "I'll be there in a few minutes, I'll be there in a few minutes," which I knew could go on forever.

I went over to a friend's house. Fred was going to meet me there, pick me up at my friend's house, and we would go out to his mother's for dinner. When I talked to him the last time, he said, "Well, it's so late, do you really want to go? If we spend the night out there, we can't sleep together." And I said, "Oh, definitely not. We cannot go." So Fred had someone come and pick me up from my friend's house and bring me back. William O'Neal either dropped me at the friend's house or picked me up from there to bring me back home.

Fred eventually came and I played like I was mad because we didn't go to his mother's house. He made an issue. "We can still go." I said, "No, that's okay. We'll stay here." So I went back to our bedroom. And Fred came back there after talking to some people for a while that were in the apartment. We talked a little bit. Then we called his mother to tell her that we're not coming, it's so late. Then we talked to her sister also on the phone. Fred at that time fell asleep in the middle of the conversation with his mother, and I couldn't wake him up. I talked to them, told them good-bye, and hung up the phone.

Mark Clark, twenty-two, leader of the Peoria chapter of the Black Panther party, and eight other party members spent the night of December 3 at Hampton's Monroe Street apartment. The FBI was familiar with the layout of the apartment.

WILLIAM O'NEAL

Well, I routinely supplied whatever floor plans or diagrams I could to the FBI. That started in June 1969. I mean, they had a floor plan and keys to the Black Panther headquarters. The specific apartment on Monroe—I supplied that floor plan. I do remember meeting with Mitchell at one point and drawing up a diagram of the apartment.

DEBORAH JOHNSON

The first thing that I remember after Fred and I had went to sleep was being awakened by somebody shaking Fred while we were laying in the bed. Saying, "Chairman, Chairman, wake up! The pigs are vamping. The pigs are vamping." About the same time, I looked up and I saw what appeared to be flashes of light going across the entranceway to the back bedroom. It looked like a million flashes of light, because the apartment was pretty much dark. I rolled over to Fred—he still hadn't moved at this point, as I recall—and then slid down to Fred's right side, so that put me closest to the wall in the bedroom. The bed was pushed against the wall. Fred at some point raised his head up, looked out towards the entranceway to the bedroom, and laid his head back down. That's all the movement that Fred Hampton had that night.

Someone else was in the room with me and kept yelling out, "Stop shooting, stop shooting, we have a pregnant sister in here." Eventually the shooting stopped and they said we could come out. I remember crossing over Fred and telling myself over and over, Be real careful. Don't stumble, they'll try to shoot you. Just be real calm. Watch how you walk. Keep your hands up. Don't reach for anything. Don't even try to close your robe.

I'm walking out of the bedroom, there are two lines of policemen that I have to walk through on my right and my left. I remember focusing on their badge numbers and their faces. Saying them over and over in my head, so I wouldn't forget. As I walked through these two lines of policemen, one of them grabbed my robe and opened it and said, "Well, what do you know, we have a broad here." Another policeman grabbed me by the hair and pretty much just shoved me—I had more hair then—into the kitchen area. It was very cold that night. I guess that it snowed.

The back door was open. Some people were on the floor in the kitchen area.

I heard a voice come from the dining room area. Someone said, "He's barely alive. He'll barely make it." The shooting, I heard some shooting start again.

> On December 4, 1969, State's Attorney Hanrahan told a press conference that the Black Panthers had mounted a "vicious, unprovoked attack" on the police who had appeared at the Monroe Street apartment at 4:45 that morning to carry out a search for illegal weapons. Hanrahan later praised the fourteen officers—nine white, five black—for their "good judgment, considerable restraint, and professional discipline," and urged all law-abiding citizens to do the same. Fred Hampton, shot in the arm, shoulder, and twice through the head, and Mark Clark, shot through the heart and lungs, were dead on arrival at the hospital. The seven survivors, including Deborah Johnson, were arrested and charged with attempted murder.

WILLIAM O'NEAL

The following day, I went directly to the office, and the office was empty, unusually empty. There was one girl sitting behind the desk, and she was on the phone, and there was just no people there. And I walked in, and I guess it was about, oh, ten o'clock in the morning. I was waiting on her to get off the phone to ask, you know, what was up. And I saw a copy of the *Sun-Times* laying there, and it had his picture on there. And it had "Panther Leader Slain" on it. And boy, I felt bad. I felt just so, I mean—I remember walking out of the office and looking through a little clearing over on the next block, which was right in front of the Monroe Street address, and seeing a lot of police cars over there. At that time, Bobby Rush came to the office. He had just come from over there, or maybe the coroner's office. In any case, we walked back over there, both of us, speechless. We just walked through that house and saw what had taken place and where he died. And it was shocking.

I think it was that morning that everything that I had done flashed before me. I began to put it all together, pretty much. And I couldn't believe it. That he had died.

You knew that something bad was gonna happen. I felt like it would be a raid. I knew it would be a raid. But I didn't feel like anyone would get killed. Especially not Fred.

I felt somewhat like I was betrayed. I felt like if anyone should have known there was going to be a raid that morning, I should have known also. I felt like I could have been caught in that raid. I was there that night, and I felt like if I would have laid down, I probably would have been a victim. So I felt betrayed. I felt like I was expendable. I felt like perhaps I was on the wrong side. Yeah. Yeah, I had my misgivings. I'm not gonna, no, I'm not gonna sit here now and take the responsibility for the raid. You know, I'm not gonna do that. I didn't pull the trigger. I didn't issue the warrant. I didn't put the guns in the apartment. So I'm not gonna take the responsibility for that. But I do feel like I was betrayed. I felt like I should have known the raid was coming down. I felt like it was probably excessive. You know, I felt like it was a surgical strike. And I was real angry for quite a few days. Quite a few days.

I refused to have any contact with Roy Mitchell at that point. But I think he pretty much understood, too. We got together and had a few drinks, and he didn't take any responsibility for it, either. He said, basically, he didn't know it was going to occur. Which at that point was hard for me to believe. I just began to understand basically how serious and deadly the game was we had all been playing for sixteen months. The reality of what we were doing just came to bear on us that morning. I think the membership was automatically decreased by three hundred members that never showed up again when that happened. I think that all of our enemies, all of the Black Panther party's enemies, came out of the woodwork to capitalize on the situation.

> Flint Taylor, a white first-year law student working with the People's Law Office in Chicago, had rushed to the apartment to gather evidence.

FLINT TAYLOR

The miracle in a sense was that the police left the apartment open so that we could go there. I think they thought they could do whatever they wanted to and get away with it as far as public opinion went. So they didn't seal the apartment. When I walked in, there was blood. It was like a Swiss-cheese type of effect, because they had ripped the apartment open with these submachine guns and automatic weapons. The walls were stitched with bullet holes. There was blood all over the place. The people who were with me had the presence of mind to get a cameraman down there, someone with a sixteen-millimeter camera. And we started to take the evidence. We didn't know what significance things had. So we took everything. We took every bullet, and there were shells all over the place.

Hanrahan had a story that Fred was up and firing away at the police in the back part of the apartment. Well, the bed that he was sleeping on had blood all over it—at the head and at other places. So obviously that totally disproved the theory that Fred was up, about, and firing away. But rather that he was murdered in his bed, which was what our people said. So we took the mattress, and we hid it. And we brought it back every day, so that people who came through the apartment could see it on the tours. So people could be shown the bed on which Fred was murdered, and here's how it proves that he's lying about Fred being involved in this serious shoot-out.

I think the police waited until the seventeenth of December to actually seal that apartment. So it was open for almost two weeks. And we spent the better part of those two weeks getting that evidence out of there. And the Panthers spent the better part of two weeks taking people who wanted to see the place through there. We would be talking to people when they went through, and while we were working, there'd be people walking through constantly. Maybe ten thousand people went through that apartment. From all over Chicago, but primarily from the black community, to see what had happened. And I'll never forget—I don't know what day it was or what—but I just remember some older black woman coming through there, shaking her head, and going, "It's nothing but a northern lynching."

On December 12, the *Chicago Sun-Times* reported that the photos released by the state's attorney's office to prove that the Panthers had shot at police depicted not bullet holes—as the *Chicago Tribune* had reported—but nail holes. This report lent credibility to the Panthers' claim that they had not attacked the police.

Almost three weeks after the killings, William O'Neal received a special payment of $300 from the FBI "for uniquely valuable services which he rendered over the past several months."

A federal grand jury that was convened in 1970 concluded that of the more than eighty shots fired during the raid, only one came from a Panther weapon. In 1982, following the longest civil rights trial in U.S. history, the survivors of the December 4 raid and the families of Fred Hampton and Mark Clark agreed to accept a settlement of $1.85 million from the federal, county, and city governments. Flint Taylor, one of the team of lawyers who represented the survivors, called the settlement "an admission of the conspiracy that existed between the FBI and Hanrahan's men to murder Fred Hampton." The U.S. attorney who argued the case said the government had settled in order to avoid another expensive trial.

28

ATTICA AND PRISONERS' RIGHTS, 1971

"THERE'S ALWAYS TIME TO DIE"

After the retaking of Attica, inmates who had attempted to take over the prison were stripped and lined up for searches.

For many movement activists, and for prison inmates from Soledad on the West Coast to Attica in the East, Angela Yvonne Davis, a young woman with a large Afro hairdo, was a symbol of black protest. Born in Birmingham in 1944, Davis was a daughter of the first black family to move into the all-white neighborhood that became known as Dynamite Hill when the Birmingham Klan attempted to drive out black families by bombing their homes.

For Davis, as a young adult, California in the late 1960s was also a testing ground. Davis, a philosopher, had studied in both the United States and Germany; one of her mentors had been the noted political philosopher and author Herbert Marcuse. She was a member of the Los

Angeles chapter of SNCC but left the organization when her membership in the Communist party became an issue. Davis was also involved in the prisoners' rights movement and worked on behalf of the Soledad Brothers, three black prisoners—George Jackson, John Clutchette, and Fleeta Drumgo—accused of murdering a white guard at Soledad Prison in California.

After August 7, 1970, Davis became one of the nation's most wanted fugitives. On that day, George Jackson's younger brother, seventeen-year-old Jonathan, staged a one-man raid on the San Rafael courthouse in Marin County, California, in an attempt to seize hostages to trade for the Soledad Brothers. Jonathan Jackson, two prisoners, and a judge were killed in the ensuing shoot-out.

Angela Davis, who was not at the scene, was accused of supplying the weapons for the raid. Two months later, Davis was arrested in New York City; eventually she was extradited to California and held for a total of sixteen months before being found not guilty of charges that included murder, kidnapping, and conspiracy.

One of the most widely circulated books of the prison movement during this period was *Soledad Brother,* a collection of prison letters by George Jackson published in 1970. Of the letters, which offered Jackson's political and personal philosophy, five were addressed to Angela Davis.

ANGELA DAVIS

I was hired to teach in the philosophy department at UCLA in the fall of 1969. I had joined the Communist party a year earlier. Before I had the opportunity to teach my first class, I was fired by the regents of the University of California, an ex officio member of which was [Governor] Ronald Reagan. As a result of the enormous amount of publicity that was focused on me by virtue of that firing, I received countless numbers of letters from prisoners all over the country. George Jackson wrote me. I began to recognize through the work that I did in the case of the Soledad Brothers that it was very important to bring into the movement of that period a consciousness of what was happening to people in prison.

Previously we had worked primarily around people who had been arrested because of their political beliefs and political activities—[Black Panthers] Huey Newton, Ericka Huggins, Bobby Seale, the New York Twenty-one, the LA Eighteen, all of those cases. But we hadn't really taken a look at the function of the prison system in our society. As a result of working to free the Soledad Brothers, I became increasingly aware of the need to integrate an understanding of the social function of the prison system into the work that we were doing calling for political equality, the work that we were doing in the community against police crimes and police brutality. So that when I fought for my right to teach on campus at UCLA, I always included in that analysis the fact that there were three young black men who were victims of the very same repression which I was confronting, but they stood to lose their lives as a result of the political work they had done within the prison system. I stood to lose my job as a result of my political activities and my work.

We began to realize that the definition of political prisoner also needed to include those who did not necessarily go to prison because they had been politically involved but who became politicized within the prison system and therefore were subjected to long prison terms and other forms of repression as a result. George Jackson, for example, who was sent to prison as a result of being convicted of a seventy-dollar robbery. When I became aware of his case and became active in the Soledad Brothers' case, he had been in prison for ten years for seventy dollars. And it was clear that they had refused to release him on parole because he was trying to organize his colleagues in prison. He was doing the kind of work that was very threatening to the prison system because he was calling for unity. He was calling upon people to demand better prison conditions, better food, the right to read whatever they wanted to read. So definitely George Jackson was a political prisoner even before he was charged with the killing of the Soledad guard.

And then we came to realize that there was a whole category of prisoners who may not have been politically active in prison, but were in prison for political reasons. They were in prison because of the function of racism in this society. They were in prison because of the function of class exploitation. We took a look at the prison system and realized that if you were wealthy, you didn't go to prison. If you did at all, you went to what we used to call the country club prisons, where you could play tennis and ride horses and that type of thing. So that expanded into a movement of support within the community, taking on the function of the prison system in general and calling for the abolition of the prison system as it exists.

Virtually every black person had some personal relationship to the prison system. In my family, I had several cousins who had spent time in jails and prisons. And that was the case with virtually everyone. However, we had not analyzed the prison system with a view towards integrating it into our overall conception of the function of racism in the society, of the function of class exploitation. We had talked about police brutality, the Black Panther party talked about the police as an occupying force in the community, but we had not really understood the extent to which the whole criminal justice system—the police, the courts, the prison system—is very much intertwined with the economic oppression of black people. There are no jobs for certain numbers of young people in our community. What happens to them? There's no recreation available. The schooling is not the kind of enlightening process that it should be. So, what happens to these young people? They might go out and get involved in petty criminal activity as a result of the lack of these facilities in the community. And then they end up, of course, spending, many of them, the rest of their lives in prison.

When *Soledad Brother* was published, the collection of George Jackson's letters, it was an extremely important moment for the prison movement, both inside and outside. For the first time, there was an attempt to develop an analysis of the relationship between what was going on in our communities, in the streets, in the factories, in the schools, on the campuses, and what was happening inside the prison. Large numbers of prisoners, of course, could relate to what George Jackson said in his letters, the stories about the horrible repression that he suffered, the fact that he was never able to spend time with his younger brother Jonathan outside of the manacles and chains that he wore. So that there was a very important emotional effect of his book on people, both inside prison and, perhaps more importantly, outside. Because those of us on the outside had generally not taken the time to try to understand what the experience was. We might have, at that time, been fighting for the freedom of political prisoners or challenging the prison system. But what George Jackson managed to do was to make that experience palpable, make it concrete, so that it became something that people could relate to as human beings.

There's always the tendency to push prisons to the fringes of our awareness so that we don't have to deal with what happens inside of these horrifying institutions. And there is the tendency also to look at the prisoners as having deserved what they have met with there. So that the criminal is a figure in our society who has very little credibility. And what George Jackson demonstrated with his letters was that prisoners are human beings. Prisoners are intelligent human beings. Prisoners have families. They have feelings. And at the same time he laid the basis for an important political analysis which was lacking.

The prisoners' rights movement was lobbying to change conditions in prisons throughout the country, many of the same conditions that George Jackson wrote about in California. In 1970, more than half the inmates of U.S. prisons were black. Sixteen prison protests, four of them reported as racially motivated, had taken place that year, including a revolt at the Manhattan House of Detention, known by most residents of New York City as the Tombs. In the state of New York, blacks constituted approximately 70 percent of the prison population.

In May 1971, several prisoners at the Attica State Correctional Facility sent a "manifesto" containing thirty demands to the new commissioner of correctional services, Russell Oswald.

Attica at that time housed more than 2,200 inmates in a facility built for 1,600. The inmate population was approximately 54 percent black, 9 percent Puerto Rican, and 37 percent white. Although Attica was located in rural Wyoming County, 77 percent of its inmates were from urban areas, primarily New York City but also Buffalo, Rochester, and Syracuse. None of Attica's 380 guards were black. Billed in a *New York Times* headline shortly before it opened in 1931 as a "Convict's Paradise," Attica forty years later had not lived up to that promise. Prisoners were confined to their cells from fourteen to sixteen hours each day. Inmates usually worked about five hours and were paid between twenty cents and one dollar for their day's labor. They were allowed one shower each week and allotted one bar of soap and one roll of toilet paper each month.

Conditions at Attica had not changed by July, when Herbert X. Blyden, Donald Noble, Frank Lott, Carl Jones-El, and Peter Butler sent an eight-page letter demanding satisfaction on twenty-seven items. The letter said in part, "The inmates of this prison have vested the power of negotiation regarding the settlement of the stipulated demands within the judgment and control of these men. All and any negotiations will be conducted by prison and state authorities with these five men. . . . These demands are being presented to you. There is no strike of any kind to protest these demands. We are trying to do this in a democratic fashion. We feel there is no need to dramatize our demands."

Herbert X. Blyden had been transferred to Attica after participating in the August 1970 rebellion at the Tombs.

HERBERT X. BLYDEN

For the most part, the consciousness of the brothers in Attica, their level was raised once they'd gotten into the writings of Malcolm X, the uprising in Watts, and definitely the Soledad Brothers' struggle, and that in turn affected conditions in the Tombs prison in New York City in 1970. So from '67 through '70 there was this uprising throughout America's prisons, from West Coast to the South, with Folsom and all the rest of the other prisons thrown in. And what we found in Attica in 1971 was the influx of prisoners from other outlying New York institutions confined in Attica. There was the Young Lords, the Panthers, the Five Percenters [an offshoot of the Nation of Islam], the Weathermen, and of course the Nation of Islam's contingent. All of these elements had their consciousness level raised, relative to the well-being of their folk as they saw it.

George Jackson was shot to death on August 21, 1971. Prison officials claimed he was attempting to escape from San Quentin prison. The next morning, at least seven hundred Attica inmates, most donning black armbands, refused to eat breakfast out of respect for Jackson.

HERBERT X. BLYDEN

George Jackson's death I think impacted on me in such a way that even Dr. King's death didn't impact on me. I remember his going to court in shackles and the brother would stand erect, proud black man that he was. And they had not broken his spirit, and these are the things that Dr. King and Malcolm talked about, the breaking down of the black man's spirit. I remember his in-cell program with the exercise and the push-ups. And then when he comes out, it would be like he was in another world while he was still in the confines of the belly of the monster. So I think what I had to do at that point was to show that we can be strong even during trials and tribulations, much as George was strong to the death.

When George Jackson died we heard it on the radio and we had the prison grapevine. The very next morning, it was interesting, because everyone was locked into their cells when we heard the news so no one had time to actually say, "Tomorrow morning at breakfast we will go in with black shoestrings as armbands in mourning and do not partake of breakfast."

Michael Smith was a prison guard at Attica.

MICHAEL SMITH

During the summer of 1971 an inmate who I had come to know quite well, Don Noble, showed me a list of demands that were still in the preparatory stage, and he asked me to review those demands and tell him what I thought. Most of the demands were of a humanitarian category. Such things as unrationed toilet paper, more showers, less censorship of mail, more visits, and less censorship of who was allowed to visit. I don't recall anything that I considered to be unreasonable. They were just asking to be treated as human beings.

Early in September, about ten days after the inmate fast in memory of George Jackson, Commissioner Oswald responded to the July demands via a tape-recorded message played over the prison radio system, saying that he would institute some reforms but they would take time. Frank Smith, nicknamed Big Black, was listening.

FRANK "BIG BLACK" SMITH

Conditions in 1971 was bad—bad food, bad educational programs, very, very low, low wages. What we called slave wages. Myself, I was working in the laundry and I was making like thirty cent a day, being the warden's laundry boy. And I'm far from a boy.

You get one shower a week. You know, a shower to us in Attica state prison is a bucket of water, and if you lucky and you get the right person outside of your cell that would bring you a second bucket, then you can wash half of your body with one bucket. What we would do is wash the top of our body with one bucket, and if we get a second bucket then we will wash the bottom part of our body. And you get one shower a week.

The books in the library was outdated. They didn't have any kind of positive recreation for us. If there was any recreation, it was minimum. It would only be on the weekends. And Attica is four prisons in one. You got A yard, B yard, C yard, and D yard and two mess hall. And the only time you would see a person that's in A block if you in B block, like I were, is when you would go to the mess hall and sometime you might run into him. "Dehumanizing," the word would be for the conditions in Attica in 1971.

After Oswald left the taped message to the brothers in Attica, we'd say, "Aw, you know, he ain't high jivin', he thinks somebody's head is screwed on." He was going with that same rhetoric, you know. This ex-commissioner of parole, he's shooting us a lot of whitewash again. He's not going to do anything. The situation that we're talking about or any manifesto that was given to him, he's not going to adhere to it. He's not going to go with any of the demands or the suggestions. He's not going to go with any of it. I thought he was going to take it as a laughing matter. The conditions in Attica—he knew. It wasn't the first time that it was thrown out there. Long before 1971, there'd been a lot of letters, even from our families, talking about the conditions in Attica—the overcrowdedness, and the slave wages, and not being able to get any kind of productive programs in Attica. The system knew we been talking about it. The Oswald tape-recorded message was a bunch of hogwash. We never took it serious because we knew he didn't take it serious. It was another dupe situation. Period.

> On the morning of Thursday, September 9, approximately twelve hundred inmates seized control of half the prison.

MICHAEL SMITH

I was in charge of the metal shop upstairs, that's located over the industrial metal shop toward the rear of the prison. The prison siren sounded and from the upstairs windows you could see inmate movement that wasn't supervised. The inmates, there were approximately thirty in the room that I was located in, were confused and didn't know what was happening either. There was only one set of double entry/exit doors in the room that I was located in. The rioting inmates gained entrance to that room through those doors. The inmates broke into the room where I was, and at that point in time I was knocked down and they moved to the rear of the room where I had secured some civilian employees. They destroyed some things in the room and broke into the room where the civilian employees were, took them hostage and on their way out, left me.

There were two particular inmates at the time when the inmates were gaining entry to that room, that protected me and in kind of spread-eagle fashion, they put their body over mine to protect me. Told the rest of the inmates that were breaking in that I was okay and to leave me alone. The rioting inmates went right past me, moved and took the civilians hostage, and went right back out of the room again and left me laying on the floor. Most of the inmates in the room at that time also left with them, with the exception of the two that had protected me. They made an attempt to get me out through the prison to safety.

I was at the rear of the prison, so I had to go through the whole complex, including the inner section in the prison called Times Square. On reaching Times Square, there was a militant group of inmates that directed the two inmates that were helping me out that all hostages had to be taken to D yard.

There was a lot of chaos in the initial takeover of the prison. I guess I was amazed at how easily the fortress fell. There was no plan. I had never been instructed in how to handle a riot situation or what to do.

HERBERT X. BLYDEN

In 1971 when the uprising occurred, we had two-thirds of the men working in their shops, making cabinets, chairs, lockers, et cetera. But I think in all fairness I should say that the evening before it, there was an altercation and an inmate was dragged out of his cell in A block, and the officials at that time were told that if anything happened to that inmate, the next day when the inmates were let out there would be some reprisals. And as a result of them not taking that statement seriously, there was a spontaneous uprising in A block which filtered out over to the remainder of the prison.

I was in the metal shops in B block, and there was a lot of running around and milling around by inmates, and the guards started to run around as if they didn't know what was happening, 'cause evidently they didn't have contingency plans for some emergency. It occurred to me that indeed there was an emergency. I left the metal plant with a group of inmates, and we proceeded through B block, where we met inmates coming from other blocks and correction officers following those inmates. We went out into D yard and inmates closed the door behind them, and the guards at that point stopped coming, because there were twelve hundred and some odd inmates confined in that yard at that point.

For the most part, right after entering D yard, the milling about and the confusion of these diverse groups from four prison blocks created what we would call pandemonium, because you had forty or fifty correction officers who no longer, it appeared, had control of the institution. So order had to be made out of this disorder, and at that point the Muslim contingent in the yard—there were thirty-five Muslim brothers—saw to it that there was no further injuries to the hostages, which were correction officers.

As a result of the Tombs uprising in 1970 and my seventy-two-count indictment for the Tombs uprising, a lot of the inmates from the Weather faction, the Muslims, the Young Lords, the Panthers, and the Five Percenters suggested that there be a fifteen-member committee set up to negotiate with the outside officials, and I was selected unanimously by that group to chair the inmate negotiating team.

> Assemblyman Arthur Eve from nearby Buffalo, one of nine black representatives in the New York state legislature, arrived at Attica that afternoon. Inmates were holding thirty-nine hostages, including Michael Smith, having earlier released eleven others.

ARTHUR EVE

I heard about the Attica inmate rebellion in my car from one of the local stations. I drove out to the radio station and they gave me the tape of the report that had come off the wire services. I went by my office and told my staff that I was going out to Attica.

Not until I got there did I find out after meeting with the commissioner that the inmates had sent for me.

When we walked into D yard it seemed like literally hundreds and thousands of people were in there. And certainly they were pleased to see some outsiders. There were some people who recognized who I was, and also Herman Schwartz, the attorney who had been handling some of their appeals. Many would then converge and the word would pass and they would all come around us. The inmates had set up a fairly elaborate speaking system, so when they spoke to you it could be heard in the whole yard, so that everyone knew what was being said. So it was all of them around you and listening for what you had to say, what kind of message that you would bring to them. But they were very pleased that we were there and that someone was listening from the outside. And that, I think, was very important.

It was very interesting. They had set up a somewhat elaborate communication system. They had certain people who were in charge of security. They had people who were in charge of dealing with human waste and garbage and some who were involved with food and other kinds of things. And any of the inmates who were ill or sick, how to deal with them. They had some of the inmates who served as medical staff. It was almost a community within a community. And it was very, very impressive that they had said, This is our home and we're now going to make it as livable as possible. There was a tremendous amount of discipline there within the yard.

When we finished the questions that may have come up, I had a sense that they for the first time felt that they were in a position to make something happen, and there was a sense that some positive things would ultimately come out of this. There was a sense of hope. No one knew where this thing would end up subsequently, but this was the first time they had to get their concerns properly addressed, concerns that they had tried to convey to the state prior to that and got absolutely no response, and in many cases they were further brutalized, harassed, whatever the case might be. So there was a sense of hope that for the first time there were some outsiders. People would now begin to listen, and hopefully some changes could be made.

LaVerne Barkley was the mother of Elliot James Barkley, a twenty-one-year-old black inmate from Rochester. Sentenced to four years in Elmira Reformatory for cashing a forged money order, he had subsequently been imprisoned at Attica for violating his parole. Barkley became one of the leading spokesmen for the inmates in D yard.

LaVerne Barkley

I think the day after I visited Elliot the uprising began. And then I saw him on television speaking out about conditions there and the treatment there. I was upset about what he was saying. But at the time I was more fearful about his life and safety. And I wanted him home. That's all I wanted, for him to come home safe and sound. And I felt, Why would you do this knowing that you will be home—the date had been set, I don't remember exactly—but he was coming home to us. So he jeopardized that in order to speak out for them. For the inmates.

He didn't like the way men were treated there. He thought that it was dehumanizing. And he felt that although the men there were paying for a crime or whatever, they were still men and should be treated like men. He felt that the guards, or some of the guards I should say, were horrible. Some of them are really horrible, the way they treated the inmates.

Russell Oswald had been appointed commissioner of correctional services on January 1, 1971, by Governor Nelson Rockefeller. Prior to that he had served as chairman of the New York State Board of Parole, and he had begun his career in corrections in Wisconsin in 1930. He was considered a prison reformer.

Thursday afternoon, Oswald entered D yard after conferring with Eve and Schwartz.

Russell Oswald

I decided to go into D yard for humanitarian reasons. I knew that the hostages were in a very difficult situation. They had been beaten, I knew that. I knew that they were harassed. I also felt that to do otherwise than to go in there would leave me with one option—that was, to go in armed. And there would be unfavorable consequences. People would be killed, invariably. So I decided that I could do better going in there and trying to talk them into reasonableness. That was my hope.

The prisoners, the leaders, were up on the stand looking down on me. And they were trying to humiliate me any way they could. They were asking for certain things and they wanted those or there would be people killed. I talked as rationally as I could with them, and listened to them for some period of time. Ultimately, they said they had an agenda of what they wanted. When I heard the demands that they made, I looked at them quickly. And I said, What are they doing? Are they taking my agenda? It was almost exactly the same things I talked with them about on the radio the week before. And I found no big difficulty with most of those demands of theirs. So that I felt, Well, we're home free now. Because if I say that I'm going to do these things, they ought to agree to release the hostages.

> But one important demand was to prove the major sticking point—"complete amnesty, meaning freedom from any physical, mental, or legal reprisals" for activities during the uprising. Other demands included improved living conditions, recruitment of black and Hispanic prison guards, and payment of the state minimum wage for all inmate labor.
>
> In addition to Arthur Eve, thirteen other observers were requested by the inmates. Tom Wicker, political columnist and associate editor of the *New York Times*, was one of them. By the time Wicker entered D yard on Friday evening with a group of observers, Commissioner Oswald had, after three tries, given up on negotiating directly with the inmates.

TOM WICKER

We went through this little passageway. I remember as if it were yesterday coming out into the actual yard where the inmates were. And there was just a vast crowd. My recollection is thirteen to fifteen hundred people in there. In the area about the size of two football fields. And there's this enormous crowd of inmates gathered there, but in front of them, and between them, between this crowd and our group of observers, there were a line of inmates that formed a human chain. That is, one facing this way and one facing that way. And they had their arms linked together. Very strong chains that I suppose would have protected us, if anyone had threatened us, which no one did. The light was a few dim electric bulbs from up on the walls, but there were trash cans with fires burning in them and so forth. A very eerie flickering light. So you wouldn't choose that experience for your ordinary weekend, I don't think, but on the other hand, I felt after that first initial feeling of being out of reach of what normally I thought of as the law—you know, the sort of protection that every citizen takes for granted until you don't have it—once I was past that shock, I felt relatively secure. I never felt particularly threatened in there in any sense. The whole situation obviously was precarious somewhat. You didn't know exactly what might happen or who might get out of hand. But I never felt that any minute now somebody's going to throttle me or drag me off to be chained, anything of that sort.

I found the inmate leaders at that point to be rather impressive. They were obviously quite strongly in control of the crowd. That was the first thing that impressed me. Secondly, they were wonderful orators. I mean, they really could turn on the oratory and fire up that crowd there. And in some ways it made a lot of sense. Other ways, it was passion. And then when we got down, they were really talking about the instant issues, the problems that the inmates wanted dealt with. And how they felt about their life in the prison. And so they were quite businesslike too. It was always true, of course, that they wanted more than they were ever likely to get. We understood that. And the main thing, the main issue, the issue that hung us up from beginning to end and never was resolved, was that they wanted amnesty. I'm not at this late stage of the game even yet prepared to pass judgment on whether that was a fair request or not. But what was clear to me from the start was that they weren't going to get it. And so what seemed to me to be necessary was, in my typical moderate intermediary position, that we should work something out that the inmates could accept as amnesty that the state didn't have to tell you was amnesty.

Eventually, more than thirty-five people, ranging from elected officials to journalists to representatives of a wide range of organizations—some invited by state officials, others who came on their own, as well as those the inmates had requested—would participate at one point or another in attempts to reach an accommodation between the state and the inmates.

James Ingram, arrested in Detroit in 1967 when he sought to buy gasoline during the disorders, was now a reporter for the *Michigan Chronicle,* a black newspaper based in Detroit. One of the observers specifically requested by the inmates, he met with the other observers in the stewards' room of the prison administration building.

JAMES INGRAM

The prison guards as well as the New York state troopers, but especially the prison guards, treated us with a great deal of hostility. They didn't say a whole lot, but the way that they would look at you, the curt responses that came if you asked them a question. The townspeople were totally hostile. I remember a civilian volunteer brought in some doughnuts and coffee, and I guess he thought that it was for the guards. When they brought it into our room, he looked up at us and he said, "Damn it, if I'd known that we were bringing it to you guys, I would have spit in it." And he in fact did spit on a couple of the doughnuts, at which point we threw half the doughnuts away and began a little discussion [*laughs*] about what if he did know in advance and had already done something to this coffee. But we'd been in there for twelve, thirteen, fourteen hours, some of us for two days, without any sustenance at all, anything to eat or drink other than occasional water down the hall. So we went on and consumed it.

But those people were extremely hostile. We'd come through a crowd assembled at the gate to the prison, and we'd hear taunts of obscenities and nigger this and nigger that. And the guards themselves almost unconsciously referred to their billy clubs as nigger sticks. And they didn't seem to even notice that they were in the presence of New York state assemblymen, at least one editor of the *New York Times,* myself a reporter, a United States congressman. They just didn't seem to care or realize how easily and loosely they flung that term "nigger" around.

On Saturday afternoon, September 11, the observer committee and Commissioner Oswald hammered out a document called "The Twenty-eight Points," a list prefaced by the remark that these were proposals "Oswald has said he will accept." The observers did not recommend the acceptance or rejection of these points but informed the inmates that they thought this list was the best agreement the state would make. The points did not include amnesty for crimes against persons.

That afternoon, William Quinn, a corrections officer injured in Thursday's takeover, died in a Rochester hospital, making total amnesty all the more important to the prisoners.

HERBERT X. BLYDEN

Upon hearing of the demise of William Quinn, the correction officer, we realized how serious a situation it was for the six hundred–plus inmates who were doing a life sentence. Because based on the existing law at the time, the death of a correction officer at the hands of an inmate made you eligible, if you will, for the electric chair. It behooved me to then tell these brothers, straight up, they're in trouble. I'll never forget their reaction once I told them, "You niggers are going to die." I said, "All you brothers are going to be slaughtered in this yard." And, you know, they were like, "Come on with it." But the position was excellent because it then created a solid core for us to be able to deal with the madness we had to deal with, with the negotiating. But we told them straight up, these were serious times and that they were going to die.

By Sunday, Commissioner Oswald was under considerable pressure to bring the uprising to an end. State police had been standing at the ready since Thursday afternoon, the hostages' families were growing increasingly desperate, and the media were following the story closely. The observers made a last-ditch appeal to Governor Rockefeller to come to Attica and meet with observers and officials.

TOM WICKER

We thought that the situation had reached a crisis. That in fact there was about to be an attempt to take the prison. We thought that there would be a lot of bloodshed. In fact, we said to the governor that if that happened, that it would be a massacre. And his response was basically that he sympathized with our position. He felt that everything had been done that could be done—anyone who remembers Governor Rockefeller will remember his effusive manner—and thanked us greatly for our efforts and that sort of thing. But the net effect of it was that he felt everything had been done that could be done. He could not grant amnesty and in fact said that "even if I could I wouldn't do it." And he felt that he should not come to Attica, which was the request we had made of him. The specific request. He thought that that wouldn't do any good. I still think that it would have. I never thought that Governor Rockefeller should come up there and involve himself with the inmates in the same way that we observers had. But I did think that if he came there and talked to his own officials, to the prison officials—maybe met with a committee of the inmates outside the yard and so forth, something like that—that his presence, his show of interest, could have helped break the deadlock. I still think that.

RUSSELL OSWALD

The observers decided that they had to make an effort to get Governor Rockefeller to come to Attica. They had failed, and so they wanted us to contact the governor and get him to come. They asked Bobby Douglass, who was his chief assistant, to get in touch with him and see if he could get the governor to come to Attica. We got him on the phone. First, Bob Douglass talked with him for some time and then hung up. And he came back and told me that the governor didn't feel he should come. And I was to go back and tell the observers' committee. But I said, "Bob, I would just as soon if you would tell them that." But, in any event, we both told them that. And they then asked us to get in touch with him again. So, I talked with him at great length, and two or three other people talked with him. And he finally asked me, "Russell, what is your true feeling? Can I help by coming?"

I said, "Well, I think that your public image would be improved if you came. But I am sincere in feeling that it's not going to change anything, because they'll insist that you come into the yard to talk with them. They will not meet you anywhere else. I'm certain of that because they wouldn't meet any of us anytime anyplace else. I often offered them an opportunity for safe passage to a separate cellblock to meet with me alone. They wouldn't do that."

And so he said, "Well, I really don't believe I can do any good." He said, "I have heard"—and I had heard the same thing—"that after they get me there, they're going to demand President Nixon coming as well." And he said, "Under those circumstances, I don't think I should come."

I didn't think if the governor came, he would have accomplished anything at all, because they were so determined that they were going to make everyone grovel. My difficulty with this whole group was that never did I run into such a group that was that obdurate, that intransigent. Never. They wanted to take everything and give nothing.

The last time the observers entered D yard was Sunday afternoon. Arthur Eve had earlier been elected chairman of the observers' committee.

ARTHUR EVE

That Sunday, the last day that we went in, Oswald had shared with us a letter that they had given to the inmates which literally had said that we, the observers, had agreed that they should accept the points and should give up. The letter misrepresented the observers' group, and as chair of it I felt we had literally been set up, that if we went back in there many of us felt we may be attacked by the inmates, and we shared that with Oswald that he had betrayed us and really jeopardized our lives. At that particular point a number of the observers did not want to go back in. And five of us agreed to go back in because we thought it was important that they know we did not lie to them and that we did not betray their trust.

When we went back into that yard, they had tears in their eyes. And they told us that they had trusted me and they trusted us collectively and we had betrayed them. The anger and the frustration was very clear, and thank God to a former Puerto Rican inmate for saying to them, "Listen, everywhere Brother Eve has gone, I have been with him. He's not had any conversation with anybody without my being present, and what you're doing is falling into a trap that if you hurt him or any of these observers they will come in and use that as a justification for killing all of us." And he said, "Don't do it. The brothers have been true." And he really played a significant role in really calming down the tensions and the animosity and obviously maybe even hatred that had been developed by the inmates in the yard for us.

TOM WICKER

When I left the yard for the last time, I had a very strong feeling that men with whom I had in a very strange and odd way developed a relationship, a relationship I never would have had before, never have had since, that these men, you know, they were going to die. There was no doubt in my mind that they were going to die.

MICHAEL SMITH

By Sunday night it was the feeling generally among the hostages and also with the inmates that we were communicating with that the negotiation process was breaking down. Governor Rockefeller had refused to come and take part in the negotiation process, and the negotiating committee didn't seem to be coming back with any positive response to the demands that were most important. Up until Sunday night, I thought positively and I guess never really considered that I might not be walking out of the yard at the end of this siege. Sunday night that feeling changed. I had the opportunity to find some paper and a pen and write my family a letter. I communicated to them that I loved them all very much and that I was sorry that this had evolved into what it had but that I was sure we'd meet again someday.

On Monday morning, September 13, state troopers and corrections officers began their assault on D yard.

FRANK "BIG BLACK" SMITH

We knew that they were going to come in, but we never knew that they were going to come in there that way. That was really a big surprise, the way that they came in the yard. We thought they were going to come in there and knock some heads and bust some heads open and that kind of way. And once we started seeing the helicopters and they start shooting the gas pellets and we start thinking the best way to protect ourself against that, we start opening up cans of milk, you know, because we got word that if you put milk on you that the gas wouldn't stick to you. And that's what we start doing. And then when they start shooting in the yard, and then when they start vamping in the yard, I mean, there's physical beings in the yard, and I start seeing people getting opened up with shotguns, you know, then I knew that they were really coming in there in a violent, violent way and it was very barbaric, man, it was very dehumanizing, you know. And it was a sad, sad, bad, bad thing to see how people could really, really—knowing that we didn't have any weapons. Yeah, we might had a shank here, I mean a butter knife or a pair of scissors that broke. But we didn't have no weapons, no guns. Why did they have to come in there like that? Why did they have to shoot from the helicopter? Why did they have to shoot from the roofs? Why did they have to shoot when they come over the wall and be right up on a person? Why did they have to shoot him with a shotgun or the .270's?

HERBERT X. BLYDEN

Monday, September 13, 1971, was indeed a blue Monday. It was a cloudy, overcast day, and we remember clearly addressing the crowd and appraising them of the urgency of the situation at hand. And to a man, with one exception, everybody decided to stay in the yard. I'll never forget this one white guy came up to me and said, "I don't want to be out here." And I told him then, "Stand behind me." And he was the only one of the one thousand two hundred eighty-one men who said they didn't want to be in the yard on September thirteenth. Fifteen minutes after that man said that, the helicopters came over and asked us to surrender, place our hands on our heads, we will not be hurt. And some of the men started to do that only to hear tear gas, pepper gas, shotguns, rifles. And again pandemonium broke out because some of them were indeed surrendering. And the chaos that was created as a result of this mass shooting into the yard, I think, to me, created the pandemonium that led to the massacre in the yard.

MICHAEL SMITH

Monday morning a number of the hostages had been taken to an elevated area in the prison called the catwalk, from which they could be observed. Each hostage was assigned inmate executioners. One of my executioners was an inmate who was in my company previously, who had protected me in the metal shop when the riot initially started. I had three executioners. Don [Noble] was located directly to my left. He had his right arm over my right shoulder and held what appeared to be a tar paper knife at my throat. I had another executioner behind me with a hammer and I had another executioner to the right side of me with a hand-fashioned spear made from parts from the metal shop. I asked Don if I made it through alive, if there were anything I could do for him. He told me who his family was and where they were located and asked me in the event of his death to get in touch with them, which I promised to do. Don said that he was sorry the situation had deteriorated to the point that it had and he asked me if there were anything that he could do for me. I said yes, that when the time came that I didn't want to suffer—just make the cut as clean and neat as possible, and he promised me that he would. He also promised me that if he made it through, he'd be in touch with my family.

Although I was blindfolded, the conversation of the inmates that surrounded me indicated that there were sharpshooters with guns on the rooftops. I recall when that helicopter flew overhead, besides being able to hear it, you could actually feel the concussion of the propellers from the helicopter overhead. I could hear the bang or the pop of the gas projectile and then the forces retaking the prison opened fire, and that seemed to last forever. It was a period of probably ten minutes, but at the time it seemed to last forever. You could hear all kinds of gunfire—shotguns, handguns, automatic weapons, rifles—and you could hear the bullets hitting around you. I can remember, as soon as the firing started, feeling a tug at my left shoulder, and I knew that Don Noble was on my left side and he pulled me off to the left. I was hit four times in the abdomen and fell to the roof of the catwalk, which was directly below me. As I lay there I didn't know what had become of one of my executioners, but one lay dead over my legs and Don Noble lay behind me. It was very painful. I can recall looking up and seeing a state trooper come up to me, and at point-blank range he pointed his gun toward me. A correction officer was not far behind and told the state trooper not to shoot, that I was okay, that I was one of them. He then raised the barrel of the gun and pointed it directly at the inmate Don Noble behind me. And Don asked me to tell him who I was, and asked me to tell them what he did for me. And I said, "His name is Don Noble and he saved my life."

TOM WICKER

We observers, to I suppose our shame in a way, we all believed—I don't know of any exceptions—we all believed that the inmates would in fact kill the hostages as they had threatened to do. And they had posted them in such a way that it looked as if they were going to do it. So, we had no more faith in the inmates than the state did. We thought they were going to kill them. It was a terrible time, because there we were cooped up in our room [the stewards' room], the gas was coming in the windows, not for us but we knew it was being used. And even though at least I couldn't hear the gunfire, we knew it was going on. And we had predicted the day before that it was going to be a massacre. People were weeping openly and not just from the gas. And [Congressman] Herman Badillo turned to me and said, "I don't know what the hurry was." He said, "There's always time to die." And I don't know what the hurry was either. You know, those guys weren't going anywhere, they were inside thirty-foot walls, it was September, it was getting cold up there, the food was running out, the sanitary conditions were bad, the place smelled awful. I mean, that sense of freedom that the guys had had to begin with for being out of their cells, that was beginning to wear away in the reality of their situation. I don't know what the hurry was, they could have waited two days, three days, four days, those guys would have given up. They didn't have to go in and kill 'em all, but they did.

A task force consisting of 211 state troopers and corrections officers retook Attica using tear gas, rifles, and shotguns. After the shooting was over, ten hostages and twenty-nine inmates lay dead or dying. At least 450 rounds of ammunition had been discharged. Four hostages and eighty-five inmates suffered gunshot wounds that they survived. After initial reports that several hostages had died at the hands of knife-wielding inmates, pathologists' reports revealed that hostages and inmates all died from gunshot wounds. No guns were found in the possession of inmates.

The McKay Commission, a body assembled in October 1971 to reconstruct the events of September 9 through 13, in its report issued nearly a year later said, "With the exception of Indian massacres in the late nineteenth century, the State Police assault which ended the four-day prison uprising was the bloodiest one-day encounter between Americans since the Civil War."

FRANK "BIG BLACK" SMITH

It was very, very barbaric, you know, very, very cruel. They ripped our clothes off. They made us crawl on the ground like we were animals. And they snatched me. And they lay me on a table, and they beat me in my testicles. And they burned me with cigarettes and dropped hot shells on me and then put a football up under my throat, and they kept telling me that if it dropped, they was going to kill me. And I really felt, after seeing so many people shot for no apparent reason, that they really were going to do this.

They set up a gauntlet in the hallway and they broke glass up in the middle of the hallway and they made people run through the gauntlet. They had police on each side with the clubs they call nigger sticks and they was beating people. It just hurt. You see another human being treating a human being this way, and they really hurt me. I never thought it would happen. I never thought so many would be treated like animals. And the way they treated me, the way they beat me and, after, they took me off the table and ran me through the gauntlet. And the way they broke my wrists, over my head. Took me to the hospital and dumped me on the floor, playing with me with shotguns, pointing it in my face and putting the barrel of the shotgun over my eyes, and telling me, "Nigger, we're going to kill you."

ARTHUR EVE

After the massacre, they took us into the yard and told us why they had to do what they did. They described an inmate cutting up the reproductive organs of a hostage and putting it in his mouth in their clear view with all of those troopers watching. They told us of another inmate that attempted to kill a hostage with a knife and they had to shoot him. They showed us the inmate on the table whom they had on his back with a football resting on his neck, Big Black, and I remembered him as the brother whom I got to know in that yard and really love, and how we had embraced and cried on the last day, that Sunday. And I said, "That doesn't seem like Big Black." But it was told to you very convincingly and to the degree that you believed it. And that's something that almost destroyed me, that I really believed the lies that they had told. And then they showed me five inmates who were spread-eagled and buck naked on the ground and said they had committed crimes against the hostages. And, as you know, subsequently the medical examiner from Rochester said it was all lies. Everything.

I thank God that I was able to keep my sanity after Attica. But it pointed up very clearly that the ruling class is a very small percentage. And as I've said to many audiences, the hostages in there, the guards, were just like the inmates. If a Rockefeller family member had been there, they never would have used the violence. And so those who work for a living are those who are in sort of a class situation, their lives are just as expendable as the inmates', be they white or black, to a great degree. But it really pointed up that racism is very heavy in New York state and that all of those men and women, all those men who were in the prison, that we had to try to do more to change what was happening in our penal institutions. That people should have an opportunity, while incarcerated, to be treated like a human being and then hopefully rehabilitated, if possible. But every chance must be given for that. It also said that how do I stop kids from going into crime? I mean, how do we stop poverty, hunger, ignorance, lack of education, poor housing? And so it sort of gave me a new resolve to try harder to prevent other Atticas from happening and people getting into situations such as Attica state prison.

During the first minute of the assault on Attica, inmate Elliot James Barkley was struck in the back by a single round from a state police .270 rifle. He died in D yard.

LAVERNE BARKLEY

He was uniquely himself, Elliot. And he would stand for himself, no matter what. And, under those conditions, and the fact that he was behind bars, that type of attitude and behavior was certainly not looked on positively. So therefore I feel as though Elliot would have a problem if you disliked a black male who is forever being himself and forever going to be no matter what happens to him. No matter what you do to him. Even if you put him in the hole, he's going to come out the same way. Because he won't change unless he feels that there's a good reason to change.

And so maybe there wasn't anything wrong to me with his being, acting, like a man and letting you know that he is someone important because he's made in God's image. He is a human being.

29

The Gary Convention, 1972

"Unity Without Uniformity"

On the weekend of March 10–12, 1972, eight thousand African-Americans gathered in Gary, Indiana, for the National Black Political Convention. Thirty-five hundred were delegates selected from forty-four states. Their purpose was to debate and ratify an extraordinary document, the National Black Political Agenda. The white media, barred from the proceedings of the convention, did not give it rave reviews. A *Time* magazine headline called it a "Frail Black Consensus." But the convention, despite the controversy it provoked in segments of the black community, heartened many. *Ebony* magazine headlined its eight-page story "National Black Political Convention Blazes New Trails for 1972 and Beyond."

"We come to Gary in an hour of great crisis and tremendous promise for Black America," the agenda declared. "While the white nation hovers on the brink of chaos, while its politicians offer no hope of real change, we stand on the edge of history and are faced with an amazing and frightening choice: We may choose in 1972 to slip back into the decadent white politics of American life, or we may press forward, moving relentlessly from Gary to the creation of our own Black life. The choice is large, but the time is very short."

The agenda described the America its writers saw in 1972: "Our cities are crime-haunted dying grounds. Huge sectors of our youth—and countless others—face permanent unemployment. Those of us who work find our paychecks able to purchase less and less. Neither the courts nor the prisons contribute to anything resembling justice or reformation. The schools are unable—or unwilling—to educate our children for the real world of our struggles. Meanwhile, the officially approved epidemic of drugs threatens to wipe out the minds and strength of our best young warriors. Economic, cultural, and spiritual depression stalk Black America, and the price for survival often appears to be more than we are able to pay."

The document summarized the movement struggles of the 1950s and 1960s. Long-term, it took its lessons from more than a century of black experience: "From the Liberty Party in the decades before the Civil War to the Republican Party of Abraham Lincoln, we trusted in white men and white politics as our deliverers. Sixty years ago, W.E.B. Du Bois said he would give the Democrats their 'last chance' to prove their sincere commitment to equality for Black people—and he was given white riots and official segregation in peace and war.

"Nevertheless, some twenty years later we became Democrats in the name of Franklin Roosevelt, then supported his successor Harry Truman, and even tried a 'non-partisan' Republican General of the Army named Eisenhower. We were wooed like many others by the superficial liberalism of John F. Kennedy and the make-believe populism of Lyndon Johnson. Let there be no more of that."

The agenda stated that "the Black Politics of Gary must accept major responsibility for creating both the atmosphere and the program for fundamental, far-ranging change in America." Among the program recommendations: the establishment of black congressional representation in proportion to the size of the black community, a bill of rights for prisoners, community control of schools in black neighborhoods, a system of national health insurance "from birth until death," a guaranteed minimum annual income, and the elimination of capital punishment.

The Gary convention was both a political and a cultural happening, a product of a growing black consciousness, of frustration with the American system and, at the same time, of a slow but steady accumulation of black political power within it.

Black members of Congress were using that political power to voice the concerns of the black community. After the deaths of Fred Hampton and Mark Clark in December 1969, eight black members of Congress had gone to Chicago to hold a special congressional hearing on the killings. In 1970, the members of what would soon become known as the Congressional Black Caucus sought to present black grievances to President Nixon. After Nixon's refusal to meet with them, the twelve black representatives boycotted his January 1971 State of the Union address, and finally achieved a meeting with the president two months later. In January 1972, the black congresswoman Shirley Chisholm, Democrat from Brooklyn, New York, had declared her candidacy for the presidency. In the years leading up to Gary, blacks had also met in convention several times—for four national conferences on Black Power between 1966 and 1969; and in Atlanta in 1970 for the first Congress of African Peoples, a meeting attended by approximately two thousand black people of many political persuasions. From this meeting, known as CAP '70, evolved the idea of holding a National Black Political Convention in order to create a Black Agenda.

In the spring of 1972, the Black Agenda at Gary encompassed issues raised in years of struggle: the antiwar movement; black impatience with calls for "law and order" as a code for racial repression; sexism; and the growing environmental crisis in America. The writers sensed that it was a historic moment and in that moment seemed to search for a moral center in the struggle for power in America. "We will have joined the true movement of history," they said, "if at Gary we grasp the opportunity to press Man forward as the first consideration of politics. Here at Gary we are faithful to the best hopes of our fathers and our people if we move for nothing less than a politics which places community before individualism, love before sexual exploitation, a living environment before profits, peace before war, justice before unjust 'order,' and morality before expediency."

Among those involved in planning for Gary early in 1972 was Ron Walters, the recently appointed chairman of the political science department at Howard University and a leading member of the black education movement. Many of the planning sessions were held at Howard.

RON WALTERS

The most important thing about 1972 was the fact that it was an election year, so it provided the environment for the politics taking place. So you had two groups of people who saw this as an opportunity to make some very important statements. One of these, of course, was the black nationalist movement led by Amiri

Baraka, Maulana Karenga, and others at that time. And a new group of elected officials had been growing since at least '67, when you had the election of Carl Stokes as mayor of Cleveland but more importantly Dick Hatcher in Gary, Indiana. So, it was this body of people who really were contending for the national leadership of the black community in the early seventies. And in the early seventies this new group of black elected officials joined the civil rights leaders and became a new leadership class, but there was sort of a conflict in outlook between them and the more indigenous, social, grass roots–oriented nationalist movement.

So now both groups saw the upcoming presidential election as an opportunity to make some new political demands and attempted to prepare the black community in their own ways to get the most out of it. What happened was that a series of meetings began to take place, coming out of the Congress of African Peoples conference in Atlanta in 1970. There was some hesitation at first about inviting Baraka and other nationalists to meet with the so-called leadership group, but they finally got together and had several joint meetings. And the notion of a large unity conference was eventually agreed upon. Now, this was a really important thing, you see, because these two groups didn't cooperate easily. And Hayward Henry [leader of the Unitarian Universalist Black Caucus] and Baraka were very much, I think, statesmen in attempting to meet with these guys on their own turf. But the leadership group understood that they had to meet with them, because the nationalist movement had this tremendous national following too. So the agreement was made to have the Gary conference.

Richard Hatcher was elected mayor of Gary, Indiana, in November 1967 and took office in January 1968. Blacks constituted approximately 55 percent of Gary's population of 180,000.

RICHARD HATCHER

At the point where there pretty much was a consensus that this convention should be held, the last meeting that I recall was in Washington, D.C. And there was a group of black leaders in that meeting. And the decision was made that there ought to be three conveners. Congressman [Charles] Diggs was at that time a very prominent member of Congress. He had founded the Congressional Black Caucus. He was a logical person to select, if you were talking about an elected official at the federal level. Amiri Baraka was clearly at that time the leader of the nationalist movement in this country, although Maulana Karenga was also very prominent and very active in that movement. So the selection of Baraka basically said that the nationalists were in. Selection of Diggs said that elected officials were in. Aside from the fact that the decision was made subsequently to hold the meeting in Gary, I'm not quite sure why I was selected as sort of a third or the in-between person, other than this feeling that I felt comfortable talking to both sides, and relating to both sides.

SNCC veteran Ivanhoe Donaldson, in the early 1970s a senior resident fellow at the Institute for Policy Studies in Washington, D.C., was called in to help coordinate the convention.

IVANHOE DONALDSON

The popular phrase was "unity without uniformity." And I think the idea was generally to accept the fact that it was possible to bring a diverse, ideological spread to the black community together and reach a consensus on the need for unified political action, while respecting that different elements of the community would approach these issues from different points of strategy and different points of tactics—but yet recognize that we're all in a common struggle, whether dealing with black liberation or control of local neighborhoods, black independent economic development, or what have you.

Michigan congressman John Conyers, a member of the Congressional Black Caucus, was one of the black elected officials instrumental in planning the convention.

JOHN CONYERS

By 1972 President Nixon had really hit his stride. He had the FBI, with J. Edgar Hoover, into their repression mode. We didn't know how many strategies were going on. That would come out later. He was attacking, very effectively, many of the social and domestic programs that had been going on. Vietnam War protesters were being characterized as unpatriotic at best, subversive at worst. The civil rights movement was almost flat on its rear end.

We were at our wits' end and I think that fueled a desire of black leadership that were not just radicals but progressive, political people, labor people, street people, intellectuals, that we come together. Mayor Hatcher's city was seen as a central spot not only by it being Midwest but that it reflected a place where we could all come together and express ourselves.

But not every black organization would be officially represented at Gary.

RICHARD HATCHER

Just before the convention opened, unfortunately, Roy Wilkins, who was then the head of the NAACP, really denounced the entire convention. He said that it was not legitimate. That the people who were involved were not the really influential people there. And there were articles, I believe in the *New York Times* and other publications, quoting him as saying this was not a good thing that this meeting was taking place. And that he would not participate. In all fairness to him, one of his major objections was that the planners made it clear that this was a convention for black people. And that whites would not be permitted to attend or to be inside the hall. And that, Roy Wilkins felt, was inconsistent with the NAACP's commitment to an integrated society.

And so he criticized it on that basis. But that criticism, interestingly enough, I think gave the convention more public exposure and caused more people to come. In other words, local members of the NAACP chapters across the country came in full force, as did members of the Urban League. Vernon Jordan himself [the new executive director of the Urban League] came to the convention. He did not play a truly active role in the convention, but he was there. And other members of the civil rights leadership of our country certainly came.

On the first day of the convention, the NAACP issued a memorandum stating that the preamble to the Black Political Agenda was at odds with NAACP principles. In a letter written after the convention, Roy Wilkins called the agenda "openly separatist and nationalist."

At the time, Gloster Current was director of branches and field administration for the NAACP.

GLOSTER CURRENT

Mr. Wilkins went on very carefully to point out that our action is taken "primarily because of a difference in ideology, as to how to win equality for the Negro minority in the United States." Then he says, "The official, announced position of the Black Political Convention favors a separate black nation or separate racial enclaves within the United States." Now I might say parenthetically that used to be one of the objectives of the Communist party, self-determination in the Black Belt. The party in the thirties advocated separate enclaves for ethnic groups, and we, as an integrationist organization, totally opposed that. Now that seems to leap out in terms of some of the things that were being said at that convention, or written into their documents. And in closing Wilkins said, "We do not believe, from a purely pragmatic standpoint, that an isolated black population of eleven percent can survive and progress in a nation where the overwhelmingly white population is eighty-nine percent. NAACP strategy, accordingly, will continue, regardless of setbacks, to be one of pressing, on all fronts, in every field of endeavor, and by every productive method for the freedom of the individual to win equality under the Constitution and the Declaration of Independence."

Baraka and his group ideologically were not in step with what we considered to be the solution to the problems of blacks of America then and now. If you take a close look at Mr. Wilkins's statement on the NAACP and the Black Political Convention, you will clearly understand why we can't become a party to these maverick groups who announce and call for a meeting and they don't have to be responsible for what they decide to do because they go out of business. You just can't create an ad hoc group and then tomorrow go in another direction. Otherwise, we [the NAACP] wouldn't have existed since 1909.

One of the convention delegates was the Reverend Ben Chavis, who had worked with SCLC in 1967 and 1968 and was now a community organizer in Wilmington, North Carolina, for the United Church of Christ's Commission on Racial Justice.

BEN CHAVIS

It was a good notion to go to Gary, Indiana, when we all knew we're not going to a funeral. I had gotten tired of going to funerals. Not that we should not go to funerals, but so much of the movement had been tragic. I have to emphasize King's assassination was a tragic blow to the movement. So four years later, March of '72, for us to be gathering up our wherewithal to go to Gary, Indiana—hey, that was a good shot in the arm for the movement. Because it meant that somehow the various forces, all these local struggles, survived that repression. Somehow we survived the grief that we all had from Dr. King's loss. And somehow we were making a statement that we were going to pick up that baton and run with it again in the 1970s. And Gary became a place for us to gather, to talk about how we were gonna wage struggle in the 1970s. To talk about how we were gonna wage struggle against Nixon. We knew '72 was an election year. We knew that we had to mobilize our people. 'Cause there'd been a lot of disillusionment again when Nixon first got elected in 1968. Keep in mind the backdrop also of this was the Vietnam War. This was the height of the Vietnam War. A lot of my friends got killed in the Vietnam War. People wanted a venue to express the struggle.

Our preparation to go to Gary, Indiana, for the convention was enormous. First of all, we had a statewide convention ourselves, in North Carolina. Thousands of people attended. And, of course, we sent delegates from across the state of North Carolina to Gary. Some went by bus, some went by car, some went by plane. We drove up. And all the way up, we were thinking about what we were going to see when we arrived in Gary.

I had never been to Gary, Indiana, before, although I had heard about Mayor Hatcher being the mayor. And I remember when we first saw the sign saying "Welcome to Gary," and we got to downtown Gary, I mean, we thought we were in a different country. To see a city in the United States, given the backdrop now of all this Nixon repression going on, all this sense of disillusionment in some quarters of the nation, to drive into Gary, Indiana, and see streamers, red, black, and green, and "Welcome, National Black Political Convention," it was a fulfillment of what a lot of our dreams were.

When we first got into Gary, we didn't know our way around, so we stopped and asked a local policeman for some help. And the police officer smiled and said, "Follow me." He not only showed us, he led us to where we needed to go to register for the convention. Keep in mind, I had just come from Wilmington, North Carolina, where the police were pointing guns at us, trying to intimidate us, keep us from having meetings, and it was a different situation with at least the law enforcement in Gary, Indiana. They had been transformed also with this convention being in Gary.

For many of the delegations that came to Gary, there was not room to stay in some of the local hotels. There were thousands of people from around the country. So a lot of the delegates, including from the North Carolina delegation, stayed in a hotel in Chicago. I remember it was the Howard Johnson's in Chicago. And there was a real stark difference between the environment of Chicago and the environment of Gary. Number one, most of us remembered while we were in Chicago the days of Daley. Daley was still the mayor then. And we had, at least I had, a remembrance of the role that Daley played in the Democratic National Convention in 1968, when all those people got their heads beat just for protesting against racism and for protesting against the Vietnam War. And I was acutely aware of the murders of Clark and Hampton, leaders of the Black Panther party in Chicago. So a lot of us were very nervous about being in a hotel in Chicago, going to a black convention in Gary, Indiana. Also there was a stillness of the environment.

When we got to Gary, it was alive. There was a lot of electricity in the air. I mean, it was truly a time in Gary, Indiana, when African-Americans were self-determined. When there was no intimidation. In fact, there was affirmation all over the place. And I would say there was a sense of pride, just to be there. To know that we'd made it out of those local struggles around the country to come into this convention to express the aspirations of the people we left back home.

Poet, playwright, and political activist Amiri Baraka was one of the three Gary conveners. Winner of an Obie Award for his play *Dutchman,* and founder of the Black Arts Repertory Theater, Baraka became a leading spokesman for black nationalism in the 1960s. Baraka, who had changed his name from LeRoi Jones, was deeply influenced by the "Kawaida," a black nationalist doctrine developed by Maulana Ron Karenga. In 1970 he was one of the key organizers in black candidate Kenneth A. Gibson's successful campaign for mayor of Newark, New Jersey.

AMIRI BARAKA

One thing that was done very well is that we had proportional representation by black people, according to the number of black people in a particular state. And those delegates were elected and they represented black people in those states. It was amazing to me. It was really impressive. Of course, Richard Hatcher was the mayor at that time, so we had complete access to the town, to the police, and to the institutions. Seeing that whole hall set up like that, with the banners for each state, like when we represented it, passionately arguing for these points, I think it filled us all with a sense of deep self-respect, knowing that ultimately the only thing keeping us down was the madman's gun, that it wasn't anything else, that we knew exactly what we wanted, and all we needed to develop was how to get there.

The convention had chosen "Unity Without Uniformity" as its theme. In addition to ratification of the Black Agenda, under consideration were formation of a third party and whether to endorse a black candidate for president.

On Saturday morning, March 11, Richard Hatcher delivered one of the keynote speeches at the overflowing West Side High School gym.

RICHARD HATCHER

That morning I still had some concern that not very many people would show up. Well, the truly wonderful thing was when I got to the hall, and came from behind the stage and out onto the platform, I saw a veritable sea of faces. It was probably one of the most glorious moments of my life when I walked out and saw all of these black people of every color, every hue, every shade. The colorful dashikis and other African garb that some of them wore, mixing with three-piece suits and so forth. It was just an incredible sight to behold. There was this wonderful sense that we had truly come together as a people, and a warm feeling of brotherhood and sisterhood that I'm not sure we've been able to duplicate since. But it was certainly there, and there was a kind of electricity in the air, and it was clear that people were there about very serious business, and really saw this as a meeting that would have a long-term, long-range impact on the lives of Black Americans.

The reception from this huge audience was pretty incredible for me. I was unused to that kind of warm—and I think very genuine—appreciative response. I had this sense that I feel sometimes when I'm in a Baptist church. There is just something about a Baptist audience that makes you feel that you've suddenly become ten feet tall, and that you are a combination of Paul Robeson, Martin Luther King, and any other great orator in the black community. A Baptist audience makes you feel that way, and that's the way this audience made me feel.

I think that many of the people who came to Gary thought that the whole purpose of the convention was to form a third party. That there was going to be a black third party, and that was just that. Gary would formalize that. However, there were many individuals, and I include myself in that number, who were not convinced that that was the best strategy for us to take. I felt at the time that we should give the Democratic party one more chance. In fact, I think somewhere in my speech, I was pointing out what the Democratic party had done to us since 1932, and talking about our being in the hip pocket of this party, and it almost being an automatic reflex to support the Democratic party on the part of blacks in this country. And yet, when you look at our role in the party and look at the benefits that we've derived from that party, they were not very substantial. But after chronicling all of that, then I said, "But I think we ought to give the Democratic party one more chance."

AMIRI BARAKA

We thought that what we were doing was providing the transitional form for a third party. And we thought about a national black assembly, national political council. In my mind I thought that what we were trying to set up was a kind of focused headquarters, if you will, a kind of developmental outpost for the beginnings of a third party.

> Jesse Jackson, executive director of the Chicago-based Operation PUSH (People United to Save Humanity), was another keynote speaker. Using the term "Nationtime" at the end of the speech, and falling just short of calling for a third party, he brought the delegates to their feet.

JESSE JACKSON

The idea of a third political party emerged because there was a sense of alienation from the Democratic party. Democrats taking us for granted, Republicans writing us off. And the agenda items for jobs and peace and justice would no longer be an afterthought for some other party or some other person. There was a sense that we had to assert this new dynamic. It's not the first time the idea had come forth, but somehow Gary gave it special meaning.

I sensed that I was speaking to the alienation but giving it some sense of direction. I had drawn much of the strength of Nationtime from a poem written by LeRoi Jones, Amiri Baraka at that time. The sense of people saying, "What's happening?" Saying, "Nothing's happening, man." Say, "What's really happening? It's Nationtime, it's time to come together. It's time to organize politically. It's time for partnership. It's time for blacks to enter into the equation, it is indeed, whether you're in California or Mississippi, it is Nationtime."

BEN CHAVIS

I think the most surprising thing about Jesse's speech was the end. No one would imagine that Reverend Jesse Jackson would affirm the nationalist call. And that was, "It's Nationtime. It's Nationtime." And I remember everybody raised their fist and stood up, literally, and repeated over and over again, "It's Nationtime. It's Nationtime." And as you looked around that auditorium, it felt like it was Nationtime. At least it sounded like it was Nationtime. And everybody expected Baraka to lead that chant.

But keep in mind Baraka was playing the role of facilitator, with African consensus. And so Jesse Jackson became the keynote in terms of lifting the emotional level of the crowd to an all-time high, with the call for Nationtime. But it was just not a hollow call. It was just not a rhetorical call. When people were repeating after Jesse, "It's Nationtime. It's Nationtime. It's Nationtime. Let the black nation rise," you could hear it reverberating Marcus Garvey. You could hear it reverberating all those proud struggles from the forties, and the thirties, and the fifties and the sixties. I mean, it came to be fulfilled in that moment, of crying that it's Nationtime, now, not next year, not next century, but now. In 1972. In Gary, Indiana.

> But the convention did not choose to form a third party. Instead, a National Black Assembly was formed "to continue permanently" after Gary.

IVANHOE DONALDSON

I think the reality of the constituency which made up the conference probably from the outset really negated forming a third party as a realistic alternative. I mean, you had many Democratic elected officials there that had ties to Democratic organizations within their own local communities. So you're bringing together a national conference. But it is made up of parts and elements of constituencies and communities from all over the United States, each with their own loyalties. Dick Hatcher was a Democratic mayor, Congressman Diggs was a Democratic congressman from out of Detroit, even Arthur Eve was a Democratic assemblyman from New York. Although these people may have had at that point in time an emotional desire to try and mount a third-party struggle, I think that they felt that from a practical point of view, neither the resources nor the will was there, outside of the emotional flirtation, to make that happen. And that to do that was really to be more anarchistic, although strong. Definitely the nationalist groups there felt that that was a possibility. But they were a minority within the conference itself. And at that point in time a minority generally within the black grass roots. And people also felt that they had invested too much energy in trying to revamp the Democratic party to just surrender it and to walk away.

> Because of the diversity of the conference delegates, there was the underlying question of whether the convention could live up to its unity theme. On Saturday, when Charles Diggs miscalled a voice vote about closing nominations for the three convention chairmen, the fragile hold on unity was threatened.

BEN CHAVIS

It was clear from the voice vote that the people wanted the nominations to stay open. The people wanted to debate this and make some other nominations. And, unfortunately, Diggs misread the crowd. Because when he said, "The chair rules that the nominations are closed," hey, pandemonium broke out. Not against him personally, but people were insulted because they didn't want the convention to start off on a point which they had just left in all the repression. We wanted an open convention, not a repressed convention. And so Diggs got himself in some hot water. And it took Amiri Baraka, Imamu Baraka, to come with his version of African consensus. I remember Baraka's statement. He said, "Now, sisters and brothers, we must use some scientific process to bring this gathering together so that we can achieve our objectives." But it was the way that Baraka said it. He didn't say it arrogantly. He said it caringly. And from all of the delegates in that room, he was shown respect, because Baraka showed respect to them.

> That evening, Baraka went from delegation to delegation.

AMIRI BARAKA

I wasn't a mayor or wasn't a congressman, but I was a black nationalist. I was an activist. And I thought a lot of those people had come to Gary because of our organizing, our pleading with people to come and be part of a whole black political development. And I thought it was important that the thing not fly apart, that we talk to the people and find out what could be done other than just walking out, just breaking down into, let's say, even worse tactics.

After those meetings people wouldn't go to sleep. They would caucus, and each state would caucus, and then there would be caucuses inside the caucuses, because then we'd have the elected officials caucusing inside the state, and then you'd have the black nationalists caucusing inside there, and a lot of times there was Marxists on the outside, they'd be caucusing. So, I'd have to get to the heads of the various kind of power focuses and find out what each thought they were going to do and whether we were going to have some kind of accord, whether there was going to be a united front or what they were going to do.

Another ongoing debate at the convention was whether it should support a black candidate for president.

RICHARD HATCHER

Shirley Chisholm, the congresswoman from New York City, had announced that she was a candidate for president of the United States. Frankly, that took a lot of black males by surprise, and shock. And many of them were not quite sure how they felt about that. Many of us tried to get Shirley Chisholm to come to Gary, to come to this convention. We were absolutely convinced that that would be the right thing for her to do. Others who were advising her apparently persuaded her that if she should come to Gary, she would run the risk of in effect being rejected by that convention, and therefore before the whole country it would appear that her own people had rejected her being a candidate for president.

SHIRLEY CHISHOLM

I was not present at the Gary convention. Even if I had the time, I might not have gone because of all the negative reports pertaining to my candidacy that were coming back to me. I didn't intend to present myself in front of a group of people who were just going to slash me right and left when I saw myself moving in an entirely different direction. The fact of the matter is many of them were very upset because they felt I should have come to them and discussed my potential candidacy before I went out there and made the announcement. But the fact of the matter is that black men are no different from white men or no different from yellow men or whatever color they may be. I knew that they would not give support to my candidacy, although people had raised some money and I had some very good support among the female population of this country and the Hispanic population. Because they would laugh at me. I knew that. And I didn't want to be wasting my time to have them laughing at me. I was on a mission. I saw myself on a mission. And that was all there was to it.

Among the convention guests were Coretta Scott King and Betty Shabazz.

Coretta Scott King

I think I may have met Betty Shabazz at another time, but I certainly had not had that much contact with her. I think the fact that we were there together, at least presented some semblance of unity. I think that sent a message to, you know, to the American people—black people and white people alike. I think that the overall significance of coming together said to us that we can, together, do a lot more than we can being separated and divided. Not that there was not some division within the group at that particular time. But I think it was a very forward step in bringing the black community and the black leadership together in a kind of family relationship. Not that we have fully achieved that. But I don't think we've attempted anything since then of that magnitude.

Betty Shabazz

I was very pleased, number one, that the organizers had the correct sensibility to have the conference. I thought it was a very good thing. I still think it's a good thing when people come together and discuss their own agenda. It was brought out at the conference that people, please, vote in terms of self-interest. And I thought, Oh, my goodness, the idea that people would come to the conference not for their own self-interest but for someone else, I found that very strange. I think that if you are a free people, and an adult and thinking about your own responsibility and you have the right of the vote, that you should vote whichever way you choose.

So that I saw nothing wrong with the conference. There was some negative press. But I thought it was healthy if there are differences, if there are questions. Why not? You know, an open forum. So I thought it was very good and said so. Some people say it failed. No. It didn't fail. Because people came together and crystallized their thinking.

> On Sunday, the delegates met to ratify the national agenda. Many of the resolutions had wide support, but two were hotly contested: one on supporting an independent Palestinian state and one on opposition to busing as a means of achieving high-quality education for blacks.
>
> At one point during the proceedings, most of the Michigan delegation, led by state legislator Coleman Young, staged a walk-out.

BEN CHAVIS

When I first saw Coleman Young attempting to lead members of the Michigan delegation out of the convention, I said, "Well, why are they doing that? I mean, this is where the action is. There's nothing going on outside the convention." And I felt that it was an incorrect move by Coleman Young. He disagreed with something that was going on in the convention. But what should have happened was to stay there and debate what you disagree about. If Gary meant anything, this was to be a time when we all hang in there and struggle over our differences, over the divisions in our community. And there was some significant divisions. It was not monolithic. It was diverse. But the point of Gary was to hang in one place at a time and to resolve some of those issues, resolve some of those things. So I was very personally hurt to see part of the Michigan delegation go up and leave the convention. I'm glad that some remained.

IVANHOE DONALDSON

I think that Coleman, of all of the elected black officials there, strongly believed that the political strength of the black community was in electoral politics. And that their principal alliance, within that context, was within the Democratic party. And he did not want to see platforms emerge, be they anti-Israeli or others, which would simply create negative publicity and fracture a very fragile alliance that then existed in 1972.

The fact that Coleman came, I think, was significant. The fact that he left was a sign that the coalition was indeed fragile. But there probably would've been times when Coleman would never have come to such a thing. So I think the victory was the gathering of the people themselves. The fact that they didn't come out in one hundred percent harmony is just a part of the political life, part of political dynamics. You're not going to get one hundred percent uniformity, unity, in something like this. And with Coleman you're talking about someone out of Detroit, deeply entrenched in Democratic politics and union politics of Michigan, and I thought it took a lot of courage and strength on Coleman's part to decide to participate. You know, he historically had dismissed a lot of these things as being useless and rabble-rousing and no benefit to anybody.

RICHARD HATCHER

It was a wonderful agenda. It addressed the issue of political parity. It was pointed out at that time that based upon our numbers, instead of having, I believe, around ten or eleven black congressmen, we should have had forty-three. And so a goal, a target, was set to achieve that level of members of Congress. We talked about the need to expand the number of local black elected officials. And people were encouraged to go back to their home communities and organize politically, and run candidates for offices like city council, mayor, and so forth. So political parity was a major thrust of this convention. But we also talked about economic parity, and the need to establish economic institutions. Discussions were occurring at that meeting about the disproportionate level of unemployment among blacks, the disproportionate level of poverty among blacks, and what to do about it. What kinds of new institutions could be created to address those problems.

I think the two agenda issues that the media spent a lot of time on was the issue of busing for the purpose of integration, and the so-called Israeli issue. The Middle East question. And the interesting thing is that the agenda was not dominated by those two questions. In fact, the first days of the convention involved the kinds of things I've talked about. Political parity, economic parity, the need to promote black pride. All of those things were very important in terms of that convention.

The last day of the convention was Sunday. We were slated to wrap up at noon. And the purpose of that last day was the adoption of the resolutions that had been agreed to by the body. Many people—I would say better than half of the people who had attended the convention—had left by the time these two resolutions, on busing for the purpose of integration and the issue of the Middle East, came up. And both of them were very, very controversial issues. And so it was the rather limited number of people who remained who debated and voted on those two issues. The vote on those issues went against busing for the purpose of integration, which was a position directly contradictory to the NAACP's position, and many other national black organizations. And then certainly the calling for a homeland for the Palestinian people at that time was a very radical position to take. Frankly, up to that point, with the exception of a very brief mention on the evening news several days prior, the media had pretty much ignored the convention because they were very angry about being locked out and not being permitted to come in. But when those two resolutions passed, they picked it up and ran with it, and that was the story that was told in the national media of the Gary convention. Interestingly, as I said, that was only a small part of the discussion acted on by less than half of the delegates to the convention, and yet that became the dominating story. At that time, there were very few blacks involved in the media, with the exception of the small weekly black newspapers and a few radio stations around the country. You did not have blacks at NBC and

ABC and so forth in any significant numbers. So it was a very hostile press that looked at what was going on in Gary and selectively decided what it would emphasize and did so in an extremely negative way.

BEN CHAVIS

On the last day of the convention, I was feeling like I had been at a revival. I mean, all I was waiting for was the benediction. So I could go home and tell all the people about the good news of what the convention decided, in terms of deciding the items on the National Black Agenda. For the first time, we will all have an agenda that we will take up, throughout the nation, to work on, together. And I was excited about that. And personally, I think it was a moment of remembrance, and also of fulfillment. I remembered all the sisters and brothers who would have liked to come to Gary, but who were no longer with us. I had a good, great feeling on the last day of the convention. But also I had a feeling of hoping that some of the sisters and brothers who had been lost in the struggle, that we were at least showing that they didn't die in vain. We were at least showing that their suffering was not in vain. And that the struggle has a sense of continuity to it. I mean, the Gary convention gave us all the step forward that was needed, to prop us up and give us the renewed energy that we needed to go back home and to continue those struggles that we were all involved in.

Mary Hightower, a community organizer with the Mississippi Freedom Democratic party, was one of the delegates. From Holmes County, she was in her mid-twenties at the time of the Gary convention.

MARY HIGHTOWER

I guess the strongest image I have about Gary is the fact that black people were able to mobilize, black people from all walks of life, from all different states, to this one focal point, and to organize, and to accomplish, to really go through even if it wasn't a hundred percent of accomplishments they set after. I think that it was the fact that people got there, that people participated. The positive image that I had was the fact that we were organized, and brought to this point. You know, it was one of the greatest mobilizations of black people that I have ever experienced in my life.

Estelle Verner-David, then known as Akiba, worked behind the scenes in coordinating the Gary convention. She was one of the leaders in the women's division of the Congress of African Peoples headed by Amiri Baraka.

ESTELLE VERNER-DAVID

It's just like Malcolm X used to say: If you're Baptist or you're Muslim, it doesn't matter. We're all being oppressed for the same reason—we're black. So the basic principle of the Gary convention was to bring different people and ideas together, come to one agreement, and work on that. There is beauty in diversity. The convention promoted "unity without uniformity." And while we didn't expect everyone to conform to the same ideological approach, the notion was, let's agree on a few things and let that be the agenda. A Black Agenda was to come out of such a convention, taken home by the participants and implemented in our own ways. So, while the diversity of people was there, it was detrimental for us not to talk and take some unified action.

IVANHOE DONALDSON

It is logical to see Gary as a historical mark. I mean, one can look at the struggle from '54, the Supreme Court decision of *Brown* versus the *Board of Education,* and Gary, as an era. Obviously, *Brown* didn't start in a vacuum. They started arguing those cases in the forties. And obviously Gary was not a termination point, because we see political struggle continuing on after it in an activist way. But clearly Gary is the culmination, in an electoral way, of all that preceded it during those previous eighteen years. And it's an era: '54 to '72 is a political era, a political chapter, in black history in the twentieth century. And it would be hard for anybody to say that wasn't true. In fact it is true.

Vietnam, the nationalist struggle, Malcolm, Martin, the civil rights movement, litigation in the courts—it's a chapter within a continuing historical story of black struggles in America. Or it might be a volume with significant chapters within it. That might be more correctly what we're talking about. You know, volumes that start from the African shores. So I would say that '54 to Gary is a volume of about maybe ten chapters. Because everything that was there you can tie back to the political events of the previous eighteen years in very specific ways. And the personalities have their roots in the activities which preceded Gary over the previous eighteen years. If it had any common denominator at all, it's the people who came out of that struggle.

A summary note to the National Black Political Agenda, published on May 19, the anniversary of Malcolm X's birth, read: "To those who say that such an Agenda is 'visionary,' 'utopian,' and 'impossible,' we say that the keepers of conventional white politics have always viewed our situation and our real needs as beyond the realm of their wildest imaginations. At every critical moment of our struggle in America we have had to press relentlessly against the limits of the 'realistic' to create new realities for the life of our people. This is our challenge at Gary and beyond, for a new Black politics demands new vision, new hope and new definitions of the possible. Our time has come. These things are necessary. All things are possible."

30

Busing in Boston, 1974–1976

"As if Some Alien Was Coming into the School"

Paul Parks and Ruth Batson of the NAACP address the Boston School Committee in 1963, in the early days of the campaign for desegregated schools.

At the Gary convention, the resolution against busing received a great deal of attention from the white media. This was true in part because the NAACP and other organizations had come out in favor of busing, and the dissent engendered by the National Black Political Agenda made for newsworthy controversy. It was also true because busing was very much in the public mind.

The previous year, the Supreme Court had sustained busing as a lawful remedy for unconstitutional segregation in public schools. By the 1970s, public schools in the North were more segregated than those in the South. And although Gallup polls showed clearly that the country favored desegregating public schools, they also showed antipathy toward busing as a remedy.

During the presidential campaign in 1972, the two hottest political topics were Vietnam (for incumbent Richard Nixon and Democrat George McGovern) and busing (for George Wallace). Wallace's antibusing stance made him a strong independent candidate. He won the Florida Democratic primary, but on May 15 he was shot while campaigning in Laurel, Maryland. The assassination attempt left him paralyzed, and he dropped out of the race.

Wallace had attracted some white voters with his antibusing stand. President Nixon stated that busing was a "classic case of the remedy for one evil creating another evil."

The responses to federally mandated busing to achieve integration varied from location to location. In the majority of cities, desegregation proceeded with few incidents. But given the controversial nature of the issue, whenever busing met with violence the media covered the stories in great detail.

One city that the country watched closely through the northern move to desegregate schools was Boston, Massachusetts. Many in Boston's black community had struggled for years to improve the quality of education for their children.

> Ruth Batson was born and raised in the Roxbury section of Boston and was living there in the late 1950s and early 1960s when her children were in school. In 1965, during a tour of Roxbury by Martin Luther King, Jr., she said, "I stand here today as a native Bostonian—a racial agitator—and I intend to continue this agitating as long as I have strength and as long as there is a need. . . . Since education represents our strongest hope of breaking out of the bond we have been placed in by discrimination and prejudice, we intend to fight with every means at our disposal to ensure the future of our children. And by ensuring our future, we also ensure the future of Boston." Ruth Batson's battle over education had begun two years earlier, even before she was named to head the NAACP's Public School Committee.

RUTH BATSON

When we would go to white schools, we'd see these lovely classrooms, with a small number of children in each class. The teachers were permanent. We'd see wonderful materials. When we'd go to our schools, we would see overcrowded classrooms, children sitting out in the corridors, and so forth. And so then we decided that where there were a large number of white students, that's where the care went. That's where the books went. That's where the money went.

We formed a negotiating team. I was chair of the team. Paul Parks and Mel King, both men who had been deeply involved in public school educational concerns, joined me, and we sat down and we decided that we would bring these complaints to the Boston School Committee. This was in 1963.

We said to them that this condition that we were talking about was called de facto segregation, and that by that we didn't mean at all that anybody on the school committee or any official was deliberately segregating students, but this was caused by residential settings and so forth, but that we felt that this had to be acknowledged and that something had to be done to alleviate the situation.

We were naive. And when we got to the school committee room I was surprised to see all of the press around. We thought this is just an ordinary school committee meeting, and we made our presentation and everything broke loose. We were insulted. We were told our kids were stupid and this was why they didn't learn. We were completely rejected that night. We were there until all hours of the evening. And we left battle-scarred, because we found out that this was an issue that was going to give their political careers stability for a long time to come.

It's important to note that the Boston School Committee was a unique political body. For one thing, it had always been used as a steppingstone to a higher office. Very seldom did you hear real educational issues discussed. Louise Day Hicks was chairperson of the school committee at that time. Some of the people on the NAACP general committee felt that she would meet our concerns favorably. She had been endorsed by the Citizens for Public Schools before. And so they thought that, Oh, Louise'll be fine. Well, Louise turned out to be not fine at all. She was an enemy from the minute that we stepped into that door. And this shocked a lot of people. Somehow she was smart enough to know that here was an issue that she can hang on to and move, just move ahead.

After that meeting we were asked to come to a private meeting with the members of the Boston School Committee. No press. Just us and them. And so we would sit down and we would talk.

At one point she said, "The word that I'm objecting to is *segregation*. As long as you talk about segregation I won't discuss this." Well, remember now, we didn't get past the de facto segregation issue. And so, we would drop these little sentences saying, "Where there is a majority of black students, these students are not being given the education that other people are given," and so forth and so on. And she'd say, "Does that mean segregation?" And so the whole thing would be dropped. We went through all these routines with her. Mrs. Hicks's favorite statement was, "Do you think that sitting a white child beside a black child, by osmosis the black child will get better?" That was her favorite statement.

And then there were black people and a lot of our friends who said, "Ruth, why don't we get them to fix up the schools and make them better in our district?" And, of course, that repelled us because we came through the separate but equal theory. This was not something that we believed in. Even now, when I talk to a lot of people, they say we were wrong in pushing for desegregation. But there was a very practical reason to do it in those days. We knew that there was more money being spent in certain schools, white schools—not all of them, but in certain white schools—than there was being spent in black schools. So therefore, our theory was move our kids into those schools where they're putting all of the resources so that they can get a better education. We never seemed to be able to get that point across.

These are the kinds of things that we were getting, plus with the press. The press came out: NAACP is wrong. This is wrong. We got very little public support and we got absolutely no political support.

We did all kinds of things outside that school committee. We made all kinds of appeals. And they would do nothing. In the meantime, Louise Day Hicks's name was spreading and she was a cult hero. They loved her. And the only person that we had on that Boston School Committee who supported us was a man named Arthur Gartland. So constantly we had these five-to-one votes. And, of course, he was vilified in this city.

It was a horrible time to live in Boston. All kinds of hate mail. Horrible stuff. I also got calls from black people in Boston. They would call up and they'd say, "Mrs. Batson, I know you think you're doing a good thing. And maybe where you came from there was segregation, but we don't have segregation in Boston." And

I would say to them, "Well, where do I come from?" And invariably they would say South Carolina or North Carolina. Of course, now, I was born in Boston. So there were people who could not accept the fact that this horrible thing was happening to Boston, the city of culture.

Among those involved in the effort to improve the schools was Thomas Atkins, an attorney working with the NAACP.

THOMAS ATKINS

One of the real problems that the black community faced was that relatively speaking it was small. We did not have a large enough community to control any political event, per se. And it showed itself in many ways. One of the ways it showed itself around the school issue is because of the rich diversity of views as to what ought to happen. One of the views was that we should just recognize that black children were going to be mistreated if white folks were in charge of them and get control of our schools, run them ourselves, hire the teachers and teach the kids ourselves. And it was an attractive notion, but I and many other people in the community concluded that it simply wasn't a practical approach, whatever your ideological views might be on integration. It depended on a notion that we were going to make a deal with somebody, the school committee, the state, whoever. But we didn't have the power to enforce the deal. If we made the deal and they broke it, what could we do about it? And so we said, separatism in Boston is not going to work.

We started dealing at the city level, because that was the most logical thing to do. And nothing succeeded. We got no support. We went to the state. By 1972, the efforts at the state level were so clearly thwarted that the feeling was if relief is going to come it will come only at the federal level. And if it's going to come at the federal level in 1972—you got Richard Nixon in the White House. I mean, he's not going to help us. So if it's going to come at the federal level, there's only one place it's going to come from. And that's out of the courts. That's why we got to the courts in the first place. It was by a simple—not very quick—process of elimination. We eliminated all of the other alternatives except filing the federal lawsuit.

In 1974, U.S. District Court Judge W. Arthur Garrity, Jr., found the city guilty of unconstitutional segregation of the city's schools. When the school committee refused to produce a desegregation plan, the judge worked with the state Department of Education. Following recent state guidelines, the plan called for integrating black and white schools that were near each other, thereby requiring little busing. Two of the communities that were paired were Roxbury and South Boston, one of the city's predominantly Irish-American enclaves.

THOMAS ATKINS

When the decision was made to file the lawsuit in the first place, there was no agreed-upon strategy as to what the solution, what the remedy, was going to be. The NAACP did not have a remedy. It didn't have a proposal in its pocket or stashed away in a drawer somewhere as to what the judge ought to do if he agreed with the lawsuit that was filed. And as a matter of law, the nature of the remedy that you get, says the Supreme Court, must be tailored by the scope of the violation you've proven in court. So you can't really start putting a remedy together, a solution together, until you have proven the dimensions of the problem you've described. The actual work in developing a remedy did not start until Garrity's decision came down in June of '74. That's the reality. People find that hard to believe. They say, "Oh, you knew what you were going to do." Well, we didn't know what we were going to do. So work began on developing a remedy.

Alan Lupo, a Boston-based journalist, was writing a book about the city when Judge Garrity's decision was handed down.

ALAN LUPO

There's a great piece of mythology in the city of Boston, and it goes like this: the schools were wonderful before desegregation.

The schools were not good before busing. The schools had been in trouble practically from the day Horace Mann pushed public schools. We're talking 1830 something. From day one, you had a class problem. You had wealthy Yankee folk saying, We don't want our kids going to school with those swamp Yankees.

You had all kinds of white Anglo-Saxon Protestants saying there were too many Irish in the schools. You had loads of Jewish and Italian people coming into the public schools in the late 1800s, scaring the heck out of teachers and administrators alike. But mainly what you had in the Boston schools was a political patronage system. Now, patronage is not a dirty word. Good patronage is fine. You also had bad patronage. It was a real tight family affair. They went to the same schools. They grew up in the same neighborhoods. They got appointed to certain jobs whether they were competent or not competent, and the people who served on the school committee, with some exceptions, were mainly a bunch of pols who were trying to either advance in their profession—that is, politics—or at least do favors for their pals.

The school committee was a bucket shop, stuff was for sale. When you ran for school committee or you ran for reelection, what you ended up doing was holding what they call a "time." A time is a political affair. And teachers would get in the mail little invitations. They were real cute. Help John Kerrigan or somebody celebrate his forty-fifth birthday. He's always been our good friend and for a fifty-dollar donation you can make him feel even better. And a lot of teachers and principals and headmasters and administrators and custodians and secretaries, et cetera, felt pressure to contribute to those things. The message being that maybe your job wouldn't be so pleasant or maybe your job wouldn't be, period, if you didn't. That's what the Boston schools were.

The hatred is almost inherited in this city. We had people, early on, who came here for religious freedom. And as soon as somebody stood up and said, Gee, I think I'll be a Quaker, they either hanged him or they banished him. That kind of set the tone, all right. And when the Irish showed up, the brutality exhibited toward them was as cruel as anything anyone has ever seen—not counting what has happened to the blacks—even more so than other immigrants. So we had a tradition of this in the city—not just in this city, in many places, but particularly poignant here because everybody was fighting for crumbs. And the economy was hardly ever good. I remember personal experiences of the early forties, into the fifties, being in a gang, happens to be a gang of Jews, self-protection. Protect your religion. Protect your class. Protect your turf, because somebody else is calling you names.

Somebody else wants to get you. So we had religious wars here. We had class wars here. Blue Hill Avenue now runs through a black neighborhood. Once upon a time it was a Jewish neighborhood and the Irish kids called it Jew Hill Avenue. And they didn't say that as a joke. Maybe to them it was a joke, but if you were Jewish, it wasn't a joke. So that's the kind of atmosphere you had here.

The real story of Boston is the story of two cities. It's a story of the traditional, alleged liberal, abolitionist Boston, the progressive Boston, the folk who sent Cesar Chavez money for his grape union. The folks who supported the Hungarian revolution in 1800 something. But the other Boston is a very hidebound, distrustful, turf-conscious, class-conscious, parochial city, full of people who did not make much progress over the years. I'm talking about white folks. They were not middle-income people. They were poor folk and they were running hardscrabble operations. And they were scared folk. And they had had plenty of things done to them. Highways had come through their living rooms. Nobody bothered to ask. Airports expanded into their neighborhoods. Nobody bothered to ask. Some of their neighborhoods had been torn down totally, two of them integrated neighborhoods. Nobody bothered to ask them. By the time busing came around, these people were ripe for revolution.

> Kevin White, son of a man who had served on the school committee for twenty-three years, had first been elected mayor of Boston in 1967, defeating Louise Day Hicks. According to the black newspaper *Bay State Banner,* "The ghetto made the difference. . . . The turnout was the highest in the city . . . more than 90 percent for White."

KEVIN WHITE

The issue in the campaign became not my qualifications but Mrs. Hicks's leadership, exacerbation of, or however you define it, of escalating the tensions between the blacks and whites over the issue of the school committee, of which she was chairman. And the battle basically in the election came down to Mrs. Hicks saying, "You know where I stand," which was a code word for saying to the hearer, "I'm antiblack, and we will not let them dislodge us from our neighborhoods or our schools or our points of power in the city government." It was a code word. I used to kid and say, If Mrs. Hicks looked like Grace Kelly, she'd've beaten me. She was not an attractive candidate, yet she came within twelve thousand votes of winning. To make a long story short, I won, with ninety-five to ninety-eight percent of the black vote. Blacks did not know me. They were afraid of Mrs. Hicks. I was an unsecured refuge for them, for the moment.

When Judge Garrity handed down his decision, the first recognition is that it's a court order, it has to be enforced by the city, that it's a final decision, that it's irrevocable, and that I'm going to be responsible at a minimum for public safety, and at a maximum for the social health, in a way it's a little exaggerated, but the morals of the town. It's a moral question, as well as a political question. What I did was respond politically. And that is I brought my staff together and I decided the first thing I had to do was to reach out to the whites. They were the ones who were going to feel threatened. And secondly, because I had beaten Mrs. Hicks, the blacks had trust in me, to a degree, with the normal skepticism reserved for all public officials, and it was the whites that I had to reach out for. So I asked them to arrange a hundred coffee hours in the city, in the homes, hosted by only antibusing mothers, in the white communities. I wanted to take it head-on. I wanted to reach out to talk to them, not to threaten them, to explain.

They were usually held in a very small living room, sometimes in the basement. A group no more than twenty, sometimes as small as six. They came to listen, they came hostile, they came suspicious. But they came hopeful that if they could only capture the mayor, if only the mayor could listen, and see that they were right, then their cause would not only be heard but would be won. Boston is an international city with sort of a small-town mentality. And the mayor is the patriarch, and because it's so political, it is a town in which the mayor is seen as all-powerful. So it's a little like capture the flag for both sides. For the blacks, if we can have the mayor as our protector, then we will achieve, and for the whites, if we have the mayor, we will not lose. And my role had to be neither a partisan for either but a protector in an odd way of both. And I began to play that role in the summer.

RUTH BATSON

When Garrity's decision came down in June of 1974, we were sunk when we heard some of the remedies, the one of busing to South Boston and Charlestown particularly, because those of us who had lived in Boston all of our lives knew that this was going to be a very, very difficult thing to pull off.

As a child I had encountered the wrath of people in South Boston. And I just felt that they were bigoted. I just felt that they made it very clear that they didn't like black people. And I was prepared for them not to want black students coming to the school. Plus which, they said it. I mean, they made it very clear. The other thing was that there was absolutely no preparation made for this transition. There were a couple of athletes and other people who would go on TV and they would say, you know, "We have this thing that we have to have happen in our city. We're going to be busing kids and so forth and so on. And we have to be brave about it." And you say to yourself, Well, what are they expecting? Here were little children that were going to a school and they were talking about being brave as if some alien from some planet was coming into the school. I never heard any public official on the state level or on the city level come and say, "This is a good thing. We should all learn together. We should all live together." There was no encouragement from anybody. I call it complete official neglect.

An antibusing group called ROAR, for Restore Our Alienated Rights, operated throughout the city's white neighborhoods under the leadership of Louise Day Hicks, by now a member of the city council. Its weekly meetings were held in the city council chambers in City Hall.

Jane DuWors was a South Boston mother and ROAR leader. She helped to organize a march and rally to protest "forced busing" on September 9, 1974, just three days before school was to open and the new plan would begin. Eight thousand demonstrators from white neighborhoods all over the city assembled at City Hall Plaza, an open space in the center of downtown, bounded on one side by City Hall and on another by the John F. Kennedy Federal Building, where Senator Edward Kennedy, first elected in 1962, had his local office.

JANE DUWORS

From South Boston we marched along Broadway over Broadway Bridge. We met people from Hyde Park at the corner of Tremont Street. People from East Boston came in by carloads through the tunnel and they met with the people of Charlestown and they marched over the bridge from Charlestown down to City Hall Plaza.

We had different speakers that were going to address the crowd. And Ted Kennedy happened to be one of them. We thought this foolish social experiment had gone on long enough and that it was time for somebody to listen to the people. We always thought that the majority ruled and that the right to redress was taken seriously and listened to seriously. But we were fast becoming aware that all we were given was lip service. People would listen to us, shake their heads. "Isn't that crazy?" they'd say. Or something that we got so sick of hearing was, "Off the record, let me tell you I wouldn't do that to my child either, but for the record I have to state that I'm for this program." So we were getting tired of hearing that and we weren't in any mood to listen to more of the same. We wanted the elected officials to tell us how to go about repealing this court law. What we would have to do to get somebody in a position to remedy it, to listen to our concerns.

Ted Kennedy got up to the microphone and Ted Kennedy was the epitome of the Boston Irish. You know, everybody loved Ted Kennedy. The Kennedy family, they were all gods. So the people thought at the time that we were fast learning that Ted Kennedy was a hypocrite. He was all for other people putting their children on buses and having them driven across town. But his children didn't even partake of public education. They were all in private schools, and we thought that somebody who had children in private schools, who didn't have to walk ten feet in our moccasins, shouldn't be chastising us and telling us to put our children on the bus. We knew that we knew what was best for our children. And not people who didn't have to live it. And we were so disenchanted with them and there were thousands of us standing there. And he got up and the people started to not boo him but hiss him, politely hiss him. And somebody yelled, "Turn your back on him when he starts to speak. Show him the same consideration that he's showing us. He's turned his back on our problems. Show him that we don't want him any longer to represent us. Turn your back on him." And we did. He started to speak, people started to turn their backs. And I was right up close to the dais so I could see. I'm a little short, and I like to see everything that's going on. And he started to speak and people started to turn around, and you could see the look of consternation appear on his face. You know, a frown, like "Why do these people do this to me? What's their problem?" Until finally the whole crowd was facing the opposite direction. We were facing the Kennedy Building instead of Ted Kennedy on the dais. And someone said, "We've heard enough. Tell him to go. He hasn't anything to say. He's not going to help us." And he started sputtering. He started losing his composure. And he kept talking, and the things he said were not making any sense whatsoever to us.

We just weren't in the mood to hear and we wanted help on how we could redress what we thought was a grievance situation. Something that was harming our children, was very detrimental to our children, which was the basic right for a parent to choose how a child should be educated and where the child should be educated. So somebody pulled the plug. And the loudspeaker went dead. And people started saying, "Go home, Ted. Go home, Ted." And he was going to speak, loudspeaker or no loudspeaker, until he finally decided that it was best for him to leave because people were really starting to get upset. And he started down off the dais and, God, he had to run across the plaza because he had a group of women, scorned women, not scorned in love, but scorned more importantly—what, how would I say it?—in the most important thing of their lives, their children. Their children were being scorned. And they chased him and they shouted at him and they——. Probably some of them were asking him for help and others were probably telling him to go home and get out. And he ran into the Kennedy Building and they locked the doors, and the women pounded on the doors to try to get in and the plate glass windows shattered, and I think we were shocked as he was when we saw the glass shatter. But the lesson that we learned that day was the lip service continues, and the bitterness and the sense of alienation continued to grow and didn't get any less, because there was no help left coming from that area.

Over the summer, the black community mobilized to try to achieve an orderly transition. Freedom House, a Roxbury community center founded by Otto and Muriel Snowden, was the focal point of activity and soon became known as the Black Pentagon. Ellen Jackson was its director. School opened on September 12.

ELLEN JACKSON

The mood in the black community was one of confusion, concern, and fear because the elected officials during that summer of 1974, after the order had been given by Judge Garrity, were very often making statements that this would not happen. And statements were coming out of certain segments of Boston, specifically out of South Boston, indicating that these students were not going to be welcomed into the schools. They would do anything that they had to do to keep students from entering the schools in South Boston. We attempted at Freedom House over the summer months to try to allay some of the fears that parents had.

By and large parents didn't know what "geocodes" were. They didn't know where these streets were that the kids were supposed to go to catch the bus. They weren't sure how the kids were going to get to school. If it was a bus, if it was going to be a taxi. If it was going to be one of the longer station wagons. They didn't know, for the children that had handicaps, what was going to happen to those particular children, how they were going to get to school. If they were a special needs student, were they to go to the same school to report to the same teacher? There was a lot of confusion. Mothers worked. What time were they going to get back into the community? Where were they supposed to go? Who was going to be there to meet them? There was a lot of concern. So we attempted to work with the school department in making sure that for each school there were pickup spots and times. And people there to accompany the children, to wait with the children when the buses came. And make sure that the children were there on time, and if not, to encourage the bus driver to wait just a few minutes because the kid may be a little late. We then began to set up with the help of the New England Telephone Company what was called the hotline. In the beginning, the hotline at Freedom House was to in a sense answer any of the questions that parents had. And it was staffed by people from various, believe it or not, agencies, various universities, various companies. We developed, my staff and I, we developed a kind of manual and we put it together for emergency numbers. We told parents about giving their children emergency numbers, pinning them on them inside their clothes or somewhere. We also made it clear that they could come and pick up this book. We tried to tell them even the bus numbers that their children would be boarding. We tried to answer and assure them that there would be plenty of people around. Many people volunteered during that time to assist parents and students during that first week of school. We kept the hotline going almost twenty-four hours a day.

Phyllis Ellison, class of '77, was one of fifty-six black students from Roxbury and Columbia Point assigned to South Boston High School.

PHYLLIS ELLISON

I didn't know much about South Boston High School at the time. I didn't know what I was getting myself into, that South Boston High School was part of busing or desegregation, I just knew that I was going to attend South Boston High School. My mother's reaction was I was *not* going to attend South Boston High School, that I would go to a Catholic school. And I let her know that my friends were going to South Boston High and I wanted to attend there. I said I would quit school if I had to go to a Catholic school, because I wanted to be with my friends and none of my friends could go to Catholic school because of affordability.

I remember my first day going on the bus to South Boston High School. I wasn't afraid because I felt important. I didn't know what to expect, what was waiting for me up the hill. We had police escorts. I think there was three motorcycle cops and then two police cruisers in front of the bus, and so I felt really important at that time, not knowing what was on the other side of the hill.

Well, when we started up the hill you could hear people saying, "Niggers go home." There were signs, they had made a sign saying, "Black people stay out. We don't want any niggers in our school." And there were people on the corners holding bananas like we were apes, monkeys. "Monkeys get out, get them out of our neighborhood. We don't want you in our schools." So at that time it did frighten me somewhat, but I was more determined then to get inside South Boston High School, because of the people that were outside.

When I got off the bus, first of all I felt important, because of the news media that was there. [Television reporter] Natalie Jacobson out in front of your school getting the story on your school. So I felt really important going through the metal detectors and making sure that no one could come into the school armed. I felt like this was a big deal to me, to attend South Boston High School.

I felt like I was making history, because that was the first year of desegregation and all the controversies and conflicts at that time. I felt that the black students there were making history.

ALAN LUPO

What sticks in my mind from the first day of busing, standing outside of Southie High School, was a sort of a rush of a crowd, verbal, not a roar really, although that's what they called themselves, ROAR. It was almost like a growl. It was scary. And I heard the word "nigger" and I saw something fly through the air, a bottle or a can, and it smacked the ground. That sticks in my mind more than anything else in terms of what I heard. But then there's what I saw. And that's more important than what I heard. What I saw was black kids looking at where they were being bused and being disappointed. Black kids smiling as if to be cocky but really nervous. Blacks walking as if to taunt the white kids but, I think, really scared. White families looking, with perhaps a combination of hatred and fear, and other whites looking with no hatred but fear and curiosity. Children looking with ignorance and awe. Their hands being held by parents who had been through a lot of hell in their white lives and were looking at a change that they couldn't understand. It was a pitiful sight for everybody.

On this first day of busing, it was quiet in Roxbury, as in most of the city. But at South Boston High School about five hundred demonstrators had stoned buses, shouted racial epithets, hurled eggs and rotten tomatoes, all in front of news cameras. Although thirteen hundred students were scheduled to attend classes, on that first day only fifty-six black students and sixty-eight white students entered the high school.

At the end of the school day, buses carrying black elementary school students out of South Boston were stoned. Nine children were injured and eighteen buses were damaged.

ELLEN JACKSON

Well, the phones, the hotlines, started ringing. And in a few minutes the official word came in that buses coming from the elementary school had been pelted and had been stoned. And they were coming directly to Freedom House. The word was from the command post, if you will, from the police, Bring those buses, do not stop at any stops. We want to see these children. There was Red Cross there, also, at Freedom House. We want to make sure they're all right and we want to talk with the children. Well, just then also we turned on the radio and the radio said that they were not going to drop the children off at their stops near their homes, they were taking them directly to Freedom House. Well, talk about the drums beating, the word went around the community and people were incensed. They were angry. And they started coming to Freedom House and forming little groups. Walking up the pathway to Freedom House demanding to know what had happened. When the kids came, everybody just broke out in tears and started crying. The kids were crying. They had glass in their hair. They were scared. And they were shivering and crying. Talking about they wanted to go home. We tried to gently usher them into the auditorium. And wipe off the little bit of bruises that they had. Small bruises and the dirt. Picked the glass out of their hair. And then we were calling parents, based on the numbers we had, to come up to Freedom House.

When the parents got there, they were as angry with me as I would have been if it had been my own child. And it sort of took me back to the days when we had problems in the sixties, when my kids were in school. And they said, "You listened to the mayor and look what happened. My kid's not going back tomorrow. I'm not letting him be, or her be, subjected to this anymore." I mean, basically parents said, "The hell with it, we're not going to do this anymore. We trusted you." And that hurt because I knew where they were coming from. I could feel their pain myself. And that feeling of trust, because I had trusted some other people who had promised me that this was not going to happen. So we talked with the parents. We asked them to give us another chance, to get to the officials and to talk with them, and they say, "You can't just talk anymore. You've got to demand for us. You've got to have them demonstrate how they're going to make sure that this day never happens again."

I went upstairs to Otto Snowden's office with two other people and I dialed. Kevin White immediately was on the phone. And he said, "Ellen, I know, I know it happened."

And I said, "You have got to come out here and talk."

And he said, "Well, I can't come right now."

I said, "Well, you've got to come, because we're not going to have any parents tomorrow. I made a promise and you made a promise. We've got to do this. We've got to have a dialogue. We've got to talk. We've got to have some assurances."

And he said, "Okay. I'll be out there around six o'clock."

Just a short half an hour after we called him, the hall began to fill up with all types of people, from all over. Parents, agency people, students, just concerned residents. And they were in a dither. It seemed an eternity before the mayor came. And I remember standing in Otto's office watching him get out of the car with his jacket thrown over his shoulder. He couldn't see the parking lot and see that many cars were there. I said, "Oh, my Lord, this man has no idea what's going to happen or what this was going to turn out to be." Nor did I at that point. So he came in the door, and I said, "We've got an auditorium full of people. Angry parents. And I don't know what we're going to do. We can't promise them anything anymore. My own credibility is on the line. I'm born and raised in this community. I'm going to be here, Kevin, when you go back to Beacon Hill. And I'm going to die here possibly. And these are my people. These are my neighbors. So I don't know if I can assure them. I'm going to need you to tell them something. So let's step into the lounge area and talk. And we want to talk to you only."

We went in the room and I said, "You put us in a hell of a position. These kids were hurt. You should have been here and seen it. You said you couldn't make it. But you had to see with your eyes and you'll understand the anger and the frustration that the parents and we all are feeling right now. So be prepared. Don't come out with one of those pat speeches. You've got to hear these parents." Kevin and I, I think, were very close. But I don't think he really even believed me then until he stepped out of that lounge and went downstairs into that auditorium and proceeded to walk up to the front and to go up onto that stage. And before he could even speak, parents were standing up and saying, "We've been betrayed again. We've been betrayed again. We put our kids out here and we take chances with our kids. We didn't want to do it, but you promised us. What are you going to do for us now, Kevin?" It was a difficult time to calm the audience down.

When he heard many of the comments, and many of the accusations, and many of the allegations, and much of the anger and the rage and the frustration from the parents, they said, "We're not going." He turned around and he said, "Wait a minute. Give me," he pleaded, he pleaded and said, "give me one more chance. Let your kids get on those buses tomorrow." He said, "I promise you this will never happen again." There was a pause in the room, and you could feel the silence. People were fighting with themselves, their consciences. Whether or not they should allow their kids to go. Should they take this chance? How could they be assured? Should they trust his word again? When that silence came, someone from the Bay State side of Columbia Point Project yelled, "No, we're not going to have it. We're going to have our own people there. If it's going to be like this, we're going to send our own people on these buses." Kevin White, frankly, was lucky to get out of there with his jacket and his skin that night.

We didn't know how many kids were going to turn out that next day, but we met all night long. And we decided then that we'd have to really form groups to follow the buses over the next morning to South Boston. And that we possibly would have to start on a regular basis from that day on to have people in a sense just watching and monitoring what was happening as the buses went up the hill. I remember we stated that to the police commissioner and he said, "Well, we don't want it. We're not going to be responsible." We said, "You haven't been responsible for us up to now, so we'll take the responsibility on our own. We'll be responsible for ourselves. At the same time, we've got to be responsible for our kids. And these are all of our kids. We may not be their biological parents, but they're our children. We've encouraged these people to participate in this process. And therefore we have a responsibility." But that was a night that changed the whole idea that this was going to be an easy, easy process. It was clear it was not.

Many black children did go to school the next day. But the city's racial climate remained confused and uncertain. In South Boston, many white parents kept their children out of the public schools.

JANE DUWORS

We asked the parents if they would go along with the boycott. The majority of people did. And in the meantime we set up schools in yacht clubs. We set up schools in veterans' posts. All over South Boston there were schools. We had them during the day at first, and then somebody complained. To this day I don't know who complained and said that you couldn't set up a school and have tutoring going on during normal school hours. So we said the hell with it. If that's the way you want to be. We'll let the kids out in the daytime to play and they'll go to school at night. And they did. We switched the tutoring hours over from daytime hours to nighttime hours. And the yacht clubs and the veterans' posts and wherever we had them agreed that we could use them at night instead of the daytime. We had teachers in the Boston public school system who were tutoring our kids at night for free. We had prospective teachers, kids going to college, tutoring our children at night. And it worked out pretty well.

South Boston mother Tracy Amalfitano, refusing to participate in the boycott, sent her two boys to their assigned schools from the first day.

TRACY AMALFITANO

My whole schedule revolved around walking both my children to school, but especially the older one, to catch the bus every morning for Columbia Point. And I also met him every afternoon. It was very difficult for us. Our whole lives, basically, became topsy-turvy, and everything revolved around making sure that the children were in school because we believed that they should be in school. But also making sure that their safety was assured. I was concerned, in my own community, if my kids would be safe. The community basically was talking about kids not being safe going into the minority communities, but because I went in and out every day myself, I knew that they were safe there. And my concern was that they were safe when they got off, when my older son got off the bus in his own community. It was very difficult for us. It was difficult for other members in the family who didn't understand what I was doing. It was almost like getting up every morning and going to war.

There were, at that point in time, many police in the community. There were police lines. There were a lot of groups congregating on street corners. And every day we walked through all of that to the bus stop. It was not easy for us but, on the other hand, I felt that as people had a right to boycott—that's a person's right—it was also my right to send my children to school. And I think I got mad as much as anything, as much as maybe being afraid. I said, Why would anyone interfere with my right to send my kids to school? And, I guess, basically, that anger also sustained me.

It was a lot of isolation for a while, though, for us. Many days I would come home and I would think about all the liberals that got on the buses and went south for sit-ins and boycotts, and I really would come home and wonder, Where were they now?

There were people out there, but for a long, long time I felt very isolated and alone in the decision, but I felt that my decision was right. My kids also became more isolated because people that were boycotting would not allow their children to play with my children anymore. And that was real. But somehow we instilled some strength in our kids so that they were sustained.

We did not get support from political leaders, although I know political leaders were meeting quite routinely with those that boycotted. But for those of us around the city that decided to support the desegregation order, it was very much a lonely place for a long time.

By 1974, Thomas Atkins was Massachusetts secretary for communities and development, a cabinet-level post under Governor Francis Sargent. He had also assumed a leadership role within the Boston NAACP.

THOMAS ATKINS

From approximately August of '74 until the end of the '74–'75 school year, because of the central role I was playing as essentially the spokesperson for the community on the school case, I was targeted for intimidation. So I started getting death threats. I was averaging about forty death threats per week. I had had that before, so it didn't particularly bother me. However, it took some rather bizarre aspects. Initially these calls were coming in to my office at the state house, to the NAACP office, and to my home. I was getting letters at all three places. And I found out, much after the fact, that some of the calls that came into my house were being answered by my children, who, like kids all over the country, I guess, tried to protect their daddy. And people would call to speak to me and to tell me that they were going to blow my head off only to find themselves being asked by one of my kids, "Why are you going to kill my daddy?" And it was an embarrassing kind of thing for them to have to try and explain this. Some of the people who started off calling for that purpose wound up calling back to talk to my kids. I got wind of this in a rather peculiar way.

One night I was home watching television. I got a call from a guy who identified himself as having called before. And he wouldn't give me his name. He said, "You know me. You'll recognize me if I give you my name." He said, "But I've talked to your kids."

I said, "What do you mean you've talked to my kids?"

He said, "Yeah, I've talked to your kids." He said, "What I want to tell you is this." He said, "There was a meeting tonight in South Boston and if those kids go over to South Boston High School tomorrow, all hell's going to break loose. They're going to stone the buses. They're going to attack the buses. They're going to turn them over. They're going to burn them."

And I said, "What are you talking about?"

And he said, "That's the message." He says, "I know what I'm talking about."

Well, I never talked to this guy before. I had no way of crediting this. And so I wasn't inclined to initially. I went back and started watching television. But the more I thought about it, the less I believed I could take the chance that he was not right.

So I called the superintendent of schools and relayed the information. The superintendent suggested that I call, and I did call, the police commissioner in Boston. I talked with him, and his information was that yes, there had been a meeting that night in South Boston and yes, something was planned for the next day. He didn't know what. He hadn't gotten the information yet. I called the person at the state level who was in charge of the state police, 'cause that's who was at that time in charge of protecting the kids in South Boston, and I passed this information on to him. And finally we concluded that we simply couldn't take the chance, that those kids had to be moved out of that school the next day.

There was no time to notify individual parents or children. So the plan was to meet the kids as they came into the Bayside Mall in South Boston, the Columbia Point–Bayside area, where typically they would be taken from the buses that brought them from home and put on buses that would take them up to the high school, in effect, in a convoy. Police cars and motorcycles on each side. That day we intercepted them and took them instead to UMass/Boston [the University of Massachusetts at Boston]. We had made arrangements to have people from the community come in and serve as freedom school teachers. So none of the kids who were supposed to go to South Boston showed up that day.

As my informant had told me, however, there was a crowd of well over fifteen hundred people, between fifteen hundred and two thousand people waiting for the buses, and when it became clear that the buses were not going to arrive, those people were very upset. Finally they broke up, and one contingent of the crowd that had broken up was going down the hill from the high school, which sits up on a hill, to Columbia Road, and as they got to Columbia Road the light changed for people to cross the street, and it happened, as fate would have it, that the second car in line, waiting for the light to change, was a car in which this black man, Haitian, was riding by himself. It was early in the morning, and one of the people in the crowd saw him and said, "There's a nigger. Let's get him." And so they attacked his car. He couldn't move his car forward. He couldn't move it backward. So he got out of the car and ran. They chased this man through the streets of South Boston, and they finally caught him on a porch trying to get into a house. Nobody would open a door for him. And he was beaten with sticks and bottles.

At South Boston High School, it was a quiet day. At UMass we had each of the kids fill out a questionnaire describing to us any problems they had had, whether anybody had mistreated them and if so, who it was. We asked them for their name and their address and the phone number and the school they had attended the year before and the names of any witnesses and so forth, and a simple description of the problem they had. It was just a one-page form. It was an eight-and-a-half-by-fourteen-inch form, legal size. And every one of the kids did fill these out, and there was so much going on I didn't have time to read them that day.

About a week later, I was sitting in my office one night and I reached into my briefcase and here were these forms. So, I took them out and I began, sort of absently, to read through them, and it was like being hit with a sledgehammer. It was an experience I'll never forget as long as I live. As I read through one after another of these forms, what I saw was that these kids couldn't spell. They could not write a simple, declaratory sentence. They couldn't spell the name of their street. They couldn't spell the name of their community. They couldn't spell *Roxbury*. They couldn't spell *Boston* as in South Boston. They couldn't spell *high* as in high school. They couldn't spell *Negro*. They couldn't spell *black,* they couldn't spell *nigger*. And as I read these forms, none of which were grammatically correct or the spelling proper, I just started to cry. It was impossible to explain the feeling of pain, on the one hand, but on the other hand, I knew we were right. We had to get those kids out of those schools and this proved it.

The beating of the Haitian man, André Yvon Jean-Louis, occurred on October 7, 1974, and served to heighten racial tensions even further. Soon after, the violence in South Boston was echoed in Roxbury, when black high school students took to the streets and hurled rocks at white passersby.

On October 9, President Gerald Ford—who had been sworn in two months earlier, when Richard Nixon resigned over the Watergate scandal—stated at a press conference that he deplored the violence in Boston. Then he added, "I have consistently opposed forced busing to achieve racial balance as a solution to quality education. And therefore, I respectfully disagree with the judge's order." The next day Mayor White told the press that he, too, opposed "forced busing." The mayor then stated, "But I believe it is the basic responsibility of any elected public official to support fully with all his resources any law as long as it is our law."

Meanwhile, the violence continued for the students who attended South Boston High School.

PHYLLIS ELLISON

On a normal day there would be anywhere between ten and fifteen fights. You could walk down the corridor and a black person would bump into a white person or vice versa. That would be one fight. And they'd try to separate us, because at that time there was so much tension in the school that one fight could just have the school dismissed for the entire day because it would just lead to another and another and another.

You can't imagine how tense it was inside the classroom. A teacher was almost afraid to say the wrong thing, because they knew that that would excite the whole class, a disturbance in the classroom. The black students sat on one side of the classes. The white students sat on the other side of the classes. The teachers didn't want to assign seating because there may be some problems in the classrooms. So the teachers basically let the students sit where they wanted to sit. In the lunchrooms, the black students sat on one side. The white students sat on the other side. And the ladies' room. It was the same thing. The black students went to the right of the ladies' room; the white students went to the left of the ladies' room. So really, it was separate. I mean, we attended the same school, but we really never did anything together. Gym classes. If the blacks wanted to play basketball, the whites wanted to play volleyball. So we never played together. They would play volleyball. We would play basketball.

Kathy Downs Stapleton was a white senior who chose to finish high school at South Boston.

KATHY DOWNS STAPLETON

I did not boycott. I stayed out of school when a majority of children stayed out of school—mostly for safety reasons on days that I didn't think that it was safe to be in the building, or it was not a good idea. But, basically, I did try to go.

There was pressure from all sorts of people, from the media as well as the civic groups. Nobody said, "Don't do this. Don't act up. This isn't nice." People wanted to see a story. People encouraged it. Nobody said, "Don't do this." Political people said, "You children should boycott. You children should not do this. This is not right." "This is the mayor or this is the police. Don't do this." And so it put pressure on everybody. No one knew the right thing to do. I mean, I wanted to go to school. I was trying to go to school, but I resented people telling me I shouldn't be in the school. I resented people telling us where we should go to school. And I hated picking up the paper every day and seeing it in the paper. It was really kind of a disgrace. I'm very proud of my community, but I did not like what I saw on the media. I think it hurt us all. The attention was negative. The kids were the ones being hurt and being told what to do. I mean, kids will do what they're told, usually. These adults say we shouldn't go to school, let's not go to school today. Or we should do this, or we should fight, or we should stand up for ourselves. But it was not coming from the kids within. I think we were all being pulled in many different directions between what was right and what was wrong.

ALAN LUPO

It was an ironic thing to watch and listen to the people actively opposing busing. A number of them said, essentially, "If Martin Luther King was a hero for sitting on the street, or blocking traffic, or picketing or demonstrating, how come we're not heroes? How come the media are treating us differently than it did the white college students who opposed Vietnam, or the blacks who had sit-ins?" Some people were very sincere when they raised that question. They felt there was no difference. They felt they were demonstrating for their homes, their neighborhoods, their children, their view of education. Their civil rights. Some people, I fear, were not so sincere—perhaps some of the leaders who thought they were being cute, and may or may not have seen any parallels, but decided to run that guilt trip on the media, and say, "Oh, so now you're discriminating against us." So you had both. You had those who honestly saw no difference and believed that their civil rights were in danger and they had a right to demonstrate. And you had those who were maybe playing it for all it was worth.

We were going up a hill one day in South Boston. I think it was probably the second or third or fourth week of busing. And I was with Bob Kiley, who was essentially the deputy mayor, sitting in one of the mayor's cars, heading up the hill. There had just been yet another incident. Cops, white cops, dealing with their white neighbors, and police screaming, "Get out of the way!" and mothers and fathers screaming, "Police brutality!" Sort of a replay of the white college kids fighting with cops earlier, or blacks dealing with cops in the street. History was repeating itself in interesting ways, and a crowd of kids were moving up the hill, and our window was open. And we clearly heard one kid say to another, "No, that'll be too late to make the six o'clock, but it'll be on the eleven o'clock news." And Kiley turned to me and shook his head and said, "Don't tell me these people aren't aware." In other words, they're out there for a principle, bad or good, but folks also get out because they want to be on TV. There's no question about it. Now, I would argue that were there no television, there would still have been fighting in the street. There still would have been hatred; there still would have been moments of accommodation. But the presence of the camera is startling, and for a lot of people who will have their names in the newspaper only when they die, and there will be a little paid death notice, almost anything, any kind of access to becoming a star, even for thirty seconds, is quite important to them, white or black.

On December 11, a white student was stabbed by a black student during a melee at South Boston High School.

PHYLLIS ELLISON

I remember the day Michael Faith got stabbed vividly, because I was in the principal's office and all of a sudden you heard a lot of commotion and you heard kids screaming and yelling and saying, "He's dead, he's dead. That black nigger killed him. He's dead, he's dead." And then the principal running out of the office. There was a lot of commotion and screaming, yelling, hollering, "Get the niggers at Southie." I was really afraid. And the principal came back into the office and said, Call the ambulance and tell all the black students that were in the office to stay there. A police officer was in there and they were trying to get the white students out of the building, because they had just gone on a rampage and they were just going to hurt the first black student that they saw. Anyone that was caught in the corridor that day would be hurt. Once that happened, it probably took about fifteen, twenty minutes for the police officers to get all the white students out. The black students were locked in their rooms and all the white students were let go out of their classrooms. I remember us going into a room, and outside you just saw a crowd of people, I mean, just so many people, I can't even count. They just looked like little bumblebees or something, there was that many. And that Louise Day Hicks was on top of the stairs saying, Let the niggers go back to Roxbury. Send them back to Roxbury. And the crowd booing her. I remember the police cars coming up the street, attempting to, and people turning over the police cars, and I was just amazed that they could do something like that. The police tried to get horses up. They wouldn't let the horses get up. They stoned the horses. They stoned the cars. And I thought that day that we would never get out of South Boston High School.

Police officials and leaders from the black community developed a plan to get the children out of the school.

ELLEN JACKSON

The plan was that some of us would go up on the bus. There would be at least four to five buses that would be going up the hill. And three of those buses were going to be decoy buses. We volunteered to go out, and we weren't asked to do it but we said here was a chance to prove to the parents and demonstrate as they had said to us sometime early back, "You need to be put in a position. You're sending our kids out there. You need to find out what those kids are going through." So some of us said yes. I was the only woman. At first they said I couldn't go. And I said, You all are going, I'm going. That's all there is to it. I don't think anybody's going to be able to stop me.

So we got on the bus and we tried to joke. We were lying on the floor. Percy Wilson, who was the head of [the Roxbury] Multi-Services [Center], said, "Oh, God, I thought I left these days in Mississippi. I didn't think I would be into this kind of situation again." But we were nervous. Frankly, we were scared. But we went up, and when we got closer to the school, we could hear the noise. And it's a hollow feeling when you go up that hill. Anytime there's a noise, it seems like it goes back to the water and it's just very echoey. And we could hear the yelling. Could hear the sirens and things.

We came around the front part of the building where the people, the mob—in a sense, crazy mob—was and they could see us. We were slouching so we would look like students. We weren't sitting straight up so they could see that we were so-called adults. And while we were trying to distract them, hopefully distracting them, the two buses with the students would take another route and get down the hill.

When we started down that hill, I tell you, they rushed past the police and started rocking those buses. I know they rocked the one I was on. And as we were going down, they started throwing everything they could get in their hands. Not rocks, they looked like boulders. Seemed like someone would have to take two hands and throw these things into the bus. And we finally got down the hill, and when we got down the hill, it was complete silence on the bus. And I think a lot of us just started crying. Fear and anger and hurt. It was a real traumatic time, when I think about it. And then we started laughing because we started picking glass out of each other. Somebody leaned down and said, "There was glass in your hair. Are you okay?" "Yeah, we're okay." And people were cheering and shouting and hugging us. And you know, one of my kids was there and said, "Mommy, you shouldn't have gone up the hill, you know that was dangerous." And somebody said, "You know you're not going to stop E.J. from doing what she wants to do." And we kind of laughed and joked about it at that point. But it was a frightening thing. And it was even more frightening when we reflected on it, because we thought of what could have happened to those kids. Because here we were adults and we were scared to death. And I know those kids would have been petrified.

The decoy was successful. The black students were evacuated from South Boston High School. As it turned out, Michael Faith's wound was not fatal, but the incident intensified resistance. Less than a week later, Judge Garrity found three members of the school committee in contempt of court when they refused to come up with a permanent desegregation plan.

With no political leaders supporting busing, desegregation limped along under court order through the remaining academic year. White parents in South Boston continued to keep the majority of their children out of the schools. Two days before the new school year, Mayor Kevin White promised that the city would pay the costs for appealing Judge Garrity's desegregation order to the U.S. Supreme Court.

Attendance during the autumn of 1975 at South Boston High School was low, but 216 white students showed up for classes the first day (three times more than the previous year). Tension remained high and the school continued to operate under tight security. White flight from the schools had intensified. Fifty-three percent of the students in the system were now nonwhite, though they represented 25 percent of the overall population.

On December 9, 1975, Judge Garrity placed South Boston High School in receivership. It would no longer be run by the school committee. Instead, it would be run by the court. The entire administrative staff at the school was to be transferred.

RUTH BATSON

I believe that putting South Boston High School into receivership was the turning point in this whole case. I had long felt that this was an important step to take. And after my first trip to South Boston High School in October 1974, I came back to our group at Freedom House and I said, "I want to write a letter to the judge saying to the judge that we have to put South Boston High School into receivership." And they said, "Oh, Ruth, he'll never do that. It's just a waste of time. He'll never do it." And I really pushed my argument. And they said, "No, we'll just aggravate the situation. They'll never do that." Well, always being the kind of person that would follow through on what I felt, I said, "Well, I'm going to write the judge on my own." So I wrote the judge a letter in October saying to him that I had been out to South Boston High School and one of the things that I believed was that this thing would never be solved at the rate it was going because the people in South Boston felt that this was their school, that they owned this building. Somehow they had paid money for it. It was their school. And as long as this was the situation, this was never going to be solved. And I pointed out to him the kinds of things that I had seen happen in the school. And so I said to him, "Judge Garrity, I really believe that this school will have to be put into receivership. Take it out of the hands of the people of South Boston, have an outside group look at it and handle it until we get over this crunch." Well, lo and behold, it was really a big day for me when the judge came out with the ruling that South Boston was going into receivership. Now, I'm not by any stretch of the imagination saying that he was influenced at all by a letter that I would have sent, but it thrilled me to have this happen, because for once, I said, somebody is looking at this situation realistically.

In the spring of 1976, President Ford and his solicitor general, Robert Bork, were considering lending the federal government's support to Boston's antibusing forces in their attempt to appeal Judge Garrity's order.

THOMAS ATKINS

In 1976 you had Gerald Ford in the White House. He wound up there by accident, and increasingly people thought he *was* an accident. But he was the president. And he was trying to bring the country together but he also wanted to stay there. He wanted to run for reelection. And it was at about the time that he was getting his campaign put together and Democrats were running around the country calling each other names, as they always do, that one of the many appeals in the Boston school desegregation case wound its way up to the Supreme Court. And the issue presented to a Supreme Court that had not yet ever accepted an appeal dealing with the Boston school desegregation issue was whether it should accept this appeal. We did not want the Supreme Court to accept the appeal. We thought that it would be the wrong message to send. So we organized, primarily under the leadership of Clarence Mitchell, who was then the NAACP's longtime lobbyist, head of its Washington bureau, and affectionately known to many as the hundred and first senator. Clarence Mitchell knew Gerald Ford from years and years of working with him. And he put together a meeting with the president, including Attorney General Edward Levi.

The meeting was a very, very tense one. I wasn't at the meeting because at that time I was trying the Columbus school desegregation case that I would ultimately argue three years later at the Supreme Court. But I got a rather copious report on the meeting. The NAACP's position was that whatever Gerald Ford's position was on busing, which he continued to say he was opposed to, that he could only have one position on the question of enforcing constitutional rights and that position had to be the same as Eisenhower had had when he sent troops into Little Rock. And Clarence Mitchell lectured Gerald Ford on the importance then of Eisenhower having done that and of how history had put him in a position to do the same thing. He said, "Mr. President, you can't support this challenge, because if you do, you send a message that the Constitution can be annulled by violent opposition." And it was an argument that both the president and the attorney general agreed overrode everything else. As a result of which the position that was taken by the United States on that issue was that the Supreme Court should not grant certiorari and it, certiorari, was not granted. The appeal was rejected.

I think it's important to note that there probably has not been another school desegregation case, either before or after Boston, in which as many individual orders have been issued. The count now is well in excess of four hundred. And the Supreme Court of the United States has never accepted an appeal from any one of those orders. Never. And it never will, for the reason that it too believes that lawlessness cannot be rewarded by making it respectable.

Phyllis Ellison graduated from South Boston High School in June 1977.

PHYLLIS ELLISON

I didn't go to my prom because I felt that it was an all-white prom. The black students had no input in the planning of the prom whatsoever. So it was as if we didn't exist. And there wasn't enough black students to vote against the white students because there was more white students attending than black. So we had no voice. We had no say-so. And we didn't want to attend. So we boycotted, and there wasn't one black student that attended the prom in '77.

If I had it to do all over again, for the civil rights part of it, I would do it over, because I felt like my rights were being violated by the white people of South Boston telling me that I could not go to South Boston High School. As far as my education, I think I could have gotten a better education if I didn't spend so much time out of school with the fighting and the violence and being dismissed from school at least once or twice a week. We were allowed to go home early because there was just so much tension inside of the school that if we didn't, someone may be killed or really seriously injured. I think that I could have gotten a better education if I'd spent more time in school than out of school at that time.

RUTH BATSON

One of the things that I was concerned about was the fact that just because you were black, you were told that you couldn't go there. "This was *my* school. This was our place. You can't come here." I thought that a great educational achievement had been made to show both white and black kids that they could go anywhere they wanted to. That there should be no school in the city of Boston that would not admit a child because of their color. So I considered it an educational achievement that that had taken place. I really did. It always used to kill me to think that I couldn't go into a place in Boston just because I was black, and that if I went there, something would happen to me.

Had I had any say in the selections of communities beforehand—at least some of us thought afterwards that it had been a mistake that we hadn't been more active—I would have said not to send them to South Boston. But after it was done and people wanted to go protest, then we thought about it and we said, "Well, they should be able to go anyplace they want, anywhere."

When you saw what the kids had to go through—I was just as proud of some of the white kids that stuck through it, because there were white families who made their kids go and stay in that school.

Kids had to go through metal detectors, and police were all over the place, and there was such ridicule in the halls. I thought that the kids who went through this were just wonderful kids. And most of them weren't kids with great marks or anything. They were just kids who were determined. There was a movement. And they felt part of a movement. We haven't seen anything like that since, I don't think.

In November 1977, Louise Day Hicks lost her seat on the city council. In that same election, John O'Bryant became the first black member of the Boston School Committee in seventy-six years.

31

Atlanta and Affirmative Action, 1973–1980

"The Politics of Inclusion"

President Lyndon Johnson, in a commencement address at Howard University on June 4, 1965, declared, "You do not take a person who, for years, has been hobbled by chains and liberate him, bring him up to the starting line of a race and then say, 'You are free to compete with the others,' and still justly believe that you have been completely fair. Thus it is not enough just to open the gates of opportunity. All our citizens must have the ability to walk through those gates. This is the next and the more profound stage of the battle for civil rights. We seek not just freedom but opportunity. We seek not just legal equity but human ability, not just equality as a right and a theory but equality as a fact and equality as a result."

In September, Johnson issued Executive Order 11246, "to promote the full realization of equal employment opportunity through a positive, continuing program in each executive department and agency." The order specified that federal contractors "will take affirmative action to ensure that applicants are employed, and that employees are treated during employment, without regard to their race, creed, color, or national origin." Included under the order were nondiscrimination provisions in federally assisted construction contracts.

Eleanor Holmes Norton, an activist attorney in the early 1970s, would later serve as chair of the Equal Employment Opportunity Commission. Reflecting on the history of affirmative action, she has said, "We would not need affirmative action if blacks had been let into the factories the way the white immigrants were. We now are making up for what we did not do when jobs were readily available, and of course the great tragedy is that blacks have gotten the right to work where only whites worked before only as the economy has become stagnant and no longer drinks up labor as it did in the late nineteenth to early twentieth century. It is a real American tragedy. The only way to make up for it now, of course, is by using what amounts to artificial means: temporary remedies, affirmative action remedies, that bring blacks in, even as they bring women in and Hispanics in who have also been excluded, and then fall away, after the entrance of these groups who were kept out—and deliberately kept out."

In the early 1970s, the population of Atlanta, Georgia, was more than 50 percent black. It was a mecca for the growing black middle class, but at the same time 29 percent of the city's black residents lived below the poverty line. In 1973, the city elected its first black mayor. It would soon become the site of one of the most aggressive local affirmative action campaigns in the country.

Maynard Jackson moved to Atlanta in 1945.

MAYNARD JACKSON

When I was seven, we moved to Atlanta from Dallas, Texas, where I was born. Atlanta is my mother's native home. It was hard-core segregation all the way, but we never bowed to it. It was against the family policy. We never walked in anybody's back door, ever. I've walked into shoe stores with my father, my grandfather, to be fitted for shoes. We would sit down and they would ask us to move to the back of the shoe store, and we'd explain we're going to spend our money, we sit anywhere we want to. They said, "Well, you gotta go to the back." We said, "I'm sorry, no, we don't have to go to the back. Our choice is to go to the back or leave, and we're leaving."

Walter Huntley moved to Atlanta in 1972.

WALTER HUNTLEY

I was just finishing up a master's degree in urban studies, and I'll never forget my professor, Dr. Earl Lewis at Trinity University in San Antonio, said, "Why do you want to do your internship in Atlanta?" I had read *Ebony* magazine, saying that Atlanta was the "black mecca." They were saying that if you were black and had a college degree, this was the best place in the world to live. It was very intriguing to me. And I just wanted to see what it was like. So I packed everything up in my car, drove from San Antonio to Atlanta, and got here in the summer of 1972.

Ethel Mae Matthews moved to Atlanta in 1950. In 1968 she became president of the Atlanta chapter of the National Welfare Rights Organization.

ETHEL MAE MATTHEWS

Atlanta is an excellent place for some black people. It is. It's an excellent place for *some* black people. But not for all black people, it's not an excellent place to live. Because if it was an excellent place to live, they would get people some jobs—all those people who sleep on the street, who eat out of the garbage can. If you're bright, the Nilla wafer color—you know what a Nilla wafer is, don't you, those kind of colored peoples what look like they're white?—if you're their color and you got long hair, sure! It's good for you. It's good for you. You can come here and get a job. But if you've been here all your life, uh-uh. If you're *black,* uh-uh. You can't get a job.

MAYNARD JACKSON

Martin Luther King, Jr., was buried the day after my first child was born, my daughter Brooke. She was born April the eighth of 1968. I went from the hospital to the grave. And I spent three days thinking about what I was going to do with my life and decided that politics, although not perfect, was the best available nonviolent means of changing how we live. That's when I know I decided to get into politics. But I thought even then I would take a long time to phase into it—two, three, four years. I wanted to build a law firm.

Lo and behold, less than two months later, after declining to run for the state house [of representatives] and telling a group of neighbors that I would not do that, I sat down to watch the Democratic returns from the California primary and saw Bobby Kennedy shot to death. When that went off finally, early in the morning hours, the late news had been delayed and came on, announcing that Herman Talmadge, then the U.S. senator from

Georgia, was going to run [for reelection]. The next day—that day, really—was the last day to qualify, June the fifth of 1968, for U.S. Senate, and apparently nobody was going to oppose Talmadge. So I went to work that morning and I resigned my job, spent all day borrowing three thousand dollars for the qualifying fee, and ran for U.S. Senate. That was twenty years ago. I was thirty years old.

> The newcomer Jackson was defeated, but the race brought him to the attention of the voters. One year later, he was elected vice mayor of Atlanta. Jackson remained in that post until 1973, when he decided to oppose the incumbent, Sam Massell, for the mayor's office.
>
> Willie Bolden, a former SCLC staffer, was an organizer for the American Federation of State, County, and Municipal Employees (AFSCME).

Willie Bolden

The black community was very supportive of Maynard. When Maynard ran for mayor, the AFSCME union, which I worked for for about five and a half years, not only supported Maynard monetarily, but we supported him physically. We were out in the streets, knocking on doors, passing out literature, making telephone calls, carrying voters to the polls, because we believed that Maynard stood for what we stood for, and for that we wanted to show him our appreciation. We got out and worked very hard for Maynard.

> Maggie Thomas was born and raised in Atlanta. She lived in the Bankhead Court Housing Project.

Maggie Thomas

I knew Maynard's grandfather. I knew him well. Dr. John Wesley Dobbs. I knew his aunt, Mattawilda Dobbs, I believe it was. And I knew Maynard. When I knew him, he was a little, small boy. You know. But Dr. Dobbs was a good man and I knew that if Maynard was anything like his grandfather, he would make a good mayor. So I campaigned for him and I also voted and encouraged people out in the neighborhood to vote for him. He's been an inspiration to me and my family, I'll say. He really has been.

MAYNARD JACKSON

The Atlanta Negro Voters' League was headed by two people: Republican John Wesley Dobbs, my grandfather, and Democrat Austin T. Walden. They were so respected and so revered and so trusted—that being the key point—that when the Atlanta Negro Voters' League made a decision and issued its ticket, at 12:01 A.M. on election day, ninety-nine percent of the black voters voted as the Atlanta Negro Voters' League recommended.

They would go, in response to the call, downtown to meet with the white leadership. And here's the way it would go, as explained to me by my grandfather. I was not there, of course. They'd walk in, they'd be seated and so forth, and exchange pleasantries, and the white leadership would say, "We have decided to back Joe Blow for mayor, and we want you all to help us out and support our candidate." The black leadership then, with the spokespersons being Dobbs and Walden, would say, "We hear you. And we'll certainly be happy to give them consideration. But first, we need a high school. We need so-and-so streets paved. We need sewers on the west side of Atlanta. We need better schools in the old fourth ward, or South Side, or south Atlanta."

They'd have to bargain for the things for which they were already paying taxes. But that's how we got Washington High School, Booker T. Washington High School, the first black high school in the city of Atlanta, in 1924. That's how we got most of the improvements in the community across time. So we're talking about a southern city that had a special edge, in my opinion. When many other southern cities put dogs and cattle prods, fire hoses in the streets, Atlanta in the sixties went to the bargaining table. It's called the Atlanta style.

You see, Atlanta is, in my opinion, truly ahead of every other major city in the country in race relations. But the problem with that is what James Baldwin warned us about: havens are high-priced, and so is the price a haven dweller has exacted of him to delude himself into believing that he's found a haven. So we were kind of believing all of our headlines and our PR too much. We're the best, but we weren't good enough. That's my point. And as mayor, what I wanted to do was to lead us—not just black people, but all people, black and white—into an era where we truly could begin to point at progress, not just for a few people, but systematic progress. Some may benefit more than others at first, but after a while, when the system begins to work, large numbers are benefited.

On October 18, 1973, Maynard Jackson defeated Sam Massell to become the first black mayor of a major southern city. In his inaugural address the following January, he spoke of his hopes for "an open door of opportunity instead of a closed door of despair" and for "good jobs, equal treatment, and fair wages for all working people."

An expert in taxation and finance, Walter Huntley joined the Jackson administration in 1974.

WALTER HUNTLEY

When Maynard took office, the level of expectation in the black community, not only in Atlanta but all over the country, was extremely high. I remember getting calls from people from back home, saying, "What's it like?" And one of the things that I remember is going in the city government and finding out that we were just besieged by calls. Everyone wanted to embrace the first black mayor of a major southern city. We were getting three to four hundred calls a day, and I remember people just saying, "Here, Walt, here are thirty calls we want you to return. Tell them that we're sorry that the mayor cannot speak with them at this time, but you were calling to see if there was something that you could do to help them out." So that's what we literally had to do when we first took office, for the first six months.

After that, we had to begin to figure out a way to include more people. Maynard ran on a platform of the politics of inclusion, and he wanted to open up the government to blacks, to women, to younger people. And one of the things that we devised, which I thought was really great, was the People's Day, whereby anybody who wanted to could come in and meet with the mayor for five minutes, with no appointment. And he had all of the commissioners and bureau directors there. And I'll never forget, there was this one woman who came in—we would have anywhere from hundreds of people that would be there waiting to see the mayor all day—but this elderly black woman came in and she walked in slowly and sat down.

And the mayor looked at her and he said, "How are you?"

She said, "I'm doing fine."

He said, "Can I help you?"

She said, "Yes."

And he said, "Well, what is it that I can do for you?"

And she said, "Well, I just wanted to see what it would be like to see a black man sitting in this chair."

And the mayor smiled very broadly and said, "Well, how'm I doing?"

And she said, "You're doing fine." And I think that kind of embodied the way that people felt. There were a lot of governmental employees that were black who had never been on the second floor of City Hall. And it was a very, very proud feeling that not only the governmental workers but black people in general, not only in the South and in Atlanta, but all over the country, felt, in terms of pride for what Maynard had achieved.

ETHEL MAE MATTHEWS

Maynard Jackson was the first black mayor we had, and that's what we was working hard for—to bring a black person in office, you know, that knew some of the plight of the poor peoples. And Maynard Jackson was good. He was good, and he did what he could. And you had to understand, I don't care who you get in office, they're going to make you promises, all kinds of promises. They're going to do this for you, they're going to do that for you. But when they get in there, it's only so much they can do for you. And some of them don't do nothing for you. But it was a challenge to us who were poor. That's why we worked hard to get him elected.

When Maynard was in there, he had jobs for uneducated peoples, you know. And peoples who had never did no work, and know how to do no work. He had jobs. They were little jobs like sweeping the streets. But that was a job. And it didn't call for you to be educated, to have two or three degrees and five or six diplomas sitting up on your wall, catching dust. But it was a job, you know. Young women and middle-aged women would have jobs sweeping streets, picking up paper and all of that. They had something to help themselves with.

When Maynard Jackson took office, much of Atlanta's public housing was in disrepair. In October 1974, Jackson decided to spend a weekend in a public housing project.

MAGGIE THOMAS

I thought it was very strange. And the strangest thing to me was that they chose me to house him. After they did that, I told them I didn't mind it, but I didn't have any place for him to sleep, me having seven children. And so they said they would arrange that. I told them it was okay with me that he come and spend the weekend.

I got up early that morning. I seen some strange people, you know, kind of hanging around my door. And I found that it was some people from the news media. I was sweeping off the porch, so they asked to come in. And I told them, no, they couldn't come in because I was getting ready to go to work. They got smart and said, "Why won't you let us in? You haven't cleaned up?" And so I said, "Well, maybe not." So I just kept sweeping, going about my activities, because I know I had to be at work at seven. Anyway, I slipped out the back door and went to work. I just left them out there. I don't know where they went to.

When I got off from work, the people were still down there on the side of the court, just cluttered outside. So I turned around. I knew I couldn't get through that crowd, so I turned around and I went all the way down through the back. And I crawled up my back steps to get in my house to avoid the news media. But when I got in the house, then I seen, you know, the mayor coming. I knew I had to open the door then. So I opened the door. And it was just a mob, really. Just a pure mob, just fell all in the door, standing all up on my furniture. I just went through with that. So when the mayor got in, he told them, you know, "Don't do that."

In Bankhead Court at that time, we was having lots of problems with the rodents. Mice, rats, and roaches. And the sewage problem was bad. I'm sure that's why he came out—to live in those conditions, you know, for a short while to really see how they were. And while he was out there, he really found out that we was having those particular problems. And another thing that they found out was that we was having heating problems, too. Where the heat supposed to be coming out, it was no hole back there for the heat to come through. So he decided that was just some false vent up against the wall.

After he came and left, things got better for a while. It really did. I know the rats, the big ol' rats that would be around the dumps—we had stopped seeing them.

Dillard Munford, like some other white businessmen, was apprehensive about the new mayor's agenda.

DILLARD MUNFORD

We were very frightened because we had nothing to go on. There had been no experience there. We never knew that the change was going to come that fast. The black population had been growing very fast. And we were having an exit from the city of the white population. The white population was going down; the black was coming up. But we had no idea that they were going to be that politically attuned to the situation then. In 1973, they surprised the white community, I'll tell you that.

Maynard Jackson was charged, as I understand, by the black power structure to get elected and to run as a young, thirty-five-year-old. And if he was defeated, he had his future ahead of him. He was a lawyer, and a good lawyer. And if he won, he would be a top man, and his charge was to convert the city from a white-majority government to black-majority government. And he did that. He did.

MAYNARD JACKSON

Being the first black mayor is what you wish on your enemy, okay? And I say that with tongue in cheek—it's a source of great pride to be mayor of Atlanta, and every black mayor who's been the first black mayor, I'm sure, has felt the same thing. But it truly is part hell. All of a sudden, I became the mayor not just of Atlanta, but of black people in Georgia and even some neighboring states. That was an extraordinary burden. But in the city of

Atlanta alone, we had to deal with that tremendous expectation in the black community. Now, equally important and equally difficult was what we found in the white community: exaggerated anxiety. That anxiety was, "Oh, my God, what are we going to do? We've got a black mayor! What does this mean? Is this the end of Atlanta?"

Where the anxiety was reflected most, strangely, was in our newspapers. I've seen bad press. But for the first two years that I was mayor, the press was almost hysterical. And not until the then-editor of the *Atlanta Constitution,* Reg Murphy, left town, two years into my first term as mayor, did things begin to settle down, and did a more objective, more dispassionate look by the newspapers occur as they reviewed our actions in the administration. We didn't expect anybody to say, "Hey, we're on your side." We just wanted fairness, evenhandedness.

REG MURPHY

I think there was initially a good deal of high hopes. Here was a very well spoken young black man, an important mayor of an important city, getting a lot of national attention, and people felt good about it. I think that after a while, people began to feel two things. Some people began to feel two things. One of them was that there was not a lot of administrative ability there, which I guess could be argued, and I candidly do not have much judgment about that. And the other thing they felt was that he had gotten himself pretty much immersed in black politics, but he hadn't gotten himself immersed in Atlanta politics. That is to say, he was very much interested in the black community but not very interested in the white or the business communities. I think that was a general attitude.

MAYNARD JACKSON

I looked at how the power structure members dealt with each other. If they disagreed, they'd say, "The hell with you, and you're a so-and-so"—but they would not walk away from the relationship. I said, "That's fair enough. I can deal with that." Because I wanted—strongly, fervently wanted—the business community to work hand in glove with me as we went through this transition.

I didn't want to do it in a confrontational way. That was not my wish. But my job was to do it, one way or the other. My preference was to do it as a team: if we stumble, we'll stumble together. If I made a mistake, fine, say I'm a dummy. But don't walk away from the relationship.

I was dead wrong. Times got hot; even some of the closest friends I had in the business community—I'm talking about the white power structure now—said, "Maynard, that was the dumbest thing I've ever seen. And good-bye." So I miscalculated.

DILLARD MUNFORD

He left a lot of people unhappy. Because, you know, the businesspeople are accustomed to when they make a phone call, they usually get a response—particularly if you're a bank president or head of a utility or something of that nature. But they got no answer. No response. And this left them asking, "Well, where do I go from here?" They had no place to go, because that was the top job in the city and they could get no response. So things were just at a standstill for a good while, and the longer they waited and didn't hear from Maynard, the madder they got.

MAYNARD JACKSON

When I became mayor, zero-point-five percent of all the contracts of the city of Atlanta went to Afro-Americans, in a city which at that time was fifty-fifty. There were no women department heads. This was not only a question of race; it was a question also of sexual discrimination and, you know, all the typical "isms." If there's one, normally there's a whole bunch of them, and they were all there. We had to change dramatically how the appointments to jobs went, normal hiring practices in city government went, the contracting process—not to reduce the quality, by the way, ever. We never ever, ever set up a lower standard. And those who say, "Well, affirmative action means you've got to lower the standard"—that's a real insult, in my opinion, to African-Americans and other minority Americans. We never did it, didn't have to do it.

Emma Darnell was commissioner of administrative services under Mayor Jackson. She was the first black woman appointed as a city commissioner.

EMMA DARNELL

The affirmative action program for the city of Atlanta, which we developed under the direction of Mayor Jackson in 1974, actually started with that first conference that I held with the mayor on the day that I was appointed. He said only one thing to me that day with respect to what he wanted done. He said words to this effect: "Emma, I want black people brought into this government. I want black people to have an opportunity to participate in not only the personnel operation with jobs, but in the purchasing and procurement operation." And, of course, this was new.

WALTER HUNTLEY

The construction of a new airport for the city of Atlanta was one of the major projects, if not the major project, in the Jackson administration. There were a number of big construction projects between 1976 and 1979 or '80. But this was the crown jewel. And the reason was because the airport plays such a major role in Atlanta's overall economy. We have one of the busiest airports in the world, and we did at that time. And this was going to be the largest public construction project that had ever been undertaken by the city.

The magnitude of it was such that it was just very difficult to comprehend. It was about a seven-hundred-fifty-million-dollar project. And the anxiety, the anticipation, was high. There were the airlines, the elected officials, the private sector. The federal government was involved, and it was something that everyone knew that we had to do, and there was a lot riding on it. It had to be done right. And when Maynard indicated that he was going to make sure that blacks participate in every element of the process from the standpoint of construction, architectural services, legal services, the whole gamut, that's when basically, I guess you would say, the whole issue came under tremendous scrutiny.

MAYNARD JACKSON

The reaction was immediate. It was not all white. It was black and white. The surprise for me was the number of black friends, well-meaning, who were frightened by the aggressiveness of this program. And who cautioned me to slow down. They were concerned there might be a reaction against the black community. Well, our studies indicated to us that for the majority of black people, things could not get any worse.

I want to emphasize that as we moved toward affirmative action, we always saw that as an issue that had to be managed. And I think this is the key point. Affirmative action is not something that just happens when you sing songs and all of a sudden it jumps off the wall. That's not it. It has to be managed, and those in charge must produce. They must have goals to meet, and they must be judged as managers by their productivity, their success. So we had to build an airport, we had to do it well. We had to do it within budget. We had to do it within the time allocation, and simultaneously, it had to be done fairly. Black people, other minorities, and women had to have an equal—not superior—but an equal opportunity to participate in the bidding, the contracting, the conception, top to bottom, of this airport. And we did.

The result was that, when we announced how we were going to approach this, from a contract compliance point of view—contract compliance meaning, oh, five, six, seven, eight different items, including but not limited to affirmative action—I would have thought the heavens were falling down. We were threatened with litigation six, seven times a day. A lot of litigation occurred. I was told that I was retarding the progress of Atlanta. Now, I'm the mayor who found an airport project that was eleven years old that nobody could do. They'd given up on it. They told me I couldn't do it. These are the longtime bureaucrats of the city, dedicated, Atlanta-loving people, but they had never sold encyclopedias, as I had, and had never trained people how to sell, and had never trained themselves in the positive attitude that is part of my life. I am a trained positive thinker. They told me, "You can't build this in that spot." I said "Why not?" They said, "Because Interstate 85 runs right through where you would have a terminal." I said, "Fine. We'll move the interstate." And they laughed at me.

Marva Brooks was an attorney in the Jackson administration.

MARVA BROOKS

Maynard was raised in very much a black aristocratic fashion, and to be unpleasant and to have people not like you was something that I'm certain that, if he had his druthers, he would have wished had not happened. But once he got committed to the program that he was on, he just would not compromise. He did not play politics with affirmative action.

Maynard was fearless. He was truly intrepid and fearless. My personal relationship with him started here; I didn't have long years of partying with him or knowing him. I'd find myself in sessions with him, and if I had known him a little better, I might have leaned over to say, "Cool it." Because I was afraid we might get shot. I don't know if I've ever seen anybody so dedicated to what he was doing.

EMMA DARNELL

More than two years before the airport expansion occurred, Maynard Jackson made it very clear, publicly and privately, to representatives of the airlines, to representatives of the architect and engineer, to the general public, that the expansion of Hartsfield International Airport would involve significant minority participation. He also stated—and this became a rather controversial point—that with respect to the status of existing contracts at the airport, there were no existing contracts. And that all contracts for the expansion of the airport would be bidded. This, of course, created a great deal of controversy with respect to the architect and the engineer, because we had done business with one architect and one engineer at Atlanta airport for more than sixteen years.

DILLARD MUNFORD

I didn't accept the affirmative action program at all, because it was unfair to white people—to white contractors. They ran this through the city council, and actually went beyond the government bounds and made a lot of unqualified black contractors very wealthy. So it was not a fair program at all. They were unfamiliar with affirmative action. Somebody in his campaign, or his office, saw it was a way to let a lot of their black supporters in on a good thing, which they did. And it was very abusive to white contractors who saw jobs going at higher prices than they were bidding, because they were black.

George Berry, who had served as chief administrative officer under Mayor Sam Massell, was assistant manager of Hartsfield Atlanta International Airport under Mayor Jackson.

GEORGE BERRY

I was one of those responsible for steering the course, and we simply took as a given that Mayor Jackson's position had to be met. That there was no alternative. That the alternative was that the project would not be done. And so we brought the architects, the engineers, the contractors in and told them that. We said, "Do you wish to do the job under these conditions? Or there will be no job at all."

There were several hundred men involved in the construction work, and as a result of our basic position, we were able to convince the architects, engineers, and contractors to modify their position and seek out minority joint-venture partners, to seek out qualified minority-owned contracting firms, and to reach his goal of twenty percent minority and another five percent small businesses. So small and minority groups together made up twenty-five percent of all construction work, which in the end, since the total construction amounted to five hundred million dollars, meant that roughly a hundred and twenty-five million dollars was done by minorities. In those days, that amount of money was historic!

Many of the critics were, in fact, correct that there were not that many experienced minority businesses and subcontractors in the Georgia area able to take on a hundred and twenty-five million dollars' worth of work in the normal and established way. So what happened was we encouraged majority-owned contractor firms to seek out smaller firms and give them more work than really those smaller firms had ever done before. And to take some risks. Many of them worked beautifully. And many contractors today owe their start to this program. AMC Mechanical is one of them that comes to mind. It's owned by a man named Tom Cordy. He is now a major mechanical contractor here in Atlanta. He has done many airport projects across the country, specializing in fueling systems, airport fueling systems. Up until that time, AMC was a very small company, but because of the experience he got under this program, he is now a major company.

TOM CORDY

We would not have been involved without the affirmative action program that was initiated by Mayor Maynard Jackson. We had recently completed a major project for Schlitz in Baldwinville, New York, and so our firm was qualified as a mechanical contractor to work out there. But the affirmative action program, then initiated by Mayor Maynard Jackson, forced the contractors to go out and actively seek minority participation.

It's very simple: you can't compete against firms that have been in business for fifty and a hundred years that have all the talent, all the financial resources, all the expertise. The reason for it is because on a major project like that, major firms will bid a lower cost to get on a project, recognizing that with all the follow-up work, they could make their money back. We just can't afford to do things like that.

EMMA DARNELL

During this period, I learned, and all of us in power learned, that being black and being in power alone is nothing about the color. It's nothing about the genetics. It's nothing about the hair or the turban or the beads or the rhetoric. What it's about is what's on the inside. You know. Have you really been deeply and permanently affected by the blood that has been shed in order for you to sit behind the desk? Do you see Martin Luther King's grave as more than a white sepulchre with a quotation on it? Do you actually feel any sensitivity and responsibility to all of those folk out there in those churches and those programs who stand up and give you big applause, believing that you stayed on the case, or are you really in there trying to hold your ground, to get your house, get your car, get your BMW, get invited to the right receptions and be considered a leader?

I spoke at thirty-two churches a year. I spoke at twenty high schools a year. I spoke to Morehouse. I spoke to white and black business and nonbusiness segments of the community, because we were, for all practical purposes, engaged in a revolution. We knew that's what it was. It was still the civil rights revolution. Those persons during the sixties laid down their lives and died to put us into these positions of power. We did not consider these positions of power to be ends in and of themselves. We were to continue the revolution until we had accomplished the goal. So the steps that we took were, many of them, sound management tasks that are taken in order to accomplish a task. But there were political tasks that had to be done. People have to know what you're doing and how you're doing it. And that consumed a large amount of my own personal time.

When you begin to move in public policy areas that involve race, you can expect a great deal of emotion. And some of the emotion is fear. We underestimated, I might add, how controversial these practices [would be]. We were extremely naive. One of the things that made this whole program so controversial was that issues involving race in the South, and indeed throughout the nation, in 1974 still created very, very strong feelings. Another reason that I think that I became very controversial is because of my own style. Number one, I was black. Number two, female. Well, both: I was black and female. And also my style is not exactly one of a shrinking violet. I'm what some people call assertive. I have very strong convictions and I express them in a very strong way. In fact, my conduct and my style was very different from what people really expected from women in a leadership position.

White businessmen reacted to me and to the program which became identified with me with a great deal of fear and alarm. First of all, because they operate in an environment that is controlled by men. Okay? So they had a lot of problems with dealing with a woman as an equal.

In early 1977, as construction of the new airport progressed, Mayor Jackson faced a labor crisis: thirteen hundred sanitation and other city workers called a strike.

MAYNARD JACKSON

I supported AFSCME. I still do. But they had bad local leadership. They called a rump strike with no local vote on issues that already had been settled. They wanted a raise. I told them we didn't have the money. We offered to pay for their accountant to find the money. We said, "If you find it, you get it." They went to look for it, couldn't find it, and still said, "It's there somewhere. So we're going to strike"—and they called a strike on the spot.

WILLIE BOLDEN

It was hard to strike Maynard, who was black. But I think it must be pointed out that we didn't strike Maynard, black mayor. We struck a system, which Maynard just happened to be the head of.

When a garbage worker goes to the store to buy a loaf of bread, he has to pay the same amount that the mayor has to pay, city council has to pay, and the department head has to pay. So what we were saying to Maynard and to the city fathers was, "Look. Our folks are the lowest on the totem pole. When we pull into a gas station, they don't say, 'Because you work for the city government, you pay X number of dollars for gas.'" Whatever the price of gas, that's what you pay. So our position was, "Maynard, we love you, we believe your heart is in the right place, but you're going to have to get your folk and you're going to make them do what is right." And we made up in our minds, even though we had a lot of respect for Maynard, that we were not going to exchange a white slave master for a black slave master. And that's not to say that we believed Maynard was trying to be a black slave master, but the message we were sending to him was we were not going to do that. And whatever it took to get for our people what they rightfully deserved, we were going to do that—including a strike. We didn't strike Maynard because he was black. We struck him because our folks were picking up garbage, working among maggots, and we felt that they needed to get paid for doing that. Seven, eight, nine thousand dollars a year, in our opinion, was not enough.

MAYNARD JACKSON

There were hundreds of striking city of Atlanta employees, who were singing "We Shall Overcome." Signs were castigating me and condemning me. That was a very rough time for me. That was a very sad decision that I made and had to make. But it was the right decision. I didn't like having to do that. For me to fire any employee—but incidentally, a thousand employees, ninety-eight percent of them being black—was something I had to pray over. I took no joy in doing it. But I also knew what my job was as mayor. And my job was to manage the city.

There's even another thing, by the way. Inability to manage is presumed to be a defect of black elected officials. The polls indicate that most white Americans think that black people in public office can't manage anyhow. To have a city with garbage piling up all over the place would hurt, as a matter of fact, the movement in black politics, not just me personally. So, after every kind of warning in the world, when they wouldn't return, we had to go on and replace many of the strikers. People understood that I was backed into a corner by an untenable, ill-timed, ill-planned, illegal strike, that I think many of the employees even understood was one that never should have been called. But I always had to be guided by what was best for Atlanta as a whole. And I was.

> The strike lasted more than three months. When it ended, the union acceded to the city's offer, and the city rehired the workers who had been fired during the strike.
>
> Maynard Jackson won reelection in 1977, defeating Emma Darnell in a landslide. In September 1980, the Midfield Terminal of Hartsfield Atlanta International Airport was completed and opened to the public. It was the world's largest air terminal.

MAYNARD JACKSON

Our transition was not just a question of race and sex and equal opportunity for women and equal opportunity for minorities. It was also a question of proving the point that we could manage well, and we did. We put new management systems in, top to bottom.

We built the Atlanta airport, biggest terminal building complex in the world, ahead of schedule and within budget—and simultaneously rewrote the books on affirmative action. Atlanta airport alone accounted for eighty-nine percent of all the affirmative action in all of America's airports. The FAA told us that; we didn't know it. So you don't have to sacrifice, and we didn't.

Postscript: The Bakke Challenge

The impact of affirmative action was not limited to the American workplace, nor was the controversy surrounding it. By 1977, after ten years of affirmative action effort at American colleges and universities, the number of black students had more than doubled. But in that year, the constitutionality of affirmative action in education became a national issue, when the U.S. Supreme Court agreed to hear *Regents of the University of California* v. *Bakke*. Allan Bakke, who had been twice rejected by the medical school at the University of California at Davis, charged that an affirmative action admissions program had unconstitutionally excluded him from medical school while giving preference to minority students with lower test scores than his own.

Luke Harris attended St. Joseph's College in Philadelphia and received a law degree from Yale University in 1977.

LUKE HARRIS

I'm deeply interested in affirmative action because I'm a product of it. I was fortunate enough to be raised by a very loving great-aunt and a great-uncle who were like a mother and father to me, and they gave me everything that you could have expected and more. But my brother and I grew up on welfare in southern New Jersey. Additionally, I spent the first six or seven years of my education in a segregated elementary school in Merchantville, New Jersey. I went to junior high school and high school in Camden. Now, by the time I was in ninth grade, I was getting signals from the guidance counselors that, you know, college is not for you. You're not the kind of guy that's ever going to learn how to do things like chemistry and calculus and physics. At the time, I had never heard of chemistry and calculus and physics, and some of it was a little bit disturbing.

For me, the whole era of affirmative action was something that I saw as representing hope, as representing encouragement, and as representing a chance that American society was giving, at least in some kind of a way, for the first time in its history to allow people of color to be in a position where their individual capabilities, their human promise, could flower and blossom in ways that had never been the case over the centuries. Without affirmative action, there is no doubt that I would not have been able to go to Saint Joe's. I worked very hard and I wound up graduating number one in my department, and that's when I wound up with the opportunity to go to Yale Law School. So I went to Yale Law School, feeling that I was part of the crest of a social movement. And that American society was finally opening up in some limited ways to allow people of color and blacks in particular to participate in all aspects of American life. And this was a first-time kind of thing. It had never happened before in America. And I felt proud and I still do feel proud to be a part of that process.

Mary Frances Berry served in President Jimmy Carter's administration from 1977 to 1980 as assistant secretary for education.

MARY FRANCES BERRY

When I went to Washington to run education in the Carter administration in 1977, one of the first things that happened was the head of my statistical agency came in to see me and she said, "Good news. The college-going rate for blacks is equal to the college-going rate for whites for the first time in American history." So, if you were black and you graduated from high school, the chances that you would go to college were as great as if you were white. And I thought to myself, Glory, Hallelujah! I almost said it out loud, because it was a goal we had been striving for for so long. We understood that even though education didn't solve all problems and even though it wouldn't pay off for us as well as other people because of discrimination, if you had education it would mean that you had more options and that you might have people move up from the poverty classes into the middle class. And so this was just wonderful news. And I thought to myself, "Boy, if we can just keep up this progress for the next few years, just think of how far we will have come."

Of course, even as I was sitting there in glee over this news, the figures were getting ready to change. In fact, that progress came about because of affirmative action and because of student aid programs and all the things we'd worked so for, and the motivation of students added to it. And those figures were changing. Little did I know that by 1978, there would be the *Bakke* case, which would have a chilling effect on the affirmative action efforts, and that there would be a redirection of the student aid programs away from the poor. And by 1979, those numbers that I'd been so happy about had started to go down again.

Toni Johnson-Chavis attended medical school at the University of California at Davis.

TONI JOHNSON-CHAVIS

I heard about Allan Bakke the very first year I was in medical school, but there was not much said other than there was a guy who wanted to get into our class and he was really angry that he didn't get into the class. So he was going to sue because he wanted a position and he didn't want to go to a foreign medical school. He was going to sue because they "let minority students in in his place." Nothing much more than that.

Allan Bakke's legal battle with the University of California had begun in 1974. In 1976, the California Supreme Court ruled that he should be admitted to the university, but the university appealed the ruling to the U.S. Supreme Court, which heard the case in October 1977. Attorney Robert Links assisted Reynold Colvin, who argued Bakke's case before the Supreme Court.

ROBERT LINKS

When the *Bakke* case was argued, the adversary was formidable indeed. The university's lawyers were fine and good and they had some of the finest constitutional scholars on their briefs, and they had Archibald Cox, who is one of America's great lawyers, as their advocate that day. And I can remember still what he said. "This case, which comes here on a writ of certiorari to the Supreme Court of California, presents a single vital issue. The answer that this court provides will determine perhaps for decades whether minorities are going to have meaningful access to higher education," or words to that effect. It was a very dramatic moment.

I also remember Reynold Colvin's first words, which I think were equally if not more moving. He said, "The first thing I think I should tell this court is that I am Allan Bakke's lawyer, and Allan Bakke is my client." And he proceeded to explain to that court who this man was, because our feeling deep down was that America had to look him in the eye and that court had to look him in the eye and say, "Do we apply one standard to you and another standard to someone else because of your race and the other person's race, or do you both get judged by the same standard?" It was a very effective and dramatic way of framing a very important part of the case.

Fundamentally, what you had in a legal sense was a debate as to whether the rights under the Constitution that we all love and enjoy and cherish are rights that come to us as individuals or are they rights that we get because we're members of particular groups. And the point we were trying to make, and I think the point we drove home and the point the court hammered out in those six different opinions, is that in America, rights belong to individuals. They do not belong to racial groups.

LUKE HARRIS

Obviously, my rights come to me as a function of being an individual. But what does it mean to be an individual of color or black in this society apart from one's racial identity? The two are inextricably intertwined. And my individuality, to a certain extent, has been determined by what it is to be a person of color in the latter part of the twentieth century in America. And, in fact, it is precisely this reality that admissions committees around the country were responding to.

What we're talking about is a range of programs that are designed to offset a specific set of institutional criteria that for generations had been discriminating against the individual potentialities of people of color. And something like that ought to be permissible in American society. I mean, those kinds of rational differentiations have been made in American society with respect to its admissions policies for much more mundane reasons. These admissions committees have distinguished between Yale alumni and non-Yale alumni. They admit that they distinguish between people from the Far West as opposed to people from the East. If they can do that, it seems to me it's much more important for them to consider whether or not someone applying is a Native American or someone who's applying is a Black American, to understand the historical context out of which their life experience grows. And these kinds of rational differentiations, it seems to me, are perfectly normal within the context of a society that's moving toward a meaningful concept of equality.

In June 1978, the Supreme Court handed down its decision in the *Bakke* case. The nine justices issued six separate opinions; no single opinion represented a majority. Though the court ordered that Bakke be admitted to medical school at the University of California, it ruled that race could be taken into account in admissions decisions. The court had taken a middle road: it declared affirmative action constitutional, but it did not require schools to institute affirmative action programs or to consider race when selecting applicants.

MARY FRANCES BERRY

One of the things that happened in the civil rights struggle and the use of remedies for the lack of opportunity was a quarrel and dispute and struggle over language. Now, if people can define you, they can confine you. Or as we say, "If you let me set the terms of the debate, I'll always win." So that when you start talking about affirmative action as being "preferential treatment," you have already set up a situation where anybody who is the beneficiary of preferential treatment will lose. If you say "reverse discrimination" against somebody, it already sounds like a bad thing is happening, and you don't focus on what the injustice was. So affirmative action was *not* preferential treatment for blacks. What it was, was trying to do something about remedying preferential treatment for whites, the injustice that had occurred in the past.

By 1979, the climate of opinion had changed almost completely in the country on issues related to civil rights and the advancement toward equality for blacks in American society—college-going rates down for black students, the unemployment rates up for blacks in general, and for youth in particular. People who had jobs and had gotten them through the civil rights and affirmative action programs found themselves stuck and stranded, not able to get promotions, under attack everywhere for complaints about things like reverse discrimination and the like. So it was a very terrible time for the black community.

You would see the reaction everywhere, the backlash against the progress that had been made. You would see rationales being used for why nothing more needed to be done. For example, people would say, "Well, we can't have equal opportunity and excellence at the same time, and since we want excellence, I guess we have to stop all of this emphasis on civil rights." And what did they mean by excellence? In many cases, it seemed that they meant an absence of black folk at every level of any importance in the society.

After she graduated from medical school, Toni Johnson-Chavis returned to her hometown to practice medicine.

TONI JOHNSON-CHAVIS

Ten years after *Bakke*, there are only two black pediatricians existing in Compton, California. [It was] considered an all-black city. It's largely Hispanic now. There are a large amount of poor people. The two black pediatricians both came from that period of time. One guy who came out of the inner city, Indianapolis, Indiana, and myself, who came from Compton, California. There is no one else who's made a selection to come in. If the two of us had not been trained in that era and were not here, who would fill the void now? Certainly Martin Luther King Hospital—that was built because of the whole post–Martin Luther King era—is now inundated with patients. And they cannot even take care of the patients. Who would fulfill that need? That's the question I asked then, and that's the question that I ask now.

EPILOGUE

FROM MIAMI TO AMERICA'S FUTURE

Arthur McDuffie, aged thirty-three, a black ex-marine, insurance agent, and father of two, slowed instead of stopped at a red light while riding his motorcycle in the city of Miami, Florida. When McDuffie failed to comply with police orders to stop, a high-speed chase involving more than a dozen police cars ensued. McDuffie, unarmed, was soon pulled over by police and beaten severely. Four days later, on December 21, 1979, in a Miami hospital, McDuffie died of his injuries. The black sections of Miami—Liberty City, the remnants of Overtown, and the small black enclave in Coconut Grove—did not erupt in violence. They waited instead for justice.

The trial of four Miami police officers accused variously of second-degree murder, manslaughter, and tampering with evidence was moved to Tampa, away from the passions that roiled around the case in Miami. At the trial, other police officers, who had been granted immunity, described the beating in bloody detail. After hearing the evidence, the all-white jury on May 17, 1980, found the police officers not guilty on all counts. Within hours, the black neighborhoods of Miami responded with the worst civil disorders the country had seen since those in Detroit in 1967. In five days of rioting in Miami, seventeen died. Ten blacks were shot to death by police and roving vigilantes. Most of the seven white victims were beaten to death by blacks, or stoned to death in their cars.

The death of black people at the hands of law enforcement officers and night riders firing from anonymous pickup trucks was an old and painful story. The death of a number of whites at black hands in an urban riot was without modern precedent, and a measure of the anger unleashed in the ghettos of Miami. A long list of grievances against the police and the courts had precipitated the violence. But more was breaking down on the streets of these communities than law and order.

Even in the quietest of times, it was evident that black Miami was in trouble. Overtown, once called Colored Town, had been set aside to house black workers when the city was first incorporated in 1896. It had never been a prosperous neighborhood, but over the years it had evolved into a true community and had become the center of black culture in south Florida, reaching its heyday in the 1940s and 1950s. Overtown was a home to blacks from all walks of life, working men and women, teachers, preachers, and other professionals. It contained numerous nightclubs, hotels, churches, and other black institutions and became the mecca for people denied access to the all-white enclaves of Miami and Miami Beach. Residents and visitors thought of it as the Harlem of the South.

By 1960, Overtown had begun a long decline. The decision to run a federal interstate highway through Overtown cut the neighborhood in two and displaced thousands of people. Many crowded into Miami's Liberty City ghetto a few miles to the north. By 1965, according to one observer, "much of Overtown had been razed for highway construction and urban renewal." Ironically, the gains made by the civil rights movement and federal affirmative action programs also cut away at what remained of the heart of Overtown. Many who could now afford to get out fled Miami's inner-city neighborhoods. With them went most of the infrastructure that had traditionally held those black neighborhoods together.

> Dewey Knight, a former deputy county manager of Dade County, witnessed the exodus and the plight of those who were left behind.

DEWEY KNIGHT

The people that were left were basically youngsters, mothers with children who couldn't get out, old people who couldn't get out, men and women with problems who couldn't get out—alcoholism, subsequently drugs. Some carryover with immigrants who could not master the language or master the cultural functioning. So there was really the bottom rung of the ladder that was left, and we've seen a growing underclass everywhere. But that does not mean that there aren't people and were not people in Overtown who stayed because they wanted to stay, but they were very limited. And that does not mean that these people didn't have great potential. But they were ignored because the upward mobility types had gone. When everyone was there, when the professionals were there and everybody, things moved up that benefited everybody. And as a consequence, the housing goes down, the streets go down, there are very few businesses, there are police problems, problems with stealing and that kind of thing. And as a consequence, the people that are left are not only limited in their mobility, but they're limited in their functioning too. And while we talk a lot about doing something about it, it is caught up in many, many plans.

Jesse McCrary, a Florida native, moved to Miami in 1965. An attorney, he is also one of four black members of the Non-Group, a Miami business fraternity.

JESSE MCCRARY

Overtown was destroyed because of government. There are some particular examples I can cite for you. The state transportation department decided that that's where Interstate I-95 should go. The county government put its administration building there. The federal government put a United States post office on the most popular social gathering place that black people had in the history of this county. The new arena is in Overtown. The mass transit has a station in Overtown. You have to understand, Overtown is adjacent to downtown Miami. Downtown Miami cannot expand southward. It can't expand westward. It can't expand eastward because they would be in the bay. And the only place it can expand is Overtown. Now, black people were easy prey. They had no political power because they didn't have any people in office. So what government did was they took a little at a time. First they cut the finger off, and then they cut the hand off, and then they cut the arm off, and pretty soon Overtown is dead. In addition to the fact that many things in Overtown were owned by whites who put up massive apartment buildings, and when government started moving in they immediately moved those tenants out because they saw chances to make huge profits from government's desire to move in.

When government moved in, people had to move out. Government moved in on a social institution and displaced that social institution, and what was cohesive at one time then became scattered. So that institution died called Overtown. And the people who lived in Overtown, who were part of Overtown, and other people who came from the outside, outlying areas, all gathered in Overtown for some reason, for church, for cultural events, for social events. And when government displaced those institutions, it displaced that society and broke it up. Overtown was not built overnight. Overtown had a history. It had the history of being our place together. We are here. We are brothers. We are businesspeople. And what you are asking, or what some would suggest, is that we'll go get forty acres somewhere and rebuild it. You can't rebuild history overnight.

Georgia Ayers, a native of Miami, is a retired social worker and longtime community activist.

GEORGIA AYERS

Overtown to blacks was what Miami Beach was to nonblacks. And that's where we went to visit and see the black entertainers when they came to Dade County—the likes of Nat King Cole, Cab Calloway, all of the big names for blacks, Harry Belafonte and those people, Ethel Waters—when they came to Dade County they'd go to the old Rockland Palace, the Sir John Hotel, the Mary Elizabeth Hotel, and that's when we got an opportunity to see them. We could not go on Miami Beach and they could not stay on Miami Beach. And when they got through performing, they would come to Overtown, and that's when we got the opportunity to see them in the early hours of the morning. When we got ready to what we call "go out," then we came to Overtown on Second Avenue.

DEWEY KNIGHT

Overtown was a viable community in which people had common causes and related to each other. There was economic development, businesses, furniture stores, a soda water bottling company. The professionals, doctors, lawyers, others, were there. It was a focal point for black people. Segregation, of course, contributed to that, but segregation caused it to be a community where people had a real sense of community. The youngsters were considered youngsters of the community, so that everyone felt some responsibility for youngsters. It was said once by a juvenile court judge that there's no such thing as a dependent black child in Dade County because the community will take care of him. And it's literally true that very few people suffered. We saw, however, some significant changes that came about, number one, because of the aspirations of black people, but more importantly, negative changes that came about because of what was supposed to be something good, something called urban renewal, which ended up being urban removal. And I-95, which was basically developed to get people from suburbia downtown and in the process destroyed Overtown and that sense of community. I say that because what did it do? It meant that people had to move. They were given very little for their property, there was no planned movement and people had to do the best they could. And as a result of that, some landlords exploited that. Liberty City—which had basically become an area for upward mobility, where you could buy a lot and work weekends and build a house—all of a sudden you saw concrete apartment houses coming up, what we call concrete monsters, simply because the demand of the pushout for Overtown was for space. There were small places that did not accommodate people, it was overcrowding areas, there was no zoning controls. These are single-family residences and next to them you had all kinds of houses. And it really literally destroyed what was the major black community in this area. And you never saw the redevelopment of that sense of community, in my estimation, that I was informed of and saw the end of over time.

The Cuban revolution of 1959 brought thousands of Cubans to Miami seeking a home away from Fidel Castro's communism. But the first major influx began in 1965, the year more than 100,000 Cuban refugees arrived via twice-daily "freedom flights." Eventually, more than half a million Cubans arrived (including 60,000 to 80,000 of the so-called Mariel refugees of 1980, named for the Cuban port from which they departed via a flotilla organized by Cuban-Americans). Additionally, approximately 100,000 exiles from other Caribbean and Central American nations, including Nicaragua and Haiti, reside in Miami.

Sonny Wright, a black real estate developer and banker, moved to Miami in the late 1950s from New York.

SONNY WRIGHT

You have to recognize that initially a lot of the Cubans that came here came with money. They came with education. They came with skills. They came away from a government that they didn't want to be subject to. So they came seeking political freedom and freedom of speech and all the things that America represents. And they came and they brought something with them. They brought their skills. They brought their wealth in a lot of instances. But there were many of them that did not have maybe great skills or great amounts of wealth. But what they've done is they've done what the black people need to do. That is, stick together, work together, pool their resources, do the things that make the difference. And what the difference is, is that when people understand that their destinies really are interwoven, and recognize that the real value of relationships, and of opportunities for that matter, is in seeing that people around you—that you are friendly with, that you have some influence with—reach the heights. Because if my friend is in a position and he has control and he has power, then at least I have an opportunity.

So we need to recognize, in my opinion at least anyway, that the idea is not to pull the other man, but push. As you make your stride to reach your goal, to do what your destiny calls for you to do, push somebody—in this case we're talking about a somebody black—in order that he might be able to reach back and pull somebody. And together we pool our resources. We learn to buy from our own community. We learn to respect one another. We learn to control our neighborhoods. And we learn to do all the things that other people have already demonstrated to us that work. I don't mean just the Cubans. What about the Jewish people? Well, when the Jewish people came here, at least when I came here, they were saying there were signs on the beach. I never saw any of the signs. But they must have been there, because I read about it, I heard about it. There were signs on Miami Beach that said "No Jews, No Dogs Allowed." That had to be very hurtful to a Jewish person to see a sign like that. It's something like, you know, "White Water Fountain—Black Water Fountain," sit at the back of the bus, same kind of thing. But today, the Jews own Miami Beach. That's what it's all about, man. I mean, now if you go to Miami Beach and you want to do something, you have to deal with them, because they understand the value of working together.

In 1980, at the time of the McDuffie trial, black unemployment was running 13.5 percent nationally, but in Overtown and Liberty City it was almost 40 percent. Among black teenagers there, it was almost 80 percent.

Maurice Ferre, born in Puerto Rico, served as mayor of Miami from 1973 to 1985.

MAURICE FERRE

The McDuffie trial was one of the critical points in the history of Miami. And the reason, of course, is that for weeks on end the newspapers and especially the television stations in the evening would report what was going on in the trial, so that the people of Miami and especially the black community were patently aware of every gruesome detail of how that poor man had died—that they had held his head, what kind of a flashlight, with how many batteries, they had beaten him with, where the blood was splattering. It was just horrible. There was no question but that this was a terrible thing that had occurred, it was tragic. I don't think anybody had any question but that there was guilt. These police officers had no right to kill that man the way he was killed. He was not resisting at that point, and yet they battered his head in. And they're all of a sudden not guilty. It was a shock.

All the things that had built up to that, all of the many problems that Miami had in the black community—poverty, the underclass, racism—all these things were coming together. The Mariel refugees coming in, the advent of economic competition between the Cubans and the blacks—or the perception of it, because a lot of times it wasn't real but just a perception of it. The lack of opportunity, the lack of jobs, the lack of upward mobility, unemployment, underemployment, single-parent homes, pregnant teenagers, drugs. All the Pandora's boxes of problems that were coming together. All of a sudden, this is the tinderbox that somebody strikes a light and all of a sudden there's an explosion. And that's exactly what occurred. There's no question but that McDuffie was a major turning point in our history. And as it occurred, those of us that had positions of responsibility were painfully aware of the potential, but frankly, I've got to tell you, it never occurred to me that those four officers on trial in Tampa would be found not guilty, totally not guilty. I thought somehow they'd end up doing some time in jail or there would be some consequences of this, but nothing. So that was a shock to me as well as to the rest of the community.

John O. Brown, an ophthalmologist, is director of the Miami chapter of the Congress of Racial Equality. He moved to Miami in 1955.

JOHN O. BROWN

My response to the McDuffie verdicts was one of anger. When you are my age, you can remember back to the days of the lynch mobs and everything, the lynchings that even sort of spurred the existence of the NAACP. There used to be a report that was given each year on the number of lynchings that occurred in the United States, and that was one of the first programs of the NAACP, to see that a federal antilynching law was passed. And, of course, in recent years we heard about Emmett Till up in Mississippi. And this was the very same thing that had happened in the Arthur McDuffie case. We knew that a black man had been killed by a policeman. We knew the policemen who were present. And yet when they had the trial of Arthur McDuffie up there, they came back with a verdict of not guilty: "These people were not guilty of murdering this man!" And it was just another lynching. So immediately there was a feeling of anger in the entire community. I belong to an organization called Sigma Pi Phi. At the time of the Arthur McDuffie verdict we were having a workshop at one of the Holiday Inns on Biscayne Boulevard, trying to work out solutions to the race problem here in Miami, the economics, the politics, discussing all of these things. And also considering the possibility of violence because of the Arthur McDuffie case. So about three o'clock that afternoon, it was announced in the workshop that the officers were not guilty. And we were certainly fearful at that moment that all hell was going to break loose in the black community.

The violence of the five days of the McDuffie riots, the destruction of businesses and the driving out of business owners, spelled even more economic trouble for black residents. Still, some saw hope for Liberty City. Some thought of returning. And some, who could have left, chose to stay.

Athalie Range owns a funeral home in Liberty City. She has served as a Miami city commissioner and as Florida secretary of community affairs.

ATHALIE RANGE

Many people have left, but Liberty City is what I consider home. Of course, I came from Overtown to begin with. I've been here in Liberty City. I serve the people in Liberty City. That is one of the main objectives of my business, to be here to serve the people in Liberty City and in neighboring areas. I feel it's a fine thing for younger people to move out, to stretch out, to go wherever they are pleased. But I am pleased to be here, to build a monument to this community. And I feel that it's necessary to remain here and to help to build Liberty City up rather than to go away and look at it in scorn. There are too many people right now who grew up right here in Liberty City, yet they get on the expressways, ride from their downtown jobs over Liberty City, go to the outlaying areas, get their cocktails, lock their door, and forget that there's a world outside of people like me who live in Liberty City.

SONNY WRIGHT

When I first came here, I remember going into what we call a Royal Castle. Royal Castle's like a Burger King or a McDonald's of today. And I made the mistake of sitting down, waiting for a hamburger that I was going to take out because I knew that you couldn't eat the hamburger there. I was told by the clerk that I had to get up. And of course I was very embarrassed because that place was full of people. And I explained that I was just waiting for the hamburger. And he explained to me that I couldn't sit down and wait for it. I had to stand up and wait for it. And that was really an experience that I think a lot of black people had at one time in their life in one way or another. But I think that the idea really is not so much the ability to eat at a hamburger place, but I think more importantly, to *buy* [a hamburger place]. And I think that's what it's all about. And I think that that's where Black America has to go. We have to try to see if we can't control the resources in the community and keep our dollars circulating among ourselves more than one time, because that's what the whole thing's all about, to be able to create opportunity for our businesspeople and to create jobs for our young people and our population in general. Not to mention the other people that we would employ. We have to begin to use our resources in a way in which it benefits us, more than what it presently does today.

The real shame and the real sadness is when are we going to learn? I mean, when are the white people going to learn that in order for everybody to live in this community and enjoy our God-given resources in this beautiful city, that everybody has to have an opportunity to share in that. When are the Cubans going to learn that the blessings they discovered in this community need to be shared with others in this community? When are the black people going to learn that we're going to have to work a little harder if we want our piece of the pie? And we're going to have to start working together.

Otis Pitts has served as a Miami police officer and as head of the Belafonte-TACOLCY Center, a multiservice social agency in Liberty City.

Otis Pitts

We have to recognize that no matter how well intentioned people are, we have to solve our own problems ultimately. I mean, at best we can receive some assistance in doing that, but the solution has to be ours, and ultimately we have to implement the solution. So, it's about us doing it for ourselves in the final analysis, maybe with the assistance of others but clearly our own effort. And so therefore, we got to look at the opportunities in our own communities to become more economically viable and to create the wherewithal out of it. I think the stuff, if you will, for doing that is already in place. I mean, it's clearly made the fortunes of others. We got to now make it a fortune for ourselves. I mean, we spend an enormous amount of money for all kinds of goods and services, but they've been spent outside this community. So therefore, jobs, wealth, et cetera, is created upon a transaction. If everything is being bought outside your community, being made outside your community, that's where the economic centers are being developed. We've got to now begin to look at creating those things in our own community with our own resources currently, not to find new money, just existing money which we currently expend in this country is sufficient to start an economic plan to revitalize our communities.

GEORGIA AYERS

All of my life—I'm sixty years old—I have been fighting for survival against racism, oppression, economically and every other way. I am fighting for a better way of life for my children. I understand now, for a fact, that my children don't have to drink in the black fountains as I did. When they go downtown, they don't have to go in the back and sit in the back of the trolley. They don't have to buy a hat and take it home because they cannot try it on. We have integration as far as the white man says it's there. My thing is to take what you have, make something of it.

A Final Note: We've Come Too Far to Turn Back Now

Mary Frances Berry, appointed to the U.S. Commission on Civil Rights by President Carter in 1980, visited Miami shortly after the McDuffie riot. She recognizes that the challenges facing Miamians, as articulated by Dewey Knight, Georgia Ayers, and others, are hardly unique to that city. Now a professor of history at the University of Pennsylvania, she told us in 1989, "In terms of the poverty and alienation that poor black people feel, you could go to any city in the country and go to any poor black neighborhood and you would find the same attitudes as in Miami, attitudes that reflect the *reality* of how little opportunity they had. . . . As far as the poverty and as far as the joblessness and so on among the poor, you would find that in almost any city. And the police brutality—you would find that too in most places."

Eleanor Holmes Norton, the first woman to chair the Equal Employment Opportunity Commission (and since 1982 a professor of law at Georgetown University Law Center), also described to us some of the problems confronting the African-American community throughout the country. "The huge deficit that is keeping us from investing in our people, especially those who have been left behind, has to be moved off so that we can once again begin to attend to our human capital. There is a large role for the government here, and there is a role that only black people can attend to. Nobody can reconstruct the black family and bring it to its historic strength except us. We've got to demand that the programs that should be available to us in undertaking this work be made available. But also ultimately this is our job and our work. . . . There are going to have to be internal changes in the black community. We've got to halt the precipitous growth of female-headed households. Not only for themselves but because most of those children are being raised in poverty. And thus we cast a pall over the next generation by not giving them a good start in life. We've got to attend to the problems that we don't yet fully understand that are resulting in far fewer black males going to college. Indeed, the whole ghetto pathology that eats up black boys when they're young is something we've got to learn to deal with. There's got to be the reinvigoration and the invention of a galaxy of new programs that originate from the government, taking up models from across the country that have seemed to work. And there's got to be an infusion of young leadership that wants to roll up its sleeves and go to work at the *hard* problems in the black community that will take more than money."

Though the authors of this book consider themselves chroniclers rather than historians, we have tried to abide by the advice of Barbara Tuchman: "If the historian will submit himself *to* his material instead of trying to impose himself on his material, then the material will ultimately speak to him and supply the answers." The answers that our interviewees have sought to the problems confronting African-Americans are perhaps found best not only in the history they have left us, but also in the lives that they now lead.

Among the problems that came to broad public attention in the 1980s is the widespread use of drugs. By mid-decade, the number of cocaine-related deaths in the United States was three and a half times the 1980 rate. Father George Clements, who worked with Fred Hampton and the Black Panther party in Chicago in the late sixties (he was called by many white people "the Black Panther priest"), is now confronting both the disintegration of the black family and the dangers of drugs in the African-American community. In 1981, he became one of the first Catholic priests to adopt a child. He has subsequently adopted two other sons. Father Clements established an adoption program called One Church/One Child, which seeks to find permanent homes for some of the nation's 100,000 black foster children. At great risk to his own life (he has received numerous death threats) he also launched an antidrug crusade focusing on retailers who sell drug paraphernalia.

Supreme Court appointments in the 1980s have caused many advocates of progressive social change to view the Court, their former ally, as an adversary. Affirmative action is but one area of civil rights legislation that has come under attack in recent decisions. Tom Cordy of Atlanta, however, is a businessman who continues to believe that affirmative action is the key to opportunities for many Black Americans. Cordy, the black developer who got his first big break on the Hartsfield International Airport project, is now one of Atlanta's most successful developers. He has maintained his belief in the importance of being responsible and responsive to his community. The developer conscientiously hires minority employees to build housing for black residents. As Cordy told us, "We've had an emergence of several firms that have had an opportunity to have access to opportunity. Therefore, they've been able to grow and develop, and they've become a part of the system. And it's good for the city, it's good for the community, it's good for business. The reason for this is that it allows minority entrepreneurs to develop and become a part of the mainstream of the business community. They can then sit at the table as equals and help to provide the vision for our community. . . . Anytime a firm has access to opportunity, then it's the business owner's responsibility to provide the infrastructure and management to take advantage of that, and to build the company. If you don't have access, you might as well close the door. If you're denied access to opportunity, then you're dead."

In the 1980s, federal support for affordable housing declined dramatically. In the mid-1970s, there were 11 million low-rent housing units available for the 9 million Americans who needed them. By the mid-1980s, the number of available housing units declined to 9 million and the number of people needing low-rent housing had increased to 12 million. The cost of home ownership increased dramatically, beyond the reach of many working families. In Cincinnati, Ohio, in 1988, the Reverend Fred Shuttlesworth, founder of the Alabama Christian Movement for Human Rights and an SCLC founder active in Birmingham in the mid-1960s, established the Shuttlesworth Housing Foundation. Using $100,000 he made through the sale of two apartment complexes, Shuttlesworth launched the foundation, which provides grants to help poor families become homeowners. Creative approaches to solving intransigent and practical problems, such as the Reverend Mr. Shuttlesworth's method of helping the poor become homeowners, are some of the ways people can, in the words of Otis Pitts of Miami, "look at the opportunities to become more economically viable and to create the wherewithal out of it."

The late 1980s witnessed numerous racial incidents on college campuses as well as in major cities. Among the best-known incidents were the 1986 attack on three black men who found themselves in the predominantly white Howard Beach section of Queens, New York (one of the victims, Michael Griffith, died), and the 1989 killing of black sixteen-year-old Yusuf Hawkins, who went to a white neighborhood in

Brooklyn to answer a classified ad for a used car. Violent displays of racial animosity are only one piece of evidence that tension continues among the races and that racial bigotry is not a thing of the past. Longtime activist the Reverend C. T. Vivian believes strongly in the need to monitor incidents of overt racism. In the late 1970s, he established the Center for Democratic Renewal, a watchdog agency that publishes statistics and reports on hate-groups. Vivian also conducts workshops for businesses and chambers of commerce to help overcome psychological problems that arise from being African-American in this society.

The percentage of black high school graduates attending college peaked in 1977 at 48 percent and by 1986 had dropped to 36.5 percent, some twenty percentage points lower than the rate for white high school graduates. Students who were able to attend college often did so under difficult conditions. The Reagan administration, which sought to abolish the U.S. Department of Education altogether, had succeeded in effectively cutting back Guaranteed Student Loans and other federal assistance programs. Between 1980 and 1987, the cost of college tuition increased by more than 75 percent. Education remains a primary concern of activist Ruth Batson, who in 1963 began her chairmanship of the NAACP Public School Committee in Boston. Today Batson runs the Ruth Batson Educational Foundation, which offers grants to students in financial need. She started the foundation in 1969 with a gift of one thousand dollars that she received from grateful parents of some of the minority students she helped through her activism over the years. Speaking of the foundation, she told us, "I think the thing that we do best is the way that we can act in an emergency situation. We don't have to go through too many chains of command in order to make a decision. For example, one Friday not long ago I received a call from a woman who was in school and thought she had her regular UN grant and had just discovered at the last minute that she did not have it—and another grant that she thought she had through some snafu was not available. She was in a panic, thinking that she might not be able to finish school. Now, this was her last year and she and her husband work as domestic workers to take care of themselves. I talked with her and talked with some school officials and found out that her story was quite accurate and that in addition she was a terrific student. The following Monday we were able to get a check to the university to get her through her first semester. This is the kind of thing that we do best."

There are no simple solutions to the problems confronting Black Americans. We asked Mary Frances Berry about the strategies she sees as necessary to meet these difficult challenges. "What one needs to have is a multifaceted approach. I don't like either/or approaches. People say, 'Well, we should have self-help.' Somebody else says, 'Well, no, we don't need self-help. What we should have is civil rights enforcement.' And somebody else says, 'We need government,' or 'No, we need private sector.' You have to have *all* of those things: private sector, government, self-help, motivation, civil rights enforcement. All these can be put together as a strategy to try to do something about the people's problems. And there's a role for every kind of institution. Individuals, churches, community groups, have to motivate people. The government has to use tax money wisely and make good policy decisions and enforce civil rights. The private sector has to use its resources and its money. Police need to make neighborhoods safe. Everybody's got a role to play."

Some activists who remain consistently engaged with social change take a long view of the present era. Marian Wright Edelman, who started her career as a lawyer working with the poor in Mississippi, now heads the Children's Defense Fund, an organization she founded in 1973 that advocates on behalf of the nation's children, particularly the poor, minority, and handicapped. "One has to remember the seasons," she told us, "that in the barest points of winter, one really does have to remember that leaves and buds are beginning to blossom now in a new recognition by the country that it is in deep trouble. That the messages of Martin twenty years ago are the messages that we have still got to answer today. But I think, paradoxically, the Reagan years, which have been very hard years, with assaults on the national role on protecting the poor and minority groups, have set the stage for the 1990s, because this country will have to confront the issues of investing in its children and families if it is going to preserve its future."

Many people throughout the country feel that to safeguard our children's future, it is important to provide an understanding of the past. Mamie Till Bradley Mobley, the mother of Emmett Till, in 1973 established the Emmett Till Players. This ever-changing troupe of mostly elementary school children has, for more than fifteen years, performed renditions of Dr. Martin Luther King, Jr.'s speeches. Mobley told *Jet* magazine, "My dream is to instill a sense of black history in the children." Ruth Batson, in addition to her foundation work, was instrumental in developing the Museum of Afro-American History in Boston. For several years she served as the museum's director. "The museum is most important to children," she told us. "Children need to know their history and understand the contributions that their forebears have made to this country and to where they live right in their community. I think the same thing holds for adults. The museum can be a place where all kinds of people can gather."

For years many activists, both black and white, have recognized a connection between the American struggle for civil rights and the international struggle for civil rights. In 1984, members of a group called TransAfrica staged a sit-in at the South African embassy in Washington, D.C., that launched daily protests there and at other South African consulates throughout the United States. The demonstrations continued for fifty-three consecutive weeks, re-energizing the anti-apartheid movement in this country. Protesters who submitted to arrest included twenty-three members of the U.S. Congress, a number of mayors, and numerous activists and celebrities. Among the first participants were Mary Frances Berry and Eleanor Holmes Norton. Norton explained to us her reasons for demonstrating against apartheid."Struggle does not begin or end at the borders of the United States. To be sure, I have some level of identification with people who are oppressed in South Africa. There is a kind of logical extension of the civil rights struggle. . . . Blacks get their moral authority not only because they were pressing for their own rights, but because they did so in a way that wrote equality lessons large. And they wrote those lessons large enough for people throughout this country and throughout the world to understand the meaning of equality. Our movement, it seems to me, is important far more for what it meant to millions of people all over the world than what it meant for twenty million Americans. Our freedom is precious and important, but in the end what gives our movement its majesty is the example it set throughout the world for people of color and for people who in any way were oppressed and found in that example a reason to hope and strive for a different life."

One of the hard-won victories of the American struggle for civil rights was the Voting Rights Act of 1965. Although the Reagan administration fought a strengthened Voting Rights Act in 1982, political gains, though still disproportionate to the black population, remain undeniable. Richard Hatcher, the mayor of Gary, Indiana, at the time of the National Black Political Convention in 1972, reminded us that "if one looks at where we were in 1965, with the passage of the Voting Rights Act, and then one looks at the end of that period with a Jesse Jackson running for president of the United States, coming in second for the Democratic nomination, you can see that tremendous progress was made. [There was a] quiet revolution at the local level, of people running for and being elected to the city council, and we grew from only two mayors in 1968 to over three hundred mayors, and mayors of some of our largest cities."

Jesse Jackson, who ran for the Democratic nomination for the presidency in 1984 and 1988, summarized the political gains similarly. "We've started further back than anybody else. After all, the Constitution designates African descendants as three-fifths human. No immigrant group had to face that mathematical equation. . . . There was another hundred years of legal apartheid, the segregation in this country. After all of this struggle—public accommodations, equal access and protection under the law, as opposed to separate but equal—came the right to vote. The most fundamental shift from slaveship en route to championship has been to be empowered, to be enfranchised with this right to vote. . . . In 1988, I got more votes than [Walter] Mondale got for the nomination in 1984. Within our lifetime this ongoing struggle will have an African-American as nominee of a major political party. Indeed, as president of the United States of America."

From 1974 to 1982, Maynard Jackson served as Atlanta's first black mayor. His two terms in office were the maximum allowed consecutively, and he was succeeded by Andrew Young. In 1989, Jackson was reelected. Shortly before this reelection, Maynard Jackson described the problems that black elected officials face. "We have all of the challenges that white elected officials have, with a major overlay in addition. That overlay is to prove—we shouldn't have to do this, it's not fair that we're expected to do this—but the reality is that we've got to prove ourselves more than others, not just to the white community but to the black community as well. There is an undercurrent in Black America that black elected officials will embarrass the black community. . . . So the challenge therefore is to manage well, to be a good public manager. But more than that, a leader who has a vision for the future and who has the guts to make that happen, but also the skill to try to build a consensus and to bring that group along. And there is no excuse that we ought to use just because we're black. We shouldn't hide behind that, shouldn't use that as a rationalization, should not try to say, 'Well, look, you've got to make special allowance for me because I'm black,' and all of this. I'm sorry, but black taxpayers want the same things as white taxpayers, and you better be able to deliver. You've got to be able to stand and deliver."

Perhaps the most obvious accomplishments of the civil rights movement are the political gains achieved and the abolition of legally sanctioned segregation. But these social transformations would not have been possible without the personal transformations of countless individual lives. Among the most powerful examples of personal and political transformation is that of Unita Blackwell, who helped lead the Mississippi Freedom Democratic party's fight during the 1964 Democratic National Convention. Twenty years later, she attended another Democratic convention, this time as a featured speaker. She was now the mayor of Mayersville, Mississippi, the same town where for much of her life she had been denied the right to vote. "I tried not to get too emotional about it," she told us, "but there was a feeling that it was worth all of it that we had been through. I remember a woman told me one time when I was running for justice of peace, 'The reason I won't vote for you is because they going to kill you.' The whites had told her that they were going to kill me, and she thought she was saving my life. And when I stood in that podium twenty years later, I was standing there for this woman, to understand that she had a right to register to vote for whomever she wanted to, and that we as a people were going to live.

Jesse Jackson spoke before me, prime time, of course. People did see me late at night, and some of those that know me know that I felt tears because Fannie Lou Hamer should have been standing there. She was standing there in us—in me, in Jesse, in all of us—because in 1964 she testified. Chaney, Schwerner, Goodman died in my state, Mississippi, for the right for me to stand there at that podium. That's what I felt, that I was standing there for all who had died, all who will live, for all the generations to come."

If it's true, as the song says, "freedom is a constant struggle," then there can be no true ending to this chronicle. But longtime Chicago activist Nancy Jefferson told us a story from her childhood that reminds us of the need to persist. "I came from the backwoods country. We used to have a big bell in Miss Burton's yard, where I had to wash the dishes. And whenever anything happened you had to pull that bell with the rope to get it to ting. Sometimes your hands would get raw from trying to get a ting out of that bell, especially on cold days. But I kept pulling. And once I had the ting, I had it made. I look at life like that. You keep pulling the bell, and you'll get a ting, and things happen. . . . I don't care who comes, they will not turn the people back to where they were. It's impossible, 'cause too many people caught on."

No matter how cold the weather, no matter how raw our hands, we must each strive to keep that bell tinging.

For Further Reading

In the course of producing this book and the "Eyes on the Prize" television series, the production teams of Blackside, Inc., have consulted literally thousands of books, periodicals, and other publications on African-American history and civil and human rights. What follows is a list of books that may be of interest to the general reader.

Civil Rights History, 1950s–1980s

Baldwin, James. *The Fire Next Time*. New York: Dial Press, 1963.

Bennett, Lerone. *Before the Mayflower: A History of Black America* (fifth edition). New York: Penguin, 1984.

Branch, Taylor. *Parting the Waters: America in the King Years, 1954–63*. New York: Simon and Schuster, 1988.

Forman, James. *The Making of Black Revolutionaries.* New York: Macmillan, 1972.

Garrow, David J. *Bearing the Cross: Martin Luther King, Jr., and the Southern Christian Leadership Conference.* New York: Vintage Books, 1986.

Giddings, Paula. *When and Where I Enter: The Impact of Black Women on Race and Sex in America.* New York: Bantam, 1984.

Grant, Joanne, ed. *Black Protest.* Greenwich, Connecticut: Fawcett Books, 1968.

Harding, Vincent. *The Other American Revolution.* Los Angeles: Center for Afro-American Studies, UCLA, 1980.

Kaufman, Jonathan. *Broken Alliance: The Turbulent Times Between Blacks and Jews in America.* New York: Charles Scribner's Sons, 1988.

King, Mary. *Freedom Song: A Personal Story of the 1960s Civil Rights Movement.* New York: William Morrow, 1987.

Kluger, Richard. *Simple Justice: The History of Brown v. Board of Education and Black America's Struggle for Equality.* New York: Vintage Books, 1975.

Lawson, Steven F. *In Pursuit of Power: Southern Blacks and Electoral Politics, 1965–1982.* New York: Columbia University Press, 1985.

Lerner, Gerda, ed. *Black Women in White America: A Documentary History.* New York: Vintage Books, 1972.

Mendelsohn, Jack. *The Martyrs: Sixteen Who Gave Their Lives for Racial Justice.* New York: Harper, 1966.

Morris, Aldon D. *The Origins of the Civil Rights Movement: Black Communities Organizing for Change.* New York: The Free Press, 1984.
Raines, Howell. *My Soul Is Rested.* New York: G. P. Putnam's Sons, 1977.
Washington, James M., ed. *A Testament of Hope: The Essential Writings of Martin Luther King, Jr.* New York: Harper and Row, 1986.
Watters, Pat, and Reese Cleghorn. *Climbing Jacob's Ladder: The Arrival of Negroes in Southern Politics.* New York: Harcourt, Brace & World, 1967.
Williams, Juan. *Eyes on the Prize: America's Civil Rights Years, 1954–65.* New York: Viking, 1987.
Zinn, Howard. *SNCC: The New Abolitionists.* Boston: Beacon Press, 1965.

1: Emmett Till

Whitfield, Stephen J. *A Death in the Delta: The Story of Emmett Till.* New York: The Free Press, 1988.

2: The Montgomery Bus Boycott

Durr, Virginia Foster. *Outside the Magic Circle: The Autobiography of Virginia Foster Durr.* Tuscaloosa: University of Alabama Press, 1985.
King, Martin Luther, Jr. *Stride Toward Freedom.* New York: Harper and Brothers, 1958.
Robinson, Jo Ann. *The Montgomery Bus Boycott and the Women Who Started It.* Knoxville: University of Tennessee Press, 1987.

3: The Little Rock Crisis

Bates, Daisy L. *The Long Shadow of Little Rock: A Memoir.* New York: David McKay, 1962.
Huckaby, Elizabeth. *Crisis at Central High: Little Rock, 1957–58.* Baton Rouge: Louisiana State University Press, 1980.

4: Student Sit-ins in Nashville

Carson, Clayborne. *In Struggle: SNCC and the Black Awakening of the 1960s.* Cambridge, Massachusetts: Harvard University Press, 1981.

5: Freedom Rides

Farmer, James. *Lay Bare the Heart: An Autobiography of the Civil Rights Movement.* New York: Arbor House, 1985.
Peck, James. *Freedom Ride.* New York: Simon and Schuster, 1962.

6: Albany, Georgia

Oates, Stephen B. *Let the Trumpet Sound: The Life of Martin Luther King, Jr.* New York: Harper and Row, 1982.

7: James Meredith Enters Ole Miss

Barrett, Russell. *Integration at Ole Miss.* New York: Quadrangle Books, 1965.

Meredith, James. *Three Years in Mississippi.* Bloomington: Indiana University Press, 1966.

8: Birmingham

King, Martin Luther, Jr. *Why We Can't Wait.* New York: Harper and Row, 1963.

9: Organizing in Mississippi

Evers, Myrlie, with William Peters. *For Us, the Living.* New York: Doubleday, 1967.

Moody, Ann. *Coming of Age in Mississippi.* New York: Dial Press, 1968.

Silver, James W. *Mississippi: The Closed Society.* New York: Harcourt, Brace & World, 1963.

10: The March on Washington

Gentile, Thomas. *March on Washington: August 28, 1963.* Washington, D.C.: New Day Publications, 1983.

11: The Sixteenth Street Church Bombing

Rowe, Gary Thomas. *My Undercover Years with the Ku Klux Klan.* New York: Bantam, 1976.

Whitehead, Don. *Attack on Terror: The FBI Against the Ku Klux Klan.* New York: Funk and Wagnalls, 1970.

12: Mississippi Freedom Summer

Belfrage, Sally. *Freedom Summer.* New York: Viking, 1965.

Cagin, Seth, and Philip Dray. *We Are Not Afraid: The Story of Goodman, Schwerner, and Chaney and the Civil Rights Campaign for Mississippi.* New York: Macmillan, 1988.

Sutherland, Elizabeth, ed. *Letters from Mississippi.* New York: McGraw-Hill, 1965.

13: Selma

Garrow, David J. *Protest at Selma: Martin Luther King, Jr., and the Voting Rights Act of 1965.* New Haven, Connecticut: Yale University Press, 1978.

Webb, Sheyann, and Rachel West Nelson with Frank Sikora. *Selma, Lord, Selma: Girlhood Memories of the Civil Rights Days.* Tuscaloosa: University of Alabama Press, 1980.

14: Malcolm X

Breitman, George, ed. *Malcolm X Speaks: Selected Speeches and Statements.* New York: Grove Press, 1965.

———, ed. *Malcolm X: By Any Means Necessary: Speeches, Interviews and a Letter by Malcolm X.* New York: Pathfinder Press, 1970.

Haley, Alex. *The Autobiography of Malcolm X.* New York: Grove Press, 1965.

Goldman, Peter Louis. *The Death and Life of Malcolm X.* New York: Harper and Row, 1973.

15: The Lowndes County Freedom Organization

Sellers, Cleveland. *The River of No Return: The Autobiography of a Black Militant and the Life and Death of SNCC.* New York: William Morrow, 1973.

16: The Meredith March

Carmichael, Stokely, and Charles V. Hamilton. *Black Power: The Politics of Liberation in America.* New York: Random House, 1967.

King, Martin Luther, Jr. *Where Do We Go from Here: Chaos or Community?* Boston: Beacon Press, 1967.

17: Chicago

Anderson, Alan B., and George W. Pickering. *Confronting the Color Line: The Broken Promise of the Civil Rights Movement in Chicago.* Athens: University of Georgia Press, 1986.

18: Muhammad Ali

Ali, Muhammad. *The Greatest: My Own Story.* New York: Random House, 1975.

Ashe, Arthur. *A Hard Road to Glory: A History of the African-American Athlete Since 1946.* New York: Amistad Books, Dodd, Mead, 1988.

19: King and Vietnam

Crane, J. David, and Elaine Crane. *The Black Soldier: From the American Revolution to Vietnam.* New York: William Morrow, 1971.

Terry, Wallace, ed. *Bloods: An Oral History of the Vietnam War by Black Veterans.* New York: Random House, 1984.

20: Birth of the Black Panthers

Cleaver, Eldridge. *Soul on Ice.* New York: Random House, 1968.

Foner, Philip S., ed. *The Black Panthers Speak.* Philadelphia: J. B. Lippincott, 1970.

Newton, Huey P. *Revolutionary Suicide.* New York: Harcourt Brace Jovanovich, 1973.

Seale, Bobby. *Seize the Time: The Story of the Black Panther Party and Huey P. Newton.* New York: Random House, 1970.

21: Detroit

Hersey, John. *The Algiers Motel Incident.* New York: Alfred A. Knopf, 1968.

Report of the National Advisory Commission on Civil Disorders. New York: Bantam, 1968.

22: The Election of Carl Stokes

Stokes, Carl B. *Promises of Power: A Political Autobiography.* New York: Simon and Schuster, 1973.

Weinberg, Kenneth G. *Black Victory: Carl Stokes and the Winning of Cleveland.* New York: Quadrangle Books, 1968.

23: Howard University

Myles, Tom. *Centennial Plus 1: A Photographic and Narrative Account of the Black Student Revolution, Howard University, 1965–68.* Washington, D.C.: Black Light Graphics, 1969.

24: King's Last Crusade

Garrow, David J. *The FBI and Martin Luther King, Jr.* New York: W. W. Norton, 1981.

Harding, Vincent, and Rosemarie Freeney. *Martin Luther King, Jr., and the Company of the Faithful.* Washington, D.C.: Sojourners, 1986.

King, Coretta Scott. *My Life with Martin Luther King, Jr.* New York: Holt, Rinehart and Winston, 1969.

25: Resurrection City

Fager, Charles. *Uncertain Resurrection.* Grand Rapids: Eerdmans Publishing, 1969.

Freeman, Jill. *Old News: Resurrection City.* New York: Grossman Publishers, 1970.

26: Ocean Hill–Brownsville

Berube, Maurice R., and Marilyn Gitell. *Confrontation at Ocean Hill–Brownsville: The New York School Strikes of 1968.* New York: Praeger, 1969.

Ravitch, Diane. *The Great School Wars, New York City, 1805–1973: A History of the Public Schools as Battlefield of Social Change.* New York: Basic Books, 1974.

27: The Black Panthers

O'Reilly, Kenneth. *Racial Matters: The FBI's Secret File on Black America, 1960–72.* New York: The Free Press, 1989.

Wilkins, Roy, and Ramsey Clark. *Search and Destroy: A Report by the Commission of Inquiry into the Black Panthers and the Police. Published by the NAACP and the Metropolitan Applied Research Center, Inc.* New York: Harper and Row, 1973.

28: Attica and Prisoners' Rights

Davis, Angela Yvonne. *An Autobiography.* New York: Random House, 1974; Bantam, 1975.

Jackson, George. *Soledad Brother: The Prison Letters of George Jackson.* New York: Coward-McCann, 1970; Bantam, 1970.

Wicker, Tom. *A Time to Die.* New York: Quadrangle Books, 1975.

29: The Gary Convention

Baraka, Amiri. *The Autobiography of LeRoi Jones/Amiri Baraka.* New York: Freundlich Books, 1984.

30: Busing in Boston

Kozol, Jonathan. *Death at an Early Age.* Boston: Houghton Mifflin, 1967.

Lukas, J. Anthony. *Common Ground: A Turbulent Decade in the Lives of Three American Families.* New York: Alfred A. Knopf, 1985; Vintage, 1986.

Lupo, Alan. *Liberty's Chosen Home: The Politics of Violence in Boston.* Boston: Little, Brown, 1977.

31: Atlanta and Affirmative Action

Berry, Mary Frances. *Black Resistance/White Law.* New York: Appleton, 1971.

Fleming, John. *The Lengthening Shadow of Slavery: A Historical Justification for Affirmative Action for Blacks in Higher Education.* Washington, D.C.: Howard University Press, 1976.

Gill, Gerald R. *Meanness Mania: The Changed Mood.* Washington, D.C.: Howard University Press, 1980.

Epilogue: From Miami to America's Future

Porter, Bruce, and Marvin Dunn. *The Miami Riot of 1980.* Lexington, Massachusetts: Lexington Books, 1984.

"Eyes on the Prize"

Project Staff and Funders

"Eyes on the Prize" was produced by Boston-based Blackside, Inc., one of the oldest minority-owned production companies in the country (founded in 1968). The series was produced over the course of twelve years by two production staffs. The first group produced programs one through six. The second group produced programs seven through fourteen.

Staff for Programs One Through Six

Executive Producer: Henry Hampton
Series Senior Producer: Judith Vecchione
Series Producer: Jon Else
Producers: Orlando Bagwell, Callie Crossley, James A. DeVinney, Judith Vecchione
Associate Producers: Prudence Arndt, Llewellyn Smith
Series Consulting Executive Producer: Michael Ambrosino
Series Writer: Steve Fayer
Series Senior Researcher: Laurie Kahn-Leavitt
Series Research Consultant: Judy Richardson
Editors: Daniel Eisenberg, Jeanne Jordan, Charles Scott
Assistant Editors: Ann Bartholomew, MJ Doherty, Victoria Garvin
Stock Footage Coordinator: Kenn Rabin
Production Manager: Jo Ann Mathieu
Production Assistant: Peter Montgomery
Editing Room Assistants: Elizabeth Carver, Eliza Gagnon, Meredith Woods
Post-Production Supervisor: Cynthia Meagher-Kuhn
Series Academic Advisers: Clayborne Carson, David Garrow, Vincent Harding, Darlene Clark Hine
Additional Academic Advisers: Wiley Branton, John Dittmer, Tony Freyer, Paul Gaston, Steven F. Lawson, Genna Rae McNeil, Aldon Morris, J. Mills Thornton, Howard Zinn

Additional Staff:
Business Manager: J. Benjamin Harris
Accountant: Lorraine Flynn Kiley
Director of Publishing: Robert Lavelle
Project Administrator: Inez Robinson
Production Secretaries: Sara Chazen, Karen Chase

STAFF FOR PROGRAMS SEVEN THROUGH FOURTEEN

Executive Producer: Henry Hampton
Producers: Sheila C. Bernard, Carroll Blue, James A. DeVinney, Madison Davis Lacy, Jr., Louis J. Massiah, Thomas Ott, Samuel Pollard, Terry Kay Rockefeller, Jacqueline Shearer, Paul Stekler
Associate Producers: Barbara Howard, Judy Richardson, Dale S. Rosen
Consulting Series Producer: Jon Else
Consulting Executive Producer: Michael Ambrosino
Consulting Producer: Judith Vecchione
Series Writer: Steve Fayer
Series Associate Producer: Judy Richardson
Production Manager: Alison Bassett
Researchers: Kirk Johnson, Susan J. Levene
Editors: Lillian Benson, Betty Ciccarelli, Thomas Ott, Charles Scott
Assistant Editors: Maia Harris, Kiki Zeldes
Stock Footage Coordinator: Janet Lawrence
Archive Consultant: Kenn Rabin
Editing and Production Assistants: Will Conroy, Bennett Singer, Noland Walker
Post-Production Supervisor: Frank Capria
Sound Editing Supervisor: John Waite
Sound Editing Assistant: Leah Mahan
Academic Advisers: Clayborne Carson, Peter Edelman, David Garrow, Vincent Harding, Darlene Clark Hine, Stan Katz, Steven F. Lawson, Aldon Morris, Kenneth O'Reilly, Diane Pinderhughes, Robert Preyer, William Strickland, Michael Thelwell, James Turner
Additional Staff:
Director of Business Affairs: Lorraine Flynn Kiley
Production Accountant: Michael King
Vice President, Publishing: Robert Lavelle
Vice President, Marketing: W. Michael Greene
Business Consultant: Janet Axelrod
Production Secretary: Valerie A. Linson

FUNDERS FOR PROGRAMS ONE THROUGH SIX

"Eyes on the Prize: Part One" was funded by Public Television Stations, the Corporation for Public Broadcasting, and major grants from the Ford Foundation, General Electric Company, Lotus Development Corporation, and Lilly Endowment, Inc.

Additional funding was provided by:

Abelard Foundation, Alabama Humanities Foundation, Ruth M. Batson Educational Foundation, Bay Packaging and Converting Co., Inc., Bird Companies Charitable Foundation, Inc., Boston Foundation, Boston Globe Foundation, Peter Buttenwieser, Ella Lyman Cabot Trust, Columbia Foundation, Cummins Engine Foundation, Maurice Falk Medical Fund, Freed Foundation, Inc., Freedom House, Inc., Friedman Family Foundation, Georgia Council on Humanities, Wallace Alexander Gerbode Foundation, Richard and Rhoda Goldman Fund, Irving I. Goldstein Foundation, Faith Griefen, Edward W. Hazen Foundation, Hillsdale Fund, Inc., Charles Evans Hughes Memorial Foundation, Hyams Foundation, H. Peter Karoff, Kraft Foundation, Sally (Mrs. Philip E.) Lillienthal, Metropolitan Foundation of Atlanta, Mississippi Humanities Council, Leo Model Foundation, New York Community Trust, PBS Program Fund, Philadelphia Foundation, Polaroid Foundation, Mary Norris Preyer Fund, Raytheon Company, Charles H. Revson Foundation, Rockefeller Foundation, Samuel Rubin Foundation, San Francisco Foundation, Sapelo Island Research Foundation, Betty J. Stebman, Sun Refining and Marketing Company, Tides Foundation, Villers Foundation, and Jerome and Laya Wiesner.

FUNDERS FOR PROGRAMS SEVEN THROUGH FOURTEEN

"Eyes on the Prize: Part Two" was funded by Public Television Stations, the Corporation for Public Broadcasting, the Public Broadcasting System, and major grants from the Ford Foundation, Lilly Endowment, Inc., the John D. and Catherine T. MacArthur Foundation, the William Penn Foundation, the Charles H. Revson Foundation, and the Rockefeller Foundation. Substantial corporate funding was provided by the Melville Corporation and the Lotus Development Corporation.

Additional funding was provided by:

Mary Reynolds Babcock Foundation, Boston Foundation (Coolidge Family Fund), Boston Foundation (Glassman Fund), Boston Foundation (Heller Fund), Cleveland Foundation, Jonathan Cohen and Eleanor

Friedman, Concord Baptist Christfund, William and Camille Cosby, Arie and Ida Crown Memorial, Cummins Engine Foundation, Digital Equipment Corporation, Fitzgerald Charitable Foundation, Richard and Rhoda Goldman Fund, Gutfreund Foundation, Phoebe W. Haas Charitable Trust, Hillsdale Fund, Inc., Eliot and Margaret Hubbard, Mate Punch and Die Company, Leo Model Foundation, Funding Exchange/National Community Funds, New York Community Trust, Philadelphia Foundation, Mary Norris Preyer Fund, Robert O. Preyer, Roger S. Ralph, Samuel Rubin Foundation, San Francisco Foundation, Betty J. Stebman, Bernard A.G. Taradash (trustee, Estate of Clyde T. Salisbury), Threshold Foundation, Andrew Tobias, Villers Foundation, Kenneth R. Walker, Jerome and Laya Wiesner, and WNYC Foundation.

"Eyes on the Prize"—the television series and related educational materials—was created and produced by Blackside, Inc., in part under contract to The Civil Rights Project, Inc., a nonprofit organization established in 1985 to research, develop, produce, and archive material relating to the American civil rights movement. President: Rev. Jack Mendelsohn. Administrator: Sabrina Perry. Coordinators: Rev. Willa Mathis and Samuel Nixon, Jr. Financial Consultant: J. Benjamin Harris.

INDEX